WRITING
WOMEN'S LIVES

ALSO BY SUSAN CAHILL

Anthologies

Growing Up Female:
Stories by Women Writers from the American Mosaic

Among Sisters: Short Stories on the Sibling Bond

Mothers: Memories, Dreams, and Reflections by Literary Daughters

Women and Fiction

Women and Fiction II

New Women and New Fiction:
Contemporary Short Stories By and About Women

Motherhood: A Reader for Men and Women

Big City Stories

The Urban Reader

Fiction

Earth Angels: Portraits from Childhood and Youth

Nonfiction

A Literary Guide to Ireland (with Thomas Cahill)

WRITING WOMEN'S LIVES

An Anthology of
Autobiographical Narratives
by Twentieth-Century
American Women Writers

Edited and with an Introduction by

SUSAN CAHILL

HarperPerennial

A Division of HarperCollinsPublishers

HarperCollins books may be purchased for educational, business, or sales promotional use. For information please write: Special Markets Department, HarperCollins Publishers, Inc., 10 East 53rd Street, New York, NY 10022.

Designed by Alma Orenstein

Library of Congress Cataloging-in-Publication Data

Writing women's lives : an anthology of autobiographical narratives by twentieth-century American women writers / edited and with an introduction by Susan Cahill. — 1st ed.
p. cm.
ISBN 0-06-096998-9
1. Women authors, American—20th century—Biography. 2. American prose literature—Women authors. 3. American prose literature—20th century. 4. Autobiography—Women authors. I. Cahill, Susan Neunzig.
PS151.W75   1994
810.9'9287'0904—dc20
[B]

93-41136

94 95 96 97 98 ❖/HC 10 9 8 7 6 5 4 3 2

For my students
whose readings and writing of autobiography
have made our English classes times of light and affection

CONTENTS

INTRODUCTION

◆

What hosannas of praise E. M. Forster might offer were he here to receive this collection of autobiographical narratives by American women writers of the twentieth century. It is as if they had taken as their collective motto his famous imperative, "Only Connect." The lives reinvented in these autobiographies and memoirs exhibit few of the fatal splits between private and public identities, between life and literature that wilt and wither many stories of emerging selfhood. The vitality of these life histories comes from their power and variety on two levels: that of primary lived experience—events like birth, childhood, poverty, desire, work and love, sickness and death—and that of narrative made about such experience. This connectedness of self and story, of contemplation and action, exposes as a worn-out fiction the perception of women's experience as essentially private, divorced from the making of history and happiness. The evidence of the written lives represented in this collection shows that American women writers' experience in the twentieth century resists such dualisms as private self vs. public identity, or essential woman vs. working artist. These fifty writers offer "testimonies of lived life," in the words of poet Denise Levertov, which "is what writers have a vocation to give, and readers have a need to receive." Beginning with Jane Addams and ending with Natalie Kusz, who were born a century apart, the writers included in this book communicate a generous feast of their experience of life and literature, selfhood and community, conscience and action. We, their readers, receive, in turn, life writings of solid and necessary nourishment.

Another theme running through this collection—a variation, perhaps, on the theme of connectedness—is that of commitment to community. The self and others are experienced as part of a single web of life: otherness is constitutive of selfhood as such. The consequence of this sense of human solidarity in many of the life histories that follow is the writers' acceptance of political responsibility and the priority of social justice over individual aggrandizement. In a century brutalized by totalitarian aggression, these women share visions and strategies of creating a wider, peaceful democracy. As they tell stories of their various responses to the chaotic modern world, they bring into focus the polarities of our century—its violent tyrannies and its popular freedom movements. Seeing the misery wrought by late nineteenth-century industrial capitalism, Jane Addams, a privileged girl fresh from the Female Seminary, opens an all-purpose shelter in Chicago's inner city. Charlotte Perkins Gilman, a child of single-parent poverty, uses Hull House as her base as she crisscrosses the country arguing, lecturing, and writing prophetically on behalf of women's economic freedom and good day care for children. Declaring herself the enemy of "this filthy rotten system," Dorothy Day's response to the Great Depression is to open a "House of Hospitality" for the urban homeless on New York's Bowery, the home base of the Catholic Worker that would become a model for other cities to follow. Mary Lee Settle, hating fascism, enlists in the RAF in 1941 and is assigned to air traffic nightwatch duty during the German air raids. Ann Cornelisen defies her privileged background to make her life's work the relief of the starving orphans left by Mussolini and Hitler in post-World War II Italy. In postwar America, Lillian Hellman, unapologetic liberal, talks back to Joe McCarthy. African-American Mary Mebane pursues an education in North Carolina before Thurgood Marshall challenged the Supreme Court to outlaw segregated schools in 1954. Remembering and accusing, Jeanne Wakatsuki Houston resurrects the war crime of the internment of the Japanese population in concentration camps on American soil. Denise Levertov, Vivian Gornick, and Patricia Hampl, immigrant, child, and grandchild of immigrants respectively, opposed to the Vietnam War, shout and write their resistance as they woman the barricades. Native American Mary Crow Dog, resisting white racism, joins AIM, the American Indian Movement, and participates in the reoccupation of Wounded Knee. Barbara Grizzuti Harrison, reporting a racial murder in her native Brooklyn, exposes the intertwined roots of racism and sexism; bell hooks, African-American academic and activist, defines her life's mission as the challenging of this same oppressive coupling. Read collectively, these stories of women writers' commitments to shaping a more inclusive national and world community may stand as correctives. As documents of moral and political courage, they contradict those theorists who interpret women's lives as plots of victimization and women themselves as existential cripples, passive and silent, conditioned to stay put on the sidelines of an oppressive history.

In addition to stories of moral recognition and political resistance, there are the autobiographical accounts of women who have challenged stereotypes of one crushing sort or another: sexual, racial, economic, classist. In this context we can place Kate Millett's heroic fight with the mental health establishment, Jane O'Reilly's realization of the destructive power of gender ideology, Joyce Johnson's scrutiny of her middle-class home and a sexist college professor, Hortense Calisher's coming to terms with the losses for women artists within some suburban family circles, Diane Glancy's recovering from divorce to finally cultivate the long-buried writing life, and Dorothy Allison's leaving home and accepting herself as "a cross-eyed working class lesbian"—"Deciding to Live," as her selection is entitled. As lighthearted as she sounds, M.F.K. Fisher challenges a legacy of lethal puritanism in the person of her grandmother. Without sensual pleasure, the granddaughter finds, the people perish. A number of other writers insist on their right to personal freedom: Ellen Glasgow stands firm against an authoritarian father; Annie Dillard ducks out from under school discipline; Jamaica Kincaid denounces empire. Also included in this protesting chorus of spitfire individualists and free—or would-be-free—spirits are May Sarton, Maureen Howard, Maxine Hong Kingston, Sandra Cisneros, and Lorene Cary. As they write their selves into stories, they take the measure of their particular culture and its impact, dissecting and refusing the myths and institutions of a crushing status quo.

The pattern of political and emotional courage in these writers' lives hardly cancels out the evidence of wasted talent and lost opportunities in women's experience to which many feminists have borne witness. The selection from Tillie Olsen's *Silences* demonstrates most vividly the crippling effects of hard circumstances—not enough money, not enough time due to the demands and interruptions of childbearing, child rearing, and exhausting low-paying jobs—on women's writing lives. When seemingly dead-end circumstances combine with a cultural ethos of low expectations for women, the consequence for some is depression. That condition is a current of varying intensity in the lives of Charlotte Perkins Gilman, Ellen Glasgow, Louise Bogan, May Sarton, Eileen Simpson, Kate Millett (who defines depression as "complicity with social disapproval"), Vivian Gornick, Jane O'Reilly, and Nancy Mairs. Their confrontations with this illness, which affects twice as many women as men, also show the salvific effects of feminist consciousness-raising and the act of writing itself, both of which counter the power of depression to waste and destroy the spirit. Other writers describe the help they received from friends and family in the chronic struggle against poverty and racism: Mary Antin's teachers, Mary Mebane's Aunt Jo, the mothers of Kate Simon and Lorene Cary, and a number of anonymous neighborhood librarians all serve as prophetic voices and keepers of the treasures of education and literature, inspiring their daughters, nieces, and students to construct rather than accept their life histories. Despite the losses and failures that Tillie Olsen details in women's fragmented literary history, many of the writers whose undefeated voices we hear in this collection testify to the possibilities of changing the course of one's life, no matter how difficult its circumstances.

Gender and gender roles are well represented in *Writing Women's Lives.* With a tough vigor, Beverly Donofrio and Mary Crow Dog recount their experiences of childbirth in harrowing circumstances; the resonance of maternal pride is strong in Audre Lorde's and Nikki Giovanni's narratives; Madeleine L'Engle writes her grief as a wife of forty years keeping watch at her beloved husband's deathbed; Bebe Moore Campbell and Shirley Abbott are loving daughters of a father and a mother respectively whom each portrays with exquisite grace and honesty; other parents—Kate Simon's, Louise Bogan's—are subjects of a more cold-eyed filial affection; lesbian identity particularizes the relationships implicit in the stories of Kate Millett, Audre Lorde, and Dorothy Allison. But perhaps because of the various difficult circumstances the majority of these writers have faced in their lives, they do not make gender or gender roles the single key element in their autobiographies. The importance of gender is not exaggerated. Women's roles as daughter, lover, wife, or mother are not devalued, but neither is gender identified as the core of selfhood or an essential handicap. Rather the experience of being women is represented as part of a larger, more complex human history.

For these fifty women writers reflect a cultural diversity that defines what it means to be an American. They come from all economic classes, from the inherited wealth of Edith Wharton to the rock-bottom poverty of Natalie Kusz; they have varying educational backgrounds and temperaments and express, therefore, strikingly different points of view. The majority, passionate believers in the possibilities of freedom and progress for themselves and others, speak their minds and change their lives with zest and conviction. A minority, however, does not protest. These writers celebrate or mourn or simply accept: Zora Neale Hurston and Kate Simon remember the world of their childhoods, at once easygoing and troubled, without judgment; Eudora Welty makes her readers see and hear her Southern youth, almost as a summer idyll. Louise Bogan charts her growth as a poet within the frame of her parents' suffering; Eileen Simpson evokes the loneliness of orphanhood without blaming anyone; Joan Didion expresses her sense of the futility of protest, and implicitly, her skepticism about the idea of change itself. In all their hybrid voices—Chinese American, Japanese American, African American, Native American, Chicana American,

Anglo-Saxon American, Jewish American, Irish American, Italian American, and many other mixings thereof—these women bear witness to lives far more complex than one-dimensional stories of gender experience. Their ethnic heritages are often infused with different religious traditions which can profoundly mark a woman's sense of herself and the world. Sandra Cisneros's Latin Catholic background, for example, contributes to her assertion of a bond between spirituality, politics, and feminism; Vivian Gornick, daughter of a Jewish Marxist family, brings to her pursuit of emotional health for her mother and herself the passion for justice of the Hebrew prophets. But the life histories of other women—Annie Dillard and Shirley Abbott, to name only two—reflect no such connection between ethnicity, religion, and gender consciousness, and this despite their childhood churchgoing as practicing Presbyterian and Baptist respectively. It is evident that many layers of past history and present circumstance shape each writer's primary experience and written story. What the autobiographical genre makes clear is that without context—the specific time and place and people whose influence on a writer is crucial—there is no individual character, no core self. Autobiography functions as the linguistic bridge between that self and its full human heritage.

One of the great pleasures of this collection is the panorama it presents of twentieth-century cultural and political history from the perspective of engaged women writers, a sort of collective American life ranging across race, class, and generation. (Florida Scott-Maxwell writes as an octogenarian; Natalie Kusz's memoir is the work of a twenty-six-year-old.) The historical events that figure here include the arrival of immigrant families in Boston and New York in the early part of the century; the execution of Sacco and Vanzetti; the Great Depression; World War II; the Holocaust; Hiroshima; school desegregation in the South; the civil rights movement; the rise of rock 'n' roll; the antiwar movement of the sixties; the founding of AIM; the beginning of Affirmative Action programs; the sexual revolution; single motherhood and the feminization of poverty; the cancer epidemic; the waning of communism in Eastern Europe; the gay and lesbian civil rights movement; and especially the resurgence of feminism in its many voices, changing the lives of such writers as Tillie Olsen, May Sarton, Barbara Grizzuti Harrison, Vivian Gornick, Audre Lorde, Kate Millett, Joyce Johnson, Jane O'Reilly, Diane Glancy, Nancy Mairs, bell hooks, Nikki Giovanni, Beverly Donofrio, and Patricia Hampl. The nightmares of twentieth-century history are real. But rather than giving in to nihilist despair, in the fashion of some postmodern European writers, many of the American women writers of this collection communicate an optimism about their lives and work and those of future generations. This comes through in the generosity and determination of spirit with which Shirley Abbott, Bebe Moore Campbell, Nikki Giovanni, and Lucille Clifton reinvent themselves and others; in the value Vivian Gornick attaches to the hard work of rebuilding her relationship with her mother, and in Nancy Mairs's gutsy personal odyssey undertaken in spite of the limitations imposed by multiple sclerosis. These women ignore neither their losses nor the cruelties of history. But they refuse to privilege their and our diminishments as absolutes. Some stories enact a dramatic dialogue between oppressive circumstances and a gathering of resources for the cause of personal emotional freedom. Beverly Donofrio's story, for instance, has this pattern. Beset by a teenage pregnancy, an impossible family, and a teenage husband, she does not cave in. She discovers a mind and a will of her own—in short, a life—and given the odds against her, this retrieval of self is a miracle. She serves it up as a harrowing comedy.

A few misconceptions about women's experience and writing are given the lie under the many wide lenses of these narratives. The first is that family is often women's nemesis, the cause of suffering and failure. The evidence of these fifty lives, taken all together, tells a more complicated story. Some writers remember their parents and elder relatives as oppressors, intentional or constitutional; others cast them as icons of strength. Mothers are no less or more noble in memory than fathers. Wharton's and Mebane's discouraging cold mothers and Fisher's dyspeptic grandmother must be read in the same collective company as Kate Simon's mother, a tough-minded humanist, and Denise Levertov's "Beatrice Levertoff," and Shirley Abbott's pioneer Southern female ancestors. Ellen Glasgow's austere Calvinist father must share the light of a writing daughter's memory with the likes of Bebe Moore Campbell's wonderful father. The writers in this book who are also parents themselves—Barbara Grizzuti Harrison, Nikki Giovanni, Audre Lorde, Mary Crow Dog, to name a few—refer explicitly to their children as life-blessings. Some do not mention their children at all because they have nothing to do with the subject of the writer's particular narrative. Husbands as well as romance don't necessarily play a major role in these stories, having little to do with how some writers understand their development as persons and artists. The narratives of Lillian Hellman, Mary McCarthy, and Maureen Howard, however, perform an ironic twentieth-century take on nineteenth-century notions of sexual liaison and marriage as romantic affairs. In short, there are simply not enough wretched relatives or relationships in evidence in these autobiographies to support any conclusions about the destructive impact of families on writing women's lives.

A second misconception concerns the assertion of definitive differences between a male autobiographical tradition—said to privilege the male ego and its egotistical adventures in the world—and a female autobiographical tradition, which, for some theorists, offers up a fissured self and a domesticated and/or cloistered life of duty. What does one make of the fact that very few, if any, contemporary autobiographies by male or female writers sustain such interpretation? How does such theory account for the tragic fissures in the autobiographical selves of Tobias Wolff, Geoffrey Wolff, Alfred Kazin, Dan Wakefield, Frank Conroy, and John Edgar Wideman or the heady individualism of Lillian Hellman, Sandra Cisneros, and many others? Autobiography, the most heterogeneous of genres—voicing its "I" and writing its history within diaries, letters, interviews, journals, essays, the narrow frame of memoir, and the full expanse of autobiography itself—does not allow such narrow readings.

The writers represented here are writing professionals of solid reputation, novelists, critics, journalists, travel writers, poets. New voices such as Lorene Cary and Natalie Kusz warrant inclusion because of the extraordinary and deserved praise given to their first books. I have introduced each writer's selection with a brief sketch, detailing some biographical and publishing information and bits of the critics' responses to their work. A list of secondary sources consulted in the composition of these sketches is appended. The selections themselves reflect America's regional diversity: important settings include the South, the Eastern seaboard, the Pacific Northwest and Alaska, New England, California, the Midwest, Texas, and the Great Plains. Jamaica Kincaid, who now lives in the United States, remembers life in Antigua; Ann Cornelisen leaves Ohio to work in southern Italy; Mary Lee Settle's wartime base in England is temporary. The diversity of place and time represented in *Writing Women's Lives* echoes the diversity of its contributors' experience.

The preparation of a comprehensive anthology always leaves the editor wishing for more, in this case more samplings of the feast that is twentieth-century American women writers' autobiography. A longer book would include selections by Susan Kenney, Martha Gellhorn, Ursula LeGuin, Septima Clark, Lorraine Hansberry, LeLy Hayslip, Jo Sinclair, Doris Grumbach, Margaret Walker, Faye Moskowitz, Ellen Gilchrist, Leslie Marmon Silko, Angela Davis, Marita Golden, Deborah Digges, Perri Klass, Judith Ortiz Cofer, Rachel Maddux (whose posthumously discovered autobiography was recently published by the University of Tennessee Press), Rosemary Mahoney, Mary Gordon, Joyce Carol Oates's "Budapest Journal," and Valerie Miner's autobiographical essay "Memory and Vision," a strong example of a new form of academic writing in which autobiography merges with scholarship. The omission of Alice Walker's "In Search of Our Mothers' Gardens," and excerpts from Margaret Mead's *Blackberry Winter* and Anais Nin's diaries is less difficult to justify, because, already widely anthologized, they have become familiar works of the canon of women writers' autobiographical literature. The choice of writers made here reflects an attempt to evoke a wide range of female identity—women portray themselves as artists, feminists, scholars, social and political activists, mothers, daughters, lovers, wives, and friends—and to assemble a selection of some of the finest storytellers and prose stylists of the century. This book derives its energy from their rich talents as writers.

For all the differences of class, ethnicity, religion, sexual identity, region, and profession reflected in these narratives, one hears a common note of irreverence. Each writer tells her story in a distinctive, confident voice, disciple to no preordained school of thought, convinced that memories contain the map of identity and that it is important to bring them back. Thumbing their collective nose at rigid and unholy boundaries and separatisms, these narratives dramatize, finally, a deeply inclusive spiritual consciousness, calling to mind the words of William Dean Howells, who, writing at the beginning of this century, called autobiography "the most democratic province in the republic of letters." We read autobiography, in part, to taste and to learn from its discoveries of freedom and meaning against the background of this long century of daunting polarities. We find much to learn in its kind humor and in the urgency of its written memories. Reading, we join the writers' retrospective journeys. We are moved to consider what they discovered: that we do not exist separately from one another; that every life story, including our own, counts; that this news is good and generative. As they quicken the pleasure of discerning significant life transformed into literature, the life stories in *Writing Women's Lives* widen our consciousness of common grounds and wonderful differences.

JANE ADDAMS
(1860–1935)

◆

JANE ADDAMS, social activist, pragmatist, and author of one of the great American autobiographies, *Twenty Years at Hull House,* was born and raised in Cedarville in north central Illinois. The eighth of nine children, she lost her mother at the age of two. She grew up to admire intensely her father, a fervent abolitionist, Quaker, and state senator, who was the dominant moral influence in her early life. After graduating from Rockford Female Seminary in 1877, she spent years seeking the vocation that would give concrete form to her high-minded Christian ideals, in particular to respond effectively to the urban misery she first saw up close in London. That period of confusion and quest is the focus of the following excerpt. Eventually, she invented her life's work, which began with the opening of a settlement house in a poor section of Chicago. When she and co-founder, Ellen Gates Starr, moved into Hull House in the Nineteenth Ward, the overcrowded neighborhood of the city's poorest immigrants, they hoped to tear down the walls between classes, creating a helping community as much for the overprivileged workers like themselves as for the poor.

The history of Hull House reflects the political savvy of the well-bred Jane Addams. Sensitive to the acute and complex problems of the neighborhood and its poverty, she organized campaigns to improve conditions in tenements and sweatshops, and to stem the abuse of child labor. As a result, child labor laws were passed, the working hours of women were legally regulated, labor unions were recognized, school attendance became compulsory, laws protecting immigrants and the safety of industrial workplaces were enacted. Assisted by accomplished co-workers like Alice Hamilton, physician and scientist, Florence Kelley, lawyer and factory inspector, and Julia Lathrop, social researcher and children's advocate, Addams emphasized the value of cultural diversity that immigrants brought to American life. Both William James and John Dewey, who volunteered at Hull House, saw her as the embodiment of their philosophical pragmatism: she learned by doing and valued the processes of work—*how* things got done—as much as the final results.

1

For many years she campaigned for women's suffrage, believing that the "moral energy of women" should be brought to bear upon social problems caused by industrial capitalism and international conflict. Chairman of the Woman's Peace Party, she worked to keep the United States out of World War I and was vilified when the United States finally entered the war in 1917 (the Daughters of the American Revolution expelled her). Alarmed by the pressure for political conformity which challenged her commitment to tolerance and diversity, she helped to found the American Civil Liberties Union in 1920.

Throughout her years of work in the Hull House community and engagement in political struggle, Addams wrote, publishing her articles and books, building a broad readership. She lectured widely. Her first book, *Democracy and Social Ethics* (1902), called for a new ethic of public responsibility to replace the private individualistic morality of a simpler, preindustrial society. Other books include *The Spirit of Youth and The City Streets* (1909), the two volumes of autobiography, *Twenty Years at Hull House* (1910) and *The Second Twenty Years at Hull House* (1930), *A New Conscience and an Ancient Evil* (1911), *The Long Road of Woman's Memory* (1916), *Peace and Bread in Time of War* (1922), *The Excellent Becomes the Permanent* (1932), and *My Friend Julia Lathrop* (1935). In 1931 she was awarded the Nobel Peace Prize. In the last years of her life, the public dropped its suspicions of her as a dangerous radical and celebrated her as a mythic figure. Born a Quaker and a practicing Presbyterian as an adult, she resisted the idolatry of her admirers. "I am a very simple person," she said.

From *Twenty Years at Hull House*

CHAPTER IV

The Snare of Preparation

The winter after I left school was spent in the Woman's Medical College of Philadelphia, but the development of the spinal difficulty which had shadowed me from childhood forced me into Dr. Weir Mitchell's hospital for the late spring, and the next winter I was literally bound to a bed in my sister's house for six months. In spite of its tedium, the long winter had its mitigations, for after the first few weeks I was able to read with a luxurious consciousness of leisure, and I remember opening the first volume of Carlyle's "Frederick the Great" with a lively sense of gratitude that it was not Gray's "Anatomy," having found, like many another, that general culture is a much easier undertaking than professional study. The long illness inevitably put aside the immediate prosecution of a medical course, and although I had passed my examinations creditably enough in the required subjects for the first year, I was very glad to have a physician's sanction for giving up clinics and dissecting rooms and to follow his prescription of spending the next two years in Europe.

Before I returned to America I had discovered that there were other genuine reasons for living among the poor than that of practicing medicine upon them, and my brief foray into the profession was never resumed.

The long illness left me in a state of nervous exhaustion with which I struggled for years, traces of it remaining long after Hull-House was opened in 1889. At the best it allowed me but a limited amount of energy, so that doubtless there was much nervous depression at the foundation of the spiritual struggles which this chapter is forced to record. However, it could not have been all due to my health, for as my wise little notebook sententiously remarked, "In his own way each man must struggle, lest the moral law become a far-off abstraction utterly separated from his active life."

It would, of course, be impossible to remember that some of these struggles ever took place at all, were it not for these selfsame note-books, in which, however, I no longer wrote in moments of high resolve, but judging from the internal evidence afforded by the books themselves, only in moments of deep depression when overwhelmed by a sense of failure.

One of the most poignant of these experiences, which occurred during the first few months after our landing upon the other side of the Atlantic, was on a Saturday night, when I received an ineradicable impression of the wretchedness of East London, and also saw for the first time the overcrowded quarters of a great city at midnight. A small party of tourists were taken to the East End by a city missionary to witness the Saturday night sale of decaying vegetables and fruit, which, owing to the Sunday laws in London, could not be sold until Monday, and, as they were beyond safe keeping, were disposed of at auction as late as possible on Saturday night. On Mile End Road, from the top of an omnibus which paused at the end of a dingy street lighted by only occasional flares of gas, we saw two huge masses of ill-clad people clamoring around two hucksters' carts. They were bidding their far-things and ha'pennies for a vegetable held up by the auctioneer, which he at last scornfully flung, with a gibe for its cheapness, to the success-ful bidder. In the momentary pause only one man detached himself from the groups. He had bidden in a cabbage, and when it struck his hand, he instantly sat down on the curb, tore it with his teeth, and hastily devoured it, unwashed and uncooked as it was. He and his fellows were types of the "submerged tenth," as our missionary guide told us, with some little satisfaction in the then new phrase, and he further added that so many of them could scarcely be seen in one spot save at this Saturday night auction, the desire for cheap food being apparently the one thing which could move them simultaneously. They were huddled into ill-fitting, cast-off clothing, the ragged finery which one sees only in East London. Their pale faces were dominated by that most unlovely of human expressions, the cunning and shrewdness of the bargain-hunter who starves if he cannot make a successful trade, and yet the final impression was not of ragged, tawdry clothing nor of pinched and sallow faces, but of myriads of hands, empty, pathetic, nerveless and workworn, showing white in the uncertain light of the street, and clutching forward for food which was already unfit to eat. . . .

For the following weeks I went about London almost furtively, afraid to look down narrow streets and alleys lest they disclose again this hideous human need and suffering. I carried with me for days at a time that curious surprise we experience when we first come back into the streets after days given over to sorrow and death; we are bewildered that the world should be going on as usual and unable to determine which is real, the inner pang or the outward seeming. In time all huge London came to seem unreal save the poverty in its East End. During the following two years on the continent, while I was irresistibly drawn to the poorer quarters of each city, nothing among the beggars of South Italy nor among the saltminers of Austria carried with it the same conviction of human wretchedness which was conveyed by this momentary glimpse of an East London street. It was, of course, a most fragmentary and lurid view of the poverty of East London, and quite unfair. I should have been shown either less or more, for I went away with no notion of the hundreds of men and women who had gallantly identified their fortunes with these empty-handed people, and who, in church and chapel, "relief works," and charities, were at least making an effort towards its mitigation.

Our visit was made in November, 1883, the very year when the *Pall Mall Gazette* exposure started "The Bitter Cry of Outcast London," and the conscience of England was stirred as never before over this joyless city in the East End of its capital. Even then, vigorous and drastic plans were being discussed, and a splendid program of municipal reforms was already dimly outlined. Of all these, however, I had heard nothing but the vaguest rumor.

No comfort came to me then from any source, and the painful impression was increased because at the very moment of looking down the East London street from the top of the omnibus, I had been sharply and painfully reminded of "The Vision of Sudden Death" which had confronted De Quincey one summer's night as he was being driven through rural England on a high mail coach. Two absorbed lovers suddenly appear between the narrow, blossoming hedgerows in the direct path of the huge vehicle which is sure to crush them to their death. De Quincey tries to send them a warning shout, but finds himself unable to make a sound because his mind is hopelessly entangled in an endeavor to recall the exact lines from the "Iliad" which describe the great cry with which Achilles alarmed all Asia militant. Only after his memory responds is his will released from its momentary paralysis, and he rides on through the fragrant night with the horror of the escaped calamity thick upon him, but he also bears with him the consciousness that he had given himself over so many years to classic learning—that when suddenly called upon for a quick decision in the world of life and death, he had been able to act only through a literary suggestion.

This is what we were all doing, lumbering our minds with literature that only served to cloud the really vital situation spread before our eyes. It seemed to me too preposterous that in my first view of the horror of East London I should have recalled De Quincey's literary description of the literary suggestion which had once paralyzed him. In my disgust it all appeared a hateful, vicious circle which even the apostles of culture themselves admitted, for had not one of the greatest among the moderns plainly said that "conduct, and not culture is three fourths of human life."

For two years in the midst of my distress over the poverty which, thus suddenly driven into my consciousness, had become to me the "Weltschmerz," there was mingled a sense of futility, of misdirected energy, the belief that the pursuit of cultivation would not in the end bring either solace or relief. I gradually reached a conviction that the first generation of college women had taken their learning too quickly, had departed too suddenly from the active, emotional life led by their grandmothers and great-grandmothers; that the contemporary education of young women had developed too exclusively the power of acquiring knowledge and of merely receiving impressions; that somewhere in the process of "being educated" they had lost that simple and almost automatic response to the human appeal, that old healthful reaction resulting in activity from the mere presence of suffering or of helplessness; that they are so sheltered and pampered they have no chance even to make "the great refusal."

In the German and French *pensions*, which twenty-five years ago were crowded with American mothers and their daughters who had crossed the seas in search of culture, one often found the mother making real connection with the life about her, using her inadequate German with great fluency, gayly measuring the enormous sheets or exchanging recipes with the German Hausfrau, visiting impartially the nearest kindergarten and market, making an atmosphere of her own, hearty and genuine as far as it went, in the house and on the street. On the other hand, her daughter was critical and uncertain of her linguistic acquirements, and only at ease when in the familiar receptive attitude afforded by the art gallery and the opera house. In the latter she was swayed and moved, appreciative of the power and charm of the music, intelligent as to the legend and poetry of the plot, finding use for her trained and developed powers as she sat "being cultivated" in the familiar atmosphere of the classroom which had, as it were, become sublimated and romanticized.

I remember a happy busy mother who, complacent with the knowledge that her daughter daily devoted four hours to her music, looked up from her knitting to say, "If I had had your opportunities when I was young, my dear, I should have been a very happy girl. I always had musical talent, but such training as I had, foolish little songs and waltzes and not time for half an hour's practice a day."

The mother did not dream of the sting her words left and that the sensitive girl appreciated only too well that her opportunities were fine and unusual, but she also knew that in spite of some facility and much good teaching she had no genuine talent and never would fulfill the expectations of her friends. She looked back upon her mother's girlhood with positive envy because it was so full of happy industry and extenuating obstacles, with undisturbed opportunity to believe that her talents were unusual. The girl looked wistfully at her mother, but had not the courage to cry out what was in her heart: "I might believe I had unusual talent if I did not know what good music was; I might enjoy half an hour's practice a day if I were busy and happy the rest of the time. You do not know what life means when all the difficulties are removed! I am simply smothered and sickened with advantages. It is like eating a sweet dessert the first thing in the morning."

This, then, was the difficulty, this sweet dessert in the morning and the assumption that the sheltered, educated girl has nothing to do with the bitter poverty and the social maladjustment which is all about her, and which, after all, cannot be concealed, for it breaks through poetry and literature in a burning tide which overwhelms her; it peers at her in the form of heavy-laden market women and underpaid street laborers, gibing her with a sense of her uselessness. . . .

It is hard to tell just when the very simple plan which afterward developed into the Settlement began to form itself in my mind. It may have been even before I went to Europe for the second time, but I gradually became convinced that it would be a good thing to rent a house in a part of the city where many primitive and actual needs are found, in which young women who had been given over too exclusively to study, might restore a balance of activity along traditional lines and learn of life from life itself; where they might try out some of the things they had been taught and put truth to "the ultimate test of the conduct it dictates or inspires." I do not remember to have mentioned this plan to any one until we reached Madrid in April, 1888. . . .

I had made up my mind that next day, whatever happened, I would begin to carry out the plan, if only by talking about it. I can well recall the stumbling and uncertainty with which I finally set it forth to Miss Starr, my old-time school friend, who was one of our party. I even dared to hope that she might join in carrying out the plan, but nevertheless I told it in the fear of that disheartening experience which is so apt to afflict our most cherished plans when they are at last divulged, when we suddenly feel that there is nothing there to talk about, and as the golden dream slips through our fingers we are left to wonder at our own fatuous belief. But gradually the comfort of Miss Starr's companionship, the vigor and enthusiasm which she brought to bear upon it, told both in the growth of the plan and upon the sense of its validity, so that by the time we had reached the enchantment of the Alhambra, the scheme had become convincing and tangible although still most hazy in detail.

A month later we parted in Paris, Miss Starr to go back to Italy, and I to journey on to London to secure as many suggestions as possible from those wonderful places of which we had heard, Toynbee Hall and the People's Palace. So that it finally came about that in June, 1888, five years after my first visit in East London, I found myself at Toynbee Hall equipped not only with a letter of introduction from Canon Fremantle, but with high expectations and a certain belief that whatever perplexities and discouragement concerning the life of the poor were in store for me, I should at least know something at first hand and have the solace of daily activity. I had confidence that although life itself might contain many difficulties the period of mere passive receptivity had come to an end, and I had at last finished with the ever-lasting "preparation for life," however ill-prepared I might be.

It was not until years afterward that I came upon Tolstoy's phrase "the snare of preparation," which he insists we spread before the feet of young people, hopelessly entangling them in a curious inactivity at the very period of life when they are longing to construct the world anew and to conform it to their own ideals. . . .

EDITH WHARTON
(1862–1937)

◆

Born in New York City, EDITH WHARTON (Edith Newbold Jones) was the youngest child in a wealthy and socially prominent family who raised her to take her place in aristocratic New York society. At the age of three, she was taken to live in Europe. She spent a lonely childhood in Italy, Germany, and France, summering in Newport, Rhode Island, reading voraciously in her father's library. Educated at home by tutors—she described herself as "much governessed and guarded"—she made her debut at seventeen. In 1885 she married Edward Wharton ("Teddy"), an amiable Bostonian who did not share her intellectual and literary interests. She began writing for publication during the early years of their marriage, though her husband disapproved. Eventually, to overcome the "paralyzing melancholy" which beset her, she sought the "rest cure" treatment of Dr. S. Weir Mitchell. By 1899, recovered from her nervous condition and having published two volumes of well-received short stories, she had committed herself to the world of literature. In 1913 her marriage ended in divorce and she settled permanently in France.

Recognized as one of America's greatest novelists, in the psychological tradition of her friend and mentor Henry James, Wharton's best fiction is marked by a preoccupation with the influence of social pressures on the development of character and with manners and morals, especially those of her female protagonists. In one of her most renowned novels, *The House of Mirth* (1905), she satirized the New York society that she knew so well, showing the destructive effect of its hypocrisies and pretensions on her heroine, Lily Bart. In *Ethan Frome* (1911) she used the New England setting of Lenox, Massachusetts, for what many consider her best and least typical work. In *The Reef* (1912), *The Custom of the Country* (1913), and *The Age of Innocence* (1920), she continued the theme of the destruction dealt unconventional women by conventional society.

In the autobiographical fragment that follows here, "Life and I," published for the first time in the Library of America's two-volume edition of her work, she provides the context of the isolation and loneliness she felt growing up in that society she would later dissect so penetratingly in fiction. In a letter to her editor in 1923, she explained that for some time she had had a plan "vaguely floating through my mind" . . . "namely, the writing of my own early memories, . . . in which I should like to interweave the recollections of my childhood and the beginnings of my literary life. . . ." According to one of her biographers, Wharton abandoned this autobiographical project when the memories of her mother's coldness, in particular, became too painful. Her official autobiography, *A Backward Glance* (1934), deals superficially with "the lonely little girl that I was," and is silent on the subject of her mother's rejection of her youngest child and only daughter. Its focus is on Wharton's indefatigable travels, her relief work in Paris during World War I for which she received the Cross of the Legion of Honor, and her friend Henry James.

At her death, she had published fifty books. Two major biographies are R. W. B. Lewis, *Edith Wharton: A Biography* (1975), and Cynthia Griffin Wolff, *A Feast of Words: The Triumph of Edith Wharton* (1977).

From "Life and I"

II

When I was nine years old I fell ill of typhoid fever, & lay for weeks at the point of death. We were at Mildbad in the Black Forest, then a small unfashionable "Bad", where my mother was taking the cure. The leading physician of the place (the only one, perhaps) had never seen a case of typhoid, & was obliged to write daily for advice to his son, also a physician, who was with the German army (it was just before the close of the Franco-Prussian war.)

This method of "absent treatment" was not successful, & at last the Dr told my parents that I was dying. That very day they happened to hear that the physician of the Czar of Russia was passing through Mildbad. In their despair they appealed to him, & on his way to the train he stopped at our hotel for five minutes, looked at me, changed the treatment—& saved my life.

This illness formed the dividing line between my little-childhood, & the next stage. It obliterated—as far as I can recall—the torturing moral scruples which had darkened my life hitherto, but left me the prey to an intense & unreasoning physical timidity. During my convalescence, my one prayer was to be allowed to read, & among the books given me was one of the detestable "children's books" which poison the youthful mind when they do not hopelessly weaken it. I must do

my mother the justice to say that, though wholly indifferent to literature, she had a wholesome horror of what she called "silly books", &
always kept them from me; but the volume in question was lent by two
little playmates, a brother & sister, who were very "nicely" brought up,
& of whom it was to be assumed that they would have only "nice" stories in their possession. To an unimaginative child the tale would no
doubt have been harmless; but it was a "robber-story", & with my
intense Celtic sense of the super-natural, tales of robbers & ghosts were
perilous reading. This one brought on a serious relapse, & again my life
was in danger; & when I came to myself, it was to enter a world
haunted by formless horrors. I had been naturally a fearless child; now I
lived in a state of chronic fear. Fear of *what?* I cannot say—& even at
the time, I was never able to formulate my terror. It was like some dark
undefinable menace, forever dogging my steps, lurking, & threatening;
I was conscious of it wherever I went by day, & at night it made sleep
impossible, unless a light & a nurse-maid were in the room. But, whatever it was, it was most formidable & pressing when I was returning
from my daily walk (which I always took with a maid or governess, or
with my father.) During the last few yards, & while I waited on the
door-step for the door to be opened, I could feel it behind me, upon
me; & if there was any delay in the opening of the door I was seized by
a choking agony of terror. It did not matter who was with me, for no
one could protect me; but, oh, the rapture of relief if my companion
had a latch-key, & we could get in at once, before It caught me!

This species of hallucination lasted seven or eight years, & I was a
"young lady" with long skirts & my hair up before my heart ceased to
beat with fear if I had to stand for half a minute on a door-step! I am
often inclined—like most people—to think my parents might have
brought me up in a manner more suited to my tastes & disposition; but
I owe them the deepest gratitude for their treatment of me during this
difficult phase. They made as light of my fears as they could, without
hurting my feelings; but they never scolded or ridiculed me for them,
or tried to "harden" me by making me sleep in the dark, or doing any
of things which are supposed to give courage to timid children. I
believe it is owing to this kindness & forbearance that my terror gradually wore off, & that I became what I am now—a woman hardly conscious of physical fear. But how long the traces of my illness lasted may
be judged from the fact that, till I was twenty-seven or eight, I could
not sleep in the room with a book containing a ghost-story, & that I
have frequently had to burn books of this kind, because it frightened
me to know that they were downstairs in the library!

Shortly after I recovered from the typhoid fever we went back to

America to live. I was keenly interested in this change in our existence, but I shall never forget the bitter disappointment produced by the first impressions of my native country. I was only ten years old, but I had been fed on beauty since my babyhood, & my first thought was: *"How ugly it is!"* I have never since thought otherwise, or felt otherwise than as an exile in America; & that this is no retrospective delusion is proved by the fact that I used to dream at frequent intervals that we were going back to Europe, & to wake from this dream in a state of exhilaration which the reality turned to deep depression.

Yet there was much to interest me in our new life, & I was always passionately interested in things! From a wandering existence in continental hotels we went to a comfortable town-house, luxuriously mounted, & a charming country-place on Narragansett Bay, in the outskirts of Newport, where I found everything to delight the heart of a happy, healthy child—cows, a kitchen-garden full of pears & quinces & straw-berries, a beautiful rose-garden, a stable full of horses (with a dear little poney of my own), a boat, a bath-house, a beautiful sheltered cove to swim in, & best of all, two glorious little boys to swim with! I wonder now that I did not forget all about Europe.

The little boys were our neighbours, the children of Mr Lewis Rutherfurd, the distinguished astronomer (father of Mrs Henry White) whose place "marched" with ours, & who was an intimate friend of my parents. The younger of the two boys, Winthrop Rutherfurd, was just my age, the elder, Lewis, three or four years older. They were two of the most beautiful young creatures it is possible to imagine, the younger espiègle, gay & audacious, the elder grave, tender-hearted & shy. Need I say that I fell in love with the former, & that the latter fell in love with me?

With these delightful companions all my days were spent; for the German governess whom we had brought from Europe having proved unsympathetic & dissatisfied, my parents sent her home, & arranged that I should study with the governess of the Rutherfurd children, who became afterward my own dear pedagogue—Anna Bahlmann. Under such conditions work was pleasant enough; but play was of course infinitely better! *How* we played! I had a poney, Lewis & Winthrop had a donkey, & *everybody* had dogs! Dogs of all ages, sizes & characters swarmed through my early years—& how I loved them! The first—a furry Spitz puppy—was given me before I was four years old, & from that moment I was never without one, except during a brief interval in Europe, when a delicious brown rabbit named "Bonaparte" ruled alone in my heart. I always had a deep, instinctive understanding of animals, a yearning to hold them in my arms, a fierce desire to protect them against pain & cruelty. This feeling seemed to have its source in a curious sense of being somehow, myself, an intermediate creature between human beings & animals, & nearer, on the whole, to the furry tribes than to homo sapiens. I felt that I *knew things about them*—their sensations, desires & sensibilities—that other bipeds could not guess; & this seemed to lay on me the obligation to defend them against their human oppressors. The feeling grew in intensity until it became a morbid preoccupation, and I passed out of the phase of physical fear that I have just described only to be possessed by a haunting consciousness of the sufferings of animals. This lasted for years, & was the last stage of imaginative misery that I passed through before reaching a completely normal & balanced state of mind. I helped to cure myself by working as hard as I could to better the condition of animals wherever I happened to be living, & above all to make the work for their protection take a practical rather than a sentimental form.

Meanwhile at Pencraig (our country place) I was developing a happy healthy young body, learning to row, to swim & to ride, & taking long walks over the rolling rocky wilderness that extended between our place & the Atlantic. Two other little boys (the step-sons of Colonel Jerôme Bonaparte), who were also our neighbours, were admitted to the band; but they were stolid ugly little animals, & played a minor part in our adventures.

Unluckily for me, none of my companions had any imagination, or any taste for books or pictures. I lived one side of life with them, gaily & thoroughly, with every drop of my blood, & every inch of my joyous little body; but of the other wonderful side they never had so much as a guess! I often wonder if any other child possessed of that "other side" was ever so alone in it as I. Certainly none in my experience. All the people I have known who have cared for "les choses de l'esprit" have found some degree of sympathy & companionship either in their families or among their youthful friends. But I never exchanged a word with a really intelligent human being until I was over twenty—& then, alas, I had only a short glimpse of what such communion might be! . . .

So I lived my two lives, the one of physical exercise & healthy natural "fun", & the other, parallel with it, but known to none but myself—a life of dreams & visions, set to the rhythm of the poets, & peopled with throning images of beauty. I cannot say that either of these lives occupied more space than the other; & perhaps the most curious thing about my youth is the equilibrium preserved between my solitary intellectual sympathies, & the sociable instincts which made me desire to be with other children, & to shine in their company. This eagerness to excel is one of the marked traits of my youth. I wanted to lead, to influence, I wanted—it must be owned!—to *épater!* There is nothing unusual in this, on the part of a clever child; but usually such strongly marked characteristics persist, & in my case the desire to be admired & to dominate died out before I was thirty.

Our return to America had brought me one untold boon—the possibility of access to a library. In the country we had few books, but in town there must have been five or six hundred, which but for me would have slumbered undisturbed behind the glass doors of the bookcases. My mother read nothing but novels & books on horticulture; my father read sermons, & narratives of Arctic exploration. But at that time every gentleman, whether he was a reader or not, possessed what was known as "a gentleman's library"; that is, a fair collection of the "standard" works in French & English. As there were *no novels* on the library shelves (except Scott & Disraeli), I was at once given free access to them, my mother's rule being that I must never read a novel without asking permission, but that "poetry & history" (her rough classification of the rest of literature) could do no harm. I must add that, having been thus put on my honour, I never once failed to observe the compact, & never read a novel without asking leave until the day of my marriage.

Oh, the rapture of my first explorations in that dear dear library! I can see now where almost every volume stood, from the beautiful old Swift & Fielding & Sterne in eighteenth century bindings (from my grandfather's library) to the white vellum Macaulay, with gold tooling & red morocco labels! I can *feel* the rough shaggy surface of the Turkey rug on which I used to lie stretched by the hour, my chin in my hands, poring over one precious volume after the other, & forming fantastic conceptions of life from the heterogeneous wisdom thus absorbed. I could make out a fairly complete list of the volumes; but instead of this, I will try to name, in the order of their importance, those from which I drew my chief intellectual sustenance. First, unquestionably, came Chambers's Encyclopaedia of English Literature, that admirable storehouse of great prose & poetry, in which I learned the cadences of the Areopagitica & the Urn-Burial, & caught fragmentary glimpses of the Elizabethan drama. Oh, how I longed for *more* of Ford & Marlowe & Webster! But the idea that they were obtainable in any other form apparently never occurred to me; & so I read & re-read the great scenes of the Duchess of Malfy, & the Broken Heart & Faustus & Edward II, & tried to write others like them ... Next came—Coleridge's "Friend". Let no one ask me why! I can only suppose it answered to some hidden need to order my thoughts, & get things into some kind of logical relation to each other: a need which developed in me almost as early as the desire to be kissed & thought pretty! It originated, perhaps, in the sense that weighed on my whole childhood—the sense of bewilderment, of the need of guidance, the longing to understand *what it was all about.* My little corner of the cosmos seemed like a dark trackless region "where ignorant armies clash by night", & I was oppressed by the sense that I was too small & ignorant & alone ever to find my way about in it . . . After Coleridge, came Sainte Beuve, Corneille, Racine, & a very good anthology of French prose & verse. Some of Macaulay's essays I enjoyed, & parts of Augustin Thierry's History. (The vivid Merovingian pictures.) I don't remember trying Gibbon, but I read bits of Carlyle without much enthusiasm (I hated his blustering, bullying tone)—& then I came upon Ruskin! His wonderful cloudy pages gave me back the image of the beautiful Europe I had lost, & woke in me the habit of precise visual observation. The ethical & aesthetical *fatras* were easily enough got rid of later, & as an interpreter of visual impressions he did me incomparable service.

There seem to have been few poets in the library, for I remember reading only Wordsworth (without enthusiasm then.) But soon after this I fell in love with our clergyman, & thereby opened wide the gates of literature. The Revd Dr Washburn, rector of Calvary Church, must have been a man of about fifty-five. He was a scholar & a linguist, & had a beautiful voice. I have always been very sensitive to qualities of intonation, & to beauty of diction, & it was ecstasy to me to sit in the dusky shadowy church, & hear him roll out: "What though I have fought with the beasts at Ephesus?" or "Canst thou loose the sweet influences of the Pleiades?" I was about thirteen when this consuming passion fell upon me, & it raged for three or four years to the exclusion of every other affection. I am not aware that it was ever known to its object; but it led to my making the acquaintance of his daughter, a queer, shy, invalid girl of twenty or so, in whom I suspect there were strong traces of degeneracy. This daughter became passionately, morbidly attached to me; & as she was extremely cultivated, & a great reader (though not really intelligent) she soon saw that I was starving for mental nourishment, & poured it out upon me in reckless profusion. There was no measure to my appetite, & as I knew French, German & Italian as well as English (having learnt them all in my babyhood in Europe), we ranged through four literatures—though chiefly absorbed in German & English. At the same time I was "studying" German literature with Miss Bahlmann, & learning to read Middle High German in order to enjoy the Niebelungen in the original. This led me to read the Edda, & then Miss Washburn suggested that I should learn Anglo-Saxon, in order to "enjoy" (ye gods!) the Saxon Chronicle & Layamon's Brut in the original. "Gesagtgethan"—I was soon fluent in Anglo-Saxon, but, apart from the pleasure derived from "The Battle of Brunanburh," which is glorious, I remember getting no especial satisfaction from this new acquirement, save the hope that Dr Washburn might fall in love with me when he knew that I had learned Anglo-Saxon!

This hope was not fulfilled—but my time was not wasted, since my studies led me naturally to philology, & Skeat, Kemble, Morris, Earle &c, admitted me to new delights. Here I was back in the realm of words, my own native country, as it were; & for the next year or two I was steeped in comparative philology—Marsh, Max Müller, & lutti quanti: all the obsolete "authorities" whose very names I have forgotten! These worthies introduced me to their protégé the Aryan, & in that elusive being & his migrations I long took a passionate interest. Meanwhile my love of poetry & letters was fed by all these studies, & I plunged with rapture into the great ocean of Goethe. At fifteen I had read every word of his plays & poems, Dichtung und Wahrheit, & Wilhelm Meister. (The other novels were *novels,* & therefore prohibited!)

Faust was one of the "epoch-making" encounters for me—another was Keats. A third was—a little volume called "Coppée's Elements of Logic," which I discovered among the books my brother Harry had brought back from Trinity Hall; & of the three, *at the time* it was Coppée who made the greatest difference to me! Here again—explain who will; I can only state the fact. I shall never forget the thrill with which my eye first lit on those arid pages, one day when, in my brother's absence, I was ferreting about in his book-shelves (carefully avoiding the *novels.*) I felt at last as if I had found the clue to life—as if nothing would ever be so dark & bewildering again! As I read, it seemed as if I had known it all before—my mind kept on saying "Of course, of course", as my fascinated eyes flew on from page to page. And when, much later, I read:

> "How charming is divine Philosophy;
> Not harsh & crabbèd, as dull fools suppose,
> But musical as is Apollo's lute,"

I thought of Coppée, & gave a full assent!

It was certainly providential that, on the same shelf with Coppée, & almost at the same moment, I found an abridged edition of Sir William Hamilton's History of Philosophy! Oh, thrice-blest discovery! Now I was going to know all about life! Now I should never be that helpless blundering thing, a mere "little girl," again! The two little black cloth volumes, with their yellow paper & small black type, were more precious to me than anything I possessed . . .

And all the while Life, real Life, was ringing in my ears, humming in my blood, flushing my cheeks & waving in my hair—sending me messages & signals from every beautiful face & musical voice, & running over me in vague tremors when I rode my poney, or swam through the short bright ripples of the bay, or raced & danced & tumbled with "the boys." And I didn't know—& if, by any chance, I came across the shadow of a reality, & asked my mother "What does it mean?" I was always told "You're too little to understand", or else "It's not nice to ask about such things" . . . Once, when I was seven or eight, an older cousin had told me that babies were not found in flowers but in people. This information had been given unsought, but as I had been told by Mamma that it was "not nice" to enquire into such matters, I had a vague sense of contamination, & went immediately to confess my involuntary offense. I received a severe scolding, & was left with a penetrating sense of "not-niceness" which effectually kept me from pursuing my investigations farther; & this was literally all I knew of the processes of generation till I had been married for several weeks—the explanation which I had meanwhile worked out for myself being that married people "had children" because God saw the clergyman marrying them through the roof of the church!

While I am speaking of this, I will add that, a few days before my marriage, I was seized with such a dread of the whole dark mystery, that I summoned up courage to appeal to my mother, & begged her, with a heart beating to suffocation, to tell me "what being married was like." Her handsome face at once took on the look of icy disapproval which I most dreaded. "I never heard such a ridiculous question!" she said impatiently; & I felt at once how vulgar she thought me.

But in the extremity of my need I persisted. "I'm afraid, Mamma—I want to know what will happen to me!"

The coldness of her expression deepened to disgust. She was silent for a dreadful moment; then she said with an effort: "You've seen enough pictures & statues in your life. Haven't you noticed that men are—made differently from women?"

"Yes," I faltered blankly.

"Well, then—?"

I was silent, from sheer inability to follow, & she brought out sharply: "Then for heaven's sake don't ask me any more silly questions. You can't be as stupid as you pretend!"

The dreadful moment was over, & the only result was that I had been convicted of stupidity for not knowing what I had been expressly forbidden to ask about, or even to think of! . . . I record this brief conversation, because the training of which it was the beautiful & logical conclusion did more than anything else to falsify & misdirect my whole life ... And, since, in the end, it did neither, it only strengthens the conclusion that one is what one is, & that education may delay but cannot deflect one's growth. Only, what possibilities of tragedy may lie in the delay! ...

Charlotte Perkins Gilman
(1869–1935)

◆

In her posthumously published autobiography *The Living of Charlotte Perkins Gilman* (1935), CHARLOTTE PERKINS GILMAN remembered a poverty-stricken and love-starved childhood. Born in Hartford, Connecticut, the great-niece of Catharine Beecher and Harriet Beecher Stowe on her father's side of the family, she and her brother were raised by their mother after their father abandoned the family. Destitute, the single-parent family moved nineteen times in eighteen years. As the early chapters of the autobiography describe, Mrs. Perkins reacted to her own loss of love by teaching her children not to expect any emotional happiness: she forbade all expressions of physical tenderness—"She would not let me caress her, and would not caress me, unless I was asleep." Her daughter grew up to suffer from depression, the focus of the following selection, and to argue throughout a lifetime of writing, lecturing, and teaching for the economic independence of women as essential to the fulfillment of their humanity. Her book *Women and Economics* (1898), repeatedly reprinted and translated into seven languages, was considered the Bible of the turn-of-the-century women's movement for its courageous and prophetic denunciation of systemic economic and social discrimination against women. Jane Addams (see page 1) called it a "masterpiece."

Gilman is best known for her short story "The Yellow Wallpaper," originally published in 1892 and later included in *Great Modern American Stories* (1920) by editor William Dean Howells, who had encouraged Gilman as a poet and fiction writer from the beginning. The excerpt from her autobiography that follows here describes the experience of her depression and breakdown, which Gilman dramatizes in the story. It also describes the "rest cure" and prescription for her mental health issued by the prominent "nerve specialist," Dr. S. Weir Mitchell, the Victorian guru of neurasthenia who treated such famous patients as Jane Addams, Edith Wharton, William Dean Howells's daughter, Winifred, and two Beecher women: "Live as domestic a life as possible. Have your child with you all the time. . . . Lie down an hour after each meal. Have but two hours' intellectual life a day. And never touch pen, brush, or pencil as long as you live."

19

Alice James remarked in her diary of "the ignorant asininity of the medical profession in its treatment of nervous disorders" and Elaine Showalter in her book *The Female Malady: Women, Madness, and English Culture, 1830–1980,* (1985) delineates the brutal treatment of psychological disorders in women. Gilman's revenge in her fiction has become part of feminist consciousness as well as literary history. After being out of print for almost fifty years, "The Yellow Wallpaper" is now, in Showalter's words, a "haunting and passionate protest against the rest cure, . . . a modern feminist classic, a paradigmatic text for critics and historians looking at the relation between sex roles, madness, and creativity."

Gilman's autobiography—called "a misleading book" by one critic because it does not admit the angst and uncertainty revealed in her diaries—has also been retrieved from obscurity and reprinted with a comprehensive introduction by Ann J. Lane, the historian and biographer of *To "Herland" and Beyond: The Life and Work of Charlotte Perkins Gilman.*

From *The Living of Charlotte Perkins Gilman*

. . . We were really very happy together. There was nothing to prevent it but that increasing depression of mine. My diary is full of thankfulness for happiness and prayers for deserving it, full of Walter's constant kindness and helpfulness in the work when I was not well—the not-wellness coming oftener and oftener.

The record dwells on delectable meals in full enumeration, as if I was a school-boy. As a note on current prices this: "Dinner vilely expensive, chops, six little chops, .50 cts.!" "Walter home about five. Brings me flowers. Dear boy!" "Walter gets most of the breakfast." "Amuse ourselves in the evenings with funny drawings." These were works of art of an unusual nature, a head and body to the waist being drawn by one of us and the paper folded back at the waistline leaving the sides indicated; and then the other finished the legs, not knowing in the least what the other part was like. The results are surprising.

I think Walter was happy. A most successful exhibition in Boston had established him more favorably and enabled him to meet domestic expenses; and an order for a set of large etchings was added.

A lover more tender, a husband more devoted, woman could not ask. He helped in the housework more and more as my strength began to fail, for something was going wrong from the first. The steady cheerfulness, the strong, tireless spirit sank away. A sort of gray fog drifted across my mind, a cloud that grew and darkened.

"Feel sick and remain so all day." "Walter stays home and does everything for me." "Walter gets breakfast." October 10th: "I have coffee in bed mornings while Walter briskly makes fires and gets breakfast." "O dear! That I should come to this!" By October 13th the diary stops altogether, until January 1, 1885. "My journal has been long neglected by reason of ill-health. This day has not been a successful one as I was sicker than for some weeks. Walter also was not very well, and stayed at home, principally on my account. He had worked for me and for us both, waited on me in every tenderest way, played to me, read to me, done all for me as he always does. God be thanked for my husband."

February 16th: "A well-nigh sleepless night. Hot, cold, hot, restless, nervous, hysterical. Walter is love and patience personified, gets up over and over, gets me warm wintergreen, bromide, hot foot-bath, more bromide—all to no purpose."

Then, with impressive inscription: "March 23rd, 1885. This day, at about five minutes to nine in the morning, was born my child, Katharine."

Brief ecstasy. Long pain.
Then years of joy again.

Motherhood means giving. . . .

We had attributed all my increasing weakness and depression to pregnancy, and looked forward to prompt recovery now. All was normal and ordinary enough, but I was already plunged into an extreme of nervous exhaustion which no one observed or understood in the least. Of all angelic babies that darling was the best, a heavenly baby. My nurse, Maria Pease of Boston, was a joy while she lasted, and remained a lifelong friend. But after her month was up and I was left alone with the child I broke so fast that we sent for my mother, who had been visiting Thomas in Utah, and that baby-worshipping grandmother came to take care of the darling, I being incapable of doing that—or anything else, a mental wreck.

Presently we moved to a better house, on Humboldt Avenue near by, and a German servant girl of unparalleled virtues was installed. Here was a charming home; a loving and devoted husband; an exquisite baby, healthy, intelligent and good; a highly competent mother to run things; a wholly satisfactory servant—and I lay all day on the lounge and cried.

CHAPTER VIII

The Breakdown

In those days a new disease had dawned on the medical horizon. It was called "nervous prostration." No one knew much about it, and there were many who openly scoffed, saying it was only a new name for laziness. To be recognizably ill one must be confined to one's bed, and preferably in pain.

That a heretofore markedly vigorous young woman, with every comfort about her, should collapse in this lamentable manner was inexplicable. "You should use your will," said earnest friends. I had used it, hard and long, perhaps too hard and too long; at any rate it wouldn't work now.

"Force some happiness into your life," said one sympathizer. "Take an agreeable book to bed with you, occupy your mind with pleasant things." She did not realize that I was unable to read, and that my mind was exclusively occupied with unpleasant things. This disorder involved a growing melancholia, and that, as those know who have tasted it, consists of every painful mental sensation, shame, fear, remorse, a blind oppressive confusion, utter weakness, a steady brain-ache that fills the conscious mind with crowding images of distress.

The misery is doubtless as physical as a toothache, but a brain, of its own nature, gropes for reasons for its misery. Feeling the sensation fear, the mind suggests every possible calamity; the sensation shame—remorse—and one remembers every mistake and misdeeds of a lifetime, and grovels to the earth in abasement.

"If you would get up and do something you would feel better," said my mother. I rose drearily, and essayed to brush up the floor a little, with a dustpan and small whiskbroom, but soon dropped those implements exhausted, and wept again in helpless shame.

I, the ceaselessly industrious, could do no work of any kind. I was so weak that the knife and fork sank from my hands—too tired to eat. I could not read nor write nor paint nor sew nor talk nor listen to talking, nor anything. I lay on that lounge and wept all day. The tears ran down into my ears on either side. I went to bed crying, woke in the night crying, sat on the edge of the bed in the morning and cried—from sheer continuous pain. Not physical, the doctors examined me and found nothing the matter.

The only physical pain I ever knew, besides dentistry and one sore finger, was having the baby, and I would rather have had a baby every week than suffer as I suffered in my mind. A constant dragging weariness miles below zero. Absolute incapacity. Absolute misery. To the spirit it was as if one were an armless, legless, eyeless, voiceless cripple. Prominent among the tumbling suggestions of a suffering brain was the thought, "You did it yourself! You did it yourself! You had health and strength and hope and glorious work before you—and you threw it all away. You were called to serve humanity, and you cannot serve yourself. No good as a wife, no good as a mother, no good at anything. And you did it yourself!". . .

The baby? I nursed her for five months. I would hold her close—that lovely child!—and instead of love and happiness, feel only pain. The tears ran down on my breast. . . . Nothing was more utterly bitter than this, that even motherhood brought no joy.

The doctor said I must wean her, and go away, for a change. So she was duly weaned and throve finely on Mellins' Food, drinking eagerly from the cup—no bottle needed. With mother there and the excellent maid I was free to go.

Those always kind friends, the Channings, had gone to Pasadena to live, and invited me to spend the winter with them. Feeble and hopeless I set forth, armed with tonics and sedatives, to cross the continent. From the moment the wheels began to turn, the train to move, I felt better. A visit to my brother in Utah broke the journey. . . .

Pasadena was then but little changed from the sheep ranch it used to be. The Channings had bought a beautiful place by the little reservoir at the corner of Walnut Street and Orange Avenue. Already their year-old trees were shooting up unbelievably, their flowers a glory.

The Arroyo Seco was then wild and clean, its steep banks a tangle of loveliness. About opposite us a point ran out where stood a huge twin live oak, still to be seen, but not to be reached by strangers. There was no house by them then, callas bloomed by the hydrant, and sweet alyssum ran wild in the grass.

Never before had my passion for beauty been satisfied. This place did not seem like earth, it was paradise. Kind and congenial friends, pleasant society, amusement, out-door sports, the blessed mountains, the long, unbroken sweep of the valley, with snow-peaks at the far eastern end—with such surroundings I recovered so fast, to outward appearance at least, that I was taken for a vigorous young girl. Hope came back, love came back, I was eager to get home to husband and child, life was bright again.

The return trip was made a little sooner than I had intended because of a railroad war of unparalleled violence which drove prices down unbelievably. It seemed foolish not to take advantage of it, and I bought my ticket from Los Angeles to Chicago, standard, for $5.00. If I had waited for a few days more it could have been bought for $1. The eastern end was unchanged, twenty dollars from Chicago to Boston, but that cut-throat competition was all over the western roads, the sleepers had every berth filled, often two in each. So many traveled that it was said the roads made quite as much money as usual.

Leaving California in March, in the warm rush of its rich spring, I found snow in Denver, and from then on hardly saw the sun for a fortnight. I reached home with a heavy bronchial cold, which hung on long, the dark fog rose again in my mind, the miserable weakness—within a month I was as low as before leaving. . . .

This was a worse horror than before, for now I saw the stark fact—that I was well while away and sick while at home—a heartening prospect! Soon ensued the same utter prostration, the unbearable inner misery, the ceaseless tears. A new tonic had been invented, Essence of Oats, which was given me, and did some good for a time. I pulled up enough to do a little painting that fall, but soon slipped down again and stayed down. An old friend of my mother's, dear Mrs. Diman, was so grieved at this condition that she gave me a hundred dollars and urged me to go away somewhere and get cured.

At that time the greatest nerve specialist in the country was Dr. S. W. Mitchell of Philadelphia. Through the kindness of a friend of Mr. Stetson's living in that city, I went to him and took "the rest cure"; went with the utmost confidence, prefacing the visit with a long letter giving "the history of the case" in a way a modern psychologist would have appreciated. Dr. Mitchell only thought it proved self-conceit. He had a prejudice against the Beechers. "I've had two women of your blood here already," he told me scornfully. This eminent physician was well versed in two kinds of nervous prostration; that of the business man exhausted from too much work, and the society woman exhausted from too much play. The kind I had was evidently beyond him. But he did reassure me on one point—there was no dementia, he said, only hysteria.

I was put to bed and kept there. I was fed, bathed, rubbed, and responded with the vigorous body of twenty-six. As far as he could see there was nothing the matter with me, so after a month of this agreeable treatment he sent me home, with this prescription:

"Live as domestic a life as possible. Have your child with you all the time." (Be it remarked that if I did but dress the baby it left me shaking and crying—certainly far from a healthy companionship for her, to say nothing of the effect on me.) "Lie down an hour after each meal. Have but two hours' intellectual life a day. And never touch pen, brush or pencil as long as you live."

I went home, followed those directions rigidly for months, and came perilously near to losing my mind. The mental agony grew so unbearable that I would sit blankly moving my head from side to side— to get out from under the pain. Not physical pain, not the least "headache" even, just mental torment, and so heavy in its nightmare gloom that it seemed real enough to dodge.

I made a rag baby, hung it on a doorknob and played with it. I would crawl into remote closets and under beds—to hide from the grinding pressure of that profound distress. . . .

Finally, in the fall of '87, in a moment of clear vision, we agreed to separate, to get a divorce. There was no quarrel, no blame for either one, never an unkind word between us, unbroken mutual affection— but it seemed plain that if I went crazy it would do my husband no good, and be a deadly injury to my child.

What this meant to the young artist, the devoted husband, the loving father, was so bitter a grief and loss that nothing would have justified breaking the marriage save this worse loss which threatened. It was not a choice between going and staying, but between going, sane, and staying, insane. If I had been of the slightest use to him or to the child, I would have "stuck it," as the English say. But this progressive weakening of the mind made a horror unnecessary to face; better for that dear child to have separated parents than a lunatic mother.

We had been married four years and more. This miserable condition of mind, this darkness, feebleness and gloom, had begun in those difficult years of courtship, had grown rapidly worse after marriage, and was now threatening utter loss; whereas I had repeated proof that the moment I left home I began to recover. It seemed right to give up a mistaken marriage.

Our mistake was mutual. If I had been stronger and wiser I should never have been persuaded into it. Our suffering was mutual too, his unbroken devotion, his manifold cares and labors in tending a sick wife, his adoring pride in the best of babies, all coming to naught, ending in utter failure—we sympathized with each other but faced a bitter necessity. The separation must come as soon as possible, the divorce must wait for conditions.

If this decision could have been reached sooner it would have been much better for me, the lasting mental injury would have been less. Such recovery as I have made in forty years, and the work accomplished, seem to show that the fear of insanity was not fulfilled, but the effects of nerve bankruptcy remain to this day. So much of my many failures, of misplay and misunderstanding and "queerness" is due to this lasting weakness, and kind friends so unfailingly refuse to allow for it, to believe it, that I am now going to some length in stating the case.

That part of the ruin was due to the conditions of childhood I do not doubt, and part to the rigid stoicism and constant effort in character-building of my youth; I was "over-trained," had wasted my substance in riotous—virtues. But that the immediate and continuing cause was mismarriage is proved by the instant rebound when I left home and as instant relapse on returning.

After I was finally free, in 1890, wreck though I was, there was a surprising output of work, some of my best. I think that if I could have had a period of care and rest then, I might have made full recovery. But the ensuing four years in California were the hardest of my life. The result has been a lasting loss of power, total in some directions, partial in others; the necessity for a laboriously acquired laziness foreign to both temperament and conviction, a crippled life.

But since my public activities do not show weakness, nor my writings, and since brain and nerve disorder is not visible, short of lunacy or literal "prostration," this lifetime of limitation and wretchedness, when I mention it, is flatly disbelieved. When I am forced to refuse invitations, to back out of work that seems easy, to own that I cannot read a heavy book, apologetically alleging this weakness of mind, friends gibber amiably, "I wish I had your mind!" I wish they had, for a while, as a punishment for doubting my word. What confuses them is the visible work I have been able to accomplish. They see activity, achievement, they do not see blank months of idleness; nor can they see what the work would have been if the powerful mind I had to begin with had not broken at twenty-four. . . .

The utter failure and loss of my marriage was bitter enough, but compensated by the blessed child; the loss of health was worse, the weakness, the dark, feeble mind. But my religion remained, and my social philosophy, that perception of the organic unity of the group which so dwarfs all individual pain. When able to think clearly I faced the situation thus:

"Thirty years old. Made a wrong marriage—lots of people do. Am heavily damaged, but not dead. May live a long time. It is intellectually conceivable that I may recover strength enough to do some part of my work. I will assume this to be true, and act on it." And I did. . . .

In that first year of freedom I wrote some thirty-three short articles, and twenty-three poems, besides ten more child-verses. Almost all the poems were given to various progressive papers, the one or two sold brought but two or three dollars. The same with the articles, though I did sell more of them, at prices like ten dollars or six dollars and seventy-five cents.

★ ★ ★

The first real success, in that first year, was my poem "Similar Cases," concerning which I received this unforgettable letter from William Dean Howells:

BOSTON, June 9th., 1890.

DEAR MADAM,

I have been wishing ever since I first read it—and I've read it many times with unfailing joy—to thank you for your poem in the April *Nationalist*. We have nothing since the Biglow Papers half so good for a good cause as "Similar Cases."

And just now I've read in *The Woman's Journal* your "Women of To-day." It is as good almost as the other, and dreadfully true.

Yours sincerely,
WM. DEAN HOWELLS.

That was a joy indeed. I rushed over to show Grace and the others. There was no man in the country whose good opinion I would rather have had. I felt like a real "author" at last. . . .

. . . Besides "Similar Cases" the most outstanding piece of work of 1890 was "The Yellow Wallpaper." It is a description of a case of nervous breakdown beginning something as mine did, and treated as Dr. S. Weir Mitchell treated me with what I considered the inevitable result, progressive insanity.

This I sent to Mr. Howells, and he tried to have the *Atlantic Monthly* print it, but Mr. Scudder, then the editor, sent it back with this brief card:

DEAR MADAM,

Mr. Howells has handed me this story.

I could not forgive myself if I made others as miserable as I have made myself!

Sincerely yours,
H. E. SCUDDER.

This was funny. The story was meant to be dreadful, and succeeded. I suppose he would have sent back one of Poe's on the same ground. Later I put it in the hands of an agent who had written me, one Henry Austin, and he placed it with the *New England Magazine*. Time passed, much time, and at length I wrote to the editor of that periodical to this effect:

DEAR SIR,

A story of mine, "The Yellow Wallpaper," was printed in your issue of May, 1891. Since you do not pay on receipt of ms. nor on publication, nor within six months of publication, may I ask if you pay at all, and if so at what rates?

They replied with some heat that they had paid the agent, Mr. Austin. He, being taxed with it, denied having got the money. It was only forty dollars anyway! As a matter of fact I never got a cent for it till later publishers brought it out in book form, and very little then. But it made a tremendous impression. A protest was sent to the Boston *Transcript,* headed "Perilous Stuff"—

TO THE EDITOR OF THE TRANSCRIPT:

In a well-known magazine has recently appeared a story entitled "The Yellow Wallpaper." It is a sad story of a young wife passing the gradations from slight mental derangement to raving lunacy. It is graphically told, in a somewhat sensational style, which makes it difficult to lay aside, after the first glance, til it is finished, holding the reader in morbid fascination to the end. It certainly seems open to serious question if such literature should be permitted in print.

The story can hardly, it would seem, give pleasure to any reader, and to many whose lives have been touched through the dearest ties by this dread disease, it must bring the keenest pain. To others, whose lives have become a struggle against an heredity of mental derangement, such literature contains deadly peril. Should such stories be allowed to pass without severest censure?

M.D.

Another doctor, one Brummel Jones, of Kansas City, Missouri, wrote me in 1892 concerning this story, saying: "When I read 'The Yellow Wallpaper' I was very much pleased with it; when I read it again I was delighted with it, and now that I have read it again I am overwhelmed with the delicacy of your touch and the correctness of portrayal. From a doctor's standpoint, and I am a doctor, you have made a success. So far as I know, and I am fairly well up in literature, there has been no detailed account of incipient insanity." Then he tells of an opium addict who refused to be treated on the ground that physicians had no real knowledge of the disease, but who returned to Dr. Jones, bringing a paper of his on the opium habit, shook it in his face and said, "Doctor, you've been there!" To which my correspondent added, "Have you ever been—er—; but of course you haven't." I replied that I had been as far as one could go and get back.

One of the *New England Magazine's* editors wrote to me asking if the story was founded on fact, and I gave him all I decently could of my case as a foundation for the tale. Later he explained that he had a friend who was in similar trouble, even to hallucinations about her wallpaper, and whose family were treating her as in the tale, that he had not dared show them my story till he knew that it was true, in part at least, and that when he did they were so frightened by it, so impressed by the clear implication of what ought to have been done, that they changed her wallpaper and the treatment of the case—and she recovered! This was triumph indeed.

But the real purpose of the story was to reach Dr. S. Weir Mitchell, and convince him of the error of his ways. I sent him a copy as soon as it came out, but got no response. However, many years later, I met some one who knew close friends of Dr. Mitchell's who said he had told them that he had changed his treatment of nervous prostration since reading "The Yellow Wallpaper." If that is a fact, I have not lived in vain. . . .

ELLEN GLASGOW
(1873–1945)

◆

ELLEN GLASGOW grew up in Richmond, Virginia, the eighth of
ten children born to a gracious, Episcopal mother of Tidewater origins
and a stern, Scotch-Irish, Presbyterian Calvinist father, the director of
the ancient Richmond foundry known as the Tredegar Iron Works.
Her house at Number One West Main Street, with its exquisite rear
garden and upstairs study where she wrote for most of her life, still
stands as an architectural gem on the map of America's literary land-
scapes. As Blair Rouse, the editor of Glasgow's Letters, tells the family
history, the daughter's sympathies "were with her mother . . . yet her
father's character and that of his people, . . . in so far as it meant . . .
stern determination . . . found its way into her work, though their narrow, even cruel, religion she rejected almost instinctively." The ancestral
iron will rings through one of her earliest letters to her publisher in
1897, the year her first book was published: "I will become a great
novelist or none at all." A paradoxical defiance and acceptance of her
ancestral Southern tradition animates the fiction that sustains her reputation, *Barren Ground* (1925), *The Sheltered Life* (1932), and *Vein of Iron*
(1935) as well as her posthumously published autobiography excerpted
here, *The Woman Within* (1954), "a beautiful and wise volume," in the
words of her friend and fellow Virginia novelist, James Branch Cabell.
Glasgow, in a note to her Literary Executors, described her memoirs as
a work "written in great suffering of mind and body," an attempt "to
make a completely honest portrayal of an interior world, . . . the life of
the solitary spirit." Her intimate experience of the interiority of the self
comes in part from her "damnable deafness," as she referred to it, an
affliction that began in her early adult years, and left her feeling always
an exile in the public world. She began *The Woman Within* in 1934,
worked on it intermittently until she presented it to her executors for
deposit in the First Bank of Richmond in 1944, a year before she died.
Though she warned them the manuscript would "need a lot of edit-
ing," the executors, finding it "a document of great psychological interest," . . . "have preferred to do as little tampering as possible." "She
appears," to quote Rouse's assessment of the autobiography, "to have
sought conscientiously to present the whole truth about herself and her

life as clearly as she could see it." That truth includes her account of the workings of her creative life as well as, in her executors' words, "the really secret life of the woman herself." A passionate lover, friend, sister, traveler, and artist, she received much recognition in her lifetime as a major American novelist from such literary colleagues and friends as Carl Van Doren, Van Wyck Brooks, H. L. Mencken, Marjorie Kinnan Rawlings, and Maxwell Perkins.

From *The Woman Within*

"Early Sorrow"

I could not have been more than ten years old when I was overtaken by a tragic occurrence which plunged my childhood into grief and anxiety, and profoundly affected, not only my mind and character, but my whole future life. In a single night, or so it seemed to us, my mother was changed from a source of radiant happiness into a chronic invalid, whose nervous equilibrium was permanently damaged. A severe shock, in a critical period, altered her so completely that I should scarcely have known her if I had come upon her after a brief absence. She, who had been a fountain of joy, became an increasing anxiety, a perpetual ache in the heart. Although she recovered her health, in a measure, her buoyant emotion toward life was utterly lost. Even now, when she has been dead so long, I cannot write of these things without a stab of that old inarticulate agony. . . .

From the mist and sunshine of those years a few stark shapes emerge. We had moved, now, into the big gray house on the corner of Main Street, and after my mother's nervous breakdown, we left Jerdone Castle forever. Mother had conceived a horror of the place I loved, and she could not stay on there without greater anguish of mind.

For Rebe, and for me, leaving the farm was like tearing up the very roots of our nature. This was the only place where I found health, where I had known a simple and natural life. It was the place where I had begun to write, and had discovered an object, if not a meaning, in the complicated pattern of my inner world. It was the place, too, where I had felt hours and even days of pure happiness, where I had rushed down the road to meet the advancing storm, while I felt in my heart the fine, pointed flame that is ecstasy.

All this was distressing, but far worse even than this was the enforced desertion of Pat, my beautiful pointer. For years, the memory of Pat, left with an overseer who might not be kind to him, would thrust up, like a dagger, into my dreams. What would they do with Pat when they moved? What would happen to him when he grew old? Why was it people made you do things that would break your heart always? Even now, I sometimes awake with a regret, that is half for Pat himself, and half a burning remorse for some act I have committed but cannot remember.

Only a delicate child, rendered morbid by circumstances, could have suffered as I suffered from that change to the city in summer. Though I went to school for a few months each year, until my health grew frail again and my nervous headaches returned, I would wonder all the way home whether I should find my mother cheerful or sad. Usually, she sent us off brightly; but the brightness would fade as soon as we turned the corner, and the deep despondency would creep over her. Once in those years she went away on her only visit to her brother, whom she had adored since she was a baby. He lived in Holly Springs, Mississippi, and the doctors advised the long trip as a diversion. Rebe went with her, and they were away several months. It was my first long separation from them, and I missed them both with an ache that was like physical pain. Most of my time was spent alone, for in our large family the three elder sisters lived in a different, and a larger, world, where they had their own interests and their own pleasures. No doubt they had their own troubles also, but they seemed, to us, creatures of a more fortunate sphere.

I still had little Toy, but, in Mother's absence, he was set apart, though I did not suspect this, as another victim. One afternoon, I could not find him when I was urged by my father to go to walk with Lizzie Patterson, and that night, after I had looked for him in vain, one of the servants told me that Father had had him put into a bag, and had given him to two men who worked at the Tredegar. They told me fearfully, wondering what "Miss Annie" (my mother) "would say when she came back"; but, without a word, I turned away and went straight to Father.

Rage convulsed me, the red rage that must have swept up from the jungles and the untamed mind of primitive man. And this rage—I have not ever forgotten it—contained every anger, every revolt I had ever felt in my life—the way I felt when I saw the black dog hunted, the way I felt when I watched old Uncle Henry taken away to the almshouse, the way I felt whenever I had seen people or animals hurt for the pleasure or profit of others. All these different rages were here; all had dissolved and intermingled with the fury of youth that is help-less. If I spoke words, I cannot recall them. I remember only that I picked up a fragile china vase on the mantelpiece and hurled it across the room. It shattered against the wall, and I can still hear the crash it made as it fell into fragments. Then I rushed into my room, and locked the door on my frightened sisters and the more frightened servants. I should never see Toy again, I knew. I had never seen Pat again. My father would not change his mind. Not once in my knowledge of him had he ever changed his mind or admitted that he was wrong—or even mistaken.

I poured out my heart in a letter to Mother. And she did not reply. Day after day, week after week, I waited, but when her letters came, they made no mention of her affection for my dog, or of the injustice from which I suffered so desperately. Not until long afterwards, when Mother was at home and ill again, did I discover the reason for her apparent neglect. Then, one afternoon, while I was studying my lessons in a corner of the library, I overheard my sister Emily, the eldest of the family, relate an amusing version of Toy's betrayal. It was a good opportunity to get rid of him, she explained, while Mother was away. He was sick and old and troublesome, and none of them liked him but Mother and Rebe and me. So they had meant to keep it a secret from Mother, and when they found that I had written, Emily had gone to the postmaster and asked him to return a letter which would give Mother a shock if she received it. And the postmaster had obligingly returned the letter from the post. An incredible incident to anyone who has not lived in a small Southern community.

The remembrance of children is a long remembrance, and the incidents often make milestones in a personal history. In those months of Mother's absence, I know that I broke forever with my childhood. For the first time I was standing alone, without the shelter and the comfort of her love and her sympathy. Her silence, inexplicable and utterly unlike her, seemed to thrust me still farther and farther into loneliness, until at last—for months may have the significance of years when one is very young—I began to love, not to fear, loneliness. During this time, and indeed through all my future life, I shrank from my father's presence; and only one of my elder sisters ever won my reluctant confidence. At the time, angry, defiant, utterly unsubdued by pleadings and rebukes, I told myself, obstinately, that if they cared nothing for my feelings, I would care nothing for theirs. For weeks I hated them all. I hated the things they believed in, the things they so innocently and charmingly pretended. I hated the sanctimonious piety that let people hurt helpless creatures. I hated the prayers and the hymns, and the red images that colored their drab music, the fountains filled with blood, the sacrifice of the lamb.

And, then, much to Father's distress, and to my sisters' consternation, I refused to attend divine service—and there was nothing left that they could do about it. My will, which was as strong as Father's, plunged its claws into the earth. Nothing, not lectures, not deprivations, not all the pressure they could bring, could ever make me again go with them to church.

If I had won nothing else, I had won liberty. Never again should I feel that I ought to believe, that older people were wiser and better than I was. Never again should I feel that I ought to pretend things were different. Dumbly, obstinately, I would stare back at them when they talked to me. I could not answer them. I could not refute my father when he opened the Bible, and read aloud, in his impressive voice, the sternest psalms in the Old Testament. All I could do was to shake my ignorant head, and reply that, even if all that was true, it made no difference to me. I was finished with that way of life before I had begun it.

And, then, in the midst of it all, while my mother was still away, I was seized, I was overwhelmed by a consuming desire to find out things for myself, to know the true from the false, the real from the make-believe. The longing was so intense that I flung myself on knowledge as a thirsty man might fling himself into a desert spring. I read everything in our library. History, poetry, fiction, archaic or merely picturesque, works on science, and even *The Westminister Confession of Faith*. Lizzie Patterson and Carrie Coleman came frequently in the afternoon; but even with them, my two closest friends, I felt that I had changed beyond understanding and recognition. They lived happy lives on the outside of things, accepting what they were taught, while I was devoured by this hunger to know, to discover some meaning, some underlying reason for the mystery and the pain of the world.

For I had ceased to be a child. My mind and the very pit of my stomach felt empty. I needed the kind of reality that was solid and hard and would stay by one.

When, at last, Mother and Rebe returned, I felt shy with them and váguely uncomfortable. It seemed to me, for the first few days at least, that they had changed, that they had seen things I had not seen, that they treasured recollections I could not share. Or perhaps I was the one who had changed. Something had gone out of me for good, and, in exchange, I had found something that, to me, was more precious. I had found the greatest consolation of my life; but I had found also an unconquerable loneliness. I had entered the long solitude that stretches on beyond the vanishing-point in the distance. . . .

MARY ANTIN
(1881–1949)

◆

"I was born, I have lived, and I have been made over." Such was the conviction with which MARY ANTIN, a Russian-Jewish immigrant to Boston just before the turn-of-the-century, began her autobiography, *The Promised Land* (1912). For her, coming to America and starting school assumed the significance of a religious conversion. The following excerpt demonstrates Antin's reverence and fervent gratitude to her new country: America is characterized by a kind of divine benevolence in contrast to the Old World of caste, pogroms, and dead-ended consciousness and experience. Her tone of absolute commitment to the New World and its egalitarian ethos recalls a similar emotional abandonment in the fiction and nonfiction of Anzia Yezierska, a Russian-Jewish immigrant to New York City. Antin arrived when she was thirteen, in the company of her mother, two sisters, and a younger brother; they were met by her father, who had gone on ahead three years before. Not long after their arrival, Antin wrote an account of the trip in Yiddish, *From Polotzk to Boston*.

Despite the poverty and bad luck of the family's early years in Boston, which Antin does not deny in her idealized account, she moved through what she represents as the holy grounds of urban public schools to eventually attend Barnard College and Columbia Teachers' College. She married a professor of paleontology and became a settlement worker at Hale House in Boston. She published two books about immigrants and immigration, the autobiographical *The Promised Land* and *They Who Knock at Our Gates: A Complete Gospel of Immigration* (1914).

Mary Dearborn, in her book *Pocahontas's Daughters: Gender and Ethnicity in American Culture* (1986), believes that Antin is not widely read today because, having thoroughly internalized the terms of the new dominant culture, including its stances toward authority, her autobiography "lack[s] any alternative, protesting voice." Werner Sollors, however, in *Beyond Ethnicity: Consent and Descent in American Culture* (1986), places Antin in the tradition of Phillis Wheatley. Both immigrants portrayed America "as a new Canaan," and Antin emphasized that the religious metaphor of the Promised Land "was especially suited to Jewish immigrants. . . . Both [women] claimed the American egalitarian promise defiantly by equating themselves with George Washington." Dearborn's analysis of the effects of public school education on the Antin children and their unacculturated parents—and the learning of English as the core experience of Americanization—recalls another later immigrant's rendering of the alienation of the generations within immigrant families—Richard Rodriguez's widely anthologized "Aria: A Memoir of a Bilingual Childhood" from his essays in his autobiography, *Hunger of Memory* (1982). So liberated does Antin feel within the new dispensation, however, that she devotes little energy to the theme of estrangement from the Old World parents, especially the father, unlike Rodriguez and other writer-immigrants and children of immigrants, Jade Snow Wong, Anzia Yezierska, and Maxine Hong Kingston (see page 347). Instead, she celebrates the possibilities that are now available to her. What has been lost, especially life in Russia, is not mourned; it's part of her new freedom.

From *The Promised Land*

Having made such good time across the ocean, I ought to be able to proceed no less rapidly on *terra firma,* where, after all, I am more at home. And yet here is where I falter. Not that I hesitated, even for the space of a breath, in my first steps in America. There was no time to hesitate. The most ignorant immigrant, on landing, proceeds to give and receive greetings, to eat, sleep, and rise, after the manner of his own country; wherein he is corrected, admonished, and laughed at, whether by interested friends or the most indifferent strangers; and his American experience is thus begun. The process is spontaneous on all sides, like the education of the child by the family circle. But while the most stupid nursery maid is able to contribute her part toward the result, we do not expect an analysis of the process to be furnished by any member of the family, least of all by the engaging infant. The philosophical maiden aunt alone, or some other witness equally psychological and aloof, is able to trace the myriad efforts by which the little Johnnie or Nellie acquires a secure hold on the disjointed parts of the huge plaything, life.

Now I was not exactly an infant when I was set down, on a May day some fifteen years ago, in this pleasant nursery of America. I had long since acquired the use of my faculties, and had collected some bits of experience, practical and emotional, and had even learned to give an account of them. Still, I had very little perspective, and my observations and comparisons were superficial. I was too much carried away to analyze the forces that were moving me. My Polotzk* I knew well before I began to judge it and experiment with it. America was bewilderingly strange, unimaginably complex, delightfully unexplored. I rushed impetuously out of the cage of my provincialism and looked eagerly about the brilliant universe. My question was, What have we here?— not, What does this mean? That query came much later. When I now become retrospectively introspective, I fall into the predicament of the centipede in the rhyme, who got along very smoothly until he was asked which leg came after which, whereupon he became so rattled that he couldn't take a step. I know I have come on a thousand feet, on wings, winds, and American machines,—I have leaped and run and climbed and crawled,—but to tell which step came after which I find a puzzling matter. Plenty of maiden aunts were present during my second infancy, in the guise of immigrant officials, school-teachers, settlement workers, and sundry other unprejudiced and critical observers. Their statistics I might properly borrow to fill the gaps in my recollections, but I am prevented by my sense of harmony. The individual, we know, is a creature unknown to the statistician, whereas I undertook to give the personal view of everything. So I am bound to unravel, as well as I can, the tangle of events, outer and inner, which made up the first breathless years of my American life. . . .

CHAPTER X
Initiation

It is not worth while to refer to voluminous school statistics to see just how many "green" pupils entered school last September, not knowing the days of the week in English, who next February will be declaiming patriotic verses in honor of George Washington and Abraham Lincoln, with a foreign accent, indeed, but with plenty of enthusiasm. It is enough to know that this hundred-fold miracle is common to the schools in every part of the United States where immigrants are received. And if I was one of Chelsea's hundred in 1894, it was only to be expected, since I was one of the older of the "green" children, and had had a start in my irregular schooling in Russia, and was carried along by a tremendous desire to learn, and had my family to cheer me on.

I was not a bit too large for my little chair and desk in the baby class, but my mind, of course, was too mature by six or seven years for the work. So as soon as I could understand what the teacher said in

---

*The village in Russia Antin came from. In the first part of her autobiography she remembers the pogroms she witnessed as a small child.

class, I was advanced to the second grade. This was within a week after Miss Nixon took me in hand. But I do not mean to give my dear teacher all the credit for my rapid progress, nor even half the credit. I shall divide it with her on behalf of my race and my family. I was Jew enough to have an aptitude for language in general, and to bend my mind earnestly to my task; I was Antin enough to read each lesson with my heart, which gave me an inkling of what was coming next, and so carried me along by leaps and bounds. As for the teacher, she could best explain what theory she followed in teaching us foreigners to read. I can only describe the method, which was so simple that I wish holiness could be taught in the same way.

There were about half a dozen of us beginners in English, in age from six to fifteen. Miss Nixon made a special class of us, and aided us so skilfully and earnestly in our endeavors to "see-a-cat," and "hear-a-dog-bark," and "look-at-the-hen," that we turned over page after page of the ravishing history, eager to find out how the common world looked, smelled, and tasted in the strange speech. The teacher knew just when to let us help each other out with a word in our own tongue,—it happened that we were all Jews,—and so, working all together, we actually covered more ground in a lesson than the native classes, composed entirely of the little tots.

But we stuck—stuck fast—at the definite article; and sometimes the lesson resolved itself into a species of lingual gymnastics, in which we all looked as if we meant to bite our tongues off. Miss Nixon was pretty, and she must have looked well with her white teeth showing in the act; but at the time I was too solemnly occupied to admire her looks. I did take great pleasure in her smile of approval, whenever I pronounced well; and her patience and perseverance in struggling with us over that thick little word are becoming to her even now, after fifteen years. It is not her fault if any of us to-day give a buzzing sound to the dreadful English *th*.

I shall never have a better opportunity to make public declaration of my love for the English language. I am glad that American history runs, chapter for chapter, the way it does; for thus America came to be the country I love so dearly. I am glad, most of all, that the Americans began by being Englishmen, for thus did I come to inherit this beautiful language in which I think. It seems to me that in any other language happiness is not so sweet, logic is not so clear. I am not sure that I could believe in my neighbors as I do if I thought about them in un-English words. I could almost say that my conviction of immortality is bound up with the English of its promise. And as I am attached to my prejudices, I must love the English language!

Whenever the teachers did anything special to help me over my private difficulties, my gratitude went out to them, silently. It meant so much to me that they halted the lesson to give me a lift, that I needs must love them for it. Dear Miss Carrol, of the second grade, would be amazed to hear what small things I remember, all because I was so impressed at the time with her readiness and sweetness in taking notice of my difficulties.

Says Miss Carrol, looking straight at me:—

"If Johnnie has three marbles, and Charlie has twice as many, how many marbles has Charlie?"

I raise my hand for permission to speak.

"Teacher, I don't know vhat is tvice."

Teacher beckons me to her, and whispers to me the meaning of the strange word, and I am able to write the sum correctly. It's all in the day's work with her; with me, it is a special act of kindness and efficiency.

She whom I found in the next grade became so dear a friend that I can hardly name her with the rest, though I mention none of them lightly. Her approval was always dear to me, first because she was "Teacher," and afterwards, as long as she lived, because she was my Miss Dillingham. Great was my grief, therefore, when, shortly after my admission to her class, I incurred discipline, the first, and next to the last, time in my school career.

The class was repeating in chorus the Lord's Prayer, heads bowed on desks. I was doing my best to keep up by the sound; my mind could not go beyond the word "hallowed," for which I had not found the meaning. In the middle of the prayer a Jewish boy across the aisle trod on my foot to get my attention. "You must not say that," he admonished in a solemn whisper; "it's Christian." I whispered back that it wasn't, and went on to the "Amen." I did not know but what he was right, but the name of Christ was not in the prayer, and I was bound to do everything that the class did. If I had any Jewish scruples, they were lagging away behind my interest in school affairs. How American this was: two pupils side by side in the schoolroom, each holding to his own opinion, but both submitting to the common law; for the boy at least bowed his head as the teacher ordered.

But all Miss Dillingham knew of it was that two of her pupils whispered during morning prayer, and she must discipline them. So I was degraded from the honor row to the lowest row, and it was many a day before I forgave that young missionary; it was not enough for my vengeance that he suffered punishment with me. Teacher, of course, heard us both defend ourselves, but there was a time and a place for religious arguments, and she meant to help us remember that point. . . .

CHAPTER XVI

Dover Street

What happened next was Dover Street.

And what was Dover Street?

Ask rather, What was it not? Dover Street was my fairest garden of girlhood, a gate of paradise, a window facing on a broad avenue of life. Dover Street was a prison, a school of discipline, a battlefield of sordid strife. The air in Dover Street was heavy with evil odors of degradation, but a breath from the uppermost heavens rippled through, whispering of infinite things. In Dover Street the dragon poverty gripped me for a last fight, but I overthrew the hideous creature, and sat on his neck as on a throne. In Dover Street I was shackled with a hundred chains of disadvantage, but with one free hand I planted little seeds, right there in the mud of shame, that blossomed into the honeyed rose of widest freedom. In Dover Street there was often no loaf on the table, but the hand of some noble friend was ever in mine. The night in Dover Street was rent with the cries of wrong, but the thunders of truth crashed through the pitiful clamor and died out in prophetic silences.

Outwardly, Dover Street is a noisy thoroughfare cut through a South End slum, in every essential the same as Wheeler Street. Turn down any street in the slums, at random, and call it by whatever name you please, you will observe there the same fashions of life, death, and endurance. Every one of those streets is a rubbish heap of damaged humanity, and it will take a powerful broom and an ocean of soapsuds to clean it out.

Dover Street is intersected, near its eastern end, where we lived, by Harrison Avenue. That street is to the South End what Salem Street is to the North End. It is the heart of the South End ghetto, for the greater part of its length; although its northern end belongs to the realm of Chinatown. Its multifarious business bursts through the narrow shop doors, and overruns the basements, the sidewalk, the street itself, in pushcarts and open-air stands. Its multitudinous population bursts through the greasy tenement doors, and floods the corridors, the doorsteps, the gutters, the side streets, pushing in and out among the pushcarts, all day long and half the night besides.

Rarely as Harrison Avenue is caught asleep, even more rarely is it found clean. Nothing less than a fire or flood would cleanse this street. Even Passover cannot quite accomplish this feat. For although the tenements may be scrubbed to their remotest corners, on this one occasion, the cleansing stops at the curbstone. A great deal of the filthy rubbish accumulated in a year is pitched into the street, often through the windows; and what the ashman on his daily round does not remove is left to be trampled to powder, in which form it steals back into the houses from which it was so lately removed. . . .

I was not unhappy on Dover Street; quite the contrary. Everything of consequence was well with me. Poverty was a superficial, temporary matter; it vanished at the touch of money. Money in America was plentiful; it was only a matter of getting some of it, and I was on my way to the mint. If Dover Street was not a pleasant place to abide in, it was only a wayside house. And I was really happy, actively happy, in the exercise of my mind in Latin, mathematics, history, and the rest; the things that suffice a studious girl in the middle teens.

Still I had moments of depression, when my whole being protested against the life of the slum. I resented the familiarity of my vulgar neighbors. I felt myself defiled by the indecencies I was compelled to witness. Then it was I took to running away from home. I went out in the twilight and walked for hours, my blind feet leading me. I did not care where I went. If I lost my way, so much the better; I never wanted to see Dover Street again.

But behold, as I left the crowds behind, and the broader avenues were spanned by the open sky, my grievances melted away, and I fell to dreaming of things that neither hurt nor pleased. A fringe of trees against the sunset became suddenly the symbol of the whole world, and I stood and gazed and asked questions of it. The sunset faded; the trees withdrew. The wind went by, but dropped no hint in my ear. The evening star leaped out between the clouds, and sealed the secret with a seal of splendor.

A favorite resort of mine, after dark, was the South Boston Bridge, across South Bay and the Old Colony Railroad. This was so near home that I could go there at any time when the confusion in the house drove me out, or I felt the need of fresh air. I liked to stand leaning on the bridge railing, and look down on the dim tangle of railroad tracks below. I could barely see them branching out, elbowing, winding, and sliding out into the night in pairs. I was fascinated by the dotted lights, the significant red and green of signal lamps. These simple things stood for a complexity that it made me dizzy to think of. Then the blackness below me was split by the fiery eye of a monster engine, his breath enveloped me in blinding clouds, his long body shot by, rattling a hundred claws of steel; and he was gone, with an imperative shriek that shook me where I stood.

So would I be, swift on my rightful business, picking out my proper track from the million that cross it, pausing for no obstacles, sure of my goal.

After my watches on the bridge I often stayed up to write or study. It is late before Dover Street begins to go to bed. It is past midnight before I feel that I am alone. Seated in my stiff little chair before my narrow table, I gather in the night sounds through the open window, curious to assort and define them. As, little by little, the city settles down to sleep, the volume of sound diminishes, and the qualities of particular sounds stand out. The electric car lurches by with silent gong, taking the empty track by leaps, humming to itself in the invisible distance. A benighted team swings recklessly around the corner, sharp under my rattling window panes, the staccato pelting of hoofs on the cobblestones changed suddenly to an even pounding on the bridge. A few pedestrians hurry by, their heavy boots all out of step. The distant thoroughfares have long ago ceased their murmur, and I know that a million lamps shine idly in the idle streets.

My sister sleeps quietly in the little bed. The rhythmic dripping of a faucet is audible through the flat. It is so still that I can hear the paper crackling on the wall. Silence upon silence is added to the night; only the kitchen clock is the voice of my brooding thoughts,—ticking, ticking, ticking.

Suddenly the distant whistle of a locomotive breaks the stillness with a long-drawn wail. Like a threatened trouble, the sound comes nearer, piercingly near; then it dies out in a mangled silence, complaining to the last.

The sleepers stir in their beds. Somebody sighs, and the burden of all his trouble falls upon my heart. A homeless cat cries in the alley, in the voice of a human child. And the ticking of the kitchen clock is the voice of my troubled thoughts.

Many things are revealed to me as I sit and watch the world asleep. But the silence asks me many questions that I cannot answer; and I am glad when the tide of sound begins to return, by little and little, and I welcome the clatter of tin cans that announces the milkman. I cannot see him in the dusk, but I know his wholesome face has no problem in it.

It is one flight up to the roof; it is a leap of the soul to the sunrise. The morning mist rests lightly on chimneys and roofs and walls, wreathes the lampposts, and floats in gauzy streamers down the streets. Distant buildings are massed like palace walls, with turrets and spires lost in the rosy clouds. I love my beautiful city spreading all about me. I love the world. I love my place in the world. . . .

The memory of my experience on Dover Street became the strength of my convictions, the illumined index of my purpose, the aureola of my happiness. And if I paid for those lessons with days of privation and dread, with nights of tormenting anxiety, I count the price cheap. Who would not go to a little trouble to find out what life is made of? Life in the slums spins busily as a schoolboy's top, and one who has heard its humming never forgets. I look forward to telling, when I get to be a master of language, what I read in the crooked cobblestones when I revisited Dover Street the other day.

Dover Street was never really my residence—at least, not the whole of it. It happened to be the nook where my bed was made, but I inhabited the City of Boston. In the pearl-misty morning, in the ruby-red evening, I was empress of all I surveyed from the roof of the tenement house. I could point in any direction and name a friend who would welcome me there. Off towards the northwest, in the direction of Harvard Bridge, which some day I should cross on my way to Radcliffe College, was one of my favorite palaces, whither I resorted every day after school.

A low, wide-spreading building with a dignified granite front it was, flanked on all sides by noble old churches, museums, and schoolhouses, harmoniously disposed around a spacious triangle, called Copley Square. Two thoroughfares that came straight from the green suburbs swept by my palace, one on either side, converged at the apex of the triangle, and pointed off, past the Public Garden, across the historic Common, to the domed State House sitting on a height.

It was my habit to go very slowly up the low, broad steps to the palace entrance, pleasing my eyes with the majestic lines of the building, and lingering to read again the carved inscriptions: *Public Library—Built by the People—Free to All.*

Did I not say it was my palace? Mine, because I was a citizen; mine, though I was born an alien; mine, though I lived on Dover Street. My palace—*mine!*

I loved to lean against a pillar in the entrance hall, watching the people go in and out. Groups of children hushed their chatter at the entrance, and skipped, whispering and giggling in their fists, up the grand stairway, patting the great stone lions at the top, with an eye on the aged policemen down below. Spectacled scholars came slowly down the stairs, loaded with books, heedless of the lofty arches that echoed their steps. Visitors from out of town lingered long in the entrance hall, studying the inscriptions and symbols on the marble floor. And I loved to stand in the midst of all this, and remind myself that I was there, that I had a right to be there, that I was at home there. All these eager children, all these fine-browed women, all these scholars going home to write learned books—I and they had this glorious thing in common, this noble treasure house of learning. It was wonderful to say, *This is mine;* it was thrilling to say, *This is ours.*

I visited every part of the building that was open to the public. I spent rapt hours studying the Abbey pictures. I repeated to myself lines from Tennyson's poem before the glowing scenes of the Holy Grail. Before the "Prophets" in the gallery above I was mute, but echoes of the Hebrew Psalms I had long forgotten throbbed somewhere in the depths of my consciousness. The Chavannes series around the main staircase I did not enjoy for years. I thought the pictures looked faded, and their symbolism somehow failed to move me at first.

Bates Hall was the place where I spent my longest hours in the library. I chose a seat far at one end, so that looking up from my books I would get the full effect of the vast reading-room. I felt the grand spaces under the soaring arches as a personal attribute of my being. . . .

Here is where I liked to remind myself of Polotzk, the better to bring out the wonder of my life. That I who was born in the prison of the Pale should roam at will in the land of freedom was a marvel that it did me good to realize. That I who was brought up to my teens almost without a book should be set down in the midst of all the books that ever were written was a miracle as great as any on record. That an out-cast should become a privileged citizen, that a beggar should dwell in a palace—this was a romance more thrilling than poet ever sung. Surely I was rocked in an enchanted cradle. . . .

FLORIDA SCOTT-MAXWELL
(1883–1979)

◆

Born in Orange Park, Florida, FLORIDA SCOTT-MAXWELL was educated at home until she was ten, briefly attended public school in Pittsburgh, then went back to lessons at home, and finally gave up schooling to go on the stage at sixteen. At twenty she gave up acting and began to write short stories. In 1910 she married and went to live in her husband's native Scotland. Until 1935 she worked for women's suffrage, wrote plays, and tended her children and flowers. Among her books are *Towards Relationships* (1939), *Women and Sometimes Men* (1957), and the plays *The Flash-point* (1914), *They Knew How to Die* (1931), and *Many Women* (1933). In 1933 she trained for another career as an analytical psychologist, studying under Carl Jung. She practiced in psychology clinics in Scotland and England. Her memoir, *The Measure of My Days,* written when she was eighty-five and the source of the following selection, is composed of her notebook meditations on the most profound themes of life and literature: the meaning of life itself, the mystery of suffering and of evil, and the losses of health and friends and certainty that mark the passage of time. Yet the small meditative essays and ruminations of her memoir are not grim. With sensitivity and grace, Florida Scott-Maxwell celebrates life as she wonders about its most incomprehensible features. She makes us feel her pleasure in rereading books long forgotten, such as Henry Adams's *Mont-Saint-Michel;* in being with friends and being alone; in writing her thoughts—the "worries of an old heart"—in her notebook. Possessed of a quiet and deep self-knowledge, especially of herself as an old woman—"There is self-pity and rancour in the old, in me"—she refuses to submit to despair or bitterness as she looks back upon the failures of her life and of a war-ravaged century. Rather, like a pilgrim, she strives to widen her consciousness and deepen her sympathies with "human-kind." Her meditations on the pursuit of meaning and value throughout a long life as she accepts its approaching end deserve a larger reputation. *The Measure of My Days* is included in Janet Varner Gunn's *Autobiography: Toward a Poetics of Experience* (1982), a study of autobiographical narratives by Augustine, Thoreau, Wordsworth, Proust, and Black Elk. Anne Morrow Lindbergh described Florida

Scott-Maxwell's visionary memoir as "pure gold, essential writing, pro-found and compassionate."

From *The Measure of My Days*

Age puzzles me. I thought it was a quiet time. My seventies were inter-esting, and fairly serene, but my eighties are passionate. I grow more intense as I age. To my own surprise I burst out with hot conviction. Only a few years ago I enjoyed my tranquility; now I am so disturbed by the outer world and by human quality in general that I want to put things right, as though I still owed a debt to life. I must calm down. I am far too frail to indulge in moral fervour. . . .

Old people are not protected from life by engagements, or pleasures, or duties; we are open to our own sentience; we cannot get away from it, and it is too much. We should ward off the problematic, and above all the insoluble. These are far, far too much, but it is just these that attract us. Our one safety is to draw in, and enjoy the simple and immediate. We should rest within our own confines. It may be dull, restricted, but it can be satisfying within our own walls. I feel most real when alone, even most alive when alone. Better to say that the liveli-ness of companionship and the liveliness of solitude differ, and the latter is never as exhausting as the former. When I am with other people I try to find them, or try to find a point in myself from which to make a bridge to them, or I walk on the egg-shells of affection trying not to hurt or misjudge. All this is very tiring, but love at any age takes every-thing you've got.

I often want to say to people, "You have neat, tight expectations of what life ought to give you, but you won't get it. That isn't what life does. Life does not accommodate you, it shatters you. It is meant to, and it couldn't do it better. Every seed destroys its container or else there would be no fruition."

But some wouldn't hear, and some would shatter themselves on principle.

A note book might be the very thing for all the old who wave away crossword puzzles, painting, petit point, and knitting. It is more restful than conversation, and for me it has become a companion, more a con-fessional. It cannot shrive me, but knowing myself better comes near to that. Only this morning—this mild, sunny morning that charmed me into happiness—I realized my cheer was partly because I was alone. I thought for an awful moment that perhaps I was essentially unloving, perhaps had never loved; but years of absorption, and of joy, yes, I have loved, but enough? Is there any stab as deep as wondering where and how much you failed those you loved? Disliking is my great sin, which I cannot overcome. It has taken me my entire life to learn not to withdraw.

I wonder why love is so often equated with joy when it is everything else as well. Devastation, balm, obsession, granting and receiving excessive value, and losing it again. It is recognition, often of what you are not but might be. It sears and it heals. It is beyond pity and above law. It can seem like truth. But what is truth? Oh this mysterious world in which we know nothing, nothing. At times love seems clarity, beyond judgement. But this is a place that can also be reached alone, an impersonal place, found and lost again.

Love is asked to carry intolerable burdens, not seen from outside. Love can be hard service, giving your all, and it may be finding your all. It is sometimes a discipline enabling you to do the impossible. It may be your glimpse of transcendence. It is even agreement. But it is all the pains as well, the small pains as well as the great. It is baffling to be loved by someone incapable of seeing you. It is pain to have your love claimed as a cloak that another may hide from himself. Love tested by its indulgence to weakness, or its blindness to unworthiness can turn to scorn. Love may have blind facets in its all-seeing eyes, but it is we who are blind to what we ask it to bear. Of course it is the heights and the depths, the follies and the glories, but being loving is not always love, and hate can be more cleansing. Why are love and hate near each other, opposite, and alike, and quickly interchangeable?

Love is honoured and hate condemned, but love can do harm. It can soften, distort, maintain the unreal, and cover hate. Hate can be nature's way of forcing honesty on us, and finding the strength to follow a truer way. But as hate is a burning poison that dehumanises us, how can I be anything but appalled by it? I am appalled. I have hated, and I know its evil. But hate is part of truth. It is not safe to forget that the Orphic World Egg had on one side the face of Eros, and on the other that of Phobus, and no one who has seen either ever forgets.

When I was young I knew inside me what I could and could not accept, but I could not express opposition. I had to bear the unacceptable a long time until I hated it. Then I could protest, but with the scalding accompaniment of hate. I know well that hate is a consuming fire poisoning every part of us, yet—yet there are times when it has to be met, for some degree of it is as cleansing as fire. Heat brings change, and so anger can be the right weapon if one is clean enough to use it.

Apparently hate and definition belong together. What differs from you, you may hate; perhaps too quickly, perhaps too slowly. It may be from fear, fear for your identity, fear of your inability to guard your weak identity. Could it be that at our archaic level we are so undifferentiated, so in a state of primal oneness that anything different feels a threat, and hate flames to protect us, is needed, as our dissolution is very possible. So the deep point in us is a dark, hot oneness, making difference a thing to dread and combat. Differing is never a cool thing, and it is the differing, not the issue that makes human beings boil, so no wonder believing what the crowd believes is a comfort and a power. Yet love, too, is a oneness, a warmth and a power, but utterly different, since it is personal, willing to face difference, and even capable of relinquishing its need. . . .

ZORA NEALE HURSTON
(1891–1960)

◆

ZORA NEALE HURSTON was born in the all-black town of Eatonville, Florida, the daughter of a seamstress who died when Zora was nine years old and a Baptist preacher who was also the three-term mayor of Eatonville. Educated at Howard University and Barnard College, Hurston was a folklorist and anthropologist (she studied with Franz Boas at Barnard) who wrote both fiction—stories, novels, and plays—and nonfiction books on folklore and black culture. Her works include a collection of folklore, *Mules and Men* (1935), the novels *Jonah's Gourd Vine* (1934), *Their Eyes Were Watching God* (1937), *Moses, Man of the Mountain* (1939), *Seraph on the Suwanee* (1948), the play *Singing Steel* (1934), and the autobiography *Dust Tracks on a Road* (1942), from which the following excerpt is taken. In the twenties she was part of the Harlem Literary Renaissance and a friend of Langston Hughes. An autobiographical piece, "How It Feels to Be Colored Me" (1928), offers evidence of her reputation as a woman of independent mind, high style, and vitality: "At certain times I have no race, I am *me*. When I set my hat at a certain angle and saunter down Seventh Avenue, Harlem City, feeling as snooty as the lions in front of the Forty-second Street Library, for instance. . . . The cosmic Zora emerges. I belong to no race nor time. I am the eternal feminine with its string of beads. . . . Sometimes, I feel discriminated against, but it does not make me angry. It merely astonishes me. How *can* any deny themselves the pleasure of my company? It's beyond me."

Though her books earned positive reviews, *Their Eyes Were Watching God* was attacked by Richard Wright as a "minstrel" novel that made black characters into objects of ridicule for white readers. (More recently, in 1990, the critic and scholar Arnold Rampersad called this story "one of the main foundations of African-American literature," where Hurston effected "her most harmonious blending of the themes of folklore and individualism.") Alain Locke, the editor of the anthology *The New Negro* (1925), dismissed her book *Moses, Man of the Mountain* as "caricature instead of portraiture." Critic Mary Helen Washington in her anthology *Invented Lives: Narratives of Black Women 1860–1960* interprets these harsh responses in the context of a sexist black literary history: "Nearly every Afro-American literary history," she writes, "reads the tradition as primarily a male tradition, beginning with the male slave narrative as the source which generates the essential texts in the canon. . . . So firmly established is this male hegemony that even men's arguments with one another (Wright, Baldwin, Ellison) get written into the tradition as a way of interpreting its development. As most feminist critics have noted, women writers cannot simply be inserted into the gaps, or be used to prefigure male writers. The tradition has to be conceptualized from a feminist viewpoint."

In the fifties, what her critics perceived as conservative politics removed Zora Neale Hurston from the world and rewards of literary recognition. She suffered poor health, eviction, poverty, and obscurity, working as a maid and receiving nothing but rejection letters from New York publishers. When she died poor and alone, after a stroke in a welfare home, she was buried in an unmarked grave. With the development of Black Studies and Women's Studies courses in American universities since the late sixties, her work has been rediscovered and interpreted by such critics and writers as Henry Louis Gates, Mary Helen Washington, her biographer Robert Hemenway, and Alice Walker, the editor of *I Love Myself When I Am Laughing . . . And Then Again When I Am Looking Mean and Impressive: A Zora Neale Hurston Reader.* Walker defines Hurston's strength as "racial health—a sense of black people as complete, complex, *undiminished* human beings."

From *Dust Tracks on a Road*

. . . I used to take a seat on top of the gate-post and watch the world go by. One way to Orlando ran past my house, so the carriages and cars would pass before me. The movement made me glad to see it. Often the white travelers would hail me, but more often I hailed them, and asked, "Don't you want me to go a piece of the way with you?"

They always did. I know now that I must have caused a great deal of amusement among them, but my self-assurance must have carried the point, for I was always invited to come along. I'd ride up the road for perhaps a half-mile, then walk back. I did not do this with the permission of my parents, nor with their foreknowledge. When they found out about it later, I usually got a whipping. My grandmother worried about my forward ways a great deal. She had known slavery and to her my brazenness was unthinkable.

"Git down offa dat gate-post! You li'l sow, you! Git down! Setting up dere looking dem white folks right in de face! They's gowine to lynch you, yet. And don't stand in dat doorway gazing out at 'em neither. Youse too brazen to live long."

Nevertheless, I kept right on gazing at them, and "going a piece of the way" whenever I could make it. The village seemed dull to me most of the time. If the village was singing a chorus, I must have missed the tune.

Perhaps a year before the old man died, I came to know two other white people for myself. They were women.

It came about this way. The whites who came down from the North were often brought by their friends to visit the village school. A Negro school was something strange to them, and while they were always sympathetic and kind, curiosity must have been present, also. They came and went, came and went. Always, the room was hurriedly put in order, and we were threatened with a prompt and bloody death if we cut one caper while the visitors were present. We always sang a spiritual, led by Mr. Calhoun himself. Mrs. Calhoun always stood in the back, with a palmetto switch in her hand as a squelcher. We were all little angels for the duration, because we'd better be. She would cut her eyes and give us a glare that meant trouble, then turn her face towards the visitors and beam as much as to say it was a great privilege and pleasure to teach lovely children like us. They couldn't see that palmetto hickory in her hand behind all those benches, but we knew where our angelic behavior was coming from.

Usually, the visitors gave warning a day ahead and we would be cautioned to put on shoes, comb our heads, and see to ears and fingernails. There was a close inspection of every one of us before we marched in that morning. Knotty heads, dirty ears and fingernails got hauled out of line, strapped and sent home to lick the calf over again.

This particular afternoon, the two young ladies just popped in. Mr. Calhoun was flustered, but he put on the best show he could. He dismissed the class that he was teaching up at the front of the room, then called the fifth grade in reading. That was my class.

So we took our readers and went up front. We stood up in the usual line, and opened to the lesson. It was the story of Pluto and Persephone. It was new and hard to the class in general, and Mr. Calhoun was very uncomfortable as the readers stumbled along, spelling out words with their lips, and in mumbling undertones before they exposed them experimentally to the teacher's ears.

Then it came to me. I was fifth or sixth down the line. The story was not new to me, because I had read my reader through from lid to lid, the first week that Papa had bought it for me.

That is how it was that my eyes were not in the book, working out the paragraph which I knew would be mine by counting the children ahead of me. I was observing our visitors, who held a book between them, following the lesson. They had shiny hair, mostly brownish. One had a looping gold chain around her neck. The other one was dressed all over in black and white with a pretty finger ring on her left hand. But the thing that held my eyes were their fingers. They were long and thin, and very white, except up near the tips. There they were baby pink. I had never seen such hands. It was a fascinating discovery for me. I wondered how they felt. I would have given those hands more attention, but the child before me was almost through. My turn next, so I got on my mark, bringing my eyes back to the book and made sure of my place. Some of the stories I had reread several times, and this Greco-Roman myth was one of my favorites. I was exalted by it, and that is the way I read my paragraph.

"Yes, Jupiter had seen her (Persephone). He had seen the maiden picking flowers in the field. He had seen the chariot of the dark monarch pause by the maiden's side. He had seen him when he seized Persephone. He had seen the black horses leap down Mount Aetna's fiery throat. Persephone was now in Pluto's dark realm and he had made her his wife."

The two women looked at each other and then back to me. Mr. Calhoun broke out with a proud smile beneath his bristly moustache, and instead of the next child taking up where I had ended, he nodded to me to go on. So I read the story to the end, where flying Mercury, the messenger of the Gods, brought Persephone back to the sunlit earth and restored her to the arms of Dame Ceres, her mother, that the world might have springtime and summer flowers, autumn and harvest. But because she had bitten the pomegranate while in Pluto's kingdom, she must return to him for three months of each year, and be his queen. Then the world had winter, until she returned to earth.

The class was dismissed and the visitors smiled us away and went into a low-voiced conversation with Mr. Calhoun for a few minutes. They glanced my way once or twice and I began to worry. Not only was I barefooted, but my feet and legs were dusty. My hair was more uncombed than usual, and my nails were not shiny clean. Oh, I'm going to catch it now. Those ladies saw me, too. Mr. Calhoun is promising to 'tend to me. So I thought.

Then Mr. Calhoun called me. I went up thinking how awful it was to get a whipping before company. Furthermore, I heard a snicker run over the room. Hennie Clark and Stell Brazzle did it out loud, so I would be sure to hear them. The smart-aleck was going to get it. I slipped one hand behind me and switched my dress tail at them, indicating scorn.

"Come here, Zora Neale," Mr. Calhoun cooed as I reached the desk. He put his hand on my shoulder and gave me little pats. The ladies smiled and held out those flower-looking fingers towards me. I seized the opportunity for a good look.

"Shake hands with the ladies, Zora Neale," Mr. Calhoun prompted and they took my hand one after the other and smiled. They asked me if I loved school, and I lied that I did. There was *some* truth in it, because I liked geography and reading, and I liked to play at recess time. Whoever it was invented writing and arithmetic got no thanks from me. Neither did I like the arrangement where the teacher could sit up there with a palmetto stem and lick me whenever he saw fit. I hated things I couldn't do anything about. But I knew better than to bring that up right there, so I said yes, I *loved* school.

"I can tell you do," Brown Taffeta gleamed. She patted my head, and was lucky enough not to get sandspurs in her hand. Children who roll and tumble in the grass in Florida, are apt to get sandspurs in their hair. They shook hands with me again and I went back to my seat.

When school let out at three o'clock, Mr. Calhoun told me to wait. When everybody had gone, he told me I was to go to the Park House, that was the hotel in Maitland, the next afternoon to call upon Mrs. Johnstone and Miss Hurd. I must tell Mama to see that I was clean and brushed from head to feet, and I must wear shoes and stockings. The ladies liked me, he said, and I must be on my best behavior.

The next day I was let out of school an hour early, and went home to be stood up in a tub of suds and be scrubbed and have my ears dug into. My sandy hair sported a red ribbon to match my red and white checked gingham dress, starched until it could stand alone. Mama saw to it that my shoes were on the right feet, since I was careless about left and right. Last thing, I was given a handkerchief to carry, warned again about my behavior, and sent off, with my big brother John to go as far as the hotel gate with me.

First thing, the ladies gave me strange things, like stuffed dates and preserved ginger, and encouraged me to eat all that I wanted. Then they showed me their Japanese dolls and just talked. I was then handed a copy of *Scribner's Magazine,* and asked to read a place that was pointed out to me. After a paragraph or two, I was told with smiles, that that would do.

I was led out on the grounds and they took my picture under a palm tree. They handed me what was to me then a heavy cylinder done up in fancy paper, tied with a ribbon, and they told me goodbye, asking me not to open it until I got home.

My brother was waiting for me down by the lake, and we hurried home, eager to see what was in the thing. It was too heavy to be candy or anything like that. John insisted on toting it for me.

My mother made John give it back to me and let me open it. Perhaps, I shall never experience such joy again. The nearest thing to that moment was the telegram accepting my first book. One hundred goldy-new pennies rolled out of the cylinder. Their gleam lit up the world. It was not avarice that moved me. It was the beauty of the thing. I stood on the mountain. Mama let me play with my pennies for a while, then put them away for me to keep.

That was only the beginning. The next day I received an Episcopal hymn-book bound in white leather with a golden cross stamped into the front cover, a copy of The Swiss Family Robinson, and a book of fairy tales.

I set about to commit the song words to memory. There was no music written there, just the words. But there was to my consciousness music in between them just the same. "When I survey the Wondrous Cross" seemed the most beautiful to me, so I committed that to memory first of all. Some of them seemed dull and without life, and I pretended they were not there. If white people like trashy singing like that, there must be something funny about them that I had not noticed before. I stuck to the pretty ones where the words marched to a throb I could feel.

A month or so after the two young ladies returned to Minnesota, they sent me a huge box packed with clothes and books. The red coat with a wide circular collar and the red tam pleased me more than any of the other things. My chums pretended not to like anything that I had, but even then I knew that they were jealous. Old Smarty had gotten by them again. The clothes were not new, but they were very good. I shone like the morning sun.

But the books gave me more pleasure than the clothes. I had never been too keen on dressing up. It called for hard scrubbings with Octagon soap suds getting in my eyes, and none too gentle fingers scrubbing my neck and gouging in my ears.

In that box were Gulliver's Travels, Grimm's Fairy Tales, Dick Whittington, Greek and Roman Myths, and best of all, Norse Tales. Why did the Norse tales strike so deeply into my soul? I do not know, but they did. I seemed to remember seeing Thor swing his mighty short-handled hammer as he sped across the sky in rumbling thunder, lightning flashing from the tread of his steeds and the wheels of his chariot. The great and good Odin, who went down to the well of knowledge to drink, and was told that the price of a drink from that fountain was an eye. Odin drank deeply, then plucked out one eye without a murmur and handed it to the grizzly keeper, and walked away. That held majesty for me.

Of the Greeks, Hercules moved me most. I followed him eagerly on his tasks. The story of the choice of Hercules as a boy when he met Pleasure and Duty, and put his hand in that of Duty and followed her steep way to the blue hills of fame and glory, which she pointed out at the end, moved me profoundly. I resolved to be like him. The tricks and turns of the other Gods and Goddesses left me cold. There were other thin books about this and that sweet and gentle little girl who gave up her heart to Christ and good works. Almost always they died from it, preaching as they passed. I was utterly indifferent to their deaths. In the first place I could not conceive of death, and in the next place they never had any funerals that amounted to a hill of beans, so I didn't care how soon they rolled up their big, soulful, blue eyes and kicked the bucket. They had no meat on their bones.

But I also met Hans Andersen and Robert Louis Stevenson. They seemed to know what I wanted to hear and said it in a way that tingled me. Just a little below these friends was Rudyard Kipling in his Jungle Books. I loved his talking snakes as much as I did the hero.

I came to start reading the Bible through my mother. She gave me a licking one afternoon for repeating something I had overheard a neighbor telling her. She locked me in her room after the whipping, and the Bible was the only thing in there for me to read. I happened to open to the place where David was doing some mighty smiting, and I got interested. David went here and he went there, and no matter where he went, he smote 'em hip and thigh. Then he sung songs to his harp awhile, and went out and smote some more. Not one time did David stop and preach about sins and things. All David wanted to know from God was who to kill and when. He took care of the other details himself. Never a quiet moment. I liked him a lot. So I read a great deal more in the Bible, hunting for some more active people like David. Except for the beautiful language of Luke and Paul, the New Testament still plays a poor second to the Old Testament for me. The Jews had a God who laid about Him when they needed Him. I could see no use waiting till Judgment Day to see a man who was just crying for a good killing, to be told to go and roast. My idea was to give him a good killing first, and then if he got roasted later on, so much the better.

In searching for more Davids, I came upon Leviticus. There were exciting things in there to a child eager to know the facts of life. I told Carrie Roberts about it, and we spent long afternoons reading what Moses told the Hebrews not to do in Leviticus. In that way I found out a number of things the old folks would not have told me. Not knowing what we were actually reading, we got a lot of praise from our elders for our devotion to the Bible.

Having finished that and scanned the Doctor Book, which my mother thought she had hidden securely from my eyes, I read all the things which children write on privy-house walls. Therefore, I lost my taste for pornographic literature. I think that the people who love it got cheated in the matter of privy houses when they were children.

In a way this early reading gave me great anguish through all my childhood and adolescence. My soul was with the gods and my body in the village. People just would not act like gods. Stew beef, fried fatback and morning grits were no ambrosia from Valhalla. Raking back yards and carrying out chamber-pots, were not the tasks of Thor. I wanted to be away from drabness and to stretch my limbs in some mighty struggle. I was only happy in the woods, and when the ecstatic Florida springtime came strolling from the sea, trance-glorifying the world with its aura. Then I hid out in the tall wild oats that waved like a glinty veil. I nibbled sweet oat stalks and listened to the wind soughing and sighing through the crowns of the lofty pines. I made particular friendship with one huge tree and always played about its roots. I named it "the loving pine," and my chums came to know it by that name. . . .

Louise Bogan
(1897–1970)

◆

LOUISE BOGAN was one of the finest lyric poets of the twentieth century: W. H. Auden said she "wrested beauty and truth out of dark places"; Theodore Roethke called her "one of the true inheritors of the great tradition. . . . [Her] best work will stay in the language as long as the language survives." She was also a distinguished critic and a brilliant stylist of an intense and personal literary genre to which belong such works as Virginia Woolf's diaries and Colette's notebooks. When Bogan died suddenly of a heart attack in 1970, she left behind an extensive collection of unpublished notebooks, papers, and letters that comprises an autobiography of sensibility. Ruth Limmer, her literary executor, assembled the journals, notebook entries, stories, excerpts from letters and criticism, and various other odds and ends to create a continuous narrative entitled *Journey Around My Room: The Autobiography of Louise Bogan,* the source of the following excerpts. From this book, aptly subtitled "A Mosaic," and from other biographical sources—Bogan's published letters, *What the Woman Lived: Selected Letters of Louise Bogan, 1920–1970,* and Elizabeth Frank's biography, *Louise Bogan: A Portrait*—come the facts of the poet's life that she transmuted into art. An intensely private woman, she exercised in these pieces a highly selective memory; her aesthetic pronouncements are austere and brilliantly original.

Born in Livermore Falls, Maine, she grew up in poverty and in an oppressive home troubled by her parents' acrimonious marriage. To escape, she threw herself into her studies at Girls' Latin School in Boston where she began to write poetry and later at Boston University where her published poems helped her win a scholarship to Radcliffe. But still in escape from her family, she dropped out of college and married. She gave birth to a daughter, and two years later, left her husband and moved to New York City. She supported herself and her child by clerking at Brentano's, at Columbia University, and by working at various branches of the New York Public Library. (As Ruth Limmer tells it, Marianne Moore worked at one of the branches also "but Bogan was too shy to introduce herself and Miss Moore was too abstracted to notice.") Throughout this early period, she was writing and publishing her poetry, poetry reviews, and film criticism. In 1931, after she had published two volumes of poetry, *Body of This Death* (1923) and *Dark Summer* (1929) and become poetry editor and reviewer for *The New Yorker,* she suffered the first of a series of depressions for which she sought hospitalization in the New York Neurological Institute. In the years that followed, she published collections of her poetry at regular intervals, received prestigious prizes and a Guggenheim Fellowship, separated from her second husband and began a relationship with the poet Theodore Roethke. (In her Introduction to *Journey Around My Room,* Limmer asserts what is obscured in the Mosaic: "With her high Irish wit . . . Bogan was one of the most amusing people of her time. To be with her was to laugh with her, and perhaps her highest accolade was, 'We laugh in the same places.'") After serving as consultant in Poetry to the Library of Congress in 1945, she received a number of professorships, literary residencies, the Bollingen Prize, and awards for her poetry as well as for five volumes of translations from the National Institute of Arts and Letters and the Academy of American Poets. Her friend May Sarton (see page 127) wrote a memoir of Bogan in *A World of Light,* emphasizing her lack of pretension: "a person . . . totally unspoiled and unworldly: 'Not bad,' she would say with a smile, when some new honor came to her, 'for an Irish girl from Camden, Maine.'" Her last volume of poetry, *The Blue Estuaries: Poems 1923–1968,* appeared a year before her death. Reviewing her posthumously published letters, Barbara Grizzuti Harrison (see page 255) said they revealed Bogan to be, "essentially, a religious ecstatic with a great deal of good common earthy sense."

From *Journey Around My Room:*
The Autobiography of Louise Bogan

6
Back Through Cities

(To the city): I came to you, a young girl, from a wooden house that shook in the autumn storms, and in the autumn I saw in *your* streets perhaps a handful of curled dry leaves.

I came at the age of the impossible heart, when the mind flew out to inhabit with warmth and compassion the rooms behind shut windows and drawn blinds; when even the advertising placards were invested with incredible possibilities of truth; when one watched the play of people's eyes and mouths, as though expecting enchanting glances, magical words, to come from them. . . .

Perhaps the beginning of my "depression" can be located at the occasion (a fall-winter morning and early afternoon) when I went back to the earliest neighborhood we lived in after coming to Boston. It was always a good distance away, in one of the drearier suburbs, to be reached by trolley car from Dudley Street. But in those days (1909) the red brick block of an apartment house (with stores below) was surrounded by empty lots, and even, at the back, within view of a wooden veranda, by a scrubby overgrown field, filled with underbrush and a few trees. A large, sunken field was visible from the row of windows, on the apartment's long side; and here boys played baseball all spring and summer. The front windows (two in the parlor, and one in the adjoining "alcove") faced the openings of two or more streets, rather nicely kept, with single wooden houses—and even some white-washed stones outlining pathways. The brand-new apartment house, more than a block long, abutted on a small, older region, with some stores and a general run-down air. A steep street forked off to the right, downhill; and at the bottom of this hill stairs went up (v. close to house-walls) to the local railway station, with infrequent trains. I sometimes walked down this unfrequented stretch of tracks, on the way to school. The neighborhood finally reached by such a walk was already a semi-slum: depressing by reason of single houses needing paint, as much as by a scattering of those three-decker wooden apartment buildings, with front and back porches, which were becoming so usual in the outer Boston suburbs.

Our own apartment was of the "railroad" kind: a center hall ran from the front door to the kitchen, with parlor, parlor alcove, the large bedroom, the dining room opening out from it. Beyond the kitchen (and its large pantry), to its right, and with the windows at the side (and at the back?), was a smaller bedroom, partially unfurnished, and dreary to a degree. My father and, often, my brother slept here. I slept with my mother, in the other bedroom, which had some respectable furniture in it, and a view over the open sunken field.

My father and mother, after a period of ghastly quarrels (and one long separation), at this time were making some effort to re-establish themselves, as a couple and as a family. New furniture and rugs had been bought for the front rooms; the piano was open and used; pictures were hung, and lace curtains veiled the windows. The woodwork of the place was, of course, dark brown, and dark green wallpaper predominated (although not in the bedroom, as I remember). There was a new brass bed. The dining room, where I came to do my lessons, had its square center table, its elaborate sideboard, a couch, and another largish table, which held some books and papers. The kitchen table was scrubbed pine. Was there a gas stove? The big black iron range functioned for major cooking—for those meals which often appeared at irregular intervals. I distinctly remember the taste of thin pieces of steak, kept warm in the overhead heating compartment, together with fried potatoes. Sunday dinner and the evening meals could be counted on to appear on time.

When I went back to this region, last fall, the whole area had slipped into true slumhood. The open field was gone; a large garage stood on its site: gray, metallic, forbidding. And the houses had crowded into the back scrubby field: a row of three-family structures, crowded as close to one another as possible. The air of a crowded necessitous place hit me like a breath of sickness—of hopelessness, of despair. The stores which had once existed in our block were gone: their windows cracked and broken. Only the old bakery, down the street, still persisted. The occasional sign was in Italian; a cheap pizza restaurant stood at the junction of the downhill street with the main thoroughfare, on which the buses now ran. I had walked down from Codman Square—the cross streets here had lost all vestige of the openness and quiet which I remembered; again crowded with run-down stores, with only the Public Library branch (where I had read my first books, in 1909) keeping a certain dignity. A large school building also abutted on the Square. This is now the Girls' Latin School, which, when I graduated from it, in 1915, was situated on the edge of the Boston Fenway.

A wave of despair seized me, after I had walked around the Library (now bedizened with cheap signs and notices but still keeping its interesting curved walls). No book of mine was listed in the catalogue. (A slight paranoid shudder passed over me.)—I felt the consuming, destroying, deforming passage of time; and the spectacle of my family's complete helplessness, in the face of their difficulties, swept over me. With no weapons against what was already becoming an overwhelming series of disasters—no insight, no self-knowledge, no inherited wisdom—I saw my father and mother (and my brother) as helpless victims of ignorance, wilfulness, and temperamental disabilities of a near-psychotic order—facing a period (after 1918) where even this small store of pathetic acquisitions would be swept away. The anguish which filled my spirit and mind may, perhaps, be said to have engendered (and reawakened) poisons long since dissipated, so that they gathered, like some noxious gas, at the v. center of my being. The modern horrors of the district also became part of this miasma; certainly the people in these newly overcrowded streets were as lost as those members of generations preceding them. Everywhere I looked, I saw *Death;* and I had to pass a strangely cluttered and disarrayed graveyard (new since my time) between the Square and my old house—(a home impermanent, it is true, for we lived there only two and a half years). But those were my first years of adolescence—and of the creative impulse—and of hard and definitive schooling. And, as I remember, in spite of the growing sense of crisis by which I was continually surrounded, they were years of a beginning variety of interests—of growth and of hope.

The thing to remember, and "dwell on," is the extraordinary *courage* manifested by those two disparate, unawakened (if not actually *lost*) souls: my mother and father. I cannot bring myself to describe the horrors of the pre-1914 lower-middle-class life, in which they found themselves. My father had his job, which kept him in touch with reality; it was his life, always. My mother had nothing but her temperament, her fantasies, her despairs, her secrets, her subterfuges. The money—every cent of it earned by my father, over all the years—came through in a thin stream, often blocked or actually exhausted. Those dollar bills—so definitive! Those quarters and ten-cent pieces—so valuable. (I went to school on a quarter a day.) Those terrible splurges on her clothes, which kept my mother going! How did they manage to keep a roof over their heads! With absolutely no plans for the future— no foresight—no practical acumen of any kind.

Yet out of this exiguous financial situation came my music lessons—my music—my Saturday money (50¢, often) for movies and even the theatre; what clothes I had—that we all had—and food. Even a woman to help with the wash. Little excursions to the beach in the summer.

No books (the library supplied those). No social expenditures. Those two people, literally cut off from any social contacts, with the exception of one or two neighbors—often as eccentric as my parents themselves.—No invitation to classmates—or perhaps one or two—in all those years. Cut off. Isolated. Strung up with a hundred anxieties. And yet they survived—and I went through my entire adolescence—in this purgatory—with an open hell in close relation. A hell which tended to blow into full being on all holidays—when my mother's multiple guilts towards her treatment of her foster mother tended to shake loose.

In the youth of a handsome woman, two currents and two demands run side by side in almost perfect accord: her own vanity's desire for praise and love, and the delight in the praise and love so easily given her. When these two currents lessen, a terrible loneliness and an hysterical disease take their place. For the energy once expended on delight and conquest now has nothing on which it can be dissipated; it is continually meeting small defeats and rebuffs; it is like a river which has made a broad bed for itself, but now has dwindled into a tiny stream that makes hardly any show among the wide sweep of pebbles that show the boundaries of its former strength.

What was the first mood in their long anger, the first item articulated in their mutual disbelief, the first lie brewed out of their passionate dissimilarity? Sometimes, she thought that she might catch a phrase, as, after a long and lucid dream, we think that we can recount to ourselves the subconscious events with which we have so recently been involved. A sharp and stimulating tone—*taste*—remains: "It was *this*," we say to ourselves; but we cannot pin it down. At our insistence the flavor as well as the substance of the dream whisks out of reach . . .

If she could have remembered with clarity one word, she thought that she could forget it all—the sound, the look, the suffering—forever.

I cannot describe or particularize. Surely all this agony has long since been absorbed into my work. Even then, it was beginning to be absorbed. For I began writing—at length, in prose—in 1909; and within a year (my last in elementary school) I had acquired the interest of one of those intelligent old maids who so often showed talented children their earliest talents—opened up their earliest efforts by the application of attention and sympathy. I went to the Girls' Latin School in the autumn of 1910, at the age of thirteen, for five most fruitful years. I began to write verse from about fourteen on. The life-saving process then began. By the age of 18 I had a thick pile of manuscript, in a drawer in the dining room—and had learned every essential of my trade.

DOROTHY DAY
(1897–1980)

———◆———

Co-founder of the Catholic Worker Movement, radical social activist and pacifist, DOROTHY DAY was born within sight of the Brooklyn Bridge and grew up in a nomadic Scotch-Irish-English family of four children who lived in Oakland and Berkeley before settling in Chicago, their most permanent home, which she left at sixteen to attend the University of Illinois. As a young woman, supporting herself as a journalist, she moved to New York, joined the socialist movement, and worked on behalf of social justice, especially women's suffrage. In 1918 she was arrested for picketing the White House with other suffragettes, the first of her twelve arrests for participation in protests against various policies of government and corporate interests. An independent and bohemian activist, friend of Eugene O'Neill, Mike Gold, and Elizabeth Gurley Flynn, she broke with her past after the birth of her daughter; she was baptized and entered the Roman Catholic Church. She left behind her common-law husband, Forster Batterham, an anarchist and atheist who would not tolerate the official ceremony required by state or church to regularize their marriage. Day wrote her life history within the context of her later conversion in several volumes of autobiography: *From Union Square to Rome* (1938); *The Long Loneliness* (1952), from which a selection follows here; and *All Is Grace,* a journal published after her death in 1980. An early novel, which she disliked, *The Eleventh Virgin* (1924), is also autobiographical. She wrote a monthly column about the Worker movement in its newspaper, *The Catholic Worker,* first published in 1932, and in such books as *House of Hospitality* (1939), *Loaves and Fishes* (1963), and *On Pilgrimage: The Sixties* (1973), detailing the community's voluntary poverty, pacifism, and care for the poor and homeless with free housing, food, and clothing at the Worker's houses of hospitality throughout the United States.

As a religious woman and activist, Day worked to make her life and ministry reflect her Church's preferential option for the poor, expressed in the gospels and in twentieth-century liberation theology. Throughout her long apostolate, she expressed her anger at "this filthy rotten system" that created the urban poverty she voluntarily embraced; she also criticized her Church's alliances with the powerful and its neglect of the weak as betrayals of its mission. Her life and autobiography have been the subjects of recent feminist studies: Patricia Meyer Spacks's "Selves in Hiding" and Mary G. Mason's "Dorothy Day and Women's Spiritual Autobiography" in Margo Culley's *American Women's Autobiography: Fea(s)ts of Memory* (1992). Author and Professor of Psychiatry and Medical Humanities at Harvard, Robert Coles in *Dorothy Day: A Radical Devotion* (1989), his volume in the Radcliffe Biography Series depicting the lives of extraordinary women, finds a profound sanity in Day's life which influenced such radical activists and writers as Michael Harrington, Thomas Merton, Daniel Berrigan, and Cesar Chavez.

From *The Long Loneliness*

Having a Baby

I was surprised that I found myself beginning to pray daily. I could not get down on my knees, but I could pray while I was walking. If I got down on my knees I thought, "Do I really believe? Whom am I praying to?" A terrible doubt came over me, and a sense of shame, and I wondered if I was praying because I was lonely, because I was unhappy.

But when I walked to the village for the mail, I found myself praying again, holding in my pocket the rosary that Mary Gordon gave me in New Orleans some years before. Maybe I did not say it correctly but I kept on saying it because it made me happy.

Then I thought suddenly, scornfully, "Here you are in a stupor of content. You are biological. Like a cow. Prayer with you is like the opiate of the people." And over and over again in my mind that phrase was repeated jeeringly, "Religion is the opiate of the people."

"But," I reasoned with myself, "I am praying because I am happy, not because I am unhappy. I did not turn to God in unhappiness, in grief, in despair—to get consolation, to get something from Him."

And encouraged that I was praying because I wanted to thank Him, I went on praying. No matter how dull the day, how long the walk seemed, if I felt sluggish at the beginning of the walk, the words I had been saying insinuated themselves into my heart before I had finished, so that on the trip back I neither prayed nor thought but was filled with exultation.

Along the beach I found it appropriate to say the *Te Deum*. When I worked about the house, I found myself addressing the Blessed Virgin and turning toward her statue.

It is so hard to say how this delight in prayer grew on me. The year before, I was saying as I planted seeds in the garden, "I *must* believe in these seeds, that they fall into the earth and grow into flowers and radishes and beans. It is a miracle to me because I do not understand it. Neither do naturalists understand it. The very fact that they use glib technical phrases does not make it any less of a miracle, and a miracle we all accept. Then why not accept God's mysteries?"

I began to go to Mass regularly on Sunday mornings.

When Freda went into town, I was alone. Forster[*] was in the city all week, only coming out week ends. I finished the writing I was doing and felt at loose ends, thinking enviously of my friends going gaily about the city, about their work, with plenty of companionship.

The fact that I felt restless was a very good reason to stay on the beach and content myself with my life as a sybaritic anchorite. For how could I be a true anchorite with such luxuries as the morning paper, groceries delivered to the door, a beach to walk on, and the water to feast my eyes on? And then the fresh fish and clams, mushrooms, Jerusalem artichokes, such delicacies right at hand. I invited Lefty to supper and discussed with him the painting of the house. I read Dickens every evening.

In spite of my desire for a sociable week in town, in spite of a desire to pick up and flee from my solitude, I took joy in thinking of the idiocy of the pleasures I would indulge in if I were there. Cocktail parties, with prohibition drinks, dinners, the conversation or lack of it, dancing in a smoky crowded room when one might be walking on the beach, the dull, restless cogitations which come after dissipating one's energies—things which struck me with renewed force every time I spent days in the city. My virtuous resolutions to indulge in such pleasure no more were succeeded by a hideous depression when neither my new-found sense of religion, my family life, my work nor my surroundings were sufficient to console me. I thought of death and was overwhelmed by the terror and the blackness of both life and death. And I longed for a church near at hand where I could go and lift up my soul.

It was pleasant rowing about in the calm bay with Forster. The oyster boats were all out, and far on the horizon, off Sandy Hook, there was a four-masted vessel. I had the curious delusion that several huge holes had been stove in her side, through which you could see the blue sky. The other vessels seemed sailing in the air, quite indifferent to the horizon on which they should properly have been resting. Forster tried to explain to me scientific facts about mirages and atmospheric condi-

---

[*]Day's common-law husband and father of her child.

tions, and, on the other hand, I pointed out to him how our senses lie to us.

But it was impossible to talk about religion or faith to him. A wall immediately separated us. The very love of nature, and the study of her secrets which was bringing me to faith, cut Forster off from religion.

I had known Forster a long time before we contracted our common-law relationship, and I have always felt that it was life with him that brought me natural happiness, that brought me to God.

His ardent love of creation brought me to the Creator of all things. But when I cried out to him, "How can there be no God, when there are all these beautiful things," he turned from me uneasily and complained that I was never satisfied. We loved each other so strongly that he wanted to remain in the love of the moment; he wanted me to rest in that love. He cried out against my attitude that there would be nothing left of that love without a faith.

I remembered the love story in Romain Rolland's *Jean Christophe,* the story of his friend and his engrossing marriage, and how those young people exhausted themselves in the intensity of their emotions.

I could not see that love between man and woman was incompatible with love of God. God is the Creator, and the very fact that we were begetting a child made me have a sense that we were made in the image and likeness of God, co-creators with him. I could not protest with Sasha about "that initial agony of having to live." Because I was grateful for love, I was grateful for life, and living with Forster made me appreciate it and even reverence it still more. He had introduced me to so much that was beautiful and good that I felt I owed to him too this renewed interest in the things of the spirit.

He had all the love of the English for the outdoors in all weather. He used to insist on walks no matter how cold or rainy the day, and this dragging me away from my books, from my lethargy, into the open, into the country, made me begin to breathe. If breath is life, then I was beginning to be full of it because of him. I was filling my lungs with it, walking on the beach, resting on the pier beside him while he fished, rowing with him in the calm bay, walking through fields and woods—a new experience entirely for me, one which brought me to life, and filled me with joy.

I had been passing through some years of fret and strife, beauty and ugliness—even some weeks of sadness and despair. There had been periods of intense joy but seldom had there been the quiet beauty and happiness I had now. I had thought all those years that I had freedom, but now I felt that I had never known real freedom nor even had knowledge of what freedom meant.

Now, just as in my childhood, I was enchained, tied to one spot, unable to pick up and travel from one part of the country to another, from one job to another. I was tied down because I was going to have a baby. No matter how much I might sometimes wish to flee from my quiet existence, I could not, nor would I be able to for several years. I had to accept my quiet and stillness, and accepting it, I rejoiced in it.

For a long time I had thought I could not bear a child, and the longing in my heart for a baby had been growing. My home, I felt, was not a home without one. The simple joys of the kitchen and garden and beach brought sadness with them because I felt myself unfruitful, barren. No matter how much one was loved or one loved, that love was lonely without a child. It was incomplete.

I will never forget my blissful joy when I was first sure that I was pregnant—I had wanted a baby all the first year we were together. When I was finally sure, it was a beautiful June day and we were going on a picnic to Tottenville to see a circus, Malcolm and Peggy, Forster and I. It was a circus in a tent, and it was Peggy who insisted on going. We brought dandelion wine and pickled eels and good home-made bread and butter. A fantastic lunch, but I remember enjoying the root beer and popcorn later, and feeling so much in love, so settled, so secure that now I had found what I was looking for.

It did not last all through my pregnancy, that happiness. There were conflicts because Forster did not believe in bringing children into such a world as we lived in. He still was obsessed by the war. His fear of responsibility, his dislike of having the control of others, his extreme individualism made him feel that he of all men should not be a father.

Our child was born in March at the end of a harsh winter. In December I had come in from the country and taken an apartment in town. My sister came to stay with me, to help me over the last hard months. It was good to be there, close to friends, close to a church where I could pray. I read the *Imitation of Christ* a great deal during those months. I knew that I was going to have my child baptized, cost what it may. I knew that I was not going to have her floundering through many years as I had done, doubting and hesitating, undisciplined and amoral. I felt it was the greatest thing I could do for my child. For myself, I prayed for the gift of faith. I was sure, yet not sure. I postponed the day of decision.

A woman does not want to be alone at such a time. Even the most hardened, the most irreverent, is awed by the stupendous fact of creation. Becoming a Catholic would mean facing life alone and I clung to family life. It was hard to contemplate giving up a mate in order that my child and I could become members of the Church. Forster would have nothing to do with religion or with me if I embraced it. So I waited.

Those last months of waiting I was too happy to know the unrest of indecision. The days were slow in passing, but week by week the time came nearer. I spent some time in writing, but for the most part I felt a great stillness. I was incapable of going to meetings, of seeing many people, of taking up the threads of my past life.

When the little one was born, my joy was so great that I sat up in bed in the hospital and wrote an article for the *New Masses* about my child, wanting to share my joy with the world. I was glad to write this joy for a workers' magazine because it was a joy all women knew, no matter what their grief at poverty, unemployment and class war. The article so appealed to my Marxist friends that the account was reprinted all over the world in workers' papers. Diego Rivera, when I met him some four years afterward in Mexico, greeted me as the author of it. And Mike Gold, who was at that time editor of the *New Masses,* said it had been printed in many Soviet newspapers and that I had rubles awaiting me in Moscow.

When Tamar Teresa—for that is what I named her—was six weeks old, we went back to the beach. It was April and, though it was still cold, it was definitely spring.

Every morning while she napped on the sunny porch, well swathed in soft woolen blankets, I went down to the beach and with the help of Lefty brought up driftwood, enough to last until next morning. Forster was home only week ends and then he chopped enough wood to last a few days. But when the wind was high and piercing it penetrated the house so that much wood was needed, and it was a pleasure to tramp up and down the beach in the bright sun and collect wood which smelled of seaweed, brine and tar. It was warmer outside than it was in the house, and on the porch Teresa was nicely sheltered. Sometimes in the afternoon I put her in her carriage and went out along the woods, watching, almost feeling the buds bursting through their warm coats. Song sparrows, woodpeckers, hawks, crows, robins, nuthatches and of course laughing gulls made the air gay with their clamor. Starlings chattered in the branches of the old pine in front of the porch. We collected azalea buds, dogwood, sassafras and apple-tree branches to decorate the room. Best of all there were skunk cabbages, gleaming mottled-green, dark red, and yellow, small enough to make a most decorative centerpiece, propped up with stones. They were never so colorful as they were that year, and spring after spring since I have watched for them thrusting up vigorously in marshy places. Skunk cabbages and the spring peepers—these tiny frogs—mean that the winter is over and gone.

There was arbutus still buried under the leaves so that one had to look carefully for it like buried treasure. There were spring beauties and adder's-tongue and dandelion greens. The year before I had been planting radishes on March first but this year gardening gave way to more delightful tasks.

Supper always was early and the baby comfortably tucked away before it was dark. Then, tired with all the activities that so rejoiced and filled my days, I sat in the dusk in a stupor of contentment.

Yet always those deep moments of happiness gave way to a feeling of struggle, of a long silent fight still to be gone through. There had been the physical struggle, the mortal combat almost, of giving birth to a child, and now there was coming the struggle for my own soul. Tamar would be baptized, and I knew the rending it would cause in human relations around me. I was to be torn and agonized again, and I was all for putting off the hard day.

Love Overflows

"Thou shalt love the Lord thy God with thy whole heart and with thy whole soul and with thy whole mind." This is the first Commandment.

The problem is, how to love God? We are only too conscious of the hardness of our hearts, and in spite of all that religious writers tell us about *feeling* not being necessary, we do want to feel and so know that we love God.

"Thou wouldst not seek Him if thou hadst not already found Him," Pascal says, and it is true too that you love God if you want to love Him. One of the disconcerting facts about the spiritual life is that God takes you at your word. Sooner or later one is given a chance to prove his love. The very word "diligo," the Latin word used for "love," means "I prefer." It was all very well to love God in His works, in the beauty of His creation which was crowned for me by the birth of my child. Forster had made the physical world come alive for me and had awakened in my heart a flood of gratitude. The final object of this love and gratitude was God. No human creature could receive or contain so vast a flood of love and joy as I often felt after the birth of my child. With this came the need to worship, to adore. I had heard many say that they wanted to worship God in their own way and did not need a Church in which to praise Him, nor a body of people with whom to associate themselves. But I did not agree to this. My very experience as a radical, my whole make-up, led me to want to associate myself with others, with the masses, in loving and praising God. Without even looking into the claims of the Catholic Church, I was willing to admit that for me she was the one true Church. She had come down through the centuries since the time of Peter, and far from being dead, she claimed and held the allegiance of the masses of people in all the cities where I had lived. They poured in and out of her doors on Sundays and holy days, for novenas and missions. What if they were compelled to come in by the law of the Church, which said they were guilty of mortal sin if they did not go to Mass every Sunday? They obeyed that law. They were given a chance to show their preference. They accepted the Church. It may have been an unthinking, unquestioning faith, and yet the chance certainly came, again and again, "Do I prefer the Church to my own will," even if it was only the small matter of sitting at home on a Sunday morning with the papers? And the choice was the Church.

There was the legislation of the Church in regard to marriage, a stumbling block to many. That was where I began to be troubled, to be afraid. To become a Catholic meant for me to give up a mate with whom I was much in love. It got to the point where it was the simple question of whether I chose God or man. I had known enough of love to know that a good healthy family life was as near to heaven as one could get in this life. There was another sample of heaven, of the enjoyment of God. The very sexual act itself was used again and again in Scripture as a figure of the beatific vision. It was not because I was tired of sex, satiated, disillusioned, that I turned to God. Radical friends used to insinuate this. It was because through a whole love, both physical and spiritual, I came to know God.

From the time Tamar Teresa was born I was intent on having her baptized. There had been that young Catholic girl in the bed next to me at the hospital who gave me a medal of St. Thérèse of Lisieux.

"I don't believe in these things," I told her, and it was another example of people saying what they do not mean.

"If you love someone you like to have something around which reminds you of them," she told me.

It was so obvious a truth that I was shamed. Reading William James' *Varieties of Religious Experience* had acquainted me with the saints, and I had read the life of St. Teresa of Avila and fallen in love with her. She was a mystic and a practical woman, a recluse and a traveler, a cloistered nun and yet most active. She liked to read novels when she was a young girl, and she wore a bright red dress when she entered the convent. Once when she was traveling from one part of Spain to another with some other nuns and a priest to start a convent, and their way took them over a stream, she was thrown from her donkey. The story goes that our Lord said to her, "That is how I treat my friends." And she replied, "And that is why You have so few of them." She called life a "night spent at an uncomfortable inn." Once when she was trying to avoid that recreation hour which is set aside in convents for nuns to be together, the others insisted on her joining them, and she took castanets and danced. When some older nuns professed themselves shocked, she retorted, "One must do things sometimes to make life more bearable." After she was a superior she gave directions when the nuns became melancholy, "to feed them steak," and there were other delightful little touches to the story of her life which made me love her and feel close to her. I have since heard a priest friend of ours remark gloomily that one could go to hell imitating the imperfections of the saints, but these little incidents brought out in her biography made her delightfully near to me. So I decided to name my daughter after her. That is why my neighbor offered me a medal of St. Thérèse of Lisieux, who is called the little Teresa.

Her other name came from Sasha's sister Liza. She had named her daughter Tamar, which in Hebrew means "little palm tree," and knowing nothing of the unhappy story of the two Tamars in the Old Testament, I named my child Tamar also. Tamar is one of the forebears of our Lord, listed in the first chapter of Matthew, and not only Jews and Russians, but also New Englanders used the name. . . .

. . . I had become convinced that I would become a Catholic; yet I felt I was betraying the class to which I belonged, the workers, the poor of the world, with whom Christ spent His life. I wrote a few articles for the *New Masses* but did no other work at that time. My life was crowded in summer because friends came and stayed with me, and some of them left their children. Two little boys, four and eight years old, joined the family for a few months and my days were full, caring for three children and cooking meals for a half-dozen persons three times a day.

Sometimes when I could leave the baby in trusted hands I could get to the village for Mass on Sunday. But usually the gloom that descended on the household, the scarcely voiced opposition, kept me from Mass. There were some feast days when I could slip off during the week and go to the little chapel on the Sisters' grounds. There were "visits" I could make, unknown to others. I was committed, by the advice of a priest I consulted, to the plan of waiting, and trying to hold together the family. But I felt all along that when I took the irrevocable step it would mean that Tamar and I would be alone, and I did not want to be alone. I did not want to give up human love when it was dearest and tenderest.

During the month of August many of my friends, including my sister, went to Boston to picket in protest against the execution of Sacco and Vanzetti, which was drawing near. They were all arrested again and again.

Throughout the nation and the world the papers featured the struggle for the lives of these two men. Radicals from all over the country gathered in Boston, and articles describing those last days were published, poems were written. It was an epic struggle, a tragedy. One felt a sense of impending doom. These men were Catholics, inasmuch as they were Italians. Catholics by tradition, but they had rejected the Church.

Nicola Sacco and Bartolomeo Vanzetti were two anarchists, a shoemaker and a fish peddler who were arrested in 1920 in connection with a payroll robbery at East Braintree, Massachusetts, in which two guards were killed. Nobody paid much attention to the case at first, but as the I.W.W. and the Communists took up the case it became a *cause célèbre*. In August, 1927, they were executed. Many books have been written about the case, and Vanzetti's prison letters are collected in one volume. He learned to write English in prison, and his prose, bare and simple, is noble in its earnestness.

While I enjoyed the fresh breeze, the feel of salt water against the flesh, the keen delight of living, the knowledge that these men were soon to pass from this physical earth, were soon to become dust, without consciousness, struck me like a physical blow. They were here now; in a few days they would be no more. They had become figures beloved by the workers. Their letters, the warm moving story of their lives, had been told. Everyone knew Dante, Sacco's young son. Everyone suffered with the young wife who clung with bitter passion to her husband. And Vanzetti with his large view, his sense of peace at his fate, was even closer to us all.

He wrote a last letter to a friend which has moved many hearts as great poetry does:

> I have talked a great deal of myself [he wrote]. But I even forget to name Sacco. Sacco too is a worker, from his boyhood a skilled worker, lover of work, with a good job and pay, a bank account, a good and lovely wife, two beautiful children and a neat little home, at the verge of a wood near a brook.
>
> Sacco is a heart of faith, a lover of nature and man.
>
> A man who gave all, who sacrificed all for mankind, his own wife, his children, himself and his own life.
>
> Sacco has never dreamed to steal, never to assassinate.
>
> He and I never brought a morsel of bread to our mouths, from our childhood to today which has not been gained by the sweat of our brows.
>
> Never.
>
> O yes, I may be more witful, as some have put it, I am a better blabber

than he is, but many many times in hearing his heartful voice ringing a faith sublime, in considering his supreme sacrifice, remembering his heroism, I felt small at the presence of his greatness and found myself compelled to fight back from my eyes the tears, and quanch my heart, trobling to my throat to not weep before him,—this man called thief, assassin and doomed. . . .

If it had not been for these things I might have lived out my life talking at street corners to scorning men. I might have died, unmarked, unknown, a failure. This is our career and our triumph.

Never in our full life could we hope to do such work for tolerance, for justice,

for man's understanding of man,

as we now do by accident.

Our words, our lives, our pains—nothing!

The taking of our lives,—lives of a good shoe maker

and a poor fish peddler—all!

That last moment belongs to us

—that agony is our triumph.

The day they died, the papers had headlines as large as those which proclaimed the outbreak of war. All the nation, mourned. All the nation, I mean, that is made up of the poor, the worker, the trade unionist—those who felt most keenly the sense of solidarity—that very sense of solidarity which made me gradually understand the doctrine of the Mystical Body of Christ whereby we are the members one of another.

Forster was stricken over the tragedy. He had always been more an anarchist than anything else in his philosophy, and so was closer to these two men than to Communist friends. He did not eat for days. He sat around the house in a stupor of misery, sickened by the cruelty of life and men. He had always taken refuge in nature as being more kindly, more beautiful and peaceful than the world of men. Now he could not even escape through nature, as he tried to escape so many problems in life.

During the time he was home he spent days and even nights out in his boat fishing, so that for weeks I saw little of him. He stupefied himself in his passion for the water, sitting out on the bay in his boat. When he began to recover he submerged himself in maritime biology, collecting, reading only scientific books, and paying no attention to what went on around him. Only the baby interested him. She was his delight. Which made it, of course, the harder to contemplate the cruel blow I was going to strike him when I became a Catholic. We both suffered in body as well as in soul and mind. He would not talk about the faith and relapsed into a complete silence if I tried to bring up the subject. The point of my bringing it up was that I could not become a Catholic and continue living with him, because he was averse to any ceremony before officials of either Church or state. He was an anarchist and an atheist, and he did not intend to be a liar or a hypocrite. He was a creature of utter sincerity, and however illogical and bad-tempered about it all, I loved him. It was killing me to think of leaving him.

Fall nights we read a great deal. Sometimes he went out to dig bait if there were a low tide and the moon was up. He stayed out late on the pier fishing, and came in smelling of seaweed and salt air; getting into bed, cold with the chill November air, he held me close to him in silence. I loved him in every way, as a wife, as a mother even. I loved him for all he knew and pitied him for all he didn't know. I loved him for the odds and ends I had to fish out of his sweater pockets and for the sand and shells he brought in with his fishing. I loved his lean cold body as he got into bed smelling of the sea, and I loved his integrity and stubborn pride.

It ended by my being ill the next summer. I became so oppressed I could not breathe and I awoke in the night choking. I was weak and listless and one doctor told me my trouble was probably thyroid. I went to the Cornell clinic for a metabolism test and they said my condition was a nervous one. By winter the tension had become so great that an explosion occurred and we separated again. When he returned, as he always had, I would not let him in the house; my heart was breaking with my own determination to make an end, once and for all, to the torture we were undergoing.

The next day I went to Tottenville alone, leaving Tamar with my sister, and there with Sister Aloysia as my godparent, I too was baptized conditionally, since I had already been baptized in the Episcopal Church. I made my first confession right afterward, and looked forward the next morning to receiving communion.

I had no particular joy in partaking of these three sacraments, Baptism, Penance and Holy Eucharist. I proceeded about my own active participation in them grimly, coldly, making acts of faith, and certainly with no consolation whatever. One part of my mind stood at one side and kept saying, "What are you doing? Are you sure of yourself? What kind of an affectation is this? What act is this you are going through? Are you trying to induce emotion, induce faith, partake of an opiate, the opiate of the people?" I felt like a hypocrite if I got down on my knees, and shuddered at the thought of anyone seeing me.

At my first communion I went up to the communion rail at the *Sanctus* bell instead of at the *Domine, non sum dignus,* and had to kneel there all alone through the consecration, through the *Pater Noster,* through the *Agnus Dei*—and I had thought I knew the Mass so well! But I felt it fitting that I be humiliated by this ignorance, by this precipitance.

I speak of the misery of leaving one love. But there was another love too, the life I had led in the radical movement. That very winter I was writing a series of articles, interviews with the workers, with the unemployed. I was working with the Anti-Imperialist League, a Communist affiliate, that was bringing aid and comfort to the enemy, General Sandino's forces in Nicaragua. I was just as much against capitalism and imperialism as ever, and here I was going over to the opposition, because of course the Church was lined up with property, with the wealthy, with the state, with capitalism, with all the forces of reaction. This I had been taught to think and this I still think to a great extent. "Too often," Cardinal Mundelein said, "has the Church lined up on the wrong side." "Christianity," Bakunin said, "is precisely the religion par excellence, because it exhibits, and manifests, to the fullest extent, the very nature and essence of every religious system, which is the impoverishment, enslavement, and annihilation of humanity for the benefit of divinity."

I certainly believed this, but I wanted to be poor, chaste and obedient. I wanted to die in order to live, to put off the old man and put on Christ. I loved, in other words, and like all women in love, I wanted to be united to my love. Why should not Forster be jealous? Any man who did not participate in this love would, of course, realize my infidelity, my adultery. In the eyes of God, any turning toward creatures to the exclusion of Him is adultery and so it is termed over and over again in Scripture.

I loved the Church for Christ made visible. Not for itself, because it was so often a scandal to me. Romano Guardini said the Church is the Cross on which Christ was crucified; one could not separate Christ from His Cross, and one must live in a state of permanent dissatisfaction with the Church.

The scandal of businesslike priests, of collective wealth, the lack of a sense of responsibility for the poor, the worker, the Negro, the Mexican, the Filipino, and even the oppression of these, and the consenting to the oppression of them by our industrialist-capitalist order—these made me feel often that priests were more like Cain than Abel. "Am I my brother's keeper?" they seemed to say in respect to the social order. There was plenty of charity but too little justice. And yet the priests were the dispensers of the Sacraments, bringing Christ to men, all enabling us to put on Christ and to achieve more nearly in the world a sense of peace and unity. "The worst enemies would be those of our own household," Christ had warned us.

We could not root out the tares without rooting out the wheat also. With all the knowledge I have gained these twenty-one years I have been a Catholic, I could write many a story of priests who were poor, chaste and obedient, who gave their lives daily for their fellows, but I am writing of how I felt at the time of my baptism.

Not long afterward a priest wanted me to write a story of my conversion, telling how the social teaching of the Church had led me to embrace Catholicism. But I knew nothing of the social teaching of the Church at that time. I had never heard of the encyclicals. I felt that the Church was the Church of the poor, that St. Patrick's had been built from the pennies of servant girls, that it cared for the emigrant, it established hospitals, orphanages, day nurseries, houses of the Good Shepherd, homes for the aged, but at the same time, I felt that it did not set its face against a social order which made so much charity in the present sense of the word necessary. I felt that charity was a word to choke over. Who wanted charity? And it was not just human pride but a strong sense of man's dignity and worth, and what was due to him in justice, that made me resent, rather than feel proud of so mighty a sum total of Catholic institutions. Besides, more and more they were taking help from the state, and in taking from the state, they had to render to the state. They came under the head of Community Chest and discriminatory charity, centralizing and departmentalizing, involving themselves with bureaus, building, red tape, legislation, at the expense of human values. By "they," I suppose one always means the bishops, but as Harry Bridges once pointed out to me, "they" also are victims of the system.

It was an age-old battle, the war of the classes, that stirred in me when I thought of the Sacco-Vanzetti case in Boston. Where were the Catholic voices crying out for these men? How I longed to make a synthesis reconciling body and soul, this world and the next, the teachings of Prince Peter Kropotkin and Prince Demetrius Gallitzin, who had become a missionary priest in rural Pennsylvania.

Where had been the priests to go out to such men as Francisco Ferrer in Spain, pursuing them as the Good Shepherd did His lost sheep, leaving the ninety and nine of their good parishioners, to seek out that which was lost, bind up that which was bruised. No wonder there was such a strong conflict going on in my mind and heart. . . .

LILLIAN HELLMAN
(1905–1984)

◆

The dramatist and memoirist LILLIAN HELLMAN was born in New Orleans to Max Hellman, a shoe merchant whose parents had migrated to Louisiana from Germany, and to Julia Newhouse, a "sweet eccentric," in her daughter's words, from a prosperous Alabama family. Hellman spent her childhood between New Orleans and New York, where she later attended New York University and Columbia University and worked as a manuscript reader for the publisher Horace Liveright. In 1934 she launched her career as a playwright with *The Children's Hour,* a highly successful debut—it ran for 691 performances on Broadway—which deals with the destructive effects of a young girl's charge that two of her teachers are lesbians. Over the next three decades came a succession of major achievements in the theater, among them *The Little Foxes, Watch on the Rhine, Another Part of the Forest, The Autumn Garden,* and *Toys in the Attic.* She twice received the New York Drama Critics Circle Award for the best play of the year, for *Watch on the Rhine* and *Toys in the Attic.* The recipient of the Gold Medal for Drama from the National Institute of Arts and Letters as well as honorary degrees from Yale, Smith, Rutgers, and other universities, she was Regents' Professor at the University of California at Berkeley, Distinguished Professor at Hunter College, and taught at Harvard, Yale, and the Massachusetts Institute of Technology.

In 1969 she began the series of memoirs that were published together as *Three* (1979), with an introduction by Richard Poirier: *An Unfinished Woman: A Memoir* (1969), the winner of the National Book Award, which describes her family background, her literary career, and her life with the writer Dashiell Hammett; *Pentimento: A Book of Portraits* (1973); and *Scoundrel Time* (1976), her account of the witch-hunting years of the 1950s, with a historical introduction by Garry Wills, in which she confesses to being more contemptuous of the intellectuals and entertainers who let themselves be used by the House Un-American Activities Committee than of Nixon and McCarthy. Collectively, these autobiographical books provide a sense of Hellman's immersion in the history of her times: the fight against fascism in Franco's Spain; the political and artistic culture of Europe and the Soviet Union during and after World War II; the anti-Communist hysteria of the McCarthy era and her refusal to cooperate with the House Un-American Activities Committee. "To hurt innocent people whom I knew many years ago in order to save myself," she told them, "is, to me, inhuman and indecent and dishonorable. . . . I cannot and will not cut my conscience to fit this year's fashions." Poirier describes these "essays in recollection" as a "clue to the beauty and substantiality of Hellman, both in her life and in her writing. . . . An understanding of her place in American letters depends on our recognizing why she chose to enter on a second career as a writer, turning from plays to prose portraiture and reminiscence. She has achieved a redirection of energies, unprecedented in our literature." Throughout Hellman's life histories, we are always, in Poirier's words, "referred back to a strong but free-moving individual presence, a spiritual presence, that suffuses the writing at every point and allows nothing to seem isolated or beyond the reach of sympathy."

From *An Unfinished Woman*

From a Diary, 1967:

Paris, April 23

For two days now I have asked myself why the French frighten me. I came here the first time when I was very young, lived here for four months, and have come back many times since. True, I am ashamed of the patois French that New Orleans taught me and won't take part in conversations with educated people, but waiters and taxi drivers think I talk just fine. I have felt more at home in Copenhagen in three days and more comfortable in a frozen outskirt of Irkutsk. I can't remember being frightened of the French when I was young and poor, so why should I be now when I am not poor? I stay at the best hotels, go to the best restaurants, can buy in good shops, can afford meals for those old friends who didn't share in the French boom. (Most intellectuals didn't.) And yet, in the last years, I am timid as I walk along the lovely streets. It's as if all of France had become a too thin lady. Very thin ladies, any age, with hand sewing on them, have always frightened me, beginning with a rich great-aunt and her underwear embroidered by nuns. The more bones that show on women the more inferior I feel.

I know my way around Paris and yet each day I get lost and it's no longer possible, as it was even three years ago, to say to hell with all that, today I go once more to see Ste. Chapelle or to the Marais or to wander around the Rue de la Université, trying to sort out all those houses that Stendhal is supposed to have lived in, and then take myself alone to a small place to eat and rest. I have, this week, bought a dress and a bag, no better and no cheaper than New York, have kept myself from the angry question of why a dress should need four fittings, and have had dinner or lunch with old friends. (I have written to Aragon and Elsa but, for the first time, they have not answered me, and yet I know they are in Paris. It is understandable: they are growing old, they work hard, and who, after a certain age, wishes to see anybody at intervals of two or three years?) The dinners and lunches were not as good as they used to be, but the talk is still good, or, at least, high class. It may be the only country in the world where the rich are sometimes brilliant.

April 24

We are at the Château Choiseul Amboise. It has been a good day: I feel at my best when somebody else drives the car, gives the orders, knows me well enough to see through the manner that, as an irritated theatre director once pointed out, was thought up early to hide the indecision, the vagueness. The hotel and gardens are charming, the dining room high and white, the dinner of Loire salmon is excellent, and I feel very close to the man opposite me. The years we have known each other have made a pleasant summer fog of the strange, crippled relationship, often ripped, always mended, merging, finally, into comfort. I am comfortable now. I feel young again on this journey that was his idea. We have a local marc in the garden, we have been talking as old friends should talk, about nothing, about everything.

R says, "I must say something to you. I should get married again. My feeling for you has kept me from marrying."

I have heard this many times before. I mumble that to myself.

"What did you say?"

"Nothing. Are you marrying a theory or a woman?"

"I met a girl in Berlin. We've been living together. I have been in a panic since she went home."

I push my chair back. I know now why this trip was arranged. It is not the first time he has done this. I go to my room, drink too much brandy, and the anger turns in against myself. The next morning we cancel the rest of the trip and drive back to Paris. I have a stinking hangover and don't speak on the ride back, don't even think much except to tell myself how much jabber there is in the name of love. The next day R sends me flowers just as the porter is carrying down my luggage for the plane to Budapest.

Budapest, April 30

Is it age, or was it always my nature, to take a bad time, block out the good times, until any success became an accident and failure seemed the only truth? I can't sleep, I have had a headache for three days, I lie on the bed telling myself that nothing has ever gone right, doubting even Hammett and myself, remembering how hard the early years sometimes were for us when he didn't care what he did or spoiled, and I didn't think I wanted to stay long with anybody, asking myself why, after the first failure, I had been so frightened of marriage, who the hell did I think I was alone in a world where women don't have much safety, and, finally, on the third night, falling asleep with a lighted cigarette and waking to a burn on my chest. Staring at the burn, I thought: That's what you deserve for wasting time on stuff proper for the head of a young girl.

Edmund Wilson's friends are nice people. Mrs. S is a bluestocking but handsome and with good manners. Her husband, much older than she, is an art expert. Bluestockings are the same the world over, but the European variety has learned a few graces: Mrs. S, of course, chose the table in the restaurant and ordered the dinner, but she pretended that her husband did and he was pleased. When I got back to the hotel I felt cheerful, for the first time in a week. I sat on the balcony outside my room and looked at the old church across the square. In the park the hotel night clerk was drinking something from a glass. I thought about Mrs. S and her husband, their age difference must be what mine was to Hammett. But Dash was not grateful, or ungrateful, either, for a much younger woman, and I didn't choose tables or food or anything very often. He used his age to make the rules.

One day, a few months after we met, he said, "Can you stop juggling oranges?"

I said I didn't know what he meant.

He said, "Yes, you do. So stop it or I won't be around to watch."

A week later, I said, "You mean I haven't made up my mind about you and have been juggling you and other people. I'm sorry. Maybe it will take time for me to cure myself, but I'll try."

He said, "Maybe it will take time for *you*. But for me it will take no longer than tomorrow morning."

And so I did stop for long periods, although several times through the years he said, "Don't start that juggling again."

Many years later, unhappy about his drinking, his ladies, my life with him, I remember an angry speech I made one night: it had to do with injustice, his carelessness, his insistence that he get his way, his sharpness with me but not with himself. I was drunk, but he was drunker, and when my strides around the room carried me close to the chair where he was sitting, I stared in disbelief at what I saw. He was grinding a burning cigarette into his cheek.

I said, "What are you doing?"

"Keeping myself from doing it to you," he said.

The mark on his cheek was ugly for a few weeks, but in time it faded into the scar that remained for the rest of his life. We never again spoke of that night because, I think, he was ashamed of the angry gesture that made him once again the winner in the game that men and women play against each other, and I was ashamed that I caused myself to lose so often.

And so I told myself that it was unjust to hold in contempt R, who is another juggler. Unjust. How many times I've used that word, scolded myself with it. All I mean by it now is that I don't have the final courage to say that I refuse to preside over violations against myself, and to hell with justice.

I have sent two cables to the Writers Union in Moscow, saying that I would arrive on Sunday night. A few hours ago, a call comes from Moscow, a man's voice makes sounds that I can't hear. I make sounds that he can't hear, I hang up, he calls again, and then Tomas comes on the phone to ask if I would like a picnic, free, no charge, with his children. I say yes, the man in Moscow goes on shouting through Tomas, an operator shouts at him in Russian, and he hangs up.

Tomas is a taxi driver whose cab I took my first day here. He speaks good English, is wry and funny, makes fancy hints about his fallen station in the world. Every morning he calls to see if I want to hire him for the day, and sometimes I do.

Yesterday, when I left him, I said, "Thank you for calling every day. It is kind of you to be so nice to a stranger."

He stared at me. "That is not it, you do not count very well. You have been giving me large amounts of forints."

"I have? How much?"

"That is for you to decide. For me, I would not like to ruin the golden goose." . . .

It has been ten days since I have slept more than a few hours or eaten more than one meal a day. I have lost eight pounds. That would usually please me, but I look tired, sad, and that does not please me. You can do and you can take almost as much as when you were young, but you cannot recover fast. I tell myself that I must forbid myself these upheavals because I can no longer afford them. But how often I have said all that before, what good does it do, how little my nature allows me to carry out the resolute wisdom of night. For a minute I wish age would strike with the bad health I have never had, then immediately frightened, superstitious, I jump from the bed, put on a coat, cross the park, and look for the first restaurant that might have coffee. On the way, I argue, I lecture, I determine. I am suddenly so sick of myself that I spit in the street. I stand staring at the spit, laughing.

I remember: Hammett and I are having breakfast with friends in the country, served on one of those ugly bar arrangements with high stools. Hammett is teasing me. He tells about a hunting trip when, in an attempt to aim at a high-flying duck, I had hit a wild lilac bush. He is saying that I have no sense of direction about anything.

I say, "Don't count on it. I could spit in your eye if I wanted to. How much says I can't do it?"

"The Jap prints," he says, meaning a rare set of Japanese art books he has just bought and loves, "fifty dollars, and anything you want to say to me for a whole night."

I spit directly into his eye and the daughter of the family screams. Hammett had a quiet laugh that began slowly and then creased his face for a long time. It begins now and is increased by the perplexed, unhappy looks of the others at the table. He says, proudly, "That's my girl. Some of the time the kid kicks through."

I turn into a restaurant, happy now at the memory of Dash's long, thin, handsome face at that spitting breakfast more than fifteen years ago. The place is crowded, the people at tables near the entrance stare at my fur-lined coat on this warm day. I move to the back and sit down at a table with two young women. I have coffee and try to order a boiled egg.

One of the young girls says in English, in an excellent accent, "The eggs are at the front bar. May I get them for you?"

She gets up and the other girl asks me in less good English if I am Australian. When her friend comes back we ask and answer questions. They are graduate students, one in English, one in French. Magda is the daughter of a history professor, Charlotte the daughter of a factory foreman. They are pleased that they know two of my plays, they ask if they can show me any part of Budapest or the countryside. I tell them I don't like gypsy music, am sick of hearing it, is there any place to hear jazz?

Magda claps her hands. "Indeed, indeed. My younger brother, if you can tolerate him, plays with a group every Saturday night. Will you come?"

★ ★ ★

It is past midnight. The apartment must once have been part of a solid private house. I am sitting in a broken chair, my back hurts. Around me are Magda and Charlotte, and Charlotte's beau Sandor, a tall young man of about twenty-four. I count the others, including the band, as eleven, and all eleven are younger, in their teens. The jazz band is not good, very imitative of us. They have been playing since nine o'clock, with few rests, but now they are tired and hungry, I guess, because two girls appear with coffee, pastry, and wine that is too sweet for me. The room having been blown with noise is now silent except for somebody who is whistling. Everybody eats or drinks and a few of them stare at me. Something is expected of me, but I don't know what, and I feel awkward. Finally, one of the younger boys says something and Sandor answers him. Then somebody else speaks and Sandor answers sharply.

He says to me, "They say 'Launch.'"

"Launch?"

"That is the translation. They mean you must have come to this country with a purpose. So launch the purpose here, now. Hungary is bad and poor, America is good and rich, et cetera, et cetera."

"Why would I do that?"

Magda laughs. "My brother says maybe you think they should enlist in Vietnam war against Communist aggressors."

I remember a Harvard seminar when two students wished to bait me. I decide on the answer I made then.

I say, "Tell your brother to go to hell."

Magda translates, and they laugh. She says, "They are young. We are not young, although there is only five or six years between us. We were the believers, they are not."

"Believers in what?"

"Socialism. We grew up believing. Now we are bitter."

Sandor, Charlotte's beau, says to Magda, "Speak for yourself, less for others. I am still a Communist. My own kind of Communist."

Charlotte puts out a hand and touches him. Timeless gesture, and timeless response when he pushes her hand away. She turns to me. "He stays with the workers. He is finding a new Communism."

He says, "Do not explain me. Not that way."

She says something to him in Hungarian. Magda whispers to me, "She is too *triste, éthérée.*"

Charlotte, as if conscious of me again, says, "My brother was to be an engineer, but now he doesn't want to be anything, except not to starve or ask favors of the government. Sandor tells him without work man is nothing."

I say to Sandor, "What do you work at?"

"I do not work." He moves about in front of me. "Something new must come, Marxism must advance. Now we leave it to the protectors of the state. It is too good for them. Something new must come."

Charlotte's brother laughs. "Lady foreigner, turn your ears away. Nothing new will come. There is nothing in this world but now for now."

Then he crosses the room, raises his arm, and the music starts again, for the first time in a kind of folk melody. The guitar player sings, and when the first verse is finished several others sing with him.

Magda brings me some wine. "The song says, 'Shut your heart against the past and the future. Now is for now.'"

After the rather sweet melody is over, the band goes back to jazz. It is two o'clock and I rise to leave. Sandor, Charlotte and Magda walk me back to my hotel, a long distance across the river. Sandor tells me that the new socialism must come from the worker, I say that was the old way, he says that's what people thought but things got off the track, and for a few minutes it seems to me I am young again and Sandor is William and Charlotte is Gertrude and the conversation is being held on the porch of a house in the Berkshires. I ask Sandor too many questions in order to hide my weariness with what he is saying, and thank them for the evening too many times. We agree that we will meet again before I leave Budapest, but the next day it is raining and I decide to fly to Moscow that afternoon. . . .

M.F.K. FISHER
(1908–1992)

◆

M(ARY) F(RANCES) K(ENNEDY) FISHER was born in Albion, Michigan, but, from the age of three, grew up in Whittier, California ("I still feel embarrassed that I was not born a native Californian because I truly think I am one.") She described her daredevil and freedom-loving youth in the autobiographical *Among Friends* and more recently in the collection *To Begin Again* from which the following piece is taken. She published sixteen books in her lifetime, many on the subject of food (*Serve It Forth; How to Cook a Wolf; Consider the Oyster; The Gastronomical Me*); she translated and annotated *The Physiology of Taste* by Jean Anthelme Brillat-Savarin. In all these books she created a genre of her own. Ostensibly writing about food—"learning to live well gastronomically"—she found another way to talk passionately about all the appetites and satisfactions of the heart, about breaking bread as an essential pleasure of the good life. At sensual family dinners, she learned, in spite of her puritanical grandmother of "Grandmother's Nervous Stomach," that there is no separation between the nourishment of the body and the soul, that happiness "seems to be connected with open enjoyment of even a badly prepared dish that could be tasted without censure of the tasting." Fisher also wrote novels and many short stories, all the products of "a richly civilized and fearless mind," in the words of one critic. Indeed, all her books are suffused with her trademark wit and intelligence. W. H. Auden called her "the best prose writer in America." (She said, "I find increasingly as I grow older that I do not consider myself a writer. . . . But by now people sometimes refer to me as a stylist, or they talk about my style, and I think this is because of my habit of putting words onto paper as much as possible as I say them in talking or telling.") For the last twenty years of her life she lived in a house set in a vineyard in the Napa Valley which included a bathroom designed as a salon, so she might entertain as she bathed. As she said in *To Begin Again,* "I have never seen any reason to be dull." Her improvisatory style, humor, and intelligence call to mind Mary Catherine Bateson's words about the wisdom of women in her remarkable book *Composing a Life:* "Usually we think of wisdom in terms of lofty abstractions, not survival skills, absolute truths, not tactful equivocations. No one expects Athena to be streetwise; even less do we expect that virgin goddess to be what you might call hearthwise, to embody a homespun wisdom of relationships and sensory richness. And yet the central survival skill is surely the capacity to pay attention and respond to changing circumstances, to learn and adapt, to fit into new environments beyond the safety of the temple precincts."

From *To Begin Again*

7
Grandmother's Nervous Stomach (1913–1920)

One of the fine feelings in this world is to have a long-held theory confirmed. It adds a smug glow to life in general.

When I was about five, I began to suspect that eating something good with good people is highly important. By the time I was ten I not only knew, for myself, that this theory was right but I had added to it the companion idea that if children are given a chance to practice it, they will stand an even better chance of being keen adults.

In my own case I was propelled somewhat precociously, perhaps, into such theorizing by what was always referred to in the family as Grandmother's Nervous Stomach, an ultimately fortunate condition that forced her to force us to eat tasteless white overcooked things like rice and steamed soda crackers in milk.

Now and then either Grandmother's stomach or her conscience drove her to a religious convention safely removed from us, and during her pious absences we indulged in a voluptuous riot of things like marshmallows in hot chocolate, thin pastry under the Tuesday hash, rare roast beef on Sunday instead of boiled hen. Mother ate all she wanted of cream of fresh mushroom soup; Father served a local wine, red-ink he called it, with the steak; we ate grilled sweetbreads and skewered kidneys with a daring dash of sherry on them. Best of all, we talked, laughed, sang, kissed, and in general exposed ourselves to a great many sensations forbidden when the matriarchal stomach rumbled among us. And I formed my own firm opinions of where gastronomy should and indeed must operate in any happy person's pattern.

A great many seemingly unrelated things can be blamed on a nervous stomach, as ladies of the middle and late years of Queen Victoria's reign well knew.

Here I am, for instance, at least ninety-five years after my maternal grandmother first abandoned herself to the relatively voluptuous fastings and lavages of a treatment for the fashionable disorder, blaming or crediting it for the fact that I have written several books about gastronomy, a subject that my ancestor would have saluted, if at all, with a refined but deep down belch of gastric protest. That I have gone further and dared link the pleasures of the table with our other basic hungers for love and shelter would outrage far more than the air around her, to be sure: kisses and comfort were suspect to such a pillar as she. They were part and parcel of the pagan connotations of "a cold bottle and a warm bird" or vice versa—wanton and therefore nonexistent.

The Nervous Stomach was to Grandmother and to her "sisters" in the art of being loyal wives and mothers of plump beardy men a heaven-sent escape.

The pattern was one they followed like the resolute ladies they were: a period of dogged reproduction, eight or twelve and occasionally sixteen offspring, so that at least half would survive the nineteenth-century hazards of colics and congestions; a period of complete instead of partial devotion to the church, usually represented in the Indian Territory where my grandmother lived by a series of gawky earnest missionaries who plainly needed fattening; and at last the blissful flight from all these domestic and extracurricular demands into the sterile muted corridors of a spa. It did not matter if the place reeked discreetly of sulphur from the baths and singed bran from the diet trays: it was a haven and a reward.

In my own grandam's gradual but sure ascent to the throne of marital freedom, she bore nine children and raised several of her sisters', loaned from the comparative sophistication of Pittsburgh for a rough winter or two in what was to be Iowa. It is not reported by any of the native or transplanted youngsters that she gave them love, but she did her duty by them and saw that the Swedish and Irish cooks fed them well and that they fell on their knees at the right moments. She raised a good half of them to prosperous if somewhat precarious maturity.

As the children left the nest, she leaned more and more in one direction as her dutiful husband leaned in another, toward long rapt sessions with the Lord. Fortunately for the social life of a village such as she reigned in, His disciples were hungry, young, and at times even attractive, on their ways to China or Mbano-Mbang.

In a Christian way things hummed during the protracted visits of these earnest boys, and everyone lived high, even my grandfather who took to retreating more and more lengthily into his library with a bottle of port and a bowl of hickory nuts.

As inevitably as in the life cycle of a female mosquito, however, my grandmother passed through the stage of replenishing the vessels of the

Lord, as she had already done through ministering to the carnal demands of her mate, and she turned to the care of her own spirit, as represented by her worn but still extremely vital body. She developed protective symptoms, as almost all women of her age and station did.

There were hushed conferences, and children were summoned from distant schools and colleges for a last faint word from her. She went on a "tour" with her husband to Ireland and the Lake Country, but for some reason it seemed to do him more good than it did her, and while he pranced off the ship in New York wearing a new Inverness cape, she left it retching and tottery.

At last she achieved what she had spent almost a lifetime practicing for, and she was sent *alone,* with no man or child to question her, to some great health resort like Battle Creek.

There the delicious routine laved her in its warm if sometimes nauseous security. Duties both connubial and maternal were shadows in her farthest heart, and even her morning prayers could be postponed if a nurse stood waiting with a bowl of strained rice water or a lavage tube.

One difference from our present substitute for this escape, the psychiatrist's low couch, is that today's refugees face few gastronomical challenges, unless perhaps the modish low-sodium-low-cholesterol diet can be counted as such. My grandmother found many such challenges in her years of flitting with her own spare crampish pleasure from one spa to another. Certainly what she could and would and did eat played a vigorous part in my own life, and most probably provided an excuse for my deciding to prove a few theories about the pleasures of the table in relation to certain other necessary functional expressions.

Grandmother did not believe in any form of seasoning, and in a period when all food was boiled for hours, whatever it was boiled in was thrown out as being either too rich (meats) or trashy (vegetables). We ate turnips and potatoes a lot, since Grandmother had lived in Iowa long before it became a state. We seldom ate cabbage: it did not agree with her, and small wonder, since it was always cooked according to her mid-Victorian recipes and would have made an elephant heave and hiccup. We ate carrots, always in a "white sauce" in little dishes by our plates, and as soon as my grandmother died I headed for the raw ones and chewed at them after school and even in the dark of night while I was growing. But the flatter a thing tasted, the better it was for you, Grandmother believed. And the better it was for you, she believed, the more you should suffer to eat it, thus proving your innate worth as a Christian, a martyr to the flesh but a courageous one.

All Christians were perforce martyrs to her, and therefore courageous, and therefore all good Christians who had been no matter how indirectly the result of Grandmother's union with Grandfather had to eat the way she learned to eat at such temples as Battle Creek.

They could eat her way, that is, or die. Several did die, and a few more simply resigned from the family, the way one does from a club, after the cook had served Grandmother's own version of white sauce once too often.

By the time she came to live with us—a custom most aging ladies followed then after their quiet withdrawn husbands, helped by gout and loneliness, had withdrawn quietly and completely—my sister and I had already been corrupted by the insidious experience of good cooking. Thanks to an occasional and very accidental stay in our big crowded house of a cook who actually cared whether the pastry was light or not, we had discovered the caloric pleasures of desserts. And thanks to an open house and heart to the south of us, where we could stay for dinner now and then while Mother was "resting," we had found that not all salad dressing need be "boiled" and not all fried things need be anathema. The mayonnaise: it was a dream, not a pallid loose something made of flour and oil and eggy water. The pineapple fritters dusted with white sugar: they were dreams, too, tiny hot sweet clouds snatched at by healthy children.

We soon learned, however, that to Grandmother's way of thinking, any nod to the flesh was a denial of her Christian duty, even to the point of putting a little butter on a soft-boiled egg, but although her own spirits as well as her guts may have benefited from the innocuous regime, ours did not.

Fortunately at least one of my grandmother's phases of development impinged upon another, so that when she felt herself hemmed in by ancestral demands, she would at one and the same time, in her late years, develop an extraordinary belch and discover that a conference was being held in a town at least thirty miles away, one in which there was a preponderance of well-heeled as well as devout dyspeptics. She would be gone a week or so, to anywhere from nearby Oceanside to a legendary religious beach-head somewhat south of Atlantic City. She picked conventions where she could drink a glass of lukewarm seawater morning and night for her innards, and it made slight difference to her whether the water was of Pacific or Atlantic vintage. It can never be known how coincidental were these secular accidents, but they were twice blessed for her and at least thrice for the rest of us: she could escape from children and grandchildren into a comfortable austere hotel, and we . . .

We? Ah! What freedom! What quiet unembarrassed silences, except for the chewings and munchings of a hundred things Grandmother would not eat!

No more rice water, opaque and unseasoned, in the guise of soup. No more boiled dressing in the guise of mayonnaise. No more of whatever it was that was pale and tasteless enough to please that autocratic digestive system.

She would start off, laced into her most rigid best, her Jane pinned firmly under the white spout of her noted pompadour. We would wave and smile, and as the Maxwell disappeared down past the college, with Father tall and dustered at the wheel, we would edge avidly toward the kitchen.

Mother would laugh only a little ashamedly, and then we'd make something like divinity fudge, a delicious memory from her boarding school days. Or if it was the cook's day off my sister would set the table crazily—ah, *la vie bohème*—with cut out magazine covers scattered over the cloth to make it crazier, and I would stand on a footstool to reach the gas burners and create.

Of course there were accidents, too revolting to detail here. But it was fine to feel the gaiety in our family, a kind of mischievous mirth, and at the same time all of us, even the small ones, sensed a real sadness that we could not share it with the short, stiff, dutiful old woman, eructating righteously over a dish of boiled carrots in a vegetarian cafeteria near her churchful of "sisters" and even "brothers."

It was magic always then to see the change in Father's and Mother's behavior at the table when Grandmother was gone. They were relaxed and easy, and they slumped in their chairs as the meal progressed. Mother would lean one elbow on the table and let her hand fall toward Father, and he would lean back in his chair and smile. And if by chance my sister or I said something, they both listened to us. In other words, we were a happy family, bathed in a rare warmth around the table.

It was then, I am sure, that I began to think of the spiritual communion of the act of peaceful eating—breaking bread. It is in every religion, including the unwritten ones of the animals, and in more ways than one, all of them basically solemn and ritual, it signifies much more than the mere nourishment of the body. When this act is most healthy, most healing to the soul, it obeys some of the basic laws: enemies do not break bread and eat salt together; one communes with others in *peace*.

And so we did, now and then when I was young. We met as if drawn together for a necessary communion as a family. The fact that we were refugees from the dietary strictures as well as the gastric rumblings of a spoiled stern matriarch added a feeling of adventure and amusement to those stolen little parties. We sipped and we dawdled, and I can still remember that occasionally we would *all* put our elbows on the table after dinner and Mother would sing, or she and Father would leave and let us stay on to indulge in the ultimate delight, in our pre-teen years, of putting a cupcake into our dessert bowls and covering it with sugar and cream. What ease, what peace, what voluptuous relaxation!

At home without Grandmother, we gobbled and laughed, and more and more I began to wonder about the meaning of happiness and why and how it seemed to be connected with the open enjoyment of even a badly prepared dish that could be tasted without censure of the tasting.

I was puzzled, of course, for I could not see why anything that made all of us so gay and contented could be forbidden by God. I did not know then, nor do I care to recognize now, the connection between self-appointed moral judging and the personal hair shirt of physical subjection, as my grandmother must have known it when she had to bear one more child and yet one more child because it was her Christian duty.

Now that I am much older, probably as old as she was when she first began to escape from her female lot by feeling dreadful pains throughout her Nervous Stomach, I can understand more of the why, but I still regret it. We escape differently now, of course, and today Grandmother would consult a couple of specialists, and perhaps stretch out on an analyst's couch, and then become a dynamic real estate broker or an airline executive or perhaps even a powerful churchwoman, which she was anyway. But she would have more fun doing it, of that I feel sure.

Of course, there was a slight element of sin, or at least of guilt, in the delightful meals we indulged in when Grandmother was not there, and as always, that added a little fillip to our enjoyment. I suppose my parents felt somewhat guilty to be doing things that Grandmother frowned on, like drinking wine or saying openly, "This is delicious!" My sister and I had not yet reached the age of remorse: we simply leaned back and sighed with bliss, like little fat kittens, unconscious of betrayal.

I think that I have been unfair to my grandmother. I realize now that what I've written about her has made many people think of her as hard and severe. She was neither. She was never a stranger in our house, and she taught me how to read and write, and I accepted her presence in my life as if she were a great protective tree. This went on until she died when I was twelve years old. I felt no sorrow for her leaving, but I missed her, and all my life I have felt some of her self-discipline and strength when I needed it.

Increasingly I saw, felt, understood the importance, especially between people who love and trust one another, of a full sharing of one of our three main hungers, which are for food, for love, and for shelter. We must satisfy them in order to survive as creatures. It is our duty, having been created.

So why not, I asked myself at what may have been a somewhat early age, why not *enjoy* it all? Since we must eat to live, why not make the best of it and see that it is a pleasure, something more than a mere routine necessity like breathing?

And if Grandmother had not been the small stout autocrat, forbidding the use of alcohol, spices, fats, tobacco, and the five senses in our household, I might never have discovered that I myself could detail their uses to my own delight. If my grandmother had not been blessed with her Nervous Stomach, I might never have realized that breaking bread together can be nourishing to more than the body, that people who can sit down together in peace and harmony will rise from the meal with renewed strength for the struggle to survive. My grandmother, who was stern and cold and disapproving of all earthly pleasure, because that was the way she had been raised to think a Christian and a lady should be, would never understand how she taught me otherwise. I revolted against her interpretations of the way to live a good life, but I honestly believe that I have come to understand as much as she of the will of God, perhaps, as Saint Teresa said, "among the pots and pipkins."

And like my grandmother, I am apparently touched with the missionary zeal, the need to "spread the word"! At least, I *suppose* that is why I began to write books about one of our three basic hungers, to please and amuse and titillate people I liked, rather as I used to invent new dishes to amuse my family. I had a feeling it might make life gayer and more fun. A Nervous Stomach can be a fine thing in a family tree, in its own way and at least twice removed.

—1971

EUDORA WELTY
(1909—)

———————◆———————

EUDORA WELTY was born and grew up in Jackson, Mississippi, where she still lives in her parents' house. In her memoir, *One Writer's Beginnings,* the source of the following excerpt, she tells us how her family, their travels, and the voices of her native place shaped her identity and her writing. The origin of this award-winning book is the set of three lectures Welty delivered at Harvard University in 1983 at the invitation of the graduate program in the History of American Civilization. Her many literary honors include O. Henry awards for her short stories (*The Collected Stories* appeared in 1980), the Howell medal of the American Academy of Arts and Letters for *The Ponder Heart* (1954), a National Book Award nomination for *Losing Battles* (1970), and a Pulitzer Prize for *The Optimist's Daughter* (1972). An unofficial prize came in the form of a letter from William Faulkner, praising her novel *The Robber Bridegroom* (1942).

In a *Paris Review* interview Welty, in the tradition of many Southern writers, talked of her love of her region: "It's my source of knowledge. It tells me the important things. It steers me and keeps me going straight, because place is a definer and a confiner of what I'm doing. It helps me to identify, to recognize and explain. . . . It saves me." She talked, too, of her kindred feeling, as a Southerner, for Chekhov: "[He's] one of us—so close to today's world, to my mind, and very close to the South. . . . He loved the singularity in people, the individuality. He took for granted the sense of family . . . there's a great love and understanding that prevails . . . and a knowledge and acceptance of each other's idiosyncracies, a tolerance of them, and also an acute enjoyment of the dramatic." In all her interviews Welty talks at length about her love of other writers, the sources of her inspiration, and the mysteries of people's lives. Because she does not discuss her private life or her friends, she has been criticized by Carolyn Heilbrun in *Writing a Woman's Life* (1988) for "camouflaging" herself, like Willa Cather, and for not recognizing or admitting the anger that she, as a woman writer, must feel within herself.

"My natural temperament is one of positive feelings," Welty said in 1972. And in *Delta Wedding* she expressed the concrete vision that defies the straitjacket of ideology: "How deep were the complexities of the everyday, of the family, what caves were in the mountains, what blocked chambers and what crystal rivers that had not yet seen light." In all her fiction, as the critics Sandra Gilbert and Susan Gubar have observed, "Welty has been particularly notable for her creation of powerfully engaging women characters, . . . explor[ing] the varieties of female experience with grace and wit."

From *One Writer's Beginnings*

Jackson's Carnegie Library was on the same street where our house was, on the other side of the State Capitol. "Through the Capitol" was the way to go to the Library. You could glide through it on your bicycle or even coast through on roller skates, though without family permission.

I never knew anyone who'd grown up in Jackson without being afraid of Mrs. Calloway, our librarian. She ran the Library absolutely by herself, from the desk where she sat with her back to the books and facing the stairs, her dragon eye on the front door, where who knew what kind of person might come in from the public? SILENCE in big black letters was on signs tacked up everywhere. She herself spoke in her normally commanding voice; every word could be heard all over the Library above a steady seething sound coming from her electric fan; it was the only fan in the Library and stood on her desk, turned directly onto her streaming face.

As you came in from the bright outside, if you were a girl, she sent her strong eyes down the stairway to test you; if she could see through your skirt she sent you straight back home: you could just put on another petticoat if you wanted a book that badly from the public library. I was willing; I would do anything to read.

My mother was not afraid of Mrs. Calloway. She wished me to have my own library card to check out books for myself. She took me in to introduce me and I saw I had met a witch. "Eudora is nine years old and has my permission to read any book she wants from the shelves, children or adult," Mother said. "With the exception of *Elsie Dinsmore*," she added. Later she explained to me that she'd made this rule because Elsie the heroine, being made by her father to practice too long and hard at the piano, fainted and fell off the piano stool. "You're too impressionable, dear," she told me. "You'd read that and the very first thing you'd do, you'd fall off the piano stool." "Impressionable" was a new word. I never hear it yet without the image that comes with it of falling straight off the piano stool.

Mrs. Calloway made her own rules about books. You could not take back a book to the Library on the same day you'd taken it out; it made no difference to her that you'd read every word in it and needed another to start. You could take out two books at a time and two only; this applied as long as you were a child and also for the rest of your life, to my mother as severely as to me. So two by two, I read library books as fast as I could go, rushing them home in the basket of my bicycle. From the minute I reached our house, I started to read. Every book I seized on, from *Bunny Brown and His Sister Sue at Camp Rest-a-While* to *Twenty Thousand Leagues under the Sea,* stood for the devouring wish to read being instantly granted. I knew this was bliss, knew it at the time. Taste isn't nearly so important; it comes in its own time. I wanted to read *immediately.* The only fear was that of books coming to an end.

My mother was very sharing of this feeling of insatiability. Now, I think of her as reading so much of the time while doing something else. In my mind's eye *The Origin of Species* is lying on the shelf in the pantry under a light dusting of flour—my mother was a bread maker; she'd pick it up, sit by the kitchen window and find her place, with one eye on the oven. I remember her picking up *The Man in Lower Ten* while my hair got dry enough to unroll from a load of kid curlers trying to make me like my idol, Mary Pickford. A generation later, when my brother Walter was away in the Navy and his two little girls often spent the day in our house, I remember Mother reading the new issue of *Time* magazine while taking the part of the Wolf in a game of "Little Red Riding Hood" with the children. She'd just look up at the right time, long enough to answer—in character—"The better to eat you with, my dear," and go back to her place in the war news.

Both our parents had grown up in religious households. In our own family, we children were christened as babies, and were taught our prayers to say at night, and sent as we were growing up to Sunday school, but ours was never a churchgoing family. At home we did not, like Grandpa Welty, say grace at table. In this way we were variously different from most of the families we knew. On Sundays, Presbyterians were not allowed to eat hot food or read the funnypapers or travel the shortest journey; parents believed in Hell and believed tiny babies could go there. Baptists were not supposed to know, up until their dying day, how to play cards or dance. And so on. We went to the Methodist Episcopal Church South Sunday School, and of course we never saw anything strange about Methodists.

But we grew up in a religious-minded society. Even in high school, pupils were used to answering the history teacher's roll call with a perfectly recited verse from the Bible. (No fair "Jesus wept.")

In the primary department of Sunday school, we little girls rose up in taffeta dresses and hot white gloves, with a nickel for collection embedded inside our palms, and while elastic bands from our Madge Evans hats sawed us under the chin, we sang songs led and exhorted by Miss Hattie. This little lady was a wonder of animation, also dressed up, and she stood next to the piano making wild chopping motions with both arms together, a chairleg off one of our Sunday school chairs in her hand to beat time with, and no matter how loudly we sang, we could always hear her even louder: "Bring them in! Bring them in! Bring them in from the fields of sin! Bring the little ones to Jesus!" Those favorite Methodist hymns all sounded happy and pleased with the world, even though the words ran quite the other way. "Throw out the lifeline! Throw out the lifeline! Someone is sinking today!" went to a cheering tune. "I was sinking deep in sin, Far from the peaceful shore, Very deeply stained within, Sinking to rise no more" made you want to dance, and the chorus—"Love lifted me! Love lifted me! When nothing else would help, Love lifted me!"—would send you leaping. Those hymns set your feet moving like the march played on the piano for us to enter Davis School—"Dorothy, an Old English Dance" was the name of that, and of course so many of the Protestant hymns reached down to us from the same place; they *were* old English rounds and dance tunes, and Charles Wesley and the rest had—no wonder—taken them over.

Evangelists visited Jackson then; along with the Red-path Chautauqua and political speakings, they seemed to be part of August. Gypsy Smith was a great local favorite. He was an evangelist, but the term meant nothing like what it stands for today. He had no "team," no organization, no big business, no public address system; he wasn't a showman. Billy Sunday, a little later on, who preached with the athletics of a baseball player, threw off his coat when he got going, and in his shirt-sleeves and red suspenders, he wound up and pitched his punchlines into the audience.

Gypsy Smith was a real Gypsy; in this may have lain part of his magnetism, though he spoke with sincerity too. He was so persuasive that, as night after night went by, he saved "everybody in Jackson," saved all the well-known businessmen on Capitol Street. They might well have been churchgoers already, but they never had been saved by Gypsy Smith. While amalgamated Jackson church choirs sang "Softly and Tenderly Jesus Is Calling" and "Just as I Am," Gypsy Smith called, and being saved—standing up and coming forward—swept Jackson like an epidemic. Most spectacular of all, the firebrand editor of the evening newspaper rose up and came forward one night. It made him lastingly righteous so that he knew just what to say in the *Jackson Daily News* when one of our fellow Mississippians had the unmitigated gall to publish, and expect other Mississippians to read, a book like *Sanctuary*.

Gypsy Smith may have been a Methodist; I don't know. At any rate, our Sunday school class was expected to attend, but I did not go up to be saved. Though all my life susceptible to anyone on a stage, I never would have been able to hold up my hand in front of the crowd at the City Auditorium and "come forward" while the choir leaned out singing "Come home! Come home! All God's children, come home, come home!" And I never felt anything like the pang of secular longing that I'd felt as a much younger child to go up onto the stage at the Century Theatre when the magician dazzlingly called for the valuable assistance of a child from the audience in the performance of his next feat of magic.

Neither was my father among the businessmen who were saved. As if the whole town were simply going through a temperamental meteorological disturbance, he remained calm and at home on Congress Street.

My mother did too. She liked reading her Bible in her own rocking chair, and while she rocked. She considered herself something of a student. "Run get me my Concordance," she'd say, referring to a little book bound in thin leather, falling apart. She liked to correct herself. Then from time to time her lips would twitch in the stern books of the Bible, such as Romans, providing her as they did with memories of her Grandfather Carden who had been a Baptist preacher in the days when she grew up in West Virginia. She liked to try in retrospect to correct Grandpa too.

I painlessly came to realize that the reverence I felt for the holiness of life is not ever likely to be entirely at home in organized religion. It was later, when I was able to travel farther, that the presence of holiness and mystery seemed, as far as my vision was able to see, to descend into the windows of Chartres, the stone peasant figures in the capitals of Autun, the tall sheets of gold on the walls of Torcello that reflected the light of the sea; in the frescoes of Piero, of Giotto; in the shell of a church wall in Ireland still standing on a floor of sheep-cropped grass with no ceiling other than the changing sky.

I'm grateful that, from my mother's example, I had found the base for this worship—that I had found a love of sitting and reading the Bible for myself and looking up things in it.

How many of us, the South's writers-to-be of my generation, were blessed in one way or another, if not blessed alike, in not having gone deprived of the King James Version of the Bible. Its cadence entered into our ears and our memories for good. The evidence, or the ghost of it, lingers in all our books.

"In the beginning was the Word.". . .

HORTENSE CALISHER
(1911—)

---◆---

Born in New York City, HORTENSE CALISHER has written about her family history: "My mother came from Oberelsbach to family already residents of Yorkville, the German community in New York. My father, old enough to be hers, was born in Richmond, Virginia, during the Civil War. They were middle-class German Jews. . . . There were thus many influences in the household. The combination was odd all round, volcanic to meditative to fruitfully dull, bound to produce someone interested in character, society and time." The Depression punctuated her college years at Barnard, but she had a part-time job in a department store and was able to graduate, unlike many of her friends. She became a social worker, married, had two children, and began to publish the stories she describes trying to write in the following excerpt from her autobiography, *Herself* (1972). Helped by numerous grants and fellowships, including a Guggenheim, she has published many volumes of fiction, including *The New Yorkers, Eagle Eye, False Entry, Queenie, Standard Dreaming,* and *Tale for the Mirror,* a collection of short stories. Critics have reviewed much of her work with strong praise: Brigid Brophy finds her talent "a naturally brilliant exotic, cutting a figure of stylish idiosyncrasy; her decorative manner is as firm and economic as rococo wrought iron." Others mention her "keen, reflective intelligence," "rich in temper," "one of our most substantial yet elusive writers." Robert Phillips admires her range and the beauty of her language: "Not since Elizabeth Bowen," he writes, "has such gorgeous prose been employed to spin a tale." Her use of language reminds novelist and critic Doris Grumbach of John Updike, Graham Greene, the Joyce of *Dubliners,* and Flannery O'Connor. Her autobiography, called a "mishmash" by one critic but appreciated by others for its "quick wit and marvelous imagination," enacts the ranging humanity of the woman whose answer to Carson McCullers's question about whether Calisher had wanted her children, knowing they would interfere with her work, was an emphatic "Yes, I did want them, and yes, they did interfere—but everything does. And everything contributes. Writers know this instinctively." In the excerpt that follows, Calisher remembers her life as a married woman before she was able to write, wide-awake and restive against the unconscious backdrop of the suburban dream. Cynthia Ozick defined the dreamers of this dream in her essay "Women and Creativity: The Demise of the Dancing Dog": "Their goals were identical. They all wanted to settle down into a perpetual and phantom coziness. . . . they had all opted . . . for the domestic life, the enclosed life, the restricted life—the life, in brief, of the daydream, into which the obvious must not be permitted to thrust its scary beams." Calisher, obviously, escaped, brains intact.

From *Herself*

Put your ear to an old faucet, do you hear the lifeblood of art drip-dripping, leaking like tapwater?—it's only the old ivory-tower blues; she hears it every day. A faucet has realms of being for everybody; that is hers.

Meanwhile, ordinary life-under-death waits at the mousehole. She tosses it theater like everybody, learns like them to build honeycomb houses for whoever shall be there with her: the flesh of her body and other guests.

With the years, so much like other peoples', this furnishment, as you know, turns to waxwork, family rooms staring shakily at time. Now and then, in spite of all she can do, one of the bodies she is in fealty with falls into death's gigantic blanket—whooshed out of a mousehole!—they sink down down, lost lost, melded to the planetary hum.

Now is the time she must speak out her life—she never told that story. Of how she has spent her life trying to learn her own name.

Is this an autobiography she writes—when you'll never get to know what she was doing that day in Wardour Street, at half-past three? Never a diary (she wrote other peoples'), partly a journal (travels with love did that), more than a memoir—for who wants to look back only?—she feeds it with fugitive soundings from a past she keeps up with, as with a correspondent more cogent than herself. If life is a minotaur to be found at the end of a confessive thread, then is this a new way of finding it?

Yes of course, it always is; you remember? This is the envelope to the life-bank, paying the interest but not the principal—not that, not yet. It's the apologia played at dawn on the boarding house piano, by the unsuccessful suicide decamping to the West. And it's the fruit carried every day to table with common bowl and knife, under the impression that someday she will fall to the floor in the fit of *grand mal* she always wanted—the great epilepsy-for-once.

"Life-talk, life-letters, that's what it is," she says. "It's what's left over after you've killed yourself laughing."

It's what the graffiti would say, on the tombstones of those who have been cremated. Or the letter one sometimes gets back from the P.O., addressed to oneself in one's own hand.

It's the note modern life leaves behind in the motel, saying "I was waiting for hope."

And it has her name on it. . . .

PART I

. . . What is the history of a writer, as a writer, outside the books? Is there an internal history, as a writer, which goes on alongside them? Is it worth talking about? I was never sure.

Not yet published, a writer lies in the womb, marvelously private as one looks back on it, but not yet born, waiting for the privilege to breathe. Outside is the great, exhaling company of those who have expressed.

First publication is a pure, carnal leap into that dark which one dreams is light. The spirit stands exposed, in what it at first takes to be the family circle of confreres. Everybody, shaped to one ear, is listening . . . but after that—one must live. . . .

. . . Behind me now are the years between, the early 1940's, spent barnstorming small industrial cities: Wilmington, Elmira, Binghamton, and larger: Rochester, Detroit—in the wake of an engineer husband. Engineers then (and perhaps now) are among the most conservative middle-class elements. As young family men, often with a holy distaste for cities, which takes no thought of what sins their own profession might be committing there, they make straight for the safer suburbs, in which all the prejudices—anti-Jew and black, anti-crowd and even anti-art—are spoken of as entirely natural. These men one collegiate step above the foundry and the furnace, have little of the rough-and-ready about them, often not even manual dexterity, and none of the individual workman's craft-guild or underdog independence. Instead, they take having a boss for granted, buy cars and houses of a grade deferentially lower, just as in the famous *Fortune* magazine study of pecking-orders in monolith industry, subscribe healthily to the theme that General Motors—or Eastman Kodak or U. S. Rubber—*is* America, and in general are the Eagle Scouts of the corporate image. (Who, by and large, seldom made it to very top executive. This daughter of a lone, cranky but never subservient small-businessman, could have told them why.)

Wives meanwhile, are to conform, up the ladder of the country clubs, which are churchgoing and hard-drinking, in the obsessive way of the American on the rise, who has no other release. As a New Yorker I am out of it in one way, as a Jew in another (almost all engineers at this time were, like my husband, Christians). And as a secret artist (for I continue writing poems in between the housework) in a third way, perhaps the most significant. Except for a "sport" like my husband, whose family was musical, and for certain foreigners in his class at school, like his friends Viscardi and Khrennikoff, all these men, met from city to city, have passed through the college mill with scarcely a trace of "the humanities" to show for it; respect for those is not yet a part of this sector of American life. (As that sector's resurgence, in each war, and in almost every President, clearly shows.)

"Art" is the property of their wives, who paint the furniture à la Peter Hunt, read the gentle *Babar* books even to their boychildren (before dreams, if not before school), press for whatever theater tickets are bought, and fill their houses with a flurry of handcraft. . . . If ever I am brought to agree that the "fine" arts and the artcrafts are the same, it will not be the art-gallery weavers and potters who have persuaded me, but the memory of those women—and myself—bent over, flecked with wool and paint and yearning, in the middle of baby's naptime, in middle America. . . .

I am not writing yet—except for those poems, flung off in brief single seizures, in trances of regret for the intellectual life I seemed to have lost. I never send the poems out. I am paralysed, not only by the house-and-child life—which is a total-flesh-draining, a catatonia of rest for the beaverish brain, that in a way is craved—but by this immersion in a society where I feel not superior to it, but at first fatally out-of-step Susie, then submerged, and ultimately lunatic-wrong. (And by my immurement in a marriage where I cannot talk of these things to a husband, however kindly, who, brought up in just this sort of life, mildly subscribes to it unless argued to otherwise, which no doubt was *his* immurement.) Again I am learning what "society" is—and again, how different.

Knowledge gotten like that, unconsciously and unphrased, unrecognized even as misery, is the deepest there is. . . .

Half the conversation of these women of the middle industrial society I am meeting comes from venoms and satisfactions of which they are unaware. In their social evenings, sitting across the living-rooms from the men, they speak of their husbands as "He" to their faces, swapping their intimate habits, always barring the sexual ones: "Oh Jim, he always, Dick, he doesn't like to, Bill, he won't ever, for him I have to—" speaking more often of what regrettably isn't than of what is, and never knowing how, in this coy chat, they take their revenge. Or for what reason it is taken. Sometimes, though, when a display of uxorious feeling is required, or even truly felt, they flirt with their husbands in a kind of sorority badinage. One never talks to another's husband except by the way, and of the most womanly preoccupations; indeed the safe topics for either sex, and the great ones, are schools-for-the-children, and redoing the house. Or the cost of dental care. . . .

As for the blacks, I never see them now. "We" never do. When they riot in the streets of Rochester in the 1960s, I will remember that. . . . Of how, once in a while up there, seated in a bus, I would see one, riding equally with us "up north here" on the aboveground railway, some old figure, dark, starched and Seminole among the white dish-clout faces. . . . At the time, the ethnic resemblance of everybody to everybody up there takes my breath away; my heart is homesick for those dirty, spittled caravans where a half dozen flaming nations jostle each other at breakfast time. All riding in that New York indifference which I now see as dignity. Into one of whose buses a lama might enter, pushing like peace against that weirdly resisting middle door (and no one will help him, nor no one comment) to stand between a bitten-off, babyface old Sally of a theater usher in her round white stock, and an eyelashed goldfish of a garment-center chick, in her racing silks. . . .

. . . The role I want to play is evermore hidden, not a role at all, but an overwhelming need. Certainly not merely to *be* a writer, for though I have a deep, natural yearning to have an honorable place in the world, co-essential with what I am in the family, and using intelligences that seem to be lying fallow—I never think of the role of the writer as other than on the printed page, have never met a writer, and somehow never expect to.

The urge I have is a personal mysticism, somehow to be worked out between external fate and this self I have been fated with, which has a physico-religious-sexual impetus to complete itself in print. As it remains thwarted, I begin to feel more and more caged off from the realm of those lucky ones who are "allowed" to do as they were meant to do, or who will it; an almost palpable wall of glass seems to be between me and them. I droop (it seems to me now) exactly like those specimen animals, rat or primate, whom the experimenter frustrates into depression or frenzy by keeping them from their natural patterns of life.

I was and am, I think, a species of human *meta* physically; since that time I have met too many in or near my pattern for it not to be so. These are the recording ones, who must forever confirm reality by

making a new piece of it—verbally, tactilely, visually, musically, kinaes-
thetically—and by doing so, bring themselves into the line of being, so
confirming themselves. Any worldly ambitions that accrete are after-
the-event even for the most greedy of these people; as artists it is only
that other hunger which will keep them truly alive. When that dies,
then the inborn pattern dies with it, exactly as all other processes in life
do—exhausted or diseased, or simply played out in a richness that is
now done. Or, more likely, in a combination of all of them. Sometimes, in a long life in-the-pattern, there are little dyings and remis-
sions; oddly, it is when this species is physically cut off from its "work"
that it feels most cut off from other people. Immersed in such work,
such a one doesn't think about reality; he or she is it. He is being
"allowed" to do what he has to. Like those others, or like the luckiest
of them.

Curiously, during all those hibernating sub-catatonic years, when at
times I cannot read good prose or poetry from sheer despair at what
could be done and I not doing it, when I dive into detective books as
into a manhole, reading ever faster and more depressively—all along I
know very well *who* is not allowing me. And that certainly it is not outward circumstance. (Certainly not because I am a woman, or a woman
busy with children and without household help; I was never able to
take that excuse route, which applies only to the surface things, and not
to that inner life which is non-exclusive for both women and men.)

Psychiatry never occurs to me, and not only because, outwardly, I
am performing conventionally. Instinctively I feel that neither the
impasse, *nor* the solution, is entirely to be found in my intrapersonal
life, present or past. This pattern I am in is, as far as possible in humans,
an impersonal phenomenon, (bound to the psyche of course, but
somewhere a-psychic), a religious one if you like, with the god-head
residing in the work done. To which the personality of the worker, a
feeder, a soma, might indeed be "everything," yet have to be so without benefit of a clergy—alone.

. . . My guess is that the best work still is done alone, safe from a
stranger's invasion of that matrix which feeds it. Safe even perhaps from
any amelioration of that madness which can also feed it, out of those
insights which a collaboration, however "freeing" to the person, cannot
give. A mind which has been freed to work by a process other than the
work, is not the same, can never be the same, as the mind which has
found its own precarious balance, murderous insight, and life celebration—within the process of itself. Psychiatry or psychoanalysis can no
doubt be an experience within that process, but for writers particularly
it perilously apes their own self-process. The examined self—*when the*

examiner is the unaided self—is different. Indeed some writers, after the psychological process, though often conventionally kinder, wiser, happier or blander than before, also seem addicted to self in a way that the still-unraveled are not. And of course they have altogether another process to go to. To resort to. Whose standard, however delicately refraining from the older, obvious norms, somewhere generalizes towards these, somewhere pities "madness" and venerates "health." Yet conversely, has no god-head of its own—except *its* process. . . .

Art is its own form of life. Psychoanalysis is. Consider Blake or Genet, Whitman, Colette, Proust, Shakespeare, Shelley, Sappho, Firbank, or Chekhov, Beckett or Poe, the Brontes or Dickinson, Turgeniev, or Joyce or Dickens—doing both. Or the qualitative changes in the work of those, in our lifetime who have.

But, by 1951, I have been writing for four years, publishing for three. What has occasioned it? We are back East. In an air I am more at home in. My parents have been dead since 1942—is it that I can now say what I will of our family life, released from both it and from being a child? Is it that my own children are now of school age? That we have a house from which we no longer move? Among friendly people, of like culture, to whose aims I am almost not ashamed to confess mine?

. . . Hoards of selfhood have had to find their spillway; I have had to burst or break. The line between the two has been very thinned. For too long, I have been in that state where one *knows* oneself to be something, someone, other than what appears. (Somebody whom no one else suspects one of being, or recognizes one as being.) This is paranoia then, unless one proves oneself by becoming what one feels one is.

Until I do write, there is a shame in confessing that I want to, so I don't confess it. And in a way, this makes a bind which helps keep me from writing, or from the posture of it—which might have helped. Most of all, to begin, I need my own self-approval—which hasn't come as easy or early or naturally as it does to some. (Yet in the writing schools, whose students are given the posture—of being a writer—on a platter, plus an immediate audience, I question whether they are not often also reduced from the rage of their own instincts, kept from that inner pressure to erupt, which has its own marvels. The attic poet, the attic soul, is often nourished by more than poverty.)

I have had plenty of approval, writing from the time I was thirteen, and through college. Once out, and into the life-shock, what I lack is my own. Even that modicum of self-approval necessary to *begin* writing, to put myself in the stance of it, does not come easy and natural. No doubt, that has its roots in family history. But also, I have been so fed on the wondrous dead of literature; it seems lèse majesté to try to align oneself at their side. Yet I can do nothing less. Harboring all this, I am gauche and private; from childhood I have known that privacy is the bourgeois' enemy.

("He's a very private person," a fashionable prates at me; they know that in "artistic" circles, this is felt to have worth. Yet an artist's privacy is an illusion. Rather, he is a fanatic, on whose scrolled flesh the marks are meant to be read. In some nations this may still be done at a respectful distance from his life. In ours, almost the last to have it so, were the Transcendentalists, in their sweet country commune. Shared barriers help. And a whole later generation revered Eliot for having fled us.)

When the courage to write finally comes, it may be simply because I have lived long enough. Perspective means having lived in a severe state of perception for some time. That I knew I had done; I had things to say; worthy or not, I had to say them. The story I write, almost the first since college, and the first published, is done in my head as I walk the younger child a long hilly mile to nursery school, call for him later—and twice in the routine walk it alone. Often on these solitary parts of the trip, as the story increases in my head, I find myself fighting for breath (though I am strong and have never fainted in my life) barely able to get to the house, where I fling myself down, and recover. Once I leave the child, no longer talking in his process, I am no longer safe. When I am walking with him, he is like an amulet by my side, while that story, which I am making about grandparents unknown to him, can go on.

I do not know that the name of my breathlessness is panic. On my occasional day-in-town, I begin to have it on the long lines waiting for the bus from New York back to Rockland County—going home, is that it? But once on the bus, thinking the story, I am safe. I fight for breath now in crowds, at parties, I who love parties and am a New York City swimmer in crowds. It begins to happen anywhere. Thought can begin unawares, anywhere; whether it *can* begin, can be permitted to, is what is at stake. The panic comes closer finally—into the house. But the story is some pages now, I can no longer hold it in my head. Writing, breath is forgotten. Finished, these are my people, me. And slowly finding other stories, I write them. I have my breath now. The process that made the panic allays it. . . .

So, in my late thirties, I began at last seriously to write—that is, as steadily as I could in time and vision, on both the hidden and the evident in the life I saw. And almost unwarily, had seen. Like many beginners, in the first work I set about understanding a family—mine, in absentia—theirs, picking my way carefully through injustices collected and just awards on both sides, making my analytic peace with them. The difference from therapy being, that each time I dove into the matrix, I retrieved a shape—a story, true—and in it a shape beyond its shape. Then suddenly, after less than a dozen such close-to-autobiographical stories, their process is over; I want out, to the wider world.

In other words, I have my health now. That long half-schizophrenia in which I am other than I seem, is over, the pane of glass gone, in a regeneration that seems to me magical; years later, when in the novella *Extreme Magic* I write in its concluding paragraphs, "For extreme cases there is sometimes extreme magic," I will be amazed to have one commentator suggest that I have perhaps venally tried to impose a "happy" ending. What I have done is to stretch a dark story toward that light which I now know can occur in life. . . .

The End of the Past

Each stage of my life has seemed to me somehow an ascent, and a surprise—since here in my country one is supposed to decline toward the grave at an acute angle, as everything in its popular civilization foretells. What has made this possible for me has been my peculiar "work," to which I have been as happily doomed as one of those children born with a religious sect, whom one sometimes glimpses on television, obscure and protected, for a time. When a child myself, I already knew I was a grudging one, thoughtless of others, yet as sensitive as if I had shingles all over, nursing all the ambitions of the envious but too easily humiliated to try my wings. In my adolescence, it was hard for me to give presents; I "forgot." Yet in the picture of me, one can see something—receptive. More open than watching, though a watcher I surely was. Waiting, rather, as if there is to be something more. There is a picture of me like that at the age of nine or ten, under the high crown and round brim of a hat that the grown have put on me, holding the reins of a pony that is not my own. I still know the feel of that cape I'm wearing. And I know that child's fortune. To be seized by work, and led through it to many loves. Perhaps the endpapers of this book, now that I'm closing it, should pose that early picture against the late one the publisher will require of me, underneath each the same invisible title: Waiting For More.

It's not death itself that I wait for. Though I expect it too will be a surprise, nothing in my heritage has taught me to await it naturally. Nothing, surely in my country, whose citizens scatter impersonal death farther than Johnny Appleseed his pips, yet to a man, and to a woman, stand affrighted to a sort of ghosthood before their time—of the personal one. No Jews I have known have been non-neurasthenic about death; whatever remains of their orthodoxy shines with the virtues of a non-acceptance which may have helped to bring them notably far in history, but does not console. As for their modern philosophies, these so far are stillborn; one may honor Buber, but find it hard to believe in the people who say they believe in him. Probably my Southern inheritance, foolish and stoic (scan how it still adheres to the gun!), looks death in the eye best—but I haven't much of it left in me.

I came on the scene, however mixed of heritage and in whatever proportion of these, half of me still from an age and a century whose thinkers, and even its bourgeoisie, took for granted (much though they talked about it) the presence in their lives of a certain rationale which no longer counts for much to my countrymen at large, or to much of a world under their influence. Call it an aesthetics of *conduct*.

History has seen so many of these, often separable even from parallel notions of "right" and "wrong." Courtly love in the middle ages, Spartan infanticide, Japanese *seppuku*—all those rituals where violence, masking as custom or honor, or even racial necessity, made use of death-attraction. The way of the pantheist or the Buddhist is milder, but still death-embracing. Western religion may see death as the door to the after-life, but doesn't much live with it. Yet one may have an aesthetic of conduct apart from any of these. Call it a sense of form, applied to life. One models one's life in the shape of something. I suspect that is what this book is about.

Any of us born in the first half of a century are in touch with the preceding one. The nineteenth century, as it left off conducting itself under the eye of Mrs. Grundy and God, or in that unholy alliance of both which confused form with conformity, bequeathed us the malaise of a noblesse gone a-wandering—how to model one's life when God is dead, as well as all the other noblemen? At least, our talk is that we are left with only the ordinary urges, to sex and politics, luxury and war. And to art too, of course. To any of which we engage ourselves only realistically, we assume—and without wonder.

Yet as far back as written work exists, one can read complaints of the shallowness of "modern" life. Nothing but death has ever put an end to that. Not all the deaths behind us have ever stopped our urge to find a light in life-as-lived—the urge toward an exemplary life, or a satisfied one. Toward—within the limits of eternity—a shapely one. Resolved. . . .

. . . How does one "finish" an account of one's life? I suppose one does that best when one intends to write no more. I have not yet engaged for that. Autobiography is often an excuse for not going on any more, along the path of whatever one has done that might make people want to read of it. I can't conclude myself like that. Not yet. But this book has its conclusions, some still projecting for me, half unknown. One, I can see clearly. Perhaps my own process is not so much my own as I thought, nor even one that only artists know—but one that we share with other Americans, other *people*. Less and less do I see any gap—in the process of us all.

Yes, my book is my blood. But all those currents in me which I have for so long kept separate, begin to seem to me no longer so. This book has pushed that on. The book and the writer, the novel and the history, the autobiography and the biographer, the journalism and the poem, no longer seem so far from one another as they used to do. It seems all—our blood. . . .

MARY MCCARTHY
(1912–1989)

◆

MARY McCARTHY began as a child of privilege in Seattle, was transferred to Minneapolis at the age of six where her mother and father died suddenly in the flu epidemic of 1918, remained in the custody of parsimonious and sadistic Minneapolis guardians until she was rescued by her maternal grandfather in 1923 and returned to spend her early adolescence in Seattle, the focus of the following excerpt from the memoir *How I Grew.* The poverty and cruelty of her orphanhood—and her three younger brothers'—is the central drama enacted in her best book, *Memories of a Catholic Girlhood* (1957), her *bildungsroman* as Carol Wrightman—author of the National Book Award-winning biography *Writing Dangerously: Mary McCarthy and Her World* (1992)—called it. After graduating from Vassar, McCarthy achieved prominence as a theater critic, book reviewer, social historian, novelist, professor at Bard College, art historian, travel writer, and political journalist, a major player through six decades of the cultural and political intrigues of the New York-based intellectual elite. Her books include the heavily autobiographical fictions *The Company She Keeps* (1942), *The Oasis* (1949), *The Groves of Academe* (1952), *A Charmed Life* (1955), *The Group* (1963), *Birds of America* (1965), *Cannibals and Missionaries* (1979), and *The Hounds of Summer and Other Stories* (1981); the collections of criticism *Cast a Cold Eye* (1950), *Sights and Spectacles, 1937–1956* (1956), and *On the Contrary* (1961); the art and social histories *Venice Observed* (1956) and *The Stones of Florence* (1959); and the memoirs *Memories of a Catholic Girlhood* (1957), *How I Grew* (1987), and *Intellectual Memoirs: New York 1936–1938* (posthumously published in 1992).

In each of her memoirs McCarthy is concerned as much with the nature and accuracy of memory as she is with the life history she recreates with all the shapeliness of fiction. The biographer and critic Jean Strouse has pointed out that she alternates the parts of the remembered story with long meditations assessing the veracity of her memories. As McCarthy wrote in the essay "The Fact in Fiction" (1960), as a writer she has an almost obsessive concern for "the world of fact, of figures, . . . the empirical element in life . . . the fetishism of fact." Her taste for clinical objectivity as well as her reputed pursuits of sexual adventure come through in the following section from her memoir of growing up under the watchful eye of her grandfather-rescuer. It brings to mind also the contemplations of one of her autobiographical fictional protagonists, Meg of *The Company She Keeps,* who wonders as she wakes up in the bed of a stranger, "How could I?" And then, "Now for the first time she saw her own extremity, saw that it was some failure in self-love that obliged her to snatch blindly at the love of others, hoping to love herself through them, borrowing their feelings, as the moon borrowed light." In the background is the sudden lovelessness of orphanhood creating a lifelong hunger for affection. Eileen Simpson, who was a friend of McCarthy, in her memoir *Orphans* (see page 177), observes that what saved her was "the strength she gained from the loving care her parents had given her during the crucial first six years of her life."

When McCarthy was awarded the National Medal for Literature at the McDowell Colony in 1984, the critic and novelist Elizabeth Hardwick said in her address on that occasion that "if [McCarthy] was, in her writing, sometimes a scourge, a Savonarola, she was a very cheerful one, lighthearted and even optimistic. I could not find in her work a trace of despair and alienation; instead she had a dreamy expectation that persons and nations should do their best." She was from the beginning, Hardwick wrote a few years later, "a prodigy," who "worked as a master of the art of writing every day of her life."

From *How I Grew*

3

In my first year at Annie Wright Seminary, I lost my virginity. I am not sure whether this was an "educational experience" or not. The act did not lead to anything and was not repeated for two years. But at least it dampened my curiosity about sex and so left my mind free to think about other things. Since in that way it was formative, I had better tell about it.

It took place in a Marmon roadster, in the front seat—roadsters had no back seats, though there was often a rumble, outside, in the rear, where the trunk is now. That day the car was parked off a lonely Seattle boulevard; it was a dark winter afternoon, probably during Thanksgiving vacation, since I was home from school. In my memory it feels like a Saturday. "His" name was Forrest Crosby; he was a Phi Delt, I understood, and twenty-three years old, a year or so out of the University and working for his family's business—the Crosby Lines, which went

back and forth across Puget Sound to points like Everett and Bremer-
ton. He was medium short, sophisticated, with bright blue eyes and
crisp close-cut ash-blond curly hair, smart gray flannels, navy-blue
jacket, and a pipe. He had a friend, Windy Kaufman, who was half-
Jewish and rode a motorcycle.

He believed I was seventeen, or, rather, that was what I had told
him. Afterwards I had reason to think that while I was adding three
years to my age he was subtracting three from his. So in reality he was
an old man of twenty-six. Probably we were both scared by what we
were doing, he for prudential reasons and I because of my ignorance,
which I could not own up to while pretending to be older. My main
aim in life, outside of school (where I could not hide the truth), was to
pass for at least sixteen.

We had met at Lake Crescent that summer. I was staying, the same
as every year, in a hotel cottage with my grandfather, who approved of
the American-plan food, the great Douglas firs, the dappled morning
walk up to misty Marymere Falls, the bridge games and poker and the
five holes of golf. I hated golf (one of the joys of growing up was that I
would not have to play it any more), but I could swim and dive in my
new "Tomboy" bathing suit (maroon-red turtleneck with a long buttoned vest that tended to rise over your head when you dove and little
separate pants underneath) and know that I was watched from pier and
porch by admiring older people awed by my long immersions in the
icy water. I could teach myself to row. I could switchback (adding a
new word to my vocabulary) up old bald-pated Storm King with my
uncle Harold and his friend Mark, eat a box lunch at the summit and
run all the way down. The changeless idyl began with a ferry ride to
Port Townsend; then there was the train ride to Port Angeles and the
opening in our compartment of an unvarying shoe box of exquisitely
packed thin chicken-liver sandwiches and deviled eggs, then the jitney
ride through the mountains to our destination, which really was cres-
cent-shaped and a bright celestial blue.

In this paradise, there were no boys for me, though—only the horrible Blethens and an ass named Warren Boole who was going to
Lawrenceville and had a nose with nostrils like a bellows. I could vamp
him, I found, in my new green tiered dress—made for me by my
grandmother's dressmaker, Mrs. Farrell—and some perfume and earrings, but it was not worth it, too disillusioning to see him "turn on"
like a wind-up toy while his indulgent parents watched. Then, with the
summer almost over, *he* came to Singer's Tavern in the Marmon, I
don't know why, possibly just as a predator, looking around. He found
only me, to judge by the result.

I would have expected him to be interested in "Missy" Lewis, a tall fair beautiful girl with braids around her head who went to the Anna Head School in California and was eighteen years old. But maybe Missy was too well protected by her married brother Richard and his stout, dark, golf-playing wife or by her own straight-browed look of virtuous reserve or simply by the fact that she stayed home in their group of cottages after supper. Anyway he danced with me the first night on the hotel porch, to the two-piece female band, and the next morning he took me rowing on the lake, down toward the steep bulk of green Sugar Loaf Mountain, till my grandfather, straining his eye-sight on the pier, angrily waved me back to the hotel landing. By lunch-time the gray car and its driver were gone (was he sizing up Rosemary Point, down the lake, supposed to be less exclusive?), but that night he danced with me again, holding his cheek closer to mine and softly singing into my ear a song that was new that summer: "Sweet Child."

"Sweet child,/ You're drivin' me wild./ That's puttin' it mild./ Sweet child, I'm wild about you." He made it "our" song, private, extremely suggestive, and I was dizzied by the thought that a liability, my age, was turning into an asset through the pulsing of his voice softly beating into my ear. Meanwhile in the big main lounge my grandfather at the poker table with Judge Alfred Battle, Mrs. Battle, Mr. Edgar Battle, Colonel Blethen, Mr. and Mrs. A. J. Singer noticed nothing wrong—he would not have been aware of the words of a popular song. Through the glass doors, if he looked, there was only ballroom dancing to be seen. To me, though, the tune "called" like the pounding of a tom-tom deep in the jungle. It needed only a bar or two hummed in his baritone to have me throbbing with excitement the next day as he walked me along a path through the woods. We were following Marymere Stream to where it emptied into the lake at a little sandy beach, which for some reason was seldom visited—the walk from Marymere Falls turned off toward the hotel a little farther up. Now I ask myself whether "Forrie" Crosby had been at Singer's before or did he find this secluded spot, protected from the wind and from prying eyes, by a natural talent, like a dowser's?

We were alone in that small sunny cove at the edge of a cool woods of maidenhair ferns and virgin spruce. His arm was around my waist; he was turning me toward him. Then, before we could kiss—he had full, rather flat, sensual lips, shirred like tight-pulled material—my grandfather came thundering down the path. He had an air of being in the nick of time and perhaps he was—compare Don Giovanni and Zerlina's fearful shriek. I was ordered back to my room in our cottage, and my grandfather, I gather, then "told the man off." I could have wept when I heard that he had "given the fellow a first-class scare"; in his high-laced shoes (or was he wearing golf knickers and the appropriate footwear?) that pillar of the bar association would have carried quite a lot of conviction.

Probably I did weep; his persistent chaperonage seemed expressly directed at robbing me of any chance in life. Though kindly and well disposed most of the time (Lewis Stone was his favorite movie-actor), he was a tinder-box when anything off-color was mooted; when I teased him one morning for helping Miss Thompson, the pretty brown-eyed violin of our duo, down from a teetery log bridge into his outstretched arms, he went red in the face and shouted. Nor was this the first time he had thundered onto the scene when I was alone with a man by the lake shore. The previous time had been with that gigolo Mr. Jones from New York, who had asked me to take his picture with a fish he had caught, and afterwards Mark Sullivan and my uncle Harold had delighted in doing imitations of the imagined scene: Mr. Jones holding the salmon-trout in one hand and my thirteen-year-old form in the other; Mr. Jones dropping the salmon and fleeing into the woods as the Honorable Harold Preston, breathing heavily and adjusting his spectacles, rounded the corner.

Still, there was a difference. I had been angry with my grandfather over the Mr. Jones episode because his absurd suspicions made himself and me ridiculous. The whole hotel was laughing. Now it was my grandfather's *interference* that made me resentful. His suspicions, possibly over-alert, were not absurd. They were well grounded in Forrie Crosby's age as compared with mine—"sweet child." I am not sure, though, whether I sensed that then, whether, amid my wails of protest, I knew in my soul what the seductive fellow was "up to." But I know it now. It seems to me also that Mark and Harold did not find this episode quite so risible as the other.

Like my grandfather, like any of the hotel guests, they were able to see that the interest of a twenty-three-year-old (or twenty-six-year-old) ordinary sensual man in a fourteen-year-old girl must have some ulterior purpose. In the earlier case, it was possible that poor Mr. Jones (suspected of being a mulatto because of his yellowish eye-whites) had really wanted to have his picture taken. But it was hard to find an innocent explanation to cover the present case. And if one could have been found, I would not have wanted to hear it. Anything that *sought an explanation* for his interest in me was too wounding to my self-love to be borne. To have people wonder about that interest, searching for clues, told me the one thing that I was closing my ears to: quite simply, that I was a juvenile. If he had taken Missy Lewis rowing on the lake, no one would have thought anything of it; her brother, *in loco parentis,* would not have been on the pier frantically waving them back.

I myself, I guess, felt no need of a theory to account for the observable data. He had fallen in love with me, I must have told myself. It happened constantly in books and films: two people danced together and immediately were "smitten"—Dan Cupid's arrows. I was a little young, but people often told me that I seemed older than my age, because of all the books I read. Just as one example, *he* thought I was seventeen.... It was typical of my grandfather's outlook to treat me purely in terms of my years. And of my sex. Although surprisingly broad-minded in some ways—about leaving me free to choose my own religion and not trying to censor my reading-matter—he had the hidebound idea that socially girls needed more control than boys. He did not stop to consider my feelings: I had not been out of sight of the hotel more than ten minutes when he came rushing out after us. And now his old man's vanity was satisfied to have driven my swain away. That afternoon, the Marmon was gone, before we could even say good-bye. But in September I would be going to Annie Wright—I had made sure on our walk that he knew. He would write to me, he had promised, holding me close. When a man declared he would write to you, that was a real sign.

Did I really believe all this? Did I dream of being "pinned" by his fraternity pin? Or did I suspect that at the first opportunity he was going to be my seducer? I had got plenty of warnings, certainly, from the *True Story* and *True Confessions* I read. Or (most likely) did I simply stop thinking and let myself be carried ahead like Maggie Tulliver on the flooding river in *The Mill on the Floss?* The fact is, I have hardly any recollection of what went through my mind between the time he left Lake Crescent and that wintry afternoon in the car with the celluloid side-curtains buttoned or snapped down. At Singer's I know that I took walks—sentimental pilgrimages—in the late afternoon to our little lonely cove, once with Mrs. Judge Battle (Madge), my favorite grown woman, in a natural-silk loose-fitting suit and wide Panama hat— strangely, I was happy, with the tall, beautiful woman in the golden light. And I can hear myself pumping out "Sweet Child" on the player piano over and over till someone complained.

In Seattle, he telephoned soon after we got back, but my grandmother, when she heard me talking to him, called out to me to hang up. Grandpa must have told her something. "Just tell him you can't see him." I hung up promptly, surprising her. I hadn't been eager to talk to him while she listened. What I really feared, however, was that he would find out, thanks to her interruptions, that I was not allowed to get telephone calls from men or boys. But then at the Seminary letters from him started coming, and I answered: "*La sfortunata rispose.*" Each girl had a list of ten approved correspondents handed in by her family, but that applied only to the letters we wrote; the authorities never bothered with any incoming mail but packages (those containing food had to be shared), and you could always give your outgoing letters to a day girl to mail or drop them into a box yourself during a school walk.

Well, it was not a flood of mail that poured in from him—a single sheet every week or so covered on two sides with round broadly spaced writing. My own letters must have been much fuller. Not only fuller but also passionate. Alas, I no longer have the packet of letters from him tied up in string that was stored in a trunk of papers in a warehouse at the time of one of my divorces and never reclaimed because I did not have the money to pay the bill. Yet it hardly matters: his letters were unrevealing, no doubt deliberately so.

He almost always ended with "*Hasta la vista*"—probably he had taken an elementary course in Spanish—which to me was the most heartfelt moment in his correspondence; I was under the spell of songs like "Marcheta" and "Valencia," of shawls and castanets, and supposed *hasta* meant "haste." It was a blow to learn from our school Spanish teacher that the phrase was a standard formula like *Au revoir* and *Auf Wiedersehen*. His letters showed a fondness, too, for such phrases as "Young feller, me lad"), addressed to himself ("Forrie, young feller, me lad"), which he used in conversation as well. The effect on me of this variant of "old man" (as I take it to be) was of a natty worldliness. He signed himself "Forrest," with a flourish, occasionally "Forrie" in smaller writing—proof, I feared, that he wrote to some other girl or girls more familiar with him than I was and did not always keep us straight. He put no return address on his envelopes and instructed me to write care of the Phi Delt house, not at home or at work. His home, I learned—from him or the telephone directory—was Federal Avenue (Capitol Hill), still a good neighborhood then. Years later, I saw the house, square, fairly well proportioned and without architectural interest.

I did not judge his letters, even if I could not help noting some mistakes in spelling, all the while I was covering the heavy white paper with kisses of joy. I was in love with him, whatever that meant. I did not let myself judge his letters and yet I knew them by heart and was extracting every drop of meaning contained in them, both what I wanted to hear and what I was afraid to. If I had been able to submit specimens to a love laboratory for tests of sincerity, I could guess what the pronouncement would have been. In other words, despite my young years, I knew too well the man who was writing to me, knew him better every week. I did not like his handwriting, so round and sloping, or the way he made his "r"s; without being a graphologist, I sensed a character deficiency in it. And I shrank almost bodily from eye contact with *"Hasta la vista,"* once I had been told what it was. None of this, however, could restrain me from hoping that my instinct—or my intelligence?—was wrong. The best means of ignoring the short-comings of those letters, which I nonetheless *hung* on as liaison with a future, was to keep reliving Lake Crescent—the past. I was able to sum-mon up the eyes, the voice in my ear, the full, flat, sensual lips, a wrist-watch, gray flannel and navy-blue worsted. His physical being and accessories (including the Marmon) had style—they matched each other and the whole entity named Forrest Crosby—and style, a quality strangely lacking in his correspondence, was for me the same as allure or even S.A., as we called it then. I was a sucker for style. The total absence of that quality from the letters I was getting may well have been the result of excessive precaution—they might have told more of their author if I had not been virtual jail bait.

In my room, after evening study hall, I wrote to him and mooned over his image. Annie Wright had assigned me as a roommate the unpopular one of our two Jewish girls, but we had asked to be sepa-rated after the first weeks. This left me free to think of him and only him; what should have been fresh impressions—different girls, teachers, food, rules, new surroundings, a new (to me) religion—barely reached me. And for the first and last time in my life I did not talk about the man I was wildly in love with. It was scarcely a matter of choice: I had nobody to confide in. I could tell my love only to him. I had no friends yet; that would come next term when I got to know girls from the class ahead. For the moment there were only my classmates, hope-lessly juvenile—their only interest was basketball.

Nonetheless, as often happens with lonely young creatures, I found companionship. In poetry. Indeed, I wonder whether poetry would have any readers besides poets if love combined with loneliness did not perform the introductions on the brink of adult life. By luck, on the study-hall shelves, I came upon Manly's *English Poetry, 1170–1892*—the volume I spoke of a while ago as turning up here in Maine and where then, in my hour of need, I encountered the Cavalier Poets. "Go and catch a falling star," "Why so pale and wan, fond lover?"—I had the conviction that Suckling, Donne (whom I took for a Cavalier), Carew, and the others were writing directly to me and about me. In Manly, later in study hall, I would find "Sister Helen" and Thomas

Lovell Beddoes, and Thomas Hood, but the insouciant Cavaliers were tied to Forrest Crosby.

The girls could not get telephone calls (calls from our families went through Miss Preston, our principal), so it must have been in one of those letters that he told me when and where to meet him. Thanksgiving would have been our first chance. At the time, the Seattle girls at the Seminary traveled by boat, a two- or three-hour trip, with a chaperon, although I once took the "interurban"—a cross between a streetcar and a train that was a little less slow—and by my senior year the new Seattle-Tacoma highway had changed all that, making weekends, even Sundays, in the bigger town possible. But in my sophomore year it was different. I remember the quantities of baggage we took with us and the effect of seeing the seniors in peppy furs like caracul and pony, topped by little hats—they were dressed to kill for the "big" football game at the University stadium and the house parties that went along with it. At home, we must have had the usual Thanksgiving bird, carved by my grandfather and preceded by Olympia oyster cocktail. Then, with palpitating heart, and pale as death, doubtless, I met Forrest Crosby, on the next afternoon. But no. I think there were two meetings, two days running: for *it* to have happened the first time, without some preliminary, would have been going too fast.

But *how* did we meet, since he could not come to my house to get me? At my age, a hotel lobby was too exposed. No, it was on a downtown street corner, after three, when the light was beginning to fade. If I was seen, I could be downtown shopping or going with a girl to a movie. It seems to me that it was on Union or University Street, not far from the Public Library, that I waited, but only for a few minutes; he was almost on time.

After that, there was nothing to do but ride around or park. He could not take me tea-dancing at the Olympic Hotel; he could not take me to the movies; he could not take me for a sundae or a toasted-cheese sandwich at one of the usual meeting-places in the University district. If it was on Saturday, he could not take me to the football game—the last of the season. In November, he could not take me swimming or rowing. Roadhouses, where we might have danced, were hardly ever open in the afternoon. The necessity of not being seen and reported to my grandmother meant that none of the ordinary ways of passing the time were open to us, which was bound to leave us in the end with no recourse but sex.

Hence I might say that what happened was my grandparents' own fault; *they* had forced me into clandestinity. If I had been free to meet him innocently, I would not have met him guiltily. This was true up to a point and in a general way. The tight rein they tried to keep on me while my contemporaries were allowed to run loose was a mistake and kept me from having any easy or natural relation with boys; I never even learned to dance with one of them properly. Moreover, the prohibitions I labored under led me into all kinds of deceptions. I lied to my grandparents about where I had been, with whom, how long, and so on. I lied to my partner in deception, in this case Forrest Crosby, because I was sure he would despise me if I avowed my inexperience, and I lied to other girls to keep them from knowing of my trammels, in short from discovering all of the above. This lying became a necessity, imposed by my grandparents in the first instance, but then the habit was formed, as the wish to appear other than I was permitted to be dominated every social relation except those with my teachers.

Yet, true as all that may be, the other truth is that my grandparents' prohibitions were far from being the cause of what happened to me on the passenger seat of that Marmon. Had they let Forrest Crosby come to the house, he would have seduced me with greater ease, probably on their own living-room sofa after they had retired.

Hold on! All the time I have been writing this, a memory has been coming back to haunt me: *he did come to my house.* In the summer-time, after Lake Crescent, and for some reason—perhaps sheer surprise at the daring of it—my grandmother let me receive him. On the living-room sofa, after she had gone up to bed. And he did start to seduce me right then and there, with the lights on. He was on top of me when something happened. Someone interrupted us. Perhaps it was my grandfather, returning from his club, who surprised us and told Forrest to get out of the house. Or Harold came in, and Forrest hastily left of his own accord. Anyway, we were on the sofa (the only time I ever was, with a man), and he fled, and after that he wrote to me at Annie Wright. I did not see him again till that wintry day, probably in Thanksgiving vacation.

On that first afternoon (I think) we drove around, we talked, we parked and kissed each other and maybe went a little bit further—I am not sure. I was wildly excited but not sexually excited. At the time, though, I was unaware of there being a difference between mental arousal and specific arousal of the genital organs. This led to many misunderstandings. In my observation, girls tend to mature as sexual performers considerably after puberty, contrary to common belief, and this is confusing for young men and for the girls themselves, especially when mental development, with its own excitement, has far outdistanced the other. I do not know the explanation but am sometimes tempted to agree with the theory that the orgasm in human females is learned from the male.

In any case, the excitement, almost ecstasy, I felt in that first embrace is hard to remember back to, since sex, by now familiar, gets in the way. Surely that bliss had more to do with love, with the tremulous persuasion that his kisses and caresses and murmured words were proofs of an eagerness for me that could only mean love on his side, than with anything like estrus. Possibly, from the signs, he himself felt that I still needed a bit more preparation, since after a while, if I recall right, he started the motor and drove me to a corner near home.

If I recall right, it was at that same corner (Union and 34th) that he picked me up the next time. And this time, the Saturday, I was more nervous. It was not that I was greatly afraid of being seen—I could lie. No, I think that I knew now what we were going to do. And I did not want to. Having finally realized what was in the cards, had been in the cards since Lake Crescent, I was scared silly. Maybe he then explained to me in so many words what we were going to do, which should have been a good move in principle; it would have made me more scared temporarily, when I saw the inexorability of what was coming, but it would also give me time to get used to the idea while he drove rapidly along the boulevards, looking for a lonely place to pull off the road. When he found one that satisfied him, he stopped the car and looked steadily at me with a faint amused smile. I must have appeared piteously tense.

As if resigned, he drew me to him, settling my head on his shoulder, and started asking me about Annie Wright and the different girls there. Like Scheherazade, I was only too pleased to talk. I must have told him about the Quevli sisters, day girls who seemed to be the prize cultivars of the school, or my desk-mate in study hall, Ellin Watts from Portland. . . . Then something prompted me to mention a small jazzy senior who wore bobbly earrings, a lot of lipstick, and a "fun" fur coat and had a peculiar name—De Vere Utter. "Lady Clara Vere de Vere", some sarcastic teacher had said. He nodded. "Windy fucked Vere Utter," he observed. The casual way he dropped that, as a datum of passing interest, froze me in his "easy" embrace. What could I answer? I was horror-struck.

Unless he was one of those men who like to talk dirty to anybody they are about to sleep with, he was exerting him self, probably, in the cheeriest way he knew, to diminish my fears of what, buttoned in his fly, lay in store for me: if a popular Annie Wright senior had done it with his friend Windy, no need for me to feel strange. He could not imagine, I suppose, that this was the first time I had heard that word, though I must have seen it scrawled on Minneapolis fences on the way to the parochial school. Of course I knew what it meant: to fuck was to do *it* straight, with no love, the way men did with prostitutes. And he was preparing to fuck me. The message had come through clear and strong.

I did not turn a hair, so far as he could see. But I felt as if I had died. I thought dimly of Vere Utter and how she would take it if she guessed that Windy had "told." I was distantly sorry for her, seeing her screwed-up little monkey face and short buck teeth with a smear of lip-stick on them and the dance step she tapped out on the forward deck of the ferryboat—poor Vere. I don't seem to have felt the same pity, in anticipation, for myself, that is, to have foreseen what Forrest would be telling Windy about me. Perhaps I was still trying to think that with me it would be different: what he was starting to do as he unbuttoned him-self and pulled aside my step-ins would not be that f---ing.

In fact, he became very educational, encouraging me to sit up and examine his stiffened organ, which to me looked quite repellent, all flushed and purplish. But in the light of the dashboard, I could not see very well, fortunately. He must have thought it would be interesting for me to look at an adult penis—my first, as by now he must have real-ized. Then, as I waited, he fished in an inside breast-pocket and took out what I knew to be a "safety." Still in an instructive mood, even with his erect member (probably he would have made a good parent), he found time to explain to me what it was—the best kind, a Merry Widow—before he bent down and fitted it onto himself, making me watch.

Of the actual penetration, I remember nothing; it was as if I had been given chloroform. How long it lasted, whether or not we were kissing—everything but the bare fact is gone. It must have hurt, but I have no memory of that or of any other sensations, perhaps a slight sense of being stuffed. Yes, there is also a faint recollection of his instructing me to move, keep step as in dancing, but I am not sure of that. What I *am* sure of is a single dreadful, dazed moment having to do with the condom. No, Reader, it did not break.

The act is over; he has slid under the steering-wheel and is standing by his side of the car and holding up a transparent little pouch resem-bling isinglass that has whitish greenish gray stuff in the bottom. I rec-ognize it as "jism." Outside it is almost dark, but he is holding the little sack up to a light source—a streetlight, the Marmon's parking lights, a lit match?—to be sure I can see it well and realize what is inside—the sperm he has ejaculated into it, so as not to ejaculate it in me. I am glad of that, of course, but the main impression is the same as with the swollen penis; the jism is horribly ugly to me, like snot or catarrh, and I have to look away.

Soon he drove me back to what was turning into "our" corner—34th and Union, at the end of the Madrona car line, near what I think was the Piggly Wiggly store. I got out of the car and quickly walked the four and a half blocks home, past Mary McQueen Street's house and the little new Catholic church with the modern stations of the cross. Nobody saw him with me, and there were no telltale traces on my step-ins for the maid to find when she washed—if the hymen was punctured, it did not bleed, then or ever. I have no memory of what story I told at home to account for my afternoon, nor of what I thought and felt that evening. Since it was Saturday, did I go with my grandparents after dinner to the current attraction at the Coliseum or the Blue Mouse—Seattle's quality movie-houses? I wonder what was playing that Thanksgiving week in the year 1926.

The next day there would have been the inevitable Sunday lunch with my married uncle, Frank, and his wife, Isabel, my uncle Harold, who had to have a special first course because he did not eat tomatoes, and maybe Aunt Alice Carr or Aunt Eva Aronson (both in fact great-aunts). We would have started with a thick slice of tomato on a bed of crabmeat and alligator pear topped by riced egg yolks and cut-up whites mimosa style and Russian or Thousand Island dressing, the whole surrounded with a chiffonade of lettuce, and we would have finished with ice-cream (possibly peppermint at that season, made with candy canes) cranked that morning on the kitchen porch by the old gardener-driver and left to ripen under burlap; in between would have been a main course of—very likely—fried chicken, and at the high point of the meal my grandfather would have said "Allee samee Victor Hugo," referring to a restaurant in Los Angeles. On this Sunday I would have been spared the after-lunch ride around Lake Washington, for I would have been driven to the dock in good season (a favorite expression with my grandfather) to catch the ferryboat back to the Seminary.

I wish I knew what was going through my head during that meal. Was I accidentally remembering parts of the day before ("WINDY FUCKED VERE UTTER") and trying to push the recollection away? Or was I feeling superior to my tablemates because I knew something they would never guess? Since yesterday afternoon I was no longer a virgin—how horrified Aunt Alice Carr with her spindly legs and old-maidish ways would be, how her frizzy head would tremble on the weak stem of her neck! For an insight into my state of mind I try thinking now of Emma Bovary at table with Charles after one of her trysts. It is not hard to guess what *she* felt. Boredom, obviously, excruciating boredom. And a Seattle Sunday at 712 35th Avenue could have given cards and spades to Yonville L'Abbaye. It was not that my grandfather, taken by himself, was uninteresting to talk to—that applied to my grandmother, too—the tedium was in their life. So, given the fact that I was old for my years and had read *Mademoiselle de Maupin,* if not yet *Madame Bovary,* I may conclude that my supreme emotion that Sunday in the bosom of my family was something between exasperated boredom and haughty disdain.

In any event I would not see them all for several weeks, not until Christmas vacation. And now comes another hiatus in my memory. Of the time in school between Thanksgiving and Christmas I remember only insignificant details having nothing to do with him, such as reading *The Merchant of Venice* after lights out in my closet by means of a bridge lamp laid on its side and shaded by a bath towel, such as Sir Roger de Coverley and isosceles triangles and Vachel Lindsay's two nieces whose parents were missionaries in China. On a more personal plane, I remember singing a new (to me) Christmas hymn, "A Virgin Unspotted," as we marched in procession into chapel, and the strange emotion that came over me as I caroled the words out, my heart singing for joy in Mary Virgin, though Mary I was and virgin I was not. In the Episcopal hymns and liturgy, I was experiencing what psychiatrists call "ideas of reference." With the Advent hymns now posted in chapel I recognized my Jewish relations and raised my voice for their safety: "Rejoice, rejoice! Em-ma-a-anuel will ransom captive I-i-israel." Without ever recovering a trace of the faith I had lost in the convent, I was falling in love with the Episcopal church. I did not believe in God's existence but, more and more, as Christmas approached, I liked the idea of Him, and chapel, morning and evening, became my favorite part of the day. . . .

MAY SARTON
(1912—)

MAY SARTON (born Eleanore Marie), poet, autobiographer, novelist, and journalist, remembers her early childhood in Belgium as the only child of historian George Sarton and the English portrait painter Mabel Sarton in the Preface to her book *A World of Light:* "I was snatched away from my mother for weeks at a time because of her illnesses, sent to stay with friends, . . . When I was two we were driven out by the war, and again I was sent to cousins in England . . . What all these uprootings did, I think, was to make the baby and small child learn to put out roots very quickly for survival. . . . We were not able to settle anywhere for the first six years of my life. Then at last we reached Cambridge, Massachusetts . . . which became home." In this same Preface, she remembers her father with affection but describes him as "an emotional cripple" and her mother, her "dearest friend," as a woman who "never made scenes" and whose cancer "of which she died might . . . have been caused by buried rage." After their deaths, she admits that she missed her parents—"the two people in the world with whom I could feel in total communion about politics, art, religion, all that really matters—yet at the same time she "felt free to be wholly myself, especially as a writer."

Her first published verse appeared in *Poetry* magazine in 1929. Since then she has published many volumes of poetry, including *Encounter in April* (1937), *Inner Landscape* (1939), *The Lion and the Rose* (1948), *The Land of Silence and Other Poems* (1953), and *Cloud, Stone, Sun, Vine: Poems, Selected and New* (1961). Among her novels are *The Single Hound* (1938), *The Small Room* (1961), *Joanna and Ulysses* (1963), and *Kinds of Love* (1970), which concern female friendships and love affairs as solutions for the problem of female loneliness. *Mrs. Stevens Hears the Mermaids Singing* (1965) is considered by many critics her most important novel. Sarton has received much critical praise for her autobiographical works: *I Knew a Phoenix: Sketches for an Autobiography* (1959); and the three volumes set in the village of Nelson, New Hampshire, concerning her buying and restoring an ancient farmhouse and living in it alone, *A Plant Dreaming Deep* (1968), *Journal of a Solitude* (1973), and *Recovering: A Journal, 1978–1979,* an account of her emotional and physical recovery from cancer that further underscores the importance of love in her life.

Journal of a Solitude, the source of the following excerpt, is a brooding work, full of dissonances, perhaps, as one critic has suggested, because recording life through journal writing may be a much darker work than the memoir softened by memory. And because the journal form often catches the writer in the midst of messy situations or dilemmas, experience is not expressed with finality; it comes across as a continuum, without comforting resolution. More than anything, this autobiography represents the poet/gardener/lecturer/friend/teacher's meditations on her identity as a woman and a writer, her desire for revelation, and her ambivalence about solitude itself. A gregarious spirit who values friendship, she represents her solitary, rural isolation as the necessary context for creation as well as prayer but also as a sometime dark night of the soul.

From *Journal of a Solitude*

September 18th

The value of solitude—one of its values—is, of course, that there is nothing to *cushion* against attacks from within, just as there is nothing to help balance at times of particular stress or depression. A few moments of desultory conversation with dear Arnold Miner, when he comes to take the trash, may calm an inner storm. But the storm, painful as it is, might have had some truth in it. So sometimes one has simply to endure a period of depression for what it may hold of illumination if one can live through it, attentive to what it exposes or demands.

The reasons for depression are not so interesting as the way one handles it, simply to stay alive. This morning I woke at four and lay awake for an hour or so in a bad state. It is raining again. I got up finally and went about the daily chores, waiting for the sense of doom to lift—and what did it was watering the house plants. Suddenly joy came back because I was fulfilling a simple need, a living one. Dusting never has this effect (and that may be why I am such a poor housekeeper!), but feeding the cats when they are hungry, giving Punch clean water, makes me suddenly feel calm and happy.

Whatever peace I know rests in the natural world, in feeling myself a part of it, even in a small way. Maybe the gaiety of the Warner family, their wisdom, comes from this, that they work close to nature all the time. As simple as that? But it is not simple. Their life requires patient understanding, imagination, the power to endure constant adversity—

the weather, for example! To go with, not against the elements, an inexhaustible vitality summoned back each day to do the same tasks, to feed the animals, clean out barns and pens, keep that complex world alive.

September 19th

The sun is out. It rose through the mist, making the raindrops sparkle on the lawn. Now there is blue sky, warm air, and I have just created a wonder—two large autumn crocuses plus a small spray of pink single chrysanthemums and a piece of that silvery leaf (artemisia? arethusa?) whose name I forget in the Venetian glass in the cosy room. May they be benign presences toward this new day!

Neurotic depression is so boring because it is repetitive, literally a wheel that turns and turns. Yesterday I broke off from the wheel when I read a letter from Sister Mary David. She is now manager of a co-op in the small town in South Carolina where she has chosen to work. Always her letters bring me the shock of what is really going on and the recognition of what one single person can do. . . .

November 9th

Home again to more radiant skies, a moon so bright last night I couldn't sleep. I found a huge box of bulbs; they have come at last. It is the eleventh hour as the ground will soon be frozen, but apparently a dock strike in Holland held them up.

The lectures went well. Both audiences, in Dallas and in Shreveport, listened intently; so at least once I experienced that marvelous stillness when I know a poem has really landed and is being heard as it can be only before a large impersonal group, because then I can "give tongue" and make whatever meaning and music is there "happen." Reading to one person, an intimate, I can never really let the poem out. I found the going hard at first because I felt *dépaysé;* after a long flight one is slightly out of balance, not really settled in, still living one's way into the new atmosphere. And because, of course, it was in Texas more than ten years ago, on a lecture trip, that I was wakened at seven thirty A.M. with a long-distance call from Judy to say that my father had died of a heart attack in a few minutes, after turning back in the taxi that was taking him to the airport to give a lecture in Montreal. That memory and also the shadow of the Kennedy assassination were much in my thoughts.

The psychological discomfort was acute at times. The women I met were kind, and apparently gentle and responsive. Then suddenly that steely look comes into their eyes, the real hatred of the Kennedys, *still,* after all the tragedies. And besides that, of course, the closed door in the mind when it comes to the race question. I know that it is there partly as a symptom of loss, the loss of a loving warmth between master and servant, the bewildering emergence of Black Power that seems to these people a betrayal of old loyalties and old graces. But how well one comes to understand in this atmosphere why many blacks have decided that all-out war is the only way to change anything. Most of this I had expected, but what upset me most was the selfishness; the perimeter was so personal and limited. Does nothing, no suffering outside it, ever break through, no need? The Kennedy assassination apparently has only closed the ring.

I felt culture in its deepest sense, what civilizes people, as only a thin veneer, like the new houses which turn out to have a brick façade pasted onto some other material. And how incredible it was, in autumn, to swing past acres and acres of fancy French provincial, Spanish, or Tudor houses where not a leaf is allowed to rest on the immaculate lawns! So beautiful in a *House and Garden* sort of way, so empty of poetry. For poetry lives in places where people work in their gardens or let them go wild and do not leave it to impersonal firms of gardeners to plant and trim.

Shreveport has far more charm, a livable town, where Dallas seems just plain inhuman, too rich, too new. A fifty-year-old building in Dallas looks antediluvian and "must be torn down." I felt the women were starved, starved for a kind of reality that does not exist in Neiman Marcus fur coats, in changes of fashion, in redecorating, in travel to the "right places." Under the polite small talk, one sensed nostalgia, the nostalgia of the bored child who does not know what he lacks, but knows he is being deprived of something essential to his well-being. These women are not disturbed, striving, anguished about the state of the world, not always guilty because they should be doing more as their equivalents in the East often are; also, they are not happy or fulfilled. It is hard to define, but under that huge sky and among so many "beautiful" things, houses, expensive cars, what I sensed was loneliness. There is too much luxury, maybe, and too little quality. Good manners are just not enough.

In the lectures I avoided politics and read no controversial poems, but at the lunches and in meeting people off the platform I said what I thought, and passionately, especially in the presence of someone gloating about a Kennedy child picked up for smoking pot!

I have an advantage in not having been born a damn Yankee, cannot be placed, in regional terms, beyond the pale, and so sometimes can say my say without giving offense.

But, oh, how marvelous it was to come home to dear shabby Cambridge, to uneven brick sidewalks, to untrimmed gardens, to lawns covered with leaves, to young people walking hand in hand in absurd clothing, to dear Judy and the pussies! We are all a little old and worn, but we are happy. And Nelson, when I drove up under a pale bright sky, looked like Heaven. I saw it freshly, saw the beauty of wooden clapboard painted white, of old brick, of my own battered and dying maples, as a shining marvel, a treasure that lifts the mind and the heart and brings everyone who sees it back to what *quality* is. . . .

December 1st

The darkness again. An annihilating review in the Sunday *Times*. I must have had a premonition, as I felt terribly low in my mind all weekend. Now it is the old struggle to survive, the feeling that I have created twenty-four "children" and every one has been strangled by lack of serious critical attention. This review is simply stupid. But what hurts is the lack of respect shown by Francis Brown in not getting a reviewer who had some knowledge of my work and would be able to get inside it with sympathetic understanding. It is odd that nonfiction appears to get a better break these days than fiction. On a deeper level I have come to believe (perhaps that is one way to survive) that there is a reason for these repeated blows—that I am not meant for success and that in a way adversity is my climate. The inner person thrives on it. The challenge is there to go deeper.

What a lonely business it is . . . from the long hours of uncertainty, anxiety, and terrible effort while writing such a long book, to the wild hopes (for it looked like a possible best seller, and the *Digest* has it for their condensed books) and the inevitable disaster at the end. I have had many good reviews and cannot really complain about that. What I have not had is the respect due what is now a considerable opus. I am way outside somewhere in the wilderness. And it has been a long time of being in the wilderness. But I would be crazy if I didn't believe that I deserve better, and that eventually it will come out right. The alternative is suicide and I'm not about to indulge in that fantasy of revenge.

Somehow the great clouds made the day all right, a gift of splendor as they sailed over our heads.

December 2nd

I opened Teilhard de Chardin (*The Divine Milieu*) to this passage this morning:

The masters of the spiritual life incessantly repeat that God wants only souls. To give those words their true value, we must not forget that the human soul, however independently created our philosophy represents it as being, is inseparable, in its birth and in its growth, from the universe into which it is born. In each soul, God loves and partly saves the whole world which that soul sums up in an incommunicable and particular way. But this summing-up, this welding, are not given to us ready-made and complete with the first awakening of consciousness. It is we who, through our own activity, must industriously assemble the widely scattered elements. The labour of seaweed as it concentrates in its tissues the substances scattered, in infinitesimal quantities, throughout the vast layers of ocean; the industry of bees as they make honey from the juices broadcast in so many flowers—these are but pale images of the ceaseless working-over that all the forces of the universe undergo in us in order to reach the level of spirit.

Thus, every man, in the course of his life, must not only show himself obedient and docile. By his fidelity he must *build*—starting with the most natural territory of his own self—a work, an *opus,* into which something enters from all the elements of the earth. *He makes his own soul* throughout his earthly days; and at the same time he collaborates in another work, in another *opus,* which infinitely transcends, while at the same time it narrowly determines, the perspectives of his individual achievement: the completing of the world.

It is only when we can believe that we are creating the soul that life has any meaning, but when we can believe it—and I do and always have—then there is nothing we do that is without meaning and nothing that we suffer that does not hold the seed of creation in it. I have become convinced since that horrible review (unimportant in itself) that it is a message, however deviously presented, to tell me that I have been overconcerned with the materialistic aspects of bringing out this novel, the dangerous hope that it become a best seller, or that, for once, I might get a leg up from the critics, the establishment, and not have once more to see the work itself stand alone and make its way, heart by heart, as it is discovered by a few people with all the excitement of a person who finds a wildflower in the woods that *he* has discovered on his own. From my isolation to the isolation of someone somewhere who will find my work there exists a true communion. I have not lacked it in these last years, and it is a blessing. It is free of "ambition" and it "makes the world go away," as the popular song says. This is what I can hope for and I must hope for nothing more or less.

Thinking of writers I cherish—Traherne, George Herbert, Simone

Weil, and the novelists Turgenev, Trollope, Henry James, Virginia Woolf, E. M. Forster, all of them modest, private, "self-actualizers"—I see that they are all outside the main stream of what is expected *now*. The moderate human voice, what might be called "the human milieu"—this is supremely unfashionable and appears even to be irrelevant. But there always have been and always will be people who can breathe only there and who are starved for nourishment. I am one of those readers and I am also one who can occasionally provide this food. That is all that really matters to me this morning. . . .

. . . This December I have been more aware than ever before of the meaning of a festival of light coming as it does when the days are so short, and we live in darkness for the greater part of the afternoon. Candlelight, tree lights—ours, tiny ones—are reflected in all the windows from four o'clock on.

Then there are the great presents of long letters from former students and friends from whom I hear only once a year. They bring me a tapestry of lives, a little overwhelming, but interesting in their conjunctions. Two of my best poets at Wellesley, two girls who had something like genius, each married and each stopped writing altogether. Now this year each is moving toward poetry again. That news made me happy. It also made me aware once more of how rarely a woman is able to continue to create after she marries and has children.

Whatever college does not do, it does create a climate where work is demanded and where nearly every student finds him- or herself meeting the demand with powers he did not know he had. Then quite suddenly a young woman, if she marries, has to diverge completely from this way of life, while her husband simply goes on toward the goals set in college. She is expected to cope not with ideas, but with cooking food, washing dishes, doing laundry, and if she insists on keeping at a job, she needs both a lot of energy and the ability to organize her time. If she has an infant to care for, the jump from the intellectual life to that of being a nurse must be immense. "The work" she may long to do has been replaced by various kinds of labor for which she has been totally unprepared. She has longed for children, let us say, she is deeply in love, she has what she thought she wanted, so she suffers guilt and dismay to feel so disoriented. Young husbands these days can and do help with the chores and, far more important, are aware of the problem and will talk anxiously about it—anxiously because a wife's conflict affects their peace of mind. But the fact remains that, in marrying, the wife has suffered an earthquake and the husband has not. His goals have not been radically changed; his mode of being has not been radically changed.

I shall copy out parts of one of these letters, as it gave me much to ponder on and I shall refer to it again in the weeks to come, no doubt. K says,

It has been a year of unusual branching out, and I feel quite young. You will laugh at that, but many of our friends now are pathetically worried about aging and full of envy for young people and regrets about wasting their own youth—and these are parents of small children, under thirty! I think it is a very destructive system indeed that worships youth the way we Americans do and gives young people no ideals of maturity to reach for, nothing to look forward to. (Adolescence is often so miserable that one needs an incentive to get through it!)

Well, I'd better stop, because I feel a harangue coming on; I'm so hopelessly out of tune with these times and it's a temptation to join the haranguers. . . .

As for the writing of poems, I'm beginning to see that *the* obstruction is being female, a fact I have never accepted or known how to live with. I wish that I could talk to you about it; I know that you are into insights that I'm only beginning to realize *exist*. (And that's why Sylvia Plath interests me; Robert Lowell describes her as "'feminine rather than female',," whatever that means; but she strikes me as breaking through the feminine to something natural that, while I suppose it still has a sex, can't be called feminine even.) At least I can see the inadequacy of that male and very Freudian psychiatrist, trying to help me accept or do something with this burden of femininity that marriage had seemed to finalize. I am grateful to all the crazies out there in the Women's Liberation; we *need* them as outrageous mythical characters to make our hostilities and dilemmas really visible. As shallow as my contact with the Women's Liberation has been, I have really seen something new about myself this year; the old stalemated internal conflict has been thrown off balance and I am surprised to understand how much of my savage hostility is against men. I have always been rejecting language because it *is* a male invention. My voice in my own poems, though coming out of myself, became a masculine voice on the page, and I felt the need to destroy that voice, that role, in making room for D in my life. It is not just my equation but a whole family tradition, which decrees a deep and painful timidity for the women; and for me this was always especially intolerable, since the personality I was born with was the very opposite of passive! It is very fortunate for me that, of all my friends, excepting you, D is the only one who seems to understand, or at least to sympathize with this—a fact which violates the principles of psychiatry since he is the one most threatened by any sexual crisis I may undergo, the target most at hand for hostilities against men, and the most disturbed by the instability that comes with my trying to readjust the balance of my mind.

This letter goes to the heart of the matter. I found it deeply disturbing. For what is really at stake is unbelief in the woman as artist, as creator. K no longer sees her talent as relevant or valid, language itself as a masculine invention. That certainly closes the door with a bang! But I believe it will open because the thrust of a talent as real as hers must finally break through an intellectual formula and assert what she now denies. What she writes eventually will be in her own voice. Every now and then I meet a person whose speaking voice appears to be placed artificially, to come not from the center of the person, but from an unnatural register. I am thinking especially of women with high, strained voices. I know nothing about voice placement in a technical sense, but I have longed to say, "For God's sake, get down to earth and speak in your own voice!" This is not so much a matter of honesty, perhaps (K is excruciatingly honest), as of self-assurance: I am who I am.

KATE SIMON
(1912–1990)

◆

Born in Warsaw and arriving in New York City at the age of four, KATE SIMON grew up in the Bronx in the years after World War I, an immigrant childhood that she portrayed in her by now classic memoir, *Bronx Primitive* (1982). She worked in publishing, and wrote book reviews and travel articles for the *Nation,* the *New Republic, Holiday, Vogue,* and the *New York Times Magazine.* Her travel books include *Italy: The Places in Between, New York: Places and Pleasures, Mexico: Places & Pleasure, Kate Simon's Paris,* and *Kate Simon's London,* all acclaimed by critics. British scholar and author J. H. Plumb's rave notice is typical: "How splendid is Kate Simon, the incomparable Kate Simon, whom no one has ever rivaled in the long, long history of guidebooks. She has made of one of the dullest forms of literature a brilliant work of art." Her other memoirs include *A Wider World* (1986), which describes her years at Hunter College during the Depression, and *Etchings in an Hourglass* (1990). In a eulogy delivered on the occasion of Simon's death in 1990, feminist scholar—and fellow Hunter College alumna—Florence Howe said that in her capacity as director of the Feminist Press she refers "would-be memoir writers to *Bronx Primitive.* It is the model I say. The effect seems effortless, but the context is as strong as the characterizations. Dazzling without show, like the author." In the chapter reprinted here, "Movies and Other Schools," Simon details her Jewish family's culture, in particular her parents' relationship, against the background of a polyglot, struggling neighborhood. Against her father's objections, her mother socialized with the Italian immigrants and other "foreign ignoramuses." She taught her children (and answered her husband), "*Es is doch a mench,*" yet these are human beings, and then the mother's daughter adds, "the only religious training we ever had, perhaps quite enough." As reviewer Elaine Kendall observed, this memoir has "a strong feminist subtext." Both Simon's parents encouraged her talents, and her mother, in particular, lectured Simon from an early age "on being a woman." Deferring marriage until she had a profession and could support herself—"or don't get married at all, better still"—was the gist of her maternal counsel.

Simon exceeded her mother's expectations considerably. "In the

137

space of her lifetime," as Florence Howe put it, "she leap[ed] out of an immigrant's world to make her way, beginning in the mid-fifties, in the male world of travel writing . . . and the publishing of memoirs likely to survive time and to break into what we in academic literary circles call the 'canon,' those books considered suitable for students." Asked to talk about her theory of writing autobiography, Simon told her friend "she had no theory." Her writing, which she defined as "revision," has earned her such critical epithets as "master of descriptive prose," "graceful and resonant," "capturing the world in language evocative, precise, and rich."

From *Bronx Primitive*

The Movies and Other Schools

Life on Lafontaine* offered several schools. School-school, P.S. 59, was sometimes nice, as when I was chosen to be Prosperity in the class play, blond, plump, dressed in a white pillow case banded with yellow and green crepe paper, for the colors of grasses and grain, and waving something like a sheaf of wheat. The cringing days were usually Fridays, when arithmetic flash cards, too fast, too many, blinded me and I couldn't add or subtract the simplest numbers. (For many years, into adulthood, I carried around a sack of churning entrails on Friday mornings.) The library, which made me my own absolutely special and private person with a card that belonged to no one but me, offered hundreds of books, all mine and no tests on them, a brighter, more generous school than P.S. 59. The brightest, most informative school was the movies. We learned how tennis was played and golf, what a swimming pool was and what to wear if you ever got to drive a car. We learned how tables were set, "How do you do? Pleased to meet you," how primped and starched little girls should be, how neat and straight boys should be, even when they were temporarily ragamuffins. We learned to look up soulfully and make our lips tremble to warn our mothers of a flood of tears, and though they didn't fall for it (they laughed), we kept practicing. We learned how regal mothers were and how stately fathers, and of course we learned about Love, a very foreign country like maybe China or Connecticut. It was smooth and slinky, it shone and rustled. It was petals with Lillian Gish, gay flags

---

*Kate Simon grew up at 2029 Lafontaine Street, "the last house on the west side of the street from 178th to 179th, a row of five-story tenements that ended at a hat factory."

with Marion Davies, tiger stripes with Rudolph Valentino, dog's eyes with Charlie Ray. From what I could see, and I searched, there was no Love on the block, nor even its fairy-tale end, Marriage. We had only Being Married, and that included the kids, a big crowded barrel with a family name stamped on it. Of course, there was Being Married in the movies, but except for the terrible cruel people in rags and scowls, it was as silky as Love. Fathers kissed their wives and children when they came home from work and spoke to them quietly and nobly, like kings, and never shouted or hit if the kids came in late or dirty. Mothers in crisp dresses stroked their children's heads tenderly as they presented them with the big ringletted doll and the football Grandma had sent, adding, "Run off and play, darlings." "Darling," "dear," were movie words, and we had few grandmothers, most of them dead or in shadowy conversation pieces reported from At Home, the Old Country. And "Run off and play" was so superbly refined, silken gauze to the rough wool of our hard-working mothers whose rules were to feed their children, see that they were warmly dressed in the wintertime, and run to the druggist on Third Avenue for advice when they were sick. Beyond that it was mostly "Get out of my way." Not all the mothers were so impatient. Miltie's mother helped him with his arithmetic homework; my mother often found us amusing and laughed with and at us a lot. From other apartments, on rainy afternoons: Joey—"What'll I do, Maaa?" His Mother—"*Va te ne! Gherradi!*" (the Italian version of "Get out of here"); Lily—"What'll I do, Maaa?" Mrs. Staviczi— "Scratch your ass on a broken bottle." I sometimes wished my mother would say colorful, tough things like that but I wasn't sure I wouldn't break into tears if she did, which would make her call me a "*pianovi chasto*" (as I remember the Polish phrase), a delicate meringue cake that falls apart easily, which would make me cry more, which would make her more lightly contemptuous, and so on. Despite my occasional wish to see her as one of the big-mouth, storming women, I was willing to settle for her more modest distinction, a lady who won notebooks in her English class at the library and sang many tunes from "Polish operettas" that, with later enlightenment, I realized were *The Student Prince* and *The Merry Widow*.

Being Married had as an important ingredient a nervous father. There must have been other kitchens, not only ours, in which at about seven o'clock, the fathers' coming-home time, children were warned, "Now remember, Papa is coming home soon. He's nervous from working in the factory all day and riding in the crowded El. Sit quiet at the table, don't laugh, don't talk." It was hard not to giggle at the table, when my brother and I, who played with keen concentration a game of mortal enemies at other times, became close conspirators at annoying Them by making faces at each other. The muffled giggles were stopped by a shout of "Respect!" and a long black look, fork poised like a sword in midair while no one breathed. After the silent meal, came the part we disliked most, the after-dinner lecture. There were two. The first was The Hard Life of the Jewish worker, the Jewish father, the deepest funereal sounds unstopped for the cost of electricity (a new and lovely toy but not as pretty as throbbing little mazda lamps) for which he had to pay an immense sum each time we switched it on and off, like the wastrels we were. Did we think butter cost a penny a pound that we slathered it on bread as if it were Coney Island mud pies? Those good expensive shoes he bought us (he was an expert shoe worker, a maker of samples, and tortured us with embarrassment when he displayed his expertise to the salesman, so don't try to fool him), which were old and scuffed and dirty within a week, did we know how much bloody sweat was paid for them? The second lecture was the clever one whose proud, sententious repetitions I listened to with shame for him, wanting to put my head down not to see my handsome father turn into a vaudeville comic whose old monologues strained and fell. This lecture was usually inspired by my brother who, in spite of the "nervous" call, dashed at my father as soon as he heard the key in the lock with "Hello, Pa. Gimme a penny?" That led it off: "You say you want a penny, *only* a penny. I've got dimes and quarters and half-dollars in my pockets, you say, so what's a penny to me? Well, let's see. If you went to the El station and gave the man four cents, he wouldn't let you on the train, you'd need another penny. If Mama gave you two cents for a three-cent ice cream cone, would Mrs. Katz in the candy store give it to you? If Mama had only forty-eight cents for a forty-nine-cent chicken, would the butcher give it to her?" And on and on, a carefully rehearsed long slow aria, with dramatic runs of words and significant questioning pauses. Once or twice I heard my mother mutter as she went out of the room, "That Victrola record again," but her usual policy was to say nothing. She was not afraid of my father, nor particularly in awe of him. (I heard him say frequently how fresh she was, but with a smile, not the way he said it to us.)

In none of my assiduous eavesdropping on the street did I ever hear any mention of unhappy marriage or happy marriage. Married was married. Although a Jewish divorce was a singularly easy matter except for the disgrace it carried, the Jewish women were as firmly imbedded in their marriages as the Catholic. A divorce was as unthinkable as adultery or lipstick. No matter what—beatings, infidelity, drunkenness, verbal abuse, outlandish demands—no woman could run the risk of making her children fatherless. Marriage and children were fate, like being skinny, like skeletal Mr. Roberts, or humpbacked, like the leering watchman at the hat factory. "*Es is mir beschert,*" "It is my fate," was a common sighing phrase, the Amen that closed hymns of woe.

My mother didn't accept her fate as a forever thing. She began to work during our school hours after her English classes had taught her as much as they could, and while I was still young, certainly no more than ten, I began to get her lecture on being a woman. It ended with extraordinary statements, shocking in view of the street mores. "Study. Learn. Go to college. Be a schoolteacher," then a respected, privileged breed, "and don't get married until you have a profession. With a profession you can have men friends and even children, if you want. You're free. But don't get married, at least not until you can support yourself and make a careful choice. Or don't get married at all, better still." This never got into "My mother said" conversations with my friends. I sensed it to be too outrageous. My mother was already tagged "The Princess" because she never went into the street unless fully, carefully dressed: no grease-stained housedress, no bent, melted felt slippers. Rarely, except when she was pregnant with my little sister, did she stop for conversations on the street. She was one of the few in the building who had gone to classes, the only mother who went out alone at night to join her mandolin group. She was sufficiently marked, and though I was proud of her difference, I didn't want to report her as altogether eccentric. In the community fabric, as heavy as the soups we ate and the dark, coarse "soldier's bread" we chomped on, as thick as the cotton on which we practiced our cross-stitch embroidery, was the conviction that girls were to marry as early as possible, the earlier the more triumphant. (Long after we moved from the area, my mother, on a visit to Lafontaine to see appealing, inept little Fannie Herman who had for many years been her charge and mine, met Mrs. Roth, who asked about me. When my mother said I was going to Hunter College, Mrs. Roth, looking both pleased and sympathetic, said, "*My* Helen married a man who makes a nice living, a laundry man. Don't worry, your Katie will find a husband soon." She knew that some of the boys of the block wound up in City College, but a girl in college? From a pretty, polite child, I must have turned into an ugly, bad-tempered shrew whom no one would have. Why else would my marrying years be spent in college?)

I never saw my mother and father kiss or stroke each other as people did in the movies. In company she addressed him, as did most of the Jewish women, by our family name, a mark of respectful distance. They inhabited two separate worlds, he adventuring among anti-

Semites to reach a shadowy dungeon called "Factory," where he labored ceaselessly. In the evening he returned to her world for food, bed, children, and fighting. We were accustomed to fighting: the boys and, once in a while, fiery little girls tearing at each other in the street; bigger Italian boys punching and being punched by the Irish gangs that wandered in from Arthur Avenue; females fighting over clotheslines— whose sheets were blocking whose right to the sun—bounced around the courtyard constantly. The Genoese in the houses near 178th Street never spoke to the Sicilians near 179th Street except to complain that somebody's barbaric little southern slob had peed against a northern tree. To my entranced ears and eyes, the Sicilians seemed always to win, hotter, louder, faster with "*Fangu*"—the southern version of "*Fa' in culo*" (up yours)—than the aristocrats who retired before the Sicilians could hit them with "*Mortacci*"—the utterly insupportable insult. My brother and I fought over who grabbed the biggest apple, who hid the skate key, and where he put my baby picture, I lying on a white rug with my bare ass showing, a picture he threatened to pass among his friends and humiliate me beyond recovery. I would have to kill him.

These sorts of fighting were almost literally the spice of daily life, deliciously, lightly menacing, grotesque and entertaining. The fighting between my mother and father was something else entirely, at times so threatening that I still, decades later, cringe in paralyzed stupidity, as if I were being pelted with stones, when I hear a man shouting. The fights often concerned our conduct and my mother's permissiveness. My father had a rich vocabulary which he shaped into theatrical phrases spoken in a voice as black and dangerous as an open sewer. The opening shot was against my brother, who was six or seven when the attacks began. He was becoming a wilderness boy, no sense, no controls, dirty, disobedient, he did badly in school (not true: with a minimum of attention he managed mediocrity). There was no doubt that he would become a bum, then a thief, wind up alone in a prison cell full of rats, given one piece of bread a day and one cup of dirty water. He would come out a gangster and wind up in the electric chair.

When it was my turn, I was disobedient and careless; I didn't do my homework when I should, I didn't practice enough, my head was always in a book, I was always in the street running wild with the Italian and Polish beasts. I didn't take proper care of my brother, I climbed with boys, I ran with boys, I skated with them on far streets. Mr. Kaplan had seen me and told him. And how would this life, this playing with boys, end? I would surely become a street girl, a prostitute, and wind up being shipped to a filthy, diseased brothel crawling with hairy tropical bugs, in Buenos Aires. My mother's response was sharp and short: we acted like other children and played like other children; it was he who was at fault, asking more of us than he should. And enough about prisons and electric chairs and brothels. He went on shouting, entranced by his gorgeous words and visions, until she left the room to wash the dishes or scrub the kitchen floor. We, of course, had heard everything from our bedroom; the oratory was as much for us as for our mother. When the big rats in the windowless cell came to our ears, my brother began to shake with terror beyond crying. I tried to comfort him, as accustomed a role as trying to maim him. I didn't know what a street girl was, and I certainly didn't know what a brothel was, but I wasn't afraid—I was too angry. If our father hated us so, why didn't he go away? I didn't examine consequences, who would feed us and pay the rent. I just wanted him out, out, dead.

Other fights were about money, and that, too, involved us. How dare she, without consulting him, change from a fifty-cent-a-lesson piano teacher to another—and who knows how good *he* was?—who charged a dollar? What about the embroidered tablecloth and the stone bowl with the pigeons that she bought from the Arab peddler, that crook. Did she realize how hard he had to work to pay for our school supplies each fall? And add to that the nickel for candy to eat at the movies every Saturday, and the ten cents each for the movie and the three cents for ice-cream cones on Friday nights. And God only knew how much money she slipped us for the sweet garbage we chewed on, which would certainly rot our teeth, and where would he get the money for dentists? Maybe she thought she was still in her shop in Warsaw, dancing and singing and spilling money like a fool. And on and on it went. These tirades, too, were answered very briefly. Our lives were meager enough. Did he ever think of buying us even the cheapest toy, like the other fathers did, instead of stashing every spare penny in the bank and taking it out only for his relatives? The ignorant Italians he so despised, they had celebrations for their children. Where were our birthday presents?

Long silences followed these fights and we became messengers. "Tell your mother to take my shoes to the shoemaker." "Aw, Pa, I'm doing my homework. Later." "Tell your mother I have no clean shirts." "Aw, Pa, I'm just sitting down to practice. I'll tell her later." We used the operative words "homework" and "practice" mercilessly while he seethed at our delays. My mother heard all these instructions but it was her role neither to notice nor to obey. Those were great days and we exploited our roles fattily, with enormous vengeful pleasure.

One constant set of squabbles that didn't circle around us concerned her relaxed, almost loose judgments of other people. She showed no sympathy when he complained about the nigger sweeper in the factory who talked back to him, when he complained about the Italian who reeked of garlic and almost suffocated him in the train. Most loudly he complained about her availability, spoiling his sleep, letting his supper get cold, neglecting her own children, to run to any Italian idiot who didn't know to take care of her own baby. Let them take care of their own convulsions or get some Wop neighbor to help. It was disgraceful that she sat on Mrs. Santini's porch in open daylight trying to teach her not to feed her infant from her own mouth. If the fat fool wanted to give it germs, let her. If it died, she'd, next year, have another; they bred like rabbits. Why didn't my mother mind her own business, what the hell did these people, these foreign ignoramuses, mean to her? The answer was short and always the same, *"Es is doch a mench,"* yet these are human beings, the only religious training we ever had, perhaps quite enough.

There were fights with no messengers, no messages, whispered fights when the door to our bedroom was shut tight and we heard nothing but hissing. The slow unfolding of time and sophistications indicated that these were fights about women, women my father saw some of those evenings when he said he was going to a Workmen's Circle meeting. There was no more "Tell your mother," "Tell your father," and except for the crying of our baby, no more evening sounds. No Caruso, no Rosa Ponselle, no mandolin practice, no lectures. My father busied himself with extra piecework, "skiving" it was called, cutting with breathtaking delicacy leaf and daisy designs into the surface of the sample shoes to be shown to buyers. She, during one such period, crocheted a beaded bag, tiny beads, tiny stitches. We watched, struck dumb by their skill, and because it was no time to open our mouths about anything, anything at all. The silence was dreadful, a creeping, dark thing, a night alley before the murderer appears. The furniture was waiting to be destroyed, the windows to be broken, by a terrible storm. We would all be swept away, my brother and I to a jungle where wild animals would eat us, my parents and the baby, separated, to starve and burn alone in a desert. School now offered the comforts of a church, the street its comforting familiarities, unchanging, predictable. We stayed out as long as we could, dashing up for a speedy supper, and down again. On rainy nights we read a lot, we went to bed early, anything to remove us from our private-faced parents, who made us feel unbearably shy.

One spring evening, invited to jump Double Dutch with a few experts, uncertain that I could leap between two ropes whipping in rapid alternation at precisely the exact moment, and continue to stay between them in small fast hops from side to side, I admitted a need, urgent for some time, to go to the toilet. I ran up the stairs to find our door locked, an extraordinary thing. Maybe they had run away. Maybe they had killed each other. Sick with panic, I kept trying the door, it wouldn't give. Then I heard the baby making squirmy, sucking baby noises. No matter what, my mother would never leave the baby, and anyway, maybe they were doing their whispering fighting again. Still uneasy, I knocked on the Hermans' door and asked to use their toilet. When I came out, I asked Fannie Herman if she knew whether my parents were at home. Yes, she said. Her door was wide open and she would have seen or heard them come out, but they hadn't. The Double Dutch on the street was finished when I got down so I joined the race, boys and girls, around the block, running hard, loving my pumping legs and my swinging arms and my open mouth swallowing the breeze. When most of the kids had gone home and it was time for us, too, I couldn't find my brother, who was hiding from me to destroy my power and maybe get me into trouble. I went up alone. The door had been unlocked, and as I walked uneasily through the long hallway of our railroad flat with wary steps, I heard sounds from the kitchen. My mother was sitting on a kitchen chair, her feet in a basin of water. My father was kneeling before her on spread newspaper. Her plump foot rested in his big hand while he cut her toenails, flashing his sharp work knife, dexterous, light, and swift. She was splashing him a little, playing the water with her free foot. They were making jokes, lilting, laughing. Something, another branch in the twisted tree that shaded our lives, was going to keep us safe for a while.

TILLIE OLSEN
(1913—)

◆

Born in Nebraska, TILLIE OLSEN has lived most of her life in San Francisco. A Depression high school dropout, she worked at "everyday" jobs, involved herself in labor-movement activism, and wrote on the side. Married in 1943, she had four children and continued to work full-time outside the home as a temp, a typist, and a transcriber, putting her writing on hold until her youngest daughter was five years old. In 1955 a Stanford University Creative Writing Fellowship saved her life as a writer. In 1961 she won the O. Henry Award for *Tell Me a Riddle,* the title novella of the collection of four stories, now considered a contemporary classic, published in 1962. In 1974, forty years after circumstances had forced her to set it aside, her "lost" novel, *Yonnondio: From the Thirties,* was published. Since her resurrection as a writer, she has taught at Amherst, Stanford, and been Writer-in-Residence at MIT and a Fellow of the Radcliffe Institute. She has received fellowships from the Ford Foundation, the Guggenheim Foundation, and the National Endowment for the Humanities as well as honorary awards from the American Academy and the National Institute of Arts and Letters.

Silences, the source of the following selection, is her first book of nonfiction, an autobiographical antiliterary history. In it, Olsen identifies the literature that has gone unwritten by women writers hobbled by circumstance—their class, color, sex, the times into which they were born. She focuses especially on the silences she has known throughout her own multilayered life, showing the connection between a woman's writing life and childbearing, mothering, and a negative literary climate. (In a generally favorable review of *Tell Me a Riddle,* Irving Howe still found it necessary to criticize the writer's "narrowness of experience.") *Silences,* as she puts it, "is not an orthodoxly written work of academic scholarship." It began as lecture notes, became articles and several published essays: "the substance herein was long in accumulation, garnered over fifty years, near a lifetime." Always the same question drove the shaping of this book: "What *are* creation's needs for full functioning? . . . I have had special need to learn all I could of this over the years, myself so nearly remaining mute and having to let writing die over and over again in me."

The writing self Olsen mourns in this book, silent out of personal necessity and cultural design, has come back from the dead. Since her return, Tillie Olsen has become a leading figure in women's literary history, a nurturer of the voiceless and a major force behind the retrieval of long-forgotten literature. Her life story calls to mind some lines (and aspects of the biography) of Dorothy Wordsworth: "Yet the lost fragments shall remain/ To fertilize some other ground."

From *Silences*

In the last century, of the women whose achievements endure for us in one way or another,* nearly all never married (Jane Austen, Emily Brontë, Christina Rossetti, Emily Dickinson, Louisa May Alcott, Sarah Orne Jewett) or married late in their thirties (George Eliot, Elizabeth Barrett Browning, Charlotte Brontë, Olive Schreiner). I can think of only four (George Sand, Harriet Beecher Stowe, Helen Hunt Jackson, and Elizabeth Gaskell) who married and had children as young women.† All had servants.

In our century, until very recently, it has not been so different. Most did not marry (Selma Lagerlof, Willa Cather, Ellen Glasgow, Gertrude Stein, Gabriela Mistral, Elizabeth Madox Roberts, Charlotte Mew, Eudora Welty, Marianne Moore) or, if married, have been childless (Edith Wharton, Virginia Woolf, Katherine Mansfield, Dorothy Richardson, H. H. Richardson, Elizabeth Bowen, Isak Dinesen, Katherine Anne Porter, Lillian Hellman, Dorothy Parker). Colette had one child (when she was forty). If I include Sigrid Undset, Kay Boyle, Pearl Buck, Dorothy Canfield Fisher, that will make a small group who had more than one child. All had household help or other special circumstances.

Am I resaying the moldy theory that women have no need, some say no capacity, to create art, because they can "create" babies? And the additional proof is precisely that the few women who have created it are nearly all childless? No.

The power and the need to create, over and beyond reproduction, is native in both women and men. Where the gifted among women (*and men*) have remained mute, or have never attained full capacity, it is because of circumstances, inner or outer, which oppose the needs of creation.

---

*"One Out of Twelve" has a more extensive roll of women writers of achievement.
†I would now add a fifth—Kate Chopin—also a foreground silence.

Wholly surrendered and dedicated lives; time as needed for the work; totality of self. But women are traditionally trained to place others' needs first, to feel these needs as their own (the "infinite capacity"); their sphere, their satisfaction to be in making it possible for others to use their abilities. This is what Virginia Woolf meant when, already a writer of achievement, she wrote in her diary:

> Father's birthday. He would have been 96, 96, yes, today; and could have been 96, like other people one has known; but mercifully was not. His life would have entirely ended mine. What would have happened? No writing, no books;—inconceivable. . . .

If I talk now quickly of my own silences—almost presumptuous after what has been told here—it is that the individual experience may add.

In the twenty years I bore and reared my children, usually had to work on a paid job as well, the simplest circumstances for creation did not exist. Nevertheless writing, the hope of it, was "the air I breathed, so long as I shall breathe at all." In that hope, there was conscious storing, snatched reading, beginnings of writing, and always "the secret rootlets of reconnaissance."

When the youngest of our four was in school, the beginnings struggled toward endings. This was a time, in Kafka's words, "like a squirrel in a cage: bliss of movement, desperation about constriction, craziness of endurance."

Bliss of movement. A full extended family life; the world of my job (transcriber in a dairy-equipment company); and the writing, which I was somehow able to carry around within me through work, through home. Time on the bus, even when I had to stand, was enough; the stolen moments at work, enough; the deep night hours for as long as I could stay awake, after the kids were in bed, after the household tasks were done, sometimes during. It is no accident that the first work I considered publishable began: "I stand here ironing, and what you asked me moves tormented back and forth with the iron."

In such snatches of time I wrote what I did in those years, but there came a time when this triple life was no longer possible. The fifteen hours of daily realities became too much distraction for the writing. I lost craziness of endurance. What might have been, I don't know; but I applied for, and was given, eight months' writing time. There was still full family life, all the household responsibilities, but I did not have to hold an eight-hour job. I had continuity, three full days, sometimes more—and it was in those months I made the mysterious turn and became a writing writer.

Then had to return to the world of work, someone else's work, nine hours, five days a week.

This was the time of festering and congestion. For a few months I was able to shield the writing with which I was so full, against the demands of jobs on which I had to be competent, through the joys and responsibilities and trials of family. For a few months. Always roused by the writing, always denied. "I could not go to write it down. It convulsed and died in me. I will pay."

My work died. What demanded to be written, did not. It seethed, bubbled, clamored, peopled me. At last moved into the hours meant for sleeping. I worked now full time on temporary jobs, a Kelly, a Western Agency girl (girl!), wandering from office to office, always hoping to manage two, three writing months ahead. Eventually there was time.

I had said: always roused by the writing, always denied. Now, like a woman made frigid, I had to learn response, to trust this possibility for fruition that had not been before. Any interruption dazed and silenced me. It took a long while of surrendering to what I was trying to write, of invoking Henry James's "passion, piety, patience," before I was able to re-establish work.

When again I had to leave the writing, I lost consciousness. A time of anesthesia. There was still an automatic noting that did not stop, but it was as if writing had never been. No fever, no congestion, no festering. I ceased being peopled, slept well and dreamlessly, took a "permanent" job. The few pieces that had been published seemed to have vanished like the not-yet-written. I wrote someone, unsent: "So long they fed each other—my life, the writing—; —the writing or hope of it, my life—; but now they begin to destroy." I knew, but did not feel the destruction.

A Ford grant in literature, awarded me on nomination by others, came almost too late. Time granted does not necessarily coincide with time that can be most fully used, as the congested time of fullness would have been. Still, it was two years.

Drowning is not so pitiful as the attempt to rise, says Emily Dickinson. I do not agree, but I know whereof she speaks. For a long time I was that emaciated survivor trembling on the beach, unable to rise and walk. Said differently, I could manage only the feeblest, shallowest growth on that devastated soil. Weeds, to be burned like weeds, or used as compost. When the habits of creation were at last rewon, one book went to the publisher, and I dared to begin my present work. It became my center, engraved on it: "Evil is whatever distracts." (By now had begun a cost to our family life, to my own participation in life as a human being.) I shall not tell the "rest, residue, and remainder" of what

I was "leased, demised, and let unto" when once again I had to leave work at the flood to return to the Time-Master, to business-ese and legalese. This most harmful of all my silences has ended, but I am not yet recovered; may still be a one-book silence.

However that will be, we are in a time of more and more hidden and foreground silences, women *and* men. Denied full writing life, more may try to "nurse through night" (that part-time, part-self night) "the ethereal spark," but it seems to me there would almost have had to be "flame on flame" first; and time as needed, afterwards; and enough of the self, the capacities, undamaged for the rebeginnings on the frightful task. I would like to believe this for what has not yet been written into literature. But it cannot reconcile for what is lost by unnatural silences. . . .

. . . How much it takes to become a writer. Bent (far more common than we assume), circumstances, time, development of craft—but beyond that: how much conviction as to the importance of what one has to say, one's right to say it. And the will, the measureless store of belief in oneself to be able to come to, cleave to, find the form for one's own life comprehensions. Difficult for any male not born into a class that breeds such confidence. Almost impossible for a girl, a woman.

The leeching of belief, of will, the damaging of capacity begin so early. Sparse indeed is the literature on the way of denial to small girl children of the development of their endowment as born human: active, vigorous bodies; exercise of the power to do, to make, to investigate, to invent, to conquer obstacles, to resist violations of the self; to think, create, choose; to attain community, confidence in self. Little has been written on the harms of instilling constant concern with appearance; the need to please, to support; the training in acceptance, deferring. Little has been added in our century to George Eliot's *The Mill on the Floss* on the effect of the differing treatment—"climate of expectation"—for boys and for girls.

But it is there if one knows how to read for it, and indelibly there in the resulting damage. One—out of twelve.

In the vulnerable girl years, unlike their sisters in the previous century, women writers go to college.* The kind of experience it may be for them is stunningly documented in Elaine Showalter's pio-

---

*True almost without exception among the writers who are women in *Twentieth Century Authors* and *Contemporary Authors.*

neering "Women and the Literary Curriculum."* Freshman texts in which women have little place, if at all; language itself, all achievement, anything to do with the human in male terms—*Man in Crises, The Individual and His World.* Three hundred thirteen male writers taught; seventeen women writers: That classic of adolescent rebellion, *A Portrait of the Artist as a Young Man;* and sagas (male) of the quest for identity (but then Erikson, the father of the concept, propounds that identity concerns girls only insofar as making themselves into attractive beings for the right kind of man).† Most, *not all,* of the predominantly male literature studied, written by men whose understandings are not universal, but restrictively male (as Mary Ellmann, Kate Millett, and Dolores Schmidt have pointed out); in our time more and more surface, hostile, one-dimensional in portraying women.

In a writer's young years, susceptibility to the vision and style of the great is extreme. Add the aspiration-denying implication, consciously felt or not (although reinforced daily by one's professors and reading) that (as Virginia Woolf noted years ago) women writers, women's experience, and literature written by women are by definition minor. (Mailer will not grant even the minor: "the one thing a writer has to have is balls.") No wonder that Showalter observes:

> Women [students] are estranged from their own experience and unable to perceive its shape and authenticity, in part because they do not see it mirrored and given resonance in literature. . . . They are expected to identify with masculine experience, which is presented as the human one, and have no faith in the validity of their own perceptions and experiences, rarely seeing them confirmed in literature, or accepted in criticism . . . [They] notoriously lack the happy confidence, the exuberant sense of the value of their individual observations which enables young men to risk making fools of themselves for the sake of an idea.

Harms difficult to work through. Nevertheless, some young women (others are already lost) maintain their ardent intention to write—fed indeed by the very glories of some of this literature that puts them down.

College English, May 1971. A year later (October 1972), *College English* published an extensive report, "Freshman Textbooks," by Jean Mullens. In the 112 most used texts, she found 92.47 percent (5,795) of the selections were by men; 7.53 percent (472) by women (One Out of Twelve). Mullens deepened Showalter's insights as to the subtly undermining effect on freshman students of the texts' contents and language, as well as the minuscule proportion of women writers.
†In keeping with his 1950s–60s thesis of a distinctly female "biological, evolutionary need to fulfil self through serving others."

But other invisible worms are finding out the bed of crimson joy.* Self-doubt; seriousness, also questioned by the hours agonizing over appearance; concentration shredded into attracting, being attractive; the absorbing real need and love for working with words felt as hypocritical self-delusion ("I'm not truly dedicated"), for what seems (and is) esteemed is being attractive to men. High aim, and accomplishment toward it, discounted by the prevalent attitude that, as girls will probably marry (attitudes not applied to boys who will probably marry), writing is no more than an attainment of a dowry to be spent later according the needs and circumstances within the true vocation: husband and family. The growing acceptance that going on will threaten other needs, to love and be loved; ("a woman has to sacrifice all claims to femininity and family to be a writer").†

And the agony—peculiarly mid-century, escaped by their sisters of pre-Freudian, pre-Jungian times—that "creation and femininity are incompatible."‡ Anaïs Nin's words.

The aggressive act of creation; the guilt for creating. I did not want to rival man; to steal man's creation, his thunder. I must protect them, not outshine them.**

The acceptance—against one's experienced reality—of the sexist notion that the act of creation is not as inherently natural to a woman as to a man, but rooted instead in unnatural aggression, rivalry, envy, or thwarted sexuality.

And in all the usual college teaching—the English, history, psychology, sociology courses—little to help that young woman understand the source or nature of this inexplicable draining self-doubt, loss of aspiration, of confidence. . . .

More and more women writers in our century, primarily in the last two decades, are assuming as their right fullness of work *and* family

---

*O Rose thou art sick./The invisible worm,
That flies in the night/In the howling storm:

Has found out thy bed/Of crimson joy:
And his dark secret love/Does thy life destroy.
—William Blake
†Plath. A letter when a graduate student.
‡*The Diary of Anaïs Nin,* Vol. III, 1939–1944.
**A statement that would have baffled Austen, the Brontës, Mrs. Gaskell, Eliot, Stowe, Alcott, etc. The strictures were felt by them in other ways.

life.* Their emergence is evidence of changing circumstances making possible for them what (with rarest exception) was not possible in the generations of women before. I hope and I fear for what will result. I hope (and believe) that complex new richness will come into literature; I fear because almost certainly their work will be impeded, lessened, partial. For the fundamental situation remains unchanged. Unlike men writers who marry, most will not have the societal equivalent of a wife—nor (in a society hostile to growing life) anyone but themselves to mother their children. Even those who can afford help, good schools, summer camps, may (*may*) suffer what seventy years ago W.E.B. Du Bois called "The Damnation of Women": "that only at the sacrifice of the chance to do their best work can women bear and rear children."†

. . . Yes, the loss in quality, the minor work, the hidden silences, are there in woman after woman writer in our century.‡ We will never have the body of work that we were capable of producing. Blight, said Blake, never does good to a tree:

> And if a blight kill not a tree but it still bear fruit, let none say that the fruit was in consequence of the blight.

As for myself, who did not publish a book until I was fifty, who raised children without household help or the help of the "technological sublime" (the atom bomb was in manufacture before the first automatic washing machine); who worked outside the house on everyday jobs as well (as nearly half of all women do now, though a woman with a paid job, except as a maid or prostitute, is still rarest of any in litera-

---

*Among those with children: Harriette Arnow, Mary Lavin, Mary McCarthy, Tess Slesinger, Eleanor Clark, Nancy Hale, Storm Jameson, Janet Lewis, Jean Rhys, Kay Boyle, Ann Petry, Dawn Powell, Meridel LeSueur, Evelyn Eaton, Dorothy Canfield Fisher, Pearl Buck, Josephine Johnson, Caroline Gordon, Shirley Jackson; and a sampling in the unparalleled last two decades: Doris Lessing, Nadine Gordimer, Margaret Laurence, Grace Paley, Hortense Calisher, Edna O'Brien, Sylvia Ashton-Warner, Paule Murray, Françoise Mallet-Joris, Cynthia Ozick, Joanne Greenberg, Joan Didion, Penelope Mortimer, Alison Lurie, Hope Hale Davis, Doris Betts, Muriel Spark, Adele Wiseman, Lael Wertenbaker, Shirley Ann Grau, Maxine Kumin, Margaret Walker, Gina Barriault, Mary Gray Hughes, Maureen Howard, Norma Rosen, Lore Segal, Alice Walker, Nancy Willard, Charlotte Painter, Sallie Bingham. (I would now add Clarice Lispector, Ruth Prawer Jhabvala, June Arnold, Ursula Le Guin, Diane Johnson, Alice Munro, Helen Yglesias, Susan Cahill, Rosellen Brown, Alta, and Susan Griffin.) Some wrote before children, some only in the middle or later years. Not many have directly used the material open to them out of motherhood as central source for their work.
†*Letters of Sarah Orne Jewett*, edited by Annie Fields.
‡Compared to men writers of like distinction and years of life, few women writers have had lives of unbroken productivity, or leave behind a "body of work." Early beginnings, then silence; or clogged late ones (foreground silences); long periods between books (hidden silences); characterize most of us. A Colette, Wharton, Glasgow, Millay, Lessing, Oates, are the exceptions.

ture); who could not kill the essential angel (there was no one else to do her work); would not—if I could—have killed the caring part of the Woolf angel, as distant from the world of literature most of my life as literature is distant (in content too) from my world:

The years when I should have been writing, my hands and being were at other (inescapable) tasks. Now, lightened as they are, when I must do those tasks into which most of my life went, like the old mother, grandmother in my *Tell Me a Riddle* who could not make herself touch a baby, I pay a psychic cost: "the sweat beads, the long shudder begins." The habits of a lifetime when everything else had to come before writing are not easily broken, even when circumstances now often make it possible for writing to be first; habits of years—response to others, distractibility, responsibility for daily matters—stay with you, mark you, become you. The cost of "discontinuity" (that pattern still imposed on women) is such a weight of things unsaid, an accumulation of material so great, that everything starts up something else in me; what should take weeks, takes me sometimes months to write; what should take months, takes years.

I speak of myself to bring here the sense of those others to whom this is in the process of happening (unnecessarily happening, for it need not, must not continue to be) and to remind us of those (I so nearly was one) who never come to writing at all. . . .

MADELEINE L'ENGLE
(1918—   )

◆

MADELEINE L'ENGLE lived her first twelve years as a lonely only child in a Manhattan apartment before she moved to Europe with her parents and entered a strict English boarding school in Switzerland. There she learned to withdraw into the world of her imagination. She was educated at Smith College and after graduation returned to New York City to write and work as an actress in Eva Le Gallienne's Civic Repertory Theatre. In 1946 she married the actor Hugh Franklin, left the theater, and began to write for publication while raising three children in an old farmhouse in Connecticut named Crosswicks. Among her highly regarded novels are *The Small Rain* (1945), *Meet the Austins* (1960), and *A Wrinkle in Time* (1962) which, rejected by many publishers, eventually won the Newberry Prize and has become a best-selling classic of children's literature. Subsequent novels for young people repeat the theme of the power of love dramatized in *Wrinkle: A Wind in the Door* (1973), *The Arm of the Starfish* (1965), *The Young Unicorns* (1968), and *Dragons in the Waters* (1976). Her autobiographical works for adults, a trilogy entitled *The Crosswicks Journal (A Circle of Quiet* [1972], *The Summer of the Great-Grandmother* [1974], and *The Irrational Season* [1977]), are compelling and personal meditations on the daily experiences of a woman narrator who lives in multiple environments in multiple roles—mother, wife, daughter, friend, godmother, writer, community volunteer, store clerk. The journals resonate with L'Engle's preoccupations with moral and theological dilemmas, told with concrete detail and common sense.

Two-Part Invention: The Story of a Marriage (1988), excerpted here, is her memoir of her marriage of more than forty years to Hugh Franklin, written after the summer of 1987 when he was suddenly hospitalized and, at the end of summer, died of cancer. L'Engle participates in her husband's dying as she simultaneously re-creates their life together in memory and continues her professional work as a writer and teacher of writing at a nearby university. Her memoir breathes with simplicity and dignity; there is no cant or easy relief taken from the promises of religion. Her tone brings to mind some words of Denise Levertov (see page 189) about death: "It is not understood that the greatest heroes and heroines are truly those who hold out the longest, or, if they do die young, do so unwillingly, resisting to the last." L'Engle interweaves this story of long love and the sorrow of her husband's last summer with the questions that have given all her books a metaphysical dimension: the conflict between good and evil, the existence of God, and the mystery of our existence in a world of tragedy and suffering.

From *Two-Part Invention: The Story of a Marriage*

... When I kiss Hugh good night at bedtime, I do not know what the next day is going to bring. I remember being on a long hike where for the last few miles uphill it was only sheer willpower that kept my legs moving, one foot in front of the other, one foot in front of the other. This summer is like that. The prognosis is still optimistic, but there is a numbness deep in my heart. The fear that preceded the China trip is still with me.

Hugh does the best he can, tries to walk, to eat, to swim. One day he hands me *The New York Times* and says, "Here. I want you to read this."

"This" is a distressing article about parents in Tennessee who want to ban textbooks because they might "stimulate" the children's imaginations, and because in history books the chapter on the Renaissance "affirms the worth and dignity of man."

The article has come to Hugh's attention because similar parents are attacking my work as un-Christian. This startles me each time it happens, and it hurts. Or used to. Right now my attention is so focused on Hugh that there is no space in it for these attackers, who seem, at best, mildly insane. But it is typical of Hugh that he has noticed the article because of me, and his concern is a return to normal. Perhaps it will even increase his appetite, make him walk a little farther. Anything that holds his interest is improvement, and I am deeply moved that it has been awakened because of something which touches me. Hugh says of the attackers, "They are afraid," and I suspect that he is right.

How could I live, endure this summer, without imagination? How can anyone even begin to have an incarnational view of the universe without an incredible leap of the imagination? That God cares for us, every single one of us, so deeply that all power is willing to come to us, to be with us, takes all the imagination with which we have been endowed. And how could I get through this summer without affirming the worth and dignity of human beings? Isn't that what the incarnation was about? It is the message for me during these long weeks of Hugh's illness. During the interminable month of June when he was in the hospital I watched the doctors and nurses struggling with all their skill to affirm the dignity and worth of the patients. On the cancer floor this is no easy task. Hugh told of one of the nurses holding his head and the basin all through the night, while he retched and retched.

But to certain Christians it is un-Christian to affirm the dignity and worth of human beings. If that is so, then I cannot be a Christian. My husband, struggling to eat, to walk, to regain strength, sharing with me an article in the *Times* that caught his interest because of his concern for me, is an example of the dignity and worth of the human being in the place of excrement.

With my imagination I try to be hopeful, not unrealistically, but still hopeful that Hugh will get through this enough so that we will have more time together. But ultimately one of us will die before the other, unless we are killed together in an accident on one of our trips—not impossible in this age of terrorism. But if Hugh dies first, would I ever be able to stop saying "we" and say "I"? I doubt it. I do not think that death can take away the fact that Hugh and I are "we" and "us," a new creature born at the time of our marriage vows, which has grown along with us as our marriage has grown. Even during the times, inevitable in all marriages, when I have felt angry, or alienated, the instinctive "we" remains. And most growth has come during times of trial. Trial by fire. Fire as an image of purification is found all through literature. Dante speaks of the fire of roses. George MacDonald's Curdie has to plunge his hands deep into the burning fire of roses. In Scripture we read, "Our God is a consuming fire." God is "like a refiner's fire." Moses saw God in a burning bush, a bush which was burned and was not consumed, as we are to be burned by this holy fire and yet not consumed. We are to be refined in the fire like silver. Shadrach, Meshach, and Abednego walked through the flames. The Spirit descended and descends in tongues of fire.

Satan has tried to take fire over as his image, teasing, tormenting us with the idea of the flames of hell. Dante understood the wrongness of this in having the most terrible circle of hell be *cold*.

Coldness of the last circle of hell; coldness of heart; lack of compassion; treating people as objects (a reasonable definition of pornography, Hugh says); pride; setting ourselves apart from the "others"—all these are cold.

It is a terrible choice: the purifying fire of the Creator or the deathly cold fire of Satan.

It is the fire this summer, and I can only pray that it will be purifying.

I spend a week going back and forth to Wesleyan University in Middletown, Connecticut, a little over an hour from Crosswicks. When I accepted the job of teaching one of the workshops at this excellent writers' conference I had expected to be there for the full five days, but with Hugh's illness this is impossible. I feel that I must honor my commitment, however, and kind friends are arranging daily transportation so that I can commute.

Even the day I leave, there is yet another setback, a massive increase in what was a slight diabetic neuropathy in Hugh's feet and lower legs, but which now makes him walk tentatively, like an old man—another side effect of the platinum chemotherapy.

My workshop is full of talented writers, but it is physically a rough week, with the commuting back and forth. As well as teaching my daily workshop, I have to give half-hour conferences to twenty-five people, which I couldn't possibly have managed on my own. With the help of my friend Jane, they are scheduled, fitted in catch-as-catch-can.

During one conference someone said, "We've been talking about your amazing optimism."

The men and women in my workshop had been told the reason for my commuting, why I could not be at the conference full-time, but this student was referring not so much to Hugh's illness as to a general attitude toward life.

And I heard myself saying, "I do not believe that true optimism can come about except through tragedy." Sometimes so casually is revelation given. . . .

. . . The student who remarked on my optimism and I talk a little further about my belief that God is not going to fail with Creation, no matter how abominably we human beings abuse free will, no matter how we keep our own self-interest in mind rather than the working out of a Grand Unified Theory. We talk about how God can come into "the flame of incandescent terror" and purify even the most terrible anguish.

It is not an easy conversation for me under the circumstances, but I learn from it.

Teaching a course in techniques of fiction involves sharing, no matter how indirectly, one's attitude toward the human endeavor. Maritain wrote that "fiction differs from every other art in one respect: it concerns the conduct of life itself." Thus any discussion of the writing of fiction is theological, even if God is never mentioned.

It is good for me to teach because it draws me out of myself and the limiting aspects of Hugh's illness. Severe illness isolates those in close contact with it, because it inevitably narrows the focus of concern. To a certain extent this can lead to healing, but not if the circle of concern is so tight that it cannot be broken into, or out of. Our circle widens with each phone call, each visitor. The workshop at Wesleyan helps me focus on the true concerns of the human endeavor. It does not lessen my love for my husband, or the deep interior prayer which goes on all the time. Rather it strengthens it, as I am forced to articulate ideas and hopes which are often latent.

I get home one afternoon and go out into the garden to pick lettuce, and hear a small sound and turn. There, caught in the net trellis which holds up the snap peas, is a small bird, a female finch. She stays very still, one wing outspread. I have brought a kitchen knife with me, and cut away the twine of the trellis until she is able to fly away, soaring, free.

Where is someone to cut us out of the net?

One thing goes wrong for Hugh after another. He still cannot swallow anything solid. Finally the gastroenterologist takes him as an outpatient to the operating room in the hospital to look down his esophagus and into his stomach and cannot look, because there is a stricture in the esophagus, almost closing it completely just at the entrance to the stomach. No wonder Hugh has not been able to eat! The doctor opens the esophagus, a very painful procedure. The peptic ulcers are healing, but the fungus is still on the esophagus and has caused the scarring which has almost closed it.

The cure seems worse than the disease.

If I feel caught in the net like that little bird, what must it be like for Hugh, with his body betraying him over and over again?

Hugh is an actor. For the actor, as for the dancer, the body is the instrument. I can walk away from the typewriter or the piano; although they seem to be part of me, in actuality they are not. But Hugh's instrument is his body, his beautiful body. He has always been tall and lean. He has felt legitimate pride in his body, and has kept it well.

When the urologist first talked to us about the procedure for Hugh's kind of cancer, and explained that it included the removal of the bladder, and the consequent use of a bag, I talked to him about this, saying that anything that changes the body is more painful and humiliating to an actor or dancer than it would be for the rest of us. I don't know whether or not he understood. He is a doctor, interested in curing disease. But curing disease is inextricably intertwined with the psyche. We are not body alone.

I wish I could take the kitchen knife and cut away the cords that are binding Hugh and free him. . . .

. . . We try to keep things as normal for Hugh as possible, have friends in for dinner. One of Laurie's colleagues, a cardiac specialist, comes on a gentle summer evening with his wife and young son. The family has been friends of Hugh's through watching him as Dr. Tyler on ABC's *All My Children*. The night Hugh had to return to the hospital with his heart galloping arrhythmically, and this gentle doctor was brought in, he greeted Hugh with affection, "Why, Dr. Tyler!"

Our tree-planting godchildren come again and of course more trees must be planted. One of our summer projects has been expanding our little terrace so that it is more functional, and Hugh has been able to watch the progress from the kitchen windows. We buy seven small hemlocks to make a tiny border, and Hugh calls instructions through the windows as we dig and plant, naming each little tree for one of the seven seas. I mostly stand and encourage while the young people do the hard work. When they come in, grubby and tired, Hugh says, "You've done a fine job. Now just move them all three inches to the right."

Laughter heals, heals those who ache for what Hugh is enduring.

Another evening Scott and Lily Peck and their son, Christopher, come for dinner. It is a beautiful evening and both before and after dinner we relax out on the expanded terrace, and Hugh is suddenly and beautifully fully there, his most real self. We are all aware that it is a special evening. Later Scotty wrote to me: ". . . but that evening in early August was quite extraordinary, as you yourself recognized. Fortunately or unfortunately, I am not one of those people given to seeing auras or whatnot. But Hugh just glowed. He glowed all over. It was one of the most extraordinary phenomenons which I have ever been privileged to witness. There were two things about it. One was the light. His whole being, despite being physically wasted, seemed to have become a being of light. The other was his absolutely extraordinary alertness. Despite his illness and disease, despite his age, despite his deafness, I have never seen any human being for a period of several hours so alert. It manifested itself in a hundred different ways. He spontaneously asked about the Foundation and how it was doing. I wouldn't even have believed that he would have remembered. He not only allowed Christopher and me to go out into the garden to have a smoke, but even wondered for us whether it wasn't time for us to do so. Et cetera, et cetera. I could go on and on, but I have never been in the presence of any human being who was, in fact, so present." . . .

EIGHT

Oh, my love.

When we first learned of Hugh's cancer I was dry as the parched land suffering drought in the Southeast. Now the tears are close to the surface. For the third time this summer I come to the Psalms for the evening of the fourth day and read, "My God, my God, why have you forsaken me?" and the tears rush out silently and stream down my face. Music, too, tends to pluck at the chords of emotion. Tears are healing. I do not want to cry when I am not alone, but by myself I don't try to hold the tears back. In a sense this solitary weeping is a form of prayer.

But things continue to go wrong. Hugh gets a bladder infection. What next?

One morning he starts uncontrollable vomiting. It goes on and on. He cannot even take the antibiotic for the urinary-tract infection, though it is in liquid form. He returns to the hospital, through the emergency room, hoping to be treated only as an outpatient until the vomiting is controlled. But despite his reluctance, it is evident that he must be admitted. The doctors are baffled and discouraged. Hugh's appetite should have returned weeks ago; he should have been gaining strength. He should have had the surgery and be recuperating by now.

John, our old friend and general practitioner, had sent a patient of his to visit Hugh when he was first in the hospital, a man in his fifties who had had the same surgery Hugh is facing, who now drives a school bus, goes fishing, considers himself, three years after surgery, to be cured. What is happening with Hugh? Where will all this end? Can I believe that he, too, will be cured? What about all those prayers with which he is surrounded? I know that these prayers are faithfully coming. I believe in them. What is happening?

The days drag on. I am overimpatient that the doctors cannot find out why Hugh cannot eat solid food. I expect too much of ordinary human beings who happen to have more training in medicine than the rest of us. They are not gods. They are doing their best. I must watch out for false expectations.

And I must have realistic but not false expectations of myself. It is all a delicate and difficult balance. Sometimes I am strong with that wonderful strength which is not my own but is given (much of it through the prayers which steadfastly keep coming); and sometimes I crumple. At four o'clock this morning I sat up in bed and wept, sitting up to weep because to cry lying down makes one's nose stuffy. And to let go, at four o'clock in the morning, is all right.

I have been looking over my old journals (something I seldom do) as I relive the volatile years of our marriage. It has been fun to relive our early years in the theatre, our courtship, stormy though it was, the birth of our babies. Sometimes I come upon unexpected things. In one entry, written during our early years at Crosswicks, I read: "They said in college that there was one housemother who was a widow and who could not go to sleep without a green velvet arm in bed with her." I think of being in bed alone and wonder if I will ever wake in the night and not stretch out foot or hand to touch the living flesh of my beloved. I ache for that strange housemother, although I know that, whatever happens, I will never want a green velvet arm. I have left behind forever the "blankie" and the favorite stuffed animal.

So I sleep alone. In the morning I swim for half an hour before breakfast, do whatever needs to be done, make myself a sandwich and a thermos of soup, and spend the rest of the day in the hospital.

One morning during my pre-breakfast swim, I remember some words Helen Waddell wrote about prayer, and go to look them up in my big brown Goody Book where I have copied them down: "They asked the abbot Macarius, saying, 'How ought we to pray?' and the old man said, 'There is no need of much speaking in prayer, but often stretch out thy hands and say, 'Lord, as Thou wilt and as Thou knowest, have mercy upon me.' But if there is war in thy soul, add, 'Help me,' and because he knoweth what we have need of he sheweth us his mercy."

Help, I cry. *Help!*

In the mail I get a loving note from Mother Ruth of the community of the Holy Spirit. She enclosed a little card from England printed with the words: "He setteth in pain the jewels of his love." They are good words. They could equally be reversed: God can provide the setting in which the pearl of pain is placed.

We learn to live in the cloud of unknowing, not only the cloud of God's mystery, but the cloud of unknowing what is going to happen from day to day. That is always true, but when things go along routinely we are less aware of it. Something unexpected seems to happen every day this summer. One problem for Hugh is cleared up, and immediately something else occurs. The doctors, who were calmly optimistic in May, are less certain as we move toward September.

In *The Irrational Season* I wrote that when two people truly love each other, each one must be willing to let the other die first. I may be reluctantly, painfully willing, but I could understand a clean death better than this nibbling away at the man I have loved for so many years.

I have a friend whose husband is being taken away from her by Alzheimer's disease, so that he is a senile wreck of what was once a handsome, virile, dominant man. That is far worse than this. There are many people in situations far more terrible than ours. But there is a quality of limbo to this unknowing. . . .

. . . My friend Tallis remarked once that cancer is the result of sin, not the sin of the person suffering from this ugly disease, but the sins of many human beings throughout the ages, making wrong choices, letting greed override wisdom.

This abuse of free will throughout the millennia does not mean that cancer is a punishment, as some people view it. No, it is a consequence of many actions by many people, often unknowing. Those first factories of the Industrial Revolution fouled the once clean sky, but it was not a conscious fouling. People did not understand what they were doing. When Hugh smoked as a young man, smoking was not yet seen as a threat to health. My grandfather smoked moderately all his life, and he lived to be a hundred and one, but our planet's air and water were far cleaner than they are now.

I have become phobic about smoking (I was one of the lucky people who never liked it), and I bitterly resent being made a "passive smoker." It is particularly bad in airports, but wherever people smoke, those of us who do not are made to suffer from the addiction and discourtesy of those who do. Even in this hospital, there is only one waiting room on all seven floors where smoking is prohibited—the meditation room on the cancer floor. When Hugh has come in as an outpatient for one procedure or another and I am told to wait in the lobby, I reply politely but firmly, "No." When I get a surprised look I say, "I will not wait where there are smokers. The smoke gets in my contact lenses and irritates my eyes. I will wait in the meditation room on the third floor. If it is occupied I will wait out in the corridor."

I am told that soon the hospital will be entirely smoke-free, and the only reason this eminently sensible decision has not already been implemented is that some of the older doctors will not give up their cigarettes.

Consequences: cancer is a result of consequences. It is not sent as a punishment. I do not have to make the repulsive theological error of feeling that I have to see cancer as God's will for my husband. I do not want anything to do with that kind of God. Cancer is not God's will. The death of a child is not God's will. The deaths from automobile accidents during this long holiday weekend are not God's will. I would rather have no God at all than that kind of punitive God. Tragedies are consequences of human actions, and the only God worth believing in does not cause the tragedies but lovingly comes into the anguish with us.

Alas, we human beings have played god throughout the centuries.

★   ★   ★

We do not play god well. Look what we have done.

What is the difference between playing god and making responsible decisions? That is always a question the doctor must ask. And so must the rest of us. How do we separate self-interest from what is right for others? How do we love without manipulating or wanting to control? Do heads of state ever completely avoid that corruption which Lord Acton warns comes from power?

Right now the doctors have absolute power over Hugh. I have to trust them to ask the right questions. I have seen some doctors let the vanity of their profession make them prolong dying or, what is even worse, abandon their patient. I trust Hugh's doctors to listen to Hugh. To listen to me when I talk to them. I trust them to take into account that sometimes death is better than keeping a patient alive just to keep him alive. I trust them not to prolong the dying when it is time for death.

Of course they see death as failure. I have to trust them to be willing to fail.

If we are not willing to fail we will never accomplish anything. All creative acts involve the risk of failure. Marriage is a terrible risk. So is having children. So is giving a performance in the theatre, or the writing of a book. Whenever something is completed successfully, then we must move on, and that is again to risk failure. . . .

. . . In Hugh's hospital room, where I spend seven or more hours a day, I am always on the alert toward my husband, even when he is sleeping. My quiet time comes in the evening, when we sit out on the terrace and wait for the stars. Most evenings I go upstairs early, at nine o'clock, to read, to think, to be quiet for a couple of hours. To unwind enough for sleep, which I need if I am to keep up my strength.

Piano time is very slim. I don't get home from the hospital in time to have that treasured hour at the piano before dinner. Writing, too, has been difficult. I have been drafting a novel, but the work has gone slowly. Although I am encouraged to use my little six-pound electronic typewriter in the hospital, I am constantly yearning toward Hugh in inner prayer. Not demanding prayer. Just a small giving of love flowing steadily to him. Most of what I have written this summer is this journal, and it, too, is a form of prayer and a source of strength.

Prayer. What about prayer? A friend wrote to me in genuine concern about Hugh, saying that she didn't understand much about intercessory prayer. I don't, either. Perhaps the greatest saints do. Most of us don't, and that is all right. We don't have to understand to know that prayer is love, and love is never wasted. . . .

MARY LEE SETTLE
(1918—)

———————◆———————

MARY LEE SETTLE was born in Charleston, West Virginia, lived for a time in Harlan County, Kentucky, where her father had a coal mine, then in Florida, and at the age of ten returned to Charleston, which remains the central home base for her fiction. At eighteen she was sent against her will to Sweet Briar College in Virginia. Two years later she left, moved to New York to work as an actress, supporting herself with modeling jobs. In 1942 she joined the Women's Auxiliary of the RAF and was stationed in Wiltshire, Herefordshire, and in Gloucestershire as part of Signals, the operation to detect the approach of German aircraft. Later she was transferred to the Office of War Information in London to escape being invalided out of the WAAF with "signals shock" due to enemy jamming. Settle's memoir of the Second World War, *All The Brave Promises: Memoirs of Aircraft Woman 2nd Class 2146391* (1966)— excerpted here—was ignored by reviewers in the United States but called "one of the best books to come out of the war" by Alan Pryce-Jones of the *Times Literary Supplement*. It was written, in Settle's words, "almost as a protest against the romanticism about the Second World War. The state of war—what the daily deprivation, grayness, drain of loss, and boredom did to people—was being forgotten. I tried to revive the memory of it, both for myself and for others."

Settle's interest in American history and its pattern of conflict between opportunity and oppression, between democracy and authoritarian government, underlies her opus, *The Beulah Quintet,* five novels spanning three centuries, from the Cromwellian English revolution to the end of the Civil Rights era, all set in the Virginia Territory, all seeking the source of continuity in the American experiment: *Prisons* (1973); *O Beulah Land* (1956); *Know Nothing* (1960); *The Scapegoat* (1980)—its heroine is Mother Jones—and *The Killing Ground* (1982) in which the central figure, the young unconventional Hannah McKarkle embodies the integrity and fearlessness of democratic idealism.

After years of neglect by the literary establishment in New York, Settle is now receiving recognition. Malcolm Cowley was an early champion of her quintet, praising its "largeness, freedom, and power" and its historical vision as "Tolstoyan in its breadth." Among the other writers and critics who admire her "courageous body of work" with its "epic dimensions" are Theodore Solotaroff, E. L. Doctorow, Walker Percy, Anne Tyler, Roger Shattuck, and George Garrett. Settle's other novels include *The Love Eaters* (1954), *The Kiss of Kin* (1955), *The Clam Shell* (1972), and *Blood Tie* (1977), the winner of the National Book Award.

Though she has taught for many years at Bard College and the University of Virginia, Settle told an interviewer that "teaching, if it is done with the dedication it requires, takes the same kind of energy as writing. One or the other must suffer. All too often the security that should enhance writing serves to destroy the capacity to write."

From *All the Brave Promises: Memoirs of Aircraft Woman 2nd Class 2146391*

Recall

We are accused of being nostalgic. We have been. What we have remembered are events. The Second World War was, for most of us, a state, a state of war, not an event. It was a permeation, a deadening, a waiting, hard to recall. What we have told about is the terrifying relief of battle or the sweet, false relief of leave.

These were not the causes of a psychic shock from which a generation of people are only now beginning to emerge. For every "historic" event, there were thousands of unknown, plodding people, caught up in a deadening authority, learning to survive by keeping quiet, by "getting by," by existing in secret, underground; conscripted, shunted, numbered. It took so many of them, so many of their gray days and their uprooted lives. It taught them evasive ways to survive. These ways, dangerous to the community and to the spirit, have been a part of the peace.

It is one small corner of this wartime life—the part of the Women's Auxiliary Air Force of the Royal Air Force in England—that I want to recall, perhaps to explain, to find out about, as I did then, step by step.

Having long since learned the lesson of "no names, no pack drill," both names and places have been "scrambled."

CHAPTER 1

By January, 1942, all women in Britain over the age of eighteen and under the age of sixty were conscripted either for factories, essential jobs and nursing or for the Armed Forces. Those of us who volunteered for the Forces were either seventeen, or Irish, or colonials, or romantics like myself who could persuade an official to let them aboard a ship.

I began trying to volunteer in Washington. In that hot summer of 1942, the diplomats and the Allied officers and the new American soldiers on leave shared taxis and talked about the war abstractly in the crowded cocktail bars or at parties on the tiny lawns in Georgetown. We saw *Mrs. Miniver* and *In Which We Serve*. Lludmilla Pavlechenka, the Russian sniper, short, square, with a heavy, boy's body and a child's face who was said to have killed five hundred Germans, sat in a box at an all-Russian concert. She wore a thick brown-blanket uniform with a tight red collar in the sweltering heat of the Washington summer. Her cheeks were painted in round, red patches like Petrouchka's. She watched us, crowded below her, as we filed into the concert hall, thin and cool in our summer evening dresses, to honor her. Whenever Russians came to the diplomatic parties, always in the background stood two officers looking exactly alike, saying nothing, only watching, with the highest polish on their boots in Washington. They were known as Tweedledum and Tweedledee.

There were little, isolated pockets of people who had been to the war. I shared a house with four code-and-cypher officers of the Women's Auxiliary Air Force of the Royal Air Force. On the hot nights, sweltering in new American underwear, they talked about Biggin Hill and the Battle of Britain. One had seen her husband killed, gone back to Canada to have her child, left the baby with her parents and come back to the WAAF. They took my attempts to join up for granted. In their atmosphere such decisions seemed normal.

Then there was a sense of war among the Allied officers, meeting at parties, sustained by the control of their manners, strolling at night under the trees, bright with light, sitting on the steps of the Lincoln Memorial—I remember all these times, constantly talking about war, and then I remembered St. Petersburg in *War and Peace*, where manners were important and gestures meant more than their action, and war was someplace else. It was what I would learn to call officer's war, with its new sense of elegance and its place for so many, its oases of comfort and dash so many would miss, forgetting or suppressing or never experiencing the rest.

At the British Embassy, the assistant military attaché, the assistant air attaché and the assistant naval attaché (they were all very tall and thin in their meticulous summer uniforms) discussed my case. They rejected me for the WRENS because I might be posted to Cairo, and the white, cotton summer stockings of their uniforms would hide my legs. They decided that in the Women's Army (the ATS) I would have no one to talk to. Then they set the unwieldy machinery of government going, almost casually, so that I could join the WAAF.

I was put aboard the train in Washington with a last bottle of champagne and an armful of roses. In my trunk were a year's supply of toilet paper, can after can of fruit juice, and evening clothes. I left what for nearly three years I would look back on as the last prewar world—a cloud cuckoo land, exciting and full of luxury. . . .

CHAPTER 2

The London of that week, as I waited to go into the WAAF, was "really" there as I had hoped, part of a language I already knew, as a memory before an event. I could still impose what I expected, comfortably, on what I saw, and it was life going on with a clung-to stability I took as normal, except for cleaned-up, neat gaps in its roofscapes, diminished against the solidity of its buildings—what was missing was less surprising than what was still there.

I lunched with a friend at Madame Prunier's in St. James's Street on the day I was to report. It had, that day, the intimacy against the cold space of October that London restaurants seem designed for, a cozy, good-smelling womb of adulthood, sweet from the pastry, a discreet tingle of glass and silver, polite murmurings, crowded but still quiet. It was a farewell lunch—small slices of good cake, Boeuf à la Bourguignonne and a rare bottle of prewar rosé from Anjou. When the bill came, my friend suggested that she pay for the food and I pay for the wine.

I walked out of Prunier's, small suitcase in hand, dressed carefully (so as not to "stand out"—this was instinctive) in an old camel's hair coat, a heavy Harris tweed suit, Pinet shoes and equipped with two hundred Balkan Sobranie cigarettes I had been given as a present and exactly one shilling. I stood staring across the road at officers' caps in Lock's, wondering how to walk to Kingsway—mapping it in my mind, damp London cold soaking through my heavy clothes. At that second a surge toward the unknown swept over me, a feeling of freedom, of guy ropes released, that can only be had once. It is an illusion that the past can be cast away so easily, as if one had only to let go for it to disappear; but, in action, that day freedom seemed pure. The feeling, and the wine, the excitement, the cold as off the end of a springboard, made me gasp, in that second, for breath.

So, light as air, I swung past St. James's Palace, sunken and small at the end of the street, and into the Mall, where across the wide, nearly deserted esplanade beyond its bordering trees St. James's Park lay veiled in the gray-green of October, air and trees almost translucent under the pale sun. Above me to my left, the elegant Regency façade of Carlton House terrace was neglected looking, disheveled by piles of sandbags soaked in damp. At the Admiralty, the huge, squat, angled monolith of a wartime building looked like it had been left from a barbarian time long before the rise of the Admiralty Arch or the delicate structure of the Horse Palace in the distance behind it.

Past the few people crisscrossing Trafalgar Square, where, in the distance, antlike dark figures in their wartime drab were strung out thinly in a late queue for the canteen below the National Gallery, I turned into the Strand. Again, at the Savoy, the same piles of stained sandbags and a lone taxi made it seem forgotten.

But as I walked fast along the Strand, all devil-may-care, I caught again the illusion of bravery, that surge of audacity, of an act well-done in some private intrigue of gallantry called "the war," was all safe, and for the last time, except in echoes I would never believe again, I stepped along with the deceptive simplicity of all romantics toward their duty in such dramatic form, a precious, innocent American Anglophile snob.

The WAAF clerk on duty at Kingsway recruiting station didn't look up when she said, "Name?" She motioned to a door. Just as she did, a military van drew up outside. Two women Military Police, with a girl in civilian clothes slung between them, poured out of the back of the van. The girl's legs were bare, filthy gray, splashed with dried dirt like the dirty face of a child finished crying. She had on heavy, solid, black Air-Force issue shoes. I resolved that if I ran away I would not wear issue shoes. The clerk saw me watching them and ordered me through the door with a twinge of impatience. I realized then that there were several girls quietly queued behind me.

I can still recall, as hearing it again, the click of that washed, bare door closing. I was committed to, caught in among, a shy, tangle of very young-faced, very small girls standing against the walls, cowed by the waiting and the silence, shrinking a little from each other, just as I was shrinking away, isolated from them. Some of them were as dirty as the girl I had seen between the MP's. There, with the women in uniform at the recruiting station, we were a flotsam of intruders swept together by an order from a sergeant who walked in with that busy, slightly impatient, woman-on-the-job walk I was to know so well.

Manipulated by the sergeant, we stood in tattered, uneasy rows, twenty or so of us. An RAF officer came in. Through the embarrassment I could hear him, vaguely, explaining the oath of allegiance. Somewhere, out of a hundred and fifty years of revolution, a stop came to my American mind. I could join their forces, fight with them, try to do my duty, but I could not, would not, say the oath of allegiance to the King of England. It seemed important to cling to this in that minute, as the impersonal mutter of voices grew around me.

There must have been a bus to take us through London. That is gone from my memory. I stand again, as I stood then, in that snaggled row of women on a long blank platform of Paddington station, under the vast skeleton of its once-glass vault, now either bare to the sky or patched with black.

We were ushered onto the train. With the feeling of safety a railway journey always engenders in the British, a feeling of being able to escape commitment at the end, the girls in the carriage began to talk, or rather, to explain themselves to each other. They had something of the air of the woman traveling by public coach in a Dickens story who keeps explaining that her "postillion" will surely come to meet her, and their whole initial pride seemed to be in the fact that they wanted it to be understood that they were "volunteers"—this meaning, as I found out later, that they had joined up before the date of their call-up, so all of them in the carriage except the girl beside me must have been seventeen years old, and all except her were from the East End of London. Seeking to stand apart, she explained to me, or to whoever would listen, that she was from the suburbs—I have forgotten which one—and that she looked after her "mum," who was far from well, and that she was ever so worried about her, leaving her alone like that. It was the first glimpse of the stratification, almost Chinese in its complication and formality, which covered everything from a hairdo to a state of health to sugar in tea and by which each Englishman holds himself apart, himself his castle, from his fellows.

Unlike the East Enders, who wore their hair in high, hard unkempt wartime pompadours, her hair was marcelled in tight ridges close to her head, self-consciously "genteel." She kept touching it, pleased, and explained that she had been to the hairdresser's that morning and had had a "perm." In contrast to her tight, thin little body, holding itself up to its place by not even taking a deep breath, the other girls in the carriage, six of them, sprawled, easy in their East End solidarity, growing more and more pleased at the train ride.

I had no idea where we were going, north, south, east or west. No one had told me. I was afraid to open my American mouth and ask, partly since I suspected they would not understand me. Except for the girl with the "perm," whose voice was as careful as her body and who still spoke with a strong tinge of what I thought of as cockney, I could understand very little—a word here and there, as of a language not well known and spoken too fast—of what the East Enders were saying.

They sounded like six small Eliza Doolittles, sitting in rows, not giving a goddamn if they never learned to speak like "ladies"—far too proud to care. What I heard was something like "Coo wa a sayo—a flippin tunup." This, with a comfortable smile, was followed by an answer, "We aynt inem fer the lolly, sa bleedin seyo. Weyo we're bleedin forut naow," with a look of complacent agreement all round.

It was only when I caught the word "Reading" and saw the girl by the window opposite lean forward to see us come toward the town that I realized we were going west. The brackish, red-brick rows of houses began to slide by the windows as we slowed down. Here was something to understand: Reading—a literary pilgrimage. I leaned forward, too, studied the dull-looking town and spoke, hardly realizing it.

"Where's the jail?"

There was a dead silence. I watched the legs of the girl opposite, with the same gray surface of no sun and no scrubbing as all the others, feeling that I had shouted.

She said, "There," proudly and pointed to, I think, a slightly higher red roof jutting above the rest.

"Know someone there?" That incredible cockney came across to me, interested.

"No. Only about someone."

"Me bruver's in there," she said and leaned back, comfortable against the seat.

The train pulled out of Reading station.

"Wot was he 'ad up for, the fellow you know about?" she asked. I could almost see her toes wiggling with pleasure at someone to talk about to bridge the gap of strangeness.

But I'm afraid Oscar Wilde had to let us down.

"I don't know," I lied.

It was the deep early twilight of a rain-sodden evening when we got to the depot. I saw, in sunken, damp meadows under the heavy sky, a huddle of sterile-looking buildings, an imposed, square wartime design. We, in our civilian clothes, outsiders, without identity in such a new world, drew closer together as we shuffled along to a huge Nissen hut; other small groups of women were shuffling with us, silent with nervousness at the unknown, so when we got inside the hut, there must have been three hundred of us, jostled together, lost.

The light inside was naked, stripped. So was a woman's voice, bawling from the end of the hut for us to take off our clothes and line up. That impersonal command, taking away even the identity of clothes, was too shocking to leave time for humiliation. Stripped down, puny under the light, I looked around me and tears gathered behind my eyelids. I had never known before how food and habit developed a human body, how rare physical beauty was. All these very young products of the dole, then the war, of white bread, "marg" and strong tea, of a hard, city life already had the shrunken upper body, the heavy-set thighs, white and doughy, of mature women. No adolescent bodies rose lightly in that room—even the taken-for-granted litheness of the young girl was a luxury there. My own body, four years older, hard from sport and protein and sun, was as different from their hardness of survival as if I had been of a different species.

We lined up for an FFI—a Free From Infection. Each copying the one before, we lifted our arms to an unspoken order as we neared the medical orderlies. My head was jerked forward, my hair parted, pulled, my shaven underarms, my pubic hair inspected closely and completely, yet without any sense of human contact. I was ordered to get dressed.

Half of the women had been isolated into a group. I heard a sob from the other queue. It was the girl from the train with her new "perm," calling out to anyone who would notice, "I must 'ave leaned me 'ead back on the train. Those carriages are filthy."

When I was dressed and waiting, I asked a WAAF what was the matter with the others, who had been quickly herded into a farther room, out of sight. She laughed. "Most of them have nits—a few crabs," she told me. "They'll get a proper 'air cut and wash—good scrub down." I could see the new careful "perm" under the impatient medical scissors, the towering 1942 cockney headdresses piled on the bare floor.

"Half of them?" I said.

"This is a bloody clean lot compared to some." She forgot me and walked on down the bench, hurrying women back into their clothes. . . .

 . . . The word was getting around that we were going to have a sex lecture, and every new girl it got to gave a short burp of a giggle. At every sound Viv, as stern that morning as an NCO, jerked around and scowled. She had taken the orientation lectures seriously since the one on God. It had been given by a tiny, handsome Scot, a Presbyterian padre who had begun by saying, "I'm no' here to talk about games, I'm here to talk about God." He had said it sternly and had proceeded to carry out his promise, with kindness and courage in the face of a Nissen hut full of agnostic girls, all larger than himself. Viv had fallen into a kind of admiring love with him and planned to go and talk to him about her problems when she could think up what they were. We talked at night, trying to help her decide. For three days she had taken the lectures seriously, thinking, from the padre, that all officers were there to help, as if his presence were somehow in all the officers' uniforms.

We were pulled to our feet by the yell "'Tension!'" Behind us I could hear the parody of a soldier's stride as the "Admin" officer marched alone down the aisle. She marched up the steps to the stage, her swagger stick thrust under her arm. Then she snapped a turn, slapped the swagger stick across her palm, creased her face into a silent smile and said, "At ease, girls," and stood to a rigid at-ease herself as she watched us slurp back into our seats.

She was spare and lean, birdlike on stalk legs; her breasts were thrust together under her meticulous tight tunic so that she presented a unilateral, slightly swollen front. Through the whole lecture she never moved her head, straight on her thin neck above her absolutely centered tie, her officer's cap straight on her pulled-back Eton crop. She looked as if the only sex she had experienced was a flipped towel in a locker room, but, oh, what jolly-brave fellow-girl would have had the nerve?

She began with a scare campaign in all its Lesbian horror which would have thrown anyone but the most passionate sensualist off sex forever, if anyone had listened. She clipped out information about disease—this was so far from the delightful subject we all had expected that I could hear the hum and fidget around me of minds wandering. She told about crabs, warned about toilet seats, skipped over prophylactics, urged antiseptics, pictured tertiary paralysis. The swagger stick kept on slapping, punishing her bad left hand with her good right hand.

"My girls"—she slapped—"are honorable [slap, slap], clean [slap, slap]." The room hummed with boredom.

"There are married women among my girls"—she slapped—"In the event of pregnancy [fire, catastrophe, act of God] you are released from active duty at the termination of three months." I looked around at Tina, who was smiling. I knew what "working one's ticket" meant.

"Many of my girls join up again after the event." The "Admin" officer said all this with the official insistence in her voice that demanded that all children be conceived after wedlock, in the "marital position," as a duty, in bed at night.

"Not bloody likely," Tina muttered.

Then the hatchet face hardened. It darkened, drew in, as if her whole face were at the mercy of her next words.

"There are foreign troops in the country," she stated, as if she had just discovered and was loath to announce that the small island was bulging with Allies. "They have more money . . . " I began to realize that she was talking about American soldiers. The room warmed toward interest.

"I can't *stop* you meeting them. But one thing I must warn you about. I absolutely forbid my girls being seen talking to American niggers."

I felt my face tense as if it had been slapped. I was stripped by that cold voice, opened, exposed, my barriers down to an inrush of terror and loss. I had run from those hard mouths all the way from America. What I had escaped from to war had followed me, the mouths grinning around "bunchajews," "bunchaniggers," to catch me, pinned there in the lecture room, that hard face—certain, secure and unjust—swimming before my eyes. I knew that there was no place, no country where I would not find it, that the brutality of mind we fight, we fight in the country of the mind. It is every place; it is not political, but is an act of darkness, sometimes in power, sometimes suppressed, always to be fought. Later I would have a middle-class English Community try to convert me by telling me that there was anti-Semitism in the Soviet Union, as if that made them "all right."

I thought that what I had done was a useless, ironic sacrifice, that I had kept my appointment in that cold, functional Nissen hut only by avoiding it at home. Almost everyone had begged of me a cheap reason to understand my action—a man, money—never knowing that however mistaken the carrying-out may be, there had been a flash, a sense of right, that can guide the minutes of one's life and make one turn. Stripped of that sense, I could only watch the woman's mouth, finishing with that assumption of ownership found in those of her class when they lack the perception to know that the core of dignity is the recognition of another's freedom.

"On the whole, I'm proud of my girls. You'll find them a jolly fine lot." Her mouth stretched into a last smile, and she snapped it into attention again. I kept paraphrasing a poem I'd heard: "The Fascist lady is so refined. She has no bosom and no behind.". . .

We stood as she processed up the aisle, forgetting us. Then, as we marched out of the lecture room to form ranks in the road, I heard one WAAF say to another, "She's not fucking well going to tell *me* 'oo to see!" I had forgotten the anarchy of the unknown people, their saving dumb insolence, that effective impotence.

At the door the sergeant told me to report to sick bay that I had fainted on parade. . . .

EILEEN SIMPSON
(1920?—)

◆

EILEEN SIMPSON had an established practice as a psychotherapist which she loved when she began writing short stories in her forties. She published them and her first novel, *The Maze* (1975), and then wrote the autobiographical works for which she is best known: *Reversals: A Personal Account of Victory over Dyslexia* (1979); *Poets in Their Youth* (1982), a much-praised memoir about her first husband, the poet John Berryman, and his friends and fellow writers Delmore Schwartz (who introduced her to Freud and Karen Horney, eventually influencing her choice of a career), Randall Jarrell, Robert Lowell, Jean Stafford, Allen Tate, and Caroline Gordon; and *Orphans, Real and Imaginary* (1987)—excerpted here—a memoir of her childhood as an orphan as well as a study of orphanhood in history and literature. Simpson lost both her parents by the age of six and lived with her older sister in a Catholic convent school run by Italian nuns. She was later transferred to a "Preventorium" institution after she was diagnosed as pretubercular. Then, as an adolescent, she went to live with her father's grudging, overburdened sister—"what Auntie loved was not children but babies. Signs of independence in budding personalities—'willfulness' she called it—made her apprehensive."

Simpson told an interviewer that the memoir *Orphans* grew out of a crisis of "aloneness" brought on by the sudden death of her second husband. Before this loss, she had never realized the effect her childhood had had on her personality. Describing the writing of these distant, long-buried memories, she said, "I almost couldn't do it. It was so painful to write! I tried, and I thought, I can't. Then I made one more very painful attempt: I really felt as though I were . . . not taking off my clothes, but taking off my skin. But there was no other way to do it." She has been surprised by how many people have told her, in response to her book, that they *felt* orphaned as children even though they grew up with their parents. The second part of the book, an interpretation of the effects of losing one's parent or parents in childhood on such writers as Tolstoy, Rousseau, Sartre, and Mary McCarthy, represents an illuminating slant on literary biography.

The critical response to this memoir suggests its emotional power.

Sheila Ballantyne, writing in the *New York Times Book Review*, referred to "the uncommon beauty" of Simpson's writing. *Psychology Today* praised the "plaintive and poignant honesty" with which "this superb book" records its "vivid and enthralling reminiscences." Cynthia Ozick, in whose fiction the memory of loss has taken on a lasting and tragic presence, called *Orphans* "a beautiful, generous, truth-telling book."

From *Orphans, Real and Imaginary*

CHAPTER 1
The Crisis

Throughout my adult life, when people asked about my childhood, and I said I was an orphan, their surprised looks made me quickly add, "A lucky one." From the long gray early years, I had emerged unscathed. Hospitable to happiness, tenacious in adversity (of neither had I been cheated), I appeared to myself, as to others, cheerful and well balanced. Even the physical weaknesses traceable to my early medical history were masked by high coloring that made me appear healthier than I was. As people said, I didn't *look* like an orphan.

Nor did I feel like one. It is true that in the past I had. Following my mother's death from tuberculosis when I was eleven months and my sister twenty-one months old, we were separated from our father except during school vacations. Shortly before I turned seven, he became ill at a dinner, was rushed to the hospital, and in three days was dead from ptomaine poisoning. It was after his death that I learned what it meant to be an orphan. But in recent years, while I thought about my childhood as frequently as others do (and even wrote about one aspect of it), I had long since ceased to think about my orphan-hood.* It had ended, I thought, when the law said it did: when I came of age. So strong was my need to believe that as an adult I was affected little by my early losses, that I was unprepared for the recent, shattering crisis that had been lying in wait for the right constellation of events. It hurtled me back through the years of my growing up to the opaline days of infancy, and forced me to reexamine the past.

The first sign I had of it (although I didn't realize it at the time) came when we learned from a routine medical examination that my

---

*And my sister and I had given up comparing notes about it. Nor did we talk about it while I was at work on this book. Although I will sometimes say "we," I have written from a single point of view, my own, based on my memories and emotions.

husband had cancer and, after surgery, that it was inoperable. During the months Bob underwent treatment, what kept me going was my inability to believe that a youthful-looking fifty-six-year-old man, who had recently been so vigorous, could have only a year to live. . . .

[Two years later, Simpson's husband died, and she entered upon a "crisis" of mourning and anguish. "For the first time in my life, I felt profoundly orphaned."]

What the crisis did was to blast through the powerful defense I'd built up of the lucky orphan. I had had to believe that my losses had not been devastating. The middle-of-the-night panics at being alone in the world, the intense anxiety and depression I suffered in the recent period of profound orphanhood, had not to do with the present. They were holdovers from the past.

Had I been as uninhibited about expressing my previously denied longings, I might have echoed Tolstoy's belated orphan cry:

Yes, yes my Maman, whom I was never able to call that because I did not know how to talk when she died. She is my highest image of love—not cold, divine love, but warm, earthly love, maternal . . . Maman, hold me, baby me! . . . All this is madness, but it is true.

(So wrote the bearded patriarch in his journal—age eighty!)

Instead, I timidly struggled to come to terms with my new knowledge about myself. I was forced to recognize that behind my cheerful façade there had always been a broad vein of sadness, and that my emotional balance had seemed equilibrated because it had never been tested at its most vulnerable point. If I was not an unlucky orphan, neither was I as lucky as I had believed. . . .

CHAPTER 2

The Convent

Green-and-white-striped awnings shaded the windows from the July sun. Against the heat they were powerless. The air was so heavy with the odor of flowers it felt as if one of the blossoms had got trapped high in my nose.

My sister and I sat side by side on folding chairs rented for the occasion, white-gloved hands clasped in our laps. To distract my attention from the queasy feeling in my stomach, I started to swing my foot in its new shoe. Thinking better of it, I turned my attention instead to the smocking on my white dress, bought in haste, like everything else I was wearing, the previous day.

The room was filled with grown-ups, strangers mostly. They were all in black but for the white handkerchiefs they used to pat their faces as they whispered to one another about the heat, the humidity. From time to time, they stole glances at Marie and me. The men looked away, as if they were embarrassed. The women put their handkerchiefs to their eyes.

When there was the signal to go, one of the women led me over to where the flowers were banked. She held me up and said, "Kiss him good-bye." I leaned over to do as I was told. When my lips touched the skin, cold and hard as stone, I retracted them in horror. I would not kiss this man, another stranger.

After a long, slow ride out of the city, we stood in a circle while a priest intoned prayers. A light breeze stirred the odor of freshly turned sod, forcing the stuck blossom farther up my nose. The ribbons hanging down the back of my leghorn hat floated in front of my eyes. They looked like swimming fish. Blue grosgrain fish.

At the sound of pebbles hitting wood, a woman cried out. Someone whispered disapprovingly, "Laura!" Laura crumpled to the ground and was carried away.

When the others started for the limousines, Auntie, who held Marie and me by the hand, took us to the next grave to say a prayer. "Now they are together again," she said. It was frightening to see grown-ups cry.

On the drive up to Dobbs Ferry, Marie and I were alone in the backseat of the old Packard. We were silent. So was Milton, the driver. At last there was the sound of gravel under the tires, and the statue of the Sacred Heart in the little glass house on the lawn. Milton rang the bell. When the door opened, he kissed us and gave us a little shove toward the nun. The dark entrance hall smelled familiarly of wax—sharp and clean, not sickly sweet like the odor of the flowers in that room.

Mother Superior came gliding toward us, her habit billowing out behind like the wings of a giant bat. Enfolding us in the wings, she cried, *"Povere orfanelle."* Behind her glasses, her eyes looked like black olives that had been rolled in oil. She led us to the chapel and told us, as we knelt, to pray that perpetual light would shine on our papa. Perpetual light sounded nice, like a sunny day at the beach.

Mother Serafina, the dormitory nun, took us to our room. She helped us change into our uniforms and straightened the kerchiefs on our middy blouses. I felt sad at having to give up my new dress so soon. After three days in the outside world, we were convent girls again.

★ ★ ★

The Convent, an Italianate villa with a crescent driveway and a handsome porte cochere, stood on a bluff overlooking the Hudson River. It was not its site, which was splendid, nor any other quality of excellence that had attracted my father to it as a school for us. He had been desperate. Following our mother's death, he kept us with one grandmother, then the other. We did not flourish. The doctor advised that with our family history, we should be sent away from New York (which had the highest incidence of tuberculosis of any city in the United States). So that we would have country air, we were boarded with a series of families in Staten Island and New Jersey. Each, before long, talked about separating us for the sake of convenience; or, equally distressing to my father, hinted at adoption. He decided it would be better to give us to the nuns. The Ursulines, at Tarrytown, who had educated his sisters, agreed to keep us temporarily in a cottage near the gatekeeper's house in the care of a baby nurse whom they supervised. It was they who suggested that Daddy look for a more permanent arrangement with the Italian nuns at Dobbs Ferry.

At the Villa Maria (so we were later told), a nun who spoke no English took the card Daddy offered her and showed him into the parlor. It was an elegantly proportioned room with floor-to-ceiling windows giving on a veranda. Furniture and draperies in rich brown velvet made the room dark, with here and there a touch of light from the antimacassars of ecru lace. Everything not velvet (even the giant rubber plants) looked and smelled as if it had been freshly waxed. On one wall hung a large wooden crucifix. On another, photographs of Pope Pius XI, and the foundress of the order, Mother Cabrini.

The rhythmic tapping of metal on wood, keys hitting against rosary beads, announced the approach of Mother Superior. She came in holding the card Daddy had handed in at the door. She was dressed like the others of her order in unrelieved black, with no touch of coquettish white around the wimple such as the Ursulines wore. She invited him to sit down and, in heavily accented English (mimicked to perfection by our aunts in the many retellings we begged for when we were growing up), asked about his trip up from the city. Her shrewd black eyes took him in at a glance: tall, boyishly slim, a straw boater in his hand.

How young he was to be a widower! she said. He was . . . ?

Twenty-seven . . .

How had he lost his wife?

She had survived the flu epidemic, but after the birth of the second child had had a relapse. He did not mention (one did not in those days) the time she had spent at the Trudeau Sanitarium at Saranac.

Mother Superior murmured something about the mysterious ways in which God works. How old were the children? He had not said over the telephone.

He had not said because he had been afraid of being rejected out of hand. The older was four, the younger three. Or almost.

Very young for boarding school. Were there no relatives?

None ideally suited to take in two little girls. And then there was the doctor's advice.

The children were not in good health then?

They were somewhat fragile.

Mother Superior clacked her tongue, whether in sympathy with his problems or at those he was posing her was not clear. She studied his card still held in her hand. His given name was Raphael. With his coloring and profile, he could be taken for an Italian. Did the children have any Italian blood? Too bad. That would have made things easier. Mother Cabrini, foundress of the Missionary Sisters of the Sacred Heart, had been sent by Holy Father to do missionary work among Italian immigrants. They were living in deplorable conditions on the Lower East Side. There were many homeless children, waifs. Every bed in the dormitories was taken.

Were there no private rooms? He could pay.

It would not be easy.

If she could take the children for just a year, give him time to make other arrangements . . .

Mother Superior patted his hand familiarly, as if he were a child. It was up to the Board of Directors, but she would see what she could do. In the meantime, would he like to be shown around a little before it was time for his train?

He followed her down the broad central hall, which was lined with sepia photographs of the Colosseum, St. Peter's, the Leaning Tower of Pisa, to the kindergarten (which had been a gymnasium in the days when the Villa had been an exclusive boys' school), to the chapel (formerly a swimming pool). She led him out onto the veranda, and through the grape arbor to the garden. They stood together on the parapet taking in the view. A Hudson River Day Line boat, its decks festooned with colored pennants, steamed by. The captain gave a blast on his comical horn, a salute to the Convent children who ran to the fence to wave, some vigorously, others with listless envy, at the families out for a day of pleasure. From below the parapet came the sound of the New York Central train as it flew along the tracks.

On feverish nights, a wakeful child could hear the band as the riverboat passed again on its way back to the city, and could imagine the couples dancing under swaying paper lanterns. Later still, the sound of a milk train's plaintive whistle would become incorporated in a nightmare.

There was no lack of subjects for nightmares, but the theme most favored was separations. There had been so many of them that the day Daddy left us in the Convent parlor may not have been more painful than the others—only the usual clutching at his neck as he held us in a simultaneous embrace, the usual promise of frequent visits, the usual wrenching apart, and, after he had gone, the tears and holding on tight to one another. . . .

In our night prayers, Marie and I prayed that the living would stay alive, and that on Sunday, visiting day, they would come to see us.

At the announcement that there was someone in the parlor for us, we raced to the dormitory to wash our hands, brush our hair, and have the silk kerchiefs on our dress uniforms rearranged by Mother Serafina. How difficult it was to stand still! The real pleasure was in these moments of anticipation, when one enjoyed the thrill of having been summoned and did not yet have to make awkward conversation. For awkward it was, especially with our maternal grandmother. We curtsied and stepped forward to receive her cool kiss. A tall, fair-haired woman with the carriage of a diva, she came dressed in mauve (still in half mourning for her husband and daughters), wearing pearl earrings, a veil tied under her chin, and a fur scarf over her arm. Since all the other grandmothers were short, plump, swarthy, wrinkled, and as enveloped in black as the nuns, her arrival always caused a stir. She brought us carefully chosen, identical, little-girl presents: tortoiseshell combs in cases, sandalwood fans, handkerchiefs of Irish linen trimmed with lace, change purses of Moroccan leather. After we'd opened our gifts and expressed our thanks for them, we could think of nothing further to say. She asked us questions. We answered. Before long, she gave up trying to make conversation with us and addressed herself instead to Mother Superior, or asked to see Mother Serafina to interrogate her about our well-being. Then, and later when I saw her on the opposite side of a courtroom, I found it difficult to believe she was *my* grandmother. Had she not lived to a good age, I might still remember her as aloof and intimidating.

The Convent did not provide the healthy environment the family doctor had prescribed. Three winters in a row the old priest was summoned to give me extreme unction. As the runny nose and cough endemic among the children turned, in my case, into pneumonia, it became harder and harder for me to lace my high shoes in the morning. At breakfast, the odor of scorched cocoa turned my stomach. Instead of playing clapping games with the others at recess, I lay on a bench curled up in a ball, the index finger of my left hand pressed against the roof of my mouth for comfort.

As chills shook me, fever burned me, and pain raked my side, I was put to bed. The pinwheel of colored disks of which I became the center turned faster, faster, faster, spun higher, higher, higher. If it slowed down for a moment, I saw a blurry ring of nuns around the crib I'd been put in and heard, as if from a great distance, the rumble of their prayers. Or, more startlingly, there was the sound of male voices. My father had arrived and was talking to the doctor. A bitter powder was put on my tongue, a mustard plaster was stuck to the pain, my drenched nightdress was changed, and the pinwheel spun again, this time carrying me down. The bed split under me. I was being sucked *down*. A scream (my own) woke me. The nuns now held candles. The priest's face as he leaned over to anoint me grew so elongated it seemed in danger of dripping, like melted wax. Disembodied hands packed me in ice. Zeppelin-shaped figures floated toward me and bounced me off their rubbery surfaces as if I were a ball.

After the crisis, I found myself in another room. My sister was not there. Nor was there the sound of other children. Mother Giovanna, a tall, large-boned woman who seemed to be of a different race from the others (a Lombardian), nursed me through weeks of convalescence. Awakening from a feverish dream, I would find her sitting by the side of my bed, one elbow resting on a massive knee, her chin in her hand, her eyes closed. (Years later, I found her image again among the massive, brooding, genderless figures in the spandrels of the Sistine ceiling.)

During the listless hours of the afternoon, as time stood still and my unstable temperature rose, she read to me from *The Lives of the Saints*. As girls who are read fairy tales daydream about becoming princesses, we who were read the lives of the saints daydreamed of becoming saints. The atmosphere in which we lived was dense with celestial spirits who existed, depending upon one's intimacy with them, from just above the right shoulder, where one's guardian angel hovered (busy, in my case, trying to keep my temperature down), all the way up to heaven. It was true that, so far, there were no American saints, but we all knew that it was only a question of time before Mother Cabrini, a naturalized American, would be canonized.

It was during one of these illnesses that I committed my first sin. Except for paroxysms of coughing, I suffered no pain during my convalescence, only terrible fatigue, and an insatiable thirst that the brandy-flavored water Mother Giovanna doled out to me in small drafts left unquenched. It was tap water (for some mysterious reason forbidden me) that I craved. One night, after a struggle with my budding conscience, I could restrain myself no longer. As Mother Giovanna sat dozing in the chair, I climbed over the crib's railing, found my way through a series of storage rooms and corridors to the dormitory, and ran down its length to the bathroom with its familiar row of sinks. Shinnying up on one of them, I diverted the water from the faucet into my mouth and drank greedily. Mother Giovanna was still asleep when I got back. I lay under my covers, panting from the effort, the forbidden water rolling heavily in my stomach. Thirst was replaced by a new and more disagreeable sensation: guilt. I had committed the sin of disobedience, and had disobeyed the nun for whom I felt the most affection. When next I was well enough to join the other children for the nightly examination of conscience, I said the *mea culpas* in earnest, and knew at last what to accuse myself of.

On afternoons when I was able to sit up, Marie was allowed to come to the door of the sickroom so that we (especially I) would be reassured the other was not far away. My father, who had felt that our security lay in our being together, had had his intuition verified the winter I had a mastoidectomy. I awakened in the middle of the night to find myself in a crib-filled ward. The light in the high-ceilinged room was the color of an ether dream, nacreous blue, the blue of a milk of magnesia bottle. It made the world look cold and indescribably sad. When I cried out, as much at the color as at the pain in my head, nuns dressed in the familiar habit, but with unfamiliar blue-white faces, said they couldn't make the color go away. In the morning, when the blue paper covers were removed from the overhead lights, the world of unfamiliar nuns, white-coated doctors, and bandaged children took on a less nightmarish aspect.

It was some time before I understood where I was. My father must have told me more than once that I had been operated on for the pain in my ear, and was in a New York hospital staffed by the same order of nuns I knew from the Convent. In a photograph of me taken at Columbus Hospital, I was shown, turban-headed, holding the teddy bear almost my size Daddy had given me for company. I loved this animal and trailed it with me to the small operating room for the changes of dressing (that were even more painful than the old earaches), to the chapel for mass, to the roof where I was taken to get the air. The teddy bear was a comfort, but it could not replace my sister. I asked for her repeatedly. When, week after week, she didn't appear, I took it that she had died.

As weeks grew into months and there was little forward movement in my convalescence, it became clear something was wrong. What explained my listlessness, tearfulness, lack of appetite? The doctor, looking for somatic causes, prescribed various tonics, to no avail. My frantic father, who had been wondering if it was the separation from my sister that was to blame, convinced the doctors, and Mother Superior, to allow Marie to come to the hospital for an extended visit. From my response to her seeming resurrection, and the spurt my convalescence took, there could be little doubt that he had been right.

Mother Superior and Daddy were so often in disagreement about our care that he was little better pleased to leave us at the Convent than he had been to board us with families. But because he could find no more satisfactory arrangement, we stayed at Dobbs Ferry not one year but five. From the time of his first visit, to see how we were settling in, until shortly before the telephone call three years later summoning us to his bedside, he and the nuns kept up a tug of war over us of which we gradually became aware. At Christmas, and in June, when he picked us up for vacation, he took us directly to Best and Company. With the resources of a Fifth Avenue department store that specialized in children's clothing, he transformed us as quickly as he could from the institutional children we had become to the daughters he had given the nuns. Pastel dresses of crepe de chine and patent-leather slippers replaced blue serge uniforms and high shoes. The store's barber was directed to cut and brush our hair the way Daddy liked it worn, parted on the side. To document that this was the way we really looked, the store's photographer recorded the metamorphosis.

Vacation over, the nuns combed our hair *their* way, removed the dresses, and put us back in uniform. So successful were they in making us over that in the black-and-white school photographs in which our fair complexions and hair don't show, we are so like our Italo-American classmates that, though we've studied the pictures long and hard, we have never made out for certain which two figures, identical in every detail as a row of paper dolls, we are.

The toys my father sent for us to play with, the food to enrich the institutional diet and help us gain weight, were expropriated for general use. We didn't know enough to complain, but our blankness when questioned—What dolls? What Ovaltine?—led to explosions of temper at home, and at the Convent, which taught us our first lessons in equivocation. Even after we caught on, we occasionally made an accidental break. For the gravest of these, I was responsible. At Christmas, Daddy's oldest sister, Auntie, who helped look after us during our vacation, decided to supervise my bath. Resisting like a frightened puppy, I ran from her and hid in a closet. When caught, I resisted being undressed. The water in the tub was rising. So was Auntie's temper. If I wouldn't take off my clothes, she would remove them for me. Ordinarily timid and lacking in spirit, I fought her off. My father was called. Between hysterical sobs, I blurted out that I could not take a bath with-out-my-bath-ing-gar-ment. It was a sin, as until this moment I thought everyone knew, to bathe naked.

My sister, who had followed our usual holiday procedure (a modest washing at the sink), was interrogated. What came out was that at the Convent bathing was a serious activity, controlled by ritual. On Saturday nights, we lined up outside the room with the row of sinks, the row of toilets, and the pair of tubs as massive and ancient-looking as sarcophagi. Mother Serafina handed us bricks of yellow soap to rub on the outside of our bathing garments, which were made of unbleached muslin. It was into the tub, scrub, out. No time for playing with the soap, or lolling about in the warm water, as we would have liked to do, to put off the moment of extreme discomfort that awaited us when we stepped out onto the bath mat and felt the air hit the water-logged muslin.

These conflicts between Daddy and the nuns provided the subjects for my earliest speculations on morality. Though I only imperfectly understood the reason for his indignation where toys and food were concerned, I was on his side. Private property didn't exist at the Convent, but it was agreeable to believe that the beautiful fire engine that all the children played with was in some remote and unclaimable way mine. On the issue of modesty, I was squarely on the side of the nuns. I submitted to the humiliating experience of being bathed at home, suffering not only from my shameful nudity, but even more painfully from my first crisis of loyalty. Nakedness was sinful. Yet here was Daddy agreeing with Auntie that the wearing of a bathing garment was medieval and unhealthful, and that it was undoubtedly to blame for my having had pneumonia every winter.

The brief vacations, two weeks at Christmas, two months in the summer, during which I was under my family's influence were no match for the endless months of uninterrupted conventual life. Holidays on Long Island in the summer, and at my paternal grandparents' brownstone in Chelsea in the winter, were brief and dreamlike. At the Hedges, a Victorian seaside hotel, Marie and I passed our days on the beach, sun-bonneted, in matching gingham dresses, pail and shovel in hand, playing in the water, collecting shells on the sandbar, building sand castles with our cousins.

The highlight of any vacation was a visit to Daddy's bachelor flat in Greenwich Village. Milton, a down-on-his-luck chauffeur who drove for my father on an erratic and informal basis, picked us up in the Packard touring car. Through the isinglass windows, we saw the pillars of the El speed by as we careened down Sixth Avenue. Indoors, the two men, who had little experience entertaining children, improvised games more suitable for boys than for girls. A seesaw, which they fashioned out of an ironing board, bounced us perilously high in the air. There were sliding races down the highly polished hall floor to the

French doors of the dining room (from the handle of which I sustained a prominent bump on my forehead that stayed with me for years). When we tired of these rowdy games, Milton made lemonade for us, Orange Blossoms for them, and tended the phonograph, while Daddy, an expert dancer, taught us the one-step, the foxtrot, and the waltz.

Did he tell us, or did we learn later, that courting as they did during the later days of Vernon and Irene Castle, he and our mother passed their time at the tea dances then fashionable at New York hotels? Among our relatives, there were those who were scandalized that my parents continued dancing during their three years of marriage, and my mother's pregnancies. In the photographs of them that I scrutinized when I was old enough to wonder what they had been like, they look static, enigmatic, sad, as if they had a premonition of what lay ahead. It is through the pictures of the Castles, and especially of Astaire and Rogers impersonating them, that my parents came alive for me. There they are together, smiling, in motion, Mother in a flowing white dress, Daddy whirling her around. It is always three o'clock in the morning and they, with the limitless energy of the young and healthy, have danced the whole night through.

What else Daddy tried to teach us in the short time he had with us I don't know, but our passion for dancing undoubtedly comes from the spins, dips, pivots, twirls, whirls, leaps, taps, feints, slides, and glides he and my mother executed when we were *in utero,* and from those holiday afternoon lessons in the Village. Today, when I hear the syncopated rhythms of ragtime, or the plaintive wail of a saxophone, I smell again the Turkish tobacco of Daddy's Murads, and feel the beaded frost of his silver cocktail shaker that, after a particularly energetic number, I rested against my burning cheek. At such moments, infrequent and evanescent, he comes to life for me again. . . .

CHAPTER 3
The Convent—Continued

The summer my father died, we did not go to the Hedges. The day after the funeral, we settled into the Convent routine as if nothing had happened. No mention was made of our loss. Our new state made us more, rather than less, like the others. Saint Roch, many of the nuns, and most of the children had been orphaned early. We said our prayers, went to mass, and, school being closed for the summer, played outdoors with the others, the homeless, who never left the Villa. The only change was that in our private prayers the litany of our dead had been increased by one. . . .

DENISE LEVERTOV
(1923—)

───────◆───────

Born and bred in Ilford, Essex, England, DENISE LEVERTOV was educated at home by her Welsh mother, whose love of telling stories nurtured her younger daughter's imagination, the point of the following memoir, "Beatrice Levertoff." Her father was a Russian Jew who later became an Anglican priest devoted to the reconciliation of Jews and Christians. During World War II, she worked as a nurse, an occupation of youth that served to develop the empathy and realism that characterize the poetry Levertov began to publish prolifically after she emigrated to the United States in 1948 with her husband, the writer Mitchell Goodman (from whom she was later divorced). Her volumes of poetry include *The Jacob's Ladder* (1961), the well-known *O Taste and See* (1964), *The Sorrow Dance* (1967), a tribute in remembrance of the death of her older sister Olga, *Relearning the Alphabet* (1970), *The Freeing of the Dust* (1975), and *Candles in Babylon* (1982). She has also published collections of essays, *The Poet in the World* (1973), *Light Up the Cave* (1981), from which the story of her youth that follows here is taken, and *New & Selected Essays* (1992), the source of "Autobiographical Sketch." The mother of one son, Levertov has taught at Stanford and Tufts, received a Guggenheim Fellowship, served as poetry editor of the *Nation,* and worked as a prominent antiwar activist during the Vietnam War, the undeclared war in El Salvador, and the Persian Gulf war. Throughout three decades, her public readings of her poems on behalf of peace reflect her commitment to the truth of human solidarity and the goodness of creation in the face of war and the lies of politicians. Many of her poems enact a mystical sense of oneness that issues in an expressed insistence on a moral politics. In her words, "Being the child of a socially conscious family, conscience and circumstance virtually forced me into the politics of the anti-war movement of the 1960s and on into the broader anti-nuclear, environmental, and social justice concerns which evolved from it. . . ." Along with a number of writers included in this collection (Addams, L'Engle, Cisneros, hooks), Levertov admits no separation between authentic spirituality and a just politics. The critic and poet M. L. Rosenthal considers Levertov's poetry as part of the body of post–World War II nontraditional verse represented

by Charles Olson, Paul Blackburn, Robert Duncan, and Robert Cree-
ley—the Black Mountain School, though, as Levertov says, "I myself
was never at Black Mountain in my life." Their poetry, according to
Rosenthal, is as intransigent as Allen Ginsberg's and Lawrence Fer-
linghetti's in its "assumption that the crack-up of values prophesied by
an older generation has completed itself." Within this group he finds
Levertov's work the most sensuous and open. Since 1965 when Rosenthal wrote this assessment, Levertov's voice has remained strong in its
insistence on the "obligation of social conscience"—"The tragic and
fearful character of our times is not something from which we can
detach ourselves; we are *in* it, as fish are in the sea . . . ," she said in her
1991 Paul Zweig Memorial Lecture in New York City.

Beatrice Levertoff*

My mother was born on June 29th 1885 and christened Beatrice Adelaide. Her father, Walter Spooner-Jones, M.D., was a grandson of
Angell Jones of Mold, the tailor, teacher, and preacher, to whom
Daniel Owen, "the Welsh Dickens" was apprenticed, and with whose
son John Angell Jones, (my great-uncle, if I am counting generations
correctly) whose shop doubled as a kind of literary and intellectual
salon in the 1870s, he subsequently worked until setting up in business
for himself. Angell Jones the elder, my great-great grandfather, is
depicted by Daniel Owens in *Rhys Lewis,* a novel I long to read but of
which the only English translation is long since out of print and unob-
tainable. My cousin Myfanwy (Mrs Illtyd Howell of Newport, Gwent)
shares this descent. She grew up in Llangefni (Anglesey) and was one of
the prime movers in Welsh language broadcasting, and later in TV also.
    My mother's parents were from Caernarvon and Llanberis. Her
father, who inherited the deft hands of several generations of master
tailors, studied medicine and surgery in Scotland, married even before
he graduated, and brought his young Llanberis bride, Miss Margaret
Griffiths, to the mining village of Abercanaid, near Merthyr (next along
the Taff valley to Aberfan), where he was employed as a junior doctor
by the mining company. Often he used to have to go down the pit to
operate at the site of an accident, when a man was pinned by a fall and

---

*This brief account of my mother's life was written in 1977 before her death, at the request of the editors
of *Poetry Wales* after they had heard me read some poems by her. Its publication in the magazine did not
take place until after her death, so she did not see it.

had to have a limb amputated there and then. He was known and trusted as an excellent surgeon, though he did not really like the practice of medicine. When my mother was two and a half her mother died in childbirth, the baby dying likewise. Dr. Spooner-Jones remarried, but was not very happy; and my mother was increasingly neglected by her step-mother. However, this very neglect gave her childhood the partial solitude which enriched it—so that all my life her memories have been to me a fascinating oral storybook. Had she grown up in the bosom of a large, happy, well-ordered household perhaps the habits of observation and reflection would not have been so well developed in her. Like New England's Sarah Orne Jewett (but at a much earlier age) she sometimes accompanied her father on his house calls (made on foot) and to this day—at ninety-two—can tell anecdotes about many of the people they went to see, describing their appearance down to details of dress. One family that has always stuck in my mind from her childhood reminiscences, kept a pub somewhere on the Nightingale Street edge of the village, and were especially musical, all singing and playing the harp, even a little girl not much older than my mother (who would have been between six and eight at this time), all having curly golden hair and beautiful milky complexions (and all, alas, riddled with T.B.). Sometimes at night, after supper, she would go with her father to visit a miner friend of his who had built himself a telescope. All along the street the men would be singing, sitting on their heels in the dusk after a long day down the pit. The music and the stars must have been mysteriously connected for the little girl, out and about when the other children of the village had been put to bed; as they were connected for me at the same age, listening to her tell about it.

When she was ten or so, there was a move into Merthyr, and not long afterwards the step-mother died. By the time she was twelve her father died too—still in his early thirties—and she was taken to live in the very different atmosphere of Holywell, Flintshire, where her maternal aunt Elisabeth—Auntie Bess—was the wife of a well-known Congregational minister, the Rev. David Oliver. Neglect and freedom were replaced by strict care and many duties, in a household from which most of the older children had gone, into marriage or career, but in which her two youngest cousins were close to her own age. The next ten years of her life gave rise to a still larger and more detailed crop of stories. Whether Holywell had more than its share of eccentrics, or whether—as I think more likely—a quiet, observant, humorous girl simply saw what others often missed or took for granted, these tales fascinated me no matter how often I heard them, and have always seemed to me distinctively Welsh in some way I can't define: I don't believe an English town of the same size at the turn of the century would have yielded anything quite comparable. It is perhaps a question of the emotional intensity involved—pent up in a besieged culture, a fervent but restrictive religious mode, a mountainous land. My memory being relatively poor and vague, I prevailed on my mother to write down some of her "Tales of Holywell" some years ago, and I treasure the many exercise books that contain them, though they present only a few of the many memories, and of course it is not quite the same thing to read them, especially the amusing ones, as to have heard them acted out, complete with imitations of people's comical speech and manners. One that comes to mind is about a man known as Man the Lifeboat; he was a devoted member of the church and had a cousin who was a famous professional singer, and so got appointed *dychraewr canu,*[*] but he really couldn't sing and when, at "socials," he would be invited to give a solo, invariably sang "Man the Liffffeboat" with a tremendous splutter on the f, from which the audience used to discreetly duck. Or the famous visiting preacher whose new false teeth were hurting him; so he slipped them quietly into his handkerchief pocket; but as his sermon developed, so did his *hwyl,* so much so that he made *himself* weep, not only the congregation—and sweeping his handkerchief out to dab his eyes, out flew the teeth, straight into a portly lady's Sunday-best lap.

In those years Beatrice went through high school and teacher training, developed her beautiful singing voice (of professional quality if she had had the opportunity to go further), played hockey, drew and painted, did a lot of housework, was deeply affected by the Revival,[†] read all the books she could get her hands on (not a wide choice) and loved the mountain with its sheep-cropped grass and tiny flowers and the sound of the distant sea you could hear in a clump of pines if you closed your eyes. And because, despite basic kindness and affection, she always felt like a "poor relation" in some ways, and hankered secretly after some of the freedom of her childhood, she always dreamed of travel. The way to travel was to teach. Her Uncle David would not let her be a governess in Paris, because Paris was a sinful and dangerous city; but he did let her take a job in Constantinople, because it was at a girls' school run by the Scotch Mission. So off she went—never having been further than Liverpool and Cardiff before—on the Orient Express. She had signed a five-year contract, but it was not long before she met my father, a young Russian Jew who had converted to Chris-

---

[*]Choir leader.
[†]The religious revival which swept Wales in the first decade of the twentieth century.

tianity and had begun his lifelong task of attempting to reconcile Jews and Christians. My mother and he were soon engaged; she broke her contract, returned to Wales to introduce him to her relations, was married in London from the house of another aunt, (also the wife of a minister), and went to live in Warsaw (then part of the Russian Empire). From Warsaw they went to Germany—were prisoners of war in Leipzig (not in a camp, but under house arrest) during WWI; "displaced persons" in Denmark after the Armistice, before being able to cross the mined North Sea to England (another cause of delay was the fact that my father was a Russian citizen still); and eventually settled for many years in the London area, in the Essex suburb of Ilford. My father was ordained in the Anglican Church in 1922. I will only summarize the next two decades of my mother's life: work as my father's amanuensis; bringing up her two children (my sister was nine years older than I though, so that in some ways my experience was that of an only child) which involved giving me daily lessons (I did not go to school); writing a novella and an (unpublished) novel for children; hard and selfless work rescuing refugees from Hitler and finding homes and work for them in Britain; reading aloud virtually all of nineteenth century fiction, and much else, to her family (and especially to me, for I was a voracious listener); reading as much history as she could manage (she should have gone to university and studied it—but then it would have been another life . . .);* surviving the drudgery of keeping house through the years of bombing and rationing; nursing my father through his painful last illness. Then, ill herself at the time, she came to live with me and my son and (now ex-) husband in New York City, a whole new adventure gamely undertaken—and soon, even more of a step into the unknown, accompanied us to Guadalajara, Mexico, where we proposed living for two years. While we were there she went at one point to Oaxaca, in the south of Mexico, to be a paying guest for a few weeks with a Mexican family. They asked her to stay longer—she did; longer still—she did; and eventually became the adopted grandmother—"Abuelita"— and in many respects the mainstay of the household, bringing up the youngest daughter (who was born after she went to live there) on Beatrix Potter and *The Wind in the Willows,* etc. She has now been in Mexico almost twenty years. And during that time she has not stood still in her life, but—reading, painting watercolors, thinking, beginning to write poems—has been constantly growing. (While, as she would add, shrinking in physical size, as people do in their eighties!)

---

*She also researched and painted a foldout panorama of first-century Jerusalem, together with a text and line-drawings, published by S.P.C.K. Press (London).

After she left Wales in 1910 to go to Constantinople she never really lived there again, though of course she visited from time to time, the last occasion being just after my father's death in 1955. But she has never lost a great love for and pride in Wales. The Welsh hymns, and secular songs like *Davydd y Garreg Wen,* sung or remembered or heard on records, never fail to bring tears to her eyes. One of her great joys in Oaxaca in the days when she was still strong and agile enough (i.e. into her eighties) was to go "for a good tramp" on the bare grassy hills just above the town, reminiscent of Welsh moorland. As I, her only surviving child, began to become well-known in America as a poet, she rejoiced, and not merely in my worldly success but more deeply in my work itself which has often moved her; but it was a special pleasure to her when I read to a Welsh audience, as I did a few years ago, and particularly on my 1976 visit when, at Barry, I really felt I had made some contact with the vital literary life of Wales, meeting a number of poets and writers. What she does not realize is that if I was given a measure of acceptance as a person less alien than a visiting American with a Russian name might be supposed to be, it was in large part because I had read to that audience a poem of *hers* about her childhood in Abercanaid.

The other thing she doesn't know—though I have told her—is that though I may have inherited from my father some of his verbal gifts (he was a prolific writer and an admired preacher) it was she who, as I have written,

> *taught me to look,*
> *to name the flowers when I was still close to the ground*
> *my face level with theirs;*
> *or to watch the sublime metamorphoses*
> *unfold and unfold*
> *over the walled back gardens of our street.*

I could not ever have been a poet without that vision she imparted.

(Beatrice Spooner-Jones Levertoff died on June 8th, 1977, a few months after this memoir was written. D.L.)

Autobiographical Sketch (1984)

"Who are you? And how did you become what you are?" are questions which, when I try to answer them honestly, increase my awareness of how strong, in my case (where in others place and community often play a dominant part), were inherited tendencies and the influence of the cultural milieu—unsupported by a community—of my own family. My father's Hasidic ancestry, his being steeped in Jewish and Christian scholarship and mysticism, his fervor and eloquence as a preacher, were factors built into my cells even though I rarely paid conscious heed to what, as a child, I mostly felt were parts of the embarrassing adult world, and which during my adolescence I rejected as restrictive. Similarly, my mother's Welsh intensity and lyric feeling for Nature were not just the air I breathed but, surely, were in the body I breathed with. Reading, at 60, the out-of-print or manuscript pages of my father's theological writings, or the poems my mother took (shyly) to writing in her late 70s and 80s, I see clearly how much they, though not dedicated to the vocation of poetry, were nevertheless protopoets.

When I say the cultural atmosphere of our household was unsupported by a community I refer to the fact that my parents—he a converted Russian Jew who, after spending the First World War teaching at the University of Leipzig (though under semi-house arrest as an "enemy alien"), settled in England and was ordained as a priest of the Anglican Church; she a Welshwoman who had grown up in a mining village and later in a North Wales country town, and subsequently travelled widely—were exotic birds in the plain English coppice of Ilford, Essex. Even though our house was semi-detached and exactly like its neighbors architecturally, it looked different because it had no half-curtains or venetian blinds like the others, only side-curtains on its large windows, so passers-by could look right in. What they could see included bookshelves in every room, while in the bay window of my father's upstairs study was an almost life-size stone statue representing Jesus preaching, which caused strangers to stare and cross the street to get a better look at it. And my mother's front garden, though more restrained than the larger back garden, was never prim like many of the others along the street but suggested a foreign opulence, especially when the California poppies—later to delight homesick G.I.s billeted down the road—were in full orange glory.

The Levertoffs lived in Ilford because my father had been given (in the mistaken supposition that he would want to proselytize a Jewish neighborhood) a church in Shoreditch that had no vicarage and no local congregation. Ilford, though in Essex, was then at the eastern extremity of London; its own western end was still country, though rapidly being "developed" into monotonous row upon row of small "mock-Tudor" houses I early learned to despise as jerry-built architectural monstrosities.

I didn't go to school, nor had my sister (nine years older) done so except briefly, another thing which set our household apart from others. Dissatisfied with my sister's one year at a convent boarding school during my infancy, and unimpressed by local day-schools, whether private or council, my mother (who had been teaching at a Constantinople high school run by the Church of Scotland when she met my father in 1910) taught me herself until at 12, enamored of the de Basil Russian Ballet to which my sister had taken me, I began daily classes at a school of ballet on the other side of London. At that point I was put on my honor to continue reading some history, and went also for weekly French, piano, and art lessons in London; my other formal education ceased.

Romantic and beautiful Wanstead and Valentines parks, frequent expeditions into the Essex countryside with my sister, and my mother's very strong sense of history, developed in me a taste for seeking-out and exploring the vanishing traces of the village Ilford which London had engulfed. The reading I did myself, and the reading aloud which was a staple of our family life, combined to give me a passion for England—for the nuances of country things, hedges and old churches and the names of wildflowers—even though part of me knew I was an outsider. Among Jews a Goy, among Gentiles (secular or Christian) a Jew or at least a half-Jew (which was good or bad according to their degree of anti-Semitism); among Anglo-Saxons a Celt; in Wales a Londoner who not only did not speak Welsh but was not imbued with Welsh attitudes; among school children a strange exception whom they did not know whether to envy or mistrust: all of these anomalies predicated my later experience. I so often feel English, or perhaps European, in the United States, while in England I sometimes feel American—and certainly as a poet have been thought of for decades as an American, for it was in the United States that I developed, though my first book had been published in England before I crossed the Atlantic. But though I was quick to scornfully protest anti-Semitic remarks, or references to the Welsh language as a "dialect," these feelings of not-belonging were positive for me, not negative. I was given such a sense of confidence by my family, *in* my family, that though I was often shy (and have remained so in certain respects) I nevertheless experienced the sense of difference as an honor, as a part of knowing (secretly) from an early age—perhaps by seven, certainly before I was ten—that I was an artist-person and had a destiny. I did not experience competitiveness, because I was alone. The age gap—nine years—between me and my sister was such that my childhood was largely that of an only child. I was given a great deal of freedom to roam about outdoors as soon as I'd learned to cross streets safely; only the loneliest depths of Wanstead Park were out of bounds. The house was full of books, many of them late seventeenth- and eighteenth-century volumes. Everyone in the family did some kind of writing; my mother and sister always seemed to be helping my father correct galley proofs. My mother sang *Lieder*, my sister was a really fine pianist. The church services I attended were, despite the frequent childish embarrassment I've mentioned and my teenage doubts, beautiful with candlelight and music, incense and ceremony and stained glass, the incomparable rhythms of the King James Bible and the Book of Common Prayer.

All of this sounds idealized *ad nauseam,* I'm afraid. There were also tremendous domestic arguments and periodic full-scale "rows" and even real tragedy (my gifted but erratic sister's life and her conflicts and reconciliations with my parents were complex). But all in all I did grow up in an extraordinarily rich environment which nurtured the imaginative, language-oriented potential I believe was an inherited gift; and gave me—or almost seduced me into—an appreciation of solitude. Since writing poetry is so essentially a solitary occupation this has always stood me in good stead and perhaps I would not have developed it if I'd gone to school (unless I'd *hated* school, of course) for I have a sociable, gregarious tendency too, that might have taken away too much time and concentration and necessary daydreaming. Or I might have become caught up in aggressive competition, to the certain detriment of my creative possibilities.

While it is true that I was not competitive because I had no peers to compete with (my playmates, whether neighbors or kids I met in the park, were altogether separate from my beginnings in literature), I did, once I'd read Keats's letters, have hopes of Fame; but I thought of this as posthumous, and thus was saved from careerist ambition. And misinterpreting, to some extent, the gists of Mann's *Tonio Kröger,* I rather luxuriated in the protagonist's wistful alienation—though it was really his friend Lisaveta Ivanovna, the painter, the artist who was getting on with *doing her art,* who most excited me; especially since when I first read the story at 13, I had the *chutzpa* to believe I would be a painter as well as a poet. (I never deeply believed I would be a dancer despite the five years of my life when I took two ballet classes a day, shedding many tears in the process.)

Though my favorite poets were all men, I had enough faith in myself, or more precisely enough awe at the magic I knew sometimes worked through me, not to worry about that. Boys seemed, in fiction, to have more adventures; but in the "pretend-games" I made up and got my sister to play with me in my later childhood, some daring

young female spies and messengers worked to combat Fascism and
Nazism and to assist the government side in the Spanish Civil War
(which was then going on). I didn't suppose my gender to be an obsta-
cle to anything I really wanted to do.

Humanitarian politics came into my life early—seeing my father on
a soapbox protesting Mussolini's invasion of Abyssinia; my father and
sister both on soapboxes protesting Britain's lack of support for Spain;
my mother canvassing long before those events for the League of
Nations Union; and all three of them working on behalf of German
and Austrian refugees from 1933 onwards. When I was 11 and 12,
unknown to my parents (who would have felt, despite their liberal
views, that it was *going too far,* and was inappropriate for my age, as
indeed it was), I used to sell the *Daily Worker* house-to-house in the
working-class streets off Ilford Lane, down towards Barking, on Saturday mornings. Oddly enough I was never questioned, despite knee-
socks and long plaits (or pigtails, as one said then) though I had many a
door slammed in my face.

I've written here only about my childhood, and not at all about the
rest of my life and all its experiences of people, places, events; nothing
about the mind's later journeys in literature and the other arts which
mean so much to me; nothing about "intellectual stance," aesthetics,
philosophy, religion. But there is, after all, no mystery about all of that:
it's either in my poems or of little interest beyond the merely anecdotal.
All that has taken place in my life since—all, that is, that has any bearing on my life as a poet—was in some way foreshadowed then. I am
surprised to sound so deterministic, and I don't mean to suggest that
the course of every life is inexorably set, genetically or by childhood
experiences, for better or worse; nor that my own life had no options.
Possibly I might have been a better person, and certainly a more effi-
cient one in several respects, if I'd had a more disciplined and methodi-
cal education, more experience of economic struggle (never rich, and
not extravagant, our household nevertheless never lacked for anything),
and had not so early felt a sense of vocation and dedication to the art of
poetry. But since I *did* have a vocation, to which some interesting genes
contributed, it seems to me that I was fortunate in an upbringing favorable to their development; and this strongly affected my response to
subsequent events and opportunities.

Poets owe to Poetry itself a loyalty which may at times be in conflict with the demands of domestic or other aspects of life. Out of those
conflicts, sometimes, poetry itself re-emerges. For example, the impulse
to reconcile what one believes to be necessary to one's human integrity
(such as forms of political action) with the necessities of one's inner life,

including its formal, aesthetic dynamic, motivates the attempt to write engaged or "political" poetry that is truly poetry, magnetic and sensuous—the synthesis Neruda said was the most difficult of any to attain (but which our strange and difficult times cry out for). Yet sometimes the poems one is able to write and the needs and possibilities of day to day life remain separate from each other.

One is in despair over the current manifestation of malevolent imbecility and the seemingly invincible power of rapacity, yet finds oneself writing a poem about the trout lilies in the spring woods. And one has promised to speak at a meeting or help picket a building. If one is conscientious, the only solution is to attempt to weigh conflicting claims at each crucial moment, and in general to try to juggle well and keep all the oranges dancing in the air at once.

ANN CORNELISEN
(1926—)

◆

ANN CORNELISEN was born in Cleveland, Ohio, and educated at Vassar College. In 1954 she went to Florence intending to study archaeology. At the invitation of an acquaintance, Giovanna Thompson, who was the organizer and director of the British Save the Children Fund, Cornelisen visited the southern Abruzzo region, which, almost a decade after the end of World War II, was still a land of poverty and starvation. Moved by the misery of the people of the south, she went to work for the Save the Children Fund for ten years, helping to set up hundreds of nursery schools in impoverished villages. Her experiences in war-torn Italy have formed the basis of her published work, which includes *Torregreca: Life, Death, Miracles* (1969), a book, according to one critic in the *New Statesman,* that "makes us proud to belong to the human race" and won for Cornelisen a special award from the National Institute of Arts and Letters. This portrait of a village offers candid appraisals of the church, of the rural Italian mentality, and of "a cycle of poverty and despair with parallels in American society," to quote the *Harper's* reviewer. Her next book, *Women of the Shadows* (1976), tells the stories of Ninetta, Peppina, Teresa, and Cettina of another southern Italian village. In the author's words, "They are women of tremendous strengths, these women of the shadows. One of their strengths, and not the least, is their silence, which outsiders have understood as submission. . . . Before they disappear to become the ghostly shadows behind a myth, I think they should have their say." In *Strangers and Pilgrims: The Last Italian Migration* (1980), she offers a moving testament to the spirit of all migrant people as she traces the tragic migrations of her friends from Torregreca to the industrialized cities of northern Italy and West Germany. Her novel, *Any Four Women Could Rob the Bank of Italy* (1983), is a romp on the surface, set in San Felice Val Gufo, a Tuscan hill town similar to the place where Cornelisen lives, but the joke comes from her recognition that Italian men don't take women seriously enough even to stop and check them carefully at police barriers. And the strictness of the female conscience finally prevents her women from pulling off a successful robbery.

Where It All Began: Italy 1954 is her memoir of her first year in Italy, of how she came to her decision to leave America and her family behind—a "renunciation of rigidity"—and become an outsider in a world so different from her own. The book, in the beginning, has the resonance of autobiography: ". . . take a young American woman in 1954, put her down in Italy, follow her steps, and the result is apt to be the wife of a stockbroker in Greenwich, Connecticut, who, if she thinks of Italy at all, confuses it with a general nostalgia for her youth. But it is thirty-five years later and I am still here." The excerpt that follows reveals the autobiographical genre as not simply the stories of selfhood but the double—or even multidimensional—inventions of "I" and "eye": the introspective witness and the public observer of life outside the self. Her retrospective of her younger self and the world it observes takes the form of what the *New York Times Book Review* critic called her "enduring portraits of a peasant society that has now all but vanished and that rivals [the books] of Ignazio Silone and Carlo Levi." Always she is the "bystander," as she refers to herself, a writer whose humor, restraint, and compassion come through in her constructs of other subjects.

From *Where It All Began: Italy 1954*

ONE

Start at the beginning, they say. All else will fall into place. *They*, whoever they are, perceive dreams and chance meetings and whole lives as clearly organized, like a recipe for meringues. "Take the whites of four eggs . . . " If each step is followed, the result is apt to be meringues (and a quart of mayonnaise. *They* are cavalier about the four innocent yolks, probably feeling that nature, sooner or later, will adapt to the commercial credo of "return the unused portion and your money will be cheerfully refunded"). On the other hand, take a young American woman in 1954, put her down in Italy, follow her steps, and the result is apt to be the wife of a stockbroker in Greenwich, Connecticut, who, if she thinks of Italy at all, confuses it with a general nostalgia for her youth.

But it is thirty-five years later and I am still here. Any beginning would be arbitrary, would leave out the imponderables—my vision of Beatrice Cenci and Lucrezia, and the visions of half-forgotten teachers, who intrigued me with Catullus, Ovid, Galileo—and archaeology, which seemed a real, grown-up treasure hunt. The Italy we invented was a country of a thousand mysteries. It still is, only now for me the mysteries are different. Or perhaps after all these years the Italy I know is simply another invention. I test my resolution of the mysteries in the only way I can, by going back to the first encounters, when, yes, the mind and eye were ignorant, but so eager. The approach may be too empirical, but Italy, more than most countries, is everything and nothing that it seems to be. There is only one certainty: its mysteries never end.

Unfortunately what I remember best about the early morning of April 15, 1954, when I crossed the border from France into Italy, is another surge of panic, which had, anyway, been boiling around the emotional sluices of my mind ever since the night before in Paris. At the station my mother had struggled through our abortive platform conversation. Over the years of boarding school and college there had been so many, always the same, details already discussed, repeated, half heard, half misunderstood, and repeated again, a verbal treading of water.

"You will remember to write? Your father worries. . . . I'll send summer clothes as soon as I get back." She was to sail on the *Ile de France* a day or so later. "About money . . . Your father . . . " She stopped, looking up and down the platform for some distraction from the end of that sentence. (Her dilemma was perennial: how to explain to my father.) Now, the decisions made, about to get on the train, with my luggage already in my compartment, I suddenly did not want to go back to Italy and study archaeology. The world off out there beyond the smoky sheds was immense and lonely, and I, at twenty-seven and recently divorced, had run out of courage.

"Mother, maybe I shouldn't . . . " She was not listening. . . .
[She travels from Paris to Rome in April, intending to begin studies at the University of Rome but finds it closed from May to September.]

FOUR

Or maybe it actually began in the Roman pension, which, off and on for the next eight years, was my substitute home, a place where I left my "good" clothes, where I always found friends to celebrate Christmas and Easter, and could always bathe and be warm and think the world civilized again. It had been a monastery and, outside the single rooms, still had the old cell numbers worked in mosaic tiles on the corridor floor. Nothing was "standard." Each room had its own, distinct personality and its own, distinct malfunctions as each season had its regular residents, who gave eager briefings on in-house gossip.

There were also certain idiosyncrasies of the place it was wise to know. Monday mornings could bring slight, or at times spectacular changes in decor—a life-size polychrome statue of Mary Magdalene come to weep over our aperitifs, or a small section of stained-glass window placed to mask the light on the landing and so make the stairs dimmer, or a bronze Cupid and Psyche, managing in the midst of their amorous contortions to support a column, a light socket and a pink silk shade, suddenly appeared on your bedside table—all because the proprietor could not resist the Sunday market at Porta Portese. His mother was inclined to take the pass keys and drift from room to room, watering her plants, making sure that taps and light switches were turned off and incidentally that her son's treasures were not being mistreated by the current occupant. She never knocked. The Patriarch of the Marian Order, who was also the landlord, took his lunch and dinner in the dining room, so the unseemly display of female flesh, be it bosom, back or arm, was discouraged. One Easter morning, when I had been given a room at the far end of a corridor, I decided to take a bath. As I sank into the hot water, I thought I heard chanting. But no, it couldn't be. I splashed around washing, then subsided to soak and read—more chanting! Up near the ceiling there was an air vent, which must have let out on the other side just above the altar of the Marian Church. Whether or not they heard me as clearly as I heard them, I never knew, but imagining how offensive the idea of a nude communicant would be to the Patriarch, I stayed very still until the Mass was over.

And of course the residents had *their* idiosyncrasies. A few were or would be fairly well known literary figures. One spent his winters in Rome because he loved horse races, especially betting on them. There were academics on sabbatical and Swedish opera buffs and middle-aged art students, living the Bohemian dream of a lifetime in comfort. Usually there was a solitary woman busy about mild self-mythology. One year it was an Englishwoman with an odd accent who claimed she was related to much of the nobility and spoke at length about candle-bras and e-peer-gnes and other even more indecipherable appurtenances of noble life. Another, it was a thoroughly middle-aged American of the sculptured hair and annealed make-up school, who babbled to anyone she could trap about her glamorous nights at the opera, night clubs and restaurants with her "young Italian beau," and about the passionate importunings of this same dashing "young Italian beau," a man famous along Via Veneto as an expensive gigolo. Several staid older ladies had their own dangerous little habits. Often after dinner they smuggled fruit for their breakfasts out of the dining room and, having wedged it down, out of sight between the arm and the cushion of an overstuffed chair in the drawing room, forgot it when they went off to bed. A slightly messier variation was soft-boiled eggs, saved this time from breakfast for lunch (after a bit more cooking in whatever water-heating apparatus they kept hidden in their wardrobes). The experienced guest never sat on the overstuffed furniture without first groping around, as nonchalantly as possible, in the crevices. But these were minor defects in an otherwise charming hotel and could be avoided with a little care and the help of an engrossing book, preferably in Italian.

From a diary, one of those intermittent flurries that have always been my antidote for loneliness and frustration, I know I spent long hours of my first week there brooding in my room. The world seemed a very perverse place indeed. In our correspondence the University of Rome had answered all my questions and could not really be blamed for not answering what I had never thought to ask, even less for not specifying what was common Italian custom. The university was closed from May to November.

What should I do until fall? Stay in Rome? Go back to Florence? I knew only two people in Rome—a priest important in the hierarchy of a large order, who instantly invited me, pressed me, to join him on a motorcycle holiday to be enjoyed without benefit of cassock or crucifix, and Mrs. Luce,* who was not apt to have much time for me. I needed to find another Italian teacher, and I had already noticed that Romans, like most people in large cities, were in too much of a hurry to dawdle in idle conversation with stammering foreigners. Florence was more relaxed, more comfortable because it was now so familiar. Tempting. The easy way out, but a reservation in a pension was *not* a reason for staying in Rome. I wavered, almost convinced.

In my diary I give myself a long lecture about the folly of rigidity, of never doing anything on the spur of the moment, of always planning and always adhering to the plan. I must do the first interesting thing that offered—not, however, go a-rambling with a randy, incognito priest. In passing I mention that an acquaintance of my mother's has asked me for a drink to meet "an English widow, a social worker, who represents the British Save the Children Fund in Italy. . . . As one gets older," I remark, "social life seems to deteriorate. Acceptance of dreariness is probably what is meant by the phrase 'settling down.'"

Giovanna Guzzeloni Thompson (later Mrs. James Mourton, M.B.E.) was not at all the bulky, earnest lady in gaslight-blue lace and ground-

*Clare Boothe Luce was the American ambassador to Italy during the Eisenhower administration.

grippers I had expected. She was the exact opposite—a dark, minute, easily amused woman in her early thirties, wearing a chic cotton damask suit of white on palest gray. Her feet were tiny, really hooves, she always claimed, and her hands, which could do the finest embroidery or lull any suffering child or animal to sleep, were small and stubby. She was birdlike in figure and in face; she had rather too long a nose and large, luminous, brown eyes, deep set under the smoothly defined brows and lids usually seen only on the silkiest of marble statues. When she talked about Italy, particularly Southern Italy, her eyes glowed with a mystic, almost fanatic passion. She cast a spell, which, quite beyond any conscious intention of hers, convinced those who heard her that they were in a saintly presence. Of course they never saw her try to feed *salame* to a donkey or crawl along the mansard roof of Zagreb's best hotel in a billowing white night-gown, nor did they ever understand one basic contradiction about her— her exterior was as completely, convincingly Italian as her interior was English.

Nature plays tricks. Gianna looked exactly like her English mother. Her father, the son of an old Milanese family, a graduate of the Naval Academy and a specialist in turbine engines, could easily have been mistaken for an English gentleman. After the First World War they had stayed in Italy—in Milan as much as necessary, in a house overlooking Lake Varese as much as possible. Gianna was born. There are pictures of a frail, winsome little girl on a pony held by her tall, slender, handsome father. Mother was tiny and frail too, steely-frail as later years would prove. Also her heart was a bit temperamental, so winters were spent in the sun of the Italian Riviera. School for Gianna meant the more rigid expectations of the Ursuline nuns and her grandmother and her aunts, who believed in drawing-room discipline and formality in all things.

Mussolini and his Fascists had settled in to govern. Her parents in their own different ways were adamantly anti-Fascist. He and the peasants who farmed the land near the house quietly smuggled people up the mountains and across the border. She took a more English and ultimately more troublesome tack. At the theater she refused to stand for the Fascist anthem. If she saw a little boy wearing a black shirt, it was hard to keep her from going up to him and sympathizing: How sad! Who had died in his family? To the locals she might be the eccentric *signora inglese,* but Fascist bureaucrats were confused by eccentrics and wary. (They could not be expected to take Violet Gibson's attack on Mussolini as a recom-mendation.) They allotted her a place on their suspect list. Her husband's name protected her from more drastic measures.

Until, when Gianna was twelve, her father died, very young, of cancer and her mother was promoted to the black list. They fled, taking what they could with them, to England. Gianna became an English schoolgirl, later went to university. At the first scare of invasion she and her friends rushed off to the south coast and helped drag farm carts and abandoned harrows into barricades they hoped would defend England. Her friends went to Dunkirk. She became an air-raid warden. School holidays she picked crops. She studied. Her subject was child development, which led finally to a job with the Ministry of Education in an experimental group for difficult children. Her résumé might almost have been invented to satisfy the Save the Children Fund's requirements for its representative in Italy.

In 1947, with a mock military kit and a bit of money, she set off across the Continent headed for the Abruzzo, an area she had never seen and knew relatively little about except the rosy bits of information supplied by the Fund's foreign relief committee. The villages had been fought over one by one, the destruction in some places was total. Water was scarce *and* dangerous. Food about the same. Housing was impossible to find (the head of the Women's Catholic Action Committee in a town high above the coast, on the first ripple of mountains, had promised her lodging). Gianna was to start feeding programs and nurseries in the rubble of villages farther back in those mountains. The Catholic Action promised to help her. The Italian government promised its complete support. The Save the Children Fund promised to send money and supplies as soon as she was settled. Promises, promises! When I met her seven years later, her knowledge of the Abruzzo was encyclopedic. So, though less freely aired, was her knowledge of the Catholic Action, the Italian government and the Save the Children Fund. Survival was an accomplishment. She had done a great deal more and showed no signs of giving up yet. . . .

[A few days later Cornelisen runs into Gianna in Piazza di Spagna and they stop for tea in Babington's English Tea Room across the Spanish Steps from Keats's house.]

I remember it all so well because it was there, after our tea and cinnamon toast, that Gianna invited me to the Abruzzo. That is, if I decided to go back to Florence, I might find it an interesting stopover for three or four days. I seemed to be curious about Italy. This was a very different one from anything I had seen or was apt to see. For once she would have the car. Usually she took the train, but the car had some complaint that could only be cured at the dealer's garage. The driver would be there early Monday morning and ready to leave again right after lunch. Another exception: she was taking the weekend off.

Normally, not to "waste" time, she traveled on weekends. By then I knew that was all of a piece with her character. The invitation seemed less so, but for me it was one more temptation to go back to Florence. There was no hurry about my decision, she reassured me. I knew there was. . . .

. . . Several days later a hurried scrawl in my diary, the last, announces that I *have* accepted the first interesting thing to come my way, that I am going to the Abruzzo—without the faintest idea where it was, *what* it was, or quite how to spell it. In preparation for this adventure I had washed my hair and all my clothes. So much for renouncing rigidity. My mother's training had won out. . . .

MAYA ANGELOU
(1928—)

◆

Born Marguerite Johnson in St. Louis, MAYA ANGELOU was sent at the age of three in the company of her older brother Bailey to Stamps, Arkansas, to live with her father's mother, her beloved grandmother, Ann Henderson. Angelou's first volume of autobiography, *I Know Why the Caged Bird Sings,* recounts her life from the age of three to sixteen, her growing up black and female in the American South during the second quarter of this century. After living in Stamps for four years, Angelou went back to her mother's house in St. Louis where she was raped by her mother's boyfriend. For the next five years she was mute, but despite her isolation, she listened and developed a voice of her own: "Language. I loved it," she told a *New York Times* interviewer. "For a long time I would think of myself, of my whole body, as an ear. . . . I never did find a voice I didn't find wonderful and beautiful. Because I really like the way we talk. I find it wonderful." At sixteen she gave birth to a son in California, the setting of the following excerpt.

She had a brief theatrical career, danced with Alvin Ailey, and at Martin Luther King, Jr.'s request, served as northern coordinator for the Southern Christian Leadership Conference. She has published three books of poetry, holds fifty honorary degrees, and is currently professor of American studies at Wake Forest University in Winston-Salem, North Carolina. She is best known, however, for the five books of her honest and joyful autobiography: *I Know Why the Caged Bird Sings* (1970)—the source of the following excerpt whose title is taken from a poem by Paul Laurence Dunbar—*Gather Together in My Name* (1974), *Singin' & Swingin' & Gettin' Merry Like Christmas* (1976), *The Heart of a Woman* (1981), and *All God's Children Need Traveling Shoes* (1986). In 1993, Angelou was the first poet since Robert Frost spoke at the inauguration of John F. Kennedy to be invited to write and read her work at a presidential inauguration. She prepared for her part in the Clinton Inaugural by reading aloud from the writers who have formed her politics—Frederick Douglass, Patrick Henry, and Thomas Paine—and trying to communicate in her inaugural poem, "On the Pulse of Morning," what she has said is the fundamental theme of all her work: "What I try to say is that as human beings we are more alike than we are unalike."

In his critical essay "Maya Angelou and the Autobiographical Statement," Selwyn R. Cudjoe addresses the profound resonance of Angelou's autobiographies:

"The Afro-American autobiographical statement is the most Afro-American of all Afro-American literary pursuits. . . . [It] remains the quintessential literary genre for capturing the cadences of the Afro-American being, revealing its deepest aspirations and tracing the evolution of the Afro-American psyche under the impact of slavery and modern U.S. imperialism." Partly in response to the distortion of Afro-American female characters and their histories by male writers, Angelou, writes Professor Cudjoe, "present[s] a powerful, authentic and profound signification of the condition of Afro-American womanhood in her quest for understanding and love rather than for bitterness and despair. Her work is a triumph in the articulation of truth in simple, forthright terms."

From *I Know Why the Caged Bird Sings*

27

In the early months of World War II, San Francisco's Fillmore district, or the Western Addition, experienced a visible revolution. On the surface it appeared to be totally peaceful and almost a refutation of the term "revolution." The Yakamoto Sea Food Market quietly became Sammy's Shoe Shine Parlor and Smoke Shop. Yashigira's Hardware metamorphosed into La Salon de Beauté owned by Miss Clorinda Jackson. The Japanese shops which sold products to Nisei customers were taken over by enterprising Negro businessmen, and in less than a year became permanent homes away from home for the newly arrived Southern Blacks. Where the odors of tempura, raw fish and *cha* had dominated, the aroma of chitlings, greens and ham hocks now prevailed.

The Asian population dwindled before my eyes.* I was unable to tell the Japanese from the Chinese and as yet found no real difference in the national origin of such sounds as Ching and Chan or Moto and Kano.

---

*See the excerpt from *Farewell to Manazanar* by Jeanne Wakatsuki Houston (see page 271) about the forced internment of Japanese-Americans in concentration camps during World War II.

As the Japanese disappeared, soundlessly and without protest, the Negroes entered with their loud jukeboxes, their just-released animosities and the relief of escape from Southern bonds. The Japanese area became San Francisco's Harlem in a matter of months.

A person unaware of all the factors that make up oppression might have expected sympathy or even support from the Negro newcomers for the dislodged Japanese. Especially in view of the fact that they (the Blacks) had themselves undergone concentration-camp living for centuries in slavery's plantations and later in sharecroppers' cabins. But the sensations of common relationship were missing.

The Black newcomer had been recruited on the desiccated farm lands of Georgia and Mississippi by war-plant labor scouts. The chance to live in two- or three-story apartment buildings (which became instant slums), and to earn two- and even three-figured weekly checks, was blinding. For the first time he could think of himself as a Boss, a Spender. He was able to pay other people to work for him, i.e. the dry cleaners, taxi drivers, waitresses, etc. The shipyards and ammunition plants brought to booming life by the war let him know that he was needed and even appreciated. A completely alien yet very pleasant position for him to experience. Who could expect this man to share his new and dizzying importance with concern for a race that he had never known to exist?

Another reason for his indifference to the Japanese removal was more subtle but was more profoundly felt. The Japanese were not whitefolks. Their eyes, language and customs belied the white skin and proved to their dark successors that since they didn't have to be feared, neither did they have to be considered. All this was decided unconsciously.

No member of my family and none of the family friends ever mentioned the absent Japanese. It was as if they had never owned or lived in the houses we inhabited. On Post Street, where our house was, the hill skidded slowly down to Fillmore, the market heart of our district. In the two short blocks before it reached its destination, the street housed two day-and-night restaurants, two pool halls, four Chinese restaurants, two gambling houses, plus diners, shoeshine shops, beauty salons, barber shops and at least four churches. To fully grasp the never-ending activity in San Francisco's Negro neighborhood during the war, one need only know that the two blocks described were side streets that were duplicated many times over in the eight- to ten-square-block area.

The air of collective displacement, the impermanence of life in wartime and the gauche personalities of the more recent arrivals tended to dissipate my own sense of not belonging. In San Francisco, for the first time, I perceived myself as part of something. Not that I identified with the newcomers, nor with the rare Black descendants of native San Franciscans, nor with the whites or even the Asians, but rather with the times and the city. I understood the arrogance of the young sailors who marched the streets in marauding gangs, approaching every girl as if she were at best a prostitute and at worst an Axis agent bent on making the U.S.A. lose the war. The undertone of fear that San Francisco would be bombed which was abetted by weekly air raid warnings, and civil defense drills in school, heightened my sense of belonging. Hadn't I, always, but ever and ever, thought that life was just one great risk for the living?

Then the city acted in wartime like an intelligent woman under siege. She gave what she couldn't with safety withhold, and secured those things which lay in her reach. The city became for me the ideal of what I wanted to be as a grownup. Friendly but never gushing, cool but not frigid or distant, distinguished without the awful stiffness.

To San Franciscans "the City That Knows How" was the Bay, the fog, Sir Francis Drake Hotel, Top o' the Mark, Chinatown, the Sunset District and so on and so forth and so white. To me, a thirteen-year-old Black girl, stalled by the South and Southern Black life style, the city was a state of beauty and a state of freedom. The fog wasn't simply the steamy vapors off the bay caught and penned in by hills, but a soft breath of anonymity that shrouded and cushioned the bashful traveler. I became dauntless and free of fears, intoxicated by the physical fact of San Francisco. Safe in my protecting arrogance, I was certain that no one loved her as impartially as I. I walked around the Mark Hopkins and gazed at the Top o' the Mark, but (maybe sour grapes) was more impressed by the view of Oakland from the hill than by the tiered building or its fur-draped visitors. For weeks, after the city and I came to terms about my belonging, I haunted the points of interest and found them empty and un-San Francisco. The naval officers with their well-dressed wives and clean white babies inhabited another time-space dimension than I. The well-kept old women in chauffeured cars and blond girls in buckskin shoes and cashmere sweaters might have been San Franciscans, but they were at most gilt on the frame of my portrait of the city.

Pride and Prejudice stalked in tandem the beautiful hills. Native San Franciscans, possessive of the city, had to cope with an influx, not of awed respectful tourists but of raucous unsophisticated provincials. They were also forced to live with skin-deep guilt brought on by the treatment of their former Nisei schoolmates.

Southern white illiterates brought their biases intact to the West from the hills of Arkansas and the swamps of Georgia. The Black ex-farmers had not left their distrust and fear of whites which history had taught them in distressful lessons. These two groups were obliged to work side by side in the war plants, and their animosities festered and opened like boils on the face of the city.

San Franciscans would have sworn on the Golden Gate Bridge that racism was missing from the heart of their air-conditioned city. But they would have been sadly mistaken.

A story went the rounds about a San Franciscan white matron who refused to sit beside a Negro civilian on the streetcar, even after he made room for her on the seat. Her explanation was that she would not sit beside a draft dodger who was a Negro as well. She added that the least he could do was fight for his country the way her son was fighting on Iwo Jima. The story said that the man pulled his body away from the window to show an armless sleeve. He said quietly and with great dignity, "Then ask your son to look around for my arm, which I left over there."

28

Although my grades were very good (I had been put up two semesters on my arrival from Stamps), I found myself unable to settle down in the high school. It was an institution for girls near my house, and the young ladies were faster, brasher, meaner and more prejudiced than any I had met at Lafayette County Training School. Many of the Negro girls were, like me, straight from the South, but they had known or claimed to have known the bright lights of Big D (Dallas) or T Town (Tulsa, Oklahoma), and their language bore up their claims. They strutted with an aura of invincibility, and along with some of the Mexican students who put knives in their tall pompadours they absolutely intimidated the white girls and those Black and Mexican students who had no shield of fearlessness. Fortunately I was transferred to George Washington High School.

The beautiful buildings sat on a moderate hill in the white residential district, some sixty blocks from the Negro neighborhood. For the first semester, I was one of three Black students in the school, and in that rarefied atmosphere I came to love my people more. Mornings as the streetcar traversed my ghetto I experienced a mixture of dread and trauma. I knew that all too soon we would be out of my familiar setting, and Blacks who were on the streetcar when I got on would all be gone and I alone would face the forty blocks of neat streets, smooth lawns, white houses and rich children.

In the evenings on the way home the sensations were joy, anticipation and relief at the first sign which said BARBECUE or DO DROP INN or HOME COOKING or at the first brown faces on the streets. I recognized that I was again in my country.

In the school itself I was disappointed to find that I was not the most brilliant or even nearly the most brilliant student. The white kids had better vocabularies than I and, what was more appalling, less fear in the classrooms. They never hesitated to hold up their hands in response to a teacher's question; even when they were wrong they were wrong aggressively, while I had to be certain about all my facts before I dared to call attention to myself.

George Washington High School was the first real school I attended. My entire stay there might have been time lost if it hadn't been for the unique personality of a brilliant teacher. Miss Kirwin was that rare educator who was in love with information. I will always believe that her love of teaching came not so much from her liking for students but from her desire to make sure that some of the things she knew would find repositories so that they could be shared again.

She and her maiden sister worked in the San Francisco city school system for over twenty years. My Miss Kirwin, who was a tall, florid, buxom lady with battleship-gray hair, taught civics and current events. At the end of a term in her class our books were as clean and the pages as stiff as they had been when they were issued to us. Miss Kirwin's students were never or very rarely called upon to open textbooks.

She greeted each class with "Good day, ladies and gentlemen." I had never heard an adult speak with such respect to teenagers. (Adults usually believe that a show of honor diminishes their authority.) "In today's *Chronicle* there was an article on the mining industry in the Carolinas [or some such distant subject]. I am certain that all of you have read the article. I would like someone to elaborate on the subject for me."

After the first two weeks in her class, I, along with all the other excited students, read the San Francisco papers, *Time* magazine, *Life* and everything else available to me. Miss Kirwin proved Bailey right. He had told me once that "all knowledge is spendable currency, depending on the market."

There were no favorite students. No teacher's pets. If a student pleased her during a particular period, he could not count on special treatment in the next day's class, and that was as true the other way around. Each day she faced us with a clean slate and acted as if ours were clean as well. Reserved and firm in her opinions, she spent no time in indulging the frivolous.

She was stimulating instead of intimidating. Where some of the other teachers went out of their way to be nice to me—to be a "liberal" with me—and others ignored me completely, Miss Kirwin never seemed to notice that I was Black and therefore different. I was Miss Johnson and if I had the answer to a question she posed I was never given any more than the word "Correct," which was what she said to every other student with the correct answer.

Years later when I returned to San Francisco I made visits to her classroom. She always remembered that I was Miss Johnson, who had a good mind and should be doing something with it. I was never encouraged on those visits to loiter or linger about her desk. She acted as if I must have had other visits to make. I often wondered if she knew she was the only teacher I remembered.

I never knew why I was given a scholarship to the California Labor School. It was a college for adults, and many years later I found that it was on the House Un-American Activities list of subversive organizations. At fourteen I accepted a scholarship and got one for the next year as well. In the evening classes I took drama and dance, along with white and Black grownups. I had chosen drama simply because I liked Hamlet's soliloquy beginning, "To be, or not to be." I had never seen a play and did not connect movies with the theater. In fact, the only times I had heard the soliloquy had been when I had melodramatically recited to myself. In front of a mirror.

It was hard to curb my love for the exaggerated gesture and the emotive voice. When Bailey and I read poems together, he sounded like a fierce Basil Rathbone and I like a maddened Bette Davis. At the California Labor School a forceful and perceptive teacher quickly and unceremoniously separated me from melodrama.

She made me do six months of pantomime.

Bailey and Mother encouraged me to take dance, and he privately told me that the exercise would make my legs big and widen my hips. I needed no greater inducement.

My shyness at moving clad in black tights around a large empty room did not last long. Of course, at first, I thought everyone would be staring at my cucumber-shaped body with its knobs for knees, knobs for elbows and, alas, knobs for breasts. But they really did not notice me, and when the teacher floated across the floor and finished in an arabesque my fancy was taken. I would learn to move like that. I would learn to, in her words, "occupy space." My days angled off Miss Kirwin's class, dinner with Bailey and Mother, and drama and dance.

The allegiances I owed at this time in my life would have made very strange bedfellows: Momma with her solemn determination, Mrs. Flowers and her books, Bailey with his love, my mother and her gaiety, Miss Kirwin and her information, my evening classes of drama and dance. . . .

MAUREEN HOWARD
(1930—)

———————◆———————

MAUREEN HOWARD was born and grew up in the Irish-Catholic part of Bridgeport, Connecticut, the setting of her best novels and the memoir that is excerpted here. She attended Smith College, has worked in publishing, written frequently in the *New York Times Book Review,* and taught at Columbia University. She is the author of the novels *Not a Word About Nightingales* (1961), *Bridgeport Bus* (1966), *Before My Time* (1975), *Grace Abounding* (1982), *Natural History* (1992), and the memoir *Facts of Life* (1978). According to the critic Suzanne Henning Uphaus, Howard's fiction has gone largely unrecognized by feminists because her work is not didactic. In her words, Howard's memoir "demonstrate[s] the power of the past in her personal life. *Facts of Life* is oblivious to chronology; it circles and recircles Howard's past in an attempt to unravel its mysteries, creating a cumulative effect." The book begins with a brilliant portrait of her mother, Loretta Burns, a lady refined but fey. More muted is Howard's reinvention of her first marriage and herself as a faculty wife, the focus of the following selection. (It brings to mind the words bell hooks confided as a girl to her mother: "I don't think I'll ever marry, seems like women just lose something in marriage" (see page 451). Frank Kermode praised the award-winning *Facts of Life,* for in it, he wrote, "Maureen Howard has solved the peculiar problems of autobiography with her usual skill, and her prose has an authentic note of self-irony and candor. She keeps her eye for the ridiculous and knows how to write the prose appropriate to a slightly painful hilarity. She also knows how to preserve her own and others' dignity while exposing affectation and vanity. Of course she can do these things because she really is an exceptionally good writer."

From *Facts of Life*

. . . In the beginning it did not seem to signify that we lived in an infirmary, an old frame building on the corner of the Williams College campus with rotted boards in the front porch, fire extinguishers at every turn of the stairs, rope ladders hung at the windows. It was called Williams Hall Annex but the structure it annexed had long since burned down. These quarters, not fit for sick boys, were now the homes of the young married faculty, each apartment a bizarre arrangement of hospital rooms. The first floor—public waiting rooms and doctors' offices—was most desirable. Above, the small sickrooms and service kitchens rambled in all directions off a dark central hallway swathed in gray linoleum. The Annex narrowed on the top floor where we lived, two apartments sealed off from the hall; it was obvious that this place was for the quarantine in the old days, before measles shots and antibiotics.

Here my married life began. My life apart from my parents. Life after the two years of marking time with those college-girl jobs in New York. Girls were made to marry and marriage was my only serious pursuit. My education and career were sham intentions, smart midcentury substitutes for the embroidery work and social graces of an earlier time. The endless dalliance of girls' waiting for a man, for the man, was my heritage. I was overdetermined (the jargon is fitting) to love and to marry, and, more's the pity, I could only respond to clever men, bright men who lived off works of art—wanting, I suppose, substance that I dared not have on my own. In memory the sighs of my first obsessive love echo through the Hall of Graduate Studies at Yale. My bridal picture tells too much: I am absolutely fierce, set in my purpose, impatient with the bouffant dress and illusion veil, the hateful lace mitts—all chosen by my parents. I would have been happier in a flour sack. I will have this thing I want. My eyes blaze out at the camera, a scornful smile on my mouth at the very idea of a bridal portrait, and my hands, twisted to arthritic grace, hold the dead waxy flowers of a studio bouquet. Even if I must sit so posed, so falsely arranged, I will have this thing I want.

The two rooms of that first apartment were small but adequate. My savings book was spent on two broadloom carpets and the reupholstering of cast-off furniture from my family's house. A barrel top found in the cellar became a quaint table—museum prints, corduroy cushions, etc. But the kitchen, all mine, faced the public stairway out in the hall. Where once the bedpans and syringes were stored, large hospital cabinets now accommodated my dishes and pots. I unpacked my wedding plates and silver, my pristine double boiler. I screwed cup hooks into the shelves and hung my cups. The trees and cows of the common Wedgwood pattern dangled over the platters and trays still dusty with excelsior. We started to eat pan-fried meat and potatoes off our plates where a shepherd lingered under a lofty willow and in the distance an English castle had fallen into romantic ruins.

The gray linoleum from the hall spread into the kitchen and an adjustable bed tray on wheels, surfaced in the same murky stuff, was abandoned in one corner. Across the hall a midwestern couple lived, both of them tall and blond, who spoke to each other only in Japanese. She, a missionary's daughter: he, a mathematician who'd been with the army of occupation in Japan. Stiff, impossible prudes, they were middle-aged at twenty-five. They disapproved of our late hours. I was exposed to them in my trousseau finery as I stood over the sink early in the morning, or, fumbling with the can opener at night, trying to throw a meal together after we'd emptied the martini pitcher.

"Please?" she would say to me in English, bowing and smiling, this bespectacled Christian girl. "Who has the money? Him or you?"

Perched in my kitchen door: "Please? Who owns the car?"

"Please? The Steuben vase?"

"You are going to prevent babies?"

I have always felt that someplace in my encounters with the Japs, as we then called them, was the beginning of the lie. The baby-blue Plymouth was mine, I replied. We used condoms because I could not be logical about matters of religion and had only recently lost my faith. There was something too amenable in my answers, a foreshadowing of the compliant young matron I would become. I wanted to say get out of my goddamn kitchen. It's not the custom of this country to ask the price of my silver tray. On Sunday morning when we lay abed their high-pitched Oriental jabbering was only a few feet from our rumpled sheets (through the fire door) as they bounded downstairs, off to the Presbyterian church.

Dining in I served up oversauced dishes, carrying them in from the hall in a French earthenware pot. The invited young couples would invite *us* one night soon for another pot. It cannot be that all we talked about was our insecurity. The husbands' precarious jobs were the one sore spot to be worried. Indictments of the men in power. We had no position, no place in the world and never stopped to take much pleasure in our youth. Our beauty and freedom were ignored while we all yearned for the goods of dissatisfied middle age. I remember defiant faces, angry voices arguing late into the night, sworn alliances, cries of betrayal, the long drone of strategies for survival. But I remember no bodies, no sexual presence on any of those evenings. One pretty wife from Akron broke the code: she wore low-cut dresses, her big creamy breasts on display. At the faculty club she pressed into the dark suits of her dance partners and let her head drop on the man's shoulder like a girl at a prom.

There lived among us one wife who danced professionally, driving over the Berkshire Hills to her teaching job. She exercised for hours on end in the Annex hallway. All her clothes were costumes. The ease of her dancer's walk was a continual surprise. Unlike the rest of us, she could not sit in rooms at dinner parties giving way to the usual, the expected. She could not hear our gossip or eat noodles and, knowing she was a figure of fun, wore her hair in a ponytail well into her thirtieth year. Oh, but she was scandalous sleeping till noon and then driving off through blizzards over the Mohawk Trail with her records of Hindemith and Cage to which her troupe of college girls would dance. No one took her seriously—we couldn't afford to—and off she went to South America and England doing what she cared for, that's what offended. The few times she got into shoes and a respectable dress to attend an official function she sputtered with laughter after one drink, listening to the important people, squinting her eyes with concentration so she would not yawn or make some odd, distracting dancelike thrust with her hips.

She kept something alive in me—the sense that I could make a choice, if not now, one day—a choice to say no to the first course, to the purse with matching shoes, real pearls, salad *after* with cheese—and to *The New Yorker* as bible. No, to keeping in my place, to joining in the adulation for the Paul Klee exhibit and heavy foreign movies and she knew, though I didn't believe it, that I might drop out of the hot competition in the hors d'oeuvres department. No—someday—to drifting through department stores and dinner table talk. I played a cowardly game waiting and watching, polishing silver, ironing napkins. The guests came up the stairs. I honored the convention of the perfectly appointed dining room, though I did not have one, and the established order of bread and butter plates: I face you over the flowers: love me for it.

I did what came my way, acted in the student plays, worked on political campaigns, typed my husband's thesis with four carbon copies to be corrected at every slip of the finger. There was no Xerox in the days of the Annex. I gave my soul to make the pages come out right. I did anything to please. In the background, like a strong sweep of dull-blue sky that we could not value in a painting, there were good people (some the hated and feared full professors) who were not substantially harmed by the world outside. And there were evenings, I must force myself to be fair, when the Annex seemed free of the rotted stench of academic politics, our soiled bandages and bloody surgical pads, and friendship was an accomplishment we all excelled at. The old skirts and sweaters from college wore out up on the third floor. After parties our cat drank what was left in the martini glasses until he staggered off to our bed. I began to push the idea of being young and pretty before it was too late, toyed with the students, developed a devastating tongue. If I seem harsh it is because I see myself as a fashionable young woman in a decorous red cocktail dress and a gamin haircut standing on the shabby porch of Williams Hall Annex ready to go out: all style and no content.

Dining out. Favored by those in power for our manners and wit, my husband and I were often invited to dine in real houses. Wine glass over the knife. Berry spoon and pudding plates—the world of Sarah Field Splint at last. To be the gayest and most knowing, what a small portion we asked for. To be indebted, from the clear soup to the assorted liqueurs, singing for our supper because we did not trust our own lives, our own fare. I said yes to the academic poetry of that time which had grown out of stale criticism and yes to the limp refined productions of Shakespeare that had begun to seep out of our new repertory theaters over the fetid landscape of high culture and yes to the staggering simplifications of all the Abstract Expressionists, because— ever aiming to please I had let myself be told.

The shame of it: I remember a lunch served up in the back bedroom of a second-story faculty flat in Ohio to Northrop Frye, the literary critic, our visiting dignitary at Kenyon College. The clothes closet turned into a china cabinet looked like a clothes closet, but I had the patched Persian rug, the colonial drop-leaf table, my mother-in-law's reglued dining room chairs, the luncheon cloth and the floral centerpiece (a ten-mile ride to the florist). I sat at the head of the table, a veritable Madame de Sévigné of central Ohio, exhausted by my labors. I cannot remember one word the great man said, yet getting up from the table I knew that I would dine out on having had him to lunch. I will not bore you with the menu which I do remember down to the last braised turnip in the grande marmite. I was charming too, always that, and knew what to ask, had "read up on," if not read his book on Blake. Myopic and proper, bending into his soup, he talked as though we had all wanted really to say something. I got the impression of a generous man, so committed to his work that he could not fathom my triviality.

My life was arranged: I wrote now: I had a calm friendly marriage, but as yet no child. I had cried when we crossed the George Washington Bridge heading out to the Midwest and I was right. The loneliness was thick in the clean air—once a day to the post office, the dry run of flirtations with the brightest students, the long wait for the weekend dinner parties with familiar faces. A colonial existence which seemed unreal even as I lived it. At the end of the spring semester when the graceful town of Gambier was suddenly lush and sultry after the gloomy winter, an insane round of parties began—a nightmare of asparagus and strawberries, trout flown into the Columbus airport from Colorado, new evening dresses ordered from the big department stores in Cleveland. The fine wines—smoky graves, full-bodied clarets—too much of that talk. The last party I remember was announced as an exercise in *de trop,* a studied decadence: dinner jackets and thick cream dessert, just the smart set on into the night and it ended in a drunken breaking of furniture, a shallow anglophile historian jumping up and down on the Dux armchairs until his hostess and his wife were in tears. It is pure accident that every witness to that joyless violence—all of us divorced.

During the day the men taught. The cramped graduate school existence was over and now they had only to prove themselves each day in the classroom and write a brilliant book. The pressures were inhuman. To some of them their profession was still of interest, but many of these men, gray-templed deans and full professors now, were too forceful for the gentlemanly world of the university they had entered. They sounded in their competitive talk like politicians or oil executives and they thrilled to power rather than ideas. Tenure, grants, jousting for position, only one or two spires of the tower were built of ivory.

At that time I wrote a mannered academic novel, actually a parody of that genre and so at a further remove from life. If there is any strength there (I will never look back to see) it can only be in what I wanted that book to reflect: a sense of order as I knew it in the late fifties and early sixties with all the forms that I accepted and even enjoyed: that was the enormous joke about life—that our passion must be contained if we were not to be fools. . . .

★ ★ ★

Theirs was a love match. I always flip back to them, my parents. Though they married late, theirs was not a marriage of accommodation watered down by the waiting. Loretta and Bill, the profanity in my use of their first names. Honor them but never wonder how he laid siege to her, why with all the girls free to go dancing he wanted this lady with her eternal gloves and hats. Cult of the Virgin. Daughter of Virtue. Mother most Holy. So restrained that when she had fun, and she did, it was so proclaimed and labeled *fun.* And that in him which had once been attracted to the rituals of the Church or to the idea of himself as an appealing choirboy: she would iron his shirts when they married and send him off to the courthouse as though in a starched alb. He would be the better for her, quite the little man.

They courted on long walks and ice cream sodas while everyone else drank bootleg booze. Forever after they would tell their children: "We didn't need liquor. Isn't that right, Mother (Dad)?" It was enough to drive me to drink in high school, rye and ginger ale, that picture of them sitting in the Big Top Coffee Shop of the Barnum Hotel slurping their better-by-far chocolate sodas. I see them in the spotlight of her virtue. Children over thirty with the circus-parade mural marching the wall behind them. Where would she have been without his coarseness, his jokes about breaking wind, his foul mouth curbed for her. "Fatty Arbuckle," he said to the waitress's backside. "Piss-elegant" he called her college friends. The running patter of his talk to everyone they met—God, she needed his glibness like his sweat and the hitch of his pants against his balls and in the nick of time there came the engagement ring set in dull platinum which was the fashion. In another instant, with her wide Celtic cheekbones and narrow chest she would have appeared forevermore in two dimensions, dissolved into her sainthood, one among many in a frieze of virgins.

Miss Burns, the teacher of Latin and algebra, was not supposed to marry and that part of herself, brilliant and stern, which had made her pupils strain beyond their limits she never showed to her husband who was a self-indulgent boy.

The unending text for me of that marriage: their first child dead at birth, then George and . . . while she was showing strangers interested in the economic design of our new 1930's elf cottage . . . her/my waterbag burst and I pressed, inconvenient, difficult from the start, into the world. . . .

MARY MEBANE
(1933—)

---◆---

MARY MEBANE was born and grew up in the back country of Durham County, North Carolina, before the Supreme Court outlawed segregation in the public schools. In her autobiography, *Mary*, excerpted here, she presents the context of her childhood and early education: "Historically, my lifetime is important because I was part of the last generation born into a world of total legal segregation in the Southern United States. . . . The [segregation] laws were meant to— and did—create a world that fixed black people at the bottom of society in all aspects of human life. It was a world without options." Yet, despite the psychological and legal barriers between Mary and the freedom that an education promised, she resisted, stayed in school, and eventually earned her doctorate in English at the University of North Carolina in Chapel Hill. She has taught English in the public high schools and colleges of North Carolina and South Carolina and at the University of Wisconsin. Her published writing, which includes two volumes of autobiography, *Mary* (1981) and *Mary Wayfarer* (1983), has been widely anthologized and praised. She has spoken to *Contemporary Authors* of the driving force behind her work: "It is my belief that the black folk [of the south] are the most creative, viable people that America has produced. They just don't know it." Her conviction recalls Albert Murray's expressed purpose in writing *The Omni-Americans,* to suggest, in his words, "the affirmative implications of [African-American] history and culture," and to do justice to the fact that "not only do [African-Americans] choose to live rather than commit suicide, but that, poverty and injustice notwithstanding, far from simply struggling in despair, they live with gusto and a sense of elegance that has always been downright enviable." Mary Mebane's life history reflects this resilience even as she represents her cultural history within a daunting narrative.

From *Mary*

1

My name is Mary.

When I first opened my eyes to the world, on June 26, 1933, in the Wildwood community in Durham County, North Carolina, the world was a green Eden—and it was magic. My favorite place in the whole world was a big rock in the backyard that looked like the back of a buried elephant. I spent a lot of time squatting on that rock. I realize now that I probably selected it because it was in the *center* of our yard, and from it, by shifting ever so slightly, this way and that, I could see *everything*. I liked to look. Mama must have told me several thousand times that I was going to die with my eyes open, looking. . . .

I would squat on that rock, my stick legs poking through the openings of my dirt-stained bloomers, my birdlike head turning from side to side, my gaze, unblinking, focusing up, down, in front of me, in back of me, now zooming in on the lower yard, then penetrating deeper into the garden, then rising up ever so slightly to where the corn was planted on the hill. I was in the center of life and I didn't miss a thing; nothing slipped by unobserved or unnoted. My problems started when I began to comment on what I saw. I insisted on being accurate. But the world I was born into didn't want that. Indeed, its very survival depended on not knowing, not seeing—and, certainly, not saying anything at all about what it was really like. . . .

For a long time I had felt a chill wind blowing through this flower-bestrewn, green, vivid Eden. I would pause in my running and ponder on it a moment; then I would dismiss it from my mind and run on, hoping it would go away. The chill was my growing knowledge that my mother, Nonnie, had no warmth, no love, no human feeling for me. When her voice spoke, it was always a rebuke and there was the absolute refusal on her part to touch me—no hugs, no kisses, no pats, nothing. I had absorbed the knowledge that she didn't want me touching her or talking to her. If I did something, she scolded me; if she asked me a question, she wanted an answer. Nothing more. I hid this secret knowledge from myself and everybody else. For it meant that I had done something very bad, and that is why my mother didn't like me. But whatever it was I had done, I would be extra good to make up for it. And if that didn't seem to be enough, I would do more and then more.

★   ★   ★

Some people find themselves in the wrong grouping of human relationships. Often it's their own fault. They marry someone and think that they know what they are doing, that they know themselves and they know the other person. Only it doesn't work out that way. For often they find out things about themselves and sometimes they find out things about the other person that let them know that they are not a natural harmonious grouping at all, that they should never have tried to form so close a human relationship with each other. They deal with this situation in various ways, two of which are separation and divorce.

But sometimes the wrong grouping is not the result of a conscious choice—of marriage with a stranger. Sometimes one is a part of the wrong grouping because he or she was born into it and, far from being a stranger, is an intimate member of the grouping, with blood ties, family memories—an association from which there is no divorce, no separation. Then what do you do? You harbor the guilty knowledge that you do not belong. But even worse, you follow the group's belief that you do not belong because there is something intrinsically the matter with you; that all family groupings are just alike, and that if you can't function in this one, you can't function in any; that since other people seem to be living harmoniously in a grouping of some kind, while you are in misery all the time, something or someone has decreed that you must be an outsider, that something being God or Fate or whatever governs human affairs; that you must be an outsider for an unspecified length of time to atone for some secret sin that you somehow, somewhere in the past, committed; that you must submit to harsh accusations, cruel judgments, uncomplainingly. For only after this suffering can you find peace and reconcilement within the grouping, whether familial or ethnic.

What do you do in such a situation? Say: I divorce you, I divorce you, I divorce you. Strong ones do. I couldn't. . . .

Nothing was ever enough; Mama's coldness never ceased and I never ceased trying to prove to be good. That is, I didn't until the third decade of my life, when I was so tired and worn out that I just didn't care one way or the other anymore.

This nightmarish relationship created a giant raw scar across my life. . . .

Aunt Jo was a tall, slim lady. She held herself very straight. She had long black hair that hung to her waist when she let it down, but she wore it parted in the middle, with a little bun in the back. She was ivory-colored and had a sharp nose. She also had a sharp temper and would cuss if you made her mad.

Aunt Jo came to live with us when she got tired of the North. She had left Durham when she was a young girl because she was disappointed in love. In her teens she had married a man, only to find out shortly afterwards that he had a wife from whom he had never been divorced. She soured on men and swore that she would never marry, and she didn't.

She adored me.

Though we couldn't have looked more unlike each other, she insisted that I was just like her. One day she called me to her.

"Let me see your hands," she said.

She took them and examined the fingers one by one.

"See, you have long, slender fingers. You are going to be a pianist.". . .

I dreamed of doing great things in life, of being famous and successful. But I knew that I wasn't being taught in school what I should have been taught. We didn't have the facilities. The high school was four rooms added on to the back of the elementary school, upstairs and downstairs. Upstairs was the ninth-grade classroom, part of which was partitioned off for the principal's office; next door was the eleventh-grade homeroom, where social studies was taught, and around the wall were books and on the sides a newspaper and magazine stand—it also served as the library. Downstairs was the tenth-grade homeroom, with a cabinet of chemicals and a sink to serve as the science laboratory. Beside it was the fourth grade. Several yards away was a barracklike building, in one half of which home economics was taught, with agriculture being taught in the other half. It also served as a rotating homeroom for seniors and other classes. I knew that I was not getting the same education as the students at the white school about two miles away; and it was not even the same education that students at the black school in town received. Yet I wanted to do great things in life. How was I going to do them when I was being crippled at the start?

I had an answer. If only I could go away to boarding school, then I would be safe. I could get a good education and I would be away from my mother, who never stopped criticizing me for reading so much and other "foolishness." But though I pined away and talked about it, I knew that I couldn't go; there was no money. . . .

12

At first I didn't know any better; I thought that people all over the world washed clothes in the backyard, cooked their supper right out of the garden, churned milk and picked blackberries, got saved and were baptized, and went to church on Sunday. If the work was sheer drudgery, as undoubtedly it was, I didn't feel it as such and perhaps never would have.

But eventually I began to perceive that I was being prepared for my life's work. That's when the trouble really got bad—when I started resisting.

I am going to do great things in life, I secretly vowed.

No, you aren't, said the world around me. You're going to accept your lot just like the rest of us. Black women have always had it hard. Who are you to be so different?

Pick up your cross, said the Sunday school and church. Everyone has a cross to bear.

Black women like me have scrubbed a hundred billion miles of tiled corridors and washed an equal number of dishes. I wasn't going to do that.

I am going to live my own life, I secretly said.

No, you aren't, said an adult. I am going to see to it that you don't. You might as well get those foolish notions out of your head, girl.

That adult was my mother.

Perhaps someday someone will discover the origin of the tension that sometimes develops between black mother and black daughter, especially when the daughter is ambitious. The spark that usually set off the conflict was my interest in things literary and cultural—worthless things for a girl like me, born black in the rural segregated American South. But that was only the tip of the iceberg. Unseen but hulking huge and more deadly was the feeling that there was some basic flaw in a personality that engaged in such pursuits.

Nonnie felt bitterly resentful and rejected when I refused to subscribe to her version of reality. She had managed to project her dislike of my interests so thoroughly into my consciousness that soon I, too, felt that there was something not quite right about valuing ideas. During intermittent periods I would self-consciously cast off the raiment of intellectuality and try on the garment of black folk culture, attempting to convince myself that it was sufficient, that to want more and—even more guilt-producing—to want better was an affectation on my part.

Nevertheless, I began to hope that music would be a way out, and I conceived the idea of becoming a concert pianist. I hadn't taken music lessons for a long time, having stopped when I could play for the Sunday school and the church choir. But I would take piano lessons and practice very hard and then one day I would be a great artist. . . .

★ ★ ★

One day I was in my room lying on my bed on my stomach, turning the pages of a magazine on the floor. I liked to read this way. The room was cluttered—the bed was unmade and there were books and records and magazines everywhere.

Nonnie had had a long day at the factory, catching the bundles of tobacco as they came down the belt and cutting off the hard-tied part. (If one of the women on the line failed to turn the bundle of tobacco the right way, the knot end might go into the machine and America would have a bitter cigarette. Nonnie had a responsible job.)

"Mary!" Nonnie yelled.

At first I didn't hear her. I continued to read my book while Beethoven was playing on the record player.

"Mary!"

I put down my book and went to the kitchen.

"What is it, Mama?"

"What is the matter with you, girl?"

"What's wrong, Mama?"

"What's wrong? The okra's burned. That's what's wrong."

"I'm sorry," I said. "It's hard to fry it without burning. I cut it up like you said, but a whole lot of slime ran out; then I rolled it in flour, but I couldn't get it to brown right. I was cooking it longer, trying to make it brown, when it burned."

"You burned up the okra."

Both Nonnie and I knew that I occasionally burned up food. I often put on supper and then got a magazine and thumbed through it while the supper cooked, or started reading a book that I had gotten out of the school library or off the bookmobile that came into the county once a week. But, either way, the results were the same: scorched chicken and leatherlike fried potatoes—not often, but sometimes.

The quarrel was all the more frustrating because we both knew that it was not really about the scorched food. It was about something else, something I would neither stop doing nor apologize for. Something in me wouldn't let me. But the scene continued.

Nonnie stood there, her glasses glinting with the faint dust that all tobacco workers were covered with. Her blue uniform had dark-brown powder in the folds, and her apron, starched white in the morning, was now slightly beige from the tobacco. From her clothing came the faint smell of tobacco dust.

"The chicken's all right, isn't it, Mama?" I said.

"I'm not talking about the chicken."

"And I fixed the biscuits all right, too."

I desperately wanted my mother's approval. I wanted to do something that would make her smile at me and say, "That's good. I'm glad that you're my daughter."

"Listen when I'm talking to you, girl."

I knew that I didn't listen. I had learned the practical use of the "tune-out." When the stimuli from the outside world came in too strongly critical of what I was doing, of what I was interested in, I tuned out. The best substitute for listening was a smile. In that way my hearer didn't know that I had long ago ceased to listen. And I had a moment's peace. But Nonnie had me right where she wanted me—in the wrong, with no alibi, and she thoroughly enjoyed her position.

"And we have some nice Jell-O and I fixed some iced tea," I said. Please, just this one time say something nice, I silently prayed. Iced tea and Jello-O were my mother's favorites.

Nonnie was not to be deterred. "You somewhere with your head in a book and you let my okra burn."

"Mama, it never seems to come out right when I fry it."

"No. You don't watch it. You always got your head in a book or you listening to those old stories or you listening to that music all the time. Burned up my food."

"I'm sorry."

"I go and work hard and when I come home my food's burned."

That hurt, for I knew that my mother worked hard.

"But Mama, I got all A's on my report card this month."

Nonnie wasn't interested in extraneous issues. "And you don't wash the clothes right, either."

I was guilty. Washing and ironing, the measure of achievement for community girls, interested me not at all. For unspoken was the knowledge that these black girls were really being trained to work as domestics, not to keep house for themselves. But they and their mothers played a game that they were learning to be good housekeepers, and their mothers and the neighborhood ladies praised them for all evidence of homemaking skills.

I was later to observe that often cooks who planned, purchased, and prepared attractive menus on their job would at home serve ill-prepared, unbalanced meals. They were too tired to fix better, they said. And women who made their living cleaning and washing and ironing for other people frequently had unironed clothing piled to the ceiling at home and sat down in the midst of untidiness. They, too, were too tired.

But I hadn't trained properly. Instinct had taught me to see through that. It was a trap.

"And my teacher said that I could go far in life, Mama."

"Marguerita makes all of her own clothes." Nonnie neglected to mention that Marguerita's mother was a seamstress herself and that she took time and showed her daughter how to do things. No one took time to show me anything. Most of what I learned, I learned from books.

"And my teacher said that I was smart. You know I can't sew, Mama."

"And Miss Pearl says that Ida Mae does all of her washing and ironing."

"I'm going to play a piece at Mrs. Shearin's piano recital. She asked me to be on the program. She can't have her whole school on the program, just a few that she thinks are playing well. And she asked me to appear."

"You keep your head in a book all the time. What is the matter with you, girl?"

"Mama, I'm sorry that I can't do anything right. I'm sorry."

"No, if I ask you to cook, you hurry up. But if you get a book, you sit back in that room all day Saturday and all day Sunday, reading it. You don't go nowhere. Just sit in that room reading a book. Those old books and those old magazines. You going to end in Goldsboro, right with those other crazy people. You going to be just like Claudia's daughter. She read those books all the time and she went crazy and they sent her to Goldsboro."

"I'm sorry, Mama. I'm sorry, Mama. Sorry that I can't do anything right."

Aunt Jo had strange, big-city ways: she smoked cigarettes on the sly, used rouge, introduced strange cuisine in the household, and put unsuitable notions in my head. Getting rid of her was a long-drawn-out campaign, but Nonnie did it—Jo moved to town and shared rooms with two maiden sisters.

When she left, the light went out for me. I never knew again the warmth, feeling, and loving concern that Aunt Jo had shown for me during those years. There was no one to whisper to me about the marvelous things that I was going to accomplish or tell me that I was meant for really great things in life: dancer, pianist, college student. But the damage had been done. In her quiet, determined way, Aunt Jo had planted the seeds so deep that no one could ever uproot them.

Nevertheless, having maneuvered Jo out of the house, Nonnie set herself the task of eradicating those unsuitable notions from her daughter's head. They were nothing but foolishness and would lead Mary to nothing but trouble. She was sorry that Ruf had let Jo stay that long, bringing those Northern ideas and ways that she had learned from rich people into her home. Anything associated with Jo's notions—my being a pianist, an intellectual—she would attack; anything not done properly in the house she would severely condemn.

On my part, I was hardheaded and stubborn. And in spite of all the fussing, I would not change. I brought a book home every day and read it between the time I got home and the time I went to bed. The okra still burned, the chicken burned, and the bread burned. Not really bad, just spots here and there, and I became adept at scraping the burned places off and putting the food back into the frying pan to brown a little more. The flour for the gravy had to be attended to every minute or it would burn so bad I'd have to throw it out and start all over, and Nonnie could not tolerate whitish gravy. So, somewhere down the line I learned about paprika, and for a while produced the reddest, spiciest gravy you ever saw. But Nonnie got wise to that—I probably put in so much that she could taste it—and I learned to cook the flour a little, then use paprika a little, not so you'd notice, but enough to speed the browning time up a bit.

If my cooking was bad, my housekeeping was worse. It would take me half the night to wash the supper dishes, for if the book I was reading was a good one, I'd read a few pages, then go wash a dish or two, then go back and read a few more. The beds got "spreaded up," not made; I took the attitude, What's the difference? You're only going to sleep in them again, anyway. And as Nonnie's fussing became sharper and the negative things she said about me got worse, I hurried even more to finish the chores and get to what I really liked. Maybe I *would* go crazy and wind up in Goldsboro. Maybe I *was* an "odd" child. But I would read that book. I know now that subconsciously I was resisting her in the only way I knew how, not by saying anything but just by not doing what she valued and wanted me to value.

One Sunday morning I had just come in from Sunday school and was sitting in the kitchen, leaning back in a straight chair propped against the wall. It was a warm day; I was slightly sweaty from walking in the heat. I lost my balance and the chair I was sitting in tipped to the left. I fell in the same direction; my head and the knob on the back of the chair hit the window, cracking the pane.

"See what you done!" Nonnie said. "I told you and told you about leaning back in that chair." I was mortified. She had told me before, but what stunned me was the rage and triumph I heard in her voice.

"I'm going to make your daddy whip you. That's what you need. A good whipping! You're getting beside yourself!"

I was too stunned to answer. Aunt Jo was gone, and though my father was sick and irritable most of the time, he let me help him in the little store that he had set up near the house, and asked me to do little things for him—so I knew he liked me. Now she wanted him to turn against me, too.

I thought that there was a magical line that separated children from grown people, that when you reached a certain age you automatically stopped acting "childish"—no longer had such traits as jealousy, spitefulness, meanness—and began acting grown, which was the way the church taught. Those who didn't act that way were sinners. The church taught: "Children, obey your parents, for this is right" and "Honor thy father and mother that thy days may be long upon the land which the Lord thy God giveth thee"; . . .

But today something snapped. Something inside said, No.

"Just wait until he comes to the house. I'm going to make him whip you," she said again.

I wanted to cry, I'm a woman now, I'm not supposed to get any more whippings. But I said nothing.

I wondered about the triumphant tone that I heard in my mother's voice and then realized that it was because at last she could confront my father with something damaging about me. He and Jesse had been bitter enemies for a long time, but my mother liked Jesse, for he had been her firstborn; so it must have been galling to her to have my father talk to him mean and try to whip him—and for Jesse to run away—while he never whipped me and seldom spoke harshly to me, let me go with him everywhere, stand right by him while he poured the steps for the back porch, and ride with him when he peddled vegetables.

I made up my mind then. I would leave and I wasn't ever coming back. Talking to me like that, trying to turn my father against me . . . She wouldn't ever see me anymore.

I went out to the store and asked my father for some money. The store was full of Sunday-school children buying cold drinks and peanuts. I looked at them all dressed up, feeling that if I could get away I'd never see them again. He gave me a quarter and I left the yard, walking with a bunch that was laughing and talking and drinking their cold drinks. One by one they dropped off, but I kept walking. I was on my way to the bus line. I had never ridden the bus, but I knew where it turned around; that was about two miles away. Aunt Jo lived in town now, and so did my father's cousins, and if I could get to them, they would help me; perhaps I could stay with them. I could finish school in town and I wouldn't have to come to Wildwood anymore.

Soon I was near the highway and alone. Everybody else was at home or at a friend's house, where they had asked permission to stop. The highway was different. There were fewer houses, but I had traveled this way hundreds of times on my father's wagon. There was one house close to Wildwood, tall and two-storied, many-windowed, with flapping shutters, that I was afraid of. People said that there was a ghost in it and the ghost made noises late at night. Farther ahead were two homes, one on either side of the highway. Both of the families were rich, but they were not friends, for one family had "old" money and one family had "new" money. Hazel and her family lived with the Richardses, the family with the "old" money, on a "farm" that was really an estate. Hazel was very proud of their house. It had running water and was well kept up, for it was practically in the Richardses' yard. The Ransoms lived in a tree-shaded park, one that occupied the full time of several yard men, practically across the street from the Richardses, but Hazel liked to tell how the people her parents worked for would have nothing to do with them, for they had no "quality."

I walked on past the long hedge that separated the Ransoms' park from the highway, wondering how it must feel to live in a big house in a grove of trees, far away from the highway, never having to do anything, with a swarm of servants doing everything. Then I looked at the four-tiered white fence that surrounded the Richardses' "farm"; it took a long time to drive past it, and I knew that by the time I walked past it, I would be near the bus line.

Once when I was visiting Hazel, she proudly showed me the farm. There was a whole garage of nothing but old cars, all kinds, that used to belong to the family. Then she showed me the swimming pool and the barn where the cows were milked and the tennis courts. She was quite proud of the place; to her it was her "home."

Near the place where the Richardses' fence stopped, but across the highway, were little houses where other white people lived, those who didn't have the money that the Richardses had. Sometimes they sat on the porch and I wondered what they thought when they looked at all the Richardses had and compared it with what they had. From then on to the bus line, there were little houses, boxlike, with little lawns and hedges; the large estate and the farm were past.

When I got to the bus stop, there was no bus. I walked on, not really minding it, for the highway had become a street and now there was a sidewalk and I liked walking; so I continued, mile after mile, passing service stations, little box houses. I met a bus going to the end of the line when I was far down the street, and still I walked—past more service stations and hot-dog stands and small businesses and more houses. I felt so good that I thought that I would walk all the way in to town, thus saving my quarter.

Near the creek at the foot of Mangum Street hill a car passed me. At first I didn't notice it, but when someone yelled I looked up.

There were three or four white boys in the car. I wondered what they had said, but I didn't really pay attention, for I was getting closer and closer to town and I was preoccupied with wondering how I was going to make out. Was someone going to invite me to stay? Would my mother let me stay? Would a new life start for me? I hoped so. I knew that my father would come and get me, and maybe then I could tell him how Nonnie hurt me by talking so mean to me all the time and he would make her stop. But then he was sick all the time and dependent on her, and besides, who would feed me, clothe me, give me money to go to school? There was nobody who could but Aunt Jo, and Nonnie wouldn't, I was sure, let me stay with her. I walked along on a bright Sunday morning—it was near noon by then—hoping that things would work out all right.

Then a black car passed me again and someone threw ice on me. I was scared, for the same car had circled around and come back up on me from behind. White people—they were the evil, the danger, that existed in the world. You avoided them like snakes. I didn't know what to do. Would they harass me from then on, constantly circling and coming up from behind? I looked back and saw the bus coming. It had gone to the end of the line and waited and now was making a return trip; it was Sunday and the buses weren't running frequently. So, never having been on a bus, I stood at the foot of the hill where there was a sign that said BUS, and when it came I got on. A brief conversation with the driver got me three tokens.

I was surprised to see Nancy on the bus; she taught the little children in Sunday school. She was surprised to see me, too. I told her that I was going to town to see my folks. She soon discovered that I knew nothing about changing buses and getting a transfer, and told me how and where to change. I went to the front and got the little pink transfer and got off at Walgreen's at Main Street.

I got to West Durham all right. I was proud of myself for finding the way, the first time on my own. I went to see Aunt Jo, but I felt so sad, for she was living in a small dark room in a house with two unmarried sisters. She didn't like it; I had heard her tell my mother that once. She asked me about everybody and I said they were all right, but I knew that she knew that something was wrong, because I had come alone. I wanted to tell her so much and I started to several times—that I wanted to come to town to live, maybe even stay with her; but I felt so bad that I would be letting her down, for she held me up as a model to her nieces and nephews, and if they knew I was running away from home it would make her look bad for having so much faith in me. I couldn't make the words come out. So we sat and talked, awkwardly, for we hadn't been alone in a long time. She spoke again of education. I must get an education.

I didn't know it then, but she was already dying of cancer. Marva, my older cousin, who lived across the street from Aunt Jo, was surprised to see me, and her daughter Jerline barely spoke—though she had been to visit us in the country—and an older male cousin took the extra token that I had put in a dish on the coffee table. I saw him take it, but he was grown and I was scared to say "Don't."

In the late afternoon I started back home. I rode the bus downtown all right, but at Five Points I didn't know how to change buses and was too scared to ask; so I started walking right on Main Street, in the heart of Durham. I walked the eight miles home.

Near the bus line Jesse met me; he was on his way to town. "Mama's gonna whip you!" He laughed in that special way he had when something bad was going to happen to somebody. I said nothing, but walked on. It was soon deep night. Wildwood was dark and quiet when I got back, with a light here and there. I passed no one.

Nonnie was angry and I was defiant. She got her switches to whip me, but I started yelling that I was going to leave again and I wasn't coming back. She did a lot of fussing, but she hit me only a time or two. I knew that I had won, for I never got another whipping. I had learned the value of protest. And I, too, put my soul on ice. I had to, if I was to survive. . . .

SHIRLEY ABBOTT
(1934—)

◆

SHIRLEY ABBOTT grew up in Hot Springs, Arkansas, and moved north to New York City after college. She has been a Fulbright scholar, an editor at *Horizon* magazine, a contributor to *Harper's, American Heritage,* and *Esquire,* the author of several books about food and antiques, and a writer for a health newsletter. The selection that follows is taken from her book *Womenfolks: Growing Up Down South* (1983), a rich blend of personal memoir and meditation on family myth and tradition. Inspired in part by feminism, she offers a moving retrospective of the mother-daughter bond as well as a tribute to the ancestral Scotch-Irish female pioneers of her family. She writes about these Southern women, present and past, with such insight and compassion that we feel until *Womenfolks* we've scarcely read anything true about the American South. It is as if we are seeing the place and its people whole for the first time. That is because Abbott invents her regional life history from the ground up. "We are all part of daily life," she has said, "which is history's foundation. I learned to respect and love history from having been born a Southerner. I draw my identity from that region, even though I have lived most of my life in New York. To come from a definable place and to seek an understanding of that place are incentives for the writer's imagination." In her second memoir of coming of age in Arkansas, *The Bookmaker's Daughter: A Memory Unbound,* she examines her difficult relationship with the most important man in her young life, her gambling, book-loving father, "Hat" Abbott. In *Listen to Their Voices: Twenty Interviews with Women Who Write,* Abbott suggests the connection between the writer's act of uncovering and writing her past and her readers: The writing of memoir, as she tells her interviewer Mickey Pearlman, depends on "trying to examine my past in such a way that it will have value for other people and will help other people examine their own past." In the same interview Abbott says that "all fiction may be autobiography, but all autobiography is of course fiction. I try very hard in [*The Bookmaker's Daughter*] to describe that process that my father taught me: He always lived by stories. Everything was a narrative. That's why we had dinner: It wasn't to eat; It was so we could tell these stories." In "Why Southern Women Leave

Home," Abbott shows her family's and her region's mythology converging on issues of race and gender to enact a complex legacy of oppression and freedom.

From *Womenfolks: Growing Up Down South*

EIGHT
Why Southern Women Leave Home

I have left the South twice in my life. The first time was against my will. When I was nine, my father decided that we had to move to California. He had somehow managed, long distance, to get himself a job as a machinist at the Navy dry dock on North Island in San Diego Bay. (Though I knew he could have dealt a dice table at Las Vegas, this was the first I had heard that he could handle battleship engines.) His essential homelessness had laid hold of him as it periodically did. He was sick of figuring bets in the casino, sick of Arkansas and the interminable Southern depression that had barely lifted even in the biggest of all wartime booms. He was determined to transplant us.

So one August, sweating like horses in our new wool traveling suits, we got on the train in Hot Springs station, with a number of trunks and suitcases, for the short run to Little Rock. There we made connections with the Choctaw Rocket, the Santa Fe's crack passenger train. Daddy knew the name of every class A train in the country and had promised me rides on all of them from the Twentieth Century Limited to the City of San Francisco. However, the Choctaw Rocket turned out to be the first and the last, for in six months we were back home. My mother and I were not transplantable.

The months in San Diego I recall in the same way I remember the bout of scarlet fever I had had a year earlier—pain and delirium mixed with boredom. In that easy port city of no discernible seasons or traditions, a tepid harbor accustomed to the ways of soldiers and sailors and the rootless and the drifting, we wore the mark of our origins too clearly. We set off every antibody in the local immune system. I might as well have been Daisy Mae Yokum from Smackover. In San Diego, I realized for the first time that some people didn't think Southerners were human. In *Sophie's Choice,* William Styron, as an emigré from North Carolina, describes how he evoked a similar reaction from Sophie's Brooklyn lover, who took him for a racist. But these Californians were just ordinary folks hating Southerners for the sport of it, back in the days before anybody cared what whites were doing to blacks.

Southerners were Arkies, Okies, clay eaters, hicks, tramps—creatures straight out of *Grapes of Wrath* and *God's Little Acre,* novels accursed under my father's roof, though at that moment he had none. To the tearful astonishment of my mother, landladies refused to rent to us. "Don't want any cracker folks around here," one said, and others shut the door as soon as we opened our mouths. Housing was scarce enough, even for people from Boston. It took us weeks to find a place to live. I set off to the local school, expecting that within a week or so I'd have installed myself, as usual, as teacher's pet. But they treated me like a yokel. Contemptuous of my hair ribbons and scrupulously ironed puffed sleeves, the principal actually checked me for head lice. A little boy asked me if I had hookworm. Were those my first pair of shoes?

Back in Arkansas in this epoch teachers harbored flat board paddles in their desks and practiced corporal punishment with grim delight. Nobody had ever hit me, but I had watched little boys undergo brutal whackings. The beatings, of course, made outlaws out of the mischievous children and prigs out of people like me, but in any case I took school very seriously and did not want to weave baskets or make pots. The California schools then were in some sort of proto-counterculture or hippie phase. Fourth grade spent most of the day doing crafts. I wanted to do long division, but these breezy young teachers wouldn't even give us homework, let alone grades. I began to put on airs and make supercilious remarks about the lack of report cards. While my classmates wove rush mats, I'd do sums or disassemble my Mickey Mouse watch.

Needless to say, I had no friends. One tropical January afternoon, to my surprise, a little girl invited me to come climb the fig trees in back of her house, two or three blocks from ours. I stayed until sunset, for the fig trees and the companionship were sweet. I thought I might like California. But then I asked permission to go indoors to the bathroom. My friend led me toward the kitchen window and called to her mother. A pink face with black curls blossoming all around it, like a bisque doll, leaned out through the fluttering curtains. Later I persistently remembered a satin bow tied under the chin but that is sheer malice. "Mommy," said my playmate, "this is the kid from Arkansas. Can she come in and use the toilet?" I went indoors. Inside the facility, as I began to wash my hands, I heard a commotion in the kitchen, and the mother's voice floated through the bathroom door: "How dare you bring that little hillbilly in here to dirty up my nice bath?" As I stood thoughtfully drying my hands, I noticed that I had made black hand prints all over the guest towel. I fled without saying good-bye, although any self-respecting hillbilly would have gone in the kitchen and beat the lady up.

Not long after that we went home. Mother had broken out in hives, and I was wan from nightmares. But California was not a wholly destructive experience. It taught me that, for some reason I had never before suspected, the South was alien, and you paid a price for coming from it. Everybody must learn this lesson somewhere—that it costs something to be what you are. I concluded that being a hillbilly was better than having no identifiable origins at all. Back on my home ground, however, taking some kind of long-range, baleful revenge against those Californians, I became a blind Southern chauvinist, beyond the wildest hopes of my father. This was when I began main-lining Margaret Mitchell, and I read volume upon volume of other partisan stuff, local colorists by the peck. The public library stocked mostly historical novels, and I read enough of these to have induced irreversible coma in a more mature brain. I even sent off to an out-of-print book supplier for Thomas Dixon's unutterable old screed, *The Clansman,* about the brave knights of the KKK. I nodded sagely as he spoke of preserving civilization in the face of the Black Menace. Ah, the Lost Cause. My head reeled with clanking swords, passionate planters, beautiful barren brides who finally managed to produce an heir to the fine old name, French kisses under Spanish moss, duels, cavalry officers, the works.

Many years and a hundred novels later, I came upon a passage in *Madame Bovary* describing the education of the heroine at a convent in mid-nineteenth-century France. The nuns carefully shielded the young ladies from any solid fact and poured on the gooey elixir of religious sentimentality. Saints, candles, heavenly bridegrooms, pious renunciations, swoonings, tears. Emma lapped it up. Flaubert clearly knew every detail of it and understood in his merciless way that adolescent women, like rhinoceroses, adore cooling their tender skins in emotionally comfortable mudholes, but that unlike rhinoceroses, they may one day be required to stand up and walk out.

Sometime, probably in my early teens, I began dimly to grasp that the glorious Southland was not what I had taken it to be. Worse than that, I was not what I had taken myself to be. I had no moment of blinding revelation. I was like an idiot trying to learn chess: each new discovery puzzled me. I do recall one autumn afternoon when I stood among the thin ranks of boosters lining Central Avenue to watch the Hot Springs High homecoming parade. Here came the marching band, all done up in black and gold, stepping smartly and playing off key as usual, followed by several convertiblefuls of princesses and queens. My girlfriends sighed with envy, but I could not manage the sigh of envy. It was a replay of my one-on-one bout with salvation in the Baptist church. I wanted to have the right feelings, but I couldn't. And then—how had they got invited?—came the marching band from Langston High, where the black kids went to school. They also played football, though not with us. Their band stepped smartly, too, and also sounded sour, which was perhaps pardonable since some of the marchers had no instruments. None of them had uniforms. They marched along in their old clothes.

Right there on the sidewalk my regional identity started to unravel. In spite of my years of rigorous training at the hands of Miss Mitchell and Mr. Dixon and the rest, I could see I wasn't turning out right. Or else the South wasn't turning out right. I began desperately trying to figure out which. The conclusion I finally reached—ambiguous as it was—drove me out of my homeland forever.

There is a whole subdivision of sociology that has devoted itself to proving that Southern society is as caste ridden as that of the Hindu, rigidly stratified by economics and by color. John Dollard's *Caste and Class in a Southern Town,* a famous work of the 1930s that is still in print, argued the point persuasively. And certainly the news, in the 1960s, of the murders of civil rights workers in Mississippi, of the bombings of black churches in Birmingham, of riots in Selma and recalcitrance in Prince Edward Country, Virginia, seemed to confirm what men like Dollard had said. Ironically, what the sociologists believed about the inviolability of the color bar was exactly what the militant segregationists wanted the outside world to believe.

But where I grew up, in darkest Arkansas, things were not ordered so neatly. There was a kind of caste system. There was segregation and a color bar. No black had the slightest hope of getting a decent education or becoming a professional. Yet such things were out of the question for most whites, too. Most of us were uniformly poor, regardless of race or creed, and tried to get along with one another without making up too many theories. It was a racist system but far less systematic than outsiders supposed.

In my own family we never used any kind of racist vocabulary. My mother would not have allowed it. According to her, pretty was as pretty did. Nobody was superior. Well, perhaps people who obeyed the law were superior to criminals, but I never heard her assert that white people as a group had any cause to feel superior to blacks.

In some situations, there was racial mixing. Hospitals, for example, hired both blacks and whites as lower-echelon help. They ate in the same dining room, and when they passed on the street, they stopped to chat, right out in the open. From our side of the fence it all seemed peaceful and right. We never stopped to think how it looked from the other side.

And yet it was all a hoax, a delicate scrim that hid—at least from me—what was really happening on the stage. In 1954, after segregated schools were declared unconstitutional, the harsh undercurrents of white supremacist thinking—hidden for so long under good manners and intellectual laziness and the unwillingness of both races to confront the truth—surfaced with terrifying force. Neighbors of ours, even relatives, kindly people I had known all my life, began to air their ugly feelings, taking it for granted that we would be of the same mind. Friends who used to drop by on a Sunday to talk fishing and politics now spent the afternoon on hot talk about integration.

Acts of bloodshed were apparently in store. Any observations of mine to the contrary were quickly shushed up by my parents. Where, I wondered, had all these bigots and sadists come from—so many, so angry? Raised from childhood on my mother's ideas of decency and common courtesy and my father's partisanship for the losing side, I had naturally concluded that integration of the schools was a fine idea, a splendid idea—high time for it. Why didn't everybody agree with me?

But alas, I can hardly claim that civil rights was the issue uppermost in my mind. Another, far stronger sense of dislocation began to overwhelm me. The closer I got to becoming a grown woman, the more inhospitable my homeland looked to me. Never having been picked as homecoming queen, I became class valedictorian, and then I went to spend four years in a women's college in east Texas, which proved to be an excellent place to contemplate the Southern feminine mystique.

East Texas, and my college in particular, were on the cusp between the West and the South. About half the students were Southerners from Louisiana and Arkansas and Mississippi, as well as the farm country of east Texas (with a few city girls from Houston and Dallas mixed in), but the rest were Texans from the high plains, and they were noticeably different from the rest of us. They were a wilder, stronger breed: beside them we Southerners looked positively dainty. They were unfeminized. They had no interest in clothes, wore their hair cropped, slept late on Sunday mornings while we were putting on our pretty little hats and waiting for the bus to go to Sunday school. (Southern Baptists go to Sunday school, or can go, from babyhood to old age.) They all played golf and tennis, fenced like masters, and had won their life-saving badges, apparently, while still in grammar school. I was frightened to death of them, but I envied them, too, because along with their life-saving badges, they seemed to have earned some magic exemption from the fate the college clearly had in mind for most of us: it wanted to turn us Southern girls into Southern ladies.

Unlike Sweet Briar or Randolph Macon and most other Southern women's colleges, Texas State College for Women had never been a female seminary or finishing school for upper-class girls. It had begun in 1903 as an industrial arts school whose mission was teaching the daughters of the poor to earn a living. When I was there, the architecture was traditional red-brick Georgian, and there was a decent liberal arts overlay to the vocational courses. But though there had never been anything remotely aristocratic about it, it was run on the Southern pattern. Gracious living was our motto and our goal. We were forbidden to be seen outdoors in blue jeans or to smoke in dormitory living rooms or other locations "where gentlemen were likely to call," in the hopeful phrase of the student handbook. Not even seniors were permitted to stay out after one, and any student who drank so much as a glass of beer could be expelled. If we had been the virginal daughters of the finest families in antebellum Savannah, our morals could hardly have been the object of more solicitude.

Yet, in fact, we were almost all first-generation college students, the daughters of farmers, white collar workers, and merchants who had sent us to this place because the tuition was cheap and the curriculum practical. Hardly one of us stood any chance of becoming a lady, but all except the most rebellious among us submissively studied the ladylike arts in anticipation of what the Dean of Women told us was "woman's only true career," marriage and motherhood. I could not help noting that the Dean of Women herself and most of the faculty were single. In any case, learning to pour tea and refraining from smoking in the living room and obeying the myriad puritanical rules that the college had devised for us did not appear to me to have much connection with marriage and motherhood.

Nor did the beauty contests. I could not understand at the time why a women's college would have beauty contests, but there they were, eight or nine of them each year. This was all part of our training, as if we were some kind of bush-league boot camp for the Miss America Pageant. We were the sister college of Texas A & M, at a safe distance of two hundred miles, and we elected several "maids," from among whom the Aggie Corps Captains selected a Sweetheart. (She had to go to all the Aggie games and stand and holler. It was against the rules for anybody, including spectators, to sit down while the team was on the field.) That was our first job each year. Then we chose a beauty from each class and an all school beauty. The winners were announced in a special assembly, and they all had full-page pictures in the yearbook, in formals and elbow-length white gloves. We also elected a Cotton Queen and her court, and a Posture Queen, whose uptilted bosom and under-tucked buttocks were to be our physical ideal. One year we even chose a Black-eyed Pea Queen, but what her function in life was I never discovered.

The best part was the Redbud Pageant, which revolved around an elected Queen and an enormous entourage of princesses, each of whom curtseyed at center stage in a cloud of pastel net as her name was uttered into a microphone—"Princess Betsy of the house of Allen" and so on—until after a weary couple of hours the end of the alphabet had been reached. Outside the administration building stood a massive statue of a pioneer woman, a strapping old party in a sunbonnet and L'il Abner shoes who was supposed to represent the spirit of the school. I often wondered why she didn't lumber across campus and burst into the Redbud Festival like Don Juan's Stone Guest, confounding all the princesses and sending the Dean of Women to hell through a trapdoor. What on earth were these rehearsals for? Obviously the final triumph for all us Princess So-and-So's was to be the wedding march. White gloves and tulle for the very last time.

I was growing increasingly pessimistic about my chances of finding a place for myself in Southern life. Outside the walls, the crisis over public school integration was building ominously. Inside, as though none of it applied to us, we maidens were industriously preparing for our futures. I was, of course, going to be a teacher, like all good girls in those days—the perfect career for a wife who might want to work, just to help her husband out, but who would certainly not want to be out of the home when her children were there.

I had no aptitude for teaching, but it sounded better than being a nurse or an occupational therapist or a nutritionist or any other possibilities offered. I spent a whole semester devising a set of lesson plans on *Macbeth,* which I was supposed to foist off on a hypothetical roomful of students as a work relevant to their daily concerns. I could not see what *Macbeth* had to do with anybody's daily life, unless we all intended to become assassins, and I could not imagine perpetrating such a fraud. That surely couldn't be steady work.

Worse than that, unlike most young women my age I was lacking not only in suitors but also in any desire to marry. I trembled when the Dean of Women spoke of this sacred mission. I didn't want a sacred mission. Oh, maybe someday, as long as it wasn't too sacred and didn't entail "helping out" by teaching *Macbeth* as if it were Hints from Heloise. None of these thoughts, of course, would be so great a solecism now as then. And even then I might have gotten away with it had

I not been so intent on making an issue of it. As Scarlett's Mammy was in the habit of saying, Southern girls of nineteen who are in need of husbands are not expected to make an issue of anything. They are supposed to be sweet-natured and tactful and to remind themselves that more flies can be caught with honey than with buttermilk.

Somehow my once-comfortable environment had been sucked through a black hole and turned into a foreign land. My immune system was working overtime again. One stifling afternoon during summer vacation before my senior year, I announced my various disinclinations to my closest relatives. My mother, my cousin June, my aunt Vera, and I still functioned as the solid bloc we had been since my childhood. June was now married and had a daughter, whom we loved all the more because she was a girl and could fit right into this proto-feminist cell of ours, this oasis where no man was admitted and where male foibles were often under examination.

We were, on this particular afternoon, at my cousin's house. The baby was napping, and since the only electric fan had been set up to blow in the direction of her crib, we made ourselves tall glasses of iced tea and sat in the backyard shade. The temperature was 105, which was nothing unusual, and the ice in the tea had melted before we got out the back door. My mother collected the laundry from the clothesline and began to fold it, pouring sweat. The grass had grown ankle high overnight and made my feet itch. There were some chiggers, too, which raised vicious little welts on my legs. A desolate boredom, more frightening than the Sahara, illimitable as the Empty Quarter of Arabia, came over me. I was sick of all this. I did not wish to be next in line to supply an heiress for this society and a back yard for it to meet in. I wanted out—of everything, permanently. I burst out saying so, in words that I cannot recall but which had the effect of nitroglycerine.

A loud and angry discussion followed, and we all began weeping. My mother wept first out of fright. What would become of me? My cousin took her part, as always, for by temperament they were more truly mother and child than Mother and I were. My aunt tried, as usual, to defend me, for like me she was a malcontent, and we often made common cause. But the best she could muster was a prediction that I would come around to another way of thinking. She was right, though on that dreadful day none of us had much expectation of it. In a rage, and on the verge of heatstroke, I began to cry, too. I knew that the only solution was to leave them—these women I loved in my body and bones—and seek my people in another country. And so one day the next spring, I did. After writing my last final exam, I packed up and headed out on a round-trip plane ticket, the other half of which I promptly cashed in as soon as I got to New York.

I did not know it, but I was part of a vast northward exodus. "I ain't good-lookin', and I doan dress fine, but I'm a travelin' woman with a travelin' mind," sang Bessie Smith many years ago, with portents both spiritual and sexual. Every year—and long before Bessie—the South has produced its small quota of travelin' women who dread the high cost of living and dying in Dixie and find they have to depart. Like many other Southern phenomena, the northward exodus has a past, rooted back in the hard earth and with special meanings for women. . . .

What lay in waiting for me at the other end of that plane ticket was a number of surprises. In the late 1950s, Southerners were still an oddity in New York, or at least white ones were. Even at large gatherings, I would be the only person with a Southern accent, and I got used to hearing people exclaim, "My God, I never met anybody from Arkansas before in my life." It was rather like being a Hottentot, but pleasantly so. At first I liked being the token Arkie. Then I discovered that all New Yorkers automatically assumed that all Southerners were lynch-mob veterans. Their hostility was usually fairly restrained, but I did have to recite my little loyalty oath: no, I had never been to a cross burning, and yes, my sentiments toward black people were entirely correct.

For a while I truly believed that theirs and mine were correct. My doubts began to take shape one day as I stood in a gallery of the Metropolitan Museum of Art surrounded by a group of well-dressed people who were eager to know what Harlem looked like and had come to an exhibition of photographs to find out. We all stood there in semidarkness as the slide projector flashed scene after scene from 125th Street, forty blocks north of the Museum. We were like Methodists at missionary circle, gawking at pictures from farthest Cathay.

At the time I was working at a publishing house where everybody was passionate about civil rights. We all sent donations to Martin Luther King and Stokely Carmichael, yet there was not one black face among us. Many of us belonged to a group that did, in fact, set foot in Harlem once a week to take part in tutoring high school students. But the gap between the races in New York City was a canyon of ice. In Alabama, people were engaging in hand-to-hand combat, which at least was newsworthy. I felt a little foolish sometimes, sitting opposite a pair of incredulous black teen-agers and explaining (in my redneck accent) how to conjugate irregular French verbs.

By then I had also wised up to the fact that to be female as well as Southern was construed as evidence of slow wits. New Yorkers assumed you were stupid, the way Californians had assumed you were diseased. I systematically reformed my speech, patterning my vowels after the typical Vassar graduate's, or as near as I could get, vainly hoping no one would find me out. Anything I had to do seemed worth it, such was my relief at finding asylum and being allowed to live in a milieu where being both unmarried and educated were not crippling disqualifications for a woman.

As escapes go, mine was ambivalent and scarcely final. I soon discovered that the mystique that drove me out—the ideal of the Southern lady—was not peculiar to the South at all, simply more flamboyantly expressed there. And in any case, it was a sort of phony overlay to begin with—the real feminine mystique of the South lay with those strong women, those drowned women of the farm and the frontier. As for racism, the Northerner brand is in some ways even less palatable than the Southern. "It isn't that we would dislike having black children in our schools," a suburban P.T.A. member remarked to me recently. "It's just that black families can't afford to buy property in this area." Are the ghettos of New York any different from what used to be called "nigger towns" of the South—except for being dirtier, more dangerous, and even more utterly walled off from the white world?

And so I have been drawn back, for brief spaces, to my homeplace, and unlike the truly displaced, I have had the chance to hang on to my cultural identity, picky about it though I have been, and to watch the fortunes of my native place fall and rise again, as they have done in the past years. From afar I watched the South remake itself (without any aid from me) nearer to my childhood image of it: a benevolent place where the outward and sometimes even the inward forms of courtesy are scrupulously observed, where people remember your grandpa with respect even though he was a chicken farmer, where there was enough decency left, after the violence ran itself out, to rebuild the Southern school system. I have had the joy of keeping in touch, of going back to the family reunions, the weddings, the funerals (which have their peculiar joy too), of showing my children where I came from and offering them the chance to love what I love. Not many refugees have such luck.

Lately I go home in panic, for fear the South is gone. According to the news magazines, the solid block of eccentricity that lives within the boundaries of the old Confederate states has been gerrymandered into a rich, bland, hateful thing called the Sunbelt, which runs from Miami Beach to Arizona and, if my painful recollection is correct, even includes Colorado and New Mexico. But when I go home, it always calms me to see that Southern cities, however slick and new, don't quite seem citified.

While the South is not as slow and introverted and land-locked as it once was, it has not vanished. The plantation South has all but disappeared, and all traces of the frontier South will soon be gone—the dirt road leading to a house with a wood stove and an oak table piled high with cornbread and fried okra, or whatever reality and symbol one grasps at. Ten years from now, perhaps they will give up opening the old churchhouses on Decoration Day. They may stop weeding the graves and decorating the headstones with plastic roses or bothering to remember the middle names of a second cousin's five children. The frontier will nevertheless survive in the attitudes a few of us inherited from it. One of those attitudes—to me a beatitude—is the conviction that the past matters, that history weighs on us and refuses to be forgotten by us, and that the worst poverty women—or men—can suffer is to be bereft of their past.

JOAN DIDION
(1934—)

◆

Novelist, essayist, journalist, and screenwriter JOAN DIDION was born in Sacramento, California, in the sixth generation of a family claiming to have traveled with the Donner Party. She majored in English at the University of California at Berkeley and edited its literary magazine. After winning a literary prize for college seniors from *Vogue* magazine, she was invited to work for *Vogue* in New York City. She also wrote on a free-lance basis for the *National Review* and *Mademoiselle* before taking a leave of absence to finish her first novel, *Run River* (1963), which established her reputation as "a fantastically brilliant writer," to quote *Esquire*. A reviewer in *Newsweek* wrote that "Joan Didion's honesty, intelligence, and skill are wonders to behold." Following the publication of her novel she married the writer John Gregory Dunne and returned to California. Her subsequent books include two collections of essays, *Slouching Toward Bethlehem* (1968)—"a rich display of some of the best prose written today" to quote Dan Wakefield—and *The White Album* (1979), from which the following piece is taken; *Salvador* (1983), a book-length essay based on a visit to war-torn El Salvador; *Miami* (1987), a study of Cuban exiles in Florida; and the novels *Play It As It Lays* (1971), which was nominated for a National Book Award, *A Book of Common Prayer* (1977), and *Democracy* (1984).

A prolific and highly praised writer, Didion explained why she writes in her Regents' Lecture at the University of California at Berkeley, reprinted in Janet Sternburg's *The Writer on Her Work*:

"In many ways writing is the act of saying *I*, of imposing oneself upon other people, of saying *listen to me, see it my way, change your mind.* It's an aggressive, even a hostile act. You can disguise its aggressiveness all you want with veils of subordinate clauses and qualifiers and tentative subjunctives, with ellipses and evasions—with the whole manner of intimating rather than claiming, of alluding rather than stating—but there's no getting around the fact that setting words on paper is the tactic of a secret bully, an invasion, an imposition of the writer's sensibility on the reader's most private space."

Didion told Linda Kuehl in an interview published in *The Paris Review Interviews* that though she wrote stories as a little girl, she didn't want to be a writer. She wanted to become an actress. "I didn't realize then that it's the same impulse. It's make-believe. It's performance." In *The White Album* she said, "We tell ourselves stories in order to live." At Berkeley, she remembers she began to understand "what writing was about, what it was for" with the help of her teacher Mark Schorer. When asked whether any writer influenced her more than others, Didion replies "Hemingway, because he taught me how sentences worked."

Didion lives now in New York City.

From *The White Album*

On the Morning After the Sixties

I am talking here about being a child of my time. When I think about the Sixties now I think about an afternoon not of the Sixties at all, an afternoon early in my sophomore year at Berkeley, a bright autumn Saturday in 1953. I was lying on a leather couch in a fraternity house (there had been a lunch for the alumni, my date had gone on to the game, I do not now recall why I had stayed behind), lying there alone reading a book by Lionel Trilling and listening to a middle-aged man pick out on a piano in need of tuning the melodic line to "Blue Room." All that afternoon he sat at the piano and all that afternoon he played "Blue Room" and he never got it right. I can hear and see it still, the wrong note in "We will thrive on/Keep alive on," the sunlight falling through the big windows, the man picking up his drink and beginning again and telling me, without ever saying a word, something I had not known before about bad marriages and wasted time and looking backward. That such an afternoon would now seem implausible in every detail—the idea of having had a "date" for a football lunch now seems to me so exotic as to be almost czarist—suggests the extent to which the narrative on which many of us grew up no longer applies.

The distance we have come from the world in which I went to college was on my mind quite a bit during those seasons when not only Berkeley but dozens of other campuses were periodically shut down, incipient battlegrounds, their borders sealed. To think of Berkeley as it was in the Fifties was not to think of barricades and reconstituted classes. "Reconstitution" would have sounded to us then like Newspeak, and barricades are never personal. We were all very personal then, sometimes relentlessly so, and, at that point where we either act or do not act, most of us are still. I suppose I am talking about just that:

the ambiguity of belonging to a generation distrustful of political highs, the historical irrelevancy of growing up convinced that the heart of darkness lay not in some error of social organization but in man's own blood. If man was bound to err, then any social organization was bound to be in error. It was a premise which still seems to me accurate enough, but one which robbed us early of a certain capacity for surprise.

At Berkeley in the Fifties no one was surprised by anything at all, a *donnée* which tended to render discourse less than spirited, and debate nonexistent. The world was by definition imperfect, and so of course was the university. There was some talk even then about IBM cards, but on balance the notion that free education for tens of thousands of people might involve automation did not seem unreasonable. We took it for granted that the Board of Regents would sometimes act wrongly. We simply avoided those students rumored to be FBI informers. We were that generation called "silent," but we were silent neither, as some thought, because we shared the period's official optimism nor, as others thought, because we feared its official repression. We were silent because the exhilaration of social action seemed to many of us just one more way of escaping the personal, of masking for a while that dread of the meaningless which was man's fate.

To have assumed that particular fate so early was the peculiarity of my generation. I think now that we were the last generation to identify with adults. That most of us have found adulthood just as morally ambiguous as we expected it to be falls perhaps into the category of prophecies self-fulfilled: I am simply not sure. I am telling you only how it was. The mood of Berkeley in those years was one of mild but chronic "depression," against which I remember certain small things that seemed to me somehow explications, dazzling in their clarity, of the world I was about to enter: I remember a woman picking daffodils in the rain one day when I was walking in the hills. I remember a teacher who drank too much one night and revealed his fright and bitterness. I remember my real joy at discovering for the first time how language worked, at discovering, for example, that the central line of *Heart of Darkness* was a postscript. All such images were personal, and the personal was all that most of us expected to find. We would make a separate peace. We would do graduate work in Middle English, we would go abroad. We would make some money and live on a ranch. We would survive outside history, in a kind of *idée fixe* referred to always, during the years I spent at Berkeley, as "some little town with a decent beach."

As it worked out I did not find or even look for the little town with the decent beach. I sat in the large bare apartment in which I lived my junior and senior years (I had lived awhile in a sorority, the Tri Delt house, and had left it, typically, not over any "issue" but because I, the implacable "I," did not like living with sixty people) and I read Camus and Henry James and I watched a flowering plum come in and out of blossom and at night, most nights, I walked outside and looked up to where the cyclotron and the bevatron glowed on the dark hillside, unspeakable mysteries which engaged me, in the style of my time, only personally. Later I got out of Berkeley and went to New York and later I got out of New York and came to Los Angeles. What I have made for myself is personal, but is not exactly peace. Only one person I knew at Berkeley later discovered an ideology, dealt himself into history, cut himself loose from both his own dread and his own time. A few of the people I knew at Berkeley killed themselves not long after. Another attempted suicide in Mexico and then, in a recovery which seemed in many ways a more advanced derangement, came home and joined the Bank of America's three-year executive-training program. Most of us live less theatrically, but remain the survivors of a peculiar and inward time. If I could believe that going to a barricade would affect man's fate in the slightest I would go to that barricade, and quite often I wish that I could, but it would be less than honest to say that I expect to happen upon such a happy ending.

1970

Barbara Grizzuti Harrison
(1934—)

─────◆─────

Journalist, essayist, memoirist, and travel writer, BARBARA GRIZ-
ZUTI HARRISON grew up in Bensonhurst, New York, attended
New Utrecht High School, lived in India and North Africa with her
husband, and returned to Brooklyn as a divorced single mother, where
she raised her two children. She has contributed as a journalist to the
New Republic, the *Nation,* the *New York Times Book Review, Harper's,
Ms.,* and the *Village Voice.* Her books include *Unlearning the Lie: Sexism
in School* (1969), *Visions of Glory; A History and a Memory of Jehovah's
Witnesses* (1978), *Off Center: Essays* (1980), *Foreign Bodies* (1984), a
novel, *Italian Days* (1989), a travel book-and-memoir, and *The Astonishing World* (1992). Harrison's nonfiction combines a tough-minded
journalism with autobiography. Her Bensonhurst Italian background
figures prominently in much of her work; indeed it is the personal
context of her reflections on present-day racism in "Women and
Blacks and Bensonhurst," the autobiographical essay from *The Astonishing World,* reprinted here. Her judgment calls, expressing a strong
sense of moral and social justice, often derive from her personal experience as a mother or a lifelong savvy city woman. She is a feminist
who knows her own mind. "The judgments I make," she writes, "are
the person I am."

When Harrison was nine years old, she converted, under her
mother's influence, to the Jehovah's Witnesses, the experience she
describes in her memoir, *Visions of Glory.* She was a devoted disciple,
but at the age of twenty-one she renounced the faith. Her book portrays the Witnesses as sexist, racist, and totalitarian; it also shows their
kindness and courage as a community of outsiders. Harrison's personal
testimony is fair—reviewers have often commented on her integrity
and emotional honesty—though, more than twenty years later when
she was writing the book, her rejection of the fundamentalist dispensation was absolute. Influenced by the writings of the theologian and
mystic Teilhard de Chardin as well as her love of her Italian heritage,
she embraced Roman Catholicism while writing the conclusion of
Visions of Glory.

Her most highly acclaimed book to date is set in Italy, an autobiographical travel journal in search of herself and the world of her parents and ancestors. Reviewing *Italian Days* in the *New York Times Book Review,* Eva Hoffman called it the encounter of a sensibility that is as "tolerant, evocative and heterogeneous as the culture it describes." "Superior in scope and spirituality to Luigi Barzini's *The Italians,*" wrote another reviewer. Of her latest book, *The Astonishing World,* one critic praised it as the work of "that rare writer who can celebrate with intelligence and without embarrassment." Asked by an interviewer where she studied writing, Harrison replied, "I didn't. I never went to college. . . . I got it (writing) the way you learn to walk, which is by doing it. . . . If anybody asked me the single best thing I've ever done for my writing, I would have to say that it was to have two children. They keep you honest, they keep you fresh, and they do provide a discipline. . . . I like the idea of cooking meals for them, I like being anchored in that way."

From *The Astonishing World*

Women and Blacks and Bensonhurst (1990)

On August 23, 1989, a sixteen-year-old black youth, Yusuf K. Hawkins, was shot to death in Bensonhurst, an almost entirely white section of Brooklyn, allegedly by Joseph Fama, a brain-damaged, neurologically impaired high school dropout with a "low normal" IQ of 72 and the academic achievement of a second to fifth-grade child. According to the prosecution, Hawkins was confronted by about thirty white youths, some of them carrying baseball bats. Fama, eighteen, and Keith Mondello, nineteen, have been charged with intentional murder. Four other whites are charged with "depraved indifference to human life" and "acting in concert with other persons" to kill Yusuf Hawkins. On September 18, pleas of Not Guilty were entered for all defendants.

Keith Mondello was once the boyfriend of eighteen-year-old Gina Feliciano, whose father, no longer living, was Puerto Rican. Feliciano, who is under round-the-clock police protection and is expected to be a key witness for the prosecution, favored black and Hispanic boyfriends; interviewed on "60 Minutes," she was not at all reluctant to talk about her preferences.

One of the defense attorneys, Benjamin Brafman, questioned why the district attorney's office had not sought to indict Feliciano, whom he called an "instigating force" in the attack.

"Was she down there and did she fire a shot? Was she armed with a baseball bat?" Judge Thaddeus Owens asked. She wasn't; but it is more than a defense strategy to implicate Feliciano: it is the prevailing feeling in Bensonhurst that she was responsible for the killing of a man.

My friend Biagio, who was brought up there, as was I, says the thing he misses most about Bensonhurst is the honeysuckle. "And pig's rind," he says. Pig's skin, pink-white and waxy, is stuffed with pine nuts and raisins and garlic and parsley, and rolled and tied with string and put—along with sweet and hot sausages, fresh pork shoulder, chuck beef, and chicken—into the "gravy," the tomato sauce for pasta. . . . Of course we never used the food-trendy word *pasta* in Bensonhurst; *macaronies* was our generic term, macaronies and gravy our Sunday ritual. . . . The pork rind gets gelatinous in the gravy, chewy, fragrant. . . .

Sometimes Biagio and I go back to Bensonhurst to buy the ingredients for gravy (nostalgia takes strange forms). Biagio patronizes a pork store on Avenue P. I like to shop on Eighteenth Avenue. I grew up in "the numbers"; Biagio grew up in "the letters"; each of us has trouble believing the other grew up in the heart of the heart of Italian Brooklyn. Bensonhurst is about territory, territory strictly defined and fiercely defended.

Besides "the numbers" and "the letters," there are "the Bays," those streets that stretch toward the Narrows. The girl who was to become my brother's wife lived on a pie-shaped block where "the letters" and "the numbers" converged; he met her at a dance in "the Bays." These facts of geography seemed to him liberating. He drove his Edsel to get to Carole's house and regarded their courtship as an event not unlike the Yalta Conference.

It isn't possible to overestimate the importance of the Sunday gravy; the amount of meat one ate was the most significant measure of affluence in Bensonhurst in the forties and fifties. You could live above a store, but if you ate meat six days a week, you counted yourself prosperous. And hospitality and generosity—character—were measured by the amount of meat you served your guests. "The kind of woman your mother was," my Uncle Pat said, summarily and succinctly defining my mother's nature, "was if four people came to dinner, there would be four pork chops." My mother was not prodigal, she was unnaturally frugal. Luigi Barzini had it that Italians in postwar Italy ate poorly, preferring to wear their money on their backs, where it showed, in the form of clothes, so as to make a *bel' figura*. But Barzini was a northern Italian. Bensonhurst's Italian immigrants came from the poverty-stricken South—from Naples and Calabria and Abruzzo—and food was both comfort and tangible proof of success, as well as justification and revenge, a way to show off to one's friends and neighbors, and a perceived way of assimilating, just as the Host (the "Communion cookie") was the way to God. We processed the world through our digestive systems. My mother served organ meat a lot, and appendages—heart stew and chicken-feet soup, many things rubbery and many things slippery; and she went comparison shopping for broccoli and fought with my maternal grandmother over whether to use the dandelions that grew in an empty lot next to us for salad or (as my grandmother wished) for wine. From such evidence I tried to assess our relative position in the world. . . . When there are internecine fights in Bensonhurst—when, for example, the new immigrants, not so impoverished as my grandparents, who came to America at the turn of the century at the time of the *grande immigrazione,* are made objects of scorn or become the source of bewilderment, Italians of my generation use the understood language of food to express uneasiness. In 1974, there was a race riot at my high school, New Utrecht, blacks having been brought in from other neighborhoods to attend. When my brother and I went back to the old neighborhood to talk to some of his friends about it, one of them said: "We got this big influx of Italians from the old country— geeps. They're not like us. They got a chip on their shoulder. Mouthy. They say, 'Blacks have been here for a hundred years and they couldn't make it; now it's our turn.' It was a geep who beat up on a black kid at Utrecht. The geeps are here three years and they got money to buy a four-family house. That's all they think of is money. They never heard of going to the movies. They never heard of anisette. They never even heard of *coffee.* What kind of Italian is that? They work two jobs, and they eat macaroni every night—pasta lenticci, pasta fazool, that's it. We're here eating steaks and drinking highballs and we hear them every night cracking macaroni into the pot—unbelievable." Food is used to signify opprobrium: a dope is called a *zhadrool,* slang for a cucumber or a squash. . . .

I am skipping rope, double-dutch, in the magic dusk. "Come in, the chicken's ready," my brother yells out the window. "Don't let the Jews down the street know what we're having for dinner," one of my aunts calls out. . . .

So embattled. The Indians were always circling around the wagons. It was that way in the Old Country, where only silence brought a measure of peace—*don't interfere*—if not of economic freedom; and it was that way in America, too. Italian immigrants of my grandparents' and my parents' generation lived in the conviction that *they*—the "Americans," the Jews, the *others*—were out to get them, cheat them, kill them. *Don't let them know anything. What they don't know can't hurt you.* In the days of his senile dementia, my grandfather believed he'd flown with Lindbergh across the Atlantic—but that *they,* the Americans, wouldn't give an Italian credit for it. When Grandpa got cancer, it was "a sin" (not "what a shame," but "what a sin"), the greater sin being to tell anybody about it. The world was malevolent, it existed to be held off and thus controlled.

As for the honeysuckle: Perhaps honeysuckle grows somewhere else in New York; if it does, I don't know about it. Or maybe—this heretical thought has occurred to me—what Biagio and I both think of as honeysuckle is the flower of the privet hedges that decorously contain Bensonhurst's tidy one- and two- and four-family houses. But I am prepared to swear that it was the sweetness of honeysuckle that threaded its way through my waking and sleeping dreams when I was young and tempestuously in love—years and years of invalidated love—in Bensonhurst.

The first man I loved was a Jew.

My first lover was a black man.

It'll kill Mommy and Daddy, I thought (not without a delicate thrill of pleasure); Mommy and Daddy will kill me, I thought (feeling what I had never felt before: a sense of latent power absurdly coupled with ennui and a sense of hopelessness).

There was a honeysuckle bush on the corner of Sixty-sixth Street and Nineteenth Avenue; its perfume restored me to a love of an enlarged world when I was desperately unhappy—and simultaneously fed the unlicensed ardors that were a source of my unhappiness.

Now I dream, not of those lost loves, but of the honeysuckle bush, which has itself become an object of intense love, flowering in my reveries.

Yusuf Hawkins was shot dead on Sixty-eighth Street and Twentieth Avenue, two blocks away from the building my parents lived in till they died. Hawkins, together with three black friends, came to Bensonhurst to look at a used car. It was an act of singular naïveté, and the timing was deadly.

Eighteen-year-old Gina Feliciano's birthday fell on August 23. The young woman had invited black and Spanish friends to celebrate with her, and she told her ex-boyfriend, Keith Mondello; perhaps she taunted him with it. According to Feliciano, Mondello and his friends called her a "spic lover," told her her "nigger friends don't belong in the neighborhood"—"stay with your own kind."

Feliciano called the celebration off. According to her, while she and her mother and a girlfriend ate potato chips and pretzels in her apartment, white kids milled around her house on the night of her birthday. By horrible accident of fate, Hawkins and his friends, unrelated in friendship to Feliciano, walked by. The white kids chased them with bats they got from a nearby schoolyard; Hawkins was killed with a shot from a .32-caliber pistol.

White residents of Bensonhurst who talked to reporters claimed that Feliciano tried to frighten them—that she said black guys were coming into the neighborhood to beat them up. She denies this. She says she knows she's being called "a prostitute, a crackhead and a liar," and she says she was "with black guys in Coney Island—a couple of them" (the implication is that she was "with" them sexually)—but that it's nobody's business, especially not the business of the "Guidos" who "wear sixty chains and have hairspray in one hand and a mirror in the other" and use "jumper cables" to style their spiked hair: "They ain't paying my rent, they ain't puttin' clothes on my back and they ain't feedin' me"—and she's not sleeping with them, she said.

Bensonhurst's response to the tragedy in their community is not monolithic. But when I hear Gina Feliciano say that they tell her she "brought Bensonhurst down," I hear a chorus of voices from the past— the immediate past, and the mythological past: *The woman made me do it.*

According to Ms. Feliciano, there is a $100,000 contract out on her life.

I ran away—as fast and as hard and as far as I could (across the bridge, to Manhattan, the emancipating city of calculated dreams); I fled from insularity and provincialism and suspicion of all that was not *us* and from familial love that was both careless and claustrophobic. I fled; and now I grieve. One cannot separate oneself from the landscape of earliest desire, the crucible, the wellspring, the source. I still want what I owned and what owned me—the honeysuckle bush on the corner. In memory I walk those streets; I look for clues, for the stuff that binds me to Yusuf Hawkins . . . and to his killers.

It is an established fact in my family that I am crazy. My Aunt Mary, who loves me, dissents—but as she is Sicilian, her word does not count for much among my Calabrian and Abruzzese aunts and uncles. Italians are tribal. Bensonhurst is tribal. My family called Aunt Mary "the Arab," Sicilians not being regarded as properly Italian.

My mother had a friend called Rosie-the-Spic. One day I answered the doorbell when Rosie-the-Spic came to visit (I can remember when doors in Bensonhurst were never locked, and so can generations of Italians. That was before, they say, "the element" moved among them). "ROSIE THE SPIC IS HERE," I shouted, having no idea whatsoever that "Thespic" was not her proper name. I didn't know about racial enmities then. I was four. Naturally Rosie-the-Spic never came back, and naturally (for whatever seemed unreasonable to me also seemed natural to me, though I made myself ill with temper tantrums trying to understand) I got a beating.

Once, lying in bed, I heard scrabbling and moaning and hoarse sounds coming from the bedroom of the apartment next door. I intuited that something I needed to know about and wanted to know about and wasn't going to be allowed to know about was going on, and, knowing also that the question was perverse, I asked my mother what the (exciting) noises were; her silence effectively anesthetized my genitals for years. . . . I wonder what questions Gina Feliciano asked her mother, and what answers she received.

Zhadrool had quasi-affectionate overtones. Blacks were called *mulanyam*—a corruption of *melanzane,* eggplant, and in that there is no affection at all—only blackness so opaque as to defy comprehension.

Sometimes we went to Prospect Park. I used—this is how, very early, I established my craziness—to run up to black people and touch their skin and tell them they were beautiful. This was an aesthetic, not an ideology. I was five years old; I don't know how or why I came to it. One of my aunts gave me a black doll and told me I could play with it if I never ever again touched a black person. It was a Little Black Sambo doll; I hated it. We never went to Prospect Park again, only to the Botanical Gardens, because the park was "full of *them.*"

It did not surprise me when black protest marchers in Bensonhurst were greeted with cries of *nigger go home,* and with watermelons. Of course the kids we used to call "gees," the kids Gina Feliciano calls "Guidos," would use the language of food.

When I went to New Utrecht High School in Bensonhurst, there was only one black student, Joan Smith. She never spoke to anyone and no one ever spoke to her. At the end of her senior year, she was nominated for most popular. I have told this story so often I believe it to be wholly true; but if it is not true, it will, as they say in Italy, "serve." It is to the point.

It is not true that Joan Smith never spoke to anyone and no one ever spoke to her. I spoke to her. I spoke to her because I was a Jehovah's Witness, and it was my (hated and hateful) duty to proselytize. I tried to convert Joan Smith. It didn't take. (I did convert Fatima Ouida, though, an Egyptian girl who kept snakes in the apartment underneath the elevated train line where she lived; Fatima used to invite people over to watch her father pray to Mecca—he became known as "the guy who prays to the West End train.") In the lunchroom at New Utrecht, I sat with a girl who had one eye, her father having knocked the other one out of her head with a broomstick; and I sat with a girl whose makeup was puddled all over her face (she was mad); and I sat with the class slut, who was stupid. I tried to convert them all. In any case no one else would have much to do with me, my religion having made me an outsider and a freak.

There are of course voyeuristic advantages to being an outsider and a freak.

I was an outsider and a freak, but I was smart. (I was pretty, too, but I didn't know that; I didn't know what my father meant when he said, "The world eats up pretty, smart girls like you." Eats them up and spits them out, he meant; he meant *Beware.*) One day a teacher approached me in the hallway of Utrecht and said—genuinely bewildered, I think—"Why do you have an Italian last name?" "Because I'm Italian," I said. He did not know what to do with this. Jews were smart—they took academic college-preparatory courses. Italians were dumb—or going immediately to be married (Jewish girls wore charm bracelets, Italian girls wore engagement rings). They took commercial or vocational courses. I took hold of this view of my world early—we all did. I can remember when Miss Silver, my third-grade teacher, a chunky woman who wore chunky Mexican silver jewelry (which jewelry I associated with lesbians, perhaps because of Miss Silver's interest in me, which my father considered untoward) came to my house rustling with sibilant *s*'s when I had viral pneumonia; she came to tell my mother I was going to skip a grade. My mother took a dim view of what she regarded as interference. Actually Miss Silver came really, I think, to say, *Look at your daughter, pay attention to her* (she held my fevered hand); and this is what my mother, who introduced herself as "Barbara's relative" and dwelt in the clouds with Jehovah, having heavenly fish to fry, took a dim view of.

In junior high school there was one black kid; and my brother, at the time of the race riots at Utrecht, said: "That kid was lucky. He was bright and good-looking. If he was just a regular black kid, he'd have had bad trouble. Every time teachers talked about black history or slavery, my word of honor I felt sorry for the kid. If they'd have talked about Italian history, there'd have been thirty of us Italians, we wouldn't be embarrassed . . . not that they ever talked about Italian history."

In high school Italian was offered as a second language. Everybody took French.

My brother got beat up bad when some kids in the Bays mouthed him and Carole, and he, gallant, answered them back. He got in his Edsel and drove to the station house all bloody, his nose broken, and several ribs. "Were the kids white or colored?" the desk sergeant asked. "White." "Go home and forget about it," the sergeant said.

The flowers in the gardens were all old-fashioned: sweet peas and sweet williams and rambling roses. Mint. Fig trees swathed in tar paper and crowned with a tin bucket all winter, undressed at the first sign of spring.

I roller-skated for my life, maintaining a difficult, thrilling balance; overhead, the winy maple trees. Alone. At sunset we were safely gathered in. We were allowed to eat ice cream only from the Good Humor truck, it was good for us, like escarole. This was before my mother became a Jehovah's Witness, before I was nine years old. Afterward, my father said, marking and ruing the day, "She never made muffins anymore."

The first day of freshman English, Utrecht: David Zeiger is our teacher; he says: "Everyone with blue eyes has to do homework." Our world is divided into three parts, Italian, Jewish, and "American." The Americans have blue eyes. They protest. "It isn't fair" . . . making his point for him. David Zeiger spent a forty-minute English period, in 1948, telling freshman English students in Bensonhurst—many of whom had never seen a Negro—why it was wrong to judge people by the color of their eyes, or their skin.

According to the dogma by which I lived, Jehovah was a god of justice and mercy, and whatever happened—including the drowning of infants in their own blood at an imminent Armageddon—was by definition fair. But I knew—I viscerally knew, I was laceratingly divided—that my world was governed by caprice, that punishments and rewards were arbitrary. I lived after all with my mother. . . .

My mother, who was beautiful, had blue eyes, like an American; she was very nearly blind. She went to a doctor, a quack, who gave her eye exercises to do; one of them involved resting her head on the windowsill while she rolled her eyes in her head. A passing motorist saw her and thought she was convulsing. I came home to a fire-engine rescue team. "Why didn't you tell them I was doing eye exercises?" she asked me, her need to place the blame a rigorous passion. I must assume that given her voracious and discordant needs she was mad; and that her religion accommodated her madness. Mad. Sad. Of course the eye exercises didn't work. Thereafter, rain or shine, she carried a red umbrella so cars could see her when she crossed the street. A beautiful woman with blue eyes carrying a red umbrella.

My mother was incapable of dual allegiances. After she fell in love with Jehovah, she no longer wanted to sleep with my father. She made me tell him so. I was ten. He cried. But he slept in the mahogany double bed with my brother and my mother slept in the twin bed next to mine. She cried. One Christmas Eve my mother went out, against my father's protests, to proselytize from door to door. My father got drunk. I washed the dishes. The doors of all the kitchen cupboards flew open and everything in them—cups, saucers, pots—came flying out. For years I remembered that poltergeist phenomenon without remembering what had directly preceded it: my father put a dish towel around my neck and, yanking it, started to strangle me; then he fell in a wet heap on the floor, and then the cupboards flew open and everything in them flew out. I was twelve. The downstairs neighbors heard the noise. Weeks later they said to me: "We mind our business." All of our neighbors minded their business. They wouldn't have heard the sound of a shot and if they had they wouldn't have done anything about it.

No matter what happened, my father needed profoundly to keep up appearances.

In particular my father hated an uncle of mine who, after coming home from the war with a Purple Heart, had been converted by my mother. This uncle worked in a doll factory. At dinner my father would say: "Did you stuff dolls today?" This is how it was: the house was hot with sex; but nobody talked about sex. "What's Tampax?" I asked my mother. She left the room.

My aunts, my godmother among them, knew that my mother and my father did not sleep together. They blamed this on "the Jehovahs." But they maintained a stony silence; it was important for them to believe that they were "nice," and "nice" people—like the "Americans"—didn't talk about sex. When I was an adult, my godmother told me that Daddy had wanted to leave my mother to marry a woman who worked in the Bargain Hats department of Gimbel's Department Store. She talked her brother out of it, my godmother said, there never having been a divorce in the family. Italians didn't get divorced and Italians didn't talk about sex.

Which was what made it possible for my mother to have a romantic affair without a guilty conscience. After the war, the Witnesses who had been imprisoned for not serving in the armed forces came home. One of them, Louis, fell in love with my beautiful mother. They went from door to door together, holding hands. They considered, having consulted various Bible concordances, that they were married in the eyes of God, the pledge being as good as the deed; they would celebrate their marriage in Jehovah's "New World," after Armageddon had disposed of my father. Future-sex. Louis painted her toenails. I'm sure they never talked about sex. They talked about the New World, when the lion and the lamb would lie down together. I was told to regard Louis, whom I loathed, as my proper father-in-the-Lord. At dinner one night: "You were seen walking *mano a mano* with that Louis," my father said, "the one who stuffs dolls with your brother." My mother cried all night long in the twin bed next to mine: "What did you tell him, oh what did you tell him?" she cried. I hadn't told him anything. Everybody in "the numbers" knew. Word gets around. What you don't want known in Bensonhurst you don't do. "You've ruined my life," my mother said.

So all in all it wasn't race relations I learned from David Zeiger (or "tolerance," which was the word we used back then) so much as the idea, new to me and radical, that lives could and should exemplify fairness, that justice wasn't exercised only by God but by human beings.

David Zeiger is still my friend, though it is hard for me to change his place in the story of my life; in reveries, he belongs to the past—the runic past I spend the present reading, the past that contains Arnold Horowitz, who is dead.

Arnold Horowitz was David Zeiger's best friend and he was my English teacher when I was fifteen. A lot of the girls—the smart girls, the point of him not being obvious to the dumb girls—had a crush on Arnold Horowitz. I myself didn't see the point of him until he wrote this sentence on the blackboard: *The beautiful girl with hair the color of ripe wheat* . . . That's as far as I got in the sentence, and then I fell in love and could not believe there was a time I hadn't been in love with Arnold Horowitz.

Almost all of my Italian neighbors were casually antisemitic; it wasn't a matter of creed. Some of my neighbors and some of my family members were virulently antisemitic. My brother brought home a loaf of Arnold's Bread from the market one day; my mother threw it out the kitchen window—but that was not so much because Arnold was Jewish but because Arnold, like Miss Silver, paid attention to me. He was more dangerous than Miss Silver. Miss Silver only taught me I was smart. Arnold told me I was good. (I have loved him all my life.)

He sent pepperoni to the gees (the hoods, the hard guys) in jail. In 1945, ahead of his time, he co-edited a book for young adults called *This Way to Unity: For the Promotion of Goodwill and Tolerance Among Races, Religions, and National Groups.* (He published it under a pseudonym, Arnold Herrick, bland and Wasp—and also *Gather Ye Rosebuds While Ye May;* the Board of Education banned it—it contained the word *womb.*) Jehovah's Witnesses are forbidden to salute the flag. Arnold came into the school auditorium at assembly time during the flag salute and held my hand; how could I not have loved him? I met a black teacher in his house on the Bays one hot summer night. It was awkward in that big living room with the window seat and the blond Danish furniture and the Picasso prints. The others—David Zeiger and his wife, Lila, and some people whose faces I cannot recall—had very little conversation. We blamed it on the heat. One treated a black person as one treated an invalid—with courtesy and caution.

Antisemitism seemed a most peculiar thing to me. The halls of all our buildings smelled ecumenically of chicken fat and gravy. The girls I had talked dirty with before talking dirty became a sin were Italian and Jewish and equally inventive and equally ignorant of sex. The girls I'd played the Ouija board with under the stairs of apartment buildings were Jewish and Italian and equally titillated (the Ouija board said I was going to marry DICK, which was my father's name) and equally scared. I'd jumped across roofs with Jewish and with Italian girls and ridden up and down dumbwaiters with Jewish and Italian girls, and what was the difference?

When the world became full of catalogued sin, both Jewish and Italian girls were remote to me, equally to be envied because they had, it seemed to me, two gifts that I had not: the freedom to play and, within limits, to choose.

On Friday evenings my Jewish neighbors gave me two cents—they gave boys three—to turn on the stove and the lights for Sabbath.

Sometimes my family and my neighbors counted the number of Jews on the subway train. They were afraid of being overwhelmed.

On Bay Parkway a self-possessed smiling young woman walked to the elevated line every morning in a silk dress underneath which there was no bra. (This was in an era when the single most potent image of freedom I cherished was that of a girl with long blond hair sitting at a lunch counter in a raincoat, her daringly unstockinged feet out of her shoes.) "She must be Jewish," the Italians said. They were afraid of sexual perdition and contagion. They wanted their daughters pink and white and girdled and pure.

Angela, one of Arnold's students, got a scholarship to Radcliffe.

The New Yorker published Harold Brodkey's short story about the love affair of a Harvard boy and a Radcliffe girl. Angela bought every copy of *The New Yorker* to be had in Bensonhurst. That was what Angela's family feared: that they *did it* there. Angela was the only Italian girl from Bensonhurst I knew who went to college. Italians didn't believe in college, it threatened family authority. (And this has not changed.)

When I was twenty-two and Arnold had not married me or asked me to marry him or for that matter declared his love for me, I fell in love—at Minton's, on 128th Street in Harlem, with a jazz drummer. It was a clever thing for me to have done; I had left my childhood religion but not the bed in the room where my mother cried at night. I wanted a baptism of fire into the world and I got it.

I had never once seen a black man walk the streets of Bensonhurst.

I loved the nights.

In those days it was safe to take the subway late at night; and full of love, replete, I'd walk at dawn to the apartment house . . . where in the lobby my father, longing for proof of what he most feared, my sexual indiscretion, lurked. (I always harbored a suspicion that the lady in the Bargain Hats department was black.) Even in Manhattan it was hard for me and G., my musician, to walk in safety; even in Birdland it was dicey to hold hands.

Once at Minton's an angry black man asked me who the Mau Mau were. "Kenyan terrorists," I said promptly. I was ignorant and innocent and did not suspect black people of laying traps. (G. laughed and laughed because I couldn't say the word *nigger,* which word he and his friends used all the time; he made me say it; I cried.) The angry black man scolded me up and down and all around. (G. was busy playing a set.) "Don't you call her no names," a whiskey voice said. "She's a woman, she's a nigger—she can be raped." The voice belonged to Billie Holiday, whom as a consequence I loved.

It would not have occurred to me to walk the streets of Bensonhurst with G. Sometimes, to test me, and, I suppose, himself, he'd stop me on a busy Manhattan street and kiss me on the lips; but it would not have occurred to him to walk the streets of Bensonhurst with me— he was very much dedicated to his own survival. Once or twice he came to my door in a car or a cab—laughing his husky laugh (Coward's Violets pastilles and Camels cigarettes), amused, defiant, proud, to think of my father waiting there. My father took to following us around Harlem. He'd crouch beneath the areaways of brownstones that housed after-hours clubs; surely there was an illicit thrill in his determined vigilance.

Arnold said: "Are you happy?"

G. was married. Three years after I fell in love with him I married a white man, a man I could take home to Bensonhurst but never took to my heart.

The thing about taking G. to Bensonhurst was: he would have been killed. That was what we understood.

Arnold taught us, echoing Camus, that people were not so much good or bad as ignorant. I don't know. I believe in good and evil; and I believe in forgiveness. What I have written here, torn from a bloody past, is not the whole truth. In the whole truth belongs the safety of the stoops in the friendly dark; trips to Ebbets Field; my growing to love my sister-in-law, Carole; the steadfast love of my grandmother Concetta who prayed for me even when I despised her Catholic prayers; "Jack Armstrong" and "The Inner Sanctum" and a linen closet full of sugar cubes that smelled of lavender; the smell of glue and new paper and old books in the library in Gravesend; Mrs. Scalia, the junior high school teacher who wanted more than anything else to see my Italian name inscribed on the marble honor roll; my meanness to my brother and his to me and the restoration of our love for each other (and the time when he hit a kid on the head with a shovel—he was four—and I packed the bleeding wound with mud); the time Mike Collura drove me to my job in the Secretariat Building of the UN in his ice truck—right to the door; the bakeries and the lemon ices and the fish carts and the kosher butchers; the bike rides to Coney Island and the parachute ride; my maternal grandfather's grapevine, the yeasty smell of his wine pervading the house; the sun room my paternal grandfather built, and Aunt Louise's tailor's dummy and the big radio, which were in it; trips to the rodeo (I cried) and the circus and to the World's Fair (I shook hands with Johnny Weissmuller); Miss Isaacs, who would not let Shirley Gottlieb play with me in eighth grade because I might convert her; Aunt Louise's death when she was twenty-three, and Dr. Greenberg, who could not bring himself to present the family with a bill; the kindness I received from strangers—all those people, Italians and Jews, whose doorbells I rang in Bensonhurst with my message of superiority and doom; the goodness of teachers and nuns and priests who listened to a wild, unhappy girl preach; the high school girls I thought despised me and who now, when I meet them, say, We remember you, you were nice. I think it is a sin to have left out all the good things and not to have told all the truth. . . . But I am thinking of Yusuf Hawkins—and of Gina Feliciano.

"It was the woman's fault." The first lie, the lie the serpent told.

Bensonhurst is full of coffee bars now—social clubs for men, they really are; and I've tried to sit in them; and I've been—even with my brother and my son and my nephews—scared. Because they don't belong to us. Bensonhurst was territorial when I grew up. It is more territorial now. It is more defended, and more frightened.

If I had told the whole truth—if I had given equal time to what is good and what I loved—I would still not feel welcome there. If I spoke of their broken dreams, of their hard working-class lives, their economic nightmares, their fear of dope and crime and invasion and change—and their guts and their love—I would still not be welcome there. Because the first survival lesson, the first thing you have to understand to live in Bensonhurst, is to honor "the blood." And when family warmth and tribal feeling have been perverted by fear and alienation, corrupted to form an incubator for hatred, the duty of "the blood" to "the blood" is silence: it is held true that even a single reproach pollutes the stream of love. "We mind our own business."

I am afraid of black men now and I am afraid of being afraid but cannot reason my way out of fear. I am different from the murderers of Yusuf Hawkins; but perhaps not so different from the people who have spun a net of protection, a net of silence, around them. All the time I have been writing this, I have fought the inclination to do the same. I have fought my will to silence.

I loved the way the girls receiving First Communion looked. I envied them. I did not understand how I would ever be married if I didn't first become a child-bride in this ceremony that prefigured marriage and looked so much like it. I loved the way their missals smelled and looked, white leather and onionskin paper; I wanted flowers in my hair. It seemed to me a kind of doom that I could not join them, a prefiguration of spinsterish loneliness.

A special mass was said for Yusuf Hawkins in Bensonhurst. Priests led their parishioners, who looked solemn, grave, frightened, in a march to protest the killing, a march to express solidarity with the people of a child shot dead. They looked as if they were in shock; count-me-among-the-just/I-am-not-worthy, their looks said. They were brave.

You'd have to have lived in Bensonhurst to know how brave. You'd have to have lived in Bensonhurst, an outsider and a freak like I was, to know how good their goodness feels.

My brother says: "Thirty years ago, honest to God, I would've been with the guys with the bats. In August, I swear to God, I would have been with the protestors." I can't tell you how hopeful that makes me feel.

On an Alitalia flight from Rome a few weeks after the killing, I sat next to an immigrant from Calabria who lived in the Bays. I asked him if he'd heard about the trouble in Bensonhurst. "You mean the Chinese?" he said. "It hasn't been the same since Chinks came to live in the Bays, making trouble."

What can you do with a man like that?

I called a friend who lives on West Fifth Street and Avenue S—"the letters." "Bensonhurst . . . " I began. "I don't live in Bensonhurst," she said, "I live in Gravesend." "All your life you've said you lived in Bensonhurst!" I said. "No more," she said. And, with what I have come to think of as characteristic Italian logic, she added: "I never lived in Bensonhurst."

Then we talked about food.

JEANNE WAKATSUKI HOUSTON
(1934—)

———————◆———————

Born in Inglewood, California, of Japanese immigrant parents, JEANNE WAKATSUKI HOUSTON at the age of seven was transported with her family to Manzanar Camp in Owens Valley, California, the first of the permanent concentration camps to open during World War II from the Sierra Nevada to the Mississippi River. They were among the 110,000 Japanese-American victims of President Roosevelt's Executive Order 9066 giving the War Department authority to define military areas in the Western states and to exclude from them anyone who might threaten the war effort. As a result of mass hysteria following the Japanese attack on Pearl Harbor (December 7, 1941), all persons of Japanese ancestry on the West Coast were forcibly evacuated and relocated in ten inland "detention centers," sparsely furnished military barracks exposed to sand and dust storms with few jobs available for adults and minimal schooling for children. One of the results of this evacuation was the destruction of the Japanese communities in San Francisco and throughout California. When the families were released in 1945, they returned to find their homes and enclaves gone: their property had been sold off to pay for storage fees and taxes. In 1988, each Japanese-American who had been interned during the war was awarded a compensatory payment of twenty thousand dollars.

Farewell to Manzanar, excerpted here, is Jeanne Wakatsuki Houston's memoir of family suffering and political injustice, written with her husband James D. Houston, as "a way of coming to terms with the impact these years have had on my entire life. But this is not a political history. It is a story, or a web of stories—my own, my father's my family's— tracing a few paths, out of the multitude of paths that led up to and away from the experience of the internment." The book begins with a quote from the historian Henry Steele Commager, written in 1947:

"It is sobering to recall that though the Japanese relocation program, carried through at such incalculable cost in misery and tragedy, was justified on the ground that the Japanese were potentially disloyal, the record does not disclose a single case of Japanese disloyalty or sabotage during the whole war."

After the war, the author returned to the West Coast where she has spent most of her life. She studied sociology and journalism at San Jose State College, where she and her husband, a Wallace Stegner Writing Fellow at Stanford, first met. With their three children they now live in Santa Cruz. The story they tell of Manzanar and Wakatsuki Houston's family is faithful to the factual horror and humiliations of the past as well as the unbroken spirits and compassionate minds that survived to write the memory.

From *Farewell to Manzanar:*
A True Story of Japanese American Experience During and After the World War II Internment

Ten Thousand Voices

As I came to understand what Manzanar had meant, it gradually filled me with shame for being a person guilty of something enormous enough to deserve that kind of treatment. In order to please my accusers, I tried, for the first few years after our release, to become someone acceptable. I both succeeded and failed. By the age of seventeen I knew that *making it,* in the terms I had tried to adopt, was not only unlikely, but false and empty, no more authentic for me than trying to emulate my Great-aunt Toyo. I needed some grounding of my own, such as Woody had found when he went to commune with her and with our ancestors in Ka-ke. It took me another twenty years to accumulate the confidence to deal with what the equivalent experience would have to be for me.

It's outside the scope of this book to recount all that happened in the interim. Suffice to say, I was the first member of our family to finish college and the first to marry out of my race. As my husband and I began to raise our family, and as I sought for ways to live agreeably in Anglo-American society, my memories of Manzanar, for many years, lived far below the surface. When we finally started to talk about making a trip to visit the ruins of the camp, something would inevitably get in the way of our plans. Mainly my own doubts, my fears. I half-suspected that the place did not exist. So few people I met in those years had even heard of it, and those who had knew so little about it, sometimes I imagined I had made the whole thing up, dreamed it. Even among my brothers and sisters, we seldom discussed the internment. If we spoke of it at all, we joked.

When I think of how that secret lived in all our lives, I remember the way Kiyo and I responded to a little incident soon after we got out of camp. We were sitting on a bus-stop bench in Long Beach, when an old, embittered woman stopped and said, "Why don't all you dirty Japs go back to Japan!" She spit at us and passed on. We said nothing at the time. After she stalked off down the sidewalk we did not look at each other. We sat there for maybe fifteen minutes with downcast eyes and finally got up and walked home. We couldn't bear to mention it to anyone in the family. And over the years we never spoke of this insult. It stayed alive in our separate memories, but it was too painful to call out into the open.

In 1966 I met a Caucasian woman who had worked for one year as a photographer at Manzanar. I could scarcely speak to her. I desperately wanted to, but all my questions stuck in my throat. This time it was not the pain of memory. It was simply her validation that all those things had taken place. Someone outside the close community of Japanese Americans had actually seen the camp, with its multitude of people and its swarm of buildings on the plain between the mountains. Something inside me opened then. I began to talk about it more and more.

It was April 1972, thirty years almost to the day, that we piled our three kids into the car and headed out there. From where we live now, in the California coast town of Santa Cruz, it's a full day's drive. We started down 101 to Paso Robles, crossed over the hummocky Diablo Range to the central valley, skirted Bakersfield, and climbed through Tehachapi Pass into the desert.

At Mojave we turned north onto the same road our bus had taken out from Los Angeles in April 1942. It is the back road to the Sierras and the main route from southern California to Reno and Lake Tahoe. We joined bikers and backpackers and the skiers heading for Mammoth. The traffic through there is fast, everyone but the bikers making for the high country. As we sped along wide roads at sixty and seventy, with our kids exclaiming at the sights we passed and our car loaded down with camping gear, it seemed even more incredible to me that a place like Manzanar could have been anywhere within reach of such a highway, such a caravan of pleasure-seeking travelers.

The bikers peeled off at Red Rock Canyon, a gorgeous bulge of pink cliffs and rusty gulches humping out of the flatlands. After that it was lovely desert but nothing much to stop for. In a hundred miles we passed two oases, the first at Olancha, the second around Lone Pine, a small, tree-filled town where a lot of mountain buffs turn off for the Mount Whitney Portal.

A few miles out of Lone Pine we started looking for another stand of trees, some tall elms, and what remains of those gnarled pear orchards. They were easy to spot. Everything else is sagebrush, tumble-weeds, and wind.

At its peak, in the summer of '42, Manzanar was the biggest city between Reno and Los Angeles, a special kind of western boom town that sprang from the sand, flourished, had its day, and now has all but disappeared. The barracks are gone, torn down right after the war. The guard towers are gone, and the mess halls and shower rooms, the hospital, the tea gardens, and the white buildings outside the compound. Even the dust is gone. Spreading brush holds it to the ground. Thirty years earlier, army bulldozers had scraped everything clean to start construction.

What you see from the road are the two gatehouses, each a small empty pillbox of a building faced with flagstones and topped, like tiny pagodas, with shingled curving roofs. Farther in, you see the elms, most of which were planted by internees, and off to the right a large green building that was once our high school auditorium, now a maintenance depot for the Los Angeles Power and Water District, who leased the land to the government during the war and still owns it.

Past the gatehouses we turned left over a cattle guard and onto a dirt perimeter road that led to the far side of the campsite. About half a mile in we spotted a white obelisk gleaming in the distance and marking a subtle line where the plain begins gradually to slope upward into the alluvial fan that becomes the base of the mountains. It seemed miraculous, as if some block of stone had fallen from the peaks above and landed upright in the brush, chiseled, solitary, twelve feet high.

Near it a dozen graves were outlined in the sand with small stones, and a barbed-wire fence surrounded them to keep back the cattle and the tumbleweed. The black Japanese script cut into the white face of the obelisk read simply, "A Memorial to the Dead."

We were alone out there, too far from the road to hear anything but wind. I thought of Mama, now seven years gone. For a long time I stood gazing at the monument. I couldn't step inside the fence. I believe in ghosts and spirits. I knew I was in the presence of those who had died at Manzanar. I also felt the spiritual presence that always lingers near awesome wonders like Mount Whitney. Then, as if rising from the ground around us on the valley floor, I began to hear the first whispers, nearly inaudible, from all those thousands who once had lived out here, a wide, windy sound of the ghost of that life. As we began to walk, it grew to a murmur, a thin steady hum.

We turned the kids loose, watched them scamper off ahead of us, and we followed what used to be an asphalt road running from the back side of the camp a mile out to the highway. The obelisk—built in

1943—and the gatehouses are all that have survived intact from internment days. The rest of the place looks devastated by a bombing raid.

The old road was disintegrating, split, weed-sprung. We poked
through the remains of hospital foundations, undermined by erosion
channels. We found concrete slabs where the latrines and shower rooms
stood, and irrigation ditches, and here and there, the small rock
arrangements that once decorated many of the entranceways. I had
found out that even in North Dakota, when Papa and the other Issei
men imprisoned there had free time, they would gather small stones
from the plain and spend hours sorting through a dry stream bed looking for the veined or polished rock that somehow pleased the most. It
is so characteristically Japanese, the way lives were made more tolerable
by gathering loose desert stones and forming with them something
enduringly human. These rock gardens had outlived the barracks and
the towers and would surely outlive the asphalt road and rusted pipes
and shattered slabs of concrete. Each stone was a mouth, speaking for a
family, for some man who had beautified his doorstep.

Vegetation gets thickest toward the center of the site, where the
judo pavilion once stood and where rows of elms planted as windbreaks
have tripled their growth since the forties. In there we came across the
remains of a small park. A stone-lined path ran along the base of a
broad mound of dirt about five feet high. Stones had been arranged on
the mound, and some low trees still shaded it and made an arch above
the path. For a moment I was strolling again, finding childish comfort
in its incongruous design.

But after ten feet the path ended in tumbleweeds. The trees were
dry and stubby, the mound was barren, and my attention was arrested
by a water faucet sticking two feet out of the sand, like some subter-
ranean periscope. One of these had provided water for each barracks.
They stuck up at intervals in every direction, strangely sharpening the
loneliness and desolation, sometimes the only sign of human presence
in an acre or two of sand.

My mood had shifted. The murmur turned to wind. For a while I
could almost detach myself from the place and its history and take pleasure in it purely as an archeological site. I saw the outlines, patterns this
city must have taken. I imagined where the buildings stood, almost as I
once did nosing around old Roman villas in Europe. We saw a low
ring of stones built up with cement and wondered who the mason was
who knelt there and studied the shapes before fitting them together.
We moved around the ring a few feet to find out. This was the old
flagpole circle, where the Stars and Stripes were hoisted every morning,

and the inscription scratched across the top said, BUILT BY WADA AND CREW, JUNE 10, 1942 A.D.

The A.D. made me shiver. I knew that the man who inscribed it had foreseen these ruins and did not want his masonry identified with the wrong era. His words coming out of the stone became a voice that merged with all the others, not a murmur this time, but low voices muttering and chattering all around me. We were crossing what used to be a firebreak, now a sandy field devoid of any growth. The wind was vicious there, with nothing to break it, and the voices grew. The firebreak was where we had talent shows and dances and outdoor movies in the summer, and where the kids played games. I heard the girls' glee club I used to sing in, way off from the other side of camp, their tiny grade-school sopranos singing, "Beautiful dreamer, wake unto me." I closed my eyes and I was ten years old again. Nothing had changed. I heard laughter. It was almost dusk, the wind had dropped, and I saw old men squatting in the dirt, Papa and some of his cronies, muttering and smoking their cigarettes. In the summertime they used to burn orange peels under gallon cans, with holes punched in the sides, to keep the mosquitoes away. Sometimes they would bring out their boards to play *goh* and *hana*. The orange peels would smolder in there, and the men would hunker down around the cans and watch the smoke seep out the holes.

From that firebreak we cut across toward the first row of pear trees, looking for what might remain of Block 28. There wasn't much to guide us but the trees themselves and a view I remembered of the blunt, bulky Inyo Range that bounds the eastern limit of the valley. When we were close enough to smell the trees we stopped. They were stunted, tenacious, tough the way a cactus has to be. The water table in that one area has kept them living through all these years of neglect, and they were ready to bloom at any moment. The heady smell was as odd in that desert setting as the little scrap of park had been, as odd yet just as familiar. We used to picnic there in blossom time, on weekends, if we got a wind-free day.

The wind blew it toward us now—chilled pear nectar—and it blew our kids around a high stand of brush. They came tumbling across the sand, demanding to know what we were going to *do* out here. Our twins were five years old at the time, a boy and a girl. Our older daughter had just turned eleven. She knew about "the evacuation," but it would be a few more years before she absorbed this part of the family history. For these three the site had been like any wreck or ruin. They became explorers, rushed around hoping the next clump of dusty trees or chunk of wall might reveal the treasure, the trinket, the exotically rusted hinge. Nothing much had turned up. The shine was wearing off the trip. Their eyes were red and their faces badly chapped. No place for kids..

My husband started walking them back to the car. I stayed behind a moment longer, first watching our eleven-year-old stride ahead, leading her brother and sister. She has long dark hair like mine and was then the same age I had been when the camp closed. It was so simple, watching her, to see why everything that had happened to me since we left camp referred back to it, in one way or another. At that age your body is changing, your imagination is galloping, your mind is in that zone between a child's vision and an adult's. Papa's life ended at Manzanar, though he lived for twelve more years after getting out. Until this trip I had not been able to admit that my own life really began there. The times I thought I had dreamed it were one way of getting rid of it, part of wanting to lose it, part of what you might call a whole Manzanar mentality I had lived with for twenty-five years. Much more than a remembered place, it had become a state of mind. Now, having seen it, I no longer wanted to lose it or to have those years erased. Having found it, I could say what you can only say when you've truly come to know a place: Farewell.

I had nearly outgrown the shame and the guilt and the sense of unworthiness. This visit, this pilgrimage, made comprehensible, finally, the traces that remained and would always remain, like a needle. That hollow ache I carried during the early months of internment had shrunk, over the years, to a tiny sliver of suspicion about the very person I was. It had grown so small sometimes I'd forget it was there. Months might pass before something would remind me. When I first read, in the summer of 1972, about the pressure Japan's economy was putting on American business and how a union in New York City had printed up posters of an American flag with MADE IN JAPAN written across it, then that needle began to jab. I heard Mama's soft, weary voice from 1945 say, "It's all starting over." I knew it wouldn't. Yet neither would I have been surprised to find the FBI at my door again. I would resist it much more than my parents did, but deep within me something had been prepared for that. Manzanar would always live in my nervous system, a needle with Mama's voice.

A gust of wind rushed through the orchard, bringing ice off the white slopes, and more blossom scent. It hurt to inhale deeply. I pulled my coat tight, ready to head for the car's warmth, but also wanting to hold this moment a little longer. I might never be back here again. I was poking around brush clumps and foundation chunks looking for something else. One more sign. Anything. I found another collection of stones, off by themselves, but so arranged that they could not have been accidental. Nearby an edge showed through the sand. I uncovered a single steppingstone, slightly worn, that led nowhere, yet lay as a subtle appendage to the small rock garden. One of these had lain outside our barracks door, a first step below three wooden ones. It could be ours. Perhaps not. Many barracks had such entrances. But this one would serve. I could call it the rock garden Papa put there. Almost the sign I wanted. Not quite. Not quite enough. There was more to all this than the lovely patience of these gathered stones. They were part of it. But there was something else, in the air. A sound. A smell. Just a whiff, hanging on that gust from the orchard, or blown down the ghostly alleyway of what used to be the street we lived on. I was hearing Mama's voice once more, but differently, louder now, right in front of me, and I smelled cork burning. That was one of Papa's remedies when her back knotted up. He would take little coins of cork and place them on the tension nodes and light them, and the cork would burn dark rings into her skin as she hunched on the porch steps groaning with relief.

They were sitting on the steps like that—Mama hunched, Papa tending the blackening rings—one morning a few days before we left camp. Now that smell and those voices in the wind from the orchard brought with them the sign I was waiting for: the image of a rekindled wildness in Papa's eyes. Twenty-seven years earlier I had carried it with me out of camp only half understanding what it meant. Remembering now, I realized I had never forgotten his final outburst of defiance. But for the first time I saw it clearly, as clearly as the gathered desert stones, and when I left today for good I would carry that image with me again, as the rest of my inheritance.

It was the day Papa suddenly came back to life and decided to go into Lone Pine and buy a car. Mama had been packing, and that brought the uncertainty of our future to such a sharp point, her back went into spasms. She didn't want to talk. She wanted to concentrate on the rings of heat. She let Papa rant a long time before she reacted.

"That's crazy, Ko," she said.

"Don't call me crazy! You think I'm going to ride that stinking bus all the way to Los Angeles?"

"It's cheaper than buying a car."

"Cheaper! What is it worth—to be packed in there like cattle? You call that cheap?"

"We don't have money to buy a car."

"I know how much money we have!"

He jumped to his feet then, rushed into the house, came out with his hat on and a shirt half-buttoned, and his walking stick and his turtleneck sweater tied around his neck, and took off striding toward the main gate, leaving Mama with her back full of smoking cork, which had done no good at all, since this new move of his merely bunched her muscles up worse than ever.

It was late afternoon when we heard the horn, still blocks away. Without looking out the door, Mama said, "Here he comes."

As the honks came closer we heard another sound, like a boxer working out on a flabby punching bag. Mama moved to the doorway. We all did—Chizu, May, me—in time to see a blue Nash four-door come around the corner, with its two front tires flat and Papa sitting up straight and proud behind the wheel, his hat cocked, his free hand punching at the horn. Heads were appearing at doorways all up and down the street.

He stopped in front, racing the engine and grinning, while he eyed Mama and fingered the shiny-knobbed dashboard gearshift. On the seat between his legs he held a half-empty quart bottle of whiskey. He yelled, "What do you think, Little Mama?"

She didn't answer. He had not been drinking much at all for about six months. She stood there waiting to see what he was going to do. He laughed and made the engine roar and demanded to know where all his boys were, he wanted to show those *yogores* what a real car looked like. Kiyo was the only son still in camp, and he had gone off to help someone else load furniture. So Papa announced that he would give all his women a ride. Mama protested, said he ought to get those tires fixed if we expected to take this car all the way into Los Angeles. Papa roared back at her, louder than the engine, and with such a terrible samurai's scowl that we all went leaping and piling into the car, Mama last, slamming the back door and climbing into the front seat next to him.

"You think it's a pretty good car?" he said, pleased by this show of power.

Mama said nothing. She sat very stiff, cool, enduring him.

Chizu was the placator now, leaning forward from the back to pat him on the shoulder. "It's a fine car, Papa."

"You watch!"

He grabbed the gear lever and rammed it into low. The Nash leaped, and we were clopperting down the street on those two flats and two good tires, with Papa laughing, sipping from the bottle. At the first corner he said, "You think I can't pick out cars?"

Softly Chizu said, "You did real good, Papa."

He stepped on the gas, hitting maybe thirty, swerving crazily. In the back seat we were all thrown around, flung from door to door like rag dolls, with Mama bouncing in front of us and Papa's hat crunching up against the ceiling.

May cried out, "Not so fast, Papa! You're going to wreck your car!"

"Think the car can't take it?" he yelled back at her. "You watch this!"

His gaiety turned ferocious again. He stomped the pedal, pushing the speedometer up to thirty-five. His right front tire had shredded and it flopped like a mangled arm. It lashed out, upending a garbage can. I started to cry. Chizu, her calm shattered, was yelling at him to slow down, Mama was too, and May was screaming. He wouldn't listen and told us to hold on, while he swung into the street, careening past emptying barracks where suitcases and duffel bags sat stacked. As we passed people standing by the baggage, Papa swerved from one side to the other, waving. He laughed, growled, made faces. In front of us, a laden family was hiking out toward the main gate. Papa swung wide, honking, and waving.

"Hey! Hey!" he shouted.

They turned, too amazed to wave back.

"Don't miss that bus!" he yelled.

At the next corner he spun off into a deserted section of barracks. These already looked like the ones we'd first moved into, sand piling up against foundation blocks, the clotheslines empty, all signs and markers gone. It made no difference to Papa that no one was out there to witness his performance. He aimed for tumbleweeds lying in the roadbed and shouted with triumph each time he squashed one. Chizu and Mama and May had quit trying to control him. I'd stopped crying. We grabbed for handholds, covered our heads, hoping simply to survive until he hit something hard or ran out of gas.

We came to a firebreak and Papa plunged into it, began to cut a twisty path across its emptiness, shouting "Hyah! Hyah!," gouging ragged tracks through the dusty sand. The way this firebreak lay, there seemed to be nothing in front of us now but sagebrush and open country, rising in the distance south of camp to the range of round, buff-colored hills rumored to be full of rattlesnakes. The few times I'd wished I could walk in one direction for as long as I wanted, the threat of those rattlesnakes deterred me. And now, farther south, beyond that visible barrier, out in the world I scarcely remembered, there loomed the dark, threatening cloud I'd heard grown-ups talk about. The way we seemed to be heading, I should have been frightened into a coma. But for this once, I was not. Watching Papa bounce and weave and shout in front of me, I was almost ready to laugh with him, with the first bubbly sense of liberation his defiant craziness had brought along with it. I believed in him completely just then, believed in the fierceness flashing in his wild eyes. Somehow that would get us past whatever waited inside the fearful dark cloud, get us past the heat, and the rattlers, and a great deal more.

At the fence he had to turn, sending up a white billow of dust. Where the fence met the highway we cornered again, heading for the bus stop. A crowd waited there, standing idly, sitting around on scattered baggage. They all turned to watch when they heard us coming. Papa tooted the horn and yelled out, "No bus for us! No bus for us!"

The young kids were mystified by this and stood open-eyed, watching. Some of the older folks smiled, waving as we hit a chuck hole and bounced. Papa swung left, and we clattered out onto the wide, empty boulevard that ran the length of the camp, back to where our own baggage waited and the final packing.

AUDRE LORDE
(1934–1992)

◆

Born and raised in Harlem, AUDRE LORDE described her childhood, her West Indian parents, and her coming of age as a lesbian in *Zami: A New Spelling of My Name* (1982), the autobiography she calls a "biomythography." As a self-described "black lesbian feminist warrior poet," she has published more than half a dozen poetry collections, which include *The First Cities* (1968), *Cables to Rage* (1970), *From a Land Where Other People Live* (1973)—nominated for a National Book Award for Poetry—*Coal* (1976), *Between Ourselves* (1976), and *The Black Unicorn* (1978). She has been Poet-in-Residence and Professor of English at Hunter College of the City of New York and also taught at Lehman College, in the SEEK program of City College, and at the John Jay College for Criminal Justice. Her honors include a National Endowment for the Arts residency grant and inclusion in the Hunter College Hall of Fame. She has written an account of her breast cancer, *The Cancer Journals* (1980), as well as the journal *A Burst of Light: Living with Cancer* (1990), from which the following excerpts are taken. After a fourteen-year battle with cancer, Audre Lorde died in 1992. Her last collection, *The Marvelous Arithmetics of Distance* (1993), was published posthumously.

In an autobiographical piece, "My Words Will Be There," included in Mari Evans's fine collection *Black Women Writers (1950–1980)*, Lorde delivered a passionate statement of her aesthetic, sexual, and racial politics:

"... love often is pain. ... we must not be afraid of pain, but ... we must not subject ourselves to pain as an end in itself. We must not celebrate victimization, because there are other ways of being Black. ...

"So much for pain; what about love? ... you can't separate loving from fighting, from dying, from hurting, but love is triumphant. ... It is powerful and strong. ... The love expressed between women is particular and powerful, because we have had to love in order to live; love has been our survival. ... I love to write love poems; I love loving. ... Women have not been taught to respect the erotic urge, the place that is uniquely female. So, just as some Black people tend to reject Blackness because it has been termed inferior, we, as women, tend to reject our capacity for feeling, our ability to love, to touch the erotic, because it has been devalued. But it is within this that lies so much of our power. . . ."

From *A Burst of Light: Living with Cancer*

though we may land here there is no other landing
to choose our meaning we must make it new.

—MURIEL RUKEYSER

Introduction

The year I became fifty felt like a great coming together for me. I was very proud of having made it for half a century, and in my own style. "Time for a change," I thought, "I wonder how I'm going to live the next half."

On February 1st, two weeks before my fiftieth birthday, I was told by my doctor that I had liver cancer, metastasized from the breast cancer for which I had had a mastectomy six years before.

At first I did not believe it. I continued with my previously planned teaching trip to Europe. As I grew steadily sicker in Berlin, I received medical information about homeopathic alternatives to surgery, which strengthened my decision to maintain some control over my life for as long as possible. I believe that decision has prolonged my life, together with the loving energies of women who supported me in that decision and in the work which gives that life shape.

The struggle with cancer now informs all my days, but it is only another face of that continuing battle for self-determination and survival that Black women fight daily, often in triumph. The following excerpts are from journals kept during my first three years of living with cancer.

January 19, 1984
New York City

I watched the movie *King* on TV tonight, and it brought those days of 1968 vividly back to me—the hope and the pain and the fury and the horror coming so close upon the possibility of change, a bare month after I'd left the Black student poets and my first meeting with Frances, at Tougaloo College in Mississippi. That night at Carnegie Hall when the Tougaloo Choir sang with Duke Ellington. A wealth of promise, of the student singers with their beautiful young Black faces, believing.

I was there to cover the concert for the Jackson, Mississippi, *Clarion Star Ledger*. "What the world needs now is love," they sang. Halfway through the song, the Master of Ceremonies interrupted to say that Dr. Martin Luther King had just been shot. "What the world needs now is love," they sang, tears lining their faces on stage catching the light, tears rolling down Mr. Honeywell's cheeks. "What the world needs now is love," they sang, his dark rhythmic arms directing the voices through all their weeping. And Dr. King is dead dead dead.

While I watched this movie I was also thinking about the course of my own life, the paths I feel bound for inside myself, the way of life that feels most real to me. And I wonder what I may be risking as I become more and more committed to telling whatever truth comes across my eyes my tongue my pen—no matter how difficult—the world as I see it, people as I feel them. And I wonder what I will have to pay someday for that privilege, and in whose coin? Will those forces which serve non-life in the name of power and profit kill me too, or merely dismember me in the eyes of whoever can use what I do?

When I stand in the radiance of a place like the Sapphires Sapphos dinner, with the elegant food and abundance of love and beautiful dark women, when I stand in that moment of sweetness, I sometimes become almost afraid. Afraid of their warmth and loving, as if that same loving warmth might doom me. I know this is not so, but it can feel like it. As if so long as I remained too different from my own time and surroundings I was safe, if terribly lonely. But now that I am becoming less lonely and more loved, I am also becoming more visible, and therefore more vulnerable. Malcolm saying to Martin in the film, "I love you Martin, and we are both dead men." . . .

May 28, 1985
Cambridge, Massachusetts

My daughter Beth's graduation from Harvard this weekend was a rite of passage for both of us. This institution takes itself very seriously, and there was enormous pomp and circumstance for three days. I couldn't help but think of all the racist, sexist ways they've tried through the last four years to diminish and destroy the essence of all the young Black women enrolled here. But it was a very important moment for Beth, a triumph that she'd survived Harvard, that she'd made it out, intact, and in a self she can continue living with. Of course, the point of so much of what goes on at places like Harvard— supposed to be about learning—is actually geared to either destroying these young people, or altering their substance into effigies that will be pliant, acceptable, and nonproblematic to the system. So I was proud of Beth standing there in the manicured garden of Adams House, wearing her broad white Disinvestment banner across her black commencement gown, but I was also very scared for her. Out there can be even more difficult, although now she knows at least that she can and did survive Harvard. And with her own style unimpaired.

I embarrassed myself because I kept trying to find secret places to cry in, but it was still a very emotionally fulfilling occasion. I feel she's on her way now in a specific sense that must leave me behind, and that is both sad and very reassuring to me. I am convinced that Beth has the stuff—the emotional and psychic wherewithal to do whatever she needs to do for her living, and I have given her the best I have to offer. I remember writing "What My Child Learns Of The Sea" when she was three months old, and it's both terrifying and wonderful to see it all coming true. I bless the goddess that I am still here to see it.

I tremble for her, for them all, because of the world we are giving them and all the work still to be done, and the gnawing question of will there be enough time? But I celebrate her, too, another one of those fine, strong, young Black women moving out to war, outrageous and resilient, plucky and beautiful.

I'm proud of her, and I'm proud of having seen her this far. It's a relief for me to know that whatever happens with my health now, and no matter how short my life may be, she is essentially on her way in the world, and next year Jonathan will be stepping out with his fine self, too. I look at them and they make my heart sing. Frances and I have done good work. . . .

December 7, 1985
New York City

My stomach x-rays are clear, and the problems in my GI series are all circumstantial. Now that the doctors here have decided I have liver cancer, they insist on reading all their findings as if that were a *fait accompli*. They refuse to look for any other reason for the irregularities in the x-rays, and they're treating my resistance to their diagnosis as a personal affront. But it's my body and my life and the goddess knows I'm paying enough for all this, I ought to have a say.

The flame is very dim these days. It's all I can do to teach my classes at Hunter and crawl home. Frances and I will leave for Switzerland as soon as school is over next week. The Women's Poetry Center will be dedicated at Hunter the night before I leave. No matter how sick I feel, I'm still afire with a need to do something for my living. How will I be allowed to live my own life, the rest of my life? . . .

December 15, 1985
Arlesheim, Switzerland

So here I am at the Lukas Klinik while my body decides if it will live or die. I'm going to fight like hell to make it live, and this looks like the most promising possibility. At least it's something different from narcotics and other terminal aids, which is all Dr. C. had to offer me in New York City in lieu of surgery when I told her how badly I hurt in my middle. "Almost every thing I eat now makes me sick," I told her. "Yes, I know," she said sorrowfully, writing me a prescription for codeine and looking at me as if there was nothing left she could do for me besides commiserate. Even though I like her very much, I wanted to punch her in her mouth.

I have found something interesting in a book here on active meditation as a form of self-control. There are six steps:

1) Control of Thought
   Think of a small object (i.e., a paper clip) for five minutes, exclusively. Practice for a month.
2) Control of Action
   Perform a small act every day at the same time. Practice, and be patient.
3) Control of Feeling (equanimity)
   Become aware of feelings and introduce equaminity into experiencing them—i.e., be afraid, not panic-stricken. (They're big on this one around here.)
4) Positivity (tolerance)
   Refrain from critical downgrading thoughts that sap energy from good work.
5) Openness (receptivity)
   Perceive even what is unpleasant in an unfettered, nonprejudiced way.
6) Harmony (perseverance)
   Work toward balancing the other five.

As a living creature I am part of two kinds of forces—growth and decay, sprouting and withering, living and dying, and at any given moment of our lives, each one of us is actively located somewhere along a continuum between these two forces. . . .

December 23, 1985, 10:30 a.m.
Arlesheim

I have cancer of the liver.

Dr. Lorenz just came in and told me. The crystallization test and the liver sonogram are all positive. The two masses in my liver are malignant. He says I should begin an increased Iscador program and antihormone therapy right away, if I decide that is the way I want to go. Well. The last possibility of doubt based on belief is gone. I said I'd come to Lukas because I trusted the anthroposophic doctors, and if they said it was malignant then I would accept their diagnosis. So here it is, and all the yelling and head-banging isn't going to change it. I guess it helps to finally know. I wish Frances were here.

I cannot afford to waste any more time in doubting, or in fury. The question is what do I do now? Listen to my body, of course, but the messages get dimmer and dimmer. In two weeks I go back home. Iscador or chemotherapy or both?

How did I ever come to be in this place? What can I use it for? . . .

November 6, 1986
New York City

Black mother goddess, salt dragon of chaos, Seboulisa, Mawu. Attend me, hold me in your muscular flowering arms, protect me from throwing any part of myself away.

Women who have asked me to set these stories down are asking me for my air to breathe, to use in their future, are courting me back to my life as a warrior. Some offer me their bodies, some their enduring patience, some a separate fire, and still others, only a naked need whose face is all too familiar. It is the need to give voice to the complexities of living with cancer, outside of the tissue-thin assurance that they "got it all," or that the changes we have wrought in our lives will insure that cancer never reoccurs. And it is a need to give voice to living with cancer outside of that numbing acceptance of death as a resignation waiting after fury and before despair.

There is nothing I cannot use somehow in my living and my work, even if I would never have chosen it on my own, even if I am livid with fury at having to choose. Not only did nobody ever say it would be easy, nobody ever said what faces the challenges would wear. The point is to do as much as I can of what I came to do before they nickel and dime me to death.

Racism. Cancer. In both cases, to win the aggressor must conquer, but the resisters need only survive. How do I define that survival and on whose terms?

So I feel a sense of triumph as I pick up my pen and say yes I am going to write again from the world of cancer and with a different perspective—that of living with cancer in an intimate daily relationship. Yes, I'm going to say plainly, six years after my mastectomy, in spite of drastically altered patterns of eating and living, and in spite of my self-conscious living and increased self-empowerment, and in spite of my deepening commitment to using myself in the service of what I believe, and in spite of all my positive expectations to the contrary, I have been diagnosed as having cancer of the liver, metastasized from breast cancer.

This fact does not make my last six years of work any less vital or important or necessary. The accuracy of that diagnosis has become less important than how I use the life I have.

November 8, 1986
New York City

If I am to put this all down in a way that is useful, I should start with the beginning of the story.

Sizable tumor in the right lobe of the liver, the doctors said. Lots of blood vessels in it means it's most likely malignant. Let's cut you open right now and see what we can do about it. Wait a minute, I said. I need to feel this thing out and see what's going on inside myself first, I said, needing some time to absorb the shock, time to assay the situation and not act out of panic. Not one of them said, I can respect that, but don't take too long about it.

Instead, that simple claim to my body's own processes elicited such an attack response from a reputable Specialist In Liver Tumors that my deepest—if not necessarily most useful—suspicions were totally aroused.

What that doctor could have said to me that I would have heard was, "You have a serious condition going on in your body and whatever you do about it you must not ignore it or delay deciding how you are going to deal with it because it will not go away no matter what you think it is." Acknowledging my responsibility for my own body. Instead, what he said to me was, "If you do not do exactly what I tell you to do right now without questions you are going to die a horrible death." In exactly those words.

I felt the battle lines being drawn up within my own body.

I saw this specialist in liver tumors at a leading cancer hospital in New York City, where I had been referred as an outpatient by my own doctor.

The first people who interviewed me in white coats from behind a computer were only interested in my health-care benefits and proposed method of payment. Those crucial facts determined what kind of plastic ID card I would be given, and without a plastic ID card, no one at all was allowed upstairs to see any doctor, as I was told by the uniformed, pistoled guards at all the stairwells.

From the moment I was ushered into the doctor's office and he saw my x-rays, he proceeded to infantilize me with an obviously well-practiced technique. When I told him I was having second thoughts about a liver biopsy, he glanced at my chart. Racism and Sexism joined hands across his table as he saw I taught at a university. "Well, you look like an *intelligent girl*," he said, staring at my one breast all the time he was speaking. "Not to have this biopsy immediately is like sticking your head in the sand." Then he went on to say that he would not be responsible when I wound up one day screaming in agony in the corner of his office!

I asked this specialist in liver tumors about the dangers of a liver biopsy spreading an existing malignancy, or even encouraging it in a borderline tumor. He dismissed my concerns with a wave of his hand, saying, instead of answering, that I really did not have any other sensible choice.

I would like to think that this doctor was sincerely motivated by a desire for me to seek what he truly believed to be the only remedy for my sickening body, but my faith in that scenario is considerably diminished by his $250 consultation fee and his subsequent medical report to my own doctor containing numerous supposedly clinical observations of *obese abdomen* and *remaining pendulous breast*.

In any event, I can thank him for the fierce shard lancing through my terror that shrieked there must be some other way, this doesn't feel right to me. If this is cancer and they cut me open to find out, what is stopping that intrusive action from spreading the cancer, or turning a questionable mass into an active malignancy? All I was asking for was the reassurance of a realistic answer to my real questions, and that was not forthcoming. I made up my mind that if I was going to die in agony on somebody's office floor, it certainly wasn't going to be his! I needed information, and pored over books on the liver in Barnes & Noble's Medical Textbook Section on Fifth Avenue for hours. I learned, among other things, that the liver is the largest, most complex, and most generous organ in the human body. But that did not help me very much.

In this period of physical weakness and psychic turmoil, I found myself going through an intricate inventory of rage. First of all at my breast surgeon—had he perhaps done something wrong? How could such a small breast tumor have metastasized? Hadn't he assured me he'd gotten it all, and what was this now anyway about micro-metastases? Could this tumor in my liver have been seeded at the same time as my breast cancer? There were so many unanswered questions, and too much that I just did not understand.

But my worst rage was the rage at myself. For a brief time I felt like a total failure. What had I been busting my ass doing these past six years if it wasn't living and loving and working to my utmost potential? And wasn't that all a guarantee supposed to keep exactly this kind of thing from ever happening again? So what had I done wrong and what was I going to have to pay for it and WHY ME?

But finally a little voice inside me said sharply, "Now really, is there any other way you would have preferred living the past six years that would have been more satisfying? And be that as it may, *should* or *shouldn't* isn't even the question. How do you want to live the rest of your life from now on and what are you going to do about it?" Time's awasting!

Gradually, in those hours in the stacks of Barnes & Noble, I felt myself shifting into another gear. My resolve strengthened as my panic lessened. Deep breathing, regularly. I'm not going to let them cut into my body again until I'm convinced there is no other alternative. And this time, the burden of proof rests with the doctors because their record of success with liver cancer is not so good that it would make me jump at a surgical solution. And scare tactics are not going to work. I have been scared now for six years and that hasn't stopped me. I've given myself plenty of practice in doing whatever I need to do, scared or not, so scare tactics are just not going to work. Or I hoped they were not going to work. At any rate, thank the goddess, they were not working yet. One step at a time.

But some of my nightmares were pure hell, and I started having trouble sleeping.

In writing this I have discovered how important some things are that I thought were unimportant. I discovered this by the high price they exact for scrutiny. At first I did not want to look again at how I slowly came to terms with my own mortality on a level deeper than before, nor with the inevitable strength that gave me as I started to get on with my life in actual time. Medical textbooks on the liver were fine, but there were appointments to be kept, and bills to pay, and decisions about my upcoming trip to Europe to be made. And what do I say to my children? Honesty has always been the bottom line between us, but did I really need them going through this with me during their final difficult years at college? On the other hand, how could I shut them out of this most important decision of my life?

I made a visit to my breast surgeon, a doctor with whom I have always been able to talk frankly, and it was from him that I got my first trustworthy and objective sense of timing. It was from him that I learned that the conventional forms of treatment for liver metastases made little more than one year's difference in the survival rate. I heard my old friend Clem's voice coming back to me through the dimness of thirty years: "I see you coming here trying to make sense where there is no sense. Try just living in it. Respond, alter, see what happens." I thought of the African way of perceiving life, as experience to be lived rather than as problem to be solved.

Homeopathic medicine calls cancer the cold disease. I understand that down to my bones that quake sometimes in their need for heat, for the sun, even for just a hot bath. Part of the way in which I am saving my own life is to refuse to submit my body to cold whenever possible.

In general, I fight hard to keep my treatment scene together in some coherent and serviceable way, integrated into my daily living and absolute. Forgetting is no excuse. It's as simple as one missed shot could make the difference between a quiescent malignancy and one that is growing again. This not only keeps me in an intimate, positive relationship to my own health, but it also underlines the fact that I have the responsibility for attending my own health. I cannot simply hand over that responsibility to anybody else.

Which does not mean I give in to the belief, arrogant or naive, that I know everything I need to know in order to make informed decisions about my body. But attending my own health, gaining enough information to help me understand and participate in the decisions made about my body by people who know more medicine than I do, are all crucial strategies in my battle for living. They also provide me with important prototypes for doing battle in all other arenas of my life.

Battling racism and battling heterosexism and battling apartheid share the same urgency inside me as battling cancer. None of these struggles are ever easy, and even the smallest victory is never to be taken for granted. Each victory must be applauded, because it is so easy not to battle at all, to just accept and call that acceptance inevitable.

And all power is relative. Recognizing the existence as well as the limitations of my own power, and accepting the responsibility for using it in my own behalf, involve me in direct and daily actions that preclude denial as a possible refuge. Simone de Beauvoir's words echo in my head: "It is in the recognition of the genuine conditions of our lives that we gain the strength to act and our motivation for change.". . .

November 15, 1986
New York City

In my office at home I have created a space that is very special to me. It is simple and quiet, with beautiful things about, and a ray of sunlight cascading through a low window on the best of days. It is here that I write whenever I am home, and where I retreat to center myself, to rest and recharge at regular intervals. It is here that I do my morning visualizations and my eurythmics.

It is a tiny alcove with an air mattress half-covered with bright pillows, and a low narrow table with a Nigerian tie-dye throw. Against one wall and central to this space is a painting by a young Guyanese woman called *The Yard*. It is a place of water and fire and flowers and trees, filled with Caribbean women and children working and playing and being.

When the sun lances through my small window and touches the painting, the yard comes alive. The red spirit who lives at the center of the painting flames. Children laugh, a woman nurses her baby, a little naked boy cuts the grass. One woman is building a fire outside for cooking; inside a house another woman is fixing a light. In a slat-house up the hill, windows are glowing under the red-tiled roof.

I keep company with the women of this place.

Yesterday, I sat in this space with a sharp Black woman, discussing the focus of a proposed piece for a Black women's magazine. We talked about whether it should be about the role of art and spirituality in Black women's lives, or about my survival struggles with current bouts of cancer. As we talked, I gradually realized that both articles were grounded in the same place within me, and required the same focus. I require the nourishment of art and spirituality in my life, and they lend strength and insight to all the endeavors that give substance to my living. It is the bread of art and the water of my spiritual life that remind me always to reach for what is highest within my capacities and in my demands of myself and others. Not for what is perfect but for what is the best possible. And I orchestrate my daily anticancer campaign with an intensity intrinsic to who I am, the intensity of making a poem. It is the same intensity with which I experience poetry, a student's first breakthrough, the loving energy of women I do not even know, the posted photograph of a sunrise taken from my winter dawn window, the intensity of loving.

I revel in the beauty of the faces of Black women at labor and at rest. I make, demand, translate satisfactions out of every ray of sunlight, scrap of bright cloth, beautiful sound, delicious smell that comes my way, out of every sincere smile and good wish. They are discreet bits of ammunition in my arsenal against despair. They all contribute to the strengthening of my determination to persevere when the greyness overwhelms, or Reaganomics wears me down. They whisper to me of joy when the light is dim, when I falter, when another Black child is gunned down from behind in Crossroads or Newark or lynched from a tree in Memphis, and when the health orchestration gets boring or depressing or just plain too much.

November 16, 1986
New York City

For Black women, learning to consciously extend ourselves to each other and to call upon each other's strengths is a life-saving strategy. In the best of circumstances surrounding our lives, it requires an enormous amount of mutual, consistent support for us to be emotionally able to look straight into the face of the powers aligned against us and still do our work with joy.

It takes determination and practice.

Black women who survive have a head start in learning how to be open and self-protective at the same time. One secret is to ask as many people as possible for help, depending on all of them and on none of them at the same time. Some will help, others cannot. For the time being.

Another secret is to find some particular thing your soul craves for nourishment—a different religion, a quiet spot, a dance class—and satisfy it. That satisfaction does not have to be costly or difficult. Only a need that is recognized, articulated, and answered.

There is an important difference between openness and naiveté. Not everyone has good intentions nor means me well. I remind myself I do not need to change these people, only recognize who they are. . . .

December 15, 1986
New York City

To acknowledge privilege is the first step in making it available for wider use. Each of us is blessed in some particular way, whether we recognize our blessings or not. And each one of us, somewhere in our lives, must clear a space within that blessing where she can call upon whatever resources are available to her in the name of something that must be done.

I have been very blessed in my life. I have been blessed to believe passionately, to love deeply, and to be able to work out of those loves and beliefs. Accidents of privilege allowed me to gain information about holistic/biological medicine and their approach to cancers, and that information has helped keep me alive, along with my original gut feeling that said, *Stay out of my body.* For me, living and the use of that living are inseparable, and I have a responsibility to put that privilege and that life to use.

For me, living fully means living with maximum access to my experience and power, loving, and doing work in which I believe. It means writing my poems, telling my stories, and speaking out of my most urgent concerns and against the many forms of antilife surrounding us.

I wish to live whatever life I have as fully and as sweetly as possible, rather than refocus that life solely upon extending it for some unspecified time. I consider this a political decision as well as a life-saving one, and it is a decision that I am fortunate to be able to make.

If one Black woman I do not know gains hope and strength from my story, then it has been worth the difficulty of telling.

[Audre Lorde died on November 17, 1992.]

KATE MILLETT
(1934—)

◆

KATE MILLETT was born and grew up in St. Paul, Minnesota, and was educated at the University of Minnesota, Oxford University, and Columbia University, where she submitted as her dissertation *Sexual Politics* (1969), a major text of feminist and cultural studies. She has exhibited her sculpture in Tokyo and New York, taught literature and philosophy in a number of universities, founded an art colony for women in Poughkeepsie, New York, and, as an essayist and autobiographer, published *The Prostitution Papers, Flying, Sita, The Basement, Going to Iran,* and *The Loony-Bin Trip* (1990), which is excerpted here.

"Not since Ken Kesey's *One Flew Over the Cuckoo's Nest* has the literature of madness emitted such a powerful anti-institutional cry"—one reviewer's response to *The Loony-Bin Trip* suggests the powerful argument it makes for the rights of mental-health patients. The book tells the story of Millett's struggle to regain control of her life after being diagnosed as manic-depressive. She survived forced hospitalization by family and friends, suicide attempts, her fight to live with her decision to go off medication and its side effects—the prescribed drug, lithium—and most painfully, her increasingly ominous doubts about her own sanity and the loyalty of her lover and friends. This memoir challenges the mental-health establishment as aggressively as Millett once took on the patriarchal sanctuary of cultural and literary studies. But because this narrative is more openly personal and the narrator immensely more vulnerable, its bravery rings with a terrible pain and fear. She says that she is telling the story of her shame and struggle for all the other people who still are shut up in their depressive silence.

The issue of women's mental health is, of course, a matter of sexual politics and has provoked much commentary. Nancy Mairs (see page 375), in writing about her own depression, cites Maggie Scarf's review of depression in women in her book *Unfinished Business: Pressure Points in the Lives of Women* (1980). Vivian Gornick (see page 305) has written in "Woman as Outsider" that "madness is in the female vein. Men shoot themselves bravely, but women go mad. . . . Our men die, but our asylums are overflowing with madwomen: women who become depressed—and go mad." Donald F. Klein, M.D., and Paul H. Wender,

M.D., authors of the recent study *Understanding Depression: A Complete Guide to Its Diagnosis and Treatment* (1993), concede that "depression, increasingly common in recent times, [is] twice as common in women as in men." But at this point they part company from the political perspectives of feminists. Without explaining why women are particularly affected, they argue that the causes of depression and manic-depression are biological rather than psychological and most cases should be treated with drug therapy prescribed by medically trained experts, the exact antithesis of Millett's point of view. As the *New York Times* reviewer put it, "there's something slightly brave-new-world-like about their apparent denial of existential unhappiness or, as they put it, 'the belief that peculiar behavior is really a sane response to an insane political and social system.'"

From *The Loony-Bin Trip*

PREFACE

This is an account of a journey into that nightmare state ascribed to madness: that social condition, that experience of being cast out and confined. I am telling you what happened to me. Because the telling functions for me as a kind of exorcism, a retrieval and vindication of the self—the mind—through reliving what occurred. It is a journey many of us take. Some of us survive it intact, others only partially survive, debilitated by the harm done to us: the temptations of complicity, of the career of "patient," the pressures toward capitulation. I am telling this too in the hope that it may help all those who have been or are about to be in the same boat, those captured and shaken by this bizarre system of beliefs: the general superstition of "mental disease," the physical fact of incarceration and compulsory drugs, finally the threat of being put away and locked up forever, or if released, stigmatized throughout the rest of one's life. A fate, after all, held before all of us through the whole course of our lives, the notion of "losing one's mind." An eventuality I once would have regarded as absurd, impossible, someone else's bad luck but not mine.

I already had a glimpse of the nether regions or at least the first circle of this dark landscape early in life: I had a summer job in St. Peter's Asylum in southern Minnesota when I was eighteen. Knowing already how terrible such places were, it never occurred to me that I would be delivered into one as an adult, when I was independent, established, a published writer. When it happened, in 1973, I was bemused and saw it as a fluke, a shameful incident, an error and misunderstanding among family members, the product of naïveté. Following my release I became profoundly depressed, my confidence broken by confinement; despite the fact that I had won my freedom through the intercession of civil rights lawyers and a trial—unusual in itself—it was accepted by those around me that I was "crazy," so I might just as well be. Moreover, there was the ominous diagnosis of manic depression, a professional scientific verdict of insanity. I began to crumble in fear and loneliness. Desperate to keep from killing myself—which seemed the logical next step, an execution I was bound by circumstances to carry out—I turned frantically to what seemed my only other option to save my life, my body anyway, and surrendered my mind, the spirit, the self: I sought "help," became a lithium patient and lived thereafter a careful existence. An unsound mind like mine must be tranquilized and occluded with a drug; left to itself it was tainted, unstable.

For seven years I lived with a hand tremor, diarrhea, the possibility of kidney damage and all the other "side effects" of lithium. Then, in the summer of 1980, I decided to go off lithium, thereby severing the control of an authority I had never entirely believed in and had reason to resent. The decision to go it on my own was a gamble for my own reason. For in accepting lithium as a remedy for depression caused by incarceration and diagnosis, I was accepting the validity of both, together with the pronouncement of my incompetence and degenerative insanity; I was confessing to an illness whose other treatments lead to the loss of one's freedom and dignity through confinement. I had been fortunate that my loss was temporary. But I had seen thousands of persons for whom it had been permanent. I dared to refuse the stigma, challenge the ascription itself. If I had kept my own counsel, maybe nothing would have come of the decision. But I imagined I was safe. This is what happened.

PART ONE

The Farm

1

At the farm in Poughkeepsie just before dinner the first evening light is soft and almost violet. Sophie and I cross the grass in the circle drive by the big locust, the gravel drive stretches just before us and beyond it the farmhouse lawn where the tables are laid for dinner under the trees. We are going to see the coop which Sophie has just fixed up as her studio. A barren New England shed, a chicken coop—she has transformed it.

It is the South now, nearly tropical, "Like a New Orleans whorehouse," I say, and we laugh. "But it's perfect." I pace the room, admiring it, remembering how they called them sporting houses, places of the afternoon. The last passionate fullness of day, Sophie's straw mats and bamboo hangings filtering the light. "How clever you are." The look between us grows into a suggestion. A quickie? "Do you suppose there's time before dinner or will the apprentices catch us in the act?" she asks. We smile and look around the room at the spectacle of light, the dark gleam inside, the light outside building, massive as water, brilliant by contrast, overwhelming like the sea around a boat.

The beauty of what Sophie has created in a few casual hours takes my breath away. I have known this place for years at nearly every hour of the day, even worked here, yet I've never seen the room in this light; Sophie has enchanted the place. This amazing woman, her intelligence, her knack, her whim and instinct conceptualized, then realized. It's genius, the way the light is caught and held by her hangings, the bamboo blinds placed at just the right junctures to filter and direct the light as it floods in at the big openings in the wall to the front of the coop on the southern and western sides. There's the old camera from her family in Canada mounted on its tripod as if in explanation, as if the camera had taken a picture and we were in it. Oceans of light in the lens of the eye opening to the masses of color in the fervent July sunset beginning now just out of reach beyond the far western wall, all the refracted yellows and reds defused in the air around us—the room has become a camera. How brilliant she is, this is beyond anything she has shown me before. Bending over me, courting me, taking me, seducing me—the whole structure a seduction, the most outrageous compliment that someone would create this and then pay me the homage of showing it as a private exhibition that would end in bedding me. The soft of her skin, her bare shoulder against my lips, the pristine blue sheets under us, cobalt, their color and the color of the golden light around us, one does not wish to close one's eyes, miss it.

And then they burst in on us, pirates of noise, Kim and Libby stumbling in the door, laughing, knowing full well what they would displace. Somehow their presence is a compliment to our love, just as they prevent it they also validate and applaud. We look at each other and cannot find resentment. "Aha, we know just what you're up to, but you're too late, the food is on the table." "Really on the table?" "Really. We give you two minutes, exactly two minutes." They both laugh. "To make yourselves decent." How they love it, being young and so full of sex themselves, its energy, its ripe invitation; sexual appetite is a presence in the room, its apprehension here is a celebration.

For they love us, as we love them, every day more so, friendship becoming a drunkenness becoming love, a love none of us define, so we call it the farm or the colony, as if it were merely an idea, an ideology of a communal something politically correct. Through it, rapturously happy. Because of how we live? Because of who we are? Sophie and I say it's because this year's bunch of apprentices is wonderful, they're treasures. Calling them the kids, though we know they are young women, young but already women.

Life has never been so good. The apprentices, the farm, the summer still ahead, only half over, spreading already to a richness, a perfection, like a peony in full bloom. Or the loosestrife around the pond. And Sophie. All, I have everything. I am even off the lithium. With no ill effect. It is six weeks now we have been keeping check on the experiment, and if it works I am whole. Either I was never crazy or I have recovered and can be sane henceforth. To be whole, not a cracked egg, not an imperfect specimen, not a deformed intellect or a mental defective—but whole. It's working, I'll make it.

"Hey, come on, you guys, the cook will have a fit." We look at each other, face to face in the circle of bodies in this wonderful light; they are by the door, between the door and the bed, their shapes already darkened against the light; leaning on an arm, you can smile up at each of them, in love. With them, with the place, with Sophie. "Come on, you're already late." Discovered now and on our way to dinner, crossing the grass with Sophie, I see the rest of them standing at the table to toast, their glasses raised, the red wine in the glasses, the last light cleansing and sparkling the glasses and plates along the straw place mats, the different, warmer light of kerosene lanterns on the wooden boards of the table, and their long brown arms above their heads, raised to toast with the pleasure of clinking glasses. "They're a wonderful bunch," I say again to Sophie as we cross the grass. "The best we ever had," she says nodding. This is the happiest summer of my life. . . .

[What follows is Millett's memoir of her forced incarceration in the United States and Ireland by her family and with the cooperation of her lover as the consequence of her refusal to go back on her medication. Her story becomes the basis of her involvement in the "antipsychiatric movement" discussed in the following excerpt from the book's Conclusion.]

CONCLUSION

I wrote *The Loony-Bin Trip* between 1982 and 1985. The last section was written first, in a hangover of penitence and self-renunciation, that complicity with social disapproval which is depression. Now, when I reread it, I find something in it rings false. True, it describes depression: the giving in, the giving up, an abnegation so complete it becomes a false consciousness. But typing it over I want to say, Wait a moment— why call this depression?—why not call it grief? You've permitted your grief, even your outrage, to be converted into a disease. You have allowed your overwhelming, seemingly inexplicable grief at what has been done to you—the trauma and shame of imprisonment—to be transformed into a mysterious psychosis. How could you?

I was trying to find my way back. Out of the unendurable loneliness of knowing. Acceptance. I could not bear to be the only one any-more. I could not pit my truth against so many, against the power of science, nor could I live without other people. I surrendered my under-standing, lost myself trying to survive and accommodate. And I went on taking lithium. It seemed a condition of parole: if I stopped taking it and were found out I might be confined again. A sort of Pascal's bet: I was terrified that without the drug I could plummet again. What if they were right after all? My own mind was too dangerous.

For years the urge to break free of lithium tugged at me, but my fear of consequences was too great: another fall, another capture? Then I was invited to attend a conference of the National Association for Rights, Protection, and Advocacy, professionals recently authorized by the federal government to protect the rights of persons with "mental illness." There is a liberal faction within the Association that has consis-tently permitted the veteran organizers of the anti-psychiatric move-ment to attend and speak out. I met them and was able to connect finally with others of my own persuasion, to discover their energy and support. I went to a few more conferences, still on lithium, deploring aloud the system and its drugs but in secret taking lithium, hedging my bets, maintaining my crutch, aware of bad faith, but frightened.

Finally my comrades Paul and Dayna asked me if I was on drugs. The movement attitude is tolerant: take them if you like; if you want to with-draw there is help and support. Dayna had withdrawn from lithium sev-eral years before. She told me to "drink lots of milk, don't get overtired, have faith, and tell no one." Paul and Dayna would be the only ones to know; they'd call me every Sunday night and I'd report.

In fact there was never anything to report. In 1988 on my birthday, September 14th, I took 600 mg of lithium instead of the usual 900, going below the therapeutic level for the first time. On January 1st, I reduced it to 300 mg, and on March 15, daring the Ides of March, I went to sleep for the first time in seven years having taken no lithium at all. Nothing happened. Nothing ever happened. None of the anger I had feared; indeed it seemed that lithium had created a stifled fury in me for years which abated and then fell away. To my surprise I had a new patience now, and serenity, was more tolerant and open, even able to fall in love again. And this time I kept my secret.

Over a year went by without incident. I still kept mum. Then one day when Sophie was visiting the farm—a flourishing place now, our trees full grown and our harvest at last able to support the art colony— it seemed the right moment; there was a great harmony between us. "I've been off lithium for over a year now, Sophie." The astonishment in her face, then relief. "What happened?" "Nothing, that's it, nothing." And then we laughed and the laughter freed us. She shook her head: had it all been for nothing?

The psychiatric diagnosis imposed upon me is that I am constitutionally psychotic, a manic-depressive bound to suffer recurrent attacks of "affective illness" unless I am maintained on prophylactic medication, specifically lithium. For a total of thirteen years I deadened my mind and obscured my consciousness with a drug whose prescription was based on a fallacy. Even discounting the possible harm of the drug's "side effects," it may seem little consolation to discover that one was sane all along. But to me it is everything. Perhaps even survival: for this diagnosis sets in motion a train of self-doubt and futility, a sentence of alienation whose predestined end is suicide. I have been close to that very death, remember its terror and logic and despair. One struggles to forgive the personal betrayals, just as one must come to analyze the forces that hemmed one in. But it is essential not to forget. In the remembering lies reason, even hope and a saving faith in the integrity of the mind.

It is the integrity of the mind I wish to affirm, its sanctity and inviolability. Of course there is no denying the misery and stress of life itself: the sufferings of the mind at the mercy of emotion, the circumstances which set us at war with one another, the divorces and antagonisms in human relationships, the swarms of fears, the blocks to confidence, the crises of decision and choice. These are the things we weather or fail to, seek council against, even risk the inevitable disequilibrium of power inherent in therapy to combat—they are the grit and matter of the human condition. But when such circumstances are converted into symptoms and diagnosed as illnesses, I believe we enter upon very uncertain ground.

The entire construct of the "medical model" of "mental illness"— what is it but an analogy? Between physical medicine and psychiatry:

the mind is said to be subject to disease in the same manner as the body. But whereas in physical medicine there are verifiable physiological proofs—in damaged or affected tissue, bacteria, inflammation, cellular irregularity—in mental illness alleged socially unacceptable behavior is taken as a symptom, even as proof, of pathology. (There are exceptions to this: brain tumors, paresis [tertiary syphilis], Huntington's chorea, and Alzheimer's disease—in each of these there is indeed physical evidence of cellular damage. However, these conditions are not what we mean by mental illness. What we generally mean—schizophrenia, manic depression, paranoia, borderline personality disorders, and so forth—are all illnesses which are established upon behavioral and not physical grounds.) Diagnosis is based upon impressionistic evidence: conduct, deportment, and social manner. Such evidence is frequently imputed. Furthermore, it may not even be experienced by the afflicted party, but instead may be observed by others who declare such a one afflicted.

For in the case of "mental illness," the petitioner for treatment is very often not the one said to be afflicted, but someone else altogether. Commitment laws are so written that the afflicted shall be deprived of judgment on the application of next of kin in conjunction with psychiatry. Their purpose is to deny the allegedly ill person the legal entitlement of any and all rights, civil, constitutional, or human. This is unlike anything we know of in physical medicine, where the prevailing attitude is compassion and respect. . . .

Ethically, and eventually legally as well, there is finally the issue of the Hippocratic Oath: one shall do no harm. The "medical model" of mental disease has taken a terrible toll on the bodies of its victims as well as on their minds and emotions. Throughout the world millions of persons now suffer from tardive dyskinesia, an iatrogenic disorder of the central nervous system brought on by the ingestion of toxic substances, the neuroleptic and antipsychotic drugs prescribed as medication. Tardive dyskinesia is an irreversible condition, resulting in (among other injuries) involuntary spasms—physical disfigurements that stigmatize and often isolate the sufferers, minimizing social interaction and opportunity. Tardive dyskinesia is produced by the entire family of neuroleptic drugs: Thorazine, Stelazine, Haldol—substances derived ultimately from chlorine and coal tar. Lithium presents a threat to the kidneys and the heart. The Physician's Desk Reference, by merely reprinting the warnings of the pharmaceutical companies themselves, makes grim reading about any psychotropic drug. It is difficult to understand how anything this physically harmful could continue to be prescribed, even for an offending mind. *Mens sana, in corpore sano.* . . .

VIVIAN GORNICK
(1935—)

---◆---

VIVIAN GORNICK, feminist, journalist, critic, and memoirist, grew up in the Bronx and attended City College, the University of California at Berkeley, and New York University. She unfolds the culture of her urban childhood, Jewish family, and early adult years in the autobiography excerpted here, *Fierce Attachments,* "a magnificent book," in the words of Phillip Lopate, "that should join the ranks of the classic American autobiographies."

Gornick's first book, *Woman in Sexist Society: Studies in Power and Powerlessness* (1971), co-edited with Barbara K. Moran, is a collection of thirty essays by feminist writers and scholars and a founding document of the women's liberation movement. Gornick's essay in the volume, "Woman as Outsider," has not dated in more than twenty years. It has the intelligence and moral courage of the writing and politics she has engaged in since the first years of the women's movement. Her second book, *In Search of Ali Mahmoud: An American Woman in Egypt* (1973), recounts her attempt to learn more about the society that had produced a close Arab friend of hers. Elizabeth Janeway praised the book's "glimpse of the chiaroscuro of Egyptian life" and the author as "one of the least obsessed or dogmatic feminists one can imagine."

Gornick's interest in the intertwining of political structures and cultural myths, generated as much by her family history as by feminism, issued next in *The Romance of American Communism* (1978).

Her most recent book, *Fierce Attachments* (1987), examines her relationship, as a girl and a woman, with her mother, who, widowed when her daughter was thirteen years old, went on to raise her two children in a chronic state of low-grade, functional depression. A *New York Times Book Review* Notable Book of the Year, this memoir of family misery and the painful passage toward rebirth has been heralded as "a landmark in American autobiography," a "brilliant" and "brave" "American classic," "marvelous," "compelling," "timeless," and "vividly real." What is particularly remarkable is the sympathy Gornick achieves for her mother without for one moment sentimentalizing her or their ethnic past. As in her other books and journalism, Gornick's moral intelligence defines this emotional journey into life history; she reconstructs it honestly, without disguising or denying the roots of bitter feeling she finds along the way. In the process, she brings to mind the words of Martin Buber: "As I create, I discover."

From *Fierce Attachments*

I'm eight years old. My mother and I come out of our apartment onto the second-floor landing. Mrs. Drucker is standing in the open doorway of the apartment next door, smoking a cigarette. My mother locks the door and says to her, "What are you doing here?" Mrs. Drucker jerks her head backward toward her own apartment. "He wants to lay me. I told him he's gotta take a shower before he can touch me." I know that "he" is her husband. "He" is always the husband. "Why? He's so dirty?" my mother says. "He feels dirty to *me*," Mrs. Drucker says. "Drucker, you're a whore," my mother says. Mrs. Drucker shrugs her shoulder. "I can't ride the subway," she says. In the Bronx "ride the subway" was a euphemism for going to work.

I lived in that tenement between the ages of six and twenty-one. There were twenty apartments, four to a floor, and all I remember is a building full of women. I hardly remember the men at all. They were everywhere, of course—husbands, fathers, brothers—but I remember only the women. And I remember them all crude like Mrs. Drucker or fierce like my mother. They never spoke as though they knew who they were, understood the bargain they had struck with life, but they often acted as though they knew. Shrewd, volatile, unlettered, they performed on a Dreiserian scale. There would be years of apparent calm, then suddenly an outbreak of panic and wildness: two or three lives scarred (perhaps ruined), and the turmoil would subside. Once again: sullen quiet, erotic torpor, the ordinariness of daily denial. And I—the girl growing in their midst, being made in their image—I absorbed them as I would chloroform on a cloth laid against my face. It has taken me thirty years to understand how much of them I understood.

My mother and I are out walking. I ask if she remembers the women in that building in the Bronx. "Of course," she replies. I tell her I've always thought sexual rage was what made them so crazy. "Absolutely," she says without breaking her stride. "Remember Drucker? She used to say if she didn't smoke a cigarette while she was having intercourse with her husband she'd throw herself out the window. And Zimmerman, on the other side of us? They married her off to him when she was sixteen, she hated his guts, she used to say if he'd get killed on the job (he was a construction worker) it would be a *mitzvah*." My mother stops walking. Her voice drops in awe of her own memory. "He actually used to take her by physical force," she says. "Would pick her up in the middle of the living-room floor and carry her off to the bed." She stares into the middle distance for a moment. Then she says to me, "The European men. They were animals. Just plain animals." She starts walking again. "Once, Zimmerman locked him out of the house. He rang our bell. He could hardly look at me. He asked if he could use our fire-escape window. I didn't speak one word to him. He walked through the house and climbed out the window." My mother laughs. "That fire-escape window, it did some business! Remember Cessa upstairs? Oh no, you couldn't remember her, she only lived there one year after we moved into the house, then the Russians were in that apartment. Cessa and I were very friendly. It's so strange, when I come to think of it. We hardly knew each other, any of us, sometimes we didn't talk to each other at all. But we lived on top of one another, we were in and out of each other's house. Everybody knew everything in no time at all. A few months in the building and the women were, well, *intimate*.

"This Cessa. She was a beautiful young woman, married only a few years. She didn't love her husband. She didn't hate him, either. He was a nice man, actually. What can I tell you, she didn't love him, she used to go out every day, I think she had a lover somewhere. Anyway, she had long black hair down to her ass. One day she cut it off. She wanted to be modern. Her husband didn't say anything to her, but her father came into the house, took one look at her cut hair, and gave her a slap across the face she saw her grandmother from the next world. Then he instructed her husband to lock her in the house for a month. She used to come down the fire escape into my window and out my door. Every afternoon for a month. One day she comes back and we're having coffee in the kitchen. I say to her, 'Cessa, tell your father this is America, Cessa, America. You're a free woman.' She looks at me and she says to me, 'What do you mean, tell my father this is America? He was born in Brooklyn.'"

My relationship with my mother is not good, and as our lives accumulate it often seems to worsen. We are locked into a narrow channel of acquaintance, intense and binding. For years at a time there is an exhaustion, a kind of softening, between us. Then the rage comes up again, hot and clear, erotic in its power to compel attention. These days it is bad between us. My mother's way of "dealing" with the bad times is to accuse me loudly and publicly of the truth. Whenever she sees me she says, "You hate me. I know you hate me." I'll be visiting her and she'll say to anyone who happens to be in the room—a neighbor, a friend, my brother, one of my nieces—"She hates me. What she has against me I don't know, but she hates me." She is equally capable of stopping a stranger on the street when we're out walking and saying, "This is my daughter. She hates me." Then she'll turn to me and plead, "What did I do to you, you should hate me so?" I never answer. I know she's burning and I'm glad to let her burn. Why not? I'm burning, too.

But we walk the streets of New York together endlessly. We both live in lower Manhattan now, our apartments a mile apart, and we visit best by walking. My mother is an urban peasant and I am my mother's daughter. The city is our natural element. We each have daily adventures with bus drivers, bag ladies, ticket takers, and street crazies. Walking brings out the best in us. I am forty-five now and my mother is seventy-seven. Her body is strong and healthy. She traverses the island easily with me. We don't love each other on these walks, often we are raging at each other, but we walk anyway.

Our best times together are when we speak of the past. I'll say to her, "Ma, remember Mrs. Kornfeld? Tell me that story again," and she'll delight in telling me the story again. (It is only the present she hates; as soon as the present becomes the past, she immediately begins loving it.) Each time she tells the story it is both the same and different because each time I'm older, and it occurs to me to ask a question I didn't ask the last time around. . . .

We're walking up Fifth Avenue. It's a bad day for me. I'm feeling fat and lonely, trapped in my lousy life. I know I should be home working, and that I'm here playing the dutiful daughter only to avoid the desk. The anxiety is so great I'm walking with a stomachache. My mother, as always, knows she can do nothing for me, but my unhappiness makes her nervous. She is talking, talking at tedious, obfuscating length, about a cousin of mine who is considering divorce.

As we near the library an Eastern religionist (shaved head, translucent skin, a bag of bones wrapped in faded pink gauze) darts at us, a copy of his leader's writings extended in his hand. My mother keeps talking while the creature in gauze flaps around us, his spiel a steady buzz in the air, competing for my attention. At last, she feels interrupted. She turns to him. "What *is* it?" she says. "What do you want from me? Tell me." He tells her. She hears him out. Then she straightens her shoulders, draws herself up to her full five feet two inches, and announces: "Young man, I am a Jew and a socialist. I think that's more than enough for one lifetime, don't you?" The pink-gowned boy-man is charmed, and for a moment bemused. "My parents are Jews," he confides, "but they certainly aren't socialists." My mother stares at him, shakes her head, grasps my arm firmly in her fingers, and marches me off up the avenue.

"Can you believe this?" she says. "A nice Jewish boy shaves his head and babbles in the street. A world full of crazies. Divorce everywhere, and if not divorce, *this*. What a generation you all are!"

"Don't start, Ma," I say. "I don't want to hear that bullshit again."

"Bullshit here, bullshit there," she says, "it's still true. Whatever else we did, we didn't fall apart in the streets like you're all doing. We had order, quiet, dignity. Families stayed together, and people lived decent lives."

"That's a crock. They didn't lead decent lives, they lived hidden lives. You're not going to tell me people were happier then, are you?"

"No," she capitulates instantly. "I'm not saying that."

"Well, what are you saying?"

She frowns and stops talking. Searches around in her head to find out what she is saying. Ah, she's got it. Triumphant, accusing, she says, "The unhappiness is so *alive* today."

Her words startle and gratify me. I feel pleasure when she says a true or a clever thing. I come close to loving her. "That's the first step, Ma," I say softly. "The unhappiness has to be made alive before anything can happen."

She stops in front of the library. She doesn't want to hear what I'm saying, but she's excited by the exchange. Her faded brown eyes, dark and brilliant in my childhood, brighten as the meaning of her words and mine penetrates her thought. Her cheeks flush and her pudding-soft face hardens wonderfully with new definition. She looks beautiful to me. I know from experience she will remember this afternoon as a deeply pleasurable one. I also know she will not be able to tell anyone why it has been pleasurable. She enjoys thinking, only she doesn't know it. She has never known it.

[When the author's father died suddenly when Gornick was thirteen years old, her mother entered upon an emotional state of permanent mourning.]

Mama and Nettie* quarreled, and I entered City College. In feeling memory these events carry equal weight. Both inaugurated open conflict, both drove a wedge between me and the unknowing self, both

---

*A close family friend who lived in the same apartment house.

were experienced as subversive and warlike in character. Certainly the conflict between Nettie and my mother seemed a strategic plan to surround and conquer. Incoherent as the war was, shot through with rage and deceit, its aims apparently confused and always denied, it never lost sight of the enemy: the intelligent heart of the girl who if not bonded to one would be lost to both. City College, as well, seemed no less concerned with laying siege, to the ignorant mind if not the intelligent heart. Benign in intent, only a passport to the promised land, City of course was the real invader. It did more violence to the emotions than either Mama or Nettie could have dreamed possible, divided me from them both, provoked and nourished an unshared life inside the head that became a piece of treason. I lived among my people, but I was no longer one of them.

I think this was true for most of us at City College. We still used the subways, still walked the familiar streets between classes, still returned to the neighborhood each night, talked to our high-school friends, and went to sleep in our own beds. But secretly we had begun to live in a world inside our heads where we read talked thought in a way that separated us from our parents, the life of the house and that of the street. We had been initiated, had learned the difference between hidden and expressed thought. This made us subversives in our own homes.

As thousands before me have said, "For us it was City College or nothing." I enjoyed the solidarity those words invoked but rejected the implied deprivation. At City College I sat talking in a basement cafeteria until ten or eleven at night with a half dozen others who also never wanted to go home to Brooklyn or the Bronx, and here in the cafeteria my education took root. Here I learned that Faulkner was America, Dickens was politics, Marx was sex, Jane Austen the idea of culture, that I came from a ghetto and D. H. Lawrence was a visionary. Here my love of literature named itself, and amazement over the life of the mind blossomed. I discovered that people were transformed by ideas, and that intellectual conversation was immensely erotic.

We never stopped talking. Perhaps because we did very little else (restricted by sexual fear and working-class economics, we didn't go to the theater and we didn't make love), but certainly we talked so much because most of us had been reading in bottled-up silence from the age of six on and City College was our great release. It was not from the faculty that City drew its reputation for intellectual goodness, it was from its students, it was from us. Not that we were intellectually distinguished, we weren't; but our hungry energy vitalized the place. The idea of intellectual life burned in us. While we pursued ideas we felt known, to ourselves and to one another. The world made sense, there was ground beneath our feet, a place in the universe to stand. City College made conscious in me inner cohesion as a first value.

I think my mother was very quickly of two minds about me and City, although she had wanted me to go to school, no question about that, had been energized by the determination that I do so (instructed me in the middle of her first year of widowhood to enter the academic not the commercial course of high-school study), and was even embattled when it became something of an issue in the family.

"Where is it written that a working-class widow's daughter should to go college?" one of my uncles said to her, drinking coffee at our kitchen table on a Saturday morning in my senior year in high school.

"Here it is written," she had replied, tapping the table hard with her middle finger. "Right here it is written. The girl goes to college."

"Why?" he had pursued.

"Because I say so."

"But why? What do you think will come of it?"

"I don't know. I only know she's clever, she deserves an education, and she's going to get one. This is America. The girls are not cows in the field only waiting for a bull to mate with." I stared at her. Where had *that* come from? My father had been dead only five years, she was in full widowhood swing.

The moment was filled with conflict and bravado. She felt the words she spoke but she did not mean them. She didn't even know what she meant by an education. When she discovered at my graduation that I wasn't a teacher she acted as though she'd been swindled. In her mind a girl child went in one door marked college and came out another marked teacher.

"You mean you're not a teacher?" she said to me, eyes widening as her two strong hands held my diploma down on the kitchen table.

"No," I said.

"What have you been doing there all these years?" she asked quietly.

"Reading novels," I replied.

She marveled silently at my chutzpah.

But it wasn't really a matter of what I could or could not do with the degree. We were people who knew how to stay alive, she never doubted I would find a way. No, what drove her, and divided us, was me thinking. She hadn't understood that going to school meant I would start thinking: coherently and out loud. She was taken by violent surprise. My sentences got longer within a month of those first classes. Longer, more complicated, formed by words whose meaning she did not always know. I had never before spoken a word she didn't know. Or made a sentence whose logic she couldn't follow. Or attempted an opinion that grew out of an abstraction. It made her crazy. Her face began to take on a look of animal cunning when I started a sentence that could not possibly be concluded before three clauses had hit the air. Cunning sparked anger, anger flamed into rage. "What are you talking about?" she would shout at me. "What *are* you talking about? Speak English, please! We all understand English in this house. Speak it!"

Her response stunned me. I didn't get it. Wasn't she pleased that I could say something she didn't understand? Wasn't that what it was all about? I was the advance guard. I was going to take her into the new world. All she had to do was adore what I was becoming, and here she was refusing. I'd speak my new sentences, and she would turn on me as though I'd performed a vile act right there at the kitchen table.

She, of course, was as confused as I. She didn't know why she was angry, and if she'd been told she was angry she would have denied it, would have found a way to persuade both herself and any interested listener that she was proud I was in school, only why did I have to be such a showoff? Was that what going to college was all about? Now, take Mr. Lewis, the insurance agent, an educated man if ever there was one, got a degree from City College in 1929, 1929 mind you, and never made you feel stupid, always spoke in simple sentences, but later you thought about what he had said. That's the way an educated person should talk. Here's this snotnose kid coming into the kitchen with all these big words, sentences you can't make head or tail of . . .

I was seventeen, she was fifty. I had not yet come into my own as a qualifying belligerent but I was a respectable contender and she, naturally, was at the top of her game. The lines were drawn, and we did not fail one another. Each of us rose repeatedly to the bait the other one tossed out. Our storms shook the apartment: paint blistered on the wall, linoleum cracked on the floor, glass shivered in the window frame. We barely kept our hands off one another, and more than once we approached disaster.

One Saturday afternoon she was lying on the couch. I was reading in a nearby chair. Idly she asked, "What are you reading?" Idly I replied, "A comparative history of the idea of love over the last three hundred years." She looked at me for a moment. "That's ridiculous," she said slowly. "Love is love. It's the same everywhere, all the time. What's to compare?" "That's absolutely not true," I shot back. "You don't know what you're talking about. It's only an idea, Ma. That's all love is. Just an idea. You think it's a function of the mysterious immutable being, but it's not! There is, in fact, no such thing as the mysterious immutable being . . . " Her legs were off the couch so fast I didn't see them go down. She made fists of her hands, closed her eyes tight, and howled, "I'll kill you-u-u! Snake in my bosom, I'll kill you. How dare you talk to me that way?" And then she was coming at me. She was small and chunky. So was I. But I had thirty years on her. I was out of the chair faster than her arm could make contact, and running, running through the apartment, racing for the bathroom, the only room with a lock on it. The top half of the bathroom door was a panel of frosted glass. She arrived just as I turned the lock, and couldn't put the brakes on. She drove her fist through the glass, reaching for me. Blood, screams, shattered glass on both sides of the door. I thought that afternoon, One of us is going to die of this attachment. . . .

JOYCE JOHNSON
(1935—)

◆

JOYCE JOHNSON (née Glassman) grew up in an utterly conventional middle-class Jewish home on the Upper West Side of New York City, attended Barnard College, and has worked as an editor for a number of New York publishers, contributed articles and reviews to various magazines, and taught creative writing in the Columbia University Graduate Writing Program. She is the author of the novels *Come and Join the Dance* (1962), *Bad Connections* (1978), and *In the Night Café* (1989). She is best known for her memoir of her years on the Beat scene, *Minor Characters,* winner of a 1983 National Book Critics Circle Award.

Johnson was twenty-one years old when she met Jack Kerouac in Greenwich Village on a blind date arranged by the poet Allen Ginsberg. It was January 1957, nine months before the publication of *On the Road.* Her book recounts her two-year love affair with Kerouac and provides an insider's impressions of Ginsberg, Gregory Corso, Peter Orlovsky, William Burroughs, Neal Cassady, and their contexts as writers and rebels in the repressive fifties. Her reflections on the minor significance of the women who were her friends in the literati's dramatic lives are particularly compelling in the light of the feminist movement that had come of age by the time Johnson wrote her story twenty-five years later. She remembers the main and the minor characters in this cultural history of artists-in-ecstasy with affection and a wise realism. As Todd Gitlin wrote in his review in the *Nation,* "The beauty of [her] book is that all the characters are for real. No one is either sentimentalized or brutalized by caricature." He interprets the girlfriends of the beats as prefiguring feminism: "[they] stayed in the shadows of their men's freedom partly because they wanted their own but had no language for the desire." The excerpt that follows concerns Johnson's pre-Kerouac memories, of growing up as an intelligent and sensitive young woman in Manhattan, with the "psychic hunger" of her generation, wanting to write and to move toward "horizons of significance," to use Charles Taylor's phrase, beyond the gender stereotyping and expectations of her parents and teachers. Reviewer Helen Chasin, writing in the *New York Times Book Review,* called this portrait of her adolescence "the true heart of the book." As a narrative that chronicles the crises of young female identity—breaking the silences of the culture's secondary characters—Johnson's memoir provides the subjective and historical evidence that psychologist Jean Baker Miller has found missing from our cultural consciousness: "[Girls'] and women's actual practice in the real world and the complex processes that those practices entail have not been drawn upon, nor elaborated on, as a basis of culture, knowledge, theory, or public policy. . . . They have been split off from official definitions of reality."

From *Minor Characters*

I'm thinking, painfully, of a room. It has a red couch with a green slipcover, a gold-upholstered chair covered in maroon, a needlepoint piano bench also covered in green—hunter green, it was called. The Oriental rug, bought just before the Depression, is red and blue and gets vacuumed every day. The table with curved bow legs—used only for important family occasions—is in the style known as French provincial. A lamp stands on it, Chinese, on little teak feet, its silk shade covered with cellophane.

The piano dominates everything—a baby grand, bought while my mother was still working, before I was born. It's a Steck, an obscure make that's supposedly every bit as good as a Steinway. For years she'd saved up for it out of her small, secretary's salary. Her picture as a young woman, placed on the polished lid that's never opened except when the piano tuner comes, is in a heavy silver frame of ornate primitive design brought by my uncle from Peru. She's slender and so pretty, graciously smiling in the long organza dress she'd made herself, white camellias pinned to the flounce on her shoulder. She could very well be what she never became, a concert singer, but she's engaged to my father, who stands beside her in a dark suit. He's a small man, round-faced like I am, with a sweet, serious look. Above the piano is an oil representation of me done by an artistic neighbor when I was eight—the golden era of my career as a daughter. I had to hold my head in one position for hours and hours, dreaming of the chocolate éclair I'd always get at the end of the session. And after all the sitting still, I never liked the portrait of the stolid child in the flowered pinafore dress with two fat blonde pigtails.

There's the terrible poignancy in this room of gratifications deferred, the tensions of gentility. It's as if all these objects—the piano, the rug, the portrait—are held in uneasy captivity, hostages to aspiration. If the slipcovers ever come off, if the heavy drapes are drawn aside letting in the daylight, everything that has been so carefully preserved will be seen to have become frayed and faded anyway.

You could just as well have gone to hell with yourself and enjoyed all that naked upholstery from the start.

I saw my first tenement apartment when I was twenty—top floor of a six-story walkup in Yorkville. Four very small rooms leading into each other railroad style, cracked walls and old tin ceilings that sagged a little. My best friend, Elise, who had just moved in there, had painted all of it white, even the linoleum on the floor. What I remember is the amazing light in that place, how it flooded in as if there was no real separation between inside and outside, and everything—what little there was—seemed to be set afloat in it. A light that was almost Mediterranean, giving the scarred, patched walls a chalky thickness like the walls of Greek villas, beatifying the mattress on the floor, the Salvation Army table, the chairs carried in from the street.

I saw that same extraordinary light in the early apartments of other friends. Why there? The defiant absence of anything over the windows, I guess. Maybe it was just as simple as that.

I sit on the needlepoint piano bench every day for two hours and play Scarlatti sonatas, Beethoven's *Für Elise,* Czerny scales. *Für Elise*—prophetically named, come to think of it—is my favorite. I play it with somewhat more pleasure and confidence than other pieces, and with it I flunk the entrance test to the High School of Music and Art.

Still my mother the optimist refuses to recognize that I am not actually musical. In any case, it isn't her plan for me to be a mere pianist. I'm to be something more exalted—a great woman composer. An eminence I'm to achieve if possible before I'm twenty-one or before I throw it all away on marriage—a state she hopes I'll avoid as long as possible. Perhaps I'll enter into it sensibly in later life, after I've written several operettas. Meanwhile, fortunately, I'm only twelve and have already composed a full-length musical comedy, both words and music. A junior Rodgers and Hammerstein combined!

As I sit at the Steck baby grand, she vacuums in another part of the apartment, the drone a counterpoint to what I'm playing. When I start picking out a new tune I'm trying to make up, she switches off the machine and listens. "That's nice, dear!" Even at twelve, I feel uneasy about my musical compositions, as if I'm getting away with something by managing to produce them. How can I become a great composer if I can never make music up in my head? I can't even read the notes in a score and have them translate into sounds. I'm confined to whatever I can wrest from the keys of the piano—and there I'm up against my limitations as a pianist. It frightens me that so far my private teacher, Mr. Bleecker, hasn't found me out. "*Lovely,* dear!" my mother calls enthusiastically. "You're on the right track!" She really believes it. She switches on the vacuum again and is perhaps at that moment perfectly happy. She is living her second life.

Unexpectedly my mother appears at my school one morning. I'm called out of history class to go down to the principal's office where she's waiting. I'm pretty scared as I run down the two flights of stairs. But I can't remember what transgression I may have committed.

She's sitting on a visitors' bench in her brown mouton coat, clutching her big handbag. She smiles at the principal's secretary as I come in—it's her gallant, times-of-crisis smile, June Allyson smiling through tears. "Thank you very much," she says in a low voice to the secretary. She takes my arm and gently hustles me out of there.

In the hallway, she whispers, "We have to go into the ladies' room." When I ask her why, her face gets very red. "I'll tell you in a minute."

In the girls' bathroom, she delivers an announcement that makes no sense to me: "I found blood in your bed this morning."

Blood? I can't remember cutting myself.

My mother's opening her handbag and taking out something wrapped up in many Kleenexes. "I brought this for you to put on." She's brought some kind of belt, too, made of pink elastic, so I figure all this has to do with Down Below.

So far this is going very badly. But my mother can't help herself. Her love for me is the all-consuming passion of her life. She recognizes no boundaries between our separate beings. She only wants to protect me from everything the way she protected me from drowning when I was little by not teaching me to swim, or from irrevocably scarring myself by discouraging me from climbing or running or riding a two-wheeler in the park. This, however, is different. There's no warding off womanhood, although she tries.

She's all flustered as she looks into my astonished face. "It's just the body's natural way of getting rid of bad blood."

I'm trying to digest this overwhelming information. I have never heard of the body doing such an alarming thing.

She tells me it's something that will happen to me now for the rest of my life. "But it's nothing you have to worry about," she says. . . .

I started at Barnard College a few weeks before my sixteenth birthday. It was the fall of 1951. Putting on a pleated Black Watch plaid skirt that fastened in front with a large safety pin, dark-green Bonnie Doon knee socks, and matching lamb's-wool (lamentably not cashmere) sweaters, I packed a small suitcase and moved across 116th Street to Hewitt Hall for three days of freshman orientation. Exhausted by my efforts to lead a double life that would not be detected by my parents, I was giving up Bohemianism, which I now saw as childish. I believed I was ready for an instant transformation in which I would become "collegiate." I did not at all want to be perceived as odd. I'd go to proms in strapless gowns of pastel tulle, and perhaps even learn to take an interest in football, though that was probably going too far, I thought. My idea of the life that would await me in college was a composite of images from three main sources: the works of F. Scott Fitzgerald, *Mademoiselle* magazine, and the campus department of Lord and Taylor.

Barnard seemed restfully quaint, almost pastoral, with its trees and bricked paths, and the delightfully overgrown area behind the tennis courts known as the Jungle, and the beau parlors in the dorms, which were miniature living rooms without doors in which girls were allowed to sit with their dates. It was like a city garden, unsuspected until you walked through its gates and stood within its walls that so mysteriously created the illusion of distance. Distance from the buses and subways rattling down Broadway to less-exalted destinations, and from the edges of Harlem only six blocks away, and from Eighth Street, where the Waldorf Cafeteria had recently been boarded up—the first of my lost landmarks. Distance even from Columbia and its troublesome men, who once a year in a rite of spring would surge across Broadway and tear down the green wooden fence surrounding the Barnard dorms, then pay to have a new fence erected.

It was the era of the ivory tower—and Barnard provided its maiden version. A retired general named Dwight D. Eisenhower was the president of Columbia University. A retired commander of the WAVES, Millicent MacIntosh, was the dean of Barnard. It was the era of Senator Joseph McCarthy, Roy Cohn, and G. David Schine. You could buy a copy of *Red Channels* in any candy store. In the house I lived in with my parents, there were rumors that the superintendent was paid by the FBI to sift through the garbage of certain professors. It was also the era of the beginning of television. A television set in operation in any shop window would draw a fascinated crowd. My aunts got a set a year or so before my parents. In the dimmed light of their living room, surrounded by bookcases full of the no-longer-read works of George Bernard Shaw and Henrik Ibsen in complete matching sets, as well as oddities such as books by Lafcadio Hearn, Balzac's *Droll Tales,* and *My Life* by Leon Trotsky, the family would gather to watch Milton Berle, and Ted Mack's *Amateur Hour.* On the campus, however, tradition reigned supreme. Prufrockian professors walked the brick paths in neutral tweeds. Every self-respecting Barnard English major claimed to be passionately interested in the seventeenth century. At Columbia it was Lionel Trilling's course in the Romantic poets that drew the brightest and most ambitious students, or Mark Van Doren's course in Shakespeare. Both men had taught Allen Ginsberg and Lucien Carr during the more turbulent wartime period. Their new crop of students—my generation—was called the Silent Generation. Our silence was common knowledge and was often cited in the pages of *Time, Life,* and the Sunday magazine of the *New York Times.* We were also called "other-directed" by David Riesman in *The Lonely Crowd.* We were considered passive, conformist, seldom individualistic or given to acts of rebellion. For us, that middle-aged line of T. S. Eliot's, "Do I dare to eat a peach?" had an especial poignancy. To our shame, we knew we usually didn't.

Just as the fifties had begun, an event had occurred of no immediate interest to the Silent Generation and of trivial importance to the reigning literati. This event—nonevent, really—was the publication of a novel called *The Town and the City* by an unknown writer named John Kerouac. In his jacket photo, John Kerouac looked much as an up-and-coming young intellectual of the time was supposed to look—well-kempt, wearing a dark suit, white shirt, and neatly knotted tie; his face was handsome and poetically melancholy, betraying a writerly intensity. The reception of his book could best be described as "mixed"—a word that to publishers means "damned by faint praise," which ultimately translates into low sales. The great reading public is not necessarily on the lookout for a "rough diamond of a book," which is what the *New York Times* reviewer called *The Town and the City;* it would rather save its money for gems with a lot of glitter.

Rough diamond is usually a term used to describe promising young men (but strangely, not young women) of working-class origins. (The young Welsh miner rescued from the pit by the efforts of the refined spinster schoolteacher in the 1940s best-seller *How Green Was My Valley* was certainly such a diamond.) It was not a particularly happy thing to be in the 1950s, when the proletarianism of the thirties and the democratic leveling of the war years had given way to a rather frantic scramble for polish.

Allen Ginsberg's former classmate Norman Podhoretz, a boy from the Jewish slums of Brownsville who had attended Columbia on a scholarship, confessed to this with a self-consciously shameless shame in his autobiography, *Making It.* Proclaiming himself a member of "the country" called the upper middle class, "less by virtue of my income than by virtue of the way my speech is accented, the way I dress, the way I furnish my home, the way I entertain and am entertained, the way I educate my children—the way, quite simply, I look and live," Podhoretz then disclosed, "It appalls me to think what an immense transformation I had to work on myself in order to become what I have become." He had evidently felt less appalled in the early fifties, when, with the encouragement of Lionel Trilling, he went all the way to Clare College at Cambridge to be polished into assimilation with WASP gentility.

Podhoretz makes the declaration that "One of the longest journeys in the world is the journey from Brooklyn to Manhattan." But Jack Kerouac (another Columbia scholarship boy) had taken a much longer journey from his French-Canadian factory workers' neighborhood in Lowell, Massachusetts, to Morningside Heights. That cultural and psychological distance was never to be fully traveled, however. The John Kerouac who could be seen in conversation with Gore Vidal and Alfred Kazin at various literary cocktail parties in the spring of 1950 was also always, both proudly and with some anguish, the Jack of Lowell. Just as it had been the Jack of Lowell, with all his conservative values and even a shy puritanical streak, who had taken the Dostoevskian midnight subway with Herbert Huncke to the low-life haunts of Times Square. While Podhoretz was obsessed with maintenance of distances, John Kerouac knew that all realities are contiguous, even life and death.

I was among the millions who didn't read *The Town and the City.* Around the time it was published, I was reading the novels of Thomas Wolfe. I read all of them, undaunted by their length. In Eugene Gant's adolescent yearnings to break free of the constricting ties of family I saw my own. Awash in the rocking sea of Wolfe's language, I was stirred by the rhythm of such phrases as "a stone, a leaf, an unfound door." I cherished the Wolfeian word *inchoate,* which suggested a chalky obscurity, and hoped there'd be a passage in my own writing where it would be apropos. But if I'd happened to come across John Kerouac's book in the public library, I might have been equally stirred by "A child, a child, hiding in a corner, peeking, infolded in veils, in swirling shrouds and mysteries," and the novel would have surprised me by being set partially in my own uncolorful neighborhood, as well as in Galloway (Lowell), and even more by its revelation of the Bohemian world you could get to so quickly in the city—the world I was now renouncing with such determination but also with a feeling of incompletion. . . .

★   ★   ★

It's a crisp September morning, the beginning of yet another academic year. The grey-haired, craggy-faced, perhaps self-consciously Lincoln-esque professor enters the small classroom where his girl students await him. There's a proper hush as he takes his place behind the oak table, circa 1910, lays out his sharpened pencils, his roll book containing their names, his two slim volumes of something or other—must be the latest in criticism. Intimidated in advance, the girl students study this man's glamorously American Gothic features, looking for signs of humor or mercy. Can he be gotten around? They will be judged by this Professor X, the big fish in the rather smallish pond that is the Barnard English Department.

Picture this middle-aged man, who no doubt wishes he were standing before a class at Harvard—*that* would count for something. There will be few compensations for the spirit here, much less the eye, in teaching this new frumpy lot of young females—rumpled, pasty girls who've dived into the laundry bag for something to wear to class. Only one slouching beauty with a tangle of auburn hair and a glory of freckles, as well as—perhaps he notices immediately—extraordinary knees, can possibly redeem this semester for him.

He wrenches his gaze away from her and begins. Ha! Let's try this question on 'em, he thinks. He rises to his full six feet, the more to heighten the little drama of this opening moment.

"Well"—his tone is as dry as the crackers in the American cultural barrel—"how many of you girls want to be writers?"

He watches with sardonic amusement as one hand flies up confusedly, then another, till all fifteen are flapping. Here and there an engagement ring sparkles.

The air is thick with the uneasiness of the girl students. Why is Professor X asking this? He knows his course is required of all creative-writing majors.

"Well, I'm sorry to see this," says Professor X, the Melville and Hawthorne expert. "Very sorry. Because"—there's a steel glint in his cold eye—"first of all, if you were going to be writers, you wouldn't be enrolled in this class. You couldn't even be enrolled in school. You'd be hopping freight trains, riding through America."

The received wisdom of 1953.

The young would-be writers in this room have understood instantly that of course there is no hope. One by one their hands have all come down.

I was one of those who'd raised hers. . . .

LUCILLE CLIFTON
(1936—)

The poet LUCILLE CLIFTON was born in Depew, New York, attended Fredonia State Teachers' College and Howard University, and has published four volumes of poetry—*Good Times* (1969), *Good News about the Earth* (1972), *An Ordinary Woman* (1974), and *Two-Headed Woman* (1980). Her memoir *Generations* (1976) is an autobiographical and genealogical portrait of her family history. "My family tends to be a spiritual and even perhaps mystical one," she has said. "That certainly influences my life and my work." She is married, the mother of six children, and the author of more than sixteen books for children. When her first book was published, she was thirty-three years old and had six children under ten years old so though she was "very happy and proud [she] had plenty of other things to think about." She has received many honorary awards and fellowships, a nomination for the Pulitzer Prize, and professorial appointments at Goucher College, Trinity College, and American University. She is engagingly relaxed and modest about her life and about the recognition she has received as a prolific African-American woman writer. In Mari Evans's collection, *Black Women Writers (1950–1980): A Critical Evaluation,* Clifton sketches a few perspectives on her identity as a writer: "I write the way I write because I am the kind of person that I am. . . . I grew up a well-loved child in a loving family and so I have always known that being very poor, which we were, had nothing to do with lovingness or familyness or character or any of that. . . . we were quite clear that what we had didn't have anything to do with what we were. . . . I am a woman and I write from that experience. I am a Black woman and I write from that experience. I do not feel inhibited or bound by what I am. That does not mean that I have never had bad scenes relating to being Black and/or a woman, it means that other people's craziness has not managed to make me crazy. . . . I draw my own conclusions and do not believe everything I am told." Writing in the same volume, the critic and poet Haki Madhubuti (formerly Don L. Lee) praises Clifton's work as "bone-strong with vision of intense magnitude" and her style as "simple and solid, like rock and granite," in the tradition of Gwendolyn Brooks, Mari Evans, and Sonia Sanchez. Critic and professor Audrey T.

McCluskey connects Clifton with Emily Dickinson, Walt Whitman, and Gwendolyn Brooks. Theirs, she believes, is a tradition of Christian optimism, a vision of the world "defined by possibility." As Clifton writes in the autobiographical *Generations,* "things don't fall apart. Things hold. Lines connect in ways that last and last and lives become generations made out of pictures and words just kept."

From *Generations*

. . . Oh she made magic, she was a magic woman, my Mama. She was not wise in the world but she had magic wisdom. She was twenty-one years old when she got married but she had had to stay home and help take care of her brothers and sisters. And she had married Daddy right out of her mother's house. Just stayed home, then married Daddy who had been her friend Edna Bell's husband after Edna Bell died. She never went out much. She used to sit and hum in this chair by the window. After my brother was born, she never slept with my Daddy again. She never slept with anybody, for twenty years. She used to tell me "Get away, get away. I have not had a normal life. I want you to have a natural life. I want you to get away."

A lot of people were always telling me to get away.

She used to sit in this chair by the window and hum and rock. Some Sundays in the summertime me and her used to go for walks over to the white folks section to look in their windows and I would tell her when I grew up I was going to take her to a new place and buy her all those things.

Once in a while we would go to the movies, me and her. But after she started having her fits I would worry her so much with Are you all right Ma and How do you feel Ma that we didn't go as often. Once I asked her if she was all right and she said she would be fine if I would leave her alone.

Mostly on Friday nights when Daddy had gone out and the other kids had gone out too we would get hamburgers and pop from the store and sit together and after we got TV we would watch TV. On New Year's Eve we would wait up until midnight and I would play Auld Lang Syne on the piano while me and my Mama sang and then we would go to bed.

Oh she was magic. If there were locks that were locked tight, she could get a little thing and open them. She could take old bent hangers and rags and make curtains and hang drapes. She ironed on chairs and made cakes every week and everybody loved her. Everybody.

When Daddy bought the house away from Purdy Street, Mama didn't know that he had been saving his money. One day he just took us to see this house he was buying. I was going away to college that fall and Punkin was off and married and we were scattering but he had bought us this house to be together in. Because we were his family and he loved us and wanted us to be together. He was a strong man, a strong family man, my Daddy. So many people knew him for a man in a time when it wasn't so common. And he lived with us, our Daddy lived in our house with us, and that wasn't common then either. He was not a common man. Now, he did some things, he did some things, but he always loved his family.

He hurt us all a lot and we hurt him a lot, the way people who love each other do, you know. I probably am better off than any of us, better off in my mind, you know, and I credit Fred for that. Punkin she has a hard time living in the world and so does my brother and Jo has a hard time and gives one too. And a lot of all that is his fault, has something to do with him.

And Mama, Mama's life was—seemed like—the biggest waste in the world to me, but now I don't know, I'm not sure any more. She married him when she was a young twenty-one and he was the only man she ever knew and he was the only man she ever loved and how she loved him! She adored him. He'd stay out all night and in the morning when he came home he'd be swinging down the street and she would look out the window and she'd say loud "Here come your crazy Daddy." And the relief and joy would make her face shine. She used to get up at five every morning to fix his breakfast for him and she one time fell down the back steps and broke her ankle and didn't see about it until after she had fixed breakfast, had gotten back up the steps and finished.

She would leave him. She would leave him and come in every morning at five o'clock to fix his breakfast because "your Daddy works hard," she would fuss, "you know you can't fix him a decent meal."

She would sit in the movies. She would leave him and sit in the movies and I would see her there and try to talk and make things right. I always felt that I was supposed to make things right, only I didn't know how, I didn't know how. I used to laugh and laugh at the dinner table till they thought I was crazy but I was so anxious to make things right.

I never knew what to do. One time they were arguing about something and he was going to hit her and my sister Punkin, who had a different mother, she ran and got the broom and kept shouting "If you hit

Mama I'll kill you" at Daddy. My brother and I didn't do anything but stand there and it was our Mama but we didn't do anything because we didn't know what to do.

Another time they were arguing and I was in the kitchen washing dishes and all of a sudden I heard my Mama start screaming and fall down on the floor and I ran into the room and she was rolling on the floor and Daddy hadn't touched her, she had just started screaming and rolling on the floor. "What have you done to her," I hollered. Then "What should I do, what should I do?" And Daddy said "I don't know, I don't know, I don't know, she's crazy," and went out. When he left, Mama lay still, and then sat up and leaned on me and whispered "Lue, I'm just tired, I'm just tired."

The last time ever I saw her alive she had been undergoing tests to find out what caused her epilepsy and I leaned over to kiss her and she looked at me and said "The doctors took a test and they say I'm not crazy. Tell your Daddy."

I wanted to make things better. I used to lay in bed at night and listen for her fits. And earlier than that, when I was younger, a little girl, I would lay awake and listen for their fights. One night they were shouting at each other and my sister Punkin whispered out of her stillness "Lue, are you awake?" "No," I mumbled. She stirred a little. "That's good," she said.

I wanted to make things right. I always thought I was supposed to. As if there was a right. As if I knew what right was. As if I knew.

My Mama dropped dead in a hospital hall one month before my first child was born. She had gone to take a series of tests to try to find out the cause of her epilepsy. I went to visit her every day and we laughed and talked about the baby coming. Her first grandchild. On this day, Friday, February 13, it was raining but I started out early because I had not gone to see her the day before. My aunt and my Uncle Buddy were standing in the reception area and as I came in they rushed to me saying "Wait, Lue, wait, it's not visiting hours yet." After a few minutes I noticed other people going on toward the wards and I started up when my aunt said "Where are you going, Lue?" and I said "Up to see my Mama," and they said all together "Lue Lue your Mama's dead." I stopped. I said "That's not funny." Nobody laughed, just looked at me, and I fell, big as a house with my baby, back into the telephone booth, crying "Oh Buddy Oh Buddy, Buddy, Buddy."

★ ★ ★

One month and ten days later another Dahomey woman was born, but this one was mixed with magic.

Things don't fall apart. Things hold. Lines connect in thin ways that last and last and lives become generations made out of pictures and words just kept. "We come out of it better than they did, Lue," my Daddy said, and I watch my six children and know we did. They walk with confidence through the world, free sons and daughters of free folk, for my Mama told me that slavery was a temporary thing, mostly we was free and she was right. And she smiled when she said it and Daddy smiled too and saw that my sons are as strong as my daughters and it had been made right.

And I could tell you about things we been through, some awful ones, some wonderful, but I know that the things that make us are more than that, our lives are more than the days in them, our lives are our line and we go on. I type that and I swear I can see Ca'line standing in the green of Virginia, in the green of Afrika, and I swear she makes no sound but she nods her head and smiles.

The generations of Caroline Donald born in Afrika in 1823
and Sam Louis Sale born in America in 1777 are
Lucille
who had a son named
Genie
who had a son named
Samuel
who married
Thelma Moore and the blood became Magic and their
daughter is
Thelma Lucille
who married Fred Clifton and the blood became whole and
their children are
Sidney
Fredrica
Gillian
Alexia four daughters and
Channing
Graham two sons,
and the line goes on.
"Don't you worry, mister, don't you worry."

JANE O'REILLY
(1937—)

◆

Journalist JANE O'REILLY grew up in a middle-class, Irish-Catholic family in St. Louis, Missouri. She moved to New York City as a divorced single mother of a young son in 1967. As the following auto-biographical essay, "Expectations," makes clear, her reevaluation of the girlish worldview she'd been schooled in coincided with the rise of the women's movement. Since the early 1970s, she has contributed provocative articles on the family, feminism, the media, money, and politics to *New York* magazine, *Ms., Atlantic Monthly, Vogue,* the *New York Times Book Review,* and the *New Republic.* She is a contributing columnist to *Time* and the author—with Barbara Ferraro and Patricia Hussey—of *No Turning Back: Two Nuns Battle with The Vatican.* Her book *The Girl I Left Behind: The Housewife's Moment of Truth, and Other Feminist Ravings* (1980) from which "Expectations" is taken is a collection of her writings from the 1970s. But, as the critic John Leonard observed in the *New York Times,* this work "is much more than a collection of her articles and columns; it is a superbly edited anthology of connections between self and society." Jane O'Reilly admits that she covered women's issues as a journalist for many years before it occurred to her that the problems she was writing about applied to her own life. Her recognition of the shape of her own experience hit her when she connected her personal life history and women's political history, when she realized that "They" are really "We." In her book she examines the personal and political issues that determine women's lives, demytholo-gizing a cultural inheritance that has much to do with loss of identity and with the high incidence of depression among middle-class women. Abigail McCarthy finds the strength of the collection in O'Reilly's "frank introspection and her clear insights into the ambivalence, long-ings, discoveries, joys and fears of the woman who has chosen to live alone. . . . her personal revelations are funny and . . . evoke a shock of recognition in her readers." A corrosively honest intelligence infuses the wit of these essays, lacing their rapid-fire insights with a saving laughter.

From *The Girl I Left Behind: The Housewife's Moment of Truth and Other Feminist Ravings*

Expectations

The women's movement, they said, was really just a bunch of radical women. Or intellectual women. Or lesbians. And then, apparently believing they had discovered the ultimate disqualification, they said the movement involved only middle-class women.

Ah! That one hit us where it hurt, an inspired accusation, one that made the women who were not middle class turn suspiciously on those who were, and flustered those who were into apologizing—always our first instinct: "So sorry, how selfish of me. I was just trying to make something of my life. My self-denial must have slipped." A female virtue, self-denial. We recovered, of course, because one of the first things we noticed—after a Click!—was that we were being dismissed not because we were or were not middle class but because we were women.

It was curious, that dismissal. The middle class, after all, is the guardian of the given, the upholder of tradition, the bedrock of perceived values, order, and predictability. The middle class is The Market; its women the unpaid Ladies' Auxiliary to our consumer economy (a role at least as important to the status quo as our "natural" role as the weaker sex). If middle-class women were dissatisfied, then surely the movement could not be dismissed?

As someone who perceived my teen-age years as seriously limited by the absence of a recreation room in my family's house, I feel competent to speak as a middle-class woman. Almost absurdly middle-class. I grew up in St. Louis, on a quiet street of middle-class houses, with a mother, a father, a sister, a brother, and a dog. Grandparents, cousins, aunts, and uncles were within walking distance. We went to Mass, raised the flag, did our best, and I enjoyed happy times, music lessons, orthodontia, dancing classes, allergy shots, and a bicycle. Jews, blacks, and, to a lesser extent, Protestants were different and did not play a large part in my consciousness, but "what people might think" did.

The Depression, the War, and the Ancestors were understood to have had an influence. There were also the usual variables: shadows, secrets, denials, disappointments—the mysteries that make, not history, but life. Every member of that household would have a different explanation of what went on there, and part of my particular situation is explained by the fact that I have no idea what those explanations might be. We did not, still do not, talk about such things to each other, of how we felt and why. Messages were oblique and seldom less than double. I grew up bewildered, slamming doors and trying to figure out what was expected of me.

It was easier to figure out what was expected of women and of me as a woman. The full weight of popular culture was devoted to providing direction. Since every woman I knew seemed to conform to specifications, it is not surprising that I failed to wonder enough if there might be a difference between me and the accepted model of "woman." Wondering about things was especially discouraged at the Convent of the Sacred Heart—an institution at that time and in that city so extreme in its dedication to the notion of genteel womanhood that it produced two extremes of reaction: Phyllis Schlafly, the antifeminist crusader, and me. I was taught and I have no doubt that Phyllis Schlafly was taught that women were incompetent and dependent and their only recourse was marriage.

Our children ask us how we could have believed that sex was sinful, that the object of a girl's life was a wedding ring, that only boys could play baseball, just as we might have asked our great grandmothers: "Why does a lady never mention pregnancy?" I believed such things (I would in fact have denied believing them if they had been put in quite that way, but they were never put quite that way—simply shown, demonstrated, assumed in every book, advertisement, and social arrangement around me) because those were what most people believed, just as they had once believed in Progress, and still believed that hard work inevitably was rewarded. To believe, to insist, that woman's place was in the home, was to ward off for a little while longer the painful adjustments of the twentieth century, which began and seems destined to end with magazine articles warning that the "new" woman will mean the end of the family. Even in Cambridge, Massachusetts, beyond the middle-class Middle West, people chose to believe those things.

I admit to a certain lack of imagination. But few of us are geniuses, able to imagine the unimaginable. (Where did Elizabeth Cady Stanton *come from?* And why was I never told about her? But that is part of the same explanation for my expectations.)

I was, in the most literal sense, unable to imagine that I was not raised to be equal.

When I graduated from college, I did not expect to receive, twenty years later, a questionnaire that would ask, among other things: "Have you met, or surpassed, the expectations you held for yourself in college?"

I responded to that question with low dread and the odd feeling that they were talking about someone else. The truth is, I could not immediately remember having any expectations at all while I was in college.

I knew we arrived as freshmen with vague notions of becoming huge successes: concert pianists, prize-winning journalists, ambassadors, poets. I remember a girl who wanted to be an archaeologist until she found out it involved a knowledge of Greek, Latin, and desert survival skills. That girl was me, but I remember her less clearly than I remember my roommate, who expected to win a Nobel Prize but dropped out to get married in her sophomore year. By the time we graduated, we all expected only to get married. And we did.

I have never really understood how it happened, that narrowing-down of expectations to the point that we believed that marriage would take care of the whole rest of our lives. It has been the great riddle and regret of our generation of women. We made a mistake, and in trying to correct it, we restarted the feminist movement. I understood it in theory, but I did not understand how it happened to me.

Last week memory came to call. A man I had not seen for years was passing through New York and came to dinner. When I opened the door to him, my life from age fifteen to eighteen passed before my eyes. During those years the arrival of that man—then boy—meant that life had arrived.

Life included movies, hamburgers, swimming parties, picnics, dances, corsages, identification bracelets, and popularity. None of those things counted (or, in the case of popularity, was acknowledged) if they came without a boyfriend.

We were in love, and after a few months we allowed ourselves a good-night kiss, which was all we ever allowed ourselves. In return for his courtesies and investment he got a princess (me) whom he would some day marry and turn into a slave or a dependent (depending on which way you now look at it) for life.

It seems a literally incredible arrangement now, but I can see that girl sitting on the porch, waiting. I can see, and feel, and hear her, riding in the front seat of a Studebaker as it turns off Lindell into Skinker. The boy asks: "Why do you want to go to Radcliffe?" And the girl, who was me, answers: "Because it will make me a better wife and mother."

But wait. There are two girls sitting in that seat, two memories in one person. I knew even then that that was not the reason I was going to Radcliffe. I simply had not thought out any other expectations. Besides, how could I tell him I wanted to be an archaeologist, when he was going to be a doctor? How could I admit to him or to me that the girl who waited on the porch was like a steel spring, coiled, waiting to be sprung, to get out of town, away from those dances and off toward her vague notions.

If there is one thing my classmates have learned, it is that there is always time for questions. After we fulfilled one set of expectations, we returned to the vague notions. My roommate had three babies, and then went to medical school. She, again, hopes for a Nobel Prize. We became doctors, journalists, and professors—but not yet ambassadors.

We first met "their" expectations (whoever "they" were), and then we surpassed our own. Perhaps it would have been better if we had been able to merge the two sooner. But I am surprised to conclude that expectations may matter less than flexibility.

The letter arrives every year. Mimeographed, with hand-drawn holly leaves around the edge, sent by someone I went to school with, it begins "Dear Friends," which presumably includes me. The letter reaches me correctly addressed and mailed early with the proper postage, despite my twenty years of wandering and two name changes. This year's letter reads:

Dear Friends,

It's hard to believe another year has passed! Time seems to grow shorter as we grow older—although not all that old, whatever the kids may think!

Speaking of the kids, they are all wonderful as ever. Timmy is 14(!) now, and doing extremely well at the new school. He's interested in track, tapes and girls . . . in that order. Bobby (11) fell off a horse this summer and spent two months in a cast. He's fine now, but the whole family feels the cast should be kept in our permanent trophy case. Sally (9) is growing up, really becoming a lady, and she seems to have all the brains in the family. Her I.Q. tests are really amazing. Linda (5) is the family devil, but we love her. And, this year's surprise is that number five will be coming along in March! Big surprise! No, seriously, the kids are our pride and joy, and watching them grow makes us feel we are growing more ourselves every day.

Other news: Roy and I spent a well-earned week in the Florida sun last March, and then came home to spend the whole summer adding a wing on the house. The kids were at camp and I sorely missed Lake Michigan, but Roy said it was better to build than buy this year, and I guess he was proved right by the grim business picture.

Roy's Dad, I'm sorry to say, died last April, very peacefully and easily. We all miss him terribly and I know many of you do, too. My mother is just fine, really amazing for "an old widder lady," as she says. She spent July traveling through the Smokies with my Aunt Martha.

This year Roy has been working too hard, but he loves it (he doesn't, he complains from across the room). I worked hard in the election last fall, and although I felt I had chosen the best man, the rest of the voters did not. Anyway, in these times, we feel everyone has to do what they can, whatever their "lights."

Every year we seem to be wishing you, our dear friends, peace and joy, and every year it seems further away. But we all, here at 6322 Pershing Avenue, wish all of you the very best for the new year, and hope to hear of your doings soon.

The Fishers

The last sentence is underlined by hand, and the same hand—of a woman I haven't seen since 1955—has written in a few details of deaths, disasters, and divorces among our classmates.

I look forward to these letters, enjoy them as messages from a more confident, complacent scheme of things, although I can read the uneasiness between the lines:

. . . Yes, we are all growing older and we never thought we would, and is this what being grown-up means? Having a teen-ager who has trouble in school, and four other kids who will be just as bewildering? We all said we would have five kids, but does anyone else wonder if we were right? Roy and I almost got divorced last spring, but we went to Florida, and a new baby and a new wing will make it all right, if his business doesn't fail. Why is the world so confusing when we did everything they taught us to do back in the convent? Please, everyone, write and tell me your life is the same! . . .

I never answer her. What would I say? I was raised for that world: babies and new houses, horses and faith in the middle class. I was supposed to be one of those women and it turned out differently. Not better, but different, and I can't explain it in a Christmas card.

If Christmas letters remind me that I was raised for a world I didn't choose to live in, they also remind me that that world had its points—especially during the holidays. Christmas was my grandmother's, and it was a peak experience. It began in November, when wrapping paper started to rustle behind locked library doors. Trees were erected, wreaths hung in every window, narcissus bloomed in Chinese pots. Seventy-five people came to sing carols on Christmas Eve, and to eat ham and turkey and baked beans and drink cocoa out of Dresden cups. Midnight Mass, jingle bells, and back to Grandmother's in the morning for . . . well, presents stacked from the mantelpiece out to the middle of the room, tangerines and silver dollars in every stocking. Buckwheat pancakes and sausage, and more presents, and then goose and three kinds of pie.

And then there was New Year's Eve. My parents said it was better when they were young, when fifty people came every year for charades and champagne. But I was allowed to stay up in my bunny slippers and red bathrobe with jingle-bell buttons and wait by the green eye of the family Philco for midnight in New York. We heard the crowd go wild in Times Square and I knew—from the cartoons in the *Saturday Evening Post*—exactly what it was like. Men wore top hats and women drank champagne from martini glasses and the whole city was a swirling, looping confetti ribbon.

There was an hour to wait until the new year swept across the time zone and midnight came to St. Louis. In my memory the years are compressed into one perfect, significant hour between eleven and twelve. My sister and brother were too small to stay up. My parents were going out, my mother extraordinarily beautiful in purple satin dancing shoes and my father wearing his black-pearl studs, but they were also home with me drinking cocoa. At midnight I opened the front door to shout Happy New Year into the middle western air.

I thought it was all real life. I also thought the world would end in 1965 because, we were told at school, the pope had been so warned by three Portuguese children who had in turn gotten the word from Our Lady of Fatima.

In 1955 my Christmas vacation was a planned peak experience. I made my debut. We were not rich, only comfortable, but I took part in the lavish charade because my grandmother was dying and the sight of me as a debutante was thought to please her, even more than the sight of me as a Radcliffe student had been known to please her. I hope it did, because it was a difficult vision to accommodate. For two weeks I went to a brunch, a lunch, a tea, a tea dance, a dinner, a dinner dance, and a ball—*every* day, except Christmas Eve, when there was no ball. I went to the St. Louis Country Club night after night and listened to Polka Bands, Gypsy Violins, Waltz Bands, Steel-Drum Bands, and Jazz Bands. I slopped through puddles of champagne left on the floor by the St. Louis youth I was coming out to meet. I wore borrowed evening gowns, glowered intellectually, and no one ever asked me to dance. A Budweiser heiress gave a ball at which a baby elephant carried trays of drinks and other people danced in the Clydesdale horses' stalls. Women from my grandmother's mysterious social past came to my own tea bringing satin petticoats and monogrammed nightgowns, initialed silver earrings and complicated evening bags. In my shame I never thanked any of them.

Because I knew, or was beginning to guess, that it would not be my real life, and that there was no need for me to come out in St. Louis because I would never go back there again.

In 1963, in Washington, I had a baby. We carried him downstairs at four o'clock Christmas morning to see the tree, and he liked it.

In 1967, I was divorced and living in New York. A man I scarcely knew called me at six o'clock on New Year's Eve to see if by any chance I was free. I was. I borrowed a dress and some very long and real pearls from a friend, and I was picked up in a limousine and taken to the annual New Year's Eve party of a Famous Broadway Producer. He lived in a house in the east sixties, with glacéed paisley walls and strobe lights in the library, and going up the stairs I tripped on Leonard Bernstein.

I stopped borrowing dresses after that party, because it was clear that Angela Lansbury, Dustin Hoffman, Burt Bacharach, Adolph Green, Lauren Bacall, and others too numerous to mention did not care what I wore. There were one or two very thin girls, in open-work crochet, who leaned against space and focused on the middle distance, and no one seemed to care what they wore either. At midnight one of them kissed me, and so did a couple of people I happened to be next to, on their way to kiss the famous people.

In 1975 I finally realized that it is impossible to pose prettily in a red velvet robe under the tree and at the same time baste a goose in the kitchen. I could not remember a single Christmas from the time it became my job to provide traditional joyousness to whoever was gathered under whatever roof when I did not at some point lie beneath the tree—usually after it had fallen over or been pushed on top of me—and sob. The very words "stocking stuffers" made me sick to my stomach. My grandmother's goose, I suddenly recalled, was basted by a cook. My grandmother also had a large family and I did not. I felt inappropriately trapped in a cultural imperative. So I sent my son to his grandmother's and went to the office on Christmas morn. There was nothing around the house unwrapped, undecorated, and unmailed to remind me of my failure to be Woman: the Organized Provider. I wasn't even around the house. It was wonderful. Everyone felt sorry for me. "Alone at Christmas? How dreadful! You must come to our house." Perhaps only other mothers will understand the absolute liberation I felt when one of the children threw up on the lace tablecloth. It was not my child, or my tablecloth, or my responsibility. I decided never to celebrate Christmas at home again.

But here I am again, whistling the "Hallelujah Chorus." Nontradition has become tradition. My friends are my family, and we will provide for each other. Gathered about the tree will be the intact family from upstairs, the broken family from across the park, an extended family from out of town, my own reconstituted family, and the various inexplicable attachments we have all acquired along the way. It is family tradition now for all the adults to fight over who will get to baste the goose.

The day will become a link in the chain of memories of where I was, and with whom, and how I felt on all the holidays that marked the change from "was" to "is." I am not, and yet I am, the person Mrs. Fisher remembers, but who she is and was is part of me and I am glad she reminds me every year. Her letter is my private rite of passage, annually raising old ghosts to be mourned a little, and sent away with relief.

My coffee table has a new book. It is *Life Goes to War*, a collection of pictures taken of World War II by *Life* magazine photographers. When my son and his friends look at the book, at the pictures of Guadalcanal, of people trampled to death on the steps of Chungking, of ships sinking and Hiroshima, and the bodies stacked up in concentration camps, they become silent and thoughtful. World War II was not, it seems, anything like "McHale's Navy."

I realize when I look at the book that I never expected to live long enough to have a coffee table, or a nearly grown son who would sit at it looking at pictures of the fires around St. Paul's Cathedral. I expected to be dead by now, killed by an atomic bomb. During my teens the word "motherhood" immediately made me imagine myself carrying a wounded child along the side of a road, part of a long line of refugees, while an enemy plane flew overhead shooting at us.

I don't think that was a particularly peculiar connection for someone of my generation to have made. What I do think is peculiar is that I seem never to have wondered about it before, and no one else seems to have brought it up.

Why, for example, did none of the expensive professionals I consulted during periods of acute depression in my life ever seem to think it worthwhile to examine the fact that I grew up during the war? I remember once trying to discover why I felt a sense of annihilating loss whenever I had to say good-bye to someone I liked. The wisdom directed toward my couch centered around an effort to learn if my mother had left me abruptly to go to the hospital to have another baby.

Perhaps she did, and perhaps she should be made to feel guilty forever because of her inconsiderate timing of labor pains. But if she did, she was no more to blame for that than she was responsible for sending her brothers off to war, or her husband off to direct local defense efforts, or for the planes passing over our house during a blackout, or for the determination that our baby-sitter was a German spy who should be deported.

My particular first memory is of the bombing of Pearl Harbor, a possibility Freud—himself overwhelmed by an evil he never imagined—did not take into account. I learned the size and shape of the world from maps covered by arrows indicating advancing and retreating troops. When I look at *Life Goes to War,* I remember my childhood as a series of days spent sitting on the floor studying pictures in *Life* magazine.

I have spent much of my life wondering what happened to the babies photographed crying in the rubble beside the bodies of their mothers. And imagining my child as one of them. What, then, explains the fact that the people my age have gone on? How was our ambition, our capacity to love, our understanding of power, affected? I don't know, and I would like to hear from anyone who thinks they know.

We are, as the saying goes, heavily into self-fulfillment now. But war is the ultimate self-fulfillment. The demagoguery, the medals, the descriptions of murder as "tactical brilliance," the closeness of working together for a common cause. Even fear is a peak experience. War can be fun.

A coffee table is the wrong place for this book. Church would be better. Some place where we can consider the fact that we are still too close to the cave.

She sat at the head of the table, a handsome woman, charming, self-absorbed, the guest of honor in her daughter's house. Her conversation ranged from the peculiar way her daughter peeled potatoes to the peculiar pictures her daughter chose to put on the walls. Her remarks were most amusingly phrased, even those—spoken within hearing of the child—about the peculiar way her granddaughter was growing up.

We were guests, and we continued to pour fresh drinks and to speak only of the cultivation of begonias. We had been specifically asked not to argue, because this was the first visit she had ever made to her daughter's house. For ten years she had not spoken at all, because she disapproved of her daughter's marriage. When the grandchild was born, she spoke, but most often to point out what a pity it hadn't been a boy.

If we had pointed out that the marriage was extraordinarily success-ful, the child a delight, and the daughter a loving, successful, competent person, it would have been considered an argument.

If we had asked why she hated her daughter, she would have been shocked. Of course she loves her daughter, all mothers love their chil-dren. No matter how disappointing children may be. She would even believe it to be true. But she gave us an answer despite herself. The talk had slipped precariously away from her, to work, and she glared at us all and said firmly: "Don't ever forget all mothers were once daughters."

As a maxim the sentence has a fine hollow ring to it. A certain bio-logical truth, perhaps, but scarcely a reliable signpost for life. But as a lament, and an accusation, it may explain why so many mothers of her generation are so angry with their daughters of my generation.

We, the daughters who have not become our mothers—not yet—comfort ourselves with generalization. We explain that mothers feel a natural ambivalence, wanting their daughters to succeed and also to fail. (I do not know why we think this is natural.) We know that too many mothers gave up their own visions, as their mothers had before them, and then expected us to fulfill all their lost hopes and dreams. Vicarious living is always disappointing.

We know that the society they grew up in was itself ambivalent, claiming to value motherhood, but at the same time shutting women out, refusing to admit them as serious contenders for jobs and power and participation, simply because they might become pregnant. No wonder our mothers complained when we did not have children, and retired to bed in depression when we did.

Perhaps the impulse to cast blame is inevitable in women who were so thoroughly blamed themselves: wrong if they took men's jobs during the Depression, wrong if they didn't during the war; wrong if they were not virtuous before marriage, wrong if they were not sexy after-ward; wrong if they coddled their babies in the twenties, wrong if they did not provide the precisely calibrated, expert-approved "right kind of love" in the thirties and forties, wrong ever after if their children took to the psychoanalytic couch "because of my mother." ("Indeed?" one wants to ask. "And where was your father?")

But generalizations are no comfort to a woman whose mother refuses to learn to spell her daughter's married name correctly. Or to another whose mother attacks her for not keeping a special drawer in which to store old wrapping paper and ribbons, in the same tone she uses to attack another daughter who drinks.

There seems to be no rational explanation (except perhaps that they never really knew us) for mothers who are not satisfied if we are intelligent, kind, and independent, but want us also to be sexy, fashionable, and more devoted. We could understand that our mothers might feel we have repudiated their lives by our efforts to change our own, but that is not the whole explanation either, because those of us who are old-fashioned are criticized for not making something of ourselves.

"We only want you to be happy," they say, and when we protest that we are happy, they quickly point out reasons we should not be. They mean: "Be happy my way." Worse, they mean: "Make me happy." And there seems no way to do that, to ever repay them for the fact that they were daughters who grew up to be mothers, to release them from the awful self-hate that came from being raised to despise and resent other women—a release we have sought for ourselves and our daughters.

They write us dunning letters, reminding us that they are our mothers. We know that. We are often enough glad of it. We would be glad to share more of our lives with them, if only we could figure out some way it would be an acceptable offering. They complain that we are holding back. And when we try to share, they say we are taking. We cannot please.

They seem to want it all back, every diaper changed, every temperature taken, every dream forestalled. But motherhood is not an investment. It is no longer a hedge against old age. We have ourselves been astonished to discover it is not even necessarily a major sacrifice. It is a reward in itself, even the diapers. Interest is not compounded with every peanut butter sandwich made.

Of course, our daughters are only beginning to grow up. It has yet to be seen if what is freely given will be given freely in return. But I hope we will remember that a little acceptance might fill up the mailboxes of our old age.

I once spent a morning trying to force a man to read a newspaper, and in the process I rediscovered some of the reasons the woman's movement causes so much confusion and anxiety.

It was a Sunday morning, and I was at another woman's house. I was sitting all alone in the living room reading the paper when another guest, a man, came downstairs and began to make himself breakfast.

The fact that he could make a cup of coffee for himself without either of us thinking that I should do it might have caused me to reflect on the great advances men and women have made in the last few years. But I didn't have time for reflection. I was too busy folding up the newspaper so the man could receive it in a pristine, unrumpled condition.

"Here is the paper," I said, carrying it into the kitchen.

"But you were reading it," he said.

"Oh, that's all right, you can have it," I said, with just the slightest trace of a sigh.

"But I don't want it, I'm going sailing," he said, adding, "Anyway, why should you stop reading it?"

I thought that was a good question. I stood in the kitchen, holding the carefully folded newspaper, and tried to figure out what I was doing there. I felt like someone coming out of a hypnotic trance.

I was there because men get the paper first. Morning papers are divided at the breakfast table: news for father, fashion for mother, and comics for children. Evening papers are refolded and placed next to father's chair. Mother and children get to read the paper when father is finished. If there is no father in the house, any available man gets priority. Even if he is going sailing and has no connection at all with the woman who really wants to read the paper. That is the way I was raised, and that is the way I respond to the problem of a newspaper and a man in the house—just like Pavlov's dog.

I was raised to defer and submit to the man in the house, which must explain why I am terrified of my friends' husbands. Whenever I visit a friend, I regress about thirty years. The friend and I may be sitting in the kitchen, drinking coffee and solving the world problems at the top of our lungs, but if The Husband should wander in, I scamper out the door feeling like an intruder.

If the friend suggests we watch a television program, and The Husband is in the room with the television set in it, I creep back out whispering that we had better not disturb him. At the dinner table I chew each mouthful twenty times and try not to spill, terrified that The Husband will start pounding the table and behaving like a scene out of *Life with Father.*

In fact, none of The Husbands I actually know would dream of pounding on the table (nor would my own father have dreamt of it). Usually they have helped cook dinner, and their wives help pay the mortgage. Probably they think I am an extremely odd person, lapsing into meek and uncharacteristic silence whenever they enter the room. They could not guess that I expect to be thrown out of the house, by virtue of the authority that I assign to them, simply because they are "the man of the house."

Most of the husbands I know deny that they feel any sense of authority. They are bewildered when their wives start stamping around the house talking about equality. It is odd, the way men suddenly discover they were raised to expect authority (and in fact do expect it) the minute their wives discover they were raised to defer and submit (and in fact defer but resent it).

The trouble is, we were not raised to be equal.

One evening I came quite late into a room on the Upper West Side of Manhattan. Within were academic people holding plastic glasses of champagne and discussing topics such as early Greek society and Marxist feminism. A few were exchanging footnotes, an activity that indicated the party had reached fever pitch.

A man on his way out of the room muttered a warning: "A woman in there," he whispered, "has just told me in all seriousness that Homer was a sexist." I grasped wildly for a remnant of my liberal education. Homer. *Odyssey.* Dido, Cassandra, Penelope, Helen. Sexist? Probably. But, frankly, just a trifle too arcane for me that evening. My life's ambition, as a matter of fact, has always been to grow up arcane, but on that particular night what I had in mind was pointless cocktail party drivel. I had exhausted my ability to find sexism lurking everywhere the night before, when I sat through the current Broadway revival of *Guys and Dolls.*

A musical inspired by the Broadway tales of Damon Runyon, *Guys and Dolls* opened in November 1950 and played 1,194 times. The revival, with an all-black cast, was very enjoyable. It was more enjoyable if you didn't go to the theater with me. I insisted on seeing it as a metaphor for the sexist society of the fifties.

"Cover your ears, close your eyes," I admonished the youths in our party as Adelaide and Sarah rendered "Marry the man today, and change his ways tomorrow." During the intermission I explained that the formative years of my generation had been spent whistling "I'll Know," the lesson of which is when your love comes along you'll know and everything will be all right forever. "Now children," I said, "you see an example of how your mothers got to be so foolish before the women's movement came along and the scales dropped from our eyes."

The children, unimpressed, slunk off for some overpriced orange drink. But I trapped them in the bus on the way home. Speaking in a style more appropriate to a Modern Language Association convention, I analyzed the lyrics of "Take Back Your Mink." A parody, rooted nonetheless in truth, of the relationship between men and women, I asserted.

Even the mothers, who until that point had been warning me against hypersensitivity, had to agree that "Adelaide's Lament" is a gruesome song, with its repeated theme that a woman can get a bad, bad cold if she fails to legally acquire a ring for the third finger, left hand.

A couple of nights later I went to see a revival of *My Fair Lady,* which originally opened in March 1956 and ran for 2,717 performances. I remembered it as charming, and wished it to remain so. But this time my companion sank into a depression. He began lecturing his children on the human relationships displayed. "Hateful, masochistic, sadistic," he muttered, as the children again crept off for an orange drink.

"Why would Eliza go back to Henry Higgins?" he demanded. "She is a strong, intelligent woman; why would she ever go back to a man who sings, 'Why can't a woman be more like a man?'" Why indeed? I have always objected to the scene where Eliza comes creeping in and picks up Professor Higgins's slippers. Even in the old English movie version of George Bernard Shaw's *Pygmalion,* from which *My Fair Lady* was drawn almost verbatim, Eliza reappears in the lamplight and we are meant to be consoled by a romantic ending, hoping that she found a soft heart where we could not.

Shaw wrote an epilogue for *Pygmalion,* and, on reading it, I discovered that what we have been seeing all these years isn't what he had in mind at all. Someone else, no doubt someone with an eye on "what the audience would stand for," assumed that a really romantic ending had to have Eliza in love with Higgins. That she would also be dominated and insulted and despised was immaterial.

Shaw himself says that Eliza knew Higgins was not a marrying man, but she also knew they would always play a strong part in each other's lives. But "Eliza has no use for the foolish romantic tradition that all women love to be mastered, if not actually bullied and beaten," Shaw wrote. His Eliza married Freddy; they opened a flower shop, and she continued to arrange everyone's lives.

Shaw's version is much more satisfactory.

I found a photograph in the back of a closet. It is a bridal portrait, large and artfully airbrushed. The girl is wearing a veil, and under it an expression of belligerent innocence. I do not remember her very well, but she is me.

I made the silk dress. It is still around somewhere in the back of another closet, and I must check sometime to see if I really finished off the hem with Scotch tape, as I remember. I did not, at the time, admit to innocence, and I did not—in time—recognize the belligerence.

I found the picture on the twentieth anniversary of that wedding. The marriage lasted only three years but, because there were no children from that one, we were spared the lifelong semiwarfare that people who share children, but not a life, suffer. After twenty years I can enjoy this anniversary when I remember it. The memory of the end has disappeared and I recall only the hope and affection of the beginning. We meant the vows at the time, and if we did not know what the vows themselves meant, or that we were a very unlikely pair to be exchanging them, well, we were not alone.

The marriage lasted such a short while that we never pasted the snapshots into books. They are still heaped up in a box. We all appear in them as buds of hope, looking younger than people have ever looked. How could we have been so young? Because we were—as our parents warned us at the time. We were not unsophisticated, but we were innocent, in the sense of being woefully ignorant. We married, all of us in those pictures, because that was what people did after they graduated from college. It had not, at that time, occurred to many people to warn us that marriage was a tricky business. It wasn't because our parents did not know; it was because no one had yet realized that there might be other choices to consider.

We are standing on the lawn looking wistful and pleased (and, yes, belligerent). There is an atmosphere of crystal patterns picked out and going-away dresses pressed. It was a ceremony of completion, social expectations met. Odd that we did not think of it as a beginning.

The bridesmaids are still my best friends. Two have been divorced and remarried and both became doctors during the divorced interim. Another one is my sister. She has been happily married for twenty years. I wonder how she achieved that? The fourth has been a perfect wife for sixteen years. Only recently did she decide to become liberated, but she did so in the most enviable way—by bringing her husband along.

The ushers are now journalists, except one who is a psychoanalyst. As I remember, they variously expected to be H. L. Mencken, president of the United States, and to die young. The groom is now eminent—as I expected. What is significant is that the women did not expect much for themselves, except to marry. The cravings came later, and it is not too much to say that we made a revolution of them.

There has been quite a long period for us when the feelings about weddings and old wedding pictures were not bittersweet, but bitter. We stood in the back of churches at first marriages, and second, and sometimes third, and muttered together cynically about "till death do us part." The young heard us, and now they are more serious about marriage, not less. They agonize about commitment and wonder if living together isn't better.

Maybe. Maybe not. There are other commitments and other ties in life that might satisfy more. In my pictures there are three old ladies.

They were my grandmother's bridesmaids, and for them their marriages were—at the end of their lives—an interval in the long tie of their friendship.

The most astonishing thing about my pictures is that so many of the people, the then young, are dead now. Life has turned out to be very short. The women have spent part of our short lives in the revolutionary struggle for independence. Maybe the greatest challenge now is to find a way to keep independence while also committing ourselves to the ties that bind people, families, and ultimately societies together.

MAXINE HONG KINGSTON
(1940—)

◆

Born in Stockton, California, the eldest child of Chinese immigrant parents who operated a number of family laundries, MAXINE HONG KINGSTON grew up to record and reinvent the cultural legacy she received in the form of her mother's stories in *The Woman Warrior: Memoirs of a Girlhood Among Ghosts* (1976). This book, "elemental," "extraordinarily rich," "savagely terrifying," "triumphant," and "utterly riveting" in the words of the critics whose unanimous acclaim led to its National Book Critics Circle Award, established Kingston as the strongest and most poetic interpreter of the Chinese-American experience from a mother and daughter's perspective. Her other books on the theme of Asian-American identity include *China Men* (1980), *Hawaii: One Summer* (1987), *Through the Black Curtain* (1988), and *Tripmaster Monkey: His Fake Book* (1989). Educated at the University of California, Berkeley, where she is now distinguished professor, Kingston has also taught English at the Mid-Pacific Institute, a private high school, at the University of Hawaii, and at The Sanctuary, an educational community project for casualties of the public school system, which she describes in a political and aesthetic meditation, "The Novel's Next Step," included in Philomena Mariani's fine and provocative collection, *Critical Fictions: The Politics of Imaginative Writing* (1991).

"No Name Woman," the first section of *The Woman Warrior* that follows here, demonstrates what Albert E. Stone has called the "terrain of contemporary autobiography which abuts the continent of fiction." Sidonie Smith defines Kingston's book as "an autobiography about women's autobiographical storytelling." In "Maxine Hong Kingston's Woman Warrior: Filiality and Woman's Autobiographical Storytelling," a chapter from Smith's book *A Poetics of Women's Autobiography* (1987), the author reads Kingston's memoir as challenging "the ideology of individualism and with it the ideology of gender. Recognizing the inextricable relationship between an individual's sense of 'self' and the community's stories of selfhood, Kingston self-consciously reads herself into existence through the stories her culture tells about women. Using autobiography to create identity, she breaks down the hegemony of formal 'autobiography' and breaks out of the silence that has bound her culturally to discover a resonant voice of her own." The agent of her personal and artistic breakthrough is her mother's powerful voice, the conservative keeper of the culture's oral narrative tradition.

from *The Woman Warrior:*
Memoirs of a Girlhood Among Ghosts

No Name Woman

"You must not tell anyone," my mother said, "what I am about to tell you. In China your father had a sister who killed herself. She jumped into the family well. We say that your father has all brothers because it is as if she had never been born.

"In 1924 just a few days after our village celebrated seventeen hurry-up weddings—to make sure that every young man who went 'out on the road' would responsibly come home—your father and his brothers and your grandfather and his brothers and your aunt's new husband sailed for America, the Gold Mountain. It was your grandfather's last trip. Those lucky enough to get contracts waved good-bye from the decks. They fed and guarded the stowaways and helped them off in Cuba, New York, Bali, Hawaii. 'We'll meet in California next year,' they said. All of them sent money home.

"I remember looking at your aunt one day when she and I were dressing; I had not noticed before that she had such a protruding melon of a stomach. But I did not think, 'She's pregnant,' until she began to look like other pregnant women, her shirt pulling and the white tops of her black pants showing. She could not have been pregnant, you see, because her husband had been gone for years. No one said anything. We did not discuss it. In early summer she was ready to have the child, long after the time when it could have been possible.

"The village had also been counting. On the night the baby was to be born the villagers raided our house. Some were crying. Like a great saw, teeth strung with lights, files of people walked zigzag across our land, tearing the rice. Their lanterns doubled in the disturbed black water, which drained away through the broken bunds. As the villagers closed in, we could see that some of them, probably men and women we knew well, wore white masks. The people with long hair hung it over their faces. Women with short hair made it stand up on end. Some had tied white bands around their foreheads, arms, and legs.

"At first they threw mud and rocks at the house. Then they threw eggs and began slaughtering our stock. We could hear the animals scream their deaths—the roosters, the pigs, a last great roar from the ox. Familiar wild heads flared in our night windows; the villagers encircled us. Some of the faces stopped to peer at us, their eyes rushing like searchlights. The hands flattened against the panes, framed heads, and left red prints.

"The villagers broke in the front and the back doors at the same time, even though we had not locked the doors against them. Their knives dripped with the blood of our animals. They smeared blood on the doors and walls. One woman swung a chicken, whose throat she had slit, splattering blood in red arcs about her. We stood together in the middle of our house, in the family hall with the pictures and tables of the ancestors around us, and looked straight ahead.

"At that time the house had only two wings. When the men came back, we would build two more to enclose our courtyard and a third one to begin a second courtyard. The villagers pushed through both wings, even your grandparents' rooms, to find your aunt's, which was also mine until the men returned. From this room a new wing for one of the younger families would grow. They ripped up her clothes and shoes and broke her combs, grinding them underfoot. They tore her work from the loom. They scattered the cooking fire and rolled the new weaving in it. We could hear them in the kitchen breaking our bowls and banging the pots. They overturned the great waist-high earthenware jugs; duck eggs, pickled fruits, vegetables burst out and mixed in acrid torrents. The old woman from the next field swept a broom through the air and loosed the spirits-of-the-broom over our heads. 'Pig.' 'Ghost.' 'Pig,' they sobbed and scolded while they ruined our house.

"When they left, they took sugar and oranges to bless themselves. They cut pieces from the dead animals. Some of them took bowls that were not broken and clothes that were not torn. Afterward we swept up the rice and sewed it back up into sacks. But the smells from the spilled preserves lasted. Your aunt gave birth in the pigsty that night. The next morning when I went for the water, I found her and the baby plugging up the family well.

"Don't let your father know that I told you. He denies her. Now that you have started to menstruate, what happened to her could happen to you. Don't humiliate us. You wouldn't like to be forgotten as if you had never been born. The villagers are watchful."

Whenever she had to warn us about life, my mother told stories that ran like this one, a story to grow up on. She tested our strength to establish realities. Those in the emigrant generations who could not reassert brute survival died young and far from home. Those of us in the first American generations have had to figure out how the invisible world the emigrants built around our childhoods fit in solid America.

The emigrants confused the gods by diverting their curses, misleading them with crooked streets and false names. They must try to confuse their offspring as well, who, I suppose, threaten them in similar ways—always trying to get things straight, always trying to name the unspeakable. The Chinese I know hide their names; sojourners take new names when their lives change and guard their real names with silence.

Chinese-Americans, when you try to understand what things in you are Chinese, how do you separate what is peculiar to childhood, to poverty, insanities, one family, your mother who marked your growing with stories, from what is Chinese? What is Chinese tradition and what is the movies?

If I want to learn what clothes my aunt wore, whether flashy or ordinary, I would have to begin, "Remember Father's drowned-in-the-well sister?" I cannot ask that. My mother has told me once and for all the useful parts. She will add nothing unless powered by Necessity, a riverbank that guides her life. She plants vegetable gardens rather than lawns; she carries the odd-shaped tomatoes home from the fields and eats food left for the gods.

Whenever we did frivolous things, we used up energy; we flew high kites. We children came up off the ground over the melting cones our parents brought home from work and the American movie on New Year's Day—*Oh, You Beautiful Doll* with Betty Grable one year, and *She Wore a Yellow Ribbon* with John Wayne another year. After the one carnival ride each, we paid in guilt; our tired father counted his change on the dark walk home.

Adultery is extravagance. Could people who hatch their own chicks and eat the embryos and the heads for delicacies and boil the feet in vinegar for party food, leaving only the gravel, eating even the gizzard lining—could such people engender a prodigal aunt? To be a woman, to have a daughter in starvation time was a waste enough. My aunt could not have been the lone romantic who gave up everything for sex. Women in the old China did not choose. Some man had commanded her to lie with him and be his secret evil. I wonder whether he masked himself when he joined the raid on her family.

Perhaps she encountered him in the fields or on the mountain where the daughters-in-law collected fuel. Or perhaps he first noticed her in the marketplace. He was not a stranger because the village housed no strangers. She had to have dealings with him other than sex.

Perhaps he worked an adjoining field, or he sold her the cloth for the dress she sewed and wore. His demand must have surprised, then terrified her. She obeyed him; she always did as she was told.

When the family found a young man in the next village to be her husband, she stood tractably beside the best rooster, his proxy, and promised before they met that she would be his forever. She was lucky that he was her age and she would be the first wife, an advantage secure now. The night she first saw him, he had sex with her. Then he left for America. She had almost forgotten what he looked like. When she tried to envision him, she only saw the black and white face in the group photograph the men had had taken before leaving.

The other man was not, after all, much different from her husband. They both gave orders: she followed. "If you tell your family, I'll beat you. I'll kill you. Be here again next week." No one talked sex, ever. And she might have separated the rapes from the rest of living if only she did not have to buy her oil from him or gather wood in the same forest. I want her fear to have lasted just as long as rape lasted so that the fear could have been contained. No drawn-out fear. But women at sex hazarded birth and hence lifetimes. The fear did not stop but permeated everywhere. She told the man, "I think I'm pregnant." He organized the raid against her.

On nights when my mother and father talked about their life back home, sometimes they mentioned an "outcast table" whose business they still seemed to be settling, their voices tight. In a commensal tradition, where food is precious, the powerful older people made wrongdoers eat alone. Instead of letting them start separate new lives like the Japanese, who could become samurais and geishas, the Chinese family, faces averted but eyes glowering sideways, hung on to the offenders and fed them leftovers. My aunt must have lived in the same house as my parents and eaten at an outcast table. My mother spoke about the raid as if she had seen it, when she and my aunt, a daughter-in-law to a different household, should not have been living together at all. Daughters-in-law lived with their husbands' parents, not their own; a synonym for marriage in Chinese is "taking a daughter-in-law." Her husband's parents could have sold her, mortgaged her, stoned her. But they had sent her back to her own mother and father, a mysterious act hinting at disgraces not told me. Perhaps they had thrown her out to deflect the avengers.

She was the only daughter; her four brothers went with her father, husband, and uncles "out on the road" and for some years became western men. When the goods were divided among the family, three of the brothers took land, and the youngest, my father, chose an education. After my grandparents gave their daughter away to her husband's family, they had dispensed all the adventure and all the property. They expected her alone to keep the traditional ways, which her brothers, now among the barbarians, could fumble without detection. The heavy, deep-rooted women were to maintain the past against the flood, safe for returning. But the rare urge west had fixed upon our family, and so my aunt crossed boundaries not delineated in space.

The work of preservation demands that the feelings playing about in one's guts not be turned into action. Just watch their passing like cherry blossoms. But perhaps my aunt, my forerunner, caught in a slow life, let dreams grow and fade and after some months or years went toward what persisted. Fear at the enormities of the forbidden kept her desires delicate, wire and bone. She looked at a man because she liked the way the hair was tucked behind his ears, or she liked the question-mark line of a long torso curving at the shoulder and straight at the hip. For warm eyes or a soft voice or a slow walk—that's all—a few hairs, a line, a brightness, a sound, a pace, she gave up family. She offered us up for a charm that vanished with tiredness, a pigtail that didn't toss when the wind died. Why, the wrong lighting could erase the dearest thing about him.

It could very well have been, however, that my aunt did not take subtle enjoyment of her friend, but, a wild woman, kept rollicking company. Imagining her free with sex doesn't fit, though. I don't know any women like that, or men either. Unless I see her life branching into mine, she gives me no ancestral help.

To sustain her being in love, she often worked at herself in the mirror, guessing at the colors and shapes that would interest him, changing them frequently in order to hit on the right combination. She wanted him to look back.

On a farm near the sea, a woman who tended her appearance reaped a reputation for eccentricity. All the married women blunt-cut their hair in flaps about their ears or pulled it back in tight buns. No nonsense. Neither style blew easily into heart-catching tangles. And at their weddings they displayed themselves in their long hair for the last time. "It brushed the backs of my knees," my mother tells me. "It was braided, and even so, it brushed the backs of my knees."

At the mirror my aunt combed individuality into her bob. A bun could have been contrived to escape into black streamers blowing in the wind or in quiet wisps about her face, but only the older women in our picture album wear buns. She brushed her hair back from her forehead, tucking the flaps behind her ears. She looped a piece of thread, knotted into a circle between her index fingers and thumbs, and ran the double strand across her forehead. When she closed her fingers as if she were making a pair of shadow geese bite, the string twisted together catching the little hairs. Then she pulled the thread away from her skin, ripping the hairs out neatly, her eyes watering from the needles of pain. Opening her fingers, she cleaned the thread, then rolled it along her hairline and the tops of her eyebrows. My mother did the same to me and my sisters and herself. I used to believe that the expression "caught by the short hairs" meant a captive held with a depilatory string. It especially hurt at the temples, but my mother said we were lucky we didn't have to have our feet bound when we were seven. Sisters used to sit on their beds and cry together, she said, as their mothers or their slave removed the bandages for a few minutes each night and let the blood gush back into their veins. I hope that the man my aunt loved appreciated a smooth brow, that he wasn't just a tits-and-ass man.

Once my aunt found a freckle on her chin, at a spot that the almanac said predestined her for unhappiness. She dug it out with a hot needle and washed the wound with peroxide.

More attention to her looks than these pullings of hairs and pickings at spots would have caused gossip among the villagers. They owned work clothes and good clothes, and they wore good clothes for feasting the new seasons. But since a woman combing her hair hexes beginnings, my aunt rarely found an occasion to look her best. Women looked like great sea snails—the corded wood, babies, and laundry they carried were the whorls on their backs. The Chinese did not admire a bent back; goddesses and warriors stood straight. Still there must have been a marvelous freeing of beauty when a worker laid down her burden and stretched and arched.

Such commonplace loveliness, however, was not enough for my aunt. She dreamed of a lover for the fifteen days of New Year's, the time for families to exchange visits, money, and food. She plied her secret comb. And sure enough she cursed the year, the family, the village, and herself.

Even as her hair lured her imminent lover, many other men looked at her. Uncles, cousins, nephews, brothers would have looked, too, had they been home between journeys. Perhaps they had already been restraining their curiosity, and they left, fearful that their glances, like a field of nesting birds, might be startled and caught. Poverty hurt, and that was their first reason for leaving. But another, final reason for leaving the crowded house was the never-said.

She may have been unusually beloved, the precious only daughter, spoiled and mirror gazing because of the affection the family lavished on her. When her husband left, they welcomed the chance to take her back from the in-laws; she could live like the little daughter for just a while longer. There are stories that my grandfather was different from other people, "crazy ever since the little Jap bayoneted him in the head." He used to put his naked penis on the dinner table, laughing. And one day he brought home a baby girl, wrapped up inside his brown western-style greatcoat. He had traded one of his sons, probably my father, the youngest, for her. My grandmother made him trade back. When he finally got a daughter of his own, he doted on her. They must have all loved her, except perhaps my father, the only brother who never went back to China, having once been traded for a girl.

Brothers and sisters, newly men and women, had to efface their sexual color and present plain miens. Disturbing hair and eyes, a smile like no other, threatened the ideal of five generations living under one roof. To focus blurs, people shouted face to face and yelled from room to room. The immigrants I know have loud voices, unmodulated to American tones even after years away from the village where they called their friendships out across the fields. I have not been able to stop my mother's screams in public libraries or over telephones. Walking erect (knees straight, toes pointed forward, not pigeon-toed, which is Chinese-feminine) and speaking in an inaudible voice, I have tired to turn myself American-feminine. Chinese communication was loud, public. Only sick people had to whisper. But at the dinner table, where the family members came nearest one another, no one could talk, not the outcasts nor any eaters. Every word that falls from the mouth is a coin lost. Silently they gave and accepted food with both hands. A pre-occupied child who took his bowl with one hand got a sideways glare. A complete moment of total attention is due everyone alike. Children and lovers have no singularity here, but my aunt used a secret voice, a separate attentiveness.

She kept the man's name to herself throughout her labor and dying; she did not accuse him that he be punished with her. To save her inseminator's name she gave silent birth.

He may have been somebody in her own household, but inter-course with a man outside the family would have been no less abhor-rent. All the village were kinsmen, and the titles shouted in loud coun-try voices never let kinship be forgotten. Any man within visiting dis-tance would have been neutralized as a lover—"brother," "younger brother," "older brother"—one hundred and fifteen relationship titles. Parents researched birth charts probably not so much to assure good fortune as to circumvent incest in a population that has but one hun-dred surnames. Everybody has eight million relatives. How useless then sexual mannerisms, how dangerous.

As if it came from an atavism deeper than fear, I used to add "brother" silently to boys' names. It hexed the boys, who would or would not ask me to dance, and made them less scary and as familiar and deserving of benevolence as girls.

But, of course, I hexed myself also—no dates. I should have stood up, both arms waving, and shouted out across libraries, "Hey, you! Love me back." I had no idea, though, how to make attraction selective, how to control its direction and magnitude. If I made myself American-pretty so that the five or six Chinese boys in the class fell in love with me, everyone else—the Caucasian, Negro, and Japanese boys—would too. Sisterliness, dignified and honorable, made much more sense.

Attraction eludes control so stubbornly that whole societies designed to organize relationships among people cannot keep order, not even when they bind people to one another from childhood and raise them together. Among the very poor and the wealthy, brothers married their adopted sisters, like doves. Our family allowed some romance, paying adult brides' prices and providing dowries so that their sons and daughters could marry strangers. Marriage promises to turn strangers into friendly relatives—a nation of siblings.

In the village structure, spirits shimmered among the live creatures, balanced and held in equilibrium by time and land. But one human being flaring up into violence could open up a black hole, a maelstrom that pulled in the sky. The frightened villagers, who depended on one another to maintain the real, went to my aunt to show her a personal, physical representation of the break she had made in the "roundness." Misallying couples snapped off the future, which was to be embodied in true offspring. The villagers punished her for acting as if she could have a private life, secret and apart from them.

If my aunt had betrayed the family at a time of large grain yields and peace, when many boys were born, and wings were being built on many houses, perhaps she might have escaped such severe punishment. But the men—hungry, greedy, tired of planting in dry soil, cuckolded—had had to leave the village in order to send food-money home. There were ghost plagues, bandit plagues, wars with the Japanese, floods. My Chinese brother and sister had died of an unknown sickness. Adultery, perhaps only a mistake during good times, became a crime when the village needed food.

The round moon cakes and round doorways, the round tables of graduated size that fit one roundness inside another, round windows and rice bowls—these talismans had lost their power to warn this family of the law: a family must be whole, faithfully keeping the descent line by having sons to feed the old and the dead, who in turn look after the family. The villagers came to show my aunt and her lover-in-hiding a broken house. The villagers were speeding up the circling of events because she was too shortsighted to see that her infidelity had already harmed the village, that waves of consequences would return unpredictably, sometimes in disguise, as now, to hurt her. This roundness had to be made coin-sized so that she would see its circumference: punish her at the birth of her baby. Awaken her to the inexorable. People who refused fatalism because they could invent small resources insisted on culpability. Deny accidents and wrest fault from the stars.

After the villagers left, their lanterns now scattering in various directions toward home, the family broke their silence and cursed her. "Aiaa, we're going to die. Death is coming. Death is coming. Look what you've done. You've killed us. Ghost! Dead ghost! Ghost! You've never been born." She ran out into the fields, far enough from the house so that she could no longer hear their voices, and pressed herself against the earth, her own land no more. When she felt the birth coming, she thought that she had been hurt. Her body seized together. "They've hurt me too much," she thought. "This is gall, and it will kill me." With forehead and knees against the earth, her body convulsed and then relaxed. She turned on her back, lay on the ground. The black well of sky and stars went out and out and out forever; her body and her complexity seemed to disappear. She was one of the stars, a bright dot in blackness, without home, without a companion, in eternal cold and silence. An agoraphobia rose in her, speeding higher and higher, bigger and bigger; she would not be able to contain it; there would be no end to fear.

Flayed, unprotected against space, she felt pain return, focusing her body. This pain chilled her—a cold, steady kind of surface pain. Inside, spasmodically, the other pain, the pain of the child, heated her. For hours she lay on the ground, alternately body and space. Sometimes a vision of normal comfort obliterated reality: she saw the family in the evening gambling at the dinner table, the young people massaging their elders' backs. She saw them congratulating one another, high joy on the mornings the rice shoots came up. When these pictures burst, the stars drew yet further apart. Black space opened.

She got to her feet to fight better and remembered that old-fashioned women gave birth in their pigsties to fool the jealous, pain-dealing gods, who do not snatch piglets. Before the next spasms could stop her, she ran to the pigsty, each step a rushing out into emptiness. She climbed over the fence and knelt in the dirt. It was good to have a fence enclosing her, a tribal person alone.

Laboring, this woman who had carried her child as a foreign growth that sickened her every day, expelled it at last. She reached down to touch the hot, wet, moving mass, surely smaller than anything human, and could feel that it was human after all—fingers, toes, nails, nose. She pulled it up on to her belly, and it lay curled there, butt in the air, feet precisely tucked one under the other. She opened her loose shirt and buttoned the child inside. After resting, it squirmed and thrashed and she pushed it up to her breast. It turned its head this way and that until it found her nipple. There, it made little snuffling noises. She clenched her teeth at its preciousness, lovely as a young calf, a piglet, a little dog.

She may have gone to the pigsty as a last act of responsibility: she would protect this child as she had protected its father. It would look after her soul, leaving supplies on her grave. But how would this tiny child without family find her grave when there would be no marker for her anywhere, neither in the earth nor the family hall? No one would give her a family hall name. She had taken the child with her into the wastes. At its birth the two of them had felt the same raw pain of separation, a wound that only the family pressing tight could close. A child with no descent line would not soften her life but only trail after her, ghostlike, begging her to give it purpose. At dawn the villagers on their way to the fields would stand around the fence and look.

Full of milk, the little ghost slept. When it awoke, she hardened her breasts against the milk that crying loosens. Toward morning she picked up the baby and walked to the well.

Carrying the baby to the well shows loving. Otherwise abandon it. Turn its face into the mud. Mothers who love their children take them along. It was probably a girl; there is some hope of forgiveness for boys.

"Don't tell anyone you had an aunt. Your father does not want to hear her name. She has never been born." I have believed that sex was unspeakable and words so strong and fathers so frail that "aunt" would do my father mysterious harm. I have thought that my family, having settled among immigrants who had also been their neighbors in the ancestral land, needed to clean their name, and a wrong word would incite the kinspeople even here. But there is more to this silence: they want me to participate in her punishment. And I have.

In the twenty years since I heard this story I have not asked for details nor said my aunt's name; I do not know it. People who can comfort the dead can also chase after them to hurt them further—a reverse ancestor worship. The real punishment was not the raid swiftly inflicted by the villagers, but the family's deliberately forgetting her.

Her betrayal so maddened them, they saw to it that she would suffer forever, even after death. Always hungry, always needing, she would have to beg food from other ghosts, snatch and steal it from those whose living descendants give them gifts. She would have to fight the ghosts massed at crossroads for the buns a few thoughtful citizens leave to decoy her away from village and home so that the ancestral spirits could feast unharassed. At peace, they could act like gods, not ghosts, their descent lines providing them with paper suits and dresses, spirit money, paper houses, paper automobiles, chicken, meat, and rice into eternity—essences delivered up in smoke and flames, steam and incense rising from each rice bowl. In an attempt to make the Chinese care for people outside the family, Chairman Mao encourages us now to give our paper replicas to the spirits of outstanding soldiers and workers, no matter whose ancestors they may be. My aunt remains forever hungry. Goods are not distributed evenly among the dead.

My aunt haunts me—her ghost drawn to me because now, after fifty years of neglect, I alone devote pages of paper to her, though not origamied into houses and clothes. I do not think she always means me well. I am telling on her, and she was a spite suicide, drowning herself in the drinking water. The Chinese are always very frightened of the drowned one, whose weeping ghost, wet hair hanging and skin bloated, waits silently by the water to pull down a substitute.

DIANE GLANCY
(1941—)

———◆———

DIANE GLANCY writes in one of her autobiographical journal entries, "I was born between two heritages," voicing the inherent tension in American identity addressed by Mary Dearborn in *Pocahontas's Daughters:* "As Americans we partake of a national identity, a communally determined and accepted sense of self; at the same time, as Americans and ethnics all, we define ourselves ancestrally." Glancy, a member of the Cherokee tribe, grew up and raised a family in Kansas and Oklahoma. She now teaches creative writing and Native American literature at Macalester College in St. Paul, Minnesota. She published her first volume of short fiction, *Trigger Dance* (1990) with the Fiction Collective Two. Her poetry has appeared in *Calyx, Cincinnati Poetry Review, Seneca Review,* the anthology *Born at the Crossroads: Voices of Mixed Heritage Women,* and *Feminist Journal. Claiming Breath,* excerpted here, her first collection of autobiographical prose, which sometimes takes the form of notes for poems, was the winner of the North American Indian Prose Award for 1991. A recipient of the Equal Opportunity Fellowship from the University of Iowa and grants from the National Endowment for the Arts and the Minnesota State Arts Board, Glancy did not begin to write regularly and for publication until after divorce and having raised her children. As she puts it in "December 1 / Fragments / Shards," "Family had covered the fissures in my life. Now I had fragments / shards / whatever the territory offered. My poems and writing were the land I cultivated. I moved toward 'being' in poetry." Read together, the journal entries in *Claiming Breath* reflect some of the basic characteristics of the ancient oral tradition of the indigenous peoples of the Americas and join this tradition with the newer evolving one of American Indian women's autobiography. In the words of critics Gretchen Bataille and Kathleen Mullen Sands, this oral tradition is characterized by "emphasis on event, attention to the sacredness of language, concern with landscape, affirmation of cultural values and tribal solidarity." Glancy's poetry and storytelling have been praised for piercing through the clichés of Native American culture, representing the unromanticized adjustment of tribal people to twentieth-century society. Her writing belongs to those works cited by Mary Dearborn, the oral histories, documents, autobiographies, and fiction, that, in her words, "give the impression that the ethnic woman's story . . . is coming out in bits and pieces." To date, says Dearborn, the studies of the most prominent ethnic scholars have not considered "what ethnic women have written."

from *Claiming Breath*

December 23 \ Alia Bowman

I could relate to her those long afternoons she talked about her husband. She'd married the wrong man, she said. There was another man she'd almost married, but for some reason at the last, chose Elmer. She relived some of their marriage with bitterness he'd not been a good husband. His disregard for her in buying the truck stop & fruit farm. It was always more work for her. He flew small planes, at one time had a fleet of school buses, drank himself stupid. I knew what she said. I had married her grandson, a hard drinking Irishman, the image of his grandfather. I knew neglect, his disregard for my feelings. She & I spent long afternoons peeling apples, rolling out dough, thinking yes, how we'd married the wrong man.

December 26

I also want to explore the breakdown of boundaries between the genres. This "communal" stance is inherent in the Native American heritage. The non-linear non-boundaried non-fenced open-prairied words. Non-creative fiction, nearly. It's something that's there. I don't have to make it up with the imagination. Just think of the relationships.

I want to explore my memories & their relational aspects to the present. I was born between 2 heritages & I want to explore that empty space, that place-between-2-places, that walk-in-2-worlds. I want to do it in a new way.

The word is important in Native American tradition. You speak the path on which you walk. Your words make the trail. You have to be careful with words. They can shape the future. For instance, when a brave hunted a bear, he first drew the bear with his arrow in it, then when he went hunting, the hunt was merely a result of what he'd already done in his drawing.

December 27 \ Delay

From the window I hear a squirrel bark at some intrusion. I think the cat must be in the tree again. Waiting to get from one place to another. A newspaper with a crease folded into it. Waiting for piano lessons & dance lessons, waiting for the kids to clear out, waiting for my time to come. What are you anxious about? He would ask. Your chance will come when you aren't expecting it. You'll have an instant to grab onto it, running with all the baggage you can't let go of. What do you have to write about anyway?

December I \ Fragments \ Shards

After the divorce, I had new territory, much like the Oklahoma land run when a piece of land was claimed & had to be settled. I had spent years hiding behind my husband, the children & housework. Now the land & sky were open. That's what's frightening about the prairie at first \ its barrenness & lack of shelter. I had always written, but now my sense of place was defined by whatever mattered. I picked up my Indian heritage & began a journey toward ani-yun-wiyu, or, translated from the Cherokee, "real people."

I read journals \ magazines. Poetry \ some fiction. I saw that feelings could be expressed in writing. Feelings of bewilderment & fear. Especially anger. It was a trend in women's writing \ the pulley I needed out of the separation & isolation I felt without the surroundings of family. I saw women come to grips with themselves. The vulnerability, the struggle, the agonizing choices. I had to find a homestead within myself, or invent one. I dug a potato cellar.

Family had covered the fissures in my life. Now I had fragments \ shards \ whatever the territory offered. My poems & writing were the land I cultivated. I moved toward "being" in poetry. A struggle for survival. My purpose was to find the truth of what I was \ my voice. What I had to offer. I could not have done it without the other voices \ the sun & rain & soil for myself as a person. The pleasure of being a woman.

I found that I weathered the prairie storms & the limitations that come with the territory. I found acceptance of myself \ the strength to travel prairie roads & talk about poetry in towns where farmers in the cafés stare. I relived the struggle to claim the land \ establish a sod house \ plow the fields \ milk the cow. The rest will come. All this is an internal land, of course. I started late with only a map given to me by other women who said the territory was there. It was a fertile landscape just inside the head. I had only to load the wagon, hitch the horses. A journey which my mother never made before she folded up her camp.

I learned to trust images. I could even experiment with words. Put muffler, glass packs on the wagon. Mud flaps if I wanted. I have what men have had \ liberty to be myself. Maybe women had it too & I just never knew. Wrong \ wright \ whatever. Now I could throw out the ice cubes \ find my severed limbs \ sew them on instead of giving heart & arms & lungs away. I have use for them on the edge of the frontier \ saw-edge after saw-edge.

The glory of the plain self in search of words to say, "the self" \ the delight of it. The birth \ the shedding of invisibility. The pursuit of she-pleasure. SHEDONISM.

The themes \ form \ experimental forms. Words as house & shed & outbuildings on the land. The urgency. The cessation of pounding myself \ hanging my separate parts to dry on low branches & rocks. It's women who influenced my work. Their courage \ their trend toward revelation. I am on the journey to the ani-yun-wiyu.

Astoria Boulevard

The cab passes a Christmas tree lot in Queens. A man arranges fir trees and wreaths, his hands the size of postal cards in fir boughs. A glimpse of him caressing trees, and those asleep on park benches along Astoria Boulevard, is all there is time for. The scrawl of graffiti decorates subway tracks on the way to La Guardia. Strings of lights and ornaments brought from attics are stiff as the cold that hovers near barrel-fires. The tree-seller warms his hands, picks a tree for the Astoria Baptist Church in the Christ-child season when hope rises like planes over the neighborhood and sends smothered messages to those asleep, small as hands.

Claiming Breath

How do you begin writing poetry? I would say after all these years I'm not sure. First of all, you read. You have to be aware of what's being written. Poetry is a conversation. Often while I'm reading, I start a poem. An image will set off another image, or I think of something I want to say.

It also helps to know the tradition of poetry, though often there's something about it that gets in the way. You strain for a rhyme without thought for the fire, the energy of the poem, the originality of voice. Yet I've heard others say that structure forces them to work in ways they would have missed on their own.

Begin by getting words down. What have you got to say? Even if you want to remain obscure there has to be coherence on some level. I remember hearing Gerald Stern say, if you get your words in order on the first row, you make room for a craziness later on, deeper in the poem, in a more important place.

Work with what you've experienced. I think sometimes, who cares about my ordinary life? But often, that's exactly what matters.

What idea, impression, image, do you want to convey? Why should I listen to you? Again, 1) read, 2) write what you have to say, & 3) read it to someone. Listen to their reaction, their criticism, & write again. So much of writing is rewriting.

Contemporary poetry says what you have to say in whatever way you want to say. Make sure you have a style, a voice, a certain way of expressing yourself. Where's your uniqueness, your individuality? You have a thumbprint different from other thumbprints. You have a way of seeing & a way of expressing what you see that is also different. Develop that difference. Take chances with unusual words & combinations. Writing is a long process. Reveal what it's like to be you.

Do you have something bothering you? Get into it. That will save the trouble of writing boring poems.

Remember imagery, the mental pictures your writing makes, usually thru metaphor & simile. Make sure they haven't been said before. They have to be new. Tell me something in a way I haven't heard it before. Let an image connect with a thought, sometimes a memory. Get rid of weak verbs. Watch tenses, make them consistent. Use DETAIL! A cotton dress printed with crocuses is usually better than "a dress." Look for the right word. The inevitable one. Ask what your poem means. What conclusion is drawn from it? Even if not a logical thought, but an impression. Good poems are sometimes simple, on at least one level.

What is life like for you? That's what you should begin writing about.

Remember also the richness of language. Make sure there's a lot in your writing. Read your words to yourself. Listen to them on a tape recorder.

The form a poem takes on the page is also integral. Experiment with line breaks, stanzas, the square or prose poem, the words wiggling over the page.

Then workshop a poem. Critiques are usually common sense. Does the poem work? Do you like it? Does it begin at the first stanza or do you really get into the poem several lines later? Do all the parts form a whole? What central thought holds the poem together? What emotion or impression is shared? What stays in your mind after you've heard it? Is it in the form it should be in? Is the poem clear? Have you said the same thing too many times? Is the reader rewarded for reading it?

Be interested in a lot of things. Be an interesting person, live a responsible life. Start keeping notes.

I think it's also important to know why you write. When I go into a bookstore & see shelves full of books, I think why do I do this? Hasn't it been done better than I can do it? That's when I have to be able to look in myself & decide, I have something to say too— These other books can move over & make room for mine.

NIKKI GIOVANNI
(1943—)

◆

NIKKI GIOVANNI was born Yolande Cornelia Giovanni, Jr., in Knoxville, Tennessee, reared in Cincinnati, Ohio, and attended Fisk University, the University of Pennsylvania, and the Columbia School of Fine Arts. She was a central figure in the African-American literary movement of the sixties during which time she was best known for her poetry and her performance readings. Her collections of poetry include *Black Feeling, Black Talk* (1968); *Black Judgement* (1969); *The Women and the Men* (1975); *Cotton Candy on a Rainy Day* (1978), and *Those Who Ride the Night Winds* (1983). Giovanni has also published two volumes of autobiography: *Gemini: An Extended Autobiographical Statement on My First Twenty-Five Years of Being a Black Poet* (1971), which was nominated for a National Book Award, and *Sacred Cows . . . and Other Edibles* (1988), a collection of autobiographical essays from which the following selection is taken. Novelist and critic Marita Golden called this latest book "quintessential Nikki Giovanni—sometimes funny, nervy and unnerving with flashes of wisdom, sparkling *and* thoughtful." The mother of a son, she has since the late sixties taught creative writing, currently at Virginia Polytechnic Institute and State University in Blacksburg.

Because her writing is often funny and glib and has explored both militant black politics and domesticated love, Giovanni has provoked some controversy among African-American critics. Perhaps she has drawn fire mostly because, as critic William J. Harris has written, "she refuses to go along with anybody's orthodoxy." Her independence of mind comes through in her statement about "How I Write" given to Mari Evans for her collection, *Black Women Writers (1950–1980):* "We write, because we believe that the human spirit cannot be tamed and should not be trained." *Gemini* ends with the down-to-earth wisdom that is key to her finest art and enduring reputation: "I think we are all capable of tremendous beauty once we decide we are beautiful or of giving a lot of love once we understand love is possible, and of making the world over in that image should we choose to. I really like to think a Black, beautiful, loving world is possible. I really do, I think."

from *Sacred Cows . . . and Other Edibles*

In Sympathy with Another Motherless Child
(One View of the Profession of Writing)

Writing is like any other profession—breakdancing, ninth grade, doctor of philosophy, surgeon—it's what I do to justify the air I breathe, the food I ingest, the time I take up on earth. I'm ever and still amazed that any artist considers himself God or in close proximity thereof. It's not like a double 0 number—it's not a license to kill, no excuse to not exercise normal courtesy in human relations, no copyright to bigotry. I suppose there is, or at least there appears to be, some human need to cull from the general stock those who should be exalted. I don't trust that instinct at all. The more you are in public life, the less likely it is that your life will be worth living, unless you exercise great care to be sure it's your life and not what someone wants your life to be that you are living. I feel as sorry for the modern politicians and rock stars as I do the Roman Claudius, who was told by his Praetorian guards that he had one of two choices: "You will be emperor or we will kill you." Ass-kissing is not a normal human posture for the kisser or the kissee.

I am not at all sure that forty is the proper age to look at a career. At forty, first of all, the body changes. No one in his right mind would ask a teenager to write or evaluate his life, because those who have been through adolescence know that every day there is another major change, another crisis, another reason to feel life sucks and there is nothing that can be done about it. I'm not sure that at forty we know much more. At sixteen we can feel there will be another sixteen and another and another; at forty you pretty well know there will not be another forty; you are pleased to think there might be another ten, and depending upon the rate of body deterioration you can hope for another twenty with the coda: If I'm healthy. Most Americans are medically indigent; I know I am. I have instructed my mother to sign nothing should I be struck with any disease more serious than cellulite. I'm probably going to die anyway and there's no point in her, my son and my dogs going into bankruptcy to stave off the inevitable. Can we talk? It's not at all that I'm interested in dying. As a matter of fact I think life is one of the more interesting propositions offered on earth; it's just that I have lived through a terminal illness and have seen.

I like my profession. I hope the telephone operators, the hamburger turner at McDonald's, the pressure checker at Kentucky Fried who sees to it that those spices and herbs get really deep in the chicken are proud, too. I know some degree of incentive is necessary to my profession. Writers are the world's biggest procrastinators and the second biggest paranoid group, being bested only by politicians. I know that we have to get some kind of seed in our craw to write, and then we only write after we have washed all the windows, cleaned the oven, weeded the garden and are threatened with either bodily harm by our publishers or imminent bankruptcy by our creditors. I have a dear friend who invites me each summer to come to her home to write. "You'll have lots of privacy," she always points out, "and there are the swimming pool and the tennis courts when you need to take a break." What she has also figured out is that her closets will be both straightened out and waxed, her silver will get polished, all repairs will be made on the porch furniture, all doorknobs will be tightened. I'm very handy. In fact, I'm a joy to have around! I paint, stain, rescreen, file crystal; the only thing I don't do well in a house is electrical work that requires the box to be turned off. I'm terribly handy with plumbing and have been known in my mother's house to repair roof shingles. Of course, we seldom mention that the books don't get written . . . To tell the truth, my secret desire is to open my own Nikki's Best Handy Girl Service. Hey! If this poetry doesn't work out, I've got my second career all planned. As you may have guessed—I'm compulsive.

Ecclesiastes teaches us there is a season and a purpose for everything under the heavens; what it fails to mention is there is a place. I really can stand dirt since in my mind there is a purpose for dirt; I cannot stand disorder. I am stupefied, amazed, that people haven't alphabetized their books and records, that clothes in the closet don't hang on proper hangers in color and length categories. An unbalanced closet is the sign of a sick mind, much more indicative of the true personality than a cluttered desk, for which there is at least one excuse. It used to be that you could tell all you needed to know about a woman by the way she kept house; the same is true of men these days. Chalk one up for the ERA.

Rage is to writers what water is to fish. A laid-back writer is like an orgasmic prostitute—an anomaly—something that doesn't quite fit. I have been considered a writer who writes from rage, and it confuses me. What else do writers write from? We are not, after all, songsters who put together a ditty because the bride is not a virgin and the groom is impotent. . . . Actually, I'm not in a rage frequently. For some reason, after all these years, meanness and stupidity still get to me. I work on it, honestly. I understand not everyone has had the advantages I have enjoyed of being able to both read and digest material and apply the lessons learned. I'm told by my young friends that experience is much more important than books. Of course Ben Franklin had something to say about experience and fools, but even Franklin thought that a fool would learn by his experience. That has proven false in the modern world. Some people are simply unwilling to learn under any circumstances, which maybe, even then, wouldn't be so bad if they weren't so damned proud of it. Doesn't it just make your skin crawl to hear somebody spout off about what they don't do and how they're never going to do it? It makes you cheer against the human race. I'm sure to be a crotchety old lady, assuming I have not yet achieved that state, because things like refusing to eat oysters will drive me up a wall. Stick one of the damned things in your mouth; then you can say, "I don't care for oysters, though I have tried them." This argument does not apply to cocaine or other hallucinogenic drugs; the experience of other people will do just fine. Isn't that the purpose of people living and sharing? So that others will at least not make the same mistake, since we seldom are able to re-create the positive things in life.

I guess one of life's experiences that I have always wanted to avoid was bitterness. Yes, I know I wrote a poem on bitterness and I know that earlier in this career critics thought I was bitter, but I am not nor was I. Just sick and tired of the same song and dance. The bitter people are as bad as the drug people because they seem to descend to a place from which no light ever emerges. . . .

. . . Now, as far as children go, I have no special insight into teenagers, save this: The fourteen-year-old personality was invented to give ulcers to otherwise calm mothers; to cause normally tranquil, proud, loving parents to snarl, growl and threaten; the fourteen-year-old personality was created, in other words, to drive forty-year-old mothers to the nuthouse.

Everyone says babies are difficult; it's just not true. Changing diapers, wiping pabulum from chins, heating bottles in the middle of the night are a snap compared to picking up your own telephone that you pay for every month and never hearing a familiar voice, either friend or relative, but rather a barbarian girl or boy demanding, "Tom home!" I was at first annoyed by the question and then by the tone, but I've trained myself to respond only to the question asked: "Why, yes, he is. How kind of you to call and inquire. I must go now." I then hang up. The barbarian response next was, "Can I speak to Tom?" to which I replied, again, as sweetly as possible: "It appears you are quite capable. I hear you very well. I must go now." Finally they reached the desired question: "May I speak to Tom?" which, unfortunately, elicits "I'm sorry, dear, but Thomas may not use the telephone until his grades improve." I don't add "Or hell freezes over."

Whichever comes first. Hell will surely win.

Why, sister mothers, do children want to fail? Is it the new high? Is there some sexual charge experienced when our ninth-graders come home with report cards full of F's and I's? What sado-psychological satisfaction is gained by them watching our hearts leap from our breasts, our eyes involuntarily tearing over, our breaths coming in short, unnatural spurts? What kick do they get standing over us watching our lives pass before our eyes? All my friends have marvelous children who clean their rooms, excel in extracurricular activities, pass their classes, get honors and awards. I've even taken, and I don't mind admitting it, to avoiding certain parents of perfect children, though I have not been a competitive parent. When little Billy Bob joined the Boy Scouts, climbed a twelve-story building and rescued a blind, paraplegic unwed mother from raging flames I never said to my son: "How come you never do anything worthwhile?" No. I smiled at the parent, congratulated the child and dutifully went back to pinning Tom's socks for the laundry and picking up the comic books that are spread across the floor, making his room a hazardous area. When little Sally Mae, in just the fifth grade, was invited to Athens to address the Senate in her fluent Greek on how stability could be obtained with Turkey, I said to her mother, my friend, "You must be very proud." I did not say to Tom, "Why is it that that little snotty-nose twerp is hailed the world over while you refuse to write a simple essay for English *in* English about the Alaskan cruise I had to mortgage the house to take you on?" I didn't even heap abuse when he replied, "Alaska wasn't so much." No. I calmly said, "Dear, I sincerely think you can improve this Incomplete by turning in your assignment." I am, however, about to be convinced that kindness, civil tone, and logic have no truck with teenagers. My son had a classmate last year who was spanked every time she brought home a B or less. Tom was appalled. "But dear," I pointed out, "look at your grades and look at hers. Surely I am the parent in the wrong." "Well," says Mister as he makes his way to the freezer to get a pizza and pop it in the oven, "she hates her mother and I love you." If this is love, folks . . .

My son, I do believe and have had demonstrated, has a lot of character. He has never lied to me. I'm told by friends with perfect children that that is because it's all the same to him. He doesn't lie because he knows I won't go off on him or stop him from doing anything he wants to do anyway. I like to think that's not true. I like to think he is truthful because (1) I *will* go crazy on him if he lies; but mostly because (2) somewhere inside that pickled fourteen-year-old mass that commonly is called a brain he has absorbed some of the values I've been trying by example to teach him. When I am hasty in my judgments or just plain wrong about something I don't mind apologizing. When I don't know something I don't mind admitting ignorance. When I don't want him to go somewhere or do something for no particular reason other than I think it's not right for him, I explain, "Mother is making an arbitrary judgment that has no logic or reason. You are right to be angry about this. I would feel the same way if the tables were turned." It may not be any easier to take, but it's honest.

I've also seen Tom come through a situation that would be difficult for a stable adult. My father developed bladder cancer following a stroke, which is the reason we moved from New York back to Cincinnati. Those years could not have been easy, living with someone who was, in fact, dying. My father was brave in the face of his impending death and so was my son. Neither complained of the burden or the pain. The night my father died Tom, my mother and I were the only ones at home. My sister was coming in from San Francisco. My nephew from Seattle* was not contacted until the day after. The hospital called that Gus had died. I had to go out to pick up his personal property and sign for the autopsy. Tom, who was then twelve, said, "I'll go with you." He went to the hospital, viewed the body, got his grandfather's walking cane, stayed while the other arrangements were made. That night he came into my room and curled up next to Wendy, my dog, and slept on the floor. The next morning we had to pick a casket. "I'll go with you," he said to my mother, my sister and me. He put his tie and jacket on and sat through the funeral arrangements. He stayed by my side as the family made calls, placed flower orders, took care of the kind of base-touching a funeral requires. For two days he looked after us as best he could. On the morning of the funeral he asked: "Mommy, when is Chris getting here?" Meaning, I think, that he had gone as far as he was capable. It was more than caring . . . it was character. . . .

. . . I really don't know what to say about myself. I like music. There is something very special about capping my headphones and drowning in a vision of sound. Someone once asked me if I played an instrument and I replied, "My stereo." It's not surprising that man's first musical instrument was a drum; the image of the heart had to be manifest. The African people made use of the ability of the drum to both inform and incite; for over two hundred years of the American experience drumming was outlawed. A people, though, are rarely stopped in

*Chris

their legitimate desire for either knowledge or pleasure. Whether the Eighteenth Amendment would outlaw alcohol or the Miss America Pageant would desire the clothing of their Black Venus, a people, through individual risk or simply aesthetic innocence, will bring word of a new day.

It is sheer folly to assume the various African cultures were without stress, frustrations, discriminations. It is only our desire to escape the challenges of our own times that leads us to envision some African Eden with fruit dripping from every branch, fish jumping in clear cool ponds, women willing with no discernible persuasion, men strong, beautiful and capable after undergoing some variation of initiation into "manhood." If the human species alone among the mammals is capable of dreaming, we are also alone in our capacity for fantasy. America did not invent the blues for Africans—it simply made us sing them in English.

The giraffe alone, among those who are warm-blooded, is without a voice. All other mammals, most insects and, as we have learned to listen to the ocean, not an inconsiderable number of fish make some sound. Among those on earth the chirping of birds is universally considered pleasant, the howl of a single wolf on a mountain ridge the most mournful. We howl with the wolf not so much in imitation of his sound as in sympathy with another motherless child. The African slave bereft of his gods, his language, his drums searched his heart for a new voice. Under sun and lash the African sought meaning in life on earth and the possibility of life hereafter. They shuffled their feet, clapped their hands, gathered a collective audible breath to release the rhythms of the heart. We affirmed in those dark days of chattel through the White Knights of Emancipation that all we had was a human voice to guide us and a human voice to answer the call.

Anthropologically speaking, humans were divided in the workforce by gender. The men became the stalkers of prey; the women tended the fire, garden and children at the home site. Men learned at a very early age the value of quiet; women learned the necessity of talk. Men learned to compete for the best spot, the biggest share; women learned to cooperate, to socialize. If there was a benefit of slavery to the slaves it was that it broke down gender barriers; men and women shared the work, learned the songs, began and ended the day together. If there was a benefit to white people during the Great Depression it was that men learned how to deal with enforced idleness; women learned having a "good marriage" would not protect them from the reality that everyone has a right, if not an obligation, to do productive work.

It is historically considered that there have been two American rev-
olutions: the one against the British for the right to tax ourselves and
the one against the South to free chattel slaves. The revisionists consider
there was perhaps a third revolution: the recovery from the Great
Depression to meld compassion with free enterprise. Those of my generation know there has been a fourth: American youth, not with fife
and bugle but with drums and boogie, headed for the twenty-first century with the battle cry: "Oo Whoop Baba Loo Boop Oo Whop Bam
Boom!"

The Coasters said they'd been "Searchin'," and once again an
African–Afro-American ritual—the Stomp—was being practiced. Any-
time that song hit the airwaves Black youngsters would pour from their
cars to form a big boss line. James Brown begged "Please Please Please"
and the Midnighters informed us "Annie Had a Baby." Sam Cooke
intoned "You Send Me," but the Dominos were only a "Sixty-Minute
Man." Jesse Belvin said "Good Night My Love" but the Dells asked
"Why Do You Have to Go?" The Brown decision was rendered by the
Supreme Court and Eisenhower had a heart attack. In the heart of Black
America it finally was made clear that no matter what we did, no matter
how much we abided by the rules and regulations, no matter how
straight our hair, correct our speech, circumscribed our behavior, no
matter *what*—we were, in the words of Moms Mabley, "still a Negro."

The advantage to a people who have clearly defined an issue is this:
The individual is relieved of the burden of carrying his people forward.
He can dance upon his own floor in his own style. Though white
Americans would try to this very day to make Black Americans responsible for each other, Black people recognize that just as individual
accomplishments open no doors, individual failures close off no
avenues. The Right Reverend Ray Charles said it best: "Tell the
Truth!" We no longer were ashamed of being Black; we no longer
wished to hide our love of chitlins and hog maws; we no longer wished
to pretend we cared. Rosa Parks in Montgomery said "No!" and
Chuck Willis asked "What Am I Living For?" Johnny Ace, who
allegedly shot himself backstage at Houston's City Auditorium, went
number one in England the next day with "Never Let Me Go;" Jesse
Belvin's car blew four tires, killing him after he played a dance in L.A.;
Chuck Willis died; Sam Cooke was murdered in L.A.; Frankie Lymon
left the Teenagers to begin his involvement with drugs; Little Willie
John was arrested for murder and died in prison; Otis Redding's plane
crashed. Don't send me Murray the K as some kind of friend, let alone
god to rhythm and blues. We paid for that music. Mr. K changed his
Cleveland station format because Black and white kids were tuned to

WCIN in Cincinnati, WDIA in Memphis, WDAS in Philadelphia and all night long WLAC in Nashville where "Randy" played and packaged the hits.

Black people had some place to run! We, like Max Schmeling, lacked a place to hide. We went "Dancin' in the Streets" behind Martin Luther King, Jr., behind Malcolm X, behind mighty mighty Sly and the Family Stone. If they snickered when Little Richard brought his painted lips, mascaraed eyes, hair piled high on his head out of his closet, they were silent when Cassius Clay echoed, "I'm Black and I'm proud." Otis Redding cried for "Respect," a coda to Chuck Berry's anthem, "Roll Over, Beethoven." And in case the message was missed, Aretha covered both Redding and Sam Cooke: "A Change Is Gonna Come." But Lady Soul, ever the lady, softened it with "A woman's only human." The Intruders replied, "Gotta let a man be a man."

I'm an old unrepentant rocker who joins with Bob Seger in demanding "Old-Time Rock and Roll." I've never been asked to do a commercial, but even if I were I couldn't demand "my MTV." No way. I like my music in my head and, when I was younger, my foot on the pedal. One of life's great thrills is putting Little Richard on the auto-reverse cassette in your car and heading from New York to Cincinnati. You don't even see the Jersey Turnpike. You pull over in Pennsylvania just before the first tunnel and get an orange sherbet ice cream from Howard Johnson's and you don't tune down until you creep through West Virginia. I liked being young and I like being not young. At the risk of being very, very dull I agree that "to everything there is a season." I think I would classify myself as happy. Which in no way means I don't go off on people, myself, situations . . . but more, that given a choice there wouldn't be too much too different in my life.

I'm finally old enough to know it would be nice to have money, but it's not all that necessary. I think I'd be a good rich person. At least I know I would enjoy my money. Nothing galls me more than somebody who's come into some sort of fortune or been born to one bitching that life is hard. I'm sure life is since the end of life for all of us is death. It just seems unfair when you keep hearing people who can call long distance and talk as long as they like, who don't worry how their children's tuition will be paid, who don't fear for their health since they are properly insured going on and on about life's difficulties. It's tacky. The very least the rich can do for the rest of us is either enjoy or shut up. But what does that have to do with what I have written? Nothing. . . .

. . . I date all my work because I think poetry, or any writing, is but a reflection of the moment. The universal comes from the particular. I like the nuts and bolts of life. I want to know everything. Sometimes, especially in the fall, if you're a morning person you wake up around five-thirty in the morning and start your coffee. The dark is just beginning to lift and in my backyard the birds come to drink and bathe. Soon they will not come so early because it will be too cold. But now they come and chirp. There's a big German shepherd that roams the neighborhood that is usually passing. But mostly you hear nothing. The sun rises in my eastern window where I am growing African violets and I just like to watch the red break and wonder about all the world. There is an ad concerning space that asks, "How long do we have to look at an organism before we recognize it?" How many little boys chunked the Rosetta Stone into the Red Sea before someone recognized that that was the key? And if there is never an answer, the quest is so worthwhile.

I like lace handkerchiefs. I like to look at those my grandmother passed to my mother; they are beautiful. Someone, perhaps Louvenia, perhaps my great-grandmother Cornelia, hand-embroidered them. They are as delicate as a spider web, as strong as a silkworm's cocoon. I cry when I watch *Little House on the Prairie*. I like to be happy. And other than an occasional response to an infrequent query I don't contemplate my work. I do try to be a good writer. I believe that I bring my best when I try to share. It's an honorable profession. There are so many pieces to my puzzle, I have no interest in trying to judge what I have done; but only to try to do more. I like my awards and honors. I love it when people say they have read my poetry. I never make the mistake of asking if they understood what I was *really* talking about or if they *really* liked what I did. I just thank them because whether I disappointed or delighted them they took the time to be involved in my effort . . . to explore with me . . . to extend themselves to me as I have extended myself to them. It's lonely. Writing. But so is practicing tennis or football runs. So is studying. So is waxing the floor and changing the baby. So is life. We are less lonely when we connect. Art is a connection. I like being a link. I hope the chain will hold.

NANCY MAIRS
(1943—)

NANCY MAIRS was born in Long Beach, California, and grew up in New Hampshire and Massachusetts. She attended Wheaton College, worked as a technical editor at the Smithsonian Astrophysical Observatory, the MIT Press, and the Harvard Law School, and in 1972 moved with her husband and two children to Tucson, Arizona, where she taught English while studying toward a Master of Fine Arts degree in creative writing and a Ph.D. in English literature. It was in the early seventies that she was diagnosed with multiple sclerosis. Her first book, *In All the Rooms of the Yellow House,* received first prize for poetry in the Western States Book Awards competition. Under the tutelage of the feminist autobiography theorist Sidonie Smith, Mairs studied and practiced unconventional narrative strategies in women's autobiographical writing. The products of that process are four volumes of personal essays that have as their subject the gutsy scrutiny of her own life: *Plaintext: Deciphering a Woman's Life* (1986), *Remembering the Bone House: An Erotics of Place and Space* (1989), *Carnal Acts* (1990), and *Ordinary Time: Cycles in Marriage, Faith and Renewal* (1993). In each book, she explores in extremely personal terms how her own life and the lives of other women have been shaped—"In defiance of the conventions of polite silence," she writes, "I've spoken as plainly and truthfully as the squirms and wriggles of the human psyche will permit." Crippled by multiple sclerosis and maddened by acute agoraphobia and chronic "unipolar" depression, which led to a suicide attempt, Mairs sifts memory for the stories that might expose the roots of her diseases, but she does not allow herself to be diminished by her illness or the prevailing cultural scripts. Indeed, Kathleen Norris described her latest book about her conversions to feminism and Catholicism as "the story of a soul, a kind of saint's autobiography." As Hilma Wolitzer put it, "Nancy Mairs' work is original, nervy, and memorable. She writes like a poet, and like a survivor." A reviewer in the *Women's Review of Books* praised her as "a funny, rebellious, chaotic woman, afflicted with the tribulations of Job, . . . without the benefit of Job's one major asset. [But] it's precisely [her] *impatience* which [is] her most heroic attribute." Francine Prose admires Mairs' "prickly astringency." The *New York Times Book Review* called *Carnal Acts*—the title essay follows here—"the story of a highly intelligent and witty woman dealing with MS, . . . living in the grip of fear . . . and pushing through the terror to find joy." Mairs' ability to see life whole, admired by many writing colleagues and critics, comes through in a passage from *Carnal Acts:* "Let's face it, life (real life, I mean, not the edited-for-television version) is a cacophonous affair from start to finish."

from *Carnal Acts*

Inviting me to speak at her small liberal-arts college during Women's Week, a young woman set me a task: "We would be pleased," she wrote, "if you could talk on how you cope with your M.S. disability, and also how you discovered your voice as a writer." Oh, Lord, I thought in dismay, how am I going to pull this one off? How can I yoke two such disparate subjects into a coherent presentation, without doing violence to one, or the other, or both, or myself? This is going to take some fancy footwork, and my feet scarcely carry out the basic steps, let alone anything elaborate.

To make matters worse, the assumption underlying each of her questions struck me as suspect. To ask *how* I cope with multiple sclerosis suggests that I *do* cope. Now, "to cope," *Webster's Third* tells me, is "to face or encounter and to find necessary expedients to overcome problems and difficulties." In these terms, I have to confess, I don't feel like much of a coper. I'm likely to deal with my problems and difficulties by squawking and flapping around like that hysterical chicken who was convinced the sky was falling. Never mind that in my case the sky really *is* falling. In response to a clonk on the head, regardless of its origin, one might comport oneself with a grace and courtesy I generally lack.

As for "finding" my voice, the implication is that it was at one time lost or missing. But I don't think it ever was. Ask my mother, who will tell you a little wearily that I was speaking full sentences by the time I was a year old and could never be silenced again. As for its being a writer's voice, it seems to have become one early on. Ask Mother again. At the age of eight I rewrote the Trojan War, she will say, and what Nestor was about to do to Helen at the end doesn't bear discussion in polite company.

Faced with these uncertainties, I took my own teacherly advice, something, I must confess, I don't always do. "If an idea is giving you trouble," I tell my writing students, "put it on the back burner and let it simmer while you do something else. Go to the movies. Reread a stack of old love letters. Sit in your history class and take detailed notes on the Teapot Dome scandal. If you've got your idea in mind, it will go on cooking at some level no matter what else you're doing." "I've had an idea for my documented essay on the back burner," one of my students once scribbled in her journal, "and I think it's just boiled over!"

I can't claim to have reached such a flash point. But in the weeks I've had the themes "disability" and "voice" sitting around in my head, they seem to have converged on their own, without my having to wrench them together and bind them with hoops of tough rhetoric. They *are* related, indeed interdependent, with an intimacy that has for some reason remained, until now, submerged below the surface of my attention. Forced to juxtapose them, I yank them out of the depths, a little startled to discover how they were intertwined down there out of sight. This kind of discovery can unnerve you at first. You feel like a giant hand that, pulling two swimmers out of the water, two separate heads bobbling on the iridescent swells, finds the two bodies below, legs coiled around each other, in an ecstasy of copulation. You don't quite know where to turn your eyes.

Perhaps the place to start illuminating this erotic connection between who I am and how I speak lies in history. I have known that I have multiple sclerosis for about seventeen years now, though the disease probably started long before. The hypothesis is that the disease process, in which the protective covering of the nerves in the brain and spinal cord is eaten away and replaced by scar tissue, "hard patches," is caused by an autoimmune reaction to a slow-acting virus. Research suggests that I was infected by this virus, which no one has ever seen and which therefore, technically, doesn't even "exist," between the ages of four and fifteen. In effect, living with this mysterious mechanism feels like having your present self, and the past selves it embodies, haunted by a capricious and meanspirited ghost, unseen except for its footprints, which trips you even when you're watching where you're going, knocks glassware out of your hand, squeezes the urine out of your bladder before you reach the bathroom, and weights your whole body with a weariness no amount of rest can relieve. An alien invader must be at work. But of course it's not. It's your own body. That is, it's you.

This, for me, has been the most difficult aspect of adjusting to a chronic incurable degenerative disease: the fact that it has rammed my "self" straight back into the body I had been trained to believe it could, through high-minded acts and aspirations, rise above. The Western tradition of distinguishing the body from the mind and/or the soul is so ancient as to have become part of our collective unconscious, if one is inclined to believe in such a noumenon, or at least to have become an unquestioned element in the social instruction we impose upon infants from birth, in much the same way we inculcate, without reflection, the gender distinctions "female" and "male." I *have* a body, you are likely to say if you talk about embodiment at all; you don't say, I *am* a body. A body is a separate entity possessable by the "I"; the "I" and the body aren't, as the copula would make them, grammatically indistinguishable.

To widen the rift between the self and the body, we treat our bodies as subordinates, inferior in moral status. Open association with them shames us. In fact, we treat our bodies with very much the same distance and ambivalence women have traditionally received from men in our culture. Sometimes this treatment is benevolent, even respectful, but all too often it is tainted by outright sadism. I think of the body-building regimens that have become popular in the last decade or so, with the complicated vacillations they reflect between self-worship and self-degradation: joggers and aerobic dancers and weightlifters all beating their bodies into shape. "No pain, no gain," the saying goes. "Feel the burn." Bodies get treated like wayward women who have to be shown who's boss, even if it means slapping them around a little. I'm not for a moment opposing rugged exercise here. I'm simply questioning the spirit in which it is often undertaken.

Since, as Hélène Cixous points out in her essay on women and writing, "Sorties,"* thought has always worked "through dual, hierarchical oppositions" (p. 64), the mind/body split cannot possibly be innocent. The utterance of an "I" immediately calls into being its opposite, the "not-I," Western discourse being unequipped to conceive "that which is neither 'I' nor 'not-I,'" "that which is both 'I' and 'not-I,'" or some other permutation which language doesn't permit me to speak. The "not-I" is, by definition, other. And we've never been too fond of the other. We prefer the same. We tend to ascribe to the other those qualities we prefer not to associate with our selves: it is the hidden, the dark, the secret, the shameful. Thus, when the "I" takes possession of the body, it makes the body into an other, direct object of a transitive verb, with all the other's repudiated and potentially dangerous qualities.

At the least, then, the body had best be viewed with suspicion. And a woman's body is particularly suspect, since so much of it is in fact hidden, dark, secret, carried about on the inside where, even with the

---

*In *The Newly Born Woman,* translated by Betsy Wing (Minneapolis: University of Minnesota Press, 1986).

aid of a speculum, one can never perceive all of it in the plain light of day, a graspable whole. I, for one, have never understood why anyone would want to carry all that delicate stuff around on the outside. It would make you awfully anxious, I should think, put you constantly on the defensive, create a kind of siege mentality that viewed all other beings, even your own kind, as threats to be warded off with spears and guns and atomic missiles. And you'd never get to experience that inward dreaming that comes when your flesh surrounds all your treasures, holding them close, like a sturdy shuttered house. Be my personal skepticism as it may, however, as a cultural woman I bear just as much shame as any woman for my dark, enfolded secrets. Let the word for my external genitals tell the tale: my pudendum, from the Latin infinitive meaning "to be ashamed."

It's bad enough to carry your genitals like a sealed envelope bearing the cipher that, once unlocked, might loose the chaotic flood of female pleasure—*jouissance,* the French call it—upon the world-of-the-same. But I have an additional reason to feel shame for my body, less explicitly connected with its sexuality: it is a crippled body. Thus it is doubly other, not merely by the homo-sexual standards of patriarchal culture but by the standards of physical desirability erected for every body in our world. Men, who are by definition exonerated from shame in sexual terms (this doesn't mean that an individual man might not experience sexual shame, of course; remember that I'm talking in general about discourse, not folks), may—more likely must—experience bodily shame if they are crippled. I won't presume to speak about the details of their experience, however. I don't know enough. I'll just go on telling what it's like to be a crippled woman, trusting that, since we're fellow creatures who've been living together for some thousands of years now, much of my experience will resonate with theirs.

I was never a beautiful woman, and for that reason I've spent most of my life (together with probably at least 95 percent of the female population of the United States) suffering from the shame of falling short of an unattainable standard. The ideal woman of my generation was . . . perky, I think you'd say, rather than gorgeous. Blond hair pulled into a bouncing ponytail. Wide blue eyes, a turned-up nose with maybe a scattering of golden freckles across it, a small mouth with full lips over straight white teeth. Her breasts were large but well harnessed high on her chest; her tiny waist flared to hips just wide enough to give the crinolines under her circle skirt a starting outward push. In terms of personality, she was outgoing, even bubbly, not pensive or mysterious. Her milieu was the front fender of a white Corvette convertible, surrounded by teasing crewcuts, dressed in black flats, a sissy blouse, and the letter sweater of the Corvette owner. Needless to say, she never missed a prom.

Ten years or so later, when I first noticed the symptoms that would be diagnosed as MS, I was probably looking my best. Not beautiful still, but the ideal had shifted enough so that my flat chest and narrow hips gave me an elegantly attenuated shape, set off by a thick mass of long, straight, shining hair. I had terrific legs, long and shapely, revealed nearly to the pudendum by the fashionable miniskirts and hot pants I adopted with more enthusiasm than delicacy of taste. Not surprisingly, I suppose, during this time I involved myself in several pretty torrid love affairs.

The beginning of MS wasn't too bad. The first symptom, besides the pernicious fatigue that had begun to devour me, was "foot drop," the inability to raise my left foot at the ankle. As a consequence, I'd started to limp, but I could still wear high heels, and a bit of a limp might seem more intriguing than repulsive. After a few months, when the doctor suggested a cane, a crippled friend gave me quite an elegant wood-and-silver one, which I carried with a fair amount of panache. The real blow to my self-image came when I had to get a brace. As braces go, it's not bad: lightweight plastic molded to my foot and leg, fitting down into an ordinary shoe and secured around my calf by a Velcro strap. It reduces my limp and, more important, the danger of tripping and falling. But it meant the end of high heels. And it's ugly. Not as ugly as I think it is, I gather, but still pretty ugly. It signified for me, and perhaps still does, the permanence and irreversibility of my condition. The brace makes my MS concrete and forces me to wear it on the outside. As soon as I strapped the brace on, I climbed into trousers and stayed there (though not in the same trousers, of course). The idea of going around with my bare brace hanging out seemed almost as indecent as exposing my breasts. Not until 1984, soon after I won the Western States Book Award for poetry, did I put on a skirt short enough to reveal my plasticized leg. The connection between winning a writing award and baring my brace is not merely fortuitous; being affirmed as a writer really did embolden me. Since then, I've grown so accustomed to wearing skirts that I don't think about my brace any more than I think about my cane. I've incorporated them, I suppose: made them, in their necessity, insensate but fundamental parts of my body.

Meanwhile, I had to adjust to the most outward and visible sign of all, a three-wheeled electric scooter called an Amigo. This lessens my fatigue and increases my range terrifically, but it also shouts out to the world, "Here is a woman who can't stand on her own two feet." At the same time, paradoxically, it renders me invisible, reducing me to the height of a seven-year-old, with a child's attendant low status. "Would she like smoking or nonsmoking?" the gate agent assigning me a seat asks the friend traveling with me. In crowds I see nothing but buttocks. I can tell you the name of every type of designer jeans ever sold. The wearers, eyes front, trip over me and fall across my handlebars into my lap. "Hey!" I want to shout to the lofty world. "Down here! There's a person down here!" But I'm not, by their standards, quite a person anymore.

My self-esteem diminishes further as age and illness strip from me the features that made me, for a brief while anyway, a good-looking, even sexy, young woman. No more long, bounding strides: I shuffle along with the timid gait I remember observing, with pity and impatience, in the little old ladies at Boston's Symphony Hall on Friday afternoons. No more lithe, girlish figure: my belly sags from the loss of muscle tone, which also creates all kinds of intestinal disruptions, hopelessly humiliating in a society in which excretory functions remain strictly unspeakable. No more sex, either, if society had its way. The sexuality of the disabled so repulses most people that you can hardly get a doctor, let alone a member of the general population, to consider the issues it raises. Cripples simply aren't supposed to Want It, much less Do It. Fortunately, I've got a husband with a strong libido and a weak sense of social propriety, or else I'd find myself perforce practicing a vow of chastity I never cared to take.

Afflicted by the general shame of having a body at all, and the specific shame of having one weakened and misshapen by disease, I ought not to be able to hold my head up in public. And yet I've gotten into the habit of holding my head up in public, sometimes under excruciating circumstances. Recently, for instance, I had to give a reading at the University of Arizona. Having smashed three of my front teeth in a fall onto the concrete floor of my screened porch, I was in the process of getting them crowned, and the temporary crowns flew out during dinner right before the reading. What to do? I wanted, of course, to rush home and hide till the dental office opened the next morning. But I couldn't very well break my word at this last moment. So, looking like Hansel and Gretel's witch, and lisping worse than the Wife of Bath, I got up on stage and read. Somehow, over the years, I've learned how to set shame aside and do what I have to do.

Here, I think, is where my "voice" comes in. Because, in spite of my demurral at the beginning, I do in fact cope with my disability at least some of the time. And I do so, I think, by speaking about it, and about the whole experience of being a body, specifically a female body, out loud, in a clear, level tone that drowns out the frantic whispers of my mother, my grandmothers, all the other trainers of wayward child-ish tongues: "Sssh! Sssh! Nice girls don't talk like that. Don't mention sweat. Don't mention menstrual blood. Don't ask what your grandfa-ther does on his business trips. Don't laugh so loud. You sound like a loon. Keep your voice down. Don't tell. Don't tell. Don't tell." Speak-ing out loud is an antidote to shame. I want to distinguish clearly here between "shame," as I'm using the word, and "guilt" and "embarrass-ment," which, though equally painful, are not similarly poisonous. Guilt arises from performing a forbidden act or failing to perform a required one. In either case, the guilty person can, through reparation, erase the offense and start fresh. Embarrassment, less opprobrious though not necessarily less distressing, is generally caused by acting in a socially stupid or awkward way. When I trip and sprawl in public, when I wet myself, when my front teeth fly out, I feel horribly embar-rassed, but, like the pain of childbirth, the sensation blurs and dissolves in time. If it didn't, every child would be an only child, and no one would set foot in public after the onset of puberty, when embarrass-ment erupts like a geyser and bathes one's whole life in its bitter stream. Shame may attach itself to guilt or embarrassment, complicating their resolution, but it is not the same emotion. I feel guilt or embarrassment for something I've done; shame, for who I am. I may stop doing bad or stupid things, but I can't stop being. How then can I help but be ashamed? Of the three conditions, this is the one that cracks and stifles my voice.

I can subvert its power, I've found, by acknowledging who I am, shame and all, and, in doing so, raising what was hidden, dark, secret about my life into the plain light of shared human experience. What we aren't permitted to utter holds us, each isolated from every other, in a kind of solipsistic thrall. Without any way to check our reality against anyone else's, we assume that our fears and shortcomings are ours alone. One of the strangest consequences of publishing a collection of per-sonal essays called *Plaintext* has been the steady trickle of letters and telephone calls saying essentially, in a tone of unmistakable relief, "Oh, me too! Me too!" It's as though the part I thought was solo has turned out to be a chorus. But none of us was singing loud enough for the others to hear.

Singing loud enough demands a particular kind of voice, I think. And I was wrong to suggest, at the beginning, that I've always had my voice. I have indeed always had *a* voice, but it wasn't *this* voice, the one with which I could call up and transform my hidden self from a naughty girl into a woman talking directly to others like herself.

Recently, in the process of writing a new book, a memoir entitled *Remembering the Bone House*, I've had occasion to read some of my early writing, from college, high school, even junior high. It's not an experience I recommend to anyone susceptible to shame. Not that the writing was all that bad. I was surprised at how competent a lot of it was. Here was a writer who already knew precisely how the language worked. But the voice . . . oh, the voice was all wrong: maudlin, rhapsodic, breaking here and there into little shrieks, almost, you might say, hysterical. It was a voice that had shucked off its own body, its own homely life of Cheerios for breakfast and seventy pages of Chaucer to read before the exam on Tuesday and a planter's wart growing painfully on the ball of its foot, and reeled now wraithlike through the air, seeking incarnation only as the heroine who enacts her doomed love for the tall, dark, mysterious stranger. If it didn't get that part, it wouldn't play at all.

Among all these overheated and vaporous imaginings, I must have retained some shred of sense, because I stopped writing prose entirely, except for scholarly papers, for nearly twenty years. I even forgot, not exactly that I had written prose, but at least what kind of prose it was. So when I needed to take up the process again, I could start almost fresh, using the vocal range I'd gotten used to in years of asking the waiter in the Greek restaurant for an extra anchovy on my salad, congratulating the puppy on making a puddle outside rather than inside the patio door, pondering with my daughter the vagaries of female orgasm, saying goodbye to my husband, and hello, and goodbye, and hello. This new voice—thoughtful, affectionate, often amused—was essential because what I needed to write about when I returned to prose was an attempt I'd made not long before to kill myself, and suicide simply refuses to be spoken of authentically in high-flown romantic language. It's too ugly. Too shameful. Too strictly a bodily event. And, yes, too funny as well, though people are sometimes shocked to find humor shoved up against suicide. They don't like the incongruity. But let's face it, life (real life, I mean, not the edited-for-television version) is a cacophonous affair from start to finish. I might have wanted to portray my suicidal self as a languishing maiden, too exquisitely sensitive to sustain life's wounding pressures on her soul. (I didn't want to, as a matter of fact, but I might have.) The truth remained, regardless of my desires, that when my husband lugged me into the emergency room, my hair matted, my face swollen and gray, my nightgown streaked with blood and urine, I was no frail and tender spirit. I was a body, and one in a hell of a mess.

I "should" have kept quiet about that experience. I know the rules of polite discourse. I should have kept my shame, and the nearly lethal sense of isolation and alienation it brought, to myself. And I might have, except for something the psychiatrist in the emergency room had told my husband. "You might as well take her home," he said. "If she wants to kill herself, she'll do it no matter how many precautions we take. They always do." *They* always do. I was one of "them," whoever they were. I was, in this context anyway, not singular, not aberrant, but typical. I think it was this sense of commonality with others I didn't even know, a sense of being returned somehow, in spite of my appalling act, to the human family, that urged me to write that first essay, not merely speaking out but calling out, perhaps. "Here's the way I am," it said. "How about you?" And the answer came, as I've said: "Me too! Me too!"

This has been the kind of work I've continued to do: to scrutinize the details of my own experience and to report what I see, and what I think about what I see, as lucidly and accurately as possible. But because feminine experience has been immemorially devalued and repressed, I continue to find this task terrifying. "Every woman has known the torture of beginning to speak aloud," Cixous writes, "heart beating as if to break, occasionally falling into loss of language, ground and language slipping out from under her, because for woman speaking—even just opening her mouth—in public is something rash, a transgression" (p. 92).

The voice I summon up wants to crack, to whisper, to trail back into silence. "I'm sorry to have nothing more than this to say," it wants to apologize. "I shouldn't be taking up your time. I've never fought in a war, or even in a schoolyard free-for-all. I've never tried to see who could piss farthest up the barn wall. I've never even been to a whorehouse. All the important formative experiences have passed me by. I was raped once. I've borne two children. Milk trickling out of my breasts, blood trickling from between my legs. You don't want to hear about it. Sometimes I'm too scared to leave my house. Not scared *of* anything, just scared: mouth dry, bowels writhing. When the fear got really bad, they locked me up for six months, but that was years ago. I'm getting old now. Misshapen, too. I don't blame you if you can't get it up. No one could possibly desire a body like this. It's not your fault. It's mine. Forgive me. I didn't mean to start crying. I'm sorry . . . sorry . . . sorry. . . ."

An easy solace to the anxiety of speaking aloud: this slow subsidence beneath the waves of shame, back into what Cixous calls "this body that has been worse than confiscated, a body replaced with a disturbing stranger, sick or dead, who so often is a bad influence, the cause and place of inhibitions. By censuring the body," she goes on, "breath and speech are censored at the same time" (p. 97). But I am not going back, not going under one more time. To do so would demonstrate a failure of nerve far worse than the depredations of MS have caused. Paradoxically, losing one sort of nerve has given me another. No one is going to take my breath away. No one is going to leave me speechless. To be silent is to comply with the standard of feminine grace. But my crippled body already violates all notions of feminine grace. What more have I got to lose? I've gone beyond shame. I'm shameless, you might say. You know, as in "shameless hussy"? A woman with her bare brace and her tongue hanging out.

I've "found" my voice, then, just where it ought to have been, in the body-warmed breath escaping my lungs and throat. Forced by the exigencies of physical disease to embrace my self in the flesh, I couldn't write bodiless prose. The voice is the creature of the body that produces it. I speak as a crippled woman. At the same time, in the utterance I redeem both "cripple" and "woman" from the shameful silences by which I have often felt surrounded, contained, set apart; I give myself permission to live openly among others, to reach out for them, stroke them with fingers and sighs. No body, no voice; no voice, no body. That's what I know in my bones.

ANNIE DILLARD
(1945—)

◆

ANNIE DILLARD, poet, prose writer, critic, autobiographer, and novelist, grew up in Pittsburgh, Pennsylvania, and was educated at Hollins College in Virginia. She lived for almost ten years in the Roanoke Valley, whose landscape inspired her Pulitzer Prize–winning book, *Pilgrim at Tinker Creek* (1974). Her poetic descriptions of the natural world, evoking a mystical connection between writer and place, led critics to compare her literary debut with the nature writing of Henry David Thoreau. Since then, she has contributed articles to *Harper's,* the *Atlantic Monthly,* and *American Scholar,* worked as writer-in-residence at Wesleyan University, and published a number of books, including a collection of poems, *Tickets for a Prayer Wheel* (1974), a volume of literary criticism, *Living by Fiction* (1982), two volumes of nature writing, *Holy the Firm* (1977) and *Teaching a Stone to Talk: Expeditions and Encounters* (1982), a discussion of writing, *The Writing Life* (1989), the autobiography excerpted here, *An American Childhood* (1987), and her first novel, *The Living* (1992).

In *An American Childhood* Dillard presents an account of her early years under the influence of her parents, and the privileges and constraints of private school until her entrance into college. What she charts is the development of her ecstatic interest in the world beyond self, the look of rock and insects under a microscope, people's moods, the sounds of prayers and poetry and church on Sundays, the thrills of disobedience and rebellion. A reviewer in *Ms.* found Dillard's memory of her adolescence, of "her evocation of a 16-year-old's floundering rage" the best part of the book. Reviewer Noel Perrin identified literary resonances: the autobiographical Dillard "is one of Blake's company. . . .—she invariably sees something beyond what is just there. . . ." The book is also her "equivalent of Wordworth's *Prelude,* an exceptionally interesting account, in semimystical prose, about the growth of her own mind, . . . an inner rather than an outer narrative." Dillard has said of the difficulties of writing one's childhood, "You can't put together a memoir without cannibalizing your own life for parts. The work battens on your memories. And it replaces them. . . . The work is a sort of changeling on the doorstep—not your baby but someone else's baby rather like it, different in some way you can't pinpoint, and yours has vanished." The reinvention that follows here reflects her resistance to convention in adolescence, an essential component of her lifelong irony and humor.

From *An American Childhood*

Now it was May. Daylight Saving Time had begun; the colored light of the long evenings fairly split me with joy. White trillium had bloomed and gone on the forested slopes in Fox Chapel. The cliffside and riverside patches of woods all over town showed translucent ovals of yellow or ashy greens; the neighborhood trees on Glen Arden Drive had blossomed in white and red.

Baseball season had begun, a season which recalled but could never match last year's National League pennant and seventh-game World Series victory over the Yankees, when we at school had been so frenzied for so many weeks they finally and wisely opened the doors and let us go. I had walked home from school one day during that series and seen Pittsburgh's Fifth Avenue emptied of cars, as if the world were over.

A year of wild feelings had passed, and more were coming. Without my noticing, the drummer had upped the tempo. Someone must have slipped him a signal when I wasn't looking; he'd speeded things up. The key was higher, too. I had a driver's license. When I drove around in Mother's old Dodge convertible, the whole town smelled good. And I did drive around the whole town. I cruised along the blue rivers and across them on steel bridges, and steered up and down the scented hills. I drove winding into and out of the steep neighborhoods across the Allegheny River, neighborhoods where I tried in vain to determine in what languages the signs on storefronts were written. I drove onto boulevards, highways, beltways, freeways, and the turnpike. I could drive to Guatemala, drive to Alaska. Why, I asked myself, did I drive to—of all spots on earth—our garage? Why home, why school?

Throughout the long, deadly school afternoons, we junior and senior girls took our places in study hall. We sat at desks in a roomful of desks, whether or not we had something to do, until four o'clock.

Now this May afternoon a teacher propped open the study hall's back door. The door gave onto our hockey field and, behind it, Pittsburgh's Nabisco plant, whence, O Lordy, issued the smell of short-bread today; they were baking Lorna Doones. Around me sat forty or fifty girls in green cotton jumpers and spring-uniform white bucks. They rested their chins on the heels of both hands and leaned their cheeks on curled fingers; their propped heads faced the opened pages of *L'Étranger, Hamlet, Vanity Fair.* Some girls leaned back and filed their nails. Some twisted stiff pieces of their hair, to stay not so much awake as alive. Sometimes in health class, when we were younger, we had all been so bored we hooked our armpits over our chairs' backs so we cut off all circulation to one arm, in an effort to kill that arm for something to do, or cause a heart attack, whichever came first. We were, in fact, getting a dandy education. But sometimes we were restless. Weren't there some wars being fought somewhere that I, for one, could join?

I wrote a name on a notebook. I looked at the study-hall ceiling and tried to see that boy's familiar face—light and dark, bold-eyed, full of feeling—on the inside of my eyelids. Failing that, I searched for his image down the long speckled tunnel or corridor I saw with my eyes closed. As if visual memory were a Marx brothers comedy, I glimpsed swift fragments—a wry corner of his lip, a pointy knuckle, a cupped temple—which crossed the corridor so fast I recognized them only as soon as they vanished. I opened my eyes and wrote his name. His depth and complexity were apparently infinite. From the tip of his lively line of patter to the bottom of his heartbroken, hopeful soul was the longest route I knew, and the best.

The heavy, edible scent of shortbread maddened me in my seat, made me so helpless with longing my wrists gave out; I couldn't hold a pen. I looked around constantly to catch someone's eye, anyone's eye.

It was a provocative fact, which I seemed to have discovered, that we students outnumbered our teachers. Must we then huddle here like sheep? By what right, exactly, did these few women keep us sitting here in this clean, bare room to no purpose? Lately I had been trying to enflame my friends with the implications of our greater numbers. We could pull off a riot. We could bang on the desks and shout till they let us out. Then we could go home and wait for dinner. Or we could bear our teachers off on our shoulders, and—what? Throw them into the Lorna Doone batter? I got no takers.

I had finished my work long ago. "Works only on what interests her," the accusation ran—as if, I reflected, obedience outranked passion, as if sensible people didn't care what they stuck in their minds. Today as usual no one around me was ready for action. I took a fresh sheet of paper and copied on it random lines in French:

Ô saisons, ô châteaux!
Is it through these endless nights that you sleep in exile
Ô million golden birds, ô future vigor?
Oh, that my keel would split! Oh, that I would go down in the sea!

I had struck upon the French Symbolists, like a canyon of sharp crystals underground, like a long and winding corridor lined with treasure. These poets popped into my ken in an odd way: I found them in a book I had rented from a drugstore. Carnegie and school libraries filled me in. I read Enid Starkie's Rimbaud biography. I saved my allowance for months and bought two paperbound poetry books, the Penguin *Rimbaud,* and a Symbolist anthology in which Paul Valéry declaimed, *"Azure! c'est moi . . . "* I admired Gérard de Nerval. This mad writer kept a lobster as a pet. He walked it on a leash along the sidewalks of Paris, saying, "It doesn't bark, and knows the secrets of the deep."

I loved Rimbaud, who ran away, loved his skinny, furious face with the wild hair and snaky, unseeing eyes pointing in two directions, and his poems' confusion and vagueness, their overwritten longing, their hatred, their sky-shot lyricism, and their oracular fragmentation, which I enhanced for myself by reading and retaining his stuff in crazed bits, mostly from *Le Bateau Ivre,* The Drunken Boat. (The drunken boat tells its own story, a downhill, downstream epic unusually full of words.)

Now in study hall I saw that I had drawn all over this page; I got out another piece of paper. Rimbaud was damned. He said so himself. Where could I meet someone like that? I wrote down another part:

There is a cathedral that goes down and a lake that goes up.
There is a troupe of strolling players in costume,
glimpsed on the road through the edge of the trees.

I looked up from the new page I had already started to draw all over. Except for my boyfriend, the boys I knew best were out of town. They were older, prep-school and college boys whose boldness, wit, breadth of knowledge, and absence of scruples fascinated me. They cruised the deb party circuit all over Pennsylvania, holding ever-younger girls up to the light like chocolates, to determine how rich their centers might be. I smiled to recall one of these boys: he was so accustomed to the glitter of society, and so sardonic and graceful, that he carried with him at all times, in his jacket pocket, a canister of dance wax. Ordinary boys carried pocket knives for those occasions which occur unexpectedly, and this big, dark-haired boy carried dance wax for the same reason. When the impulse rose, he could simply sprinkle dance wax on any hall or dining-room floor, take a girl in his arms, and whirl her away. I had known these witty, handsome boys for years, and only recently understood that when they were alone, they read books. In public, they were lounge lizards; they drank; they played word games, filling in the blanks desultorily; they cracked wise. These boys would be back in town soon, and my boyfriend and I would join them.

Whose eye could I catch? Everyone in the room was bent over her desk. Ellin Hahn was usually ready to laugh, but now she was working on something. She would call me as soon as we got home. Every day on the phone, I unwittingly asked Ellin some blunt question about the social world around us, and at every question she sighed and said to me, "You still don't get it"—or often, as if addressing a jury of our incredulous peers, "She still doesn't get it!"

Looking at the study-hall ceiling, I dosed myself almost fatally with the oxygen-eating lines of Verlaine's "The long sobs / of the violins / of autumn / wound my heart / with a languor / monotone."

This unsatisfying bit of verse I repeated to myself for ten or fifteen minutes, by the big clock, over and over, clobbering myself with it, the way Molly, when she had been a baby, banged the top of her head on her crib.

> Ô world, ô college, ô dinner . . .
> Ô unthinkable task . . .

Funny how badly I'd turned out. Now I was always in trouble. It felt as if I was doing just as I'd always done—I explored the neighborhood, turning over rocks. The latest rocks were difficult. I'd been in a drag race, of all things, the previous September, and in the subsequent collision, and in the hospital; my parents saw my name in the newspapers, and their own names in the newspapers. Some boys I barely knew had cruised by that hot night and said to a clump of us girls on the sidewalk, "Anybody want to come along for a drag race?" I did, absolutely. I loved fast driving.

It was then, in the days after the drag race, that I noticed the ground spinning beneath me, all bearings lost, and recognized as well that I had been loose like this—detached from all I saw and knowing nothing else—for months, maybe years. I whirled through the air like a bull-roarer spun by a lunatic who'd found his rhythm. The pressure almost split my skin. What else can you risk with all your might but your life? Only a moment ago I was climbing my swing set, holding one cold metal leg between my two legs tight, and feeling a piercing oddness run the length of my gut—the same sensation that plucked me when my tongue touched tarnish on a silver spoon. Only a moment ago I was gluing squares of paper to rocks; I leaned over the bedroom desk. I was drawing my baseball mitt in the attic, under the plaster-stain ship; a pencil study took all Saturday morning. I was capturing the flag, turning the double play, chasing butterflies by the country-club pool. Throughout these many years of childhood, a transparent sphere of timelessness contained all my running and spinning as a glass paperweight holds flying snow. The sphere of this idyll broke; time unrolled before me in a line. I woke up and found myself in juvenile court. I was hanging from crutches; for a few weeks after the drag race, neither knee worked. (No one else got hurt.) In juvenile court, a policeman wet all ten of my fingertips on an ink pad and pressed them, one by one, using his own fingertips, on a form for the files.

Turning to the French is a form of suicide for the American who loves literature—or, as the joke might go, it is at least a cry for help. Now, when I was sixteen, I had turned to the French. I flung myself into poetry as into Niagara Falls. Beauty took away my breath. I twined away; I flew off with my eyes rolled up; I dove down and succumbed. I bought myself a plot in Valéry's marine cemetery, and moved in: cool dirt on my eyes, my brain smooth as a cannonball. It grieves me to report that I tried to see myself as a sobbing fountain, apparently serene, tall and thin among the chill marble monuments of the dead. Rimbaud wrote a lyric that gently described a man sleeping out in the grass; the sleeper made a peaceful picture, until, in the poem's last line, we discover in his right side two red holes. This, and many another literary false note, appealed to me.

I'd been suspended from school for smoking cigarettes. That was a month earlier, in early spring. Both my parents wept. Amy saw them weeping; horrified, she began to cry herself. Molly cried. She was six, missing her front teeth. Like Mother and me, she had pale skin that turned turgid and red when she cried; she looked as if she were dying of wounds. I didn't cry, because, actually, I was an intercontinental ballistic missile, with an atomic warhead; they don't cry.

Why didn't I settle down, straighten out, shape up? I wondered, too. I thought that joy was a childish condition that had forever departed; I had no glimpse then of its return the minute I got to college. I couldn't foresee the pleasure—or the possibility—of shedding sophistication, walking away from rage, and renouncing French poets.

While I was suspended from school, my parents grounded me. During that time, Amy began to visit me in my room.

When she was thirteen, Amy's beauty had grown inconspicuous; she seemed merely pleasant-looking and tidy. Her green uniform jumper fit her neatly; her thick hair was smoothly turned under; her white McMullen collars looked sweet. She had a good eye for the right things; people respected her for it. I think that only we at home knew how spirited she could get. "Oh, no!" she cried when she laughed hard. "Oh, no!" Amy adored our father, rather as we all did, from afar. She liked boys whose eyebrows met over their noses. She liked boys, emphatically; she followed boys with her big eyes, awed.

In my room, Amy listened to me rant; she reported her grade's daily gossip, laughed at my jokes, cried, "Oh, no!" and told me about the book she was reading, Wilkie Collins, *The Woman in White*. I liked people to tell me about the books they were reading. Next year, Amy was going to boarding school in Philadelphia; Mother had no intention of subjecting the family to two adolescent maelstroms whirling at once in the same house.

Late one night, my parents and I sat at the kitchen table; there was a truce. We were all helpless, and tired of fighting. Amy and Molly were asleep.

"What are we going to do with you?"

Mother raised the question. Her voice trembled and rose with emotion. She couldn't sit still; she kept getting up and roaming around the kitchen. Father stuck out his chin and rubbed it with his big hands. I covered my eyes. Mother squeezed white lotion into her hands, over and over. We all smoked; the ashtray was full. Mother walked over to the sink, poured herself some ginger ale, ran both hands through her short blond hair to keep it back, and shook her head.

She sighed and said again, looking up and out of the night-black window, "Dear God, what are we going to do with you?" My heart went out to them. We all seemed to have exhausted our options. They asked me for fresh ideas, but I had none. I racked my brain, but couldn't come up with anything. The U.S. Marines didn't take sixteen-year-old girls.

Outside the study hall that May, a cardinal sang his round-noted song, and a robin sang his burbling song, and I slumped at my desk with my heart pounding, too harried by restlessness to breathe. I collected poems and learned them. I found the British war poets—World War I: Rupert Brooke, Edmund Blunden, Siegfried Sassoon, and especially Wilfred Owen, who wrote bitterly without descending to sarcasm. I found Asian and Middle Eastern poetry in translation—whole heaps of lyrics fierce or limp—which I ripped to fragments for my collection. I wanted beauty bare of import; I liked language in strips like pennants.

Under the spell of Rimbaud I wrote a poem that began with a line from *Une Saison en Enfer,* "Once, if I remember well," and continued, "My flesh did lie confined in hell." It ended, slantingly, to my own admiration, "And in my filth did I lie still." I wrote other poems, luscious ones, in the manner of the Song of Songs. One teacher, Miss Hickman, gave her lunch hour to meet with us about our poems.

It galled me that adults, as a class, approved the writing and memorization of poetry. Wasn't poetry secret and subversive? One sort of poetry was full of beauty and longing; it exhaled, enervated and helpless, like Li Po. Other poems were threats and vows. They inhaled; they poured into me a power I could not spend. The best of these, a mounted Arabic battle cry, I recited to myself by the hour, hoping to trammel the teachers' drone with hoofbeats.

I dosed myself with pure lyricism; I lived drugged on sensation, as I had lived alert on sensation as a little child. I wanted to raise armies, make love to armies, conquer armies. I wanted to swim in the stream of beautiful syllables until I tired. I wanted to bust up the Ellis School with my fists.

One afternoon at Judy Schoyer's house, I saw a white paperback book on a living-room chair: Lucretius, *On the Nature of Things.* Lucretius, said the book's back cover, had flourished in the first century B.C. This book was a prose translation of a long poem in Latin hexameters, the content of which was ancient physics mixed with philosophy. Why was this book in print? Why would anyone read wrong science, the babblings of a poet in a toga—why but from disinterested intellectual curiosity? I regarded the white paperback book as if it had been a meteorite smoldering on the chair's silk upholstery.

It was Judy's father's book. Mr. Schoyer loaned me the book when he was finished with it, and I read it; it was deadly dull. Nevertheless, I admired Judy's lawyer father boundlessly. I could believe in him for months at a time. His recreation proceeded from book to book, and had done so all his life. He had, I recalled, majored in classical history and literature. He wanted to learn the nature of things. He read and memorized poetry. He quizzed us about current events—what is your opinion of our new Supreme Court justice? On the other hand, his mother's family were Holyokes, and he hadn't raised a hand to rescue Judy from having to come out in Salem, Massachusetts. She had already done so, and would not talk about it.

Judy was tall now, high-waisted, graceful, messy still; she smiled forgivingly, smiled ironically, behind her thick glasses. Her limbs were thin as stalks, and her head was round. She spoke softly. She laughed at anything chaotic. Her family took me to the ballet, to the Pittsburgh Symphony, to the Three Rivers Arts Festival; they took me ice skating on a frozen lake in Highland Park, and swimming in Ohiopyle, south of town where the Youghiogheny River widens over flat rock outcrops.

After school, we piled in Judy's jeep. Out of the jeep's open back I liked to poke the long barrel of a popgun, slowly, and aim it at the drivers of the cars behind us, and shoot the cork, which then swung from its string. The drivers put up their hands in mock alarm, or slumped obligingly over their wheels. Pittsburghers were wonderful sports.

All spring long I crawled on my pin. I was reading *General Semantics*—Alfred Korzybski's early stab at linguistics; I'd hit on it by accident, in books with the word "language" in their titles. I read Freud's standard works, which interested me at first, but they denied reason. Denying reason had gotten Rimbaud nowhere. I read without snobbery, excited and alone, wholly free in the indifference of society. I read with the pure, exhilarating greed of readers sixteen, seventeen years old; I felt I was exhuming lost continents and plundering their stores. I knocked open everything in sight—Henry Miller, Helen Keller, Hardy, Updike, and the French. The war novels kept coming out, and so did John O'Hara's. I read popular social criticism with Judy and Ellin—*The Ugly American, The Hidden Persuaders, The Status Seekers.* I thought social and political criticism were interesting, but not nearly so interesting as almost everything else.

Ralph Waldo Emerson, for example, excited me enormously. Emerson was my first crack at Platonism, Platonism as it had come bumping and skidding down the centuries and across the ocean to Concord, Massachusetts. Emerson was a thinker, full time, as Pasteur and Salk were full-time biologists. I wrote a paper on Emerson's notion of the soul—the oversoul, which, if I could banish from my mind the thought of galoshes (one big galosh, in which we have our being), was grand stuff. It was metaphysics at last, poetry with import, philosophy minus the Bible. And Emerson incited to riot, flouting every authority, and requiring each native to cobble up an original relation with the universe. Since rioting seemed to be my specialty, if only by default, Emerson gave me heart.

★ ★ ★

Enervated, fanatic, filled long past bursting with oxygen I couldn't use, I hunched skinny in the school's green uniform, etiolated, broken, bellicose, starved, over the back-breaking desk. I sighed and sighed but never emptied my lungs. I said to myself, "O breeze of spring, since I dare not know you, / Why part the silk curtains by my bed?" I stuffed my skull with poems' invisible syllables. If unauthorized persons looked at me, I hoped they'd see blank eyes.

On one of these May mornings, the school's headmistress called me in and read aloud my teachers' confidential appraisals. Madame Owens wrote an odd thing. Madame Owens was a sturdy, affectionate, and humorous woman who had lived through two world wars in Paris by eating rats. She had curly black hair, rouged cheeks, and long, sharp teeth. She swathed her enormous body in thin black fabrics; she sat at her desk with her tiny ankles crossed. She chatted with us; she reminisced.

Madame Owens's kind word on my behalf made no sense. The headmistress read it to me in her office. The statement began, unforgettably, "Here, alas, is a child of the twentieth century." The headmistress, Marion Hamilton, was a brilliant and strong woman whom I liked and respected; the school's small-minded trustees would soon run her out of town on a rail. Her black hair flared from her high forehead. She looked up at me significantly, raising an eyebrow, and repeated it: "Here, alas, is a child of the twentieth century."

I didn't know what to make of it. I didn't know what to do about it. You got a lot of individual attention at a private school.

My idea was to stay barely alive, pumping blood and exchanging gases just enough to sustain life—but certainly not enough so that anyone suspected me of sentience, certainly not enough so that I woke up and remembered anything—until the time came when I could go. . . .

PATRICIA HAMPL
(1946—)

"I suppose I write about all the things I intended to leave behind, to grow out of, or deny: being a Midwesterner, a Catholic, a woman." So said PATRICIA HAMPL some years ago to *Contemporary Authors*. She grew up in St. Paul, Minnesota, in the fifties, the grandchild of Czech immigrants on her father's side of the family, attended a Catholic convent school run by the Madames of the Sacred Heart, majored in English at the University of Minnesota, and received a Master of Fine Arts from the Writers' Workshop of the University of Iowa. A published poet and memoirist, she is currently on the faculty of the English department of the University of Minnesota and has received numerous grants and fellowships from the Guggenheim Foundation, the Ingram-Merrill Foundation, the John D. and Catherine T. MacArthur Foundation, and the National Endowment for the Arts. A contributor to *American Poetry Review, The New Yorker, Paris Review,* and *Iowa Review,* her volumes of poetry include *Woman Before an Aquarium* (1978) and *Resort and Other Poems* (1983). Her first prose memoir, *A Romantic Education* (1981)—excerpted here—a winner of a Houghton Mifflin Literary Fellowship, is the story of her northern Midwestern childhood, of coming of age in the sixties and connecting with both feminism and the anti-Vietnam War movement, and of her journey in the seventies to the Prague of her family's past. Paul Zweig detected in the book's mixture of personal and cultural history a "mourning" for what he called "the greened America of her adolescence: the failed communes, the moral fervor of the anti-war movement," written in a "strong, at times even brilliant" prose, "a quarry of richly imagined lines." Pat Conroy called the memoir "astonishing and marvelous," "written in an elegant style that glitters like water and light. It is a moving search for one's own identity, for the burden of history, and for the beauty and poetry that illuminate that history." Terence Des Pres praised Hampl's evocation of "the roots and mystery of place; her way of joining poetic perception with history and political awareness is rare and welcome." Her second memoir, *Virgin Time* (1992), continues her contemplation and reinvention of her Catholic tradition in the context of her travels to religious foundations at Assisi, Lourdes, and Rosethorn, a Cistercian retreat in northern California important to Thomas Merton. In search of the meaning of religious experience in general and her own religious culture in particular, Hampl remains, in both books, a poet with a sense of humor and the desire to construct her own spirituality. Her journeys bring to mind the thesis of Gerda Lerner's most recent history, *The Creation of Feminist Consciousness,* that throughout the centuries, religious culture has enabled many literary and resilient women to resist patriarchal indoctrination and create alternate spiritual worlds for themselves.

From *A Romantic Education*

I was five and was sitting on the floor of the vestibule hallway of my grandmother's house where the one bookcase had been pushed. The bookcase wasn't in the house itself—ours wasn't a reading family. I was holding in my lap a book of sepia photographs bound in a soft brown cover, stamped in flaking gold with the title *Zlatá Praha.* Golden Prague, views of the nineteenth century.

The album felt good, soft. First, the Hradčany Castle and its gardens, then a close-up of the astronomical clock, a view of the baroque jumble of Malá Strana. Then a whole series of photographs of the Vltava River, each showing a different bridge, photograph after pale photograph like a wild rose that opens petal by petal, exposing itself effortlessly, as if there were no such thing as regret. All the buildings in the pictures were hazy, making it seem that the air, not the stone, held the contour of the baroque villas intact.

I didn't know how to read yet, and the Czech captions under the pictures were no more incomprehensible to me than English would have been. I liked the soft, fleshlike pliancy of the book. I knew the pictures were of Europe, and that Europe was far away, unreachable. Still, it had something to do with me, with my family. I sat in the cold vestibule, turning the pages of the Prague album. I was flying; I was somewhere else. I was not in St. Paul, Minnesota, and I was happy.

My grandmother appeared at the doorway. Her hands were on her stout hips, and she wanted me to come out of the unheated hallway. She wanted me to eat coffee cake in the kitchen with everybody else, and I had been hard to find. She said, "Come eat," as if this were the family motto.

As she turned to go, she noticed the album. In a second she was down on the floor with me, taking the album carefully in her hands, turning the soft, felt pages. "Oh," she said, "Praha." She looked a long time at one picture, I don't remember which one, and then she took a white handkerchief out of her pinafore apron pocket, and dabbed at the tears under her glasses. She took off the wire-rim glasses and made a full swipe.

Her glasses had made deep hollows on either side of her nose, two small caves. They looked as if, with a poke, the skin would give way like a ripe peach, and an entrance would be exposed into her head, into the skull, a passageway to the core of her brain. I didn't want her head to have such wounds. Yet I liked them, these unexpected dips in a familiar landscape.

"So beautiful," she was crying melodramatically over the album. "So beautiful." I had never seen an adult cry before. I was relieved, in some odd way, that there was crying in adulthood, that crying would not be taken away.

My grandmother hunched down next to me in the hallway; she held the album, reciting the gold-stamped captions as she turned the pages and dabbed at her eyes. She was having a good cry. I wanted to put my small finger into the two little caves of puckered skin, the eye-less sockets on either side of her large, drooping nose. Strange wounds, I wanted to touch them. I wanted to touch her, my father's mother. She was so *foreign*.

Looking repeatedly into the past, you do not necessarily become fascinated with your own life, but rather with the phenomenon of memory. The act of remembering becomes less autobiographical; it begins to feel tentative, aloof. It becomes blessedly impersonal.

The self-absorption that seems to be the impetus and embarrassment of autobiography turns into (or perhaps always was) a hunger for the world. Actually, it begins as hunger for *a* world, one gone or lost, effaced by time or a more sudden brutality. But in the act of remembering, the personal environment expands, resonates beyond itself, beyond its "subject," into the endless and tragic recollection that is history.

We look at old family photographs in which we stand next to black, boxy Fords and are wearing period costumes, and we do not gaze fascinated because there we are young again, or there we are standing, as we never will again in life, next to our mother. We stare and drift because there we are . . . historical. It is the dress, the black car that dazzle us now and draw us beyond our mother's bright arms which once caught us. We reach into the attractive impersonality of something more significant than ourselves.

We embrace the deathliness and yet we are not dead. We are impersonal and yet ourselves. The astonishing power and authority of memory derive from this paradox. Here, in memory, we live *and* die. We do "live again" in memory, but differently: in history as well as in biography. And when these two come together, forming a narrative, they approach fiction. The imprecision of memory causes us to create, to extend remembrance into narrative. It sometimes seems, therefore, that what we remember is not—could not be—true. And yet it is *accurate*. The imagination, triggered by memory, is satisfied that this is so.

We trust memory against all the evidence: it is selective, subjective, cannily defensive, unreliable as fact. But a single red detail remembered—a hat worn in 1952, the nail polish applied one summer day by an aunt to her toes, separated by balls of cotton, as we watched—has more real blood than the creatures around us on a bus as, for some reason, we think of that day, that hat, those bright feet. That world. This power of memory probably comes from its kinship with the imagination. In memory each of us is an artist: each of us creates. The Kingdom of God, the nuns used to tell us in school, is within you. We may not have made a religion of memory, but it is our passion, and along with (sometimes in opposition to) science, our authority. It is a kingdom of its own.

Psychology, which is somehow *our* science, the claustrophobic discipline of the century, has made us acknowledge the value of remembering—even at the peril of shame. But it is especially difficult to reach back into the merely insignificant, into a family life where, it seemed, nothing happened, where there wasn't the ghost of a pretension. That is a steelier resistance because to break through what is unimportant and as anonymous as dirt a greater sense of worthlessness must be overcome. At least shame is interesting; at least it is hidden, the sign of anything valuable. But for a past to be overlooked, discarded because it was not only useless but simply without interest—that is a harsher heritage. In fact, is it a heritage?

It seems as if I spent most of my twenties holding a lukewarm cup of coffee, hunched over a table, talking. Innumerable cups of coffee, countless tables: the booths of the Gopher Grill at the University of Minnesota where, probably around 1965, I first heard myself use the word *relationship;* a little later, the orange formica table of a federal prison where "the man I live with" (there still is no other term) was serving a sentence for draft resistance; and the second-hand tables of a dozen apartments, the wooden farmhouse table of a short-lived commune—table after table, friend after friend, rehashing our hardly ended (or not ended) childhoods. I may have the tables wrong; maybe the formica one was in the farmhouse, the oak one in the prison, maybe the chairs in the prison were orange and the table gray. But they are fixtures, nailed down, not to be moved: memories.

This generation has written its memoirs early; we squeezed every childhood lemon for all it was worth: my mother this, my father that. Our self-absorption was appalling. But I won't go back—not yet—on that decade. It was also the time when my generation, as "a generation," was most political, most involved. The people I sat with, picking at our individual pasts, wearing nightgowns till noon as we analyzed within a millimeter our dreams and their meanings (that is, how they proved this or that about our parents), finally put on our clothes, went outside and, in various ways that are too easily forgotten, tried to end a war which we were the first, as a group, to recognize was disastrous. In fact, our protest against the war is what made us a generation, even to ourselves.

Perhaps no American generation—certainly not our parents who were young during the Depression—had a childhood as long as ours. The war kept us young. We stayed in school, endlessly, it seemed, and our protest kept us in the child's position: we alternately "rebelled" against and pestered the grownups for what we wanted—an end to the war. Those who fought the war had no such long, self-reflective youths. Childhood belonged to us, who stayed at home. And we became the "sixties generation."

Our certainty that the war was wrong became entangled with our analysis of our families and our psyches not only because we were given to self-reflection and had a lot of time on our hands. We combed through our dreams and our childhoods with Jung's *Man and His Symbols* at the ready, and were looking for something, I now think, that was neither personal nor familial and perhaps not even psychological. We had lost the national connection and were heartsick in a cultural way. I don't think we knew that; I didn't, anyway. But at home I didn't talk psychology, I talked politics, arguing with a kind of angry misery whose depths confused me and made my family frightened for me, and probably of me. But there was no real argument—I did all the talking; my family, gathered for Sunday dinner, looked glumly at the gravy on their plates as if at liquid Rorschach blots that might suggest why I, the adored child, had come to this strange pass. They weren't "for the war," but the belligerent way I was against it dismayed them and caused them to fall silent, waiting for me to stop. I had opinions, I spoke of my "position" on things.

One night my uncle, trying to meet me halfway, said, "Well, when I was in Italy during the War . . . "

"How do you defend that analogy?" I snapped at him, perhaps partly because for them "the War" was still the Second World War. My family couldn't seem, for a long time, to *focus* on Vietnam. But my uncle retreated in the face of the big guns of my new English-major lingo.

On Thanksgiving one year I left the table to find *I. F. Stone's Weekly* and read parts of it to the assembled family in a ringing, triumphantly angry voice. "But," my father said when I finished, as if I. F. Stone had been compiling evidence about me and not the Johnson administration, "you used to be so *happy*—the happiest person I ever met."

"What does that have to do with anything?" I said.

Yet he was right. My unhappiness (but I didn't think of myself as unhappy) was a confusion of personal and public matters, and it was made more intense by the fact that I had been happy ("the happiest person!") and now I couldn't remember what that happiness had been—just childhood? But many childhoods are miserable. And I couldn't remember exactly how the happiness stopped. I carry from that time the feeling that private memory is not just private and not just memory. Yet the resistances not against memory but against the significance of memory remain strong.

I come from people who have always been polite enough to feel that nothing has ever happened to them. They have worked, raised families, played cards, gone on fishing trips together, risen to grief and admirable bitterness and, then, taken patiently the early death that robbed them of a brother, a son. They have not dwelt on things. To dwell, that appropriate word, as if the past were a residence, faintly morbid and barbaric: the dwellings of prehistoric men. Or, the language of the Bible: "The Word was made flesh, and dwelt amongst us."

I have dwelt, though. To make a metaphor is to make a fuss, and I am a poet, though it seems that is something one cannot claim for oneself; anyway, I write poetry. I am enough of them, my kind family, to be repelled by the significance of things, to find poetry, with its tendency to make connections and to break the barriers between past and present, slightly embarrassing.

It would be impossible to look into the past, even a happy one (especially a happy one), were it not for the impersonality that dwells in the most intimate fragments, the integuments that bind even obscure lives to history and, eventually, history to fiction, to myth.

I will hold up negative after family negative to the light. I will dwell. Dwell in the house of the dead and in the living house of my relatives. I'm after junk. I want to make something out of what my family says is nothing. I suppose that is what I was up to when my grandmother called me out of the vestibule, away from the bookcase and the views of Prague, to eat my dinner with everybody else. . . .

III
Prague The Castle

"Are you going to write a 'Letter from Prague'?" Jaromil asked me one day as we walked along together.

"I'll write something," I said.

"I've read a lot of these 'Letters from Prague,'" he said. "What does it mean? A person comes, stays a week; he walks around and then he writes an article and says, 'The people seem contented—or discontented. Fresh vegetables appear to be plentiful, but the lines in stores are long—or the lines are short, but the vegetables are wilted. The people are well dressed—or the women don't have any sense of style.' Whether we stand in line, vegetables, what we wear—that's it. What do you think?"

"I noticed, as I rode by on the tram this morning, that a vegetable stand seemed to have wilted vegetables, mostly just kohlrabi and radishes—but it's only May. And the well-dressed women seem to be West German tourists. And I've noticed lines."

"That's what I mean," he said, shaking his head.

"I was joking," I said.

"Yes," he said, but he didn't laugh. We walked along together in silence.

What *is* it possible to know? I mean, beyond the fact that there are or are not wilted vegetables, and that the women do or do not have nice clothes (is it possible to know even that?). This is the question that haunts modern times: *did you know?* Did you know about Auschwitz? ("Only a few people knew." "We didn't know.") Did you know about My Lai? Did you know about the CIA in Chile? Did we know? When did we find out?

There is, in this question, the lingering nerve of an ethical culture: if we know, then we are responsible. We still feel we must answer for our knowledge. But clearly, it is necessary, at times, for whole nations to be sure they do not know certain things. East Germany, for example, has worked out its relation to Second World War history in a way that acknowledges *and* denies reality: yes, the horrors of the camps existed, but the cause was Fascism, which has been boldly routed by Socialism. As a result, East Germany, unlike West Germany, does not pay reparations to Jewish survivors.

As for us, who knows what more, exactly, will emerge from the Vietnam years? Was America really surprised by My Lai? It strikes me that I, an ordinary citizen in the Midwest with no special information, was not surprised. Horrified—yes, I was sickened; I remember the pictures. But I wasn't surprised. The whole business stank to high heaven for years. Years before My Lai, *Life* magazine ran that full-color picture of a GI wearing a string of ears slung around his waist. That, I think, is when I knew—knew all a person needs to know. I knew then that it was worse than war; it was a perversion of the national self, as well as the destruction of another nation.

It was not necessary to be told much to come to the realization that I *knew*. Apparently, moral intelligence is subtle and wily; it finds the news. We do not need to be told that there are concentration camps dotting Central and Eastern Europe, and they are located here and here. We do not need the U.S. Army or the American press to give the "facts" about My Lai. Atrocities cannot be hidden. They appear first in language: *We had to destroy the village in order to save it.*

But in order "not to know," large groups of people, whole nations, have to find a way to blunt their intelligence. A way must be found not to know. The cost must be enormous. History is traduced, but perhaps it always is. Worse than that, people must deny over and over the intelligence of their senses. It is a denial of the most ancient poetic intelligence. It is a denial of reality. At its most extreme, it is madness.

We are haunted by history because we denied its reality when it was the present. It keeps coming back, as Kundera says. It will keep coming back until we get the story straight. "During the war," Muriel Rukeyser says in *The Life of Poetry*, "we felt the silence in the policy of the governments of English-speaking countries. That policy was to win the war first, and work out the meanings afterward. The result was, of course, that the meanings were lost. You cannot put these things off." And therefore, the hunger for meaning increases.

But to answer my question, at least for now: what is it possible to know? Apparently, just about everything we need to know. This fact must be acknowledged: we do know when something vile and gigantically evil is happening among us. We may not know the names: Auschwitz, Buchenwald, Terezin (the "artists' concentration camp" that wasn't far from Prague), My Lai. But we know. It is impossible to believe otherwise.

Still, I often feel *wrong* to be approaching this history as I am—I who have been untouched by this kind of suffering. I go cold at the thought that silence *is* the only response, as so many of the real witnesses have said. I have felt, vaguely, that if I could get permission (I think of it that way) for this inquiry from the man in the luggage shop in London,* that I would have my justification, my right to speak at all.

Why such timidity? It comes, I think, from the peculiar relation the "untouched," such as myself, must have to the Holocaust. It remains the central episode of our history, the horror against which all other atrocities are measured, even previous ones, and by which innocence is gauged. My relation to it is not one of personal or even national guilt (as, say, a young German might feel). Mine is the confusion, the search, of someone unmarked. *Nothing bad has ever happened to me.* Nothing impersonally cruel and ruinous—and that is an odd, protected history or nonhistory to have in this century. I can only proceed, assuming that to be untouched has some significance in the presence of the deeply touched life of this city.

Or perhaps I must be more emphatic: the value of my inquiry *is* that I am unmarked. I have no "story," no documentation of the camps, the tortures, the cruelties. I have not lived in the post-War world Milosz describes as "a hard school, where ignorance was punished not by bad marks but by death." Such a world (and it is a world where the War and the peace that followed must be seen as one thing) forced the intellectuals here "to think sociologically and historically." People like me are entirely different.

We are part of the evidence that all that raw material from survivors and witnesses has gone out of journalism, even out of the testament of history, and has plunged into the psychic life of all of us. The horrors and the sadness, the endless mourning, is floating there, careening in the imagination, looking for a place. Looking for some way to be transformed. Looking, in a word, for culture. As I am.

---

*A shopkeeper Hampl talked with en route to Prague.

DOROTHY ALLISON
(1949—)

◆————————◆

DOROTHY ALLISON grew up in Greenville, South Carolina, in the heart of a poor, extended, eccentric family. She left them behind, as she says in the autobiographical piece that follows, to escape their legacy of abuse and waste and "inevitable death by misadventure." Currently living in Monte Rio, California, Allison has received strong critical praise for her recent novel, *Bastard Out of Carolina* (1992), which was a finalist for the National Book Award. But she has been publishing poetry, short fiction, and essays since the seventies in such anthologies as *High Risk, Women on Women, Pleasure and Danger,* and *Naming the Waves.* In 1989 *Trash,* a collection of short stories, received two Lambda Literary Awards. The Preface to that collection, reprinted here, is the closest Allison has come to writing a memoir. When an interviewer asked her if the sexually charged material she deals with in her fiction could be handled as a memoir, Allison responded, "Oh yes, I will do that someday. But for now, fiction is a lot easier. You can build in a lot of hope that you don't have in real life. If [*Bastard Out of Carolina*] had been autobiographical, it would have been a lot meaner."

Critics and reviewers have assigned Allison a distinguished place on the American literary landscape. "[She] joins the ranks of such enduring Southern writers as Flannery O'Connor, Walker Percy, Tennessee Williams, and Faulkner, creating a significant moral vision of the world," is just one of many such responses to her work. *The Women's Review of Books'* reviewer, Amber Hollibaugh, observes that Allison's writing, in capturing the life of a "cross-eyed working-class lesbian" and of the people she came from, goes back to the "earliest days of the women's movement and speaks bitterness, letting the weight of what her readers already know come together with the power of her vision. [She] isn't easy to read, but neither are our lives." George Garrett, writing in the *New York Times Book Review,* marks the moral courage of her vision. The literary territory that she explores "is dangerous turf. [Her] people are what some would call white trash, rednecks, crackers, . . . members of the white working poor." What is dangerous, says Garrett, "is the whole Southern thing. Terminal cuteness is the dread disease of too much new Southern writing. . . . [Allison] . . . is often funny, never cute, . . . never sentimental." She does not dodge "the pain of felt experience." In the words of Barbara Kingsolver, her writing resonates "like a gospel choir."

From *Trash*

Preface: Deciding to Live

There was a day in my life when I decided to live.

After my childhood, after all that long terrible struggle to simply survive, to escape my stepfather, uncles, speeding Pontiacs, broken glass and rotten floorboards, or that inevitable death by misadventure that claimed so many of my cousins; after watching so many die around me, I had not imagined that I would ever need to make such a choice. I had imagined the hunger for life in me was insatiable, endless, unshakable.

I became an escapee—one of the ones others talked about. I became the one who got away, who got glasses from the Lions Club, a job from Lyndon Johnson's War On Poverty, and finally went to college on a scholarship. There I met the people I had always read about: girls whose fathers loved them—innocently; boys who drove cars they had not stolen; whole armies of the middle and upper classes I had not truly believed to be real; the children to whom I could not help but compare myself. I matched their innocence, their confidence, their capacity to trust, to love, to be generous against the bitterness, the rage, the pure and terrible hatred that consumed me. Like many others who had gone before me, I began to dream longingly of my own death.

I began to court it. Cowardly, traditionally—that is, in the tradition of all those others like me, through drugs and drinking and stubbornly putting myself in the way of other people's violence. Even now, I cannot believe how it was that everything I survived became one more reason to want to die.

But one morning I limped into my mama's kitchen and sat alone at her dining table. I was limping because I had pulled a muscle in my thigh and cracked two ribs in a fight with the woman I thought I loved. I remember that morning in all its details, the scratches on my wrists from my lover's fingernails, the look on my mama's face while she got ready to go to work—how she tried not to fuss over me, and the way I could not meet her eyes. It was in my mama's face that I saw myself, my mama's silence, for she behaved as if I were only remotely the daughter she had loved and prayed for. She treated me as if I were in a way already dead, or about to die—as unreachable, as dangerous as one of my uncles on a three-day toot. *That* was so humiliating, it broke my pride. My mouth opened to cry out, but then I shut it stubbornly. It was in that moment I made my decision—not actually the decision to live, but the decision not to die on her. I shut my mouth on my grief and my rage and began to pretend as if I would live, as if there were reason enough to fight my way out of the trap I had made for myself—though I had not yet figured out what that reason was.

I limped around tightlipped through the months it took me to find a job in another city and disappear. I took a bus to that city and spoke to no one, signed the papers that made me a low-level government clerk, and wound up sitting in a motel room eating peanut butter sandwiches so I could use the per diem to buy respectable skirts and blouses—the kind of clothes I had not worn since high school. Every evening I would walk the ten blocks from the training classes to the motel where I could draw the heavy drapes around me, open the windows, and sit wrapped around by the tent of those drapes. There I would sit and smoke my hoarded grass.

Part of me knew what I was doing, knew the decision I was making. A much greater part of me could not yet face it. I was trying to make solid my decision to live, but I did not know if I could. I had to change my life, make baby steps into a future I did not trust, and I began by looking first to the ground on which I stood, how I had become the woman I was. By day I played at being what the people who were training me thought I was—a college graduate and a serious worker, a woman settling down to a practical career with the Social Security Administration. I imagined that if I played at it long enough, it might become true, but I felt like an actress in a role for which she was truly not suited. It took all my concentration not to laugh at inappropriate moments and keep my mouth shut when I did not know what to say at all.

There was only one thing I could do that helped me through those weeks. Every evening I sat down with a yellow legal-size pad, writing out the story of my life. I wrote it all: everything I could remember, all the stories I had ever been told, the names, places, images—how the blood had arched up the wall one terrible night that recurred persistently in my dreams—the dreams themselves, the people in the dreams. My stepfather, my uncles and cousins, my desperate aunts and their more desperate daughters.

I wrote out my memories of the women. My terror and lust for my own kind; the shouts and arguments; the long, slow glances and slower approaches; the way my hands always shook when I would finally touch the flesh I could barely admit I wanted, the way I could never ask for what I wanted, never accept it if they offered. I twisted my fingers and chewed my lips over the subtle and deliberate lies I had told myself and them, the hidden stories of my life that lay in disguise behind the mocking stories I did tell—all the stories of my family, my childhood, and the relentless deadening poverty and shame I had always tried to hide because I knew no one would believe what I could tell them about it.

Writing it all down was purging. Putting those stories on paper took them out of the nightmare realm and made me almost love myself for being able to finally face them. More subtly, it gave me a way to love the people I wrote about—even the ones I had fought with or hated. In that city where I knew no one. I had no money and nothing to fill the evenings except washing out my clothes, reading cheap paperbacks, and trying to understand how I had come to be in that place. I was not the kind of person who could imagine asking for help or talking about my personal business. Nor was I fool enough to think that could be done without risking what little I'd gained. Still, though I knew the danger of revealing too much about my life, I did not imagine anyone reading my rambling, ranting stories. I was writing for myself, trying to shape my life outside my terrors and helplessness, to make it visible and real in a tangible way, in the way other people's lives seemed real—the lives I read about in books. I had been a child who believed in books, but I had never really found me or mine in print. My family was always made over into caricatures or flattened into saint-like stock creatures. I never found my lovers in their strength and passion. Outside my mother's stubbornness and my own outraged arrogance, I had never found any reason to believe in myself. But I had the idea that I could make it exist on those pages.

Days, I went to training sessions, memorized codes, section numbers, and memo formats. Nights, I wrote my stories. I would pull out scraps of paper at work to make notes about things I wanted to write about, though most of those scraps just wound up tucked in my yellow pad. What poured out of me could not be planned or controlled; it came up like water under pressure at its own pace, pushing my fear ahead of it. By the end of the month, I'd taken to sitting on the motel roof—no longer stoned, but still writing. By then I was also writing letters to all the women I didn't really expect to see again, explaining the things that writing out my stories had made real to me. I did not intend to mail those letters, and never did. The letters themselves were stories—mostly lies—self-justifying, awkward, and desperate.

I finished that month, got assigned to a distant city, put away my yellow papers, and moved—making sure no one who knew me from before could find me. I threw myself into the women's community, fell in love every third day, and started trying to be serious about writing—poems and essays and the beginnings of stories. I even helped edit a feminist magazine. Throughout that time I *told* stories—mostly true stories about myself and my family and my lovers in a drawl that made them all funnier than they were. Though that was mostly a good time for me, I wrote nothing that struck me as worth the trouble of actually keeping. I did not tuck those new stories away with the yellow pads I had sealed up in a blanket box of my mother's. I told myself the yellow pads were as raw and unworked as I felt myself to be, and the funny stories I was telling people were better, were the work of someone who was going to be a "real" writer. It was three years before I pulled out those old yellow sheets and read them, and saw how thin and self-serving my funny stories had become.

The stuff on those yellow pads was bitter. I could not recognize myself in that bitchy whiny hateful voice telling over all those horrible violent memories. They were, oddly, the same stories I'd been telling for years, but somehow drastically different. Telling them out loud, I'd made them ironic and playful. The characters became eccentric, fascinating—not the cold-eyed, mean and nasty bastards they were on the yellow pages, the dangerous frightened women and the more dangerous and just as frightened men. I could not stand it, neither the words on the page nor what they told me about myself. My neck and teeth began to ache, and I was not at all sure I really wanted to live with that stuff inside me. But holding onto them, reading them over again, became a part of the process of survival, of deciding once more to live—and clinging to that decision. For me those stories were not distraction or entertainment; they were the stuff of my life, and they were necessary in ways I could barely understand.

Still, I took those stories and wrote them again. I made some of them funny. I made some of them poems. I made the women beautiful, wounded but courageous, while the men disappeared into the background. I put hope in the children and passion in the landscape while my neck ached and tightened, and I found myself wanting nothing so much as a glass of whiskey or a woman's anger to distract me. None of it was worth the pain it caused me. None of it made me or my people real or understandable. None of it told the truth, and every lie I wrote proved to me I wasn't worth my mother's grief at what she thought was my wasted life, or my sister's cold fear of what I might tell other people about them.

I put it all away. I began to live my life as if nothing I did would survive the day in which I did it. I used my grief and hatred to wall off my childhood, my history, my sense of being part of anything greater than myself. I used women and liquor, constant righteous political work, and a series of grimly endured ordeals to convince myself that I had nothing to decide, that I needed nothing more than what other people considered important to sustain me. I worked on a feminist journal. I read political theory, history, psychology, and got a degree in anthropology as if that would quiet the roar in my own head. I watched women love each other, war with each other, and take each other apart while never acknowledging the damage they did—the damage we all did to each other. I went through books and conferences, CR groups and study groups, organizing community actions and pragmatic coalition fronts. I did things I did not understand for reasons I could not begin to explain just to be in motion, to be trying to do something, change something in a world I wanted desperately to make over but could not imagine for myself.

That was all part of deciding to live, though I didn't know it. Just as I did not know that what I needed had to come up from inside me, not be laid over the top of my head. The bitterness with which I had been born, that had been nurtured in me, could not be eased with a lover or a fight or any number of late-night meetings and clumsily written manifestoes. It may never be eased. The decision to live when everything inside and out shouts death is not a matter of moments but of years, and no one has ever told me how you know when it is accomplished.

But a night finally came when I woke up sweaty and angry and afraid I'd never go back to sleep again. All those stories were rising up my throat. Voices were echoing in my neck, laughter behind my ears, and I was terribly, terribly afraid that I was finally as crazy as my kind was supposed to be. But the desire to live was desperate in my belly, and the stories I had hidden all those years were the blood and bone of it. To get it down, to tell it again, to make sense of something—by god just once—to be real in the world, without lies or evasions or sweet-talking nonsense. I got up and wrote a story all the way through. It was one of the stories from the yellow pages, one of the ones I'd rewritten, but it was different again. I wasn't truly me or my mama or my girl-friends, or really any of the people who'd been there, but it had the feel, the shit-kicking anger and grief of my life. It wasn't that whiny voice, but it had the drawl, and it had, too, the joy and pride I sometimes felt in me and mine. It was not biography and yet not lies, and it resonated to the pulse of my sisters' fear and my lovers' teeth-shaking shouts. It began with my broken ribs and my desperate shame, and it ended with all the questions and decisions still waiting—most of all the decision to live.

It was a rough beginning—my own shout of life against death, of shape and substance against silence and confusion. It was most of all my deep abiding desire to live fleshed and strengthened on the page, a way to tell the truth as a kind of magic not cheapened or distorted by a need to please any damn body at all. Without it, I cannot imagine my own life. Without it, I have no way to know who I am.

One time, twice, once in a while again, I get it right. Once in a while, I can make the world I know real on the page. I can make the women and men I love breathe out loud in an empty room, the dreams I dare not speak shape up in the smoky darkness of other people's imaginations. Writing these stories is the only way I know to make sure of my ongoing decision to live, to set moment to moment a small piece of stubbornness against an ocean of ignorance and obliteration.

I write stories. I write fiction. I put on the page a third look at what I've seen in life—the condensed and reinvented experience of a cross-eyed working-class lesbian, addicted to violence, language, and hope, who has made the decision to live, is determined to live, on the page and on the street, for me and mine.

JAMAICA KINCAID
(1949—)

◆

JAMAICA KINCAID was born and grew up in St. John's, Antigua, a ten-by-twelve-mile island in the British West Indies. She immigrated to the United States as a young woman and now lives in Vermont with her husband and children. She is the author of several highly praised works of fiction, originally published in part in *The New Yorker: At the Bottom of the River* (1983), which won the Morton Dauwen Zabel Award of the American Academy and Institute of Arts and Letters; *Annie John* (1985); and *Lucy* (1990). Her first book of nonfiction, *A Small Place,* is the source of the excerpt that follows here, a somewhat modified section taken from the book and given as an oral presentation by the author at a California conference on the topic of the political imagination of contemporary writers. *A Small Place* is a long essay, interfaced with autobiographical details, about the poverty and political corruption of the author's native country, conditions which, in Kincaid's view, are the legacy of British colonialism and the current empire of tourism fueled by the money of her adopted country. The book brings to life the consciousness of the postcolonial woman who, with confidence and anger, points her finger at the despoilers of her original home and earliest identity. Unlike the immigrants of the early twentieth century (see Mary Antin, page 37, or Denise Levertov, page 189), Kincaid does not celebrate her memory of the Old World or the possibilities of the new country. Rather she focuses on what has been lost in a Swiftian mode that cannot help but amplify our vision of one small poor place and its history of racist domination. Kincaid remembers and writes as a representative new immigrant from the Third World, expressing an interpretation of history and place that is searingly political rather than conventionally nostalgic or bittersweet. Salman Rushdie called *A Small Place* "a jeremiad of great clarity and a force that one might have called torrential were the language not so finely controlled."

From *A Small Place*

About a month ago, I went to England with a friend. We spent time in London and the English countryside. Now I have millions of opinions about the English, but they are rather long opinions. Actually, these opinions are prejudices, but the reason they remain opinions is because I come from a poor country and I cannot back them up. For instance, I thought that it was horrible the way the English kept their countryside, that it was just a lot of hedges. It was too neat. It might reflect something about the culture, perhaps that they have problems with constipation. I, for instance, might be in the position of saying to them, "I bet you don't shit easily," and this might actually be true. But this can only remain my opinion.

This may be a good thing. I believe it is a good thing. One shouldn't have these prejudices. But a very interesting thing happened between my friend and me which I will now tell you about.

My husband is a composer and he often performs in public and he likes to wear a very nice shirt when he does. So I thought, well, I will take him back a present of a nice shirt. So I went to Turnbull and Asser to get him a nice shirt. Afterwards, we needed a tie to go with the shirt, and one of the salespersons showed us a lot of ties in different colors but all with the same pattern. And he described the ties in tones perhaps only the Pope uses when silently or privately praying to God. He said, "Look at these ties, they have the Prince of Wales crest on them. Aren't they beautiful? This pattern is very exclusive to us. The Prince of Wales has never allowed his crest to be used in this way. It's such a marvelous thing." Now, I was incredibly horrified and just said, "My God, we hate princes in my family. My husband would never wear a tie with the Prince of Wales crest on it." The man was truly upset, which I was glad about. I thought that he should know that there was at least one person in England at that moment who did not like the Prince of Wales.

Well, I thought that was the end of it, but I had not considered that, as odious as the idea of the Prince of Wales is to me, that this is in fact my friend's tradition. This is in fact her country. And she correctly realized that I was in fact horrified by this country and this experience, that I was close to things that, when described, had always mentally ended the sentence with "And then it all burned down." Westminster Abbey, for instance. We were in Westminster Abbey, and we saw all the tombs. And it was really amazing that it had all been kept. You know, such as the piece of stone that is used in coronations—and it is actually a very unattractive piece of stone. If one saw it in one's yard, one would be likely to put it out of the way. But it is a very precious thing to the English. It is part of the coronation ritual, a stone that had been taken from Scotland because the English had heard that every king of Scotland had been crowned on that stone. So the stone represents an incredible act of conquest, a symbolic conquest of the Scots. When I see the stone, I think how much like something of me that stone is, and the end of the sentence involving the stone is, "and then it was blown up, and they never saw it again." And so the end of every sentence for me in England is: "And then it vanished." Everything.

Now, as I said, my friend sensed this and so got quite upset about my insulting this man about his Prince of Wales tie. She said, "But you know, this is my culture and my tradition." She really made me feel that I should have some sympathy and respect for where she comes from, and I thought about it and came to the conclusion that she is right as far as it goes. But on the whole, I think that the end of all sentences about England for me is: "And it didn't exist anymore."

I am from Antigua. The Antigua that I knew, the Antigua in which I grew up, is not the Antigua you, a tourist, would see now. That Antigua no longer exists partly for the usual reason, the passing of time, and partly because the bad-minded people who used to rule over it, the English, no longer do so.

In the Antigua that I knew, we lived on a street named after an English maritime criminal, Horatio Nelson, and all the other streets around us were named after some other English maritime criminals. There was Rodney Street, there was Hood Street, there was Hawkins Street, and there was Drake Street. There were flamboyant trees and mahogany trees lining East Street. Government House, the place where the Governor, the person standing in for the Queen, lived, was on East Street. Government House was surrounded by a high white wall—and to show how cowed we must have been, no one ever wrote bad things on it; it remained clean and white and high. There was the library on lower High Street, above the Department of the Treasury, and it was in that part of High Street that all colonial government business took place. In that part of High Street, you could cash a check at the Treasury, read a book in the library, post a letter at the post office, appear before a magistrate in court. It was in that same part of High Street that you could get a passport in another government office. In the middle of High Street was the Barclays Bank. The Barclay brothers, who started Barclays Bank, were slave-traders. That is how they made their money. When the English outlawed the slave trade, the Barclay brothers went into banking. It made them even richer. It's possible that when they saw how rich banking made them, they gave themselves a good beating for opposing an end to slave trading (for surely they would have opposed that), but then again, they may have been visionaries and agitated for an end to slavery, for look at how rich they became with their banks borrowing from (through their savings) the descendants of the slaves and then lending back to them. But people just a little older than I am can recite the name of and the date the first black person was hired as a cashier at this very same Barclays Bank in Antigua. Do you ever wonder why some people blow things up? I can imagine that if my life had taken a certain turn, there would be the Barclays Bank, and there I would be, both of us in ashes. Do you ever try to understand why people like me cannot get over the past, cannot forgive and cannot forget? There is the Barclays Bank. The Barclay brothers are dead. The human beings they traded, the human beings who to them were only commodities, are dead. It should not have been that they came to the same end, and heaven is not enough of a reward for one and hell enough of a punishment for the other. People who think about these things believe that every bad deed, even every bad thought, carries with it its own retribution. So you see the queer thing about people like me? Sometimes we hold your retribution.

And then there was another place, called the Mill Reef Club. It was built by some people from North America who wanted to live in Antigua but who seemed not to like Antiguans (black people) at all, for the Mill Reef Club declared itself completely private, and the only Antiguans (black people) allowed to go there were servants. People can recite the name of the first Antiguan (black person) to eat a sandwich at the clubhouse and the day on which it happened; people can recite the name of the first Antiguan (black person) to play golf on the golf course and the day on which the event took place. In those days, we Antiguans thought that the people at the Mill Reef Club had such bad manners, like pigs. There they were, strangers in someone else's home, and then they refused to talk to their hosts or have anything human, anything intimate, to do with them. And what were these people from North America, these people from England, these people from Europe, with their bad behavior, doing on this little island? For they so enjoyed behaving badly, as if there were pleasure immeasurable to be had from not acting like a human being. Let me tell you about a man. Trained as a dentist, he took it on himself to say he was a doctor, specializing in treating children's illnesses. No one objected—certainly not us. He came to Antigua as a refugee (running away from Hitler) from Czechoslovakia. This man hated us so much that he would send his wife to inspect us before we were admitted into his presence, and she would make sure that we didn't smell, that we didn't have dirt under our fingernails, and that nothing else about us—apart from the color of our skin—would offend the doctor.

Then there was a headmistress of a girls' school, hired through the colonial office in England and sent to Antigua to run this school, which only in my lifetime began to accept girls who were born outside a marriage; in Antigua it had never dawned on anyone that this was a way of keeping black children out of this school. This woman was twenty-six years old, not too long out of university, from Northern Ireland, and she told these girls over and over again to stop behaving as if they were monkeys just out of trees. No one ever dreamed that the word for any of this was *racism*. We thought these people were so ill-mannered, and we were so surprised by this, for they were far away from their home, and we believed that the farther away you were from your home the better you should behave. We thought they were un-Christian-like; we thought they were small-minded; we thought they were like animals, a bit below human standards as we understood these standards to be. We felt superior to all these people; we thought that perhaps the English among them who behaved this way weren't English at all, for the English were supposed to be civilized, and this behavior was so much like that of an animal, the thing we were before the English rescued us, that maybe they weren't from the real England at all but from another England, one we were not familiar with, not at all from the England we were told about, not at all from the England we could never be from, the England that was so far away, the England that not even a boat could take us to, the England that, no matter what we did, we could never be of. We felt superior, for we were so much better behaved and we were full of grace, and these people were so badly behaved and they were completely empty of grace. We were taught the names of the kings of England. In Antigua, the twenty-fourth of May was a holiday—Queen Victoria's official birthday. We didn't say to ourselves, Hasn't this extremely unappealing person been dead for years and years? Instead, we were glad for a holiday.

I cannot tell you how angry it makes me to hear people from North America tell me how much they love England, how beautiful England is, with its traditions. All they see is some frumpy, wrinkled-up person passing by in a carriage waving at a crowd. But what I see is the millions of people, of whom I am just one, made orphans: no motherland, no fatherland, no gods, no mounds of earth for holy ground, no excess of love which might lead to the things that an excess of love sometimes brings, and worst and most painful of all, no tongue. For isn't it odd that the only language I have in which to speak of this crime is the language of the criminal who committed the crime? And what can that really mean? For the language of the criminal can contain only the goodness of the criminal's deed. The language of the criminal can explain and express the deed only from the criminal's point of view. It cannot contain the horror of the deed, the injustice of the deed, the agony, the humiliation inflicted on me. When I say to the criminal, "This is wrong, this is wrong, this is wrong," or "This deed is bad, and this other deed is bad, and this one is also very, very bad," the criminal understands the word *wrong* in this way: it is wrong when "he" doesn't get his fair share of the profits from the crime just committed; he understands the word *bad* in this way: a fellow criminal betrayed a trust. That must be why, when I say, "I am filled with rage," the criminal says, "But why?" And when I blow things up and make life generally unlivable for the criminal, the criminal is shocked, surprised. But nothing can erase my rage—not an apology, not a large sum of money, not the death of the criminal—for this wrong can never be made right, and only the impossible can make me still: can a way be found to make what happened not have happened?

I attended a school named after a Princess of England. Years and years later, I read somewhere that this Princess made her tour of the West Indies (which included Antigua, and on that tour she dedicated my school) because she had fallen in love with a married man, and since she was not allowed to marry a divorced man she was sent to visit us to get over her affair with him. How well I remember that all of Antigua turned out to see this Princess person, how every building that she would enter was repaired and painted so that it looked brand-new, how every beach she would sun herself on had to look as if no one had ever sunned there before, and how everybody she met was the best Antiguan body to meet, and no one told us that this person we were putting ourselves out for on such a big scale, this person we were getting worked up about as if she were God Himself, was in our midst because of something so common, so everyday: her life was not working out the way she had hoped, her life was one big mess.

Have you ever wondered to yourself why it is that all people like me seem to have learned from you is how to imprison and murder each other, how to govern badly, and how to take the wealth of our country and place it in Swiss bank accounts? Have you ever wondered why it is that all we seem to have learned from you is how to corrupt our societies and how to be tyrants? You will have to accept that this is mostly your fault. Let me just show you how you looked to us. You came. You took things that were not yours, and you did not even, for appearances' sake, ask first. You could have said, "May I have this, please?" and even though it would have been clear to everybody that a yes or no from us would have been of no consequence you might have looked so much better. Believe me, it would have gone a long way. I would have had to admit that at least you were polite. You murdered people. You imprisoned people. You robbed people. You opened your own banks, and you put our money in them. The accounts were in your name. The banks were in your name. There must have been some good people among you, but they stayed home. And that is the point. That is why they are good. They stayed home. But still, when you think about it, you must be a little sad. The people like me, finally, after years and years of agitation, made deeply moving and eloquent speeches against the wrongness of your domination over us, and then finally, after the mutilated bodies of you, your wife, and your children were found in your beautiful and spacious bungalow at the edge of your rubber plantation—found by one of your many house servants—you say to me, "Well, I wash my hands of all of you, I am leaving now," and you leave, and from afar you watch as we do to ourselves the very things you used to do to us. And you might feel that there was more to you than that, you might feel that you had understood the meaning of the Age of Enlightenment; you loved knowledge, and wherever you went you made sure to build a school, a library. But then again, perhaps as you observe the debacle in which I now exist, the utter ruin that I say is my life, perhaps you are remembering that you had always felt people like me cannot run things, people like me will never grasp the idea of Gross National Product, people like me will never be able to take command of the thing the most simple-minded among you can master, people like me will never understand the notion of rule by law, people like me cannot really think in abstractions, people like me cannot be objective, we make everything so personal. You will forget your part in the whole setup, that bureaucracy is one of your inventions, that Gross National Product is one of your inventions, and all the laws that you know mysteriously favor you. Do you know why people like me are shy about being capitalists? Well, it's because we, for as long as we have known you, *were* capital, like bales of cotton and sacks of sugar, and you were the commanding, cruel capitalists, and the memory of this is so strong, the experience so recent, that we can't quite bring ourselves to embrace this idea that you think so much of. As for what we were like before we met you, I no longer care. No periods of time over which my ancestors held sway, no documentation of complex civilizations, is any comfort to me. Even if I really came from people who were living like monkeys in trees, it was better to be that than what happened to me, what I became after I met you.

BEBE MOORE CAMPBELL
(1950—)

◆

BEBE MOORE CAMPBELL, freelance journalist, recipient of a National Endowment for the Arts and Literature grant, and author of *Successful Women, Angry Men* (1987), the prize-winning play *Old Lady Shoes*, the memoir *Sweet Summer: Growing Up With and Without My Dad* (1989), and the novel *Your Blues Ain't Like Mine* (1992), currently lives in Los Angeles with her husband and daughter. In an engaging interview she gave to Lisa See for *Publishers Weekly* she discusses the origin and context of her memoir *Sweet Summer,* the first chapter of which appears here. She conceived the book after receiving an overwhelming response to a piece she did for the *Washington Post* celebrating Father's Day. The book is her story of growing up as the daughter of divorced parents, one of whom stayed in the South while the other moved North to Philadelphia. The child went North with her mother, but Bebe Moore spent the summers with her paraplegic father in North Carolina and in her narrative she lovingly details the bond that developed between the father and daughter separated by divorce. During the school year she was raised in a doubly female-headed household by a fiercely responsible mother and grandmother, and a host of aunts, uncles, teachers, friends, and pastors of the Faith Tabernacle Baptist Church. As she put it in her interview, "Things that might have destroyed me didn't, because my family had empowered me. There's strength in that which can help you rise above circumstance." (On her word processor she has stuck a note to herself: "Trust your hopes, not your fears.") She wrote *Sweet Summer* to give others her experience of being cherished as a child, especially by her father, whose weaknesses she came to recognize and accept as she got older; she also wanted to challenge the negative stereotypes of black fathers with her own life history. That personal experience helped her to understand that "in every community, the traditional responsibility for the father is to be the breadwinner, but it's often hard for black men to be breadwinners. There's a stereotype that black fathers are deserters, but it's not because they're bred to walk away." Novelist Paule Marshall, in response to this book's implicit compassionate plea on behalf of all fathers and their capacity for nurturing love, described *Sweet*

Summer as "a deeply moving autobiography of a woman-child coming of age in the promised land, as well as a praise poem to a very special father and to the strong black men who shaped her being." Poet Nikki Giovanni (see page 365) praised this memoir as "one of the more overdue books about and for the black community." The author's reverence toward that community rings especially strong in her conclusion: "Long ago I realized that love is all that is required of fatherhood, that love will spark the action that it takes to mold a child. I have grown strong and whole from the blessings of my many fathers. . . . I was given a rich and privileged childhood, an American childhood, a solid foundation on which to stand and, yes, even go forward. I was guided by good men, powerful men. I was raised right."

From *Sweet Summer:*
Growing Up With and Without My Dad

When my father died, old men went out of my life. From the vantage point of my girlhood, he and his peers had always been old to me, even when they were not. In his last years, the reality of his graying head began to hit home. I no longer boogied the weekends away in smoke-clogged rooms that gyrated all night with Motown sounds, where I'd take a breather from the dancing by leaning up against the wall, sipping a sloe gin fizz and spewing out fire-laced rhetoric of "death to the pigs." I was a mature young wife, a mother even, three rungs from thirty, a home owner, a meal planner, who marched for an end to apartheid in front of the South African embassy only often enough to feel guilty. I made vague plans to care for him in his dotage. Care for him on a teacher's salary, in the middle of a marriage that was scratching against the blackboard with its fingernails, in a two-bedroom brick fixer-upper my husband, daughter and I had outgrown the moment we moved in. That was the plan.

When he died in 1977, I suppose, a theoretical weight was lifted, since Daddy was a paraplegic because of a car accident he'd had when I was ten months old. No doubt his senior-citizen years would have been expensive and exhausting for me. And then too, I had other potential dependents. I mused about the future, fantasized about my role as a nurturer of old people, feeling vaguely smug and settled, maybe a little bourgeois.

The afternoon was muggy as only a D.C. summer afternoon can be. The humidity and my afro were duking it out on the tiny sun porch of our home, the ring being the area immediately above the base of my neck, the hair coffee-colored grandmamas laughingly call the "kitchen." It is the hair I hated most as a child. The rest of my head was covered with a wavy-frizzy mixture that proclaimed my black ancestry had been intruded upon. My "kitchen" has always been hard-core naps, straight from the shores of Dahomey. Benin, they call it now. From time to time I'd tug my fingers haphazardly through the tight web of kinks, trying to make my recalcitrant hair obey me and separate into manageable clumps of curls. The hair was simply too dense back there. I would need my big black comb with the wide-spaced prongs, something heavy like that to pry my rebellious locks apart. All I was doing was hurting my fingers. I raised the window higher for more air. The faint smell of roses wafted in on a thin, damp breeze.

"I am not your responsibility, darling," Mommy had said in a brisk, businesslike tone of voice that still managed to sound loving when, on one of my frequent visits to Philly, I broached the subject of my caring for her when she got old. Each word my mother uttered stood at attention, like a soldier doing battle in the war for improved communication. But what should I have expected from a woman who was absolutely savage about enunciation, pronunciation, speaking co-rrectly, so that *they* would approve. My mother viewed speaking impeccably proper English as a strategy in the overall battle for civil rights. "Bebe, we've got to be prepared," she'd say briskly.

When as a child I said, "He be going," my mother's eyes would widen as big as silver dollars and the corners of her mouth would get dry and chalky-looking. She'd clench her throat with wide, splaying fingers and spring into action, like a fireman sniffing a cigarette in a forest and dousing it before flames erupt. "Don't say that." Her voice would be firm and patiently instructive. "That's a Negro colloquialism. Totally incorrect. They'll think you're dumb if you talk like that." They, always they.

She was sitting at her small mahogany desk in the dining room, her glasses propped on her nose, sorting papers into neat little stacks, bundling them together with rubber bands. Glancing down I saw that the papers were related to her church work, Alpha Kappa Alpha sorority, her volunteer work with a senior citizens' group and her membership on the grievance board of Holmesburg Prison, all overwhelmingly dignified pursuits. Although she was no longer a social worker for the city, my dear mother's retirement consisted of running feverishly from one volunteer gig to the next one, all for the uplifting of the race. My mother has always been and will always be a very lift-every-voice-and-sing type of sister, a woman who takes her Christian duty very seriously. Under the desk she crossed her short, brown legs and tapped her foot a little. "Clara and I will probably take a fabulous apartment together, one of those new complexes with everything inside, a laundry, a grocery store, cleaners, everything. Or by that time, my goodness, the church's senior-citizen complex will be ready and I'll just move in there. Or I'll stay here." She smiled serenely at me for a brief moment, her smooth brown face full of sunshine, then excused herself to continue working on the church bulletins.

"Senior citizens' complex!" I let my words explode in the air. "You *want* to live in an old folks' home? Mommy, that's not our culture." I finished, totally disgusted.

Mommy looked at me, her eyes squinched up in laughter, a grin spreading across her face. She loves for me to mess with her, gets a big kick out of my tongue-in-cheek assaults on her dignity. As if anything could ever put a dent in her dignity.

"Here I am, offering you a secure place in your old age, nutritious hot meals, no abuse, make sure you get your high-blood-pressure medicine. All you have to do is sign over the ole pension, SS check, bonds, CDs, deed to your property, and you get the run of the place. Do whatever you want to do. Want to have the AKAs over? The sorors can come. You get to have a boyfriend. All the sex you want! I'm talking about the best the black extended family has to offer. And you want to go . . . "

"I don't have high blood pressure," my mother said, chuckling and dabbing at her eyes.

"Yet, yet . . . "

My mother whooped.

"What about your arthritis?" I asked in an aha! kind of tone, truly alarmed at the notion of my aged mother hobbling to a dingy basement laundromat, sorting faded bras and well-worn girdles while her ancient sidekick, Clara, threw her yellowed undies into the motley heap.

Doris looked at me as if the word "lunatic" had suddenly become emblazoned on my forehead. Her shoulders and her full upper lip went stiff; the nostrils in her wide nose flared slightly. "What are you talking about, girl? I don't have any arthritis. If you're referring to the occasional stiffness in my knees, I've had that since I was a young girl and it's not going to get any worse. Darling," she said, her tone softening a little, her hands still busily sorting, stacking, writing, "you have your family to look after. A baby. Don't worry about me. I'll go right on, the same as always."

So that was that; my mother was immortal. However, if by some fluke lightning struck or the rapture came and my divine mother was sent soaring away from this earth on diaphanous wings, merrily pumping her way to heaven with stiff knees, then, then I'd be duty-bound to take in Nana.

My feisty grandmother could talk the naps out of any black child's kitchen. Mouth all mighty. Mouth's mammy. I was Nana's sole choice for a caretaker, since her only other children, my Aunt Ruth and my namesake, Aunt Bebe, were dead and her only other grandchild, my cousin Michael, was engaged in a perennial search—finding himself—that made his life-style suspect. Nana wasn't into living with anyone whose phone was on one day and off the next. "Hell, I might as well have stayed in Virginia and picked cotton if I didn't want to do any better," she told me with a snort, referring to her and her parents' migration from the grips of the sharecropping South, aeons ago when she was a baby. For the record, Nana had never picked cotton a day in her life, but all the same, she was fervent about black economic progress and she found Michael's gypsy ways appalling. What was worse, what was intolerable was that her only grandson didn't have a job, at least not a steady one.

"The boy is mad," she said one day as we were snapping string beans in her kitchen. Her large almond-shaped eyes flashed. Nana's eyes were bright, the white part startlingly clear. She was small and plump, the color of a lemon wafer. "Gorgeous in my day, honey," she'd tell you in a minute. "I had all the men frothing at the mouth." Gold hoop earrings dangled at her ears. She gave off subtle whiffs of Estée Lauder, and when she spoke I could smell Doublemint chewing gum. "Smart boy like that. Nice-looking," she said disgustedly. "They need to put him in some government work camp or something." Nana's "they" was different from my mother's. More all-encompassing. Whoever made the rules, set the tone, that was Nana's "they."

"The depression is over, sweetheart. There are no work camps anymore."

"Well, then they should put his ass in the Army!" she snapped.

"Who is 'they'?" I asked, just for fun. Nana laughed. "Anyway, you can't force someone to be in the Army. And besides, he's too old."

Nana put down her beans. Her fingers were motionless in front of her. "You think he's ever gonna get himself together?" Nana's eyes were brimming with concern.

"What do you think?"

Nana sighed and began rubbing at her temples, where her hair was mostly gray, with the base of her thumbs so as to keep her fingers clean. Her eyes stared right into mine as she pulled her hands away from her hair and reached across the table and grabbed my wrist, squeezing it tightly with her thick fingers. "If anything happens to your mother you'll have to take me, Bebe," she whispered.

I simply nodded, too surprised at the sudden serious turn her outburst about Michael had taken. If I had been thinking, I would have
said flippantly, "Nuh unh, honey. Sending your butt straight to the old
folks' home with your daughter. Come see you every Tuesday." I could
have lightened the moment a little, but I chose not to, probably because
deep inside I didn't think Nana would outlive Mom. She didn't want
to. Nana was seventy-five when we had this little talk and was beginning to show unmistakable signs of a disenchantment with life. Her old
folks' blues would become increasingly more sorrowful as she
approached her eighties. The older she got, the clearer it was that she
was ready to "pass."

At seventy-nine, she called me one late afternoon and wailed into
the telephone. "I don't like it anymore. I can't even go out in the winter; I'm so scared I'll fall on the ice and break my ass. And I don't even
have a boyfriend," she cried, her voice high and piercing, plaintive.
"What kind of life is that?"

A life with no rustling taffeta dresses, no fire-engine-red toes and
fingers, no mambo nights, no baritones calling on the phone. For my
jazzy grandmother (I still thought of her that way), no life. No life at all.

Whatever frailties owned her, she still possessed the strength to will
herself right on out of this world. Seven years after my father's death, I
believe she did just that. Only days after her eightieth birthday and a
few weeks before the first Philadelphia snowstorm of 1984 could trap
her for yet another season, Nana slipped off her red velvet bedroom
slippers, lay down on the sofa in the living room of the house I grew
up in, and fell into a dreamless, endless sleep.

When I thought about my father I realized that he had a strong will
too, and maybe more reasons not to want to live to be older than Nana.
You could see that will in the way he jutted out his chin, the quick way
he moved and drove. He liked speed because it was powerful, as strong
as he always wanted to be. I knew George Moore's mental powers
would never be used to precipitate his leaving this earth any sooner
than absolutely necessary. Right after the accident the doctors told him
he wouldn't live out the year because of the damage that had been
done to his kidneys. He made the decision right then. Put away the
razor blade he'd been clutching and pressing to his throat when he saw
his toes would never move again. Made a decision right then and there.
Started drinking gallons of water a day. Doing his exercises. Praying.
How he forced the sadness from his eyes I do not know. Only one time
did I witness him mourning the life he might have had. It was a terrible
moment, but a healing one. That split second taught me that the best
part of my father, the jewel stuck deep inside his core, was determina-

tion. George Moore was about living life until it was gone, wrested from him, snatched out of his clenched fist. He would play out the hand that had been dealt. My potbellied daddy wouldn't roll off resolutely to some senior citizen's palace to sip tea and play canasta, and he sure as hell didn't know any old guy he'd want for a roommate. Unmarried men living together, unless they were in the Army or Navy or something, seemed weird to him. No, he'd see his old age, his infirmities as something quite naturally to be shared with his only child. He wouldn't want to be a burden; he'd pay his way, share his little Social Security check so he would have a legitimate gripe when there weren't any pork chops in the house. And he'd be very useful; all the Moore men, my father and my seven uncles, have always had a tendency toward workaholism. They get up early and get busy; that's in their blood. Daddy would fix all the broken radios, clocks and televisions in the house. He'd do the plumbing and put in new electrical outlets. And of course, Daddy would tend the garden, since he could make anything grow. And much as he loved children, I'd have had a super built-in baby-sitter. If there was no work, no ball game on television and he couldn't get a decent conversation going, he'd just leave, go for a ride or something. He had a car with hand controls for the accelerator and brakes. Icy streets wouldn't keep Daddy inside a house where there was nothing to do, nobody to chew the fat and trade stories with. And he wouldn't be rushing off to attend some important, purposeful meeting called by the NAACP, the Neighborhood Association, the Coalition of 100 Black Men, or even Omega Psi Phi fraternity, of which he was a very nonactive member. He'd left behind those kinds of gatherings in his other life, the one I knew nothing about, the one he titled "Before I got hurt." No, Daddy would go riding just to hang out. And not alone, either. At least that's what I thought on that day in Washington as the fragrant, moist air mixed in my hair, rendering my kitchen absolutely impassable to my wandering fingers.

I remembered the sweet North Carolina summers of my childhood, my father's snappy "C'mon, kiddo. Let's go for a ride," when life was boring sitting in Grandma Mary's house or the yard. There was a ritual my father had to endure before he and I could zoom away down the one-car-wide dirt lane that led to the larger tar road. He'd roll his wheelchair right up between his open car door and the driver's seat and hoist himself from his chair to the car seat with one powerful thrust of his body. Then he'd clutch his leg, which would invariably start twitching with involuntary muscle spasms. When the shaking stopped, he'd lean out of his car seat, snatch his chair closed, press his body into the steering wheel, pulling the back of his seat up so that he could lift his chair into the backseat of the car. This done, he'd take out a white handkerchief, wipe his drenched forehead and look over at me and grin. Then I'd hop into the seat next to his and we'd take off. In those days I was his partner, his roadie, his little minimama homegirl. In the summer he hardly went anywhere without me. And I believed, as I engaged in my humid, sun-porch reverie, my probing fingers struggling inside the tangle of my kitchen, that I would be all those things again, that when my father got old he would need me.

The thought of our living together for the first time since I was a child delighted me, since it was in such stark contrast to the female-centered home I'd grown up in after my parents separated and my mother and I moved from North Carolina to Nana's house in Philadelphia. Realistically, though, living with my father would present special challenges. There were, of course, the implications of his paralysis, and his lack of mobility was complicated by his size. There were over two hundred pounds of him sitting in that chair. He was the black man's Chief Ironside. Well, maybe Raymond Burr had a couple of pounds on him. He tried to play it off when I teased him about his gut. Daddy would pat his belly, grin and say, "The chippies' playground, baby girl." Still, Daddy would be no fun to heave up and down stairs or in and out of a bathtub, although periodically, when he set his mind on losing weight, my father dieted quite successfully and could knock off thirty or forty pounds. When he was on a diet, I don't care how many pork chops you floated under George Moore's nose, the boy wasn't eating. That kind of doggedness enabled him in his later years finally to cut loose the Winstons he had inhaled with passion when he was younger. When he set his mind on something, that was it. Nobody had more determination than Daddy. So maybe the weight wouldn't have been a problem. What would have irritated me, though, was his innate ability to run the helpless bit into the ground at times, at least with me. Maybe only with me.

The summer before he died I drove from D.C. to the outskirts of Richmond for a visit and stayed with him at the home where he boarded with an elderly widow named Mrs. Murphy. He had only recently begun working for the federal government in personnel. He was, in affirmative-action terms, a twofer: black and disabled. Finally he was beginning to make decent money. He was sick the day I came to see him, something that rarely happened to him. Aside from his useless legs, he was robust. He rarely even got so much as a cold, although, of course, from time to time he had to go into the McGuire VA Hospital for a stay to have his damaged kidneys checked out. The day I went to visit him he had the flu and was coughing like crazy, drinking water like a fiend, snorting, trying to let out his Big Daddy Jumbo Pasquotank County farts on the sly and rattling on and on about the stock market, his latest in a long line of plans to become wealthy. To his dying day he never saw his becoming rich as something out of the realm of ordinary possibilities. His was the American dream: to work hard and have it pay off big. "Yeah, baby. Your ole daddy's gonna make us some money." He tossed off the titles of stocks and prices per share, totally losing me amid the names and numbers. Sensing my disinterest, he said disgustedly, "You ought to listen to this, girl. I'm telling you, we can make us some money." When my only response was to shrug my shoulders, Daddy shook his head. His mood turned bossy. "Bebe, go get Daddy some more cough syrup." "Bebe, go get Daddy a big ole glass of ice water." "Bebe, go empty this urine duct for your ole sick Daddy." Which was pushing it, because I hated rinsing out his urine ducts. And he knew it. But I did it that day, holding way out ahead of me the rubber duct that contained the acrid-smelling waste he could no longer control. I turned my head in the small, cramped bathroom that held his toothbrush at one end of the sink and Mrs. Murphy's teeth in a cup at the other, as I emptied the urine into the toilet, and again as I rinsed the containers out in the special buckets Mrs. Murphy kept right next to the small commode.

When I returned to his bedroom, Daddy was laid up in the bed like some imperial royal highness, flashing me a slightly wan but still very dazzling smile as I handed him his duct; I turned my head as he fiddled under the covers, attaching the thing to himself. The room needed ten shots of Air-Fresh. He cleared his throat when he finished. Then he grinned at me.

My daddy had a killer of a smile and I think he knew it. I know he knew it. His teeth were so white, so perfectly straight they were startling. Big, white, even teeth. Chiclets. And his grin was just a little crooked, and that's what made him such a charming smiler. On that particular day, I wasn't falling for his charm. "Don't ask me to do one more thing, old man," I said, as sourly as I could.

"BebebebebebeMoore," Daddy sang out, throwing his big, heavy arm around my shoulder when I stopped fussing. I was sitting on the side of his bed, one leg under me, the other leg swinging, my big toe just brushing the floor as I looked at a magazine, my hips against his very still legs. The air had returned to normal and I thought to myself, George Linwood Peter Moore, please do not funk up this room with another one of those jumbo farts. I looked up and he was smiling that killer smile. "Don't bother me, old man," I said.

What can I say? Daddy would have run my ass raggedy, but he was so charming I wouldn't have minded. To have my father at the dinner table every night, to watch television with him in the early evening, to discuss books and politics, what Ted Koppel said, to go shopping with him and take rides in his car, I would have emptied his urine ducts to have all that.

But this is what I really wanted to see: Daddy and Maia being crazy about each other. He saw his granddaughter only once before he died. She was an infant at the time and I remember he took her out of my arms because I wasn't burping her right. He showed me how to do it, which didn't surprise me because whenever my father took me to visit people there were usually little kids or babies around. The children would jump up in his lap or climb on the back of his chair. He was used to burping babies. "Where'd you get this little red thing from anyway?" he teased, propping Maia up on his lap and smiling at her, lifting her up and down and shaking her gently. "Hey there, baby girl. Hey, little bit. What her got to say to ole Grandad, huh?"

They would have loved each other. I can see Maia sitting in Granddad's lap for hours, falling asleep in his arms, waking up and giggling as he rolled his wheelchair back and forth to amuse her. I can see her standing on the bracers on the back of his chair, placing her tiny arms around his neck. And when she was older, what a pair they would have made: a little brown-skinned girl and the heavyset man in the chair, she pushing him into the park near the water when they went for rides there. Daddy would go to her school plays and to open house and watch Maia as she pirouetted across the stage or recited a Paul Laurence Dunbar poem in church, his applause the loudest in the audience, his smile the brightest.

And my uncles, my father's seven brothers, would come to visit when Daddy came to live with us. John. Elijah. Eddie. Cleat. Joe. Sammy. Norman. On Sundays my husband and I would have to put the two leaves in the dining room table to accommodate two or three of my uncles and maybe their families. And my father's men friends would visit also. It wasn't such a long ride from North Carolina or Richmond to D.C. I imagine Tank Jackson, who was also paralyzed, but from World War II, driving his block-long Lincoln to our door and the two men rolling their chairs into the backyard to have beer and pretzels and me baking something whenever my uncles or Tank came to visit, a potato pie or a coconut cake, and making lemonade too, even in the winter. It would be easy enough to tear out one of the rose bushes and have a ramp put in that would lead right to the door. When Daddy pulled himself up the ramp, as he got older, I'd stand behind him and say, "Can you make it all right, old man?"

The day before my father died I was a bridesmaid in my best friend's wedding and was staying with friends in Pittsburgh. My hostess awakened me around three or four o'clock Sunday morning and told me my uncle was on the phone. Uncle Norman's signature has always been brevity, an innate ability to get to the point with a minimum of fanfare or bullshit. When I picked up the phone he said, "Bebe, this is Norman. Your father died in a car accident this morning." Just like that. Then, "Did you hear me? Honey, did you hear Uncle Norman?"

A car accident, I thought, the phone still in my hand, Uncle Norman still talking, another car accident. That wasn't supposed to happen, is what ran through my mind. How did that happen twice in one life? Twice in two lives? Somehow, with the room spinning and my head aching, I listened to the rest of his instructions. I was to return home the next day and Uncle Cleat would take me to Richmond to identify the car and sign papers at the police station. We'd get Daddy's things at Mrs. Murphy's. Uncle Johnny, the eldest of Grandma Mary's eleven children, was having my father's body transported to North Carolina, where he would be buried in the family plot behind Grandma Mary's house. "He was coming to see you, Bebe," Uncle Norman said. "He didn't know you were out of town. You know your daddy, he just hopped in the car and got on the road. He was bringing a camera to take pictures of the baby."

When Uncle Norman said that, I remembered the pictures I'd promised to send Daddy weeks before and felt the first flicker of pain course through my body. Something swept through me, hot as lightning. All at once I was shaking and crying. God. He shouldn't have died like that, all alone out on a highway, slumped over the wheel like some fragile thing who couldn't take a good hard knock. God.

It was cool and dim in the funeral parlor, and filled with a strange odor I'd never smelled before. There were three rooms full of caskets—bronze, dark wood, light wood, pastels. A dizzying array. The funeral director was a friend of the family. Mr. Walson had an uncanny affinity for professional solemnity. He referred to Daddy as "the body." Did I wish to see the body? Was I satisfied with the appearance of the body? Did I care for knotty pine or cherry wood? He said this, his dark face devoid of all emotion, his expansive belly heaving threateningly against the dangerously thin belt around his waist. The same odd smell that filled the room clung to Mr. Walson. What was that smell? I leaned against Uncle Johnny and felt his hand on my shoulder. Upon learning that my grief was buttressed by a healthy insurance policy, Mr. Walson urged me to choose the cherry wood. I looked at Uncle Johnny questioningly; he has always known how to take charge. Maybe it comes from being the oldest. If he tells you to do something, you do it. "We'll take the cherry," he told the funeral director, who assured me he would take care of everything. But he could not, of course, take care of me. My grief was private and not covered.

As we left the funeral parlor, Uncle Johnny took my hand. "Do you know what your big-head daddy wanted to do?"

I shook my head.

"After I retired and moved down here next to Mama, he tried to talk me into doing some hog farming with him. Said we could make a lot of money. I told that joker, 'Man, I came down here to rest.'" Uncle Johnny looked at me. He was smiling. "Your daddy loved making money, didn't he, girl?"

"Loved it."

The cars rolled slowly up the unpaved lane that led to Grandma Mary's house, a fleet of Cadillacs, shiny, long and black, moving quietly, and stirring up dust that flew everywhere, clinging to everyone, coating shoes and suits and dresses, blowing in hair and on faces, where particles finally lodged in eyes that blinked, blinked, blinked then looked away.

It is still cool in North Carolina in April, a perfect time for a family reunion. Crowded in Grandma's yard were all the faces that looked like her face, the resemblance lying somewhere between the chin and the character lines that ran straight across high foreheads. There were others standing next to the ones who looked like her, so many people that their feet would have crushed Grandma's zinnias had they been in bloom.

The people looked up when the Cadillacs drove into the yard. They broke away from the joyous hugs of reunion, of North once again meeting South, put their cameras back into their bags and stood silently, at attention. The gray-haired old ladies fanned themselves with miscellaneous bits of paper, the backs of magazines, newspapers, napkins, even though it wasn't warm. All of a sudden there was a circle, shoulders touching, everyone's breath mingling into a giant sigh. Somebody, my daddy's first cousin, the preacher from New York, was praying, offering to the Lord brief, familiar words that the occasion called for: higher ground, no more suffering, home. The words fell around the crowd like soft pieces of flower petals. An old woman began to sing. The lyrics came back to the people who'd taken that long-ago bus ride from Pasquotank County to Philly, Jersey, New York, in heady rushes. All wiped the dust from their eyes and joined in. The last note had scarcely disappeared before Mr. Walson's assistants began calling the names of immediate family members and leading them to the limousines: ". . . Mr. and Mrs. John Moore, Mr. and Mrs. Elijah Moore." Grandma Mary gripped my fingers as I helped her into the car where my husband and daughter were waiting. I was about to sit down when I felt a hand on my back. I turned around. "How ya making out, kiddo?" It was Sammy, my Marine uncle, the hero of my childhood. Whenever I saw him I thought of starched uniforms, even though he hadn't been in the service for years.

"Okay, so far," I said. I took his hand.

He squeezed my fingers and helped me into the car. "I'm here if you need me," he said.

Later, when I was looking into the layers of expensive satin, blinking frantically as the top of the smooth cherry-wood coffin closed, it occurred to me that more than my father had passed away. Not only had I lost a treasured friend, but gone was the ease with which I could connect to his brothers, his male friends.

After he was buried, Grandma Mary's old friend Miss Lilly or Miss Lizzy, Miss Somebody, whose face had floated in and out of my childhood summers, a wiry woman with lines like railroad tracks on skin the color of a paper bag, put her hand in mine and whispered, "Baby, you sho' put him away nice. Yes you did, chile," then, even more quietly, "God knows best, baby." She gave my arm three hard pats. Be . . . all . . . right. Don't . . . you . . . cry. Hush . . . baby . . . hush. I nodded to her, but later when I was alone I had a singular contemplation: his death wasn't for the best. That clear knowing hit me square upside my head after the last of the heavy North Carolina loam had covered the cherry-wood coffin, after Aunt Edith, my father's youngest sister, had heaved a final mournful wail that pierced through the surrounding fields of soybeans and corn that bordered my grandmother's house, then slowly faded. And what I felt wasn't even pain or grief. Just regret, gripping me like a steel claw.

In a way, it was like the end of an ordinary family reunion. I stood at the edge of the lane with Grandma Mary and watched the last of the out-of-town license plates careen down that narrow dirt road, leaving behind a cloud of dust. Pennsylvania. New Jersey. New York. Tomorrow would be another work day, regular and hard.

In the kitchen my father's mother looked tired, every one of her eighty-six years filling her eyes. She held onto the small table as she walked.

"Grandma, why don't you go to bed," I said.

"I reckon I will," she replied. I kissed her on the cheek. She stumbled and grabbed my shoulder to get her balance. "Is you gone get your daddy's car fixed?"

Her question jolted me. I hadn't given my father's Cadillac any thought since Uncle Cleat and I had left it at the mechanic's in Richmond. Soon I would be whipping around doing a "Detroit lean" out the window of George Moore's hog. Wouldn't he love to see that, I thought. "It's being fixed now, Grandma," I said.

"He sure did like that car," she mused almost to herself. "That boy loved pretty cars." She looked straight at me. "Don't bring it up the lane when you come. Hear?" I had to smile to myself. Grandma was loyal to the end. She stubbornly reasoned it was the machine at fault, and not her beloved son. I understood.

So I cleaned the kitchen, mourning my loss with each sweep of Grandma Mary's broom, each swipe of the battered dish cloth, and thought about this father whose entire possessions had fit neatly into the trunk of his yellow Cadillac, which now was mine.

I took my father's wheelchair back to D.C., even though Aunt Edith asked me if I wanted to give it to one of the old ladies in the neighborhood who was having a hard time getting around. I remember I said, "No, I want it," so fast and maybe so fiercely that Edith blinked and stepped away from me. Though why I wanted it, who knows. I put Daddy's chair in my basement and let it collect dust. Sometimes when I was washing clothes I'd look at it. The most I ever did was touch it occasionally.

In the months that followed, the fat insurance checks my father left me transformed my life-style, but at that moment I could feel his death reshaping my life, or at least the life I thought I was entitled to. There are gifts that only a father can give a daughter: his daily presence, his daily molding, his thick arm across thin girlish shoulder, his solemn declaration that she is beautiful and worthy. That her skin is radiant, the flare of her nostrils pretty. *Yeah, and Daddy's baby sure does have some big, flat feet, but that's all right. That's all right now. Come here, girl, and let Daddy see those tight, pretty curls, them kitchen curls.* I was all prepared to receive a daily ration of such gifts, albeit belatedly, but it was not to be. I would never serve beer and pretzels in the yard to Daddy and Tank. I would never have his company as I cleaned the dishes. He wouldn't see Maia's plays or her recitals. That was the way the cards had been dealt. I would go to my uncles, they wouldn't come to me. And the time for even those visits would later be eroded by obligations and miles. After April 1977 the old men in my life just plain thinned out.

For one thing, I got divorced and later remarried and moved far away to Los Angeles. After Grandma died, Uncle Johnny and Aunt Rena moved to Georgia near Aunt Rena's people. "You come see us," he told me before he left. "Don't forget; I'm your pop now." My Uncle

Eddie finally sold his grocery store and moved from Philly to North Carolina, so I couldn't conveniently drop in at his market and chew the fat with him when I came to town to see Mom and Nana. Uncle Elijah died and I couldn't even go to his funeral, because my money was real funny that month. I sent flowers and called his wife, but what could I say? I should have been there.

My Marine uncle became a preacher. Uncle Sammy doesn't whoop and holler; his message is just plain good-sense gospel. He can even get scientific on you. When I hear his message I am thinking the whole time.

Uncle Norman and I still talk, but mostly on the telephone. My youngest uncle would call me up in hell, just to find out how I was getting treated. He is busy with his family and business. We don't see each other often.

The last time I saw Tank was a few weeks after the funeral, when he picked me up at the Greyhound bus station in Richmond and took me to get my father's car. Tank's skin is like a country night—no moon, no stars. You don't know what black is until you look in his face. Daddy always told me he wasn't much of a talker, and he's not, but he was just so nice and polite, sitting up in that big Lincoln, being my chauffeur. "Just tell me where you want to go," he said when I got into the car. We drove all over Richmond. Tank took me to where my father worked, to Mrs. Murphy's, everywhere.

Around two o'clock we pulled into McDonald's and he bought hamburgers, french fries and sodas for our lunch; the car was filled with the aroma of greasy food. We were both famished and we ate without talking at first. All you could hear was our lips smacking against our Big Macs. Al Green was singing, "Love will make a waaay . . ." on the radio. Tank looked at me and said, "Ole Be Be," as though astonished that little girls grow up and become women. He said my name the way older southerners are wont to, two distinct syllables. I love the sound. But it was weird, because as soon as he said my name like that, I caught sight of his wheelchair in the rearview mirror and at the same time thought about Maia, whom I'd left in D.C. with a girlfriend. I was still nursing her and I immediately felt pins and needles in my breasts, and when I looked at my blouse there were two huge wet milk rings. Tank looked, he looked away, then he looked again. Then he said, as if thinking aloud, "That's right. Moore's a grandaddy."

Tank's chair was very shiny in the mirror. His words hung between us real softly for a minute before I started up, which I'd sworn I wasn't going to do. I put my head on his shoulder and I just cried and cried and cried. Tears wouldn't stop. "George was right crazy about you, Be

Be. Talked about you all the time. All the time," Tank said shyly. He offered up these words as the gift they were. I just nodded.

There have never been enough idle moments really to straighten out those tight, tight curls at the nape of my neck. Untangling a kitchen calls for a protracted, concentrated effort. You have to be serious. It is not a job for weak fingers on a summer's afternoon. Still, daydreaming fingers, even those caught up in tangles, reveal much.

It has proved to be true, what I felt looking into my father's satin-lined casket: my loss was more than his death, much more. Those men who used to entice me with their storytelling, yank my plaits, throw me quarters and tell me what a pretty girl I was are mostly beyond my reach now. But that's all right. When they were with me they were very much with me. My father took to his grave the short-sleeved, beer-swilling men of summer, big bellies, raucous laughter, pipe smoke and the aroma of cigars. My daddy is really gone and his vacant place is my cold, hard border. As always, my life is framed by his absence. . . .

BEVERLY DONOFRIO
(1950—)

———————◆———————

BEVERLY DONOFRIO grew up in Wallingford, Connecticut, in a conventional and sexist Italian-American family. When she was in the tenth grade, her mother told her she would not be going to college. She urged her smart daughter, who wanted to go the University of Connecticut and had the grades, to become a typist.

"Somebody would have to pay," thought the daughter.

Riding in Cars with Boys: Confessions of a Bad Girl Who Makes Good, excerpted here, is a memoir of growth and transcendence of teenage rebellion against the sexual stereotyping of a dominating policeman-father and subservient housewife-mother. In her senior year of high school, Beverly Donofrio turned up pregnant. She married and a short time later divorced. Her autobiographical narrative charts the zigzags of her growing up alongside her young son during the era of the Vietnam War, in and out of patterns of self-destruction and self-invention. As a single mother, she constructed her salvation out of education, the old dream of the sassy tenth-grader. She went to a community college, then transferred to Wesleyan University, scholarship and son in hand, and after graduation moved to New York, became a freelance writer, saw her son through Stuyvesant High School, and drove him off to college.

This story of teenage pregnancy and single motherhood offers a darkly comic and painful angle on "family values" in the context of small-town working-class America. In an article in the *Village Voice*, "Bad Girls Like Me" (January 21, 1992), Donofrio writes of the relevance of her life history to contemporary teenagers:

"Back in 1968, I became one of those infamous girls who got pregnant in high school. The experience was so traumatic I spent ten years sorting out my feelings then spilling them on paper to write a memoir of my life as a teen mother and hippie on welfare who hits rock bottom before she finds a way to get herself to college. The book came out last year, and a little later I received a phone call from a woman with a distinct Long Island accent who introduced herself as Joanne Savio and told me she'd read *Riding in Cars with Boys* and wanted to invite me to read at her school. The school is called EPPPA, Educational Program for Pregnant and Parenting Adolescents."

What Donofrio told the students is the core wisdom of her book: "'Let's face it,' I said. 'You're handicapped, so you need to give yourself an edge.' Basically, I told them that edge was education. . . . Education had saved my life.'"

And though she doesn't mention it, so had Donofrio's sense of humor. Phyllis Theroux's comment is especially apt to the childbirth scene excerpted here: "This book will be a classic. Unless you hate to laugh, read it now." Susan Minot reviewed *Riding in Cars with Boys* as a "wonderful book! Her story has all the bad girl freshness and vitality to make it true to the bone."

This memoir also suggests the psychological context explored in a popular text of Women's Studies programs, *Women's Ways of Knowing: The Development of Self, Voice, and Mind,* in particular its profile of women who change from passivity to action, from acceptance of external authority to "a protesting inner voice and infallible gut":

"Our reading of . . . women's stories," write authors Mary Belenky, Blythe Clinchy, Nancy Goldberger, and Jill Tarule, "leads us to conclude that as a woman becomes more aware of the existence of inner resources for knowing and valuing . . . she finds an inner source of strength. A major developmental transition follows that has repercussions in her relationships, self-concept and self-esteem, morality, and behavior. Women's growing reliance on their intuitive processes is, we believe, an important adaptive move in the service of self-protection, self-assertion, and self-definition. Women become their own authorities."

That discovery is the bracing plot of *Riding in Cars with Boys.*

From *Riding in Cars with Boys:* *Confessions of a Bad Girl Who Makes Good*

CHAPTER 5

Labor started on a Sunday night in the middle of September. It was so hot that week that the neighborhood dogs had taken to roaming in packs in a flurry of heat madness. Cats dived under cars and into open cellar windows to escape them. One day I saw the dogs toss a doll in the air and rip it limb from limb, a cloud of white foam clinging to their coats. I was almost two weeks late, and if I didn't deliver soon, I was planning to throw myself in the middle of that pack of mangy dogs and be done for.

We went for macaroni at my mother's on Sunday, a ritual I'd missed maybe a half dozen times in my entire life, only this time I felt a pain after dinner while we were watching *The FBI* and eating lemon meringue pie, but I didn't say anything. Raymond wanted to stay for the Sunday night movie, but I told him I didn't feel too well and wanted to go home. As soon as we walked into our house, a slimy liquid drooled down the inside of my thigh. "Oooh, gross! Raymond!" I yelled. "I think I'm in labor."

"You're kidding," he said.

We tossed my overnight bag into the backseat of our Chevelle (my father had found it for five hundred dollars and co-signed for the loan), and I suggested we take a ride once around the duck pond before we went to the hospital. The new Beatles song "Hey Jude" came on the radio.

"That's it!" I said. "That's what we'll name her—June." I'd misheard the lyrics.

Ray drummed his thumbs on the dashboard, jerked his chin in and out, and said, "Cool."

I was scared to death in the labor room. First they shaved me, then they gave me an enema, then after I waddled out of the bathroom and back into the room, they laid me in a crib like a beached whale. Immediately, the nurse poked some fingers in. I was three fingers, the middle circle. Five fingers was the biggest. When you stretched that wide it was bingo, birth. The Puerto Rican women came in and left within half an hour, screaming, "*Mama! Mama! Mama!*"

There was a pretty woman lying in the crib across from me. "Hi," she said after the nurse left.

"Hi."

"I'm Louise Baker. This is my first baby. You too?"

"Yeah. My name's Beverly Bouchard."

"If I scream like those ladies, shoot me, okay?"

"You think it's gonna really hurt?"

"I'm sure it does, but it can't hurt that much."

"How long you been here?"

"About an hour. I haven't seen a doctor yet. I go to the clinic."

"So do I. I never saw you."

"That place is the pits." She pulled back her long blond hair and began making a braid. "I go to Central Connecticut College. I mean, I did. After I was six months, I quit. My boyfriend still goes there. I'll probably go back after the baby."

"What were you going to school for?"

"My major? Anthropology."

I wasn't sure I knew what that was, but I'd rather die than ask her. I noticed her legs weren't shaved. I wished I'd seen her at the clinic. Everybody else spoke Spanish, and there never were enough folding chairs to go around. I'd had to wait a minimum of four hours every time, and if I'd met Louise there, we could've talked for whole mornings. By now we'd be good friends. But, probably, a person who went to college would think I was too stupid.

"Do you have medical insurance?" she asked.

"No. You?"

"Do you realize if you don't marry, your boyfriend's insurance won't cover you? We refused to marry. We put our politics in action. Art and I believe it's an archaic formality binding you together by law. My parents don't even . . . oh boy. Here comes one."

My pains had stopped altogether. I told the nurse. A doctor came in. He was young and handsome. His hands were slender and long. I'd never laid eyes on him before. "Hello," he said. He looked at my chart. "Mrs. Bouchard, I hear your pains have stopped."

"Yes."

"We're going to give you a little something to get them started again, speed things up."

The nurse handed him a needle and he stuck it in my ass. Within ten minutes, I was in agony and there was no breather between contractions. The doctor came back and said, "Okay, Mrs. Bouchard, we're moving right along. Now, I'm going to give you some Demerol to ease it up a bit." He gave me another shot in the ass. Before I passed out, I had a hallucination. I saw the kitten I'd had when I was a kid. It was jumping up over and over again, trying to get in the crib with me.

I don't know how long I was out before I awoke to Louise screaming, "Oh God, oh God, oh God. Ah ah ah ah *aaaahhhhhh!*"

Sweat started raining from every pore of my body. When she stopped screaming, she saw me looking at her through the bars and said, "I'm sorry, but it hurts so much," then she started crying.

I wished I could die.

Louise was long gone when the nurse rolled me onto my back, put my ankles in my hands, and told me to push. It was too humiliating. I kept thinking how even Jacqueline Kennedy must've held her ankles in the air and grunted like she was taking a shit. The next time the nurse appeared, she looked between my legs and started breathing heavily. "Okay, Mrs. Bouchard, I'd like you to stop pushing now. We're paging your doctor. Don't worry, everything's fine."

"I can't help it," I cried. "I have to."

"Please, Mrs. Bouchard, try not to push," she said as she wheeled my cot into the delivery room. I felt betrayed by every living mother. Why hadn't they warned me?

"This is horrible." I started crying. "Where's the gas? Give me the gas," I yelled. "Don't I get gas?" The nurse strapped my knees into stirrups, then positioned a round mirror above to distract me. "Look, Mrs. Bouchard, look. You can see the head." It was slimy green and protruding. I covered my eyes and yelled, "Take it away, I can't stand it, I don't want to!" Finally, an Oriental intern walked in. They clamped a gas mask on my face and it was over.

When I awoke, the nurse held a wrinkled, ugly red baby in a white cloth out to me. "Congratulations, Mrs. Bouchard, you have a healthy eight-and-a-half-pound baby boy."

"Boy!" I screamed. His head was huge and shaped like a football. "What's the matter with his head? He has blond hair!" The nurse blanched. I covered my face with my hands and sobbed. It was as though my daughter had died. The baby girl with the pretty round head who'd been hiccupping, rolling over, and kicking inside me—the daughter who'd been my best friend for months—had been a boy all along. What would I do with him? I didn't even like boys anymore. He'd have army men and squirt guns and baseball cards and a *penis*. What would we talk about?

My mother brought me a strawberry milkshake and kissed me on the cheek, then sat down and settled her pocketbook on her lap. "So, how does it feel to be a mother?" she asked.

I shrugged.

"Hurt, huh?"

I bit my lips to keep from crying.

Later, I took a walk to the nursery and saw him, a little lump under a white blanket. I thought if it weren't for his name on the bassinet, I wouldn't even know he was mine.

My mother came back at the next visiting hour and brought my father and my sisters, Rose and Phyllis, with her. Ray's mother came too, and so did three of my girlfriends. Everybody sat on my bed or the windowsills. Rose sat on my father's lap. When Ray came by after work, there was no place for him. He seemed like an outsider, and I felt sorry. He handed me a bunny with an ivy plant in its back, and the first opening he got, he rocked forward and back and said, "Hey, Bev, you know something? The song's 'Hey Jude,' not 'June.'"

Since the Beatles had been singing about a boy all along, maybe having a boy wouldn't be too bad. Besides, if the fortune-teller had been wrong about the sex of my baby, then she was probably wrong about the other two kids and the split-level house, too. "Do you think we should name him Jude instead of Jason?" I asked Ray.

"I guess."

"Jude?" my mother said. "What kind of a name's that?"

I'd never heard of St. Jude or *Jude the Obscure,* and the name reminded me of Judas, Jesus' traitor. I changed my mind. "Let's call him Jason," I said.

"Cool." Ray dragged on his cigarette.

The next day, when Jason came to my room, he was soft and warm and smelled sweet like baby, but he moved his head like a dinosaur in a Japanese movie. I was scared of him. Then he got the hiccups after half an ounce of milk and started crying.

He was still crying when I gave him back to the nurse. "Only half an ounce?" she said.

"He got the hiccups," I explained.

She shook her head as if to say, Stupid teenage mother.

The next time he came to my room, I made myself be braver. I shut the door, then took off his undershirt and memorized exactly how his diaper was pinned so I could duplicate it, then took it off too. I'd never seen an uncircumsised penis before. It looked like an elephant's trunk. I kissed it. I nuzzled his stomach, his armpit, his neck. I put his whole foot in my mouth.

The day we left the hospital, I dressed Jason in a blue suit with a plastic Tweety Bird glued on the chest. Ray carried him to the car like he was a tank of nitroglycerin. At a traffic light, when I noticed his head being led around by his mouth, I stuck my finger in. He sucked on it.

My mother was at our house when we got there and it looked like she'd been there for weeks. For one thing, it was spic-and-span, and for another, she'd moved the kitchen table from kitty-corner to flush against the wall. She was sitting at it with a tray of pastries and a pot of coffee in front of her. "You have more room this way," she said. I sat down and said, "Ma, look." I stuck my finger in.

"Take that finger out of his mouth! Are you crazy?" she said.

"Why? He likes it."

"You got germs on your hands. Everything that passes that baby's lips has to be sterilized. Come on, Jason." She held out her arms. I handed him over. "How you doin', little fella? What a big boy you are." She pinched his cheeks. "How you doing? How you doing? How you doing?" she shouted at him, nodding her head every time, poking his chin with her finger. "Look at those fat cheeks. I could eat him up. Your mother's tired, so your Mimi's taking over, let her get her strength back. Isn't that right?"

"Your *Mimi?*"

"It's cute, don't you think?"

"I like it," Ray said, taking off his jacket and sitting on the couch.

"Raymond, hang it up," my mother said. "Your wife just had a baby, she can't be picking up after you."

"I think Mimi's stupid."

"What's the matter with it?"

"It sounds like a dog."

"I like it. It'll be easier to pronounce."

I figured either she wanted to be called Mimi because she was only forty-five and embarrassed to be a grandmother or because Mimi sounded more like Mommy than Grandma did.

My mother came over for hours every single day. I hardly had to do anything, and when I did do something, she watched me like a hawk. "Watch out for his head, Beverly, don't forget the soft spot. His neck isn't strong yet, he could snap it. . . . Better put him on his stomach, he might spit up and suffocate if you lie him on his back."

By the time she started bringing my fat aunt Alma with her, I'd had it. They perked a pot of coffee, broke open an Entenmann's coffee cake and gave detailed infant histories of every one of their children. "Jerry was colicky, kept me up six months straight, but Willie, God bless'm, slept eight hours the first night."

"That's like Beverly. You were the best baby. Never a peep. Loved to sleep. You're lucky Jason's like that. You don't know. Your brother—up every night. I didn't mind, though. You get attached. Wait. You'll see."

One day, around the same time I first smelled winter in the air, I sat at the table with my mother and aunt and Jason, who was in his little seat on top of the table. I watched my aunt's fat fingers roll a cake crumb on her plate and couldn't take them another minute. I stood up and said, "I'm bringing Jason to the library."

"You can't," my mother said. "You can't take a baby in public until he's had all his shots."

"You said I could after six weeks. I'm going crazy."

"Then you go. I'll watch him."

"No."

"You can't take him, and that's the end of it."

"He's *my baby.*"

"It's awfully breezy," my aunt said. "Might be hard to catch his breath." She shrugged and bit her lips.

I ignored her, put a jacket and bonnet on Jason, then made a triangle out of a blanket and wrapped him up.

At the library, I checked out *David Copperfield,* and when I returned, my mother had lost her stand as big chief the baby expert. I invited my girlfriends over every night. Virginia was commuting to college. The rest had jobs, except for Fay, who was pregnant and still living down in New London. I felt sorry for Fay, but I figured it was my duty not to deceive her and to tell her the truth about the horrors of childbirth when she visited. "It hurts like hell," I said to Fay and Beatrice and Virginia as we drank coffee one night in the kitchen. "That miracle shit is a bunch of propaganda. I'll never, no matter what, have another one as long as I live. And Jason? He's all right. I love him, but it's not what you imagine. It's more like you'd love an abandoned puppy you found on the street."

With my friends around, I liked to make fun of Jason. I took off his clothes, strapped him to his changing table, then imitated Diana Ross in my "Love Child" routine. "Started his life in old cold run-down tenement slum . . . love child, always second best, love child, different from the rest." I swung my hips, spun around, and pointed at him to the beat.

If we laughed too loud, Raymond called from the living room for us to keep it down.

By winter, Ray was working four to twelve and leaving me alone every night. And just about every night, Virginia came by to keep me company after she'd finished her homework. She gave me all her books to read as soon as she'd finished them, like *The Ego and the Id,* from Psychology 101, and some Hemingway, Fitzgerald, and Ford Madox Ford books from a course called "The Jazz Age." I joined the Literary Guild and got four more books by Hemingway, four by Steinbeck, and four by Faulkner, which I read whenever Jase went down for a nap or I could get him to shut up in his playpen for a while. I was trying to make myself smart to make up for not going to college.

The thing V and I liked to do best, besides talk about her classes, was to play with the Ouija board. Usually, we asked it questions like if I'd ever get divorced; when Raymond would die; if Jason would go to college; when Bobby and Virginia would marry; how many children they'd have; and if Bobby would make it home from Vietnam in one piece. Then one night we contacted a spirit. Her name was Nancy and she told us her history: she'd died at the age of eighteen, had three brothers still alive and one sister dead, lived somewhere in Michigan, and was a B student in high school. We carried on a dialogue with Nancy for a couple of nights before she turned nasty.

It was early spring and one of those moonless nights when little puffs of wind pushed the shades away from the window, leaving a black gap where someone could peek in. We were a little scared to begin with, but then when the magic indicator started jerking around the board spelling out profanities, I thought my heart would beat a hole through my chest. "Nancy, is that you?" I said.

Fuck, bitch, bastard, asshole.

"Why are you swearing?" Virginia asked.

Dirty twat, scum, cunt.

Then we heard a crash behind us. We jerked our hands off the magic indicator. The utensil rack was swinging from one screw in the wall and the utensils were strewn all over the floor.

We walked over to the wall to get a good look. Here's the thing. The rack was made in such a way that you had to squeeze it together to pull the round holes over the screws. The only way it could be swinging there would be if the other screw had fallen out of the wall or if someone had squeezed the rack together, then pulled it off. Both screws were still in the wall.

V and I looked at each other, screamed, ran up the stairs, and locked ourselves in the bathroom. We sat on the floor with our backs pressed against the door. "What about Jason?" V said.

"Oh God," I said. "We have to get him." We ran across the hall on our toes, went into his room, locked the door, and peeked in his crib. He was lying on his back. His eyes were wide open with only the whites showing.

We ran back into the bathroom. "He's possessed," I said.

"Oh, Mary, Mother of God." V was my only religious friend. She went to mass every morning—she said it was for the peace and quiet, but I knew she probably prayed for Bobby. Just then we heard banging at the front door. We stopped breathing. Then we heard banging at the back door, next the cellar hatchway being pulled open, then footfalls on the stairs. By the time the door opened from the cellar to the living room, we were weeping. "Bev," I heard. It was Raymond. He'd lost his keys.

We ran down the stairs and told him everything. He looked at the baby and said his eyes were normal. Then I looked, too, and they were.

Virginia was too spooked to drive home, so she slept on the sofa. The next night, she was back in our kitchen. "Nancy went nuts because of Bobby," she said. "He's dead."

"What?"

"Shrapnel. They said he didn't feel a thing. His mother called. It'll take a couple of days for his body to come home."

"You're kidding," I said.

"Right. I made it up. It's a big joke."

"I'm sorry. I didn't mean . . . " I said.

Virginia started crying. I couldn't think of a single thing to say. I wished I could cry too. I hugged her and we rocked, stretched between our seats. When Ray came home, he sat in the rocker to take off his work boots, and we told him the news. He threw a boot across the floor, then flung himself back, pressed the heels of his hands into his eyes, and said, "My buddy. My buddy."

The night before the funeral, Ray and I didn't put Jase to bed at six o'clock as usual. We sat on our steps, and Jason, eight months old now, pushed a dump truck around our feet. We put the "White Album" on and, one by one, as if they'd been invited, people began to pull into our driveway and park on the road. There were about a dozen of us sitting on our steps and lying on our lawn that night, listening to the Beatles, reminiscing about Bobby. He'd gone to Dag Hammarskjold with me and had been responsible for the rash of bomb scares one freezing fall. The whole school had to stand outside while the cops searched every locker and desk in the building. A guy named Lenny flicked a cigarette into the night and told us how he'd been waiting for his turn outside the vice-principal's office when Bobby called the vice-principal an ape, then decked him. Bobby was expelled for that one. Rather than face his father, he ran away to Maine and got a severe case of frostbite. But then in high school, he'd joined the football team, and made more touchdowns than anyone. His father was proud of him. Which was Virginia's theory of why he joined the marines: to keep his father that way.

On leave after boot camp, Bobby'd come over for Sunday dinner. He hardly ate any macaroni, then he drank so much he puked in the living room. After he'd come downstairs from washing his face, I'd asked him if he was scared to go to war.

"Bev," Ray said.

"What?"

"You don't ask a guy those questions."

"Oh," I'd said, and Bobby turned his face away.

Sitting on the steps, I pictured Bobby the way he'd looked at my wedding, wearing a shirt with huge polka dots and maroon bell-bottoms. Then I pictured him in the photo he'd sent me from Nam. He had a rifle slung over his shoulder and his hair cut like a Mohican. He was standing on a hill and looked like a statue. I wondered if I'd still remember Bobby when I was thirty or forty. I'd be an adult, but in my memory he'd still be a kid. I wondered if Bobby would've always been wild or if he'd have calmed down, settled in a job somewhere, had a couple of kids, a bald head, a beer belly. I wondered if Bobby was the lucky one. I looked at the back of my son's neck—he was passed out on the grass. It looked so delicate, so tender. Finally, I wept.

"Blackbird" was playing in the background, and I thought how Bobby would never get the chance to spread his wings and learn to fly. I wondered if any of us would. . . .

BELL HOOKS
(1952—)

◆

BELL HOOKS grew up as Gloria Watkins in Kentucky. As she explains in the Introduction to her book *Talking Back,* from which the following autobiographical essay is taken, she chose to write using the pseudonym of her great-grandmother, bell hooks, in order to "construct a writer-identity that would challenge and subdue all impulses leading me away from speech into silence." Her great-grandmother was remembered as a "sharp-tongued woman, a woman who spoke her mind, a woman who was not afraid to talk back." Her great-granddaughter invented her ancestor as "my ally, my support."

bell hooks was educated at Stanford University and is currently Professor of English and Women's Studies at Oberlin College. She has lectured extensively on the issues of race, class, and gender, insisting always on the connection between racism and sexism. She is the author of such works as *Ain't I Woman: Black Women and Feminism* (1981), *Feminist Theory from Margin to Center* (1984), *Talking Back: Thinking Feminist, Thinking Black* (1988), *Yearning: Race and Gender in the Cultural Marketplace* (1990), and *Sisters of the Yam: Black Women and Self-Recovery* (1993). She is the co-author, with Cornel West, of *Breaking Bread: Insurgent Black Intellectual Life* (1991). In that dialogue, her colleague and friend, Cornel West, has described her prodigious literary production as work "in search of a beloved community whose members will come from . . . [the] margins of the academy and the Black community." Her books, as he puts it in his "Introduction to bell hooks," "help us not only to decolonize our minds, souls, and bodies; on a deeper level, they touch our lives. It is difficult to read a bell hooks essay or text without enacting some form of self-examination or self-inventory. To look exclusively for argument and evidence in her work is to remain within one dimension of it. As with a Chekhov play or Billie Holiday solo, one must also probe into the complex interplay of circumstance, pain, and resistance. For bell hooks, the unexamined life is not worth living, yet the examined life is full of yearnings, hurts, and hope." A multi- dimensional thinker passionately committed to constructing new solidarities rather than forcing stale separatisms, she is, as West has said, "like a jazz musician, not afraid of or apologetic for the hybrid character of Black culture," knowing that, in America, to quote Henry Louis Gates, "mixing and hybridity are the rule, not the exception." Yet she never minimizes the struggle of the Black woman writer: "Each time I begin work on a new piece of writing," she says, "a theoretical essay, a critical book, fiction, autobiography, I confront within myself extreme dread that the subjectivity that I have fought so hard to claim will not assert itself. Paralyzed by the fear that I will not be able to name or speak words that fully articulate my experience or the collective reality of struggling black people, I am tempted to be silent." Women have been socialized to back off, believing that "our words are not important." From life she has learned the importance of claiming one's health or wholeness: "Living as we do in a white-supremacist capitalist patriarchal context that can best exploit us when we lack a firm grounding in self and identity, choosing 'wellness' is an act of political resistance."

From *Talking Back*

writing autobiography

To me, telling the story of my growing up years was intimately connected with the longing to kill the self I was without really having to die. I wanted to kill that self in writing. Once that self was gone—out of my life forever—I could more easily become the me of me. It was clearly the Gloria Jean of my tormented and anguished childhood that I wanted to be rid of, the girl who was always wrong, always punished, always subjected to some humiliation or other, always crying, the girl who was to end up in a mental institution because she could not be anything but crazy, or so they told her. She was the girl who sat a hot iron on her arm pleading with them to leave her alone, the girl who wore her scar as a brand marking her madness. Even now I can hear the voices of my sisters saying "mama make Gloria stop crying." By writing the autobiography, it was not just this Gloria I would be rid of, but the past that had a hold on me, that kept me from the present. I wanted not to forget the past but to break its hold. This death in writing was to be liberatory.

Until I began to try and write an autobiography, I thought that it would be a simple task this telling of one's story. And yet I tried year after year, never writing more than a few pages. My inability to write out the story I interpreted as an indication that I was not ready to let go of the past, that I was not ready to be fully in the present. Psychologically, I considered the possibility that I had become attached to the wounds and sorrows of my childhood, that I held to them in a manner that blocked my efforts to be self-realized, whole, to be healed. A key message in Toni Cade Bambara's novel *The Salteaters,* which tells the story of Velma's suicide attempt, her breakdown, is expressed when the healer asks her "are you sure sweetheart, that you want to be well?"

There was very clearly something blocking my ability to tell my story. Perhaps it was remembered scoldings and punishments when mama heard me saying something to a friend or stranger that she did not think should be said. Secrecy and silence—these were central issues. Secrecy about family, about what went on in the domestic household was a bond between us—was part of what made us family. There was a dread one felt about breaking that bond. And yet I could not grow inside the atmosphere of secrecy that had pervaded our lives and the lives of other families about us. Strange that I had always challenged the secrecy, always let something slip that should not be known growing up, yet as a writer staring into the solitary space of paper, I was bound, trapped in the fear that a bond is lost or broken in the telling. I did not want to be the traitor, the teller of family secrets—and yet I wanted to be a writer. Surely, I told myself, I could write a purely imaginative work—a work that would not hint at personal private realities. And so I tried. But always there were the intruding traces, those elements of real life however disguised. Claiming the freedom to grow as an imaginative writer was connected for me with having the courage to open, to be able to tell the truth of one's life as I had experienced it in writing. To talk about one's life—that I could do. To write about it, to leave a trace—that was frightening.

The longer it took me to begin the process of writing autobiography, the further removed from those memories I was becoming. Each year, a memory seemed less and less clear. I wanted not to lose the vividness, the recall and felt an urgent need to begin the work and complete it. Yet I could not begin even though I had begun to confront some of the reasons I was blocked, as I am blocked just now in writing this piece because I am afraid to express in writing the experience that served as a catalyst for that block to move.

I had met a young black man. We were having an affair. It is important that he was black. He was in some mysterious way a link to this past that I had been struggling to grapple with, to name in writing. With him I remembered incidents, moments of the past that I had completely suppressed. It was as though there was something about the passion of contact that was hypnotic, that enabled me to drop barriers and thus enter fully, rather re-enter those past experiences. A key aspect seemed to be the way he smelled, the combined odors of cigarettes, occasionally alcohol, and his body smells. I thought often of the phrase "scent of memory," for it was those smells that carried me back. And there were specific occasions when it was very evident that the experience of being in his company was the catalyst for this remembering.

Two specific incidents come to mind. One day in the middle of the afternoon we met at his place. We were drinking cognac and dancing to music from the radio. He was smoking cigarettes (not only do I not smoke, but I usually make an effort to avoid smoke). As we held each other dancing those mingled odors of alcohol, sweat, and cigarettes led me to say, quite without thinking about it, "Uncle Pete." It was not that I had forgotten Uncle Pete. It was more that I had forgotten the childhood experience of meeting him. He drank often, smoked cigarettes, and always on the few occasions that we met him, he held us children in tight embraces. It was the memory of those embraces—of the way I hated and longed to resist them—that I recalled.

Another day we went to a favorite park to feed ducks and parked the car in front of tall bushes. As we were sitting there, we suddenly heard the sound of an oncoming train—a sound which startled me so that it evoked another long-suppressed memory: that of crossing the train tracks in my father's car. I recalled an incident where the car stopped on the tracks and my father left us sitting there while he raised the hood of the car and worked to repair it. This is an incident that I am not certain actually happened. As a child, I had been terrified of just such an incident occurring, perhaps so terrified that it played itself out in my mind as though it had happened. These are just two ways this encounter acted as a catalyst breaking down barriers enabling me to finally write this long-desired autobiography of my childhood.

Each day I sat at the typewriter and different memories were written about in short vignettes. They came in a rush, as though they were a sudden thunderstorm. They came in a surreal, dreamlike style which made me cease to think of them as strictly autobiographical because it seemed that myth, dream, and reality had merged. There were many incidents that I would talk about with my siblings to see if they recalled them. Often we remembered together a general outline of an incident but the details were different for us. This fact was a constant reminder of the limitations of autobiography, of the extent to which autobiography is a very personal story telling—a unique recounting of events not so much as they have happened but as we remember and invent them. One memory that I would have sworn was "the truth and nothing but the truth" concerned a wagon that my brother and I shared as a child. I remembered that we played with this toy only at my grandfather's house, that we shared it, that I would ride it and my brother would push me. Yet one facet of the memory was puzzling, I remembered always returning home with bruises or scratches from this toy. When I called my mother, she said there had never been any wagon, that we had shared a red wheelbarrow, that it had always been at my grandfather's house because there were sidewalks on that part of town. We lived in the hills where there were no sidewalks. Again I was compelled to face the fiction that is a part of all retelling, remembering. I began to think of the work I was doing as both fiction and autobiography. It seemed to fall in the category of writing that Audre Lorde, in her auto-biographically-based work *Zami,* calls bio-mythography. As I wrote, I felt that I was not as concerned with accuracy of detail as I was with evoking in writing the state of mind, the spirit of a particular moment.

The longing to tell one's story and the process of telling is symbolically a gesture of longing to recover the past in such a way that one experiences both a sense of reunion and a sense of release. It was the longing for release that compelled the writing but concurrently it was the joy of reunion that enabled me to see that the act of writing one's autobiography is a way to find again that aspect of self and experience that may no longer be an actual part of one's life but is a living memory shaping and informing the present. Autobiographical writing was a way for me to evoke the particular experience of growing up southern and black in segregated communities. It was a way to recapture the richness of southern black culture. The need to remember and hold to the legacy of that experience and what it taught me has been all the more important since I have since lived in predominately white communities and taught at predominately white colleges. Black southern folk experience was the foundation of the life around me when I was a child; that experience no longer exists in many places where it was once all of life that we knew. Capitalism, upward mobility, assimilation of other values have all led to rapid disintegration of black folk experience or in some cases the gradual wearing away of that experience.

Within the world of my childhood, we held onto the legacy of a distinct black culture by listening to the elders tell their stories. Autobiography was experienced most actively in the art of telling one's story. I can recall sitting at Baba's (my grandmother on my mother's side) at 1200 Broad Street—listening to people come and recount their life experience. In those days, whenever I brought a playmate to my grandmother's house, Baba would want a brief outline of their autobiography before we would begin playing. She wanted not only to know who their people were but what their values were. It was sometimes an awesome and terrifying experience to stand answering these questions or witness another playmate being subjected to the process and yet this was the way we would come to know our own and one another's family history. It is the absence of such a tradition in my adult life that makes the written narrative of my girlhood all the more important. As the years pass and these glorious memories grow much more vague, there will remain the clarity contained within the written words.

Conceptually, the autobiography was framed in the manner of a hope chest. I remembered my mother's hope chest, with its wonderful odor of cedar and thought about her taking the most precious items and placing them there for safekeeping. Certain memories were for me a similar treasure. I wanted to place them somewhere for safekeeping. An autobiographical narrative seemed an appropriate place. Each particular incident, encounter, experience had its own story, sometimes told from the first person, sometimes told from the third person. Often I felt as though I was in a trance at my typewriter, that the shape of a particular memory was decided not by my conscious mind but by all that is dark and deep within me, unconscious but present. It was the act of making it present, bringing it into the open, so to speak, that was liberating.

From the perspective of trying to understand my psyche, it was also interesting to read the narrative in its entirety after I had completed the work. It had not occurred to me that bringing one's past, one's memories together in a complete narrative would allow one to view them from a different perspective, not as singular isolated events but as part of a continuum. Reading the completed manuscript, I felt as though I had an overview not so much of my childhood but of those experiences that were deeply imprinted in my consciousness. Significantly, that which was absent, left out, not included also was important. I was shocked to find at the end of my narrative that there were few incidents I recalled that involved my five sisters. Most of the incidents with siblings were with me and my brother. There was a sense of alienation from my sisters present in childhood, a sense of estrangement. This was reflected in the narrative. Another aspect of the completed manuscript that is interesting to me is the way in which the incidents describing adult men suggest that I feared them intensely, with the exception of my grandfather and a few old men. Writing the autobiographical narrative enabled me to look at my past from a different perspective and to use this knowledge as a means of self-growth and change in a practical way.

In the end I did not feel as though I had killed the Gloria of my childhood. Instead I had rescued her. She was no longer the enemy within, the little girl who had to be annihilated for the woman to come into being. In writing about her, I reclaimed that part of myself I had long ago rejected, left uncared for, just as she had often felt alone and uncared for as a child. Remembering was part of a cycle of reunion, a joining of fragments, "the bits and pieces of my heart" that the narrative made whole again.

SANDRA CISNEROS
(1954—)

◆

SANDRA CISNEROS was born and grew up in Chicago, the daughter of a Mexican father and Mexican-American mother, and sister to six brothers. She began her writing career in poetry—"I think you have to learn how to build a room before you build a house"—and studied at the Iowa Writers' Workshop where she learned "what I didn't want to be, how I didn't want to write." Later, she returned home and spent time in the barrio: "I became fascinated by the rhythms of speech, this incredible deluge of voices." She gives her mother credit for nurturing her love of language. A self-educated woman, Cisneros's mother got her seven children library cards long before they could actually read. This autobiographical detail as well as her confessed love of the sound of local people's voices—"My original love, the rhythm of the spoken word"—recalls the early life histories of Eudora Welty (see page 95) and Maya Angelou (see page 209). Cisneros has worked as a teacher of high school dropouts—like Maxine Hong Kingston, whose "wonderful book," *The Woman Warrior* (see page 347), "gave me permission to keep going with what I started in *The House on Mango Street*"—and as writer-in-residence at California State University at Chico, the University of California at Berkeley and Irvine, and the University of New Mexico. The recipient of two NEA fellowships for poetry and fiction, as well as the Lannan Literary Award for 1991, she is the author of *My Wicked Wicked Ways,* (1987) a volume of poetry, *The House on Mango Street* (1984), and *Woman Hollering Creek* (1991), a volume of twenty-two stories about the experiences of Chicanas, women born in the United States whose heritage lies south of the Mexican border. The critic Peter S. Prescott has praised Cisneros's "feminist, Mexican-American voice [as] not only playful and vigorous, it's original—we haven't heard anything like it before." She has been called the most powerful of the young Chicana writers to emerge in the 1980s. Cisneros has said she writes "the kind of stories I didn't get growing up. Stories about . . . people I knew and loved, but never saw in the pages of the books I borrowed from the Chicago Public Library. Now that I live in the southwest, I'm even more appalled by the absence of brown people in mainstream literature and more committed than ever to populating the Texas literary landscape, the American literary landscape with stories about mexicanos, Chicanos, and Latinos."

In the autobiographical interview that follows Cisneros talks about herself as a writer, about her cultural conflicts as well as her love of other writers. Her equation of "the spiritual and political" brings to mind Jane Addams's (see page 1) insistence on the solidarity of all classes as the political and spiritual imperative of an authentic democratic society.

From *Interviews with Writers of the Post-Colonial World*

CONDUCTED AND EDITED BY FEROZA JUSSAWALLA AND REED WAY DASENBROCK.

F.J.: You've . . . touched on something I see as a key theme of yours, which is the conflict of cultures. What is very interesting in this for me is that it isn't between Chicano and Anglo as much as inside "Hispanic" culture. I don't know whether that's the right word to use; I have a lot of students who don't like being called "Hispanic."

Cisneros: I hate Hispanic. One day that word just appeared! Just like *USA Today.* One day we were sleeping, we woke up and saw that. "How'd that get there?" (*Laughter*) I don't know where that word came from. It's kind of an upwardly mobile type word. That word to me came out of Washington, D.C. I only use it when I apply for a grant. But something I've learned is not to feel superior when people want to call themselves Hispanic. You have a right to call yourself what you want, and I have to respect that if I want to be called what I want to be called. So, I no longer get so hysterical anymore if someone wants to call themselves that. But you wouldn't find me going out with a Hispanic. (*Laughter*) Anyway, we had a word, no one asked us! I like the word Latino. It groups me with the other Latino groups in Chicago.

F.J.: Yet even in *House on Mango Street,* one gets a sense of conflicts within that Latino culture in Chicago. In one of the stories, the male character brings a wife from "back home," as it were. She comes with a baby, doesn't step out, stays locked up and doesn't come out of her apartment, doesn't speak anything but Spanish, and doesn't even try. There seems to be a voice criticizing her.

Cisneros: I just wanted to talk there about peoples' fear of the English language and also why they want to keep their own language. The language, for a lot of people, was a link back; it meant that you were going to get back eventually. That's why some people refused to learn English because they were assuming, as so many immigrants did, that there was a road back. And it's a frightening thing when you let go of a language because you've let go your tiny thin string back home. . . .

F.J.: It strikes me as you are describing your new novel that one of the things it is about is class politics. What would you say your politics are now?

Cisneros: I have lived in socialist countries, so I can't call myself a socialist, because I know that doesn't work. When I travelled in Europe for a year, I went from country to country and I met women and men, and women helped me and men helped me, but it turned out to be too expensive when you got anything free from a man *(laughter)*, so I realized I'd only depend on women. Women helped me and they asked for nothing in return, and they gave me great compassion and love when I was feeling lost and alone. I, in turn, listened to their stories, and I think I made so many friendships that crossed borders. It was like we all came from the same country, the women; we all had the same problems. I don't know what my politics are, except my stories tell it to you. I can't give it to you as an -ism or an -ist.

F.J.: How about as feminist?

Cisneros: Well, yes—it's a feminism, but it's a feminism that is very different from the feminism of upper-class women. It's a feminism that's very much tied into my class.

R.D.: What would be the difference?

Cisneros: I guess my feminism and my race are the same thing to me. They're tied in one to another, and I don't feel an alliance or an allegiance with upper-class white women. I don't. I can listen to them and on some level as a human being I can feel great compassion and friendships; but they have to move from their territory to mine, because I know their world. But they don't know mine. Then I moved to Texas, and that made me so angry. I don't know why Texas did that to me. Texas made me angry. In some way that I never had before, I started getting racist towards white people. I was wandering around like this colonized fool before, trying to be like my women friends in school. I didn't have any white women friends when I was in Texas. Once, Norma Alarcón came to visit me when I was working in San Antonio and she said, "Don't you have any white friends?" It suddenly occurred to me that she hadn't met one and I thought, "I don't!" You know, that's because I was working in the barrio, I was doing community arts, I didn't have time. White people never came to the neighborhood where I worked. I wasn't about to go into their neighborhood and start telling them about Chicano art. I was creating Chicano art, and I was bringing Chicano writers to the neighborhood. I was up to my elbows in work. I didn't have time to be going off to UTSA [University of Texas, San Antonio] telling them where Chicano writers are.

I was committed to the neighborhood; I was committed to creating a small press book fair—the first one that was there. And if people were scared of my neighborhood, well, they better start thinking what our cultural center was all about to begin with and who we were supposed to serve first. Something ugly happened during that time that I didn't realize. I have to say now that I'm in a more balanced place than I was at that period. And so my politics have been changing, and some of my white women friends who have come into my life—I think it was divine providence that put them there—have taught me a lot. Those white women friends who have bothered to learn about my culture have entered into my life now and have taught me something. Maybe a little sliver of glass of the Snow Queen in my heart has dissolved a bit. But I'm still angry about some things, and those issues are going to come up in my next book.

F.J.: What are those?

Cisneros: I'm really mad at Mexican men, because Mexican men are the men I love the most and they disappoint me the most. I think they disappoint me the most because I love them the most. I don't care about the other men so much. They don't affect my personal politics because they're not in my sphere whereas Latino men, and specifically Mexican men, are the ones that I want to be with the most. And they keep disappointing me. I see so many intelligent Mexican women in Texas and they can't find a Mexican man because our Mexican men are with white women. What does that say about Mexican men? How do they feel about themselves if they won't go out with Mexican women, especially professional Mexican women? What does that say about themselves? They must not love themselves or, like someone said, "You must not love your mama." You know? You must not. That's an issue we talk about only among ourselves— the Latina women. That's really hard for me to tell my white women friends and make them understand without offending them. And these issues have to come up, and they will come up. Now these are some of the things on my agenda that I didn't get to in this book, but I'll get to in the next one.

F.J.: Could it be that you are an exception among Latina women?

Cisneros: No! I'm not the exception! I came to Texas, I met so many major mountain movers here, especially in Texas. The Chicanas I met in Texas, my God they're something! They're like nopalitos. And I think it's because they're like the landscape. But it's hard to be a woman in Texas.

F.J.: They are not women who want to assume the traditional Mexican female role?

Cisneros: I have to say that the traditional role is kind of a myth. I think the traditional Mexican woman is a fierce woman. There's a lot of victimization but we are also fierce. We are very fierce. Our mothers had been fierce. Our women may be victimized but they are still very, very fierce and very strong. I really do believe that.

R.D.: Is the same kind of gender politics involved in writing?

Cisneros: How specifically?

R.D.: Certainly, male Chicano writers were recognized and published before the women. Do you think that's a function of some of the same kinds of things you've been talking about?

Cisneros: The men who were published first, Tomás Rivera, Rudolfo Anaya, Rolando Hinojosa, they were all in universities, no? Whereas with the women, it's taken us this long to get educated. Or some of them have educated their husbands first. It's taken us a while to get to this level where we are educated enough so that we can feel confident enough to even compete. It's taken us this long to take care of our sense of self. There's a lot of stuff going on with women, as far as getting your education, and as far as figuring out you don't have to go the route that society puts on you. Men are already in a privileged position. They don't have to fight against patriarchy; it put them in a great place. But the women did; it took us a little while to figure out, "I don't have to get married just yet," or "Wait a second, I don't have to have a baby now." And some of us figured it out a few babies later.

I think it took a little while for the women who wanted to get their education, and to fight for that education, because our fathers didn't want us to go to school or they wanted us to go to school to get married. As for me, I went through great trauma in my twenties trying to figure out that my life had no role model, so I had to invent that. I don't know if Rolando Hinojosa went through the trauma of wondering if he should have children in his twenties and should he get married. I don't think he did. He had other pressures, supporting his family, sure, but I had pressures too. You know, we all did. I wasn't even applying for a job in a university with an MFA. Imagine that. With an MFA from one of the famous writing schools, and even with an NEA I didn't dare apply for a job at a university. I was making $12,000 a year working at an alternative high school in inner-city Chicago when I came out of Iowa. Why? Because as women, we think we're not good enough. Because as people of color, we have been led to believe, we're colonized to think, we're not smart enough, we're not good enough, we have nothing to share at the university. And where would I have gone at the university had I gone into the schools that I left? Would I be teaching *Moby Dick*? You know I don't want to teach *Moby Dick*! *(Laughter)*

F.J.: You said yesterday in your talk that your consciousness of yourself as being a thoroughly colonized person developed while you were working in Chicago with underprivileged students. I'm trying to think of what it means to you to have been a thoroughly colonized person.

Cisneros: My consciousness of growing up, the consciousness of myself, the subjects that I write about, the voice that I write in—I suppose all of that began in Iowa in a seminar class. The madeleine—to use Proust's term—was Bachelard's poetics of space. The house. The house! Everyone was talking about the house the way they'd always been talking about everything. It was at that moment I realized, "I don't have a house—these things don't matter to me!" *(Laughter)* I don't have a house, how could I talk about house! With people from my neighborhood, you'd be talking about a very different house than the one Bachelard was talking about—the wonderful house of memory. My house was a prison for me; I don't want to talk about house.

F.J.: You treat that in *House on Mango Street*. There is a little interlude where the child runs into one of the nuns who teaches at her school and the nun points up to a window and asks, "Do you live there?"

Cisneros: I used to be ashamed to take anyone into that room, to my house, because if they saw that house they would equate the house with me and my value. And I know that house didn't define me; they just saw the outside. They couldn't see what was inside. I wrote a poem that was a precursor, or perhaps the same story—about an apartment, a flat. I wrote it for the workshop after that experience of being in that seminar, and *House on Mango Street* began that night, that same night. It was an incredible moment. It all began at that same time. I can't tell you whether the poems came first or the stories; they all came like a deluge. It had been as if all of the sudden I realized, "Oh my God! Here's something that my classmates can't write about, and I'm going to tell you because I'm the authority on this—I can tell you."

F.J.: So after the seminar you were not ashamed of that house anymore. You wouldn't be ashamed of your background, you'd say, "This is the background that empowered me."

Cisneros: At that moment I ceased to be ashamed because I realized that I knew something that they could never learn at the universities. It was all a sudden that I realized something that I knew that I was the authority on.

R.D.: What was that?

Cisneros: It was the university of the streets, the university of life. The neighbors, the people I saw, the poverty that the women had gone through—you can't learn that in a class. I could walk in that neighborhood, and I knew how to walk in that neighborhood, and they didn't. So to me it began there, and that's when I intentionally started writing about all the things in my culture that were different from them—the poems that are these city voices—the first part of *Wicked Wicked Ways*—and the stories in *House on Mango Street*. I think it's ironic that at the moment when I was practically leaving an institution of learning, I began realizing in which ways institutions had failed me. It was that moment in Iowa when I realized my difference from the other classmates as far as our class differences, our cultural differences, my color difference—all of which I had acknowleged but I couldn't articulate as such until that moment in that seminar class: I began intentionally addressing the issues and using the voice that I'm now known for; I began searching out writers who were writing the types of stories that I wanted to read; I began, in essence, trying to piece together those parts of my education that my education had missed, to fill that void so to speak. I can't pretend that I came out of the Iowa corn fields whole and complete like an Athena from Zeus' head. But I knew where I wanted to go.

R.D.: Who are the writers who have influenced your work significantly?

Cisneros: A whole generation of the Chicano writers were influenced by the Latin American male boom because that's all we got. Borges was an influence, but the ones I really stay with are Manuel Puig and Juan Rulfo, Rulfo obviously for his rhythms and what he's doing with voices. And, of course, you know Rulfo influenced that story I wrote last night, very much so. Manuel Puig for his compassion, always looking out for these underdogs. So I have to say we were influenced by the Latino male writers, and it's only recently that we are gaining access to the women's work and that we're getting influenced by the women. I think the writers that influenced me the most in this last collection were—well the one I can name the most is Merce Rodoreda. She's Catalan. She's taught me a lot about voices and monologues and following that kind of emotions that she does. Her writing is very emotional and I like that. She taught me a lot in writing this last book.

But there are also a lot of American working class women writers. They can be white women writers if they're working-class women writers—Pat Ellis Taylor in Austin, Texas, I love her work very much.

F.J.: And the Asian women?

Cisneros: I love Maxine Hong Kingston. *The Woman Warrior* (see page 347)—what a wonderful book that was for me. That gave me permission to keep going with what I'd started with *House on Mango Street*.

R.D.: So not just Latino writers, but also other minority writers—

Cisneros: Yes, I'm not that familiar with the black women writers, but I'm much more interested in some black feminist women writers as opposed to the mainstream black women writers.

R.D.: Why is that?

Cisneros: I'm not saying that I prefer one over the other, but I think that small presses are more fearless about things that they take.

F.J.: And that's why you say your neighborhood then is among those people who are publishing with the women's presses and the minor presses rather than the major—

Cisneros: I didn't realize that was my neighborhood until I was serving on an NEA panel. Anytime a book came up that was by a women's press or a feminist press or a working class press, I knew those writers. When they mentioned the writers who were publishing with New York I didn't know who they were (*laughter*), but anytime a name that was from a small press or Southwest or minority came up, I usually knew it.

I just have to say personally I haven't read the black women writers to the degree that I've read some of the smaller presses. And that's because I'll read their works, but I haven't kept up with them. For some reason, they're not making me do mental backflips like some of the other writers I'm reading. They're wonderful writers, but we have to work as writers to the ones that are somehow doing something for us in our own agenda. My companera, Helena Maria Viramontes, loves the black women writers—the big press ones that we're talking about, the handful.

F.J.: You mean Gloria Naylor and Paule Marshall—

Cisneros: Naylor, Paule Marshall, Toni Morrison, Alice Walker. I'll read their stories, and they don't do to me what Merce Rodoreda does to me. Something happens when I read Rodoreda and Puig. I don't know what it is. And I think that you have to stay with those writers that are somehow touching those passion buttons in you. I don't know what it is that they do for me.

And it may be that I'm just not taken by the linear novel form, that I'm much more interested in something new happening to the literature. I'm saying this all now, as I'm speaking to you, for the first time. That may be why some of the black women writers who are working in traditional forms, even though I can recognize the craft—but that's not the kind of story that appeals to me. I'm much, much more excited by a writer who is doing something with the form, like Rulfo or Borges or Puig. Just from my own personal taste, I like somebody doing something new.

R.D.: So now you're writing a novel, your first novel. Many Chicano writers seem to have taken small forms and built up a kind of mosaic, have worked with a group of short stories rather than a continuous narrative. This is true, of course, of *House on Mango Street,* but I'm also thinking of Tomás Rivera's *y no se lo tragó la tierra* and Ana Castillo's *The Mixquiahuala Letters* and Denise Chavez's *The Last of the Menu Girls.* Why do you think this is so?

Cisneros: For one thing, you have to talk about where we are as far as our careers as writers. We're young writers, and you don't start out by building a house if you haven't learned how to build a room. Some writers have done that, and I don't think that they've done a very good job of building their houses. I'm much more interested in carpentry and getting my walls done so that all the joints meet. I'm a very, very meticulous carpenter. So, I think that at this point in our career and our craft we're learning how to build the rooms before we can build a house. And also, maybe we don't want the house—

R.D.: Yes, that would be my question—

Cisneros: I didn't know what I was writing when I wrote *House on Mango Street,* but I knew what I wanted. I didn't know what to call it, but I knew what I was after. It wasn't a naive thing, it wasn't an accident. I wanted to write a series of stories that you could open up at any point. You didn't have to know anything before or after and you would understand each story like a little pearl, or you could look at the whole thing like a necklace. That's what I always knew from the day that I wrote the first one. I said, "I'm going to do a whole series of these, and it's going to be like this, and it'll all be connected." I didn't know the order they were going to come in, but I wasn't trying to write a linear novel.

R.D.: But now you are?

Cisneros: Well, no. I'm writing a novel; I don't know if it's linear. I don't decide the shape. It really decides itself. I don't know the shape of this novel. I don't know it yet. All I have is pages of it, and I have some parts of it, and I know some of the agendas and the issues, and I have some parts written—but I don't know the shape.

F.J.: It's going to be about your family, right?

Cisneros: Yes, it'll start out with that foundation, but it's not going to be autobiographical. It'll start out with an autobiographical foundation of taking my father and my mother and their situation at that time in history, but I have to do research about that time so I can fill in the gaps of what family doesn't speak about or what my father doesn't know. And it's going to be my agenda, you know?

F.J.: You keep saying agenda; it's almost as though you were doing some cause writings. Starting with a position—

Cisneros: That's right! That's right, we do. That's how fiction is different from poetry. I don't have an agenda when I write poetry. I don't know what I'm going to write about.

R.D.: But you do when you write fiction?

Cisneros: Absolutely. Absolutely. I've got some things that have got to get said, and this is how I'm going to get it out. I have to sometimes ask my two editors, my Random House editor and my personal editor, is my axe too sharp here? Do I need to hold back? Because I do have some things I really want to do.

R.D.: Do you see that as a difference between minority writers and Anglo writers, white writers?

Cisneros: I think that the work of women and minorities and working-class people has spiritual content and political content, and that's their strength. I really do. I see so much writing by mainstream people that is well written but it doesn't have anything to say. So, it's not going to be substantial, not going to stand. And I would much rather have work that's not quite as clean and finished, but that has some spiritual content. I see the spiritual and political in some ways being the same thing.

MARY CROW DOG
(1955—)

———————◆———————

MARY CROW DOG, née Mary Brave Bird, grew up fatherless in a one-room cabin, without plumbing or electricity, on a Sioux reservation in South Dakota. Her autobiography, *Lakota Woman,* records her memories of growing up female and Native American on the impoverished margins of a racist mainstream America; it also celebrates her liberation from this legacy of despair through activist politics, Native American religion, and childbirth during the occupation of Wounded Knee in 1973. In giving her private and public history a voice, Mary Crow Dog exemplifies the American Indian women who, in the words of Dexter Fisher, "have been a part of the storytelling tradition—both oral and written—from its inception, passing on stories to their children and their children's children and using the word to advance those concepts crucial to cultural survival." Her life history shows her determination against all odds to save herself in a world that has been hostile to America's First Peoples for centuries. Reviewing her narrative in the *Atlantic,* Phoebe-Lou Adams defined the source of Mary Crow Dog's change from a passive, exploited girl into a brave young woman: "As the wife of Leonard Crow Dog, the author knows a great deal about the revival of traditional religious practices which he leads, and her explanations of the purposes and effects of Indian rites are invariably interesting, because they introduce the reader to a system of belief that is, however unfamiliar, coherent and attractively generous." Activist lawyer William Kunstler, who defended members of the American Indian Movement led by Leonard Crow Dog after the incident at Oglala—the trial was the basis of the documentary film *Incident at Oglala*—has also identified traditional Native American culture as the force behind Mary Crow Dog's deliverance, calling *Lakota Woman* "the moving story of a Native American woman who fought her way out of despair and bitterness to find the righteous ways of her ancestors." As a storyteller of her own life and culture, Mary Crow Dog represents the tradition of American Indian women's autobiography as Gretchen M. Bataille and Kathleen Mullen Sands describe it in their book *American Indian Women: Telling Their Lives.* "It is based on storytelling" and shares with oral forms of expression "a concern for communal welfare [and] the subordination of the individual to the collective needs of the tribe. [But] the conservative roots of the Euro-American literary tradition provide the [autobiographical] tribal narrator with a new element essential to the process of personal narration—egocentric individualism." *Lakota Woman* affirms the ancient tribe, the modern collective known as AIM, and the individual self who voices an unconquered spirit.

From *Lakota Woman*

CHAPTER 1
A Woman from He-Dog

*A nation is not conquered until the hearts of its women are on the ground.
Then it is done, no matter how brave its warriors nor how strong their weapons.*
—CHEYENNE PROVERB

I am Mary Brave Bird. After I had my baby during the siege of Wounded Knee they gave me a special name—Ohitika Win, Brave Woman, and fastened an eagle plume in my hair, singing brave-heart songs for me. I am a woman of the Red Nation, a Sioux woman. That is not easy.

I had my first baby during a firefight, with the bullets crashing through one wall and coming out through the other. When my newborn son was only a day old and the marshals really opened up upon us, I wrapped him up in a blanket and ran for it. We had to hit the dirt a couple of times, I shielding the baby with my body, praying, "It's all right if I die, but please let him live."

When I came out of Wounded Knee I was not even healed up, but they put me in jail at Pine Ridge and took my baby away. I could not nurse. My breasts swelled up and grew hard as rocks, hurting badly. In 1975 the feds put the muzzles of their M-16s against my head, threatening to blow me away. It's hard being an Indian woman.

My best friend was Annie Mae Aquash, a young, strong-hearted woman from the Micmac Tribe with beautiful children. It is not always wise for an Indian woman to come on too strong. Annie Mae was found dead in the snow at the bottom of a ravine on the Pine Ridge Reservation. The police said that she had died of exposure, but there was a .38-caliber slug in her head. The FBI cut off her hands and sent them to Washington for fingerprint identification, hands that had helped my baby come into the world.

My sister-in-law, Delphine, a good woman who had lived a hard life, was also found dead in the snow, the tears frozen on her face. A drunken man had beaten her, breaking one of her arms and legs, leaving her helpless in a blizzard to die.

My sister Barbara went to the government hospital in Rosebud to have her baby and when she came out of anesthesia found that she had been sterilized against her will. The baby lived only for two hours, and she had wanted so much to have children. No, it isn't easy.

When I was a small girl at the St. Francis Boarding School, the Catholic sisters would take a buggy whip to us for what they called "disobedience." At age ten I could drink and hold a pint of whiskey. At age twelve the nuns beat me for "being too free with my body." All I had been doing was holding hands with a boy. At age fifteen I was raped. If you plan to be born, make sure you are born white and male.

It is not the big, dramatic things so much that get us down, but just being Indian, trying to hang on to our way of life, language, and values while being surrounded by an alien, more powerful culture. It is being an iyeska, a half-blood, being looked down upon by whites and full-bloods alike. It is being a backwoods girl living in a city, having to rip off stores in order to survive. Most of all it is being a woman. Among Plains tribes, some men think that all a woman is good for is to crawl into the sack with them and mind the children. It compensates for what white society has done to them. They were famous warriors and hunters once, but the buffalo is gone and there is not much rep in putting a can of spam or an occasional rabbit on the table.

As for being warriors, the only way some men can count coup nowadays is knocking out another skin's teeth during a barroom fight. In the old days a man made a name for himself by being generous and wise, but now he has nothing to be generous with, no jobs, no money; and as far as our traditional wisdom is concerned, our men are being told by the white missionaries, teachers, and employers that it is merely savage superstition they should get rid of if they want to make it in this world. Men are forced to live away from their children, so that the family can get ADC—Aid to Dependent Children. So some warriors come home drunk and beat up their old ladies in order to work off their frustration. I know where they are coming from. I feel sorry for them, but I feel even sorrier for their women.

To start from the beginning, I am a Sioux from the Rosebud Reservation in South Dakota. I belong to the "Burned Thigh," the Brule Tribe, the Sicangu in our language. Long ago, so the legend goes, a small band of Sioux was surrounded by enemies who set fire to their tipis and the grass around them. They fought their way out of the trap but got their legs burned and in this way acquired their name. The Brules are part of the Seven Sacred Campfires, the seven tribes of the Western Sioux known collectively as Lakota.

The Eastern Sioux are called Dakota. The difference between them is their language. It is the same except that where we Lakota pronounce an *L,* the Dakota pronounce a *D.* They cannot pronounce an *L* at all. In our tribe we have this joke: "What is a flat tire in Dakota?" Answer: "A b*d*owout." . . .

CHAPTER 9
The Siege

Coming to Wounded Knee was just the most natural thing in the world to do.
—CHIEF FRANK FOOLS CROW

I am not afraid to die.
If I die at Wounded Knee,
I will go where Crazy Horse
and Sitting Bull
and our grandfathers are.

—CROW DOG

. . . Wounded Knee lasted seventy-one long days. These days were not all passed performing heroic deeds or putting up media shows for the reporters. Most of the time was spent in boredom, just trying to keep warm and finding something to eat. Wounded Knee was a place one got scared in occasionally, a place in which people made love, got married Indian style, gave birth, and died. The oldest occupants were over eighty, the youngest under eight. It was a heyoka place, a place of sacred clowns who laughed while they wept. A young warrior standing up in the middle of a firefight to pose for the press; Russel Means telling the photographers, "Be sure to get my good side."

We organized ourselves. The biggest room in the store became the community hall. A white man's home, the only house with heat and tap water, became the hospital, and women were running it. The museum became the security office. We all took turns doing the cooking, sewing shirts, and making sleeping bags for the men in bunkers. We embroidered the words "Wounded Knee" on rainbow-colored strips of cloth. Everybody got one of those as a badge of honor, "to show your grandchildren sometime," as Dennis said. We shared. We did things for each other. At one time a white volunteer nurse berated us for doing the slave work while the men got all the glory. We were betraying the cause of womankind, was the way she put it. We told her that her kind of women's lib was a white, middle-class thing, and that at this critical stage we had other priorities. Once our men had gotten their rights and their balls back, we might start arguing with them about who should do the dishes. But not before.

Actually, our women played a major part at Wounded Knee. We had two or three pistol-packing mamas swaggering around with six-shooters dangling at their hips, taking their turns on the firing line, swapping lead with the feds. The Indian nurses bringing in the wounded under a hail of fire were braver than many warriors. The men also did their share of the dirty work. Bob Free, our first chief of engineers, had a crew which built twelve fortified bunkers, made an apartment house out of the trading post, dug latrines and constructed wooden privies, kept the juice going, repaired cars, operated the fork-lift and an earth-moving bulldozer. The men also formed a sanitary squad, picking up garbage and digging trenches to bury all that crap. One day Bob laid down the law: "Okay, that's it. The only electricity we keep is for the freezers to store the meat, for the gas pumps and three lights. That's all!" And he enforced it.

For a while I stayed at the trading post. But it was too much for me. Too many people and too little privacy. I figured that I would have my baby within two weeks. I moved into a trailer house at the edge of Wounded Knee. By then daily exchanges of fire had become common-place. The bullets were flying as I got bigger and bigger. One day the government declared a cease-fire so that the women and children could leave. One of the AIM leaders came up to me: "You're leaving. You're pregnant, so you've got to go." I told him, "No, I won't. If I'm going to die, I'm going to die here. All that means anything to me is right here. I have nothing to live for out there."

"It doesn't matter whether you want to or not, you've got to go. All the women and children are going."

But we were not going. I stayed, all the older women stayed, most of the young mothers with children stayed, the sweethearts of the warriors stayed. Only a handful took advantage of the cease-fire and left. The deadline passed. The firing started again. Heavy MGs, automatic rifles, trip-wire flares, single shots from the government sniper experts. Some of our men burned the wooden bridge over the creek so the feds couldn't sneak up on us across it. Somebody said, "Now we've burned our bridge behind us." . . .

CHAPTER 11

Birth Giving

Ho! Sun, Moon, and Stars,
All you that move
In the Sky,
Listen to me!
Into your midst
New Life has come.
Make its path smooth.
—OMAHA PRAYER FOR A NEWBORN CHILD

On Friday, April 5, Crow Dog left Wounded Knee for about one week. He had been chosen to go on a four-man embassy to Washington in the hope of being able to see the president in order to reach a settlement we could live with. As it turned out, trying to reach a settlement in Washington was just as futile as at Wounded Knee. At this time Crow Dog was not yet my husband and lover, but I had great confidence in him, believing in his powers as a medicine man, and I had hoped he would be around when I had my baby. Now he was leaving just when I was about to give birth and I felt let down. I was very self-centered, or rather belly-centered. Washington and Nixon could have been swallowed up by a flood or an earthquake as far as I was concerned. My baby seemed a helluva lot more important.

The Sioux language has a number of words for pregnancy. One of them means "growing strong." Another means "to be overburdened." I felt both strong and overburdened at the same time. I wanted to have my baby at Wounded Knee, but was not sure whether that could be, because sometimes a person would come and say, "Negotiations are coming on real good. We'll all be out of here in a day or two. We're all gonna go home." I always answered, "We'll either be out of here or we'll die. Whatever, I'm going to have my baby right here, the Indian way." But I was a lot less confident than I sounded.

I was determined not to go to the hospital. I did not want a white doctor looking at me down there. I wanted no white doctor to touch me. Always in my mind was how they had sterilized my sister and how they had let her baby die. My baby was going to live! I was going to have it in the old Indian manner—well, old, but not too old. In the real ancient tradition our women stuck a waist-high cottonwood stick right in the center of the tipi. Squatting, holding on to that stick, they would drop the baby onto a square of soft, tanned deer hide. They themselves cut the umbilical cord and put puffball powder on the baby's navel. Sometimes a woman friend was squatting behind them, pressing down on their stomach, or working the baby down with some sort of belt.

They would rub the baby down with water and sweetgrass and then wipe it clean with buffalo grease. I did not think that I was quite that hardy or traditional to do it exactly in that way. And where would I have gotten buffalo grease?

Somebody should also have given me a fully beaded and quilled cradleboard and two turtle or lizard amulets to put the navel cord in— one to hide somewhere in the cradleboard and the other to display openly so that the bad spirits would think the navel cord was in that one, and they would try to bewitch it and would be fooled. Keha, the turtle, and Telanuwe, the sand lizard, are hard to kill. They live long. Their hearts go on beating long after they are dead. So these fetishes protect and give long life. My aunt, Elsie Flood, the turtle woman, would have made such a charm for me, but that was not to be.

I should have found a winkte, that is a gay person, to give my baby a secret name. Winktes were believed to always live to a great old age. If they gave the newborn such a hidden name, not the one everybody would know him by, then the winkte's longevity would rub off on the little one. Such a winkte name was always funnily obscene, like for instance Che Maza, meaning Iron Prick, and you had to pay the name-giver well for it. Well, I had no money and how was I going to find a winkte at Wounded Knee? I could not very well go to every warrior and ask him, "Are you by any chance gay?" This is not to criticize winktes. We Sioux have always believed that a person is free to be what he or she wants to be. I know a winkte who is incredibly brave. At the Sun Dance he chooses the most painful way of self-inflicted suffering. He pierces at the same time in two places in front and two spots in the back. Then he stands fastened between four poles with little space to move. He cannot tear himself loose by running a few steps and then making a sudden jump. He has to work the skewers through his flesh slowly, excruciatingly. But somehow, I cannot believe in the winktes' power of longevity. In the old days the winkte lived so long because he wore women's clothes and was tanning and beading and cooking while the other men went on a war party and got themselves killed. I have a suspicion that nowadays the winktes live no longer than anybody else.

So I could not be quite as traditional as all that. When I say that I was determined to have my baby the Sioux way, I simply meant with an Indian prayer and the burning of sweetgrass and with the help of Indian women friends acting as midwives, having it the natural way without injections or anesthesia. I did intend to have my baby inside the ceremonial tipi, but was persuaded not to. It was too exposed and often under fire.

I did not always have lofty thoughts about traditional birth giving on my mind during the last week before I went into labor. More often I was preoccupied with much more earthly things such as getting safely to the toilet. Being in my ninth month I had to urinate frequently. The women had cleaned out a garage and with the help of some men made it into a four-way ladies' room. It was really weird. You always met a number of girls lined up, waiting their turn. Seeing my big belly they usually let me go ahead. Sometimes tracers were all around us like lightning bugs as the bullets kicked up the dust at our feet. Somehow or other this shooting did not seem real. The girls remained standing in line, chatting and giggling. There was never any panic. Somebody would come and shout, "Is everybody all right? Anybody need tranquilizers?" Imagine being in a place where you needed tranquilizers to go to the can! We did not take them anyway. My problem was that in my condition I had to go two or three times as often as the others, and I was in more of a hurry.

One evening I was inside the trading post. I had just cleaned up when that Pine Ridge man came in and sat down. He kept looking and looking at me and finally said, "Are you gonna have your baby here?"

I told him, "Yeah, if I have to. Are you going to stay to the end?"

He said, "No. I got work to do on the outside."

"Gee," I told him, "you're an Oglala. This is your land. You're supposed to stick it out. I'm from the next reservation, Rosebud, a Brule woman and pregnant. But I'm staying. You're not going to accomplish much."

He gave me a long look. "Wow! You're gonna have your baby here the Indian way. That's pretty heavy." I had to agree with him.

On another occasion my brother told me, "You shouldn't be here, pregnant as you are. I should put you across my knee and spank you for having come." I told him to mind his business, and did he have a cigarette.

There was another pregnant woman with me at the Knee, Cheryl Petite. She also planned to have her baby inside the perimeter. She was a great big woman. Some of the guys were betting which of us would pop first. She went into labor on Sunday, three days before I did. Her husband was a loudmouth and he came to tell me, "She beat you. We're gonna have our baby first."

I answered him that I did not care who was having her baby first. This was no sports event. I wasn't in a race. But he kept on bragging all over the village that Cher was going to beat me to it. She was in labor for two hours. When her pains were about ten minutes apart he started worrying: "Maybe it would be better to go to the hospital. Maybe she's too small. Maybe he's not in the right position. Maybe it's gonna be a breach baby." So they got themselves all worried and he started negotiating at the roadblock, and the marshals let them through to have their baby at the Pine Ridge Hospital. The people inside the village felt bad. Many came to me saying, "Mary, you're our last chance now to have a baby born at Wounded Knee." I did not want to disappoint them.

Shortly before Crow Dog left for Washington, he put on a peyote meeting. I was glad to be able to participate in it just when I was on the point of giving birth—exactly a week before I went into labor, as it turned out. I took medicine. When the sacred things were passed around I took hold of the staff and prayed with it, prayed that my child and I would come through it all safely. And at the time of midnight water Leonard stood up and said, "It's gonna be all right. Good things will happen to you." And I told him how much strength the meeting was giving me. While I was praying it had rained, a sort of foggy, misty-white rain. But then it stopped and when the meeting ended the sky was clear. I left confident, feeling good.

Monday, just as the morning star came out, my water broke and I went down to the sweat lodge to pray. I wanted to go into the sweat but Black Elk would not let me. Maybe there was a taboo against my participating, just as a menstruating woman is not allowed to take part in a ceremony. I was disappointed. I did not feel that the fact that my water had burst had made me ritually unclean. As I walked away from the vapor hut, for the third time, I heard that ghostly cry and lamenting of a woman and child coming out of the massacre ravine. Others had heard it too. I felt that the spirits were all around me. I was later told that some of the marshals inside their sandbagged positions had also heard it, and some could not stand it and had themselves transferred.

After that nothing happened until Tuesday morning when some stuff came out of me. At four o'clock in the afternoon I began having spasms at intervals of half an hour. They made me lie down then. At nine o'clock at night the cramps became severe. The pains lasted all night. On Wednesday morning they became harder. A firefight started, but I was too preoccupied to pay it any attention. My friends kept me strong. Pedro Bissonette, who was later killed by BIA police, was pacing the floor, pacing and pacing. Every now and then he would look in on me to see how I was doing, trying to reassure me: "An ambulance is waiting for you. Just in case anything should go wrong. It's ready to take you through the roadblock to the hospital. Just give the word."

"No," I said, "it's all right." But it wasn't. The pains were bad and they lasted so long. And they were so real, blotting out everything else. I was too tired to push, too tired to live. Then I got lonesome. I missed my mother with whom I had never gotten along, missed my sisters, missed Grandma. I wished that there had been a father waiting for me and the baby. And yet I was so lucky in having such devoted women friends standing by, helping me. Josette Wawasik acted as the chief midwife. She was a seventy-two-year-old Potawatomy lady from Kansas who had been at the Knee from the very beginning and had also taken part in the BIA building takeover half a year before. Ellen Moves Camp and Vernona Kills Right were assisting her, and naturally Annie Mae Aquash was there, too. Mrs. Wawasik had delivered thirteen babies before and Ellen Moves Camp had delivered three or four, so they knew what they were doing. Ellen's case was tragic; she was such a strong-hearted woman, and later had to see a son turn into an informer against us. Their hands were gentle. I had no injections, or knockout medicine, just water. I gave birth inside a trailer house. As I said, I had wanted to deliver inside the tipi but that would have been risking all our lives. Well, my labor lasted until 2:45 P.M. and then it went zip, easy, just like that.

A couple of hours before Pedro was born a cow gave birth to a calf. The old-style Sioux are proverbial gamblers and they had been betting which would come in first, the cow or me. And the cow had beaten me by a length.

When the baby was born I could hear the people outside. They had all come except the security manning the bunkers, and when they heard my little boy's first tiny cry all the women gave the high-pitched, trembling brave-heart yell. I looked out the window and I could see them, women and men standing there with their fists raised in the air, and I really thought then that I had accomplished something for my people. And that felt very, very good, like a warmth spreading over me.

Dennis Banks came in and hugged me, saying, "Right on, sister!" and he was crying, and that made me cry, too. And then Carter Camp and Pedro Bissonette came in with tears streaming down their faces. All those tough guys were weeping. And then my girl friends came in, taking turns holding the baby. Grandma Wawasik went to the window and held up the baby and a great cheer went up. They were beating the big drum and singing the AIM song. And that led to another song, many songs, and my heart beat with the drum. They wrapped my baby up and laid him beside me. They brought in the pipe and we prayed with it, prayed for my little boy whom I named Pedro. I am glad I did because this way Pedro Bissonette's name is living on. And right away after my son was born he lifted up his little, soft head and so I knew that I had a strong child, because they don't do that until they are two weeks old. And the macho Sioux men said, "For sure, that's a warrior." As I looked at him I knew that I was entering a new phase of my life and that things would not, could not ever be the same again. More and more people crowded in, pumped my hand, and snapped my picture, and I wasn't even done yet. Grandma Wawasik and Ellen Moves Camp had to throw them all out so that I could have my afterbirth. Out of the window I could see smoke. The feds were burning off the sagebrush to deprive our guides of cover. The whole prairie around Wounded Knee was burning. Vernona said, "They're sending up a smoke signal for you." I was very, very tired and finally slept a little.

LORENE CARY
(1956—)

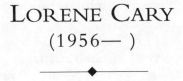

LORENE CARY grew up in Philadelphia and as a high school student was offered a scholarship to St. Paul's School in Concord, New Hampshire, a private white male prep school for the rich and socially secure which was recruiting blacks and girls. Cary, naive, intellectually ambitious, and curious, accepted. *Black Ice* (1991), excerpted here, is her memoir of the changes of mind and heart this new world seemed to demand and her adolescent confusion and equilibrium in the face of them. Later, as an adult, she returned to St. Paul's as a teacher and a trustee; the memoir also offers her seasoned retrospective insight into what she had come through.

Phillip Lopate, writing in the *New York Times Book Review,* praised her story, told in "a wry, reflective, unpreachy voice all her own," of "the ache of the minority or immigrant scholarship student, who keeps trying to straddle two worlds and lose neither." Scholar and critic Houston Baker reads Cary's memoir as representing an original contribution to American letters: in his words, it "refines and redefines an entire tradition of Afro-American autobiographical writing. Much more than a compelling personal narrative, the book is a journey into selfhood that resonates with sober reflection, intelligent passion, and joyous love. . . . Cary's authorial mastery—like the book that represents it—signals a black triumph." Arnold Rampersad has called *Black Ice* "probably the most beautifully written and the most moving African-American autobiographical narrative since Maya Angelou's celebrated *I Know Why the Caged Bird Sings.*" (See page 209.) Like Angelou, Cary narrates her pilgrimage with a tonal spiritual dignity that Stanley Crouch in *Notes of a Hanging Judge* (1990) delineates as "the voice of the Negro, . . . the vernacular sound of majestic human engagement, whether personal or social, political or spiritual, . . . provid[ing] us with the most sterling sense of tragedy and . . . prov[ing] that human beings need not be reduced to lower forms of animal life by great suffering. . . . what is most important in the Negro story is not the loss of life to murder, to mistreatment, to madness, but the sense of heroic optimism . . . , the source of the willingness to take the field, to do battle, to struggle up from the sink holes of self-pity that exist just beneath the cynicism so many would encourage in Negroes and in all Americans, assuring them all that there is no hope within 'the system.'"

Cary graduated from St. Paul's in 1974 and received a B.A. and M.A. from the University of Pennsylvania in 1978. She has worked as an editor at *TV Guide* and as a writer for *Time* and *Newsweek*. Her short fiction has been published in *Obsidian*. She currently lives in Philadelphia with her husband and daughter and is working on a novel.

From *Black Ice*

> *Shall it any longer be said of the daughters of Africa, they have no ambition . . . ?*
> —MARIA W. STEWART IN THE LIBERATOR, *1831*

> *. . . There is a grace in life. Otherwise we could not live.*
> —PAUL TILLICH, THE SHAKING OF THE FOUNDATIONS

> *"Skin, skin, ya na know me?"*
> —WEST INDIAN FOLKTALE

June 1989

I could see them from the dais: families and friends sitting on the risers, young students spilling out onto the grass, black-robed faculty members standing in front of their seats—all watching for the first graduates to begin their march down the grassy aisle between the folding chairs on the green. Someone let out a whoop as they appeared, the girls in their white dresses and the boys in their jackets and ties.

Fifteen years before I had walked down the same aisle as a graduate, and nine years later as a teacher. Now I was ending my term as a trustee.

I watched the black and Hispanic students, "my kids," come to the podium to receive their diplomas and awards from the Rector. One young man named Harlem winked at me as he passed. His shoulders still rocked a little, just a little, like the shoulders of black men in cities, and he held himself up on the balls of his feet like the ballet dancer he had become while at St. Paul's School. I remembered him as a Fourth Former, his head cocked to one side, asking, "I'd like to know: would you send *your* daughter to St. Paul's?"

The other students had laughed in that way that teenagers do when an adult is forced to reveal herself. But we also laughed together as black people alone, safe for the moment within the group, the collective tensions and harmonic humor of it, relieved for an hour or so from our headlong rush toward individual achievement.

"My daughter will have to decide that for herself," I said. "Don't you roll your eyes. I mean it. My parents did not make me come here. I was bound and determined. They *let* me, and it was not an easy thing to do.

"It won't be the same for my daughter. Neither my parents nor I really knew what we were getting into. Once you've made the journey, you can't pretend it didn't happen, that everything's like it was before except now you play lacrosse."

I had pretended, myself; many of us had. I had acknowledged my academic debt to the boarding school I'd attended on scholarship for two years. But I would not admit how profoundly St. Paul's had shaken me, or how damaged and fraudulent and traitorous I felt when I graduated. In fact, I pretended for so long that by the time I was twenty-six years old, I was able to convince myself that going back to school to teach would be the career equivalent of summering with distant, rich relatives.

Instead, I found my own adolescence, in all its hormonal excess, waiting for me at St. Paul's: old rage and fear, ambition, self-consciousness, love, curiosity, energy, hate, envy, compulsion, fatigue. I saw my adolescence in my students, and I felt it burbling inside me, grown powerful by long silence. I lost control of it one night when a black boy came to me nearly weeping because a group of white friends had told a racist joke in his presence. He hated himself, he said, because he hadn't known how to react. "It was like I couldn't move. I couldn't *do* anything," he said.

I too had known that terrible paralysis, and when the boy left, I wept with remembering. I could no longer forget, not with Westminster chimes ringing out the quarter hours, the piney mist that rolled off the pond in the morning, and the squeaking boards under our feet as we crossed Upper Common Room to the dining hall. I remembered the self-loathing, made worse by a poised bravado, as close as my own skin, that I wore over it. I remembered duty and obligation—to my family, to the memory of dead relatives, to my people. And I remembered confusion: was it true that these teachers expected less of me than of my white peers? Or had I mistaken kindness for condescension? Were we black kids a social experiment? If we failed (or succeeded too well) would they call us off? Were we imported to help round out the white kids' education? Did it make any difference if we were?

In the aftermath of Black Is Beautiful, I began to feel black and blue, big and black, black and ugly. Had they done that to me? Had somebody else? Had I let them? Could I stop the feelings? Or hide them?

I knew that I was to emerge from St. Paul's School changed, but I did not know how, and I did not trust my white teachers and guardians to guide me. What would this education do to me? And what was I to do with it?

A couple years after I taught at St. Paul's, I was asked to serve as a trustee. During my term, I visited the school for board meetings, and I talked with the students. I could feel their attention one fall evening when I told them to try to think of St. Paul's as their school, too, not as a white place where they were trespassing. The next fall a boy told me: "I *had* been thinking of it as their school. It was like I had forgotten that this is my life."

Two years later that boy's formmates elected him class president. At his graduation, Eric smiled broadly at me as he walked to the podium to receive the President's Medal. So did a girl, an excellent and feisty writer, who was awarded the Rector's Medal. I wondered if they knew, or if they would learn, that just as St. Paul's was theirs, because they had attended the school and contributed to it, so, too, was American life and culture theirs, because they were black people in America.

Sitting on the dais, I recalled how wary I'd been of John Walker, the first black teacher at St. Paul's, its first black trustee, and the first black Bishop of the Washington, D.C. diocese of the Episcopal Church. I remembered watching him walk with other board members and trying to deduce from his gait and the way he inclined his head whether the small man with the tiny eyes was traitor or advocate.

He was still on the board during my tenure, a quiet-spoken man who affected people deeply by his presence. John Walker spoke wisely and from experience, but more than that, he emanated both judgment and compassion. I saw him affect my colleagues. I felt him. He filled me with hope for my own racial and spiritual healing, and courage to look back. (John Walker died in September, 1989.)

I began writing about St. Paul's School when I stopped thinking of my prep-school experience as an aberration from the common run of black life in America. The isolation I'd felt was an illusion, and it can take time and, as they say at St. Paul's, "the love and labor of many," to get free of illusions. The narratives that helped me, that kept me company, along with the living, breathing people in my life, were those that talked honestly about growing up black in America. They burst into my silence, and in my head, they shouted and chattered and whispered and sang together. I am writing this book to become part of that unruly conversation, and to bring my experience back to the community of minds that made it possible.

"You must really love the school to be on the board." The students wanted to know each time I visited. Each time I answered yes.

"Did you like it when you were here?"

I made a sour face. They looked relieved. . . .

[What follows is Cary's story of her three years as a high school student at St. Paul's. This excerpt ends with her memory of graduation.]

The day of graduation dawned sunny with clouds. We glared at the clouds every half-hour to hold them back. We arrived onto the grounds just before the Chapel service ended. Chapel Road was lined with expensive cars. My school did not look like itself. I went into the Chapel with my mother. It was packed. We stood in the entryway with other latecomers. I remembered running to Chapel and sitting in the entry, where everyone could see that I was late. I remembered Mr. Tolliver, whom we called Toad, because of his solid body and bad posture, putting his finger into my shoulder. "Girl," he said. "You were late to Chapel."

I was late again, and ashamed, now that I'd stepped through the doors, that I had not had the sense to get there on time. I remembered how the last services of the term had never failed to move me, to help me pass from one phase of my life at St. Paul's to the next. Already, the Rector's voice was intoning the closing prayer. I knew it by heart:

"O God, who through the love and labor of many hast built us here a goodly heritage in the name of thy servant St. Paul, and hast crowned our school with honor and length of days: For these thy gifts, and for thyself, we thank thee, and for past achievements and future hopes; beseeching thee that both we and all who follow after us may learn those things on earth, of which the knowledge continues in thy Heaven. . . .

"Bless the work of this School undertaken for thy glory and continued in thy fear. Make this to be in deed and in truth a Christian school, that none who come here may go away unimproved, that none may be afraid or ashamed to be thy faithful servants."

We sang the *Salve Mater,* which we pulled out only on graduation day, and the traditional closing hymn. The Chapel rang with music. Mr. Wood at the organ, the choir filing out past the throng, singing the song I had sung, dressed in the robes I had worn, the acolytes and the priests, the banners and standards. They filed out smiling, nodding at old students, parents, friends, and singing:

Ye watchers and ye holy ones,
Bright seraphs, cherubim, and thrones,
Raise the glad strain, Alleluia!
Cry out, dominions, princedoms, powers,
Virtues, archangels, angels' choirs,
Alleluia! Alleluia! Alleluia! Alleluia! Alleluia!

It was high-church at its best, and I knew it as well as I knew my mother's voice. I ached with the sound and the sight of it. Distant gobbledegook at first, the seraphs, cherubim, and thrones resonated deeply now. How many times had I argued with that song? Why was it that this rich, rich school had to get dominions, princedoms, and powers to praise their God? Why were our worshippers "disconsolate" while theirs were "gracious" and "bright"? Who had told them that God was pleased with them? Was it the "goodly heritage"? Was that the proof of God's love? Well, what about the rest of the world, whom they asked God not to forget? What about them? What about the dirty, ragged, cramped, stupid, ugly motherfuckers? When would they be crowned with honor and length of days? What made St. Paul's so cocksure? What about the rest of us? What about me?

I cried then because the music was so beautiful and I loved it so, because loving it was treachery, because I had scribbled the words on scraps of paper and looked them up in the dictionary to learn them, because I could not bear to be so far away from a God who smiled on such exquisite praise. I have read the word of the Lord our God until my eyes burned like the very fires of hell. And still you have not found grace? Still not made Tillich's "leap of faith"?

I wanted to leap right then. I wanted to leap into a big, big faith: big as the sky on a black night, big enough to hold Ward A.M.E. and the Chapel of St. Peter and St. Paul within it. I wanted an infinity inside me that could hold it all. I wanted to fly out of my skin, to leave it draped over the chair by the window and fly up into the welcoming night.

I had come to St. Paul's to fly, and I had failed. What had I become that was worthy of so much effort and money?

We went to lunch at the Upper for the traditional poached salmon on red-and-white school plates. At two o'clock I ran to the green behind the Chapel to get in line for graduation.

No music plays as the paired lines move down the hill behind the Chapel and onto the green. The faculty in their caps and gowns proceeded first, and at the end of the faculty file, the Vice-Rectors, the

trustees, and the Rector. Then the students. We walked in pairs alpha-
betically. The clapping rose to a roar as we entered between bleachers
arranged in a U facing the dais. We four officers walked at the end of
line. My relatives had been waiting, watching for me while more than a
hundred students walked past, and they rushed to hoist their cameras to
their faces.

The brass ensemble played the *Salve Mater.* We sang it for the second time that day. The Rector and then a guest speaker made speeches.
The sun was hot on the top of my head. Prizes and awards lined the
long table on the dais. The Rector read the dedication of each before
he awarded it to a student. Then, the Vice-Rector stepped to a microphone on the side of the dais opposite the Rector and began calling
names of graduating Sixth Formers in flights of four. I was called early,
because my last name begins with C. I did not graduate with Honors,
not even in English, and I sat stupidly for a moment waiting. There was
nothing more. I had simply graduated: no honors.

The Vice-Rector read the diplomas awarded cum laude, magna
cum laude, and summa cum laude. I sat still. The sun and my shame
made me sweat.

Finally the Rector announced the final awards, those that are given
only to graduates. It seemed as if this would never end. I would never
get out of the sun and away from the long, long list of students who
had done what I had claimed I had come to St. Paul's to do.

"The Rector's Award," said Mr. Oates, "is made at the discretion of
the Rector to graduating Sixth Formers whose selfless devotion to
School activities has enhanced all our lives and improved the community we share here at St. Paul's School.

"The two students to whom the Rector's Awards are made this
afternoon represent a wide variety of characteristics. To be a moment
merry, I am going to combine and deliberately mix up comments on
their skills and qualities in such a way that I may possibly obscure from
you who these students are. Of course, if you care to, you may sort
these out as I go, and readily ascertain who they are."

I pursed my lips. "To be a moment merry" indeed. Typical graduation humor. Ha, ha.

"Poised and attractive, determined and responsible, these students
have established superior records academically, been an officer of the
Sixth Form, become skilled in karate, been outstanding in athletics,
sung in the chorus, written for *The Pelican,* been a member of the Missionary Society, joined the Astronomy Club."

My ears perked up at "officer of the Sixth Form." That was one of
us four sitting in pairs on either side of the aisle in the front row. I had

written articles for *The Pelican*. I shushed the greedy girl within. Starved for some special notice, she stood inside my skin jumping up and down. In the seconds while Mr. Oates read the list, I heard her clamor. I heard how deeply she had been hurt to receive nothing, nothing at all but a diploma. No honors, no cum laude, nothing. Nothing for me, nothing for my work? Not a farthing for my trouble? Nothing for the family who had traveled so far? Nothing to compensate for what they don't even know they have lost—my confidence, my trust? Not one little gift to give the people who have given up a daughter? "I've given her to God," my mother sometimes said. I didn't believe it, because it felt as if she were holding on tighter than ever, but she'd lost me. No matter how dutifully I hid it, it was true.

". . . joined the Astronomy Club."

That was it. None of the other three had ever come out to the observatory. The Astronomy Club was a tiny club. Some of my friends had begun to smile at me. They sought out my eyes. Peter tossed me a happy look. I could not face their eyes. The girl inside was too immodest, too grasping and loud. I looked down into my lap as if folded hands could save me from the discomfiting need within.

"Even-tempered, talented, conscientious, well-mannered, he and he, or he and she, or she and she are students of sterling character and high integrity. St. Paul's is deeply indebted to them."

The Rector called my name. He used all three names, as was the graduation custom. And he called Tom Painchaud's name, too.

I heard clapping, and I got up. Painchaud was coming behind. He and I stood together and received our small white boxes tied in red ribbons. Mr. Oates shook hands with each of us and kissed me. He was beaming as he told us congratulations. I thought of the plane tickets when my mother had been sick. I looked at Painchaud and remembered the friendship he had so freely given on the night of the Sixth-Form elections. After that afternoon I might never see him again. Why had I not talked more with him as we had that night? Why had I been so afraid of his eyes?

I had not loved enough. I'd been busy, busy, so busy, preparing for life, while life floated by me, quiet and swift as a regatta.

I had not loved enough. The greedy girl inside me clutched at the little white box with its red ribbons. She was heartbreaking to look upon, a spoiled child at a party grabbing up expensive gifts, no sooner opened than found wanting, grabbing up new ones, hoping for one that would seep into and fill up her soul.

I had not loved enough.

The old people sang a song in church: "Just As I Am, Without One

Plea." We'd sing it as the preacher stood at the altar, in front of the pul- pit, calling one, just one, to make the decision to come to God today. "Are you ready?" he asked. "If you had to meet your Maker today, could you say, 'I'm ready, Lord, just as I am? Not as I *hope* to be. Not tomorrow, not tomorrow, brothers and sisters, please. Because tomor- row may never come. 'Just as I am, Thou wilt receive, Wilt pardon, cleanse, relieve.' He wants us as we are. Only one in the world'll take me just as I am! Thank you, Jesus. *Just* as I am. *He'll* make you ready. He can do it. Isn't there one?"

The old people would wave their arms in the air, and I'd never understood. I'd cried and cried at the vision. Just as I was? How I longed to believe it. I'd cried and joined the church. I'd joined the gospel choir—they'd let me, too, at eleven, and I sang with all the adults, hoping that He would fill my soul with belief.

"In every spiritual experience, Tillich says," Reverend Ingersoll had told us, "there must be in the worshipper a 'leap of faith.'"

I had leapt and leapt and leapt, and here I stood, my big feet in white pumps, standing on the ground. How could you leap at the sky?

The Chapel tolled three. The Sixth Form would depart in half an hour. It said so on the program. The program always said so. It always would. For the first time that year, I was not ready to leave St. Paul's. I had had all my time, all my chances. I could never do it again, never make it right. I had not loved enough.

In the bleachers I saw Nana Jackson, her hands folded in her lap. She was watching the Rector give the last awards. She looked peaceful in her blue and white suit. I remembered how she'd let me play in her hair when I was little, before she cut it, when she took out the hairpins and let it hang down her back. For the last two years, she had sent pear nectar and crackers; cards and money for holidays, even Halloween and Valentine's Day. Pop-Pop had written me faithfully and had ordered sta- tionery for me, white paper with my name and address—ST. PAUL'S SCHOOL—in red.

I was glad of the award in my lap, even though I was no longer sat- isfied with it. The Rector's Medal—there was only one of those awarded each year, and he was reading it now—carried more prestige. I told myself to be grateful for my award, even though I suspected that it was a booby prize, maybe even the badge of a Tom, a palliative to the selfless-devotion types who fell short of the mark.

Graduation ended abruptly, as always, and we filed past our teach- ers. We cried and said thank-you. We hugged and walked on to the next teacher. I cried bitterly. I could barely speak to Sr. Fuster, Sr. Ordoñez, Miss Clinton, Mr. Buxton, Mr. Hawley, Miss Deane, Mr.

Price, Mr. Shipman, Mr. Oates. Love and gratitude, hate, resentments, shame, admiration, loss. They sloshed on deck in big waves; I could only hold onto the hands that were passing me along the line. Mr. Oates was last. He said things to me, but I could not hear them by now. I could only grasp the last hand, embrace the last body, and let go to step onto the green. . . .

NATALIE KUSZ
(1962—)

◆

NATALIE KUSZ was born in California but moved to Alaska when she was six years old and grew up there. She is a graduate of the University of Alaska and now lives with her daughter in St. Paul, Minnesota. On the basis of her first published writing, the memoir *Road Song*—a portion of which follows here—she was awarded a 1989 Whiting Writers Award and the 1990 General Electric Younger Writers Award. Her story begins with the family of four children and two parents moving from Los Angeles to Alaska where they hoped to create an alternative life as homesteaders. Her parents had developed a "distaste for civilization—for its . . . self-absorbed borders." They had the "roaming urge" and the times confirmed their desire to head out for the territory: "it was the spirit of the day"—1969—"to abandon certainty." In Alaska they found unrelenting hard times—a harsh environment, poverty, and personal tragedy. As a first-grader, Natalie, the oldest child, was attacked by a neighbor's sled dog, who tore away one side of her face, causing, among other injuries, the loss of an eye. She was not expected to survive, but did; she underwent years of painful reconstructive surgery, and anguish, in high school turning to drugs and becoming pregnant, in college having the responsibility of being a single parent without much money. She recounts these experiences with no self-pity. The tone is calm and meditative, almost prayerlike; her memory has a radiance. "Adversity," she says, is "the small, hard seed of courage." Her narrative comes across more as a testament to the power of family love, humor, and courage to pull a child through her suffering than as a personal history of pain. It has earned the highest praise. Novelist Alice McDermott found it "elegant and courageous; a wise, sad, beautifully written book. Kusz turns a highly personal and quintessentially American story into a tale that speaks to, and for, us all." In the words of the *Bloomsbury Review*, "the story of her life is told with astonishing skill for so young a writer. . . . her prose is as simple and unadorned as the language of Job, the Proverbs, and Ecclesiastes. It is the kind of prose that will endure, for it speaks the truth resonantly." Memoirist, poet, and critic Patricia Hampl (see page 397) wrote, "A truly great memoir requires not only a powerful story but an absolutely authentic voice. *Road Song* has both. Natalie Kusz has written a master-ful contemporary reprise of the classic American pioneer story with flawless candor, grace, and discretion. I wept and I laughed out loud. I didn't simply read about her family, I became part of it."

Road Songs

Our first months in Alaska, that one long summertime before I was hurt, were hard—in the way, I think, that all immigrants' lives must be hard—but they were also very grand, full of wood fires and camp-grounds, full of people and the stories they told at night when we ate all together, full of clean dust that we washed from our bodies with water carried home from cold springs. My family—Mom and Dad and we four children—had driven up from Los Angeles in a green Rambler station wagon, our clothes and plants and water jugs packed and pulled behind us in a twelve-foot travel trailer with two beds. We were going for an adventure, Mom and Dad had told us, to a place where we could play as loud as we wanted to, where neighbors were far away and everyone minded their own kinds of business. During the 1968 reces-sion, my father had been laid off from his computer job, and he and my mother had seen this as their chance to break away, to act upon wishes we had made among ourselves for years, there at our table in the city. No more feeling jealous when Mom's sisters wrote from Oregon and Idaho, telling of apples in the trees and cows in the barn. We would write them now from country more raw and more our own than any Sheryl or Cara could tell of. And though the new place we came to was hard, we had come to it exhilarated and hopeful, expecting rough-ness and finding it, when we arrived, more to our taste than all we had relinquished behind us.

These were the things my parents had shed us of, shrugging up out of them like clothing grown too small around their shoulders: a house on southeast L.A.'s Chester Street, tall and white from its days as a farm-house, sitting on a double city lot with outbuildings, a playhouse, a gar-den, magnolias and roses and fenced-in grass; blackberry vines I hunted through for ripeness while Mom talked to a neighbor over the fence; chinning bars hung from the trees where Leslie and I played, shouting our voices over car sounds on the boulevard one block over; a mortgage that Mom and Dad paid by having one or two jobs each, working differ-ent shifts when they could to save sending their children into the care of my grandmother; city people with good clothes and white teeth and deftly styled hair, smiling in church and mixing about afterward, speaking of dishwashers and diets and how to keep oil stains off the driveway.

We were gone from these things long before we moved away, living our days through my father's Polish songs and my mother's spoken dreams, through stories Dad told at night of Europe, of the war, of times when people survived picking mushrooms and roasting whole pigs to render off the fat of them. He protected us children, in those early days, from the hard parts of war, referring instead to the land. He spoke his father's name, and those of his brothers, telling of the trees outside the prison camps, the berries growing at their feet, the times when, after escaping one camp or another, he and his brothers grabbed handfuls of these, filling their mouths and sucking their fingers clean. And the people there, he said, the people of the land . . . Far back in the woods, with no one but family nearby, a man might walk the yard in his underwear, just because he could. Through the stories my mother, and then we all, had turned nostalgic for places we had never seen, countries full of trees and cold rivers and neighbors far apart. My father's privilege as an airline worker was to fly us low-cost just about anywhere, and we went as often as we could, and as far. Dad showed us France, and England, even Germany, visiting small villages there to give thanks to the one or two masters who had been kind to him back when he had been a Polish boy-prisoner on their farms. I played there on brick pavement with children who spoke none of my language but who could teach me their games just as well. My special friend in Germany was Heidi, a blond child with a face like a heart, wearing pointed shoes and old jeans and a checked flannel shirt tucked in. She was the granddaughter of the man who had used Dad's brother Pietrek on his farm—the only man in the village, Dad told us later, who had not been a Nazi then.

In the middle of hopscotch, Heidi would tell her friends to wait, and pull me down the alley. "Come on," she said, for it seemed to me then that I understood her speech, and we went into a candy store with glass counters taller than I was, and lights shining down on licorice and hard candy and more chocolates than I had ever seen in my life. Heidi knew the shopkeeper there, standing in his thick white apron and belly, and she spoke to him, grabbing my arm and pointing to me, making the introductions. I held up a hand and waved, and Heidi flashed a hand toward the glass case. What did I want, she asked. I pointed out my choice, and the round man packed up a pile of chocolate disks with white sprinkles, and later, when I showed the bag to my father, he murmured, "Ah, *bon-bons*. I remember." We sat on the bed and shared them, my father biting down and beginning a new story—telling, not of the beatings he received as a prisoner there, but about candy, about *bon-bons* snuck into the hay and eaten there in secret with his brother.

Later, back in the States, when my mother drove the freeway at rush hour, she said to me, or to herself, I couldn't tell, "It's hard to get used to this again, isn't it. This enormous number of people." Young as I was, I understood her, wondered how she had heard me thinking of Europe, of Heidi's tall brick house and its trees, the goats wandering there, the flowers not planted but wild. So, over time, my parents' hunger to leave the city became my own, appeased but never satisfied by short trips and by stories of lives they had led long ago. . . .

They had come, my parents said later, to distaste for civilization—for its people, its small and self-absorbed borders—and to impatience as well, a churning in their bellies to be elsewhere, in places much newer and still greatly older than this. Over years, they had observed in themselves a continuing unlikeness to their society, a growing unease during pinochle parties or church potlucks. Before we children had arrived, they had sampled and cast aside all the lives they could find in that place, and by the time we left for Alaska, my parents had run through what options the city had for them, performing light opera and theater, going to college, training in computers and business and even—for Mom—flight attendance. My father had played handball but hated to talk it with his friends. "A game," he would say, "is not a religion." My mother had shocked the neighbors by bearing a child one evening and coming home to weed the pomegranates and to tend her other children next morning. She said, "It's the women giving birth in the rice paddies and getting on with the job. They're putting us to shame." She despised sewing and cleaning and housewife domesticity, and she furnished the house with secondhand things, again to the shock of the churchfolk. . . .

. . . For us, the children of the family, who remembered Mom and Dad only since they began traveling away with us, songs on the road were tradition, as much our habit as were stories from my parents' growing up, or the huge illustrated Bible they read to us at nap time. A song began with one voice—Mom's or Dad's opening out for two notes. By the third, the rest of us had it and added our parts, Mom switching to alto and taking me sometimes with her, the children's voices and the adults' mixing and widening out, a cappella. My father's head dipped side to side, like a swimmer leaning into his strokes, bellowing out tenor and baritone from the deep, ringing caverns of himself. Mom lifted up her face, taking in air, moving back into the melody, and from her we children learned our own sopranos, the true and unmuffled phrasings, the tones directed by breath and sustained until our very bones and their hollows resonated and increased with the joy of them.

And as the stories all along had kept us whole in ourselves, the songs and the words in my father's own tongues drew in now, it seemed, the rest of the world, those alike and those unlike, but all somehow familiar friends. In Alberta, having driven one hundred miles with the trailer hitch barely holding on, we pulled up to a machinist's shop in a Polish mining town, and while a man welded another full brace onto the tongue, my father stood in the street and spoke loud hilarity with his countrymen. The town, it seemed, had not changed in five decades, and the men there spoke of "renting" local women at the saloon, paying them cash on the spot if they would dance and drink for the evening. "They wear nice clothes," the men said. "And hair, too. A man needs that kind of company." In the end, the machinist charged just eight dollars, and was astonished that my parents had expected to pay much more. "I only charge what's fair," he huffed. "I'm not some guy from the States, sticking it to you like a thief. That hitch should get you where you're going now."

Elsewhere on the way, there were Slavic shopkeepers and German grocers, many of whom handed candy to us children and accepted no payment, all of whom were glad enough to talk to my father, to speak their old language out loud. My mother listened for the words she could recognize, keeping up as best she could with the conversation, and what she didn't get, my father filled in for us later as we drove.

But there were other good people, too, English-speakers not drawn to us by language, or by song, or by anything visible we could name; and soon it was clear that this fresh sort of kindness was new, not to the world, but only to us, and that my parents were seeing what they had imagined in their stories all along: people more our kind than we were ourselves. There were young men alone in small trucks who pulled us up steep hills or fiddled under the hood when our engine gave out, waving us on our way and grinning. At Liard Hot Springs, we met a Cherokee man named Bob with degrees in mining and geology, who spent summers in Alaska and winters in Florida and who lived year-round in a camper on back of his pickup. He would tell us anything we wanted to know about the road, and offer any help, but he would refuse my parents' offer of a tiny heater for his camper; it was as if, my mother wrote later, a cup of coffee he could accept as hospitality, but a slice of bread might obligate him, or give one the right to tell him what to spread on it. My parents' hearts warmed to him, and much later he would drink coffee with us again at the Fairbanks campground, and would drive with us out to see the land we had bought, scouting it over with my father and approving it with a grand gesture of his arm. . . .

★ ★ ★

[The family arrived in Alaska in May. They spent the summer looking for land which they finally found and bought, 258 acres in Delta Junction. Before winter set in, they built temporary housing, "a plywood wanigan with a tarpaper roof," attached to a tiny trailer.]

. . . My mother described the next months as the time she learned winter. At twenty below, she found, Jell-O set in half an hour, but it would freeze inward from the edges at −40°. Metal clung to the hands at that temperature and left burn marks on skin at −60°. Propane would still flow to the stove even at fifty below if you wound heat tape around its tank or built around it a box with a 100-watt bulb inside. The same gas dryer you put in your car's tank would keep heating oil flowing from its barrel. And some of the best places to find winter clothes were the Salvation Army and the Army Surplus Store. Oscar had said, and other friends had agreed, that in winter every person should keep a full set of clothes in the car in case of a breakdown, and bags of sand in the trunk for extra traction. All of these came from thrift stores, too, and even with the summer money running out, Mom and Dad seemed glad to buy them, because it made our stake in this place appear somehow more substantial.

Still, there was nervousness in the looks my parents gave each other, and in the breathless way my dad hurried to the car every morning on his way to the union hall in town. Our summer friends had said to prepare for a jobless winter, to earn what we could before snowfall, because no one built houses or put through any roads in the cold. Yet our own building materials and car repairs had cost my parents most of what they had had to spare, and now that November had come, and the thermometer read −41°, there was almost nothing left for stove oil or for food. During this time, I was the only one of us sure of getting a fully balanced meal every day; my first-grade teacher had sent home an application for free hot lunch after she had noticed me asking for credit several days in a row. Leslie and Ian learned to be happy with any-thing—oatmeal, egg noodles, fresh rabbit when there was some—and while they ate, Mom put powdered milk in Bethel's bottle, and fed her the soft food with a spoon.

Our nearest neighbors through the trees were the Horners, two cabins of cousins whose sons went to my school. Paul was in my class, Kevin was a year ahead, and both their families had moved here, as we had, from California, escaping the city and everything frightening that lived there. Kevin had a grown brother in L.A. who was comatose now since he'd been hit on the freeway; his mother, Geri, had come with her brother-in-law's family to Alaska to get well, she hoped, from her own mental breakdown, and to keep herself as far as she could from automobiles.

Paul and Kevin Horner were my best friends then, and we played with our dogs in the cousins' houses, or in the wide snowy yard in between. On weekends or days off from school, my parents took us sledding and to the gravel pit with our skates. Sometimes, if the day was long enough, Paul and Kevin and I followed rabbit tracks through the woods, careful not to step right on the trails for fear of leaving our scent there—for fear, that is, that the rabbits would abandon them. We mapped all the new trails we could find, and my mother gave me orders about when to be home. Bears, she said, and we laughed, said didn't she know they were asleep, and we could all climb trees anyway. We were not afraid, either, when Mom warned of dog packs. Dogs got cabin fever, too, she said, especially in the cold. They ran through the woods, whole crowds of them, looking for someone to gang up on.

That's okay, I told her. We carried pepper in our pockets in case of dogs: sprinkle it on their noses, we thought, and the whole pack would run away.

In December, the day before my birthday, when the light was dim and the days shorter than we had known before, Dad got a break at the union hall, a job at Prudhoe Bay that would save us just in time, before the stove oil ran out and groceries were gone. Mom convinced us children that he was off on a great adventure, that he would see foxes and icebergs, that we could write letters for Christmas and for New Year's, and afford new coats with feathers inside. In this last, I was not much interested, because I had my favorite already—a red wool coat that reversed to fake leopard—but I would be glad if this meant we could redeem from the pawnshop Dad's concertina, and his second violin, and mine, the half-size with a short bow, and the guitar and mandolin and rifles and pistol that had gone that way one by one. Whether I played each instrument or not, it had been good to have them around, smelling still of campfires and of songfests in the summer.

It was cold after Dad left, cold outside and cold in our house. Ice on the trailer windows grew thick and shaggy, and Leslie and I melted handprints on it and licked off our palms. There had been no insulation when the add-on went up, so frost crawled the walls there, too, and Mom had us wear long johns and shoes unless we were in our beds. Paul and Kevin came for my birthday, helped me wish over seven candles, gave me a comb and a mirror. They were good kids, my mother said, polite and with good sense, and she told me that if I came in from school and she was not home, I should take Hobo with me and walk to their house. You're a worrywart, Mommy, I said. I'm not a baby, you know.

I wish now I had been tolerant of her fears, and perhaps even shared them. Alaska was a young place when we moved to it, much larger than it seems now, with more trees and thicker ice fog, and with its few people more isolated in the midst of them. During the very deep cold, car exhaust came out in particles rather than as gas, and it hung low and thick in the air, obscuring everything, so that even traffic lights were invisible to the car which was stopped right beneath them. In the middle of ice fog, a person was isolated, muffled and enclosed apart from anyone else on the road. Radio stations ran air-quality bulletins, warning asthmatics and old people to stay indoors, and most folks stayed home anyway, knowing how easily a fan belt would shatter in the cold. To us California-bred children, the rolling dense fog that billowed in our open door was a new and thrilling thing; but to my mother, who siphoned stove oil into the fuel barrel five gallons at a time, and who scavenged deadwood and sticks from under snow, that fog must have seemed formidable, the visual symbol of all one must fight against in this place. She kept the lock fastened even when we were home, and she looked and listened with her head out the door for long seconds each time she had to go out to the ice box. I remember her steps outside, slow and controlled on the bottom stairs, hitting faster and harder toward the top, and I remember her gasp as she lurched inside, her glasses clouding up with frost, Baggies of frozen berries falling down from her arms.

The morning after my birthday, Mom woke up and couldn't stand. She shivered and sweated, and when I helped her sit up she said the room was tilting away from her, and could I mix Bethel up a bottle. It was her tonsils, she said. They were tight in her throat and she couldn't swallow around them. Her skin was hot and wet under my hand; the sweat sat on her forehead and soaked into hairs that fell into it when she tried to lift her neck. "Stay there and I'll make some Russian Tea," I said. "Okay, Mommy? Maybe you can drink some tea?" Mom moved her head. She made a grunting noise as she swallowed, and her lips drew far back from her teeth.

Bethel had been sucking air from an empty bottle, and now she started to cry, dangling the nipple from her teeth and pulling herself up onto Mom's bed. Mom's eyes stayed closed, but her hand lifted off the mattress and patted limply at Bethel's shoulder. I breathed hard, and my eyes stung inside their lids. I picked my sister up and carried her into the trailer room, telling her, "Come on in here, Bethel. Let's make some milk and tea."

Leslie and Ian had their treasure chests out on the floor, and Leslie looked up. "Mommy's really sick, isn't she," she asked. I said yes, she was really sick.

I stayed home all week from school, making macaroni from boxes and saying everyone's prayers at night. Mom moved from bed to honey-bucket and back and had me read Psalms at bedtime until she was strong enough again to see the words. The honeybucket in the corner was a five-gallon plastic paint can with a toilet seat on top, and under its red cloth drape it filled up, for Mom was too weak to carry it to the out-house pit. I poured in more Pine Sol than usual each time someone used it, and the cabin filled with the fecund smell of pine oil and waste, a scent we would still loathe years later when we got a real toilet and electricity and began to boycott pine cleaners. The days got shorter all the time, and with no windows in the wanigan, we seemed to move in twilight, squinting at one another between four dark walls. I felt snap-pish and breathless, and I bossed Leslie and Ian until they cried. Finally, my mother was better and I went back to school, and she met me at the bus stop afternoons, walking me home down the road, shining the flash-light ahead of us.

Christmas passed, and Mom went into town every day—for water, or to do laundry, or to get the mail—but no check arrived from my father. He wrote often, including short notes to each of us, and he said he had sent his first paycheck down just two weeks after he started work. It was good money, he wrote, enough for stove oil and groceries and for the instruments in hock. When he came home, we would fin-ish my violin lessons, and we'd start on the younger kids, too, and we would play together the same songs we had sung on the way up the Alcan and then after that at the campgrounds all summer long.

That first check never did come. Mom wrote back that it must have been lost, and could he get them to print another. When was the next one due, she asked. She would try to stretch things out until it came.

The redemption time was running out on all our things at the pawnshop. We had one violin left to pawn, the one my grandfather had given to Dad before I was born, when Dad had driven from L.A. to New York and brought the old man home with him. In Polish, it was a *Benkarty*, a wide, barrel-chested French violin, aged reddish-brown under its lacquer. It was for a master, made to play fast and ring loudly, its neck rounded and thinner than most, the back of its body all a single piece of maple. The wood and varnish had aged and crystallized so smoothly that when my father tuned it and began to play, each string he stroked resonated acutely with the sounds of the others. To pay the interest on the other things in hock, my mother took the *Benkarty* in to the pawnbroker, telling him she would be back for it soon. "It's my husband's," she said, trusting this Russian man to keep the violin safe, if only for sake of the old country and my father's Slavic tongue. She could not know then that the man would sell the *Benkarty* before its redemption date, or that she and my father would never get it back. At the time, the clearest thing for her was the extra cash she got for it, and the powdered milk and the gas she was able to buy that afternoon.

Mom arranged her days carefully around the hours I was in school. Her glasses had broken across the bridge one morning when she had come inside and set them to thaw on the woodstove, so she walked me to the bus stop wearing prescription sunglasses and then fastened my sisters and brother into the truck and drove into town, scraping ice from the windshield as she steered. I know from her journal that she was afraid, that she padlocked the cabin door against the vandalism recently come into town, that she counted her time out carefully so she would be home in time to meet my afternoon bus. She reminded me and made me promise that, should she be late one day, I would take Hobo to Paul and Kevin's and wait there until she came for me. "Okay, Mommy," I said then, and turned to pull Hobo's ears.

"No, listen to me, Natalie." Mom held my arm until I looked up. Behind the dark lenses her eyes were invisible, but her cheeks were white, and her lips very nearly the same color. "This is not a joke," she said. "Now don't forget what I'm saying. You must go to the boys' if I'm late. This is very important."

"It's okay," I repeated. I looked into her glasses. "I'll remember."

On January 10, only Hobo met me at the bus stop. In the glare from school-bus headlights, his blue eye shone brighter than his brown, and he watched until I took the last step to the ground before tackling me in the snow. Most days, Hobo hid in the shadow of the spruce until Mom took my bag, then he erupted from the dark to charge up behind me, run through my legs and on out the front. It was his favorite trick. I usually lost my balance and ended up sitting in the road with my feet thrown wide out front and steaming dog tongue all over my face.

Hobo ran ahead, then back, brushing snow crystals and fur against my leg. I put a hand on my skin to warm it and dragged nylon ski pants over the road behind me. Mom said to have them along in case the bus broke down, but she knew I would not wear them, could not bear the plastic sounds they made between my thighs.

No light was on in our house.

If Mom had been home, squares of yellow would have shown through the spruce and lit the fog of my breath, turning it bright as I passed through. What light there was now came from the whiteness of snow, and from the occasional embers drifting up from our stovepipe. I laid my lunchbox on the top step and pulled at the padlock, slapping a palm on the door and shouting. Hobo jumped away from the noise and ran off, losing himself in darkness and in the faint keening dog sounds going up from over near the Horners' house. I called, "Hobo. Come back here, boy," and took the path toward Paul's, tossing my ski pants to the storage tent as I passed.

At the property line, Hobo caught up with me and growled, and I fingered his ear, looking where he pointed, seeing nothing ahead there but the high curve and long sides of a Quonset hut, the work shed the Horners used also as a fence for one side of their yard. In the fall, Paul and Kevin and I had walked to the back of it, climbing over boxes and tools and parts of old furniture, and we had found in the corner a lemmings' nest made from chewed bits of cardboard and paper, packed under the curve of the wall so that shadows hid it from plain sight. We all bent close to hear the scratching, and while Paul held a flashlight I took two sticks and parted the rubbish until we saw the black eyes of a mother lemming and the pink naked bodies of five babies. The mother dashed deeper into the pile and we scooped the nesting back, careful not to touch the sucklings, for fear that their mama would eat them if they carried scent from our fingers.

It seemed that we had spent most of the fall looking out just like that for shrews and lemmings. Oscar and Vic had cats, and Paul and Kevin had three German shepherds, and one or another of them usually found a rodent to play with. Oscar's cats would catch a shrew in their teeth, holding tight to skin behind its neck until its eyes swelled out and it stopped breathing. The boys and I squeezed the cats' jaws, screaming, "You're not even *hungry*," until the teeth parted and the shrew dropped into our palms. If we were fast enough, it was still alive, and we pushed its eyes back in and let it go. The dogs worried a lemming in their mouths, dropping it out on occasion and catching it back into the air, over and over again until it couldn't move and was no longer any fun. When we caught the dogs doing this, we beat their ears with walking sticks, but usually we were too late and had to bury the thing under moss.

The dogs were loud now beyond the Quonset, fierce in their howls and sounding like many more than just three. Hobo crowded against my legs, and as I walked he hunched in front of me, making me stumble into a drift that filled my boots with snow. I called him a coward and said to quit it, but I held his neck against my thigh, turning the corner into the boys' yard and stopping on the edge. Paul's house was lit in all its windows, Kevin's was dark, and in the yard between them were dogs, new ones I had not seen before, each with its own house and tether. The dogs and their crying filled the yard, and when they saw me they grew wilder, hurling themselves to the ends of their chains, pulling their lips off their teeth. Hobo cowered and ran and I called him with my mouth, but my eyes did not move from in front of me.

There were seven. I knew they were huskies and meant to pull dogsleds, because earlier that winter Paul's grandfather had put on his glasses and shown us a book full of pictures. He had turned the pages with a wet thumb, speaking of trappers and racing people and the ways they taught these dogs to run. They don't feed them much, he said, or they get slow and lose their drive. This was how men traveled before they invented snowmobiles or gasoline.

There was no way to walk around the dogs to the lighted house. The snow had drifted and been piled around the yard in heaps taller than I was, and whatever aisle was left along the sides was narrow, and pitted with chain marks where the animals had wandered, dragging their tethers behind. No, I thought, Kevin's house was closest and out of biting range, and someone could, after all, be sitting home in the dark.

My legs were cold. The snow in my boots had packed itself around my ankles and begun to melt, soaking my socks and the felt liners under my heels. I turned toward Kevin's house, chafing my thighs together hard to warm them, and I called cheerfully at the dogs to shut up. Oscar said that if you met a wild animal, even a bear, you had to remember it was more scared than you were. Don't act afraid, he said, because they can smell fear. Just be loud—stomp your feet, wave your hands—and it will run away without even turning around. I yelled "Shut up" again as I climbed the steps to Kevin's front door, but even I could barely hear myself over the wailing. At the sides of my eyes, the huskies were pieces of smoke tumbling over one another in the dark.

The wood of the door was solid with cold and even through deer-skin mittens it bruised my hands like concrete. I cupped a hand to the window and looked in, but saw only black—black, and the reflection of a lamp in the other cabin behind me. I turned and took the three steps back to the ground; seven more and I was in the aisle between doghouses, stretching my chin far up above the frenzy, thinking hard on other things. This was how we walked in summertime, the boys and I, escaping from bad guys over logs thrown across ditches: step lightly and fast, steady on the hard parts of your soles, arms extended outward, palms down and toward the sound. That ditch, this aisle, was a river, a torrent full of silt that would fill your clothes and pull you down if you missed and fell in. I was halfway across. I pointed my chin toward the house and didn't look down.

On either side, dogs on chains hurled themselves upward, choking themselves to reach me, until their tethers jerked their throats back to earth. I'm not afraid of you, I whispered; this is dumb.

I stepped toward the end of the row and my arms began to drop slowly closer to my body. Inside the mittens, my thumbs were cold, as cold as my thighs, and I curled them in and out again. I was walking past the last dog and I felt brave, and I forgave him and bent to lay my mitten on his head. He surged forward on a chain much longer than I thought, leaping at my face, catching my hair in his mouth, shaking it in his teeth until the skin gave way with a jagged sound. My feet were too slow in my boots, and as I blundered backward they tangled in the chain, burning my legs on metal. I called out at Paul's window, expecting rescue, angry that it did not come, and I beat my arms in front of me, and the dog was back again, pulling me down.

A hole was worn into the snow, and I fit into it, arms and legs drawn up in front of me. The dog snatched and pulled at my mouth, eyes, hair; his breath clouded the air around us, but I did not feel its heat, or smell the blood sinking down between hairs of his muzzle. I watched my mitten come off in his teeth and sail upward, and it seemed unfair then and very sad that one hand should freeze all alone; I lifted the second mitten off and threw it away, then turned my face back again, overtaken suddenly by loneliness. A loud river ran in my ears, dragging me under.

My mother was singing. *Lu-lee, lu-lay, thou little tiny child,* the song to the Christ Child, the words she had sung, smoothing my hair, all my life before bed. Over a noise like rushing water I called to her and heard her answer back, Don't worry, just sleep, the ambulance is on its way. I drifted back out and couldn't know then what she prayed, that I would sleep on without waking, that I would die before morning. . . .

ACKNOWLEDGMENTS

◆

Grateful acknowledgment is made for permission to reprint the following:

CURTIS BROWN LTD.: Excerpts from *Generations* by Lucille Clifton. Copyright © 1976 by Lucille Clifton. Reprinted by permission of Curtis Brown, Ltd.

DELL BOOKS: Excerpts from *Silences* by Tillie Olsen. Copyright © 1965, 1972, 1978 by Tillie Olsen. Used by permission of Delacorte Press/Seymour Lawrence, a division of Bantam Doubleday Dell Publishing Group, Inc.

DONADIO & ASHWORTH, INC.: Excerpts from *Herself* by Hortense Calisher. Reprinted by permission of Donadio & Ashworth, Inc. Copyright © 1972 by Hortense Calisher.

FARRAR, STRAUS & GIROUX, INC.: Excerpts from *Two-Part Invention* by Madeline L'Engle. Copyright © 1988 by Crosswicks Ltd. Reprinted by permission of Farrar, Straus & Giroux, Inc. Jamaica Kincaid's conference presentation at Dia Center for the Arts, May 1990, partially excerpted from *A Small Place,* copyright © 1988, 1991 by Jamaica Kincaid. Reprinted by permission of Farrar, Straus & Giroux, Inc. "On the Morning After the Sixties" from *The White Album* by Joan Didion. Copyright © 1970 by Joan Didion. Excerpts from *Fierce Attachments* by Vivian Gornick. Copyright © 1987 by Vivian Gornick. Excerpts from *Road Song* by Natalie Kusz. Copyright © 1990 by Natalie Kusz. Reprinted by permission of Farrar, Straus & Giroux, Inc.

FIREBRAND BOOKS: "Deciding to Live" by Dorothy Allison, from *Trash.* Copyright © 1988 by Dorothy Allison. Reprinted by permission of Firebrand Books, Ithaca, New York. Excerpts from *A Burst of Light* by Audre Lorde. Copyright © 1988 by Audre Lorde. Reprinted by permission of Firebrand Books, Ithaca, New York 14850.

GROVE PRESS: From the book *Orphans: Real and Imaginary* by Eileen Simpson. Copyright © 1987 by Eileen Simpson. Used by permission of Grove/Atlantic Monthly Press. Paperback available through Plume c/o Penguin USA, 374 Hudson Street, New York, NY 10014. From the book *Lakota Woman* by Mary Crow Dog with Richard Erdoes. Copyright © 1990 by Mary Crow Dog and Richard Erdoes. Used by permission of Grove/Atlantic Monthly Press. Paperback available through HarperCollins, 10 East 53rd Street, New York, NY 10022.

HARCOURT BRACE & COMPANY: Excerpts from *The Woman Within* by Ellen Glasgow. Copyright © 1954 and renewed 1982 by Harcourt Brace & Company. Excerpt from *How I Grew* by Mary McCarthy. Copyright © 1986,

1987 by Mary McCarthy. Reprinted by permission of the publisher.

HARPERCOLLINS PUBLISHERS, INC.: Excerpts from *Dust Tracks on a Road* by Zora Neale Hurston. Copyright 1942 by Zora Neale Hurston. Copyright © renewed 1970 by John C. Hurston. Excerpt from *Carnal Acts* by Nancy Mairs. Copyright © 1991 by Nancy Mairs. Excerpt from *The Long Loneliness* by Dorothy Day. Copyright © 1952 by Harper & Row, Publishers, Inc. Excerpt from *An American Childhood* by Annie Dillard. Copyright © 1987 by Annie Dillard. Reprinted by permission of HarperCollins Publishers, Inc.

HARVARD UNIVERSITY PRESS: From *One Writer's Beginnings* by Eudora Welty. Copyright © 1983, 1984 by Eudora Welty. Reprinted by permission of Harvard University Press, Cambridge, Massachusetts.

HOUGHTON MIFFLIN COMPANY: "Women and Blacks and Bensonhurst (1990)" from *The Astonishing World* by Barbara Grizzuti Harrison. Copyright © 1992 by Barbara Grizzuti Harrison. Reprinted by permission of Ticknor & Fields/Houghton Mifflin Co. All rights reserved. From *Minor Characters* by Joyce Johnson. Copyright © 1983 by Joyce Johnson. Reprinted by permission of Houghton Mifflin Co. All rights reserved. From *Farewell to Manzanar* by James D. Houston and Jeanne Wakatsuki Houston. Copyright © 1973 by James D. Houston. Reprinted by permission of Houghton Mifflin Co. All rights reserved. From *Womenfolks: Growing Up Down South* by Shirley Abbott. Copyright © 1983 by Shirley Abbott. Reprinted by permission of Ticknor & Fields/Houghton Mifflin Co. All rights reserved.

ALFRED A. KNOPF, INC.: From *Black Ice* by Lorene Cary. Copyright © 1991 by Lorene Cary. Reprinted by permission of Alfred A. Knopf, Inc. From *The Measure of My Days* by Florida Scott-Maxwell. Copyright © by Florida Scott-Maxwell. From *to Begin Again* by M.F.K. Fisher. Copyright © 1993 by the M.F.K. Fisher Literary Trust. Reprinted by permission of Pantheon Books, a division of Random House, Inc. From *The Woman Warrior* by Maxine Hong Kingston. Copyright © 1975, 1976 by Maxine Hong Kingston. Reprinted by permission of Alfred A. Knopf, Inc.

RUTH LIMMER, Executor: From *Journey Around My Room* by Louise Bogan. Copyright © 1980 by Ruth Limmer, Trustee, Estate of Louise Bogan. All rights reserved.

LITTLE, BROWN AND COMPANY: From *An Unfinished Woman* by Lillian Hellman. Copyright © 1969 by Lillian Hellman. From *Facts of Life* by Maureen Howard. Copyright © 1975, 1978 by Maureen Howard. By permission of Little, Brown and Company.

WILLIAM MORROW & COMPANY, INC.: From *Riding in Cars with Boys* by Beverly Donofrio. Copyright © 1988 by Beverly Donofrio. Excerpts from *Sacred Cows . . . and Other Edibles* by Nikki Giovanni. Copyright © 1988 by Nikki Giovanni. By permission of William Morrow & Company, Inc.

NEW DIRECTIONS PUBLISHING CORPORATION: "Autobiographical Sketch" by Denise Levertov: *New and Selected Essays.* Copyright © 1992 by Denise Levertov. "Beatrice Levertoff" by Denise Levertov: *Light Up the Cave.* Copyright © 1981 by Denise Levertov. Reprinted by permission of New Directions Publishing Corp.

W. W. NORTON & COMPANY, INC.: Reprinted from *Journal of a Solitude* by May Sarton by permission of W. W. Norton & Company, Inc. Copyright © 1973 by May Sarton.

PENGUIN USA: From *Where It All Began* by Ann Cornelisen. Copyright © 1990 by Ann Cornelisen. Used by permission of the publisher, Dutton, an imprint of New American Library, a division of Penguin Books USA Inc. From *Mary* by Mary Mebane. Copyright © 1981 by Mary Elizabeth Mebane. Used by permission of Viking Penguin, a division of Penguin Books USA Inc. From *Bronx Primitive* by Kate Simon. Copyright © 1982 by Kate Simon. Used by permission of Viking Penguin, a division of Penguin Books USA Inc.

THE PUTNAM PUBLISHING GROUP: From *Sweet Summer: Growing Up With and Without My Dad* by Bebe Moore Campbell. Copyright © 1989 by Bebe Moore Campbell. Reprinted by permission of The Putnam Publishing Group.

RANDOM HOUSE, INC.: From *I Know Why the Caged Bird Sings* by Maya Angelou. Copyright © 1969 by Maya Angelou. Reprinted by permission of Random House, Inc.

THE SCHLESINGER LIBRARY, Radcliffe College: From *The Living of Charlotte Perkins Gilman: An Autobiography* by Charlotte Perkins Gilman. Reprinted by permission of The Schlesinger Library, Radcliffe College, Cambridge, MA 02138.

MARY LEE SETTLE: From *All the Brave Promises: Memories of Aircraft Woman 2nd Class 2146391.* Copyright © 1966 by Mary Lee Settle. Reprinted by permission of the author.

SIMON & SCHUSTER, INC.: From *The Loony-Bin Trip* by Kate Millett. Copyright © 1990 by Kate Millett. Reprinted by permission of Simon & Schuster, Inc.

SOUTH END PRESS: "writing autobiography" by bell hooks. From *Talking Back: Thinking Feminist, Thinking Black* by bell hooks. Copyright © 1989 by Gloria Watkins. Reprinted by permission of South End Press.

UNIVERSITY OF MISSISSIPPI PRESS: Interview with Sandra Cisneros from *Interviews with Writers of the Post-Colonial World*, edited by Feroza Jussawalla and Reed Way Dasenbrock, University of Mississippi Press, 1992. Reprinted by permission of the publisher.

UNIVERSITY OF NEBRASKA PRESS: Excerpts from Claiming Breath by Diane Glancy. Copyright © 1992 by the University of Nebraska Press.

WALLACE LITERARY AGENCY, INC.: "Expectations" from *The Girl I Left Behind* by Jane O'Reilly. Used by permission of the Wallace Literary Agency, Inc.

WATKINS/LOOMIS AGENCY, INC.: "Life and I" by Edith Wharton. Reprinted by permission of the Watkins/Loomis Agency, agents for the Edith Wharton Estate.

RHODA WEYR AGENCY: From the book *A Romantic Education* by Patricia Hampl published by Houghton Mifflin Company. Copyright ©1981 by Patricia Hampl. Reprinted by permission of the Rhoda Weyr Agency.

WORKS CITED

———————◆———————

Bataille, Gretchen M., and Kathleen Mullen Sands. *American Indian Women: Telling Their Lives*. Lincoln: University of Nebraska Press, 1984.

Bateson, Mary Catherine. *Composing a Life*. New York: Atlantic Monthly Press, 1989.

Belenky, Mary Field, Blythe McVicker Clinchy, Nancy Rule Goldberger, and Jill Mattuck Tarule. *Women's Ways of Knowing: The Development of Self, Voice, and Mind*. New York: Basic Books, 1986.

Coles, Robert. *Dorothy Day: A Radical Devotion*. Radcliffe Biography Series. Reading, MA.: Addison-Wesley Publishing Company, Inc., 1987.

Crouch, Stanley. *Notes of a Hanging Judge: Essays and Reviews 1979–1989*. New York: Oxford University Press, 1990.

Culley, Margo, ed. *American Women's Autobiography: Fea(s)ts of Memory*. Madison: University of Wisconsin Press, 1992.

Dearborn, Mary. *Pocahontas's Daughters: Gender and Ethnicity in American Culture*. New York: Oxford University Press, 1985.

Evans, Mari, ed. *Black Women Writers (1950–1980): A Critical Evaluation*. New York: Doubleday, 1984.

Gornick, Vivian, and Barbara K. Moran, eds., *Woman in Sexist Society: Studies in Power and Powerlessness*. New York: Basic Books, 1971.

Gunn, Janet Varner. *Autobiography: Towards a Poetics of Experience*. Philadelphia: University of Pennsylvania Press, 1982.

Howe, Florence. "Memories of Kate Simon." *Women's Studies Quarterly*. Fall/Winter 1990.

Jelinek, Estelle C., ed. *Women's Autobiography: Essays in Criticism*. Bloomington: Indiana University Press, 1980.

Kuehl, Linda. *Interviews with Joan Didion and Eudora Welty. In Women Writers at Work: The Paris Review Interviews*. George Plimpton, ed. New York: Viking Penguin, 1989.

Lerner, Gerda. *The Creation of Feminist Consciousness*. New York: Oxford University Press, 1993.

Levertov, Denise. *New & Selected Essays*. New York: New Directions, 1992.

Mariani, Philomena, ed. *Critical Fictions: The Politics of Imaginative Writing*. Seattle: Bay Press, 1991.

Mason, Mary G., "Dorothy Day and Women's Spiritual Autobiography," in *American Women's Autobiography: Fea(s)ts of Memory*. Ed. Margo Culley. Madison: University of Wisconsin Press, 1992.

Miller, Jean Baker, "The Development of Women's Sense of Self," in *Women's*

Growth in Connection: Writings from the Stone Center. New York: Guilford Press, 1991.

Murray, Albert. *The Omni Americans: Black Experience & American Culture.* New York: Da Capo Press, 1970.

Ozick, Cynthia, "Women and Creativity: The Demise of the Dancing Dog," in *Women in Sexist Society: Studies in Power and Powerlessness.* Vivian Gornick and Barbara K. Moran, eds. New York: Basic Books, 1971.

Pearlman, Mickey. *Listen to Their Voices: Twenty Interviews with Women Who Write.* New York: Norton, 1993.

Rosenthal, M. L. *The Modern Poets.* New York: Oxford University Press, 1965.

Showalter, Elaine. *The Female Malady: Women, Madness, and English Culture, 1830–1980.* New York: Viking Penguin, 1985.

Smith, Sidonie. *A Poetics of Women's Autobiography: Marginality and the Fictions of Self-Representation.* Bloomington: Indiana University Press, 1987.

Sollors, Werner. *Beyond Ethnicity: Consent and Descent in American Culture.* New York: Oxford University Press, 1986.

Spacks, Patricia Meyer. "Selves in Hiding," in *Women's Autobiography: Essays in Criticism.* Estelle C. Jelinek, ed. Bloomington: Indiana University Press, 1980.

Sternburg, Janet, ed. *The Writer on Her Work.* New York: Norton, 1980.

Tompkins, Jane, "Me and My Shadow," in *Feminisms: An Anthology of Literary Theory and Criticism.* Robyn R. Warhol and Diane Price Herndl, eds. Rutgers University Press, 1991.

Washington, Mary Helen, ed. *Invented Lives: Narratives of Black Women 1860–1960.* New York: Doubleday, 1987.

West, Cornel, and bell hooks. *Breaking Bread: Insurgent Black Intellectual Life.* Boston: South End Press, 1991.

Wolff, Cynthia Griffin. *A Feast of Words: The Triumph of Edith Wharton.* New York: Oxford University Press, 1977.

Wrightman, Carol. *Writing Dangerously: Mary McCarthy and Her World.* New York: Clarkson Potter Publishers, 1992.

ABOUT THE EDITOR

◆

Susan Cahill is the author of the autobiographical novel *Earth Angels: Portraits from Childhood and Youth*. She has edited many anthologies of fiction and nonfiction by women writers. She teaches at Fordham University in New York City.